T0226269

Lecture Notes in Computer Science   11127

Commenced Publication in 1973
Founding and Former Series Editors:
Gerhard Goos, Juris Hartmanis, and Jan van Leeuwen

More information about this series at http://www.springer.com/series/7409

Khalid Saeed · Władysław Homenda (Eds.)

Computer Information Systems and Industrial Management

17th International Conference, CISIM 2018
Olomouc, Czech Republic, September 27–29, 2018
Proceedings

 Springer

Editors
Khalid Saeed 🆔
Białystok University of Technology
Białystok
Poland

Władysław Homenda 🆔
Warsaw University of Technology
Warsaw
Poland

ISSN 0302-9743   ISSN 1611-3349   (electronic)
Lecture Notes in Computer Science
ISBN 978-3-319-99953-1   ISBN 978-3-319-99954-8   (eBook)
https://doi.org/10.1007/978-3-319-99954-8

Library of Congress Control Number: 2018952481

LNCS Sublibrary: SL3 – Information Systems and Applications, incl. Internet/Web, and HCI

This Springer imprint is published by the registered company Springer Nature Switzerland AG
The registered company address is: Gewerbestrasse 11, 6330 Cham, Switzerland

Preface

CISIM 2018 was the 17th of a series of conferences dedicated to computer information systems and industrial management applications. The conference was supported by Springer LNCS Information Systems. This year it was held during September 27–29, 2010, in Olomouc, Czech Republic, at Palacký University Olomouc. More than 70 papers were submitted to CISIM by researchers and scientists from a number of reputed universities around the world. These scientific and academic institutions belong to Australia, Chile, Colombia, Czech Republic, France, Germany, India, Italy, Japan, Lithuania, Luxembourg, Malaysia, Mexico, New Zealand, Peru, Poland, Portugal, South Korea, Tunisia, and the USA. Most of the papers were of high quality, but only 69 of them were sent for peer review. Each paper was assigned to at least two referees initially, and the accept decision was taken after receiving two positive reviews. In the case of conflicting decisions, another expert's review was sought for the respective papers. In total, about 150 reviews and comments were collected from the referees for the submitted papers. In order to maintain the guidelines of Springer's *Lecture Notes in Computer Science* series, the number of accepted papers was limited. Furthermore, a number of electronic discussions were held by the Program Committee (PC) chairs to decide about papers with conflicting reviews and to reach a consensus. After the discussions, the PC chairs decided to accept for publication in the proceedings book the best 42 of the total submitted papers. The main topics covered by the chapters in this book are biometrics, security systems, multimedia, classification and clustering, and industrial management. Besides these, the reader will find interesting papers on computer information systems as applied to wireless networks, computer graphics, and intelligent systems.

We are grateful to the four esteemed speakers for their keynote addresses. The authors of the keynote talks were Profs. Anna Bartkowiak, Wroclaw University, Poland; Nabendu Chaki, University of Calcutta, India; Jan Mielniczuk, Institute of Computer Science, Polish Academy of Science; and Kaori Yoshida, Kyushu Institute of Technology, Japan. All the keynote abstracts are published in the proceedings book.

We would like to thank all the members of the PC and the external reviewers for their dedicated efforts in the paper selection process, particularly Profs. Kateřina Slaninová, Jan Martinovič, and Pavel Moravec, all from the Technical University of Ostrava, Czech Republic. Special thanks are extended to the members of the Organizing Committee both the international and local members, namely, to Prof. Vít Voženílek and Jitka Doležalová, both from Palacký University Olomouc, Czech Republic; and the Springer team for their great efforts to make the conference a success. We are also grateful to Andrei Voronkov, whose EasyChair system eased the submission and selection process and greatly supported the compilation of the proceedings. The proceedings editing was managed by Prof. Jiří Dvorský (Technical University of Ostrava, Czech Republic), to whom we are indeed very grateful.

We hope that the reader's expectations will be met and that the participants enjoyed their stay in the beautiful city of Olomouc.

September 2018

Khalid Saeed
Władysław Homenda

Organization

Conference Patrons

Lech Dzienis   Białystok University of Technology, Poland
Václav Snášel   VŠB-Technical University of Ostrava, Czech Republic

General Chair

Khalid Saeed   Białystok University of Technology, Poland

Conference Co-chairs

Rituparna Chaki   University of Calcutta, India
Agostino Cortesi   Ca' Foscari University of Venice, Italy
Marek Krętowski   Białystok University of Technology, Poland
Vít Vondrák   VŠB-Technical University of Ostrava, Czech Republic
Vít Voženílek   Palacký University Olomouc, Czech Republic

Program Committee

Chairs

Władysław Homenda   Warsaw University of Technology, Poland
Jan Martinovič   VŠB-Technical University of Ostrava, Czech Republic
Khalid Saeed   Białystok University of Technology, Poland

Members

Waleed Abdulla   University of Auckland, New Zealand
Raid Al-Tahir   The University of the West Indies, St. Augustine, Trinidad and Tobago
Adrian Atanasiu   Bucharest University, Romania
Aditya Bagchi   Indian Statistical Institute, India
Anna Bartkowiak   Wrocław University, Poland
Rahma Boucetta   National Engineering School of Gabes, Tunisia
Nabendu Chaki   University of Calcutta, India
Rituparna Chaki   University of Calcutta, India
Agostino Cortesi   Ca' Foscari University of Venice, Italy
Dipankar Dasgupta   University of Memphis, USA
Pierpaolo Degano   University of Pisa, Italy
Jan Devos   Ghent University, Belgium
Andrzej Dobrucki   Wrocław University of Technology, Poland
Jiří Dvorský   VŠB-Technical University of Ostrava, Czech Republic

Additional Reviewers

Marcin Adamski	Białystok University of Technology, Poland
Katarzyna Borowska	Białystok University of Technology, Poland
Jitka Doležalová	Palacký University Olomouc, Czech Republic
Dorota Duda	Białystok University of Technology, Poland
Grzegorz Góra	University of Warsaw, Poland
Ekaterina Grakova	VŠB-Technical University of Ostrava, Czech Republic
Wiktor Jakowluk	Białystok University of Technology, Poland
Dariusz Jankowski	Białystok University of Technology, Poland
Kateřina Janurová	VŠB-Technical University of Ostrava, Czech Republic
Tomáš Karásek	VŠB-Technical University of Ostrava, Czech Republic
Adam Klimowicz	Białystok University of Technology, Poland
Michal Krumnikl	VŠB-Technical University of Ostrava, Czech Republic
Miloš Kudělka	VŠB-Technical University of Ostrava, Czech Republic
Eliška Ochodková	VŠB-Technical University of Ostrava, Czech Republic
Mirosław Omieljanowicz	Białystok University of Technology, Poland
Walenty Oniszczuk	Białystok University of Technology, Poland
Antoni Portero	VŠB-Technical University of Ostrava, Czech Republic
Janusz Rafałko	Warsaw University of Technology, Poland
Lukáš Rapant	VŠB-Technical University of Ostrava, Czech Republic
Lubomír Říha	VŠB-Technical University of Ostrava, Czech Republic
Mariusz Rybnik	University of Białystok, Poland
Andrzej Skowron	University of Warsaw, Poland
Marek Tabędzki	Białystok University of Technology, Poland
Lukáš Vojáček	VŠB-Technical University of Ostrava, Czech Republic

Keynotes

Assessing Data Variables by Some Collective Intelligence Methods

Anna Bartkowiak

Institute of Computer Science, University of Wroclaw, Poland
anna.bartkowiak@ii.uni.wroc.pl

Abstract. Statistically, since Pearson, data are recorded as matrices of size $n \times p$, where rows contain n subjects (individuals, cases), and columns are values of the p variables (attributes) characterizing the subjects. When performing traditional multivariate analysis of the recorded data, the crucial problem is: should all the p recorded variables be taken for the analysis; may be less of them will be sufficient and some of them are not relevant, or even an impediment. The old saying: "the more the better" has become questionable nowadays: too many non-relevant variables may be disturbing by introducing some random effects into the data.

The problem to solve is composite. I will consider it in the context of regression or classification analysis, when dealing with directly recorded 'variables' (no 'features' derived from them). I will concentrate on group of methods referred to as Collective Intelligence (contains, among others, Ensemble Learning, Decision trees and Random Forests). Specifically, I will concentrate on the Random Forests (RFs) methodology. RFs offer some non-conventional indices of importance of variables in the context of regression and clustering. They work directly on original variables (not on new features derived from them). They can work on mixed type variables, that is quantitative (numeric) or qualitative (categorial). They work without assumption on the probability distribution of the variables. They yield an internal unbiased estimate of the generalization error. It has been shown that RFs are resistant to outliers, however not all of them are universally consistent. I intend to show – on real data examples – how all this works in practice.

A Data-Driven Approach Towards Forecasting Generalized Mid-Term Energy Requirement for Industrial Sector Users of Smart Grid

Nabendu Chaki

Department of Computer Science and Engineering, University of Calcutta, India
nchaki@cucse.org

Abstract. One of the major improvements that Smart Grid offers over traditional power grid is a balanced supply demand ratio. As electricity is hard to store for future usage, it is important to be aware of the demand in order to generate enough electicity for uninterrupted power supply. Thus, forecasting plays a vital role in Smart Grid. However, with various range of rapidly fluctuating parameters that influence electricity consumption patterns, it is next to impossible to design a single forecasting model for different types of users. Typically, electricity usage depends on demographic, socio-economic and climatic environment of any region. Besides, the dependencies between influencing parameters and consumption varies over different sectors, like, residential, commercial and industrial. In this paper, our main goal is to develop a generalized mid-term forecasting model for industrial sector, that can accurately predict quarterly energy usage of a large geographic region with diverse range of influencing parameters. The proposed model is designed and tested on real life datasets of industrial users of various states in the U.S.

Selection of Active Predictors
for Misspecified Binary Model

Jan Mielniczuk[1,2]

[1] Department of Artificial Intelligence, Institute of Computer Science,
Polish Academy of Science, Poland
[2] Faculty of Mathematics and Information Science,
Warsaw University of Technology, Poland
j.mielniczuk@ipipan.waw.pl

Abstract. Selection of active predictors in high dimensional regression problems plays a pivotal role in contemporary data mining and statistical inference. However, properties of frequently applied selection procedures such as consistent choice of an active set usually strongly rely on assumption that data follows a specific model.

In the presentation we address this problem and discuss general setups when estimation procedures can appproximately recover the direction of the true vector of parameters and estimate its support consistently. This explains sometimes observed phenomenon that certain procedures work well even when the underlying data generating mechanism is misspecified; e.g. methods constructed for linear models are applied to binary regression. The basic reasoning was discovered long ago by D. Brillinger and P. Rudd but it is scarcely known in data mining community.

As a particular application we introduce a two-stage selection procedure which first screens predictors using LASSO method for logistic regression and then choses the final model via optimization of Generalized Information Criterion on ensuing hierarchical family. We discuss its properties and in particular the fact that in the case of misspecification it picks with large probability a model which approximates Kullback-Leibler projection (in the average sense) onto the family of logistic regressions.

Kansei Information Processing and Its Applications

Kaori Yoshida

Department of Human Intelligence Systems,
Kyushu Institute of Technology, Japan
kaori@brain.kyutech.ac.jp

Abstract. Kansei Information Processing is a part of Human-Computer Interaction research. "Kansei" is a Japanese word that covers the meanings of sensitivity or sensibility. Kansei studies is an interdisciplinary research field. It intends to understand what Kansei is, how Kansei works, and how to apply an understanding of Kansei in the design of new products and services. I would like to introduce Kansei studies and its applications in my talk.

Contents

Computer Information Systems

Industrial Management and Other Applications

Machine Learning and High Performance Computing

Modelling and Optimization

Various Aspects of Computer Security

Biometrics and Pattern Recognition Applications

Multi-muscle Texture Analysis for Dystrophy Development Identification in Golden Retriever Muscular Dystrophy Dogs

Dorota Duda[1($\boxtimes$)], Noura Azzabou[2], and Jacques D. de Certaines[2]

[1] Faculty of Computer Science, Bialystok University of Technology,
Wiejska 45a, 15-351 Bialystok, Poland
d.duda@pb.edu.pl

[2] Institute of Myology, Nuclear Magnetic Resonance Laboratory, Paris, France

Abstract. The study assesses the suitability of multi-muscle texture analysis (TA) for the dystrophy development characterization in Golden Retriever Muscular Dystrophy (GRMD) dogs. Textural features, statistical and model-based, are derived from T2-weighted Magnetic Resonance Images (MRI) of canine hindlimb muscles. Features obtained from different types of muscles (EDL, GasLat, GasMed, and TC) are analyzed simultaneously. Four phases of dystrophy progression, including the "zero phase" – the absence of the disease, are differentiated. Two classifiers are applied: Support Vector Machines (SVM) and Adaptive Boosting (AdaBoost). A Monte Carlo-based feature selection enables to find features (and the corresponding muscle types) that are the most useful in identifying the phase of dystrophy. The simultaneous consideration of several muscles improves the classification accuracy by maximum 12.5% in comparison to the best corresponding result achieved with single-muscle TA. A combination of 17 textural features derived from different types of muscles provides a classification accuracy of approximately 82%.

Keywords: Duchenne Muscular Dystrophy · DMD
Golden Retriever Muscular Dystrophy · GRMD dog model · MRI T2
Tissue characterization · Texture analysis
Monte Carlo feature selection · Classification

1 Introduction

Duchenne muscular dystrophy (DMD) is a severe genetic disorder, resulting in progressive degeneration of all the striated muscles [1]. It is found predominantly in male children and young men. Affected individuals typically die in their second or third decade due to either respiratory failure or cardiomyopathy. So far, many extensive attempts have been made to develop therapies for DMD [2], however,

© Springer Nature Switzerland AG 2018
K. Saeed and W. Homenda (Eds.): CISIM 2018, LNCS 11127, pp. 3–15, 2018.
https://doi.org/10.1007/978-3-319-99954-8_1

there is still no effective cure for this disease. Various healthcare practices can only improve the life expectancy. In this context, the search for effective therapies has become the subject of research by many scientists worldwide. It is also crucial to elaborate reliable approaches for evaluating the quality of therapy. Testing therapeutic methods is often performed using animal models. The most popular of them is the canine model known as the *Golden Retriever Muscular Dystrophy* (GRMD) [3], reflecting both the genotype and phenotype of DMD.

Several protocols for the assessment of treatment effects have been developed. They are based, for example, on biochemical studies, muscular strength evaluation or histological examination of biopsy specimens [4]. Choosing the right measure is not a trivial task since none of the methods is definitely satisfactory. Recent advances in ultrasound and Magnetic Resonance Imaging (MRI) have made these techniques play an increasing role in the evaluation of patients with neuromuscular disorders. Nevertheless, muscle imaging is still used as a supplement to clinical and electrophysiological examination. Its role could be improved by using computer-aided techniques for analysis and interpretation of muscle images. Here, great hope is placed in texture analysis (TA) [5,6], that provides valuable information about muscular tissue properties. Such properties change under the DMD disease progression and/or its response to treatment.

The general objective of our research is to develop strategies for texture-based analysis of MRI muscle images and to assess their potential in characterizing dystrophy development. This work is carried out within the European COST project (Action BM1304, MYO-MRI) aimed at improving diagnosis and therapy evaluation in neuromuscular diseases. The database which we use, includes different sequences of MRI images acquired from GRMD and healthy dogs, at three phases of canine growth and/or disease progression [5]: 2–4 months (the first phase), 5–6 months (the second phase), 7 months and more (the third phase). Up to four types of muscles in canine pelvic limbs are identified on every image: the *Extensor Digitorum Longus* (EDL), the *Gastrocnemius Lateralis* (GasLat), the *Gastrocnemius Medialis* (GasMed), and the *Tibial Cranialis* (TC).

In our preliminary work [7] we evaluated the potential of MRI texture analysis in distinguishing healthy and GRMD dogs. The experiments were performed separately for each type of muscles and for each phase of canine growth. Results demonstrated that some of TA methods (e.g. based on co-occurrence matrices [8] and run-length matrices [9–11]) could be considerably efficient. In addition, the usefulness of each analyzed muscle (in terms of discrimination process) turned out to be different in each phase of canine growth and/or disease development.

In our next research [12] a modified Monte Carlo (MC) feature selection [13] was used to assess the relative importance of various textural features in the dystrophy identification process. In total, 39 textural features derived from 8 TA methods were analyzed. Like in the previous work, classification experiments were conducted separately for each muscle type. Apart from the two-class discrimination tasks (healthy vs. GRMD dogs), we also faced the problem of differentiating three phases of dystrophy progression in GRMD dogs. The latter task proved to be much more difficult, resulting in classification accuracy worse by 20–30%, compared to the two-class results. Moreover, the group of the most discriminative features was different for different types of muscles.

This study focuses on the four-class classification problem. The first three classes of muscle tissue reflect three phases of dystrophy development in GRMD dogs. The fourth one corresponds to healthy muscles of dogs at different ages, hence it is called the "zero phase". In this work, for the first time, texture characteristics derived from several types of muscles, EDL, GasLat, GasMed, and TC, are analyzed simultaneously (we refer to this as a "multi-muscle" texture analysis). It is examined whether and how the consideration of several muscles at a time improves the recognition of dystrophy phases in comparison to that achieved with each muscle separately ("single-muscle" TA). Moreover, feature selection allows us to determine which textural features, as well as derived from which muscle, are the most useful in identifying considered dystrophy phases.

The next section includes an overview of related studies performed by other researchers. Section 3 describes the methods proposed for the present study and gives details of the experimental setup for their validation. Next, the results are presented and discussed. Conclusions and future work are outlined in Sect. 5.

2   Related Work

To the best of our knowledge, a system for a texture-based differentiation among several phases of muscular dystrophy development in GRMD dogs has not yet been proposed. However, some works evaluated the TA potential in recognition of healthy and affected muscles at different dog's ages. For example, Wang et al. [14] worked on a semiautomated system to quantify MRI biomarkers of GRMD. The system was applied to a database of T2-weighted and T2-weighted fat-suppressed images, derived from 10 GRMD and 8 normal dogs. Six proximal pelvic limb muscles were scanned at approximately 3, 6, and 9 months of age. For each of the segmented muscles, several characteristics were considered: the MRI biomarkers of muscle volume, the intensity statistics over MRI biomarker maps, and statistical image texture features. The latter were obtained from a gray-level histogram (one feature – standard deviation) and from the run length matrices (5 commonly used features [9]). In their work, differentiation between groups of dystrophic and healthy muscles was performed separately for each phase of canine growth and/or disease development. Experiments (using the paired two tailed t-test) showed obvious group differences between normal and affected muscles for each considered textural feature.

Another study, aiming at differentiation between GRMD and healthy dogs at different dog's ages, was presented in [15]. This work was performed on a database similar to that used in the previous study. Several MRI imaging biomarkers and three texture analysis biomarkers were quantified in seven muscles. Three textural features were used: a gray-level histogram-based entropy, and two run-length matrix-based features: short run emphasis (referring to the small lesion index) and run-length non-uniformity (referring to the heterogeneity index). The last of them performed best giving statistically different values (according to the Mann-Whitney-Wilcoxon test) for GRMD and healthy dogs at each phase of canine growth. Moreover, classification performed with Linear Discriminant Analysis (LDA) and evaluated by Receiver Operating Characteristic (ROC) curves, showed better potential of textural features, in comparison to other (non-texture-based) tested biomarkers.

Some attempts to distinguishing healthy and affected GRMD muscles were also undertaken by Yang *et al.* [16]. Their work focused on the use of moment-based TA methods applied to T2-weighted MRI images. Two moment functions were investigated: Legendre and Zernike. Although several canine hindlimb muscles (EDL, GasLat, GasMed, and TC) were identified in the database, the potential difference between considered muscles was not taken into account. Recognition of dystrophic and healthy tissue was performed at 7 different dog's ages: 2, 3, 4, 5, 6, 7 months, and 9 months and more. As a classifier, Support Vector Machines [17] with second degree polynomial kernel were used. The application of several moment-based textural features resulted in a good differentiation between healthy and affected muscles only at the second phase of canine growth and/or dystrophy development (defined in their work as a period lasting from around 4 to 6 months). The differences between considered features in healthy and GRMD muscles were not observed at first phase of canine growth. The results were also unsatisfactory at the third phase.

3   Methodology and Experimental Setup

Three groups of experiments were planned. The aim of the first one was to investigate whether and how the simultaneous analysis of textural features derived from different muscles (EDL, GasLat, GasMed, TC) improves the recognition of dystrophy phase (from the "zero", first, second and third one). The potential of multi-muscle texture analysis was compared to that achieved when each type of muscle was considered separately. The single-muscle texture analysis was always performed on the same set of images as the set used for the multi-muscle texture analysis. During the second experiment, the usefulness of various textural features in the dystrophy development identification was assessed. Features were ranked according to their frequency of selection in a modified Monte Carlo procedure. In the third group of experiments, the classification accuracies obtained with different groups of the most frequently selected features were compared. This allowed to determine how many top-ranked features would be sufficient to ensure the best possible differentiation among considered dystrophy phases.

3.1   Database

The database (including images and segmented muscles) was provided by the Nuclear Magnetic Resonance Laboratory of the Institute of Myology in Paris, France. Images were acquired from 5 GRMD dogs and 5 healthy controls. Each dog was examined from 3 to 5 times over a maximum 14 months. In total, 38 examinations were carried out. Each examination was assigned to one of the three

Table 1. Numbers of examinations available for each phase of canine growth and/or dystrophy development. The dogs' age is given in months.

phase →	Phase 1				Phase 2		Phase 3							
dogs' age →	1	2	3	4	5	6	7	8	9	10	11	12	13	14
GRMD dogs	-	3	-	4	3	2	-	3	1	-	2	-	-	-
Healthy dogs	-	3	2	2	3	1	-	5	-	-	2	1	-	1

Table 2. Total numbers of ROIs considered for each muscle, while analyzing simultaneously the textural features corresponding to pairs, triples, and quadruples of muscles

cohort type →	GRMD	GRMD	GRMD	Healthy dogs
combination of muscles\phase →	Phase 1	Phase 2	Phase 3	"zero phase"
EDL + GasLat	7	18	25	48
EDL + GasMed	20	24	41	95
EDL + TC	88	73	91	286
GasLat + GasMed	67	36	43	160
GasLat + TC	19	30	38	100
GasMed + TC	33	37	54	149
EDL + GasLat + GasMed	7	17	23	48
EDL + GasLat + TC	6	18	25	47
EDL + GasMed + TC	17	24	42	91
GasLat + GasMed + TC	19	28	36	95
EDL + GasLat + GasMed + TC	6	17	23	47

typical phases of canine growth and/or dystrophy development. The numbers of examinations available for each phase are given in Table 1.

Acquisitions were performed on a 3T Siemens Magnetom Trio TIM scanner. All details on the acquisition protocols can be found in [18]. Only T2-weighted Spin Echo sequences were considered. They were performed with the following parameters: repetition time $TR = 3,000$ ms, echo time $TE1 = 6.3$ ms, and $TE2 = 50$ ms. The in-plane resolution was 0.56 mm × 0.56 mm, the slice thickness was 3 mm, and the inter-slice gap was 7.5 mm. Each acquisition provided a series of 12 to 14 images. All images had a size of 240 × 320 pixels.

At least three *Regions of Interest* (areas of images to be analyzed, abbreviated ROIs) per image series were initially available for each type of considered muscles: EDL, GasLat, GasMed, and TC. However, there were not many images on which all four types of muscles could be seen at the same time. Due to this reason, further simultaneous analysis of multi-muscle textures was also based on triples and pairs of muscles. Only ROIs larger than 50 pixels and having each dimension greater than five pixels were finally accepted. Average sizes of ROIs used in our experiments were: 174, 172, 324, and 227 pixels for the EDL, GasLat, GasMed, and TC muscle, respectively. Table 2 shows the total numbers of ROIs considered for each muscle, while analyzing simultaneously pairs, triples, and quadruple of muscles.

3.2   Single-Muscle Texture Analysis

Single-muscle texture analysis was performed with the home-made application *Medical Image Processing* (MIP) [19]. In total, 34 textural features were calculated for each of the four types of muscles. The following groups of features were considered:

- first order statistics (FOS) obtained from a gray-level histogram: Avg (average), Var (variance), $Skew$ (skewness), $Kurt$ (kurtosis),
- based on the co-occurrence matrices (COM) [8]: $AngSecMom$ (angular second moment), $InvDiffMom$ (inverse difference moment), $Entr$ (entropy), $SumAvg$ (sum average), $SumVar$ (sum variance), $SumEntr$ (sum entropy), $DiffAvg$ (difference average), $DiffVar$ (difference variance), $DiffEntr$ (difference entropy), $Corr$ (correlation), $Contrast$ (contrast),
- based on the run length matrices (RLM) [9–11]: $ShortEmp$ (short run emphasis), $LongEmp$ (long run emphasis), $LowGlrEmp$ (low gray level runs emphasis), $HighGlrEmp$ (high gray level runs emphasis), $RlNonUni$ (run length non-uniformity), $GlNonUni$ (gray level non-uniformity), $Fraction$ (fraction of image in runs), $RlEntr$ (run length entropy),
- based on the gray level difference matrices (GLDM) [20]: $gAngSecMom$ (angular second moment), $gInvDiffMom$ (inverse difference moment), $gAvg$ (average), $gEntr$ (entropy), $gContrast$ (contrast),
- based on the gradient matrix (GM) [21]: $GradAvg$ (average), $GradVar$ (variance), $GradSkew$ (skewness), $GradKurt$ (kurtosis), $GradNonZero$ (percentage of non-zero gradients),
- based on the fractional Brownian motion model (FB) [22]: $FractalDim$ (fractal dimension).

When applying the COM, RLM, and GLDM methods, the number of image gray levels was reduced to 64, and four standard directions of pixel runs ($0°$, $45°$, $90°$ and $135°$) were considered. Due to the relatively small size of the ROIs, and due to their narrow and irregular shape, only the smallest distances between pixels in pairs (1 and 2) were taken into account for the COM, GLDM, and FB methods. If the same feature was calculated at several directions or distances between pixels in pairs, its average value was used in further analysis.

3.3   Multi-muscle Texture Analysis

The creation of a multi-muscle feature vector was presented schematically in Fig. 1. Each ROI outlined in the image refers to a different muscle: EDL, GasLat,

GasMed, or TC. First, the texture of each muscle was characterized independently from the others. However, each muscle/ROI was characterized using the same set of textural features, calculated with the same methods. Then, features corresponding to different muscles were combined in one vector, characterizing a set of muscles. In our experiments, each vector was assigned a label referring to a phase of dystrophy development (the "zero", first, second, or third phase).

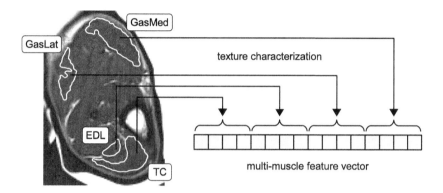

Fig. 1. Creation of a multi-muscle feature vector, characterizing a set of canine hindlimb muscles. Here, four muscles are taken into account: EDL, GasLat, GasMed, and TC. The size of the MRI image section is 97×133 pixels.

3.4   Evaluation of the Usefulness of Different Sets of Features

The usefulness of features calculated with different TA methods and derived from different muscles, as well as the benefits of simultaneous consideration of several muscle types, were assessed on the basis of the classification accuracy obtained with tested feature vectors. Classification was performed with the *Weka* [23] software. The classification accuracies were estimated using 10-fold cross-validation, repeated 10 times. Two classifiers were applied: (i) a nonlinear Support Vector Machines (SVM) with a second degree polynomial kernel, and (ii) an adaptive boosting (AdaBoost) [24] using the C4.5 Decision Tree [25] as the underlying algorithm.

3.5   Search for the Most Discriminative Textural Features

The search for the most discriminative textural features was based on a modified Monte Carlo feature selection procedure described in our previous work [12]. It was performed on a data set composed of labeled multi-muscle feature vectors comprising 34 features for each considered muscle. In total, $4 \times 34 = 136$ features were examined. The entire experiment consisted in multiple repetitions of a single execution of a selection procedure performed on a "truncated data set". Such a truncated data set was created by a random choice of 2/3 observations form the initial data set, which were described by a randomly chosen subset of initial textural features (here – 28 features, which constituted approximately 20% of 136 features initially used). Different random choices were applied for each repetition. The relative importance of each feature in identifying the phase of dystrophy was assessed by its "incidence frequency rate" (IFR), that was the ratio between the number of cases in which the feature was selected and the number of times it occurred in the subsets of features describing the truncated data sets (subjected to the selection).

A single selection procedure was executed 200,000 times, using the *Weka* tool. For each execution, each candidate subset of features was evaluated by a supervised wrapper method (called *WrapperSubsetEval* in *Weka*) combined with a C4.5 (*J48* in Weka) classifier. Classification accuracies were assessed by a 10-fold cross-validation. The space of subsets of features was searched using the *BestFirst* strategy with the *Forward* searching direction.

4   Results

4.1   Multi-muscle vs. Single-Muscle Texture Analysis

Table 3 summarizes the best classification results obtained for single-muscle texture analysis and corresponding results for multi-muscle texture analysis. Each row of the table refers to the same set of images in which either one muscle (single-muscle TA) or a group of muscles (multi-muscle TA) was considered at a time. We limit ourselves to show only the results obtained with two best texture analysis methods, the COM- and RLM-based, as very often they outperformed the other methods, such as the FOS, GM-, or GLDM-based ones.

It can be observed that, regardless of the texture analysis method, regardless of the combination of muscles, and regardless of the classifier used, better classification results were always achieved when pairs, triples or quadruple of muscles were analyzed together. If multi-muscle texture analysis was applied, the improvements in the classification accuracy ranged from 2.9% to 12.5%, compared to the corresponding results for the single-muscle analysis. When looking for the best combination of muscles, it should be remembered that sets of images used in the experiments were different in size for each muscle combination. The most numerous sets were available for two-muscle cases, the smallest set was used for the four-muscle case. In general, the larger the set of objects (here – images), the better classifier could be found. Moreover, the numbers of textural features describing each image slice were also different – proportional to the number of muscles analyzed simultaneously. Paradoxically, too many features in relation to the number of objects may worsen the quality of a classifier. This might explain why better improvements in the classification quality were sometimes observed for pairs or triples of muscles and not for the quadruple. Different improvements obtained for various muscle combinations can also suggest that textural features corresponding to different muscles do not contribute in the same way to the dystrophy development identification. For example, the COM-based features provided better classification accuracies when derived from the

Table 3. Classification accuracy [%] (and standard deviation) achieved after application of single-muscle and multi-muscle texture analysis. The results were obtained with the SVM and AdaBoost classifiers, and for the COM- and RLM-based TA methods. For each TA method, the first column of results contains the best result among the two, three, or four obtained separately for single-muscle cases. The name of the muscle for which the best result was achieved is given next to the result. The next column, titled "multi-m", contains the result obtained with the multi-muscle TA.

	TA method →	COM		RLM	
	combination\TA type →	single-muscle	multi-m	single-muscle	multi-m
SVM	EDL + GasLat	68.4 (5.5) EDL	71.7 (6.9)	66.4 (6.1) GasLat	69.7 (7.3)
	EDL + GasMed	69.9 (4.0) EDL	73.2 (4.1)	65.4 (4.1) EDL	73.0 (4.2)
	EDL + TC	68.9 (2.2) EDL	73.4 (2.3)	69.8 (2.1) EDL	75.1 (2.3)
	GasLat + GasMed	65.5 (3.1) GasLat	69.6 (2.9)	69.1 (3.2) GasMed	72.8 (3.3)
	GasLat + TC	67.3 (3.4) GasLat	70.4 (3.7)	68.9 (3.2) GasLat	77.1 (4.0)
	GasMed + TC	59.4 (2.5) GasMed	71.1 (3.1)	64.9 (2.6) TC	76.9 (3.7)
	EDL + GasLat + GasMed	67.8 (6.2) EDL	72.8 (6.4)	66.1 (5.7) GasLat	74.3 (6.4)
	EDL + GasLat + TC	67.2 (5.8) EDL	74.8 (5.9)	67.0 (6.3) TC	74.2 (6.1)
	EDL + GasMed + TC	69.7 (3.7) EDL	74.6 (4.6)	73.3 (5.0) TC	78.7 (4.2)
	GasLat + GasMed + TC	67.6 (3.9) GasLat	72.6 (4.2)	69.0 (3.8) GasLat	79.2 (4.4)
	EDL + GasLat + GasMed + TC	66.8 (7.6) EDL	72.4 (6.6)	69.5 (6.7) TC	77.8 (6.6)
AdaBoost	EDL + GasLat	64.9 (6.9) EDL	67.8 (6.4)	64.3 (7.3) EDL	71.9 (6.5)
	EDL + GasMed	69.8 (5.0) EDL	72.8 (4.6)	67.9 (5.2) EDL	73.8 (5.2)
	EDL + TC	66.2 (2.6) EDL	72.9 (2.8)	68.7 (2.8) EDL	78.9 (2.6)
	GasLat + GasMed	66.1 (4.1) GasMed	70.6 (4.0)	67.1 (3.6) GasMed	73.6 (3.4)
	GasLat + TC	64.3 (5.0) TC	71.2 (4.4)	67.0 (4.6) GasLat	73.2 (3.9)
	GasMed + TC	65.8 (4.3) TC	77.6 (3.8)	69.7 (3.8) TC	78.9 (3.5)
	EDL + GasLat + GasMed	67.5 (6.6) EDL	70.6 (6.6)	65.0 (6.4) EDL	75.6 (5.9)
	EDL + GasLat + TC	68.1 (6.9) TC	78.0 (6.4)	68.3 (7.2) EDL	77.5 (5.8)
	EDL + GasMed + TC	69.9 (4.9) EDL	80.1 (4.5)	74.8 (4.5) TC	80.9 (4.3)
	GasLat + GasMed + TC	62.9 (4.9) TC	72.6 (3.8)	66.9 (5.1) TC	77.1 (4.6)
	EDL + GasLat + GasMed + TC	69.1 (7.8) TC	74.7 (7.2)	68.3 (6.7) TC	80.8 (5.7)

EDL muscle. This was especially noticeable when the SVM classifier was used. In turn, with the AdaBoost classifier, the TC muscle also turned out to provide the effective COM-based texture descriptors. As for the RLM-based features, the best ones were derived from the TC and EDL muscle, a little worse – from the GasLat muscle. Finally, the GasMed muscle seemed to provide the least useful information, regardless of the TA method.

4.2   Ranking of Features

The table 4 presents the 20 most often selected features in a modified Monte Carlo selection procedure. Features are sorted in descending order of their incidence frequency rate in the entire MC selection experiment. It could be seen that the most frequently selected features (the top ranked) were these derived from the TC and GasLat muscles. Features extracted from the EDL muscle, still quite often selected, start to appear a bit further in the ranking. This could suggest that, along with the considered TA methods, more useful information (for identifying the phase of dystrophy development) could be derived mainly from the TC and GasLat muscles, and a little less from the EDL muscle. As in the previous part of experiments, the best texture analysis methods turned out to be the RLM- and COM-based ones. Relatively good was also the *Avg* feature, derived from a gray-level histogram. These results coincide, to some extent, with findings of other research [7, 14, 15], proving that the use of certain RLM-, COM-, and histogram-based textural features could be advantageous for the dystrophy development identification.

Table 4. Ranking of features according to their incidence frequency rate (IFR) obtained with the modified Monte Carlo method. Only the first 20 features are considered. For each feature the corresponding texture analysis method is given in brackets. This is followed by the name of the muscle being characterized by the feature.

Rank	Feature (TA method)	Muscle	IFR	Rank	Feature (TA method)	Muscle	IFR
1	HighGLREmp (RLM)	TC	51.43	11	LowGLREmp (RLM)	EDL	34.03
2	SumAvg (COM)	TC	50.44	12	RLNonUni (RLM)	EDL	33.01
3	SumAvg (COM)	GasLat	43.76	13	Entr (COM)	GasMed	29.83
4	Avg (FOS)	TC	43.56	14	InvDiffMom (COM)	TC	29.17
5	LowGLREmp (RLM)	TC	41.90	15	gInvDiffMom (GLDM)	TC	28.99
6	LowGLREmp (RLM)	GasLat	36.62	16	Avg (FOS)	EDL	28.88
7	RLNonUni (RLM)	TC	36.43	17	GLNonUni (RLM)	TC	26.05
8	HighGLREmp (RLM)	GasLat	35.05	18	SumAvg (COM)	EDL	25.99
9	Avg (FOS)	GasLat	34.56	19	GradAvg (GB)	GasMed	25.41
10	AngSecMom (COM)	TC	34.41	20	FractalDim (FB)	TC	24.66

4.3   Assessment of a Sufficient Number of the Top-Ranked Features

The plots in Fig. 2 show the relation between the classification quality, obtained with the SVM and AdaBoost classifiers, and the number of the top-ranked features (from the feature incidence frequency ranking), used as tissue descriptors in the classification task. It could be seen that extending the set of features with consecutive features from the ranking, results initially in a relatively fast improvement of classification qualities. Nevertheless, for both classifiers, the classification quality starts to decrease slowly in an irregular way after exceeding

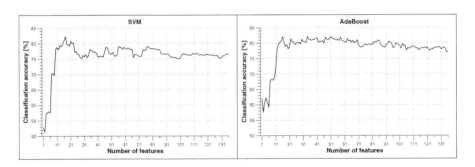

Fig. 2. Accuracy of classification (based on multi-muscle texture analysis), achieved with different numbers of the most frequently selected features. The results were obtained using the SVM and AdaBoost classifiers.

about 17 features in the set. One could therefore conclude that the use of 17 most-selected features could be the relatively best solution in the considered problem. It should be remembered, however, that this set may be one of many possible solutions of similar quality, and for initial set of 136 features, $2^{136} \approx 8.71 * 10^{40}$ subsets of features would have to be tested to find the best solution. Finally, the classification accuracy obtained with the set of 17 top-ranked features was 81.6% and 82.1%, for the SVM and AdaBoost classifiers, respectively.

5 Conclusions and Future Work

The aim of the study was to assess the potential of multi-muscle texture analysis in identifying phases of dystrophy progression in GRMD dogs. Proposed approach consists in a simultaneous analysis of textural features derived from several muscles. In the work, four types of canine hindlimb muscles were characterized: EDL, GasLat, GasMed, and TC. 34 textural features derived from 6 texture analysis methods were calculated for each muscle. Apart from the three typical phases of dystrophy development in GRMD dogs, the "zero phase", corresponding to healthy muscles of dogs at different ages, was also considered in the classification task. Experiments with two classifiers, SVM and AdaBoost, showed that a simultaneous analysis of textural features derived from several muscles can improve (by a maximum 12.5%) the recognition of dystrophy phases, in comparison with the best results achieved for each muscle separately.

With the applied TA methods, the most useful piece of information (in terms of discrimination process) was generally provided by the TC and GasLat muscles, a little less useful – by the EDL muscle. Conducting a Monte Carlo-based feature selection allowed to identify features that could be the most effective in differentiating dystrophy phases. They were mainly based on run-length and co-occurrence matrices. Comparison of the classification results achieved with different numbers of the most frequently selected features revealed that a set of the top-ranked 17 features could provide the best possible solution for analyzed problem. Finally, it was possible to correctly recognize the dystrophy phase in approximately 82% of cases, with both the SVM and AdaBoost classifier.

The obtained results prove that multi-muscle texture analysis could be a promising tool for identifying the phase of dystrophy and, consequently, for evaluation of tested dystrophy therapies. However, to apply it in practice, more experiments would have to be carried out, certainly on a larger data set. It would be interesting to analyze MRI images of other series, e.g. T1-weighted ones. Other texture analysis methods, particularly model- and filter-based, could also be tested. It would be desirable to find textural features that evolve with the individual's growth (and not with the dystrophy development) and eliminate them from further analyses. Finally, a model describing the texture evolution under dystrophy progression is worth elaborating.

Acknowledgments. This work was performed under the auspices of the European COST Action BM1304, MYO-MRI. It was also supported by grant S/WI/2/18 (from the Bialystok University of Technology, Bialystok, Poland), founded by the Polish Ministry of Science and Higher Education.

The authors would like to thank Prof. M. Kretowski for his valuable comments and advice.

References

1. Guiraud, S., Aartsma-Rus, A., Vieira, N.M., Davies, K.E., van Ommen, G.J., Kunkel, L.M.: The pathogenesis and therapy of muscular dystrophies. Annu. Rev. Genomics Hum. Genet. **16**, 281–308 (2015)
2. Shieh, P.B.: Duchenne muscular dystrophy: clinical trials and emerging tribulations. Curr. Opin. Neurol. **28**(5), 542–546 (2015)
3. Kornegay, J.N.: The golden retriever model of Duchenne muscular dystrophy. Skelet Muscle **7**(9), 1–21 (2017)
4. European Medicines Agency (EMA): Committee for Medicinal Products for Human Use (CHMP). Guideline on the clinical investigation of medicinal products for the treatment of Duchenne and Becker muscular dystrophy (2015). http://www.ema.europa.eu/docs/en_GB/document_library/Scientific_guideline/2015/12/WC500199239.pdf. Last Accessed 4 Apr 2018
5. De Certaines, J.D., Larcher, T., Duda, D., Azzabou, N., Eliat, P.A.: Application of texture analysis to muscle MRI: 1-What kind of information should be expected from texture analysis? EPJ Nonlinear Biomed. Phys. **3**(3), 1–14 (2015)
6. Lerski, R.A., de Certaines, J.D., Duda, D., Klonowski, W., Yang, G.: Application of texture analysis to muscle MRI: 2 - technical recommendations. EPJ Nonlinear Biomed. Phys. **3**(2), 1–20 (2015)
7. Duda, D., Kretowski, M., Azzabou, N., de Certaines, J.D.: MRI texture analysis for differentiation between healthy and golden retriever muscular dystrophy dogs at different phases of disease evolution. In: Saeed, K., Homenda, W. (eds.) CISIM 2015. LNCS, vol. 9339, pp. 255–266. Springer, Cham (2015). https://doi.org/10.1007/978-3-319-24369-6_21
8. Haralick, R.M., Shanmugam, K., Dinstein, I.: Textural features for image classification. IEEE Trans. Syst. Man Cybern. SMC **3**(6), 610–621 (1973)
9. Galloway, M.M.: Texture analysis using gray level run lengths. Comput. Graph. Image Process. **4**(2), 172–179 (1975)
10. Chu, A., Sehgal, C.M., Greenleaf, J.F.: Use of gray value distribution of run lengths for texture analysis. Pattern Recognit. Lett. **11**(6), 415–419 (1990)
11. Albregtsen, F., Nielsen, B., Danielsen, H.E.: Adaptive gray level run length features from class distance matrices. In: Sanfeliu, A., Villanueva, J.J., Vanrell, M., Alqukzar, R., Crowley, J., Shirai, Y. (eds.) 15th International Conference on Pattern Recognition 2000, vol. 3, pp. 738–741. IEEE Press, Los Alamitos, CA, USA (2000)
12. Duda, D., Kretowski, M., Azzabou, N., de Certaines, J.D.: MRI texture-based classification of dystrophic muscles. A search for the most discriminative tissue descriptors. In: Saeed, K., Homenda, W. (eds.) CISIM 2016. LNCS, vol. 9842, pp. 116–128. Springer, Cham (2016). https://doi.org/10.1007/978-3-319-45378-1_11
13. Draminski, M., Rada-Iglesias, A., Enroth, S., Wadelius, C., Koronacki, J., Komorowski, J.: Monte Carlo feature selection for supervised classification. Bioinformatics **24**(1), 110–117 (2008)

14. Wang, J., Fan, Z., Vandenborne, K., Walter, G., Shiloh-Malawsky, Y.: A computerized MRI biomarker quantification scheme for a canine model of Duchenne muscular dystrophy. Int. J. Comput. Assist. Radiol. Surg. **8**(5), 763–774 (2013)
15. Fan, Z., Wang, J., Ahn, M., Shiloh-Malawsky, Y., Chahin, N.: Characteristics of magnetic resonance imaging biomarkers in a natural history study of golden retriever muscular dystrophy. Neuromuscul. Disord. **24**(2), 178–191 (2014)
16. Yang, G., Lalande, V., Chen, L., Azzabou, N., Larcher, T.: MRI texture analysis of GRMD dogs using orthogonal moments: a preliminary study. IRBM **36**(4), 213–219 (2015)
17. Vapnik, V.N.: The Nature of Statistical Learning Theory, 2nd edn. Springer, New York (2000). https://doi.org/10.1007/978-1-4757-3264-1
18. Thibaud, J.L., Azzabou, N., Barthelemy, I., Fleury, S., Cabrol, L.: Comprehensive longitudinal characterization of canine muscular dystrophy by serial NMR imaging of GRMD dogs. Neuromuscul. Disord. **22**(Suppl. 2), S85–S99 (2012)
19. Duda, D.: Medical image classification based on texture analysis. Ph.D. thesis, University of Rennes 1, Rennes, France (2009)
20. Weszka, J.S., Dyer, C.R., Rosenfeld, A.: A comparative study of texture measures for terrain classification. IEEE Trans. Syst. Man Cybern. **6**(4), 269–285 (1976)
21. Lerski, R., Straughan, K., Shad, L., Boyce, D., Bluml, S., Zuna, I.: MR image texture analysis - an approach to tissue characterization. Magn. Reson. Imaging **11**(6), 873–887 (1993)
22. Chen, E.L., Chung, P.C., Chen, C.L., Tsai, H.M., Chang, C.I.: An automatic diagnostic system for CT liver image classification. IEEE Trans. Biomed. Eng. **45**(6), 783–794 (1998)
23. Hall, M., Frank, E., Holmes, G., Pfahringer, B., Reutemann, P., Witten, I.H.: The WEKA data mining software: an update. SIGKDD Explor. **11**(1), 10–18 (2009)
24. Freund, Y., Shapire, R.: A decision-theoretic generalization of online learning and an application to boosting. J. Comput. Syst. Sci. **55**(1), 119–139 (1997)
25. C4.5: Programs for Machine Learning. Morgan Kaufmann, San Francisco, CA, USA (1993)

Tissue Recognition on Microscopic Images of Histological Sections Using Sequences of Zernike Moments

Aneta Górniak$^{(\boxtimes)}$ and Ewa Skubalska-Rafajłowicz

Wrocław University of Science and Technology, Wrocław, Poland
{aneta.gorniak,ewa.skubalska-rafajlowicz}@pwr.edu.pl

Abstract. In this paper, we propose an approach in microscopic image classification for histological sections of human tissues. The method is based on image descriptors composed of vectors of accumulated Zernike moments. The goal is to construct a robust and precise method of image recognition and classification that can be applied in the case of histological tissue samples. Thanks to their properties Zernike moments fit these requirements. Additionally, processed Zernike moments can be made scale, translation, and rotation invariant. In a series of experiments, we verify the effectiveness of the method and its application to the presented problem of medical image classification. The results are obtained with the help of predefined classifiers provided by dedicated software. The paper presents a comparison of results and proposes an example method of improving the approach.

Keywords: Image processing · Microscopic image · Image matching
Histological sections · Tissue images · Classification · Zernike moments

1 Introduction

Study of medical images is an expansive field of research that finds application in many disciplines like diagnosis, planning, treatment or monitoring disease progression [6]. The very domain of the subject varies on its own both in the sphere of image source material and image registration problems.

The subject of medical images vary. It covers images obtained in a CT scanning or MR imaging system, through a microscope survey and many more [2,11]. Obtained images can have different levels of complexity: from simple, little-detailed objects to very elaborate structures. Inherent qualities of medical subjects cause differences to occur in objects of the same nature or during the acquisition process. Distortions appearing during processing may result in different positioning of the object in the image through rotation, translation or scaling.

One category of medical images are histological sections. They provide useful information for diagnosis or the study of a pathology. They have numerous applications at both the microscopic and macroscopic levels. Histological sections are

© Springer Nature Switzerland AG 2018
K. Saeed and W. Homenda (Eds.): CISIM 2018, LNCS 11127, pp. 16–26, 2018.
https://doi.org/10.1007/978-3-319-99954-8_2

complex structures considered both on the morphology level and the phenotype of its constitute cells [8].

Problems concerning medical images often require complex and customized methods of solving; there is no common approach that would apply to all the cases. Depending on the goal the problems may pertain to classification, pattern matching, image registration and recognition, and many more.

Zernike moments and derivative Zernike-based image descriptors have the potential to be an easily-obtained method of image recognition.

Zernike moments do not carry redundant data because each Zernike moment contains a non-replicated piece of information from the image. This property allows for good control of the amount of information from the image we need to get processed. Due to their orthogonality, their invariants can be calculated independently of high orders without the need to recalculate low order invariants. Depending on the number of moments used we can obtain a generalized or a detailed image characteristic. These are some of the properties that make them suitable for image description. After further processing, Zernike moments can be made invariant to rotation, translation, and scaling. Their magnitude of the moment is rotation invariant. They can be made invariant to scaling in the process of mapping the image into the unit disk.

In [5] the Zernike and Orthogonal Fourier-Mellon (OFM) moments are used in representation and recognition of printed digits. The moments were chosen because of their invariance properties with scale, translation, and rotation. Zernike-based methods are used in geometry invariant texture [10] and object classification [1,4], image recognition [7].

This paper presents a method of microscopic image recognition and classification for histological sections of tissue samples. The basis of the method comprises Zernike moments. The proposed method creates image descriptors with accumulated sequences of Zernike moments. In this paper it is shown how well such descriptors can be used for image recognition of microscopic tissue samples. The method extrapolates on the previously presented paper on image classification with Zernike moments.

The paper is organized as follows. Section 2 contains the definitions of Zernike moments and Zernike polynomials and the necessary image transformations. Next Sect. 3 shows the application of Zernike moments to the proposed method of image description. Section 4 covers performed experiments and the discussion of obtained results. Finally, Sect. 5 contains a brief summary and conclusions.

2   Zernike Moments

Zernike polynomials are a finite set of complex radial polynomials that are orthogonal in a continuous fashion over the interior of the unit disk in the polar coordinate space [3,9]. Let $V_{nm}(\rho, \theta)$ be the Zernike polynomial of order n and repetition m defined as

$$V_{nm}(\rho, \theta) = R_{nm}(\rho) \exp{(jm\theta)} \qquad \rho \leq 1, \tag{1}$$

where R_{nm} is a polynomial orthogonal in the unit circle and ρ and θ are polar coordinates. The value of n is a positive integer and m is an integer that is subject to constraints

$$\begin{cases} |m| \leq n \\ (n - |m|)/2 \text{ is even.} \end{cases} \tag{2}$$

The orthogonal polynomial $R_{nm}(\rho)$ is given by

$$R_{nm}(\rho) = \sum_{s=0}^{(n-|m|)/2} (-1)^s \frac{(n-s)!}{s!(\frac{n+|m|}{2} - s)!(\frac{n-|m|}{2} - s)!} \rho^{n-2s}, \tag{3}$$

where $R_{nm}(\rho) = R_{n(-m)}(\rho)$.

Let $f(\rho, \theta)$ be the image intensity function stretched over the unit circle. The two-dimensional complex Zernike moment of order n and repetition m is defined as

$$A_{nm} = \frac{n+1}{\pi} \int_0^{2\pi} \int_0^1 f(\rho, \theta)[V_{nm}(\rho, \theta)]^* d\rho d\theta, \quad \rho \leq 1 \tag{4}$$

where $[V_{nm}(\rho, \theta)]^*$ is the complex conjugate of Zernike polynomial $V_{nm}(\rho, \theta)$ that follows $[V_{nm}(\rho, \theta)]^* = V_{n(-m)}(\rho, \theta)$.

A discrete two-dimensional Zernike moment of a computer digital image $f(x, y)$ is defined as [9]

$$A_{nm} = \frac{n+1}{\pi} \sum_x \sum_y f(x, y)[V_{nm}(x, y)]^*. \tag{5}$$

The discrete intensity function $f(x, y)$ needs to be converted from the Cartesian coordinate system into the polar coordinate system for further processing. The transformation follows

$$\begin{cases} \rho = \sqrt{x^2 + y^2} \\ \theta = \tan^{-1}(y/x). \end{cases} \tag{6}$$

We assume that the point of origin of $f(x, y)$ lays in the center of the image and that the area boundary of $f(x, y)$ is removed from the center symmetrically in every direction θ along the x and y -axis.

3   Image Description with Zernike Moments

In this section, we present an approach to image identification previously mentioned in [4]. The proposed method establishes image descriptors using sequences of accumulated Zernike moments. The assumption is that images representing similar objects will have similar image descriptors. It would potentially allow for identification, recognition or classification of these images.

The proposed image descriptors are constructed with sequences of accumulated Zernike moments. These sequences can be described by vectors of size

$n_{max} \times 1$, where n_{max} is the maximum order of the Zernike moments used in calculations. Each component of the vector contains the absolute accumulated value of all Zernike moments of order n, where $n = 1, \ldots, n_{max}$. Thus the image descriptor D is defined as

$$D = [Z_1 \ Z_2 \ \ldots \ Z_{n_{max}}]^{\mathrm{T}}, \tag{7}$$

where components Z_i are accumulated values of Zernike moment of the order i

$$Z_i = |\sum_j A_{ij}|. \tag{8}$$

To calculate the singular Zernike moment the formula from (5) was used.

Each vector component Z_i carries a different portion of image information. The information isn't repeated across Zernike moments and that notion propagates to the accumulated values. The module of the sum was introduced to make the descriptor rotation invariant.

The purpose of accumulating Zernike moments is the reduction of the amount of information without losing too much data quality. The solution allows for easier processing of the data. The descriptor retains some of the properties of original Zernike moments, but the reconstruction of the image from that form becomes impossible.

4   Experiments and Discussion

The proposed approach was tested for the problem of medical tissue classification. The problem, in this case, concerns histological samples of medical tissues. The goal is to classify this sample images into predefined classes using the Zernike moment descriptors. To verify the suitability of the proposed approach we perform a series of experiments that differ in parameters.

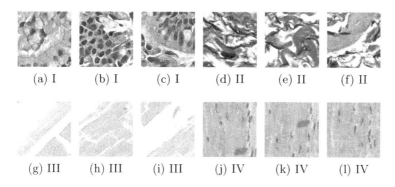

| (a) I | (b) I | (c) I | (d) II | (e) II | (f) II |

| (g) III | (h) III | (i) III | (j) IV | (k) IV | (l) IV |

Fig. 1. Sample images from microscopic image data: I - benign bronchial epithelium, II - normal visceral pleura of lung, III - anucleate striated muscle, IV - tendon.

The dataset used in experiments consists of microscopic histological samples (as seen in Fig. 1). Original images that served as base templates for samples were sourced from Wikimedia Commons under the CC-BY-SA-3.0 license. We derive four classes of tissues that are numbered in Roman numerals from I to IV. The class series consists of images depicting slices of tissues: I - benign bronchial epithelium, II - normal visceral pleura of a lung, III - anucleate striated muscle and IV - tendon. Series I and II represent sections of the human lung system. The data sets III and IV are sections of human skeletal muscles. The number of samples in a series varies. The actual numbers are 160 for class I, 105 - II, 168 - III and 145 - IV.

Images are written in grayscale format, where the pixel value ranges from 0 (black) to 1 (white). The images are not normalized. The original size of the sample image is 600×600 px. Sample images were resized to 120×120 px for the purposes of Zernike moment calculations.

Sample images from the data sets need to be preprocessed. For less time-consuming calculations images were resized to 120×120 px size. A series of Zernike moments has to be calculated for each image separately. In the experiment we set the maximum order of the Zernike moment to the value $n_{max} = 40$. The moment A_{nm} of order n and repetition m is calculated according to the definition from (5). The obtained sequence is further processed to get the image descriptor D (7). The vector of accumulated Zernike moments is calculated using the formula from (7) and presented as the image descriptor D.

In experiments we used the built-in classification tools provided by *Mathematica* software. The classifiers used to evaluate the proposed method were Random Forest (RF), Neural Network (NN), Naive Bayes (NB), Support Vector Machine (SVM), Nearest Neighbors (NNB) and Logistic Regression (LR). The methods require the creation of the training data sets that serve as templates for further image recognition and classification. The samples that are not used in training sets are put in testing sets that evaluate the method.

The evaluation criterion is the **classification error** - a scalar value that describes the percentage of samples classified into the correct class. Another form of assessment is the **classification matrix** that shows a graphic depiction of how the samples from the testing set are distributed across the classes. It's the graph of actual classes versus predicted classes and the number of samples that fall into each category.

We performed the test suit of 11 experiments numbered from 0 to 10. We modified parameters pertaining to the number of class and series used, and the size of the training dataset. The purpose of this modification was to have a more thorough picture of the method's capabilities. We also propose a way of improving the general classification parameters of the proposed method in the form of combining results from multiple classifiers in the form of majority voting.

Test 0. This experiment is performed on the complete dataset containing all the image classes, that is {I, II, III, IV}. The number of class is 4. The training set consists of 70% of the samples from each image series. The remaining samples were put in the testing set. This gives us the 70% to 30% ratio which is 112/48 samples for I, 73/32 - II, 118/50 - III and 102/43 - IV. The classification error for all methods is visible in Table 1 and the classification matrix for chosen methods is in Fig. 2.

Table 1. The classification error for *Test 0* to *Test 4* with different classifiers.

Test	RF	NN	NB	SVM	NNB	LR
Test 0	0.849711	0.867052	0.849711	0.901734	0.786127	0.820809
Test 1	0.955224	0.958955	0.955224	0.966418	0.902985	0.94403
Test 2	0.952	0.944	0.968	0.952	0.968	0.944
Test 3	0.964539	0.978723	0.971631	0.971631	0.964539	0.964539
Test 4	0.959538	0.982659	0.976879	0.976879	0.971098	0.959538

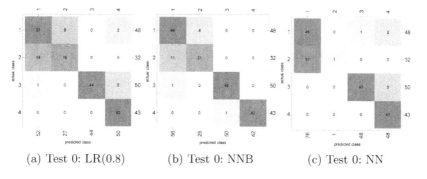

(a) Test 0: LR(0.8)   (b) Test 0: NNB   (c) Test 0: NN

Fig. 2. Graphic presentation of classifications results for chosen classifiers from *Test 0*. The number next to LR is the threshold level value used.

Test 1. This experiment is performed on the dataset consisting of the sample series {II, II, IV}. There are 3 classes. We excluded class I, because of its similarity to class II. We are testing whether the results improve. The size of the training dataset for all series is 50 samples. The remaining samples were put into respective training sets. The classification error is presented in Table 1 and the classification matrix in Fig. 3.

Test 2. In this experiment, we use the same dataset as in *Test 1* that is {II, III, IV}. There are 3 classes. The training set uses 70% of available samples and so for II it is 73, III - 118 and IV - 102. The remaining samples are put in the test set. The classification error for this setup is featured in Table 1.

Test 3. The dataset consists of the series {I, III, IV}. There are 3 classes. We excluded series II this time to see if the results improve. This experiment keeps using 70% of samples in the training set (the numbers are the same as in previous tests). The remaining samples are put in the test set. The classification error can be viewed in Table 1 and the classification matrix in Fig. 3.

Test 4. In this experiment, we join series I and II into one category since they both represent lung tissue. The data sets used are {I+II, III, IV} and there are

3 classes. The training set consists of 70% of samples from each dataset that is for I+II - 112+73, III - 118 and IV - 102. The remaining samples are put into the testing set. The classification error is shown in Table 1 and the classification matrix in Fig. 3.

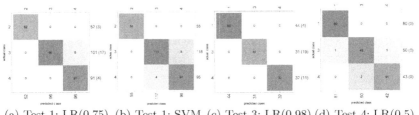

(a) Test 1: LR(0.75) (b) Test 1: SVM (c) Test 3: LR(0.98) (d) Test 4: LR(0.5)

Fig. 3. Graphic presentation of classifications results for chosen classifiers from *Test 1* to *Test 4*. The number next to LR is the threshold level value used.

Table 2. The classification error for *Test 5* to *Test 10* with different classifiers.

Test	RF	NN	NB	SVM	NNB	LR
Test 5	0.8	0.7375	0.7375	0.8	0.6125	0.7875
Test 6	0.747899	0.789916	0.756303	0.781513	0.756303	0.823529
Test 7	0.982659	0.988439	0.988439	0.99422	0.988439	0.99422
Test 8	0.849711	0.83237	0.803468	0.895954	0.820809	0.83237
Test 9	0.83237	0.878613	0.751445	0.919075	0.820809	0.867052
Test 10	0.953757	0.947977	0.82659	0.942197	0.971098	0.924855

Test 5. This experiment starts the series where we use only 2 classes. Its purpose is to evaluate how the method discriminates between similar groups of tissue. The dataset consists of series {I, II}, both series depict lung tissue. The size of the training set is 70% of samples out of each series: I - 112 and II - 73. The remaining samples are put into the testing set. The classification error is viewed in Table 2.

Test 6. This experiment uses the same dataset as in *Test 5*. There are 2 classes. As the training set we used 70% of samples from series II - 73, the training size of class I is also set to 73. The remaining samples are put into the testing set. The classification error is seen in Table 2, the classification matrix is in Fig. 4.

Test 7 The number of classes in this experiment is 2. The dataset consists of two pairs of series {I+II, III+IV}. We grouped separately lung tissue samples and skeletal muscles tissue samples. The size of the training set is the 70% out of each sample series. The remaining samples are put into the testing set. The classification error is shown in Table 2 and the classification matrix is in Fig. 4.

Test 8. The number of classes is 2. The dataset consists of all series grouped into 2 classes, where series I is a separate class and series II to IV are the second class. The dataset is {I, II+III+IV}. The size of the training dataset is 112 for I, 73 - II, 113 - III, 103 - IV. The remaining samples are put into the testing set. The classification error is in Table 2.

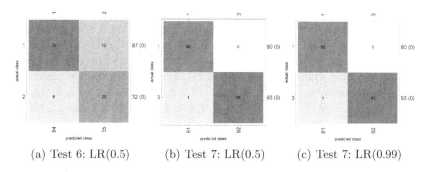

(a) Test 6: LR(0.5)   (b) Test 7: LR(0.5)   (c) Test 7: LR(0.99)

Fig. 4. Graphic presentation of classifications results for chosen classifiers from *Test 5* to *Test 10*. The number next to LR is the threshold level value used.

Test 9. This experiment is very similar to *Test 8*, but the dataset consists of series II forming a separate class and series I, III and IV making up the second class. The number of class is 2. The dataset is {II, I+III+IV}. The training set and the testing set are created analogically to the ones from *Test 8*. The classification error is in Table 2.

Test 10. This experiment is similar to the two previous ones (*Test 8* and *Test 9*). The separate class is series III, the remaining series composes the second class. The dataset is {III, I+II+IV}. The number of class is 2. The sizes of the training set and the test set are the same as in *Test 8* and *Test 9*. The classification error is in Table 2.

The classification error for the complete dataset from *Test 0* comes in the range from 0.79 (NNB) to 0.90 (SVM). Most often it is on the level of 0.84. That means that depending on the method from 21% to 10% of the test samples have been misclassified. The most commonly mistaken with each other are classes I and II. Both are sections of lung tissues.

As a result the next set of experiments (from *Test 1* to *Test 4*) investigates how these two classes influence the results and what the removal of one of them from the dataset causes. *Test 1* and *Test 2* have series I removed from the data sets (they differ in sizes of the training and test sets). The classification error in this case is between 0.94 (NN, LR) and 0.97 (NB, NNB) for *Test 2* (we omitted from the conclusion *Test 1* due to its small training set size). In *Test 3* we remove series II from the dataset. The value of classification error is 0.96 (RF, NNB, LR) to 0.98 (NN). For *Test 4*, where series I and II are merged into one class, the classification error is 0.96 (RF, LR) to 0.98 (NN). There is a very noticeable improvement of classification after some management of available classes. The classification error changed from the lower range of $0.79 - 0.90$ to $0.94 - 0.98$ in the modified data sets. The misclassification concerns only the $2 - 6\%$ of the test samples.

The next set of experiments is meant to evaluate how the proposed method differentiates between similar classes of tissue. For that in *Test 5* we focus only on series I and II. The classification error is between 0.61 (NNB) and 0.8 (RF, SVM). That is a very wide misclassification range where between the 20% to 39% of the test samples was classified incorrectly. *Test 6* contains similar parameters to *Test 5* and returns similar results; it is therefore omitted. In *Test 7* we pair up classes that come from the same category of tissues. Classes I and II containing lung sections are put into one class and classes III and IV containing skeletal muscle sections are put into a class of their own. This experiment tests how the method differentiates between two groups of tissue. The classification error is in the range from 0.98 (RF) to 0.99 (SVM, LR). The test results for differentiating within the same group of tissue are rather low: the percentage of samples classified correctly is between 20–39%. Differentiating between two groups of tissues yields much better results. The misclassification of test samples is between 1–2%.

The last set of experiments tests if the method can recognize one class out of the complete dataset. We performed this type of experiment for classes I (*Test 8*), II (*Test 9*), III (*Test 10*). The remaining classes make up the other category. The classification error for those tests is respectively 0.80 (NB) - 0.89 (SVM), 0.75 (NB) - 0.92 (SVM) and 0.83 (NB) - 0.97 (SVM). The results show that depending on the classifier the misclassification of samples can be minimized to a $3 - 11\%$ range. A class can be recognized in the worst case scenario with 75% accuracy and using the appropriate tools with 90% accuracy and above. Misclassification in the case of these tests comes from the interference of tissue coming from the same source (see the differentiation of lung tissue in *Test 5* and *Test 6*). If the tissues have a different source of origin as in the case of classifying groups of lung and skeletal muscle tissues, the misclassification is minuscule.

Table 3. The output of classification results for the test set of class I in *Test 0* and associated errors.

Classifier	Test samples of class I	Err
RF	1 1 1 1 1 1 1 1 1 2 1 1 1 2 1 1 1 2 1 1 1 1 1 1 1 1 1 1 1 1 1 1 1 1 1 1	0.9167
NN	1 1 2 1 1 1 1 1 1 1 2 1 1 2 1 1 1 1 1 1 1 1 1 1 1 1 1 1 1 1 2 2 1 1 1 1	0.8611
NNB	1 1 1 1 1 1 1 1 1 1 1 1 1 2 1 1 1 1 1 1 1 1 2 1 1 1 1 1 1 2 1 1 1 1 1 1	0.9167
SVM	1 1 1 1 1 1 1 1 1 1 1 1 1 2 1 1 1 1 1 1 1 1 2 1 1 1 1 1 1 2 1 1 1 1 1 1	0.9167
NB	1 1 1 1 1 1 1 1 4 1 1 1 1 1 1 1 1 1 1 1 1 1 1 1 1 1 1 1 1 3 1 1 1 1 1 1	0.9444
LR	1 1 2 1 1 1 1 1 1 2 2 1 1 2 1 1 1 2 1 2 2 1 1 1 1 1 1 1 1 1 2 1 1 1 1 1	0.7778
Multi	1 1 1 1 1 1 1 1 1 1 1 1 1 2 1 1 1 1 1 1 1 1 1 1 1 1 1 1 1 1 1 1 1 1 1 1	0.9722

The prediction powers of the featured approach may be increased. We propose combining outputs from multiple classifiers to create a single stronger classifier. The final classification result would be an outcome of the majority vote from all classifiers.

Table 4. The output of classification results for the test set of class II in *Test 0* and associated errors.

Classifier	Test samples of class II	Err
RF	2 1 2 2 2 2 1 1 2 1 1 2 1 1 2 1 1 1 2 1 2 2 2 1 2 2 1 1 1 1 2 1	0.4688
NN	1 2 2 2 2 2 2 1 2 2 2 2 1 1 2 1 1 1 2 2 2 2 2 2 2 2 2 1 1 1 1 2	0.6563
NNB	2 1 2 2 2 2 2 1 2 1 2 2 1 2 2 1 1 1 2 2 2 2 2 1 2 1 2 2 1 1 2 2	0.6563
SVM	2 2 2 2 2 2 1 1 2 1 2 2 1 2 2 1 1 1 2 2 2 2 2 2 2 2 1 1 1 1 2 2	0.6563
NB	1 1 1 1 1 1 1 1 1 1 1 1 1 1 1 1 1 1 1 1 1 1 1 1 2 1 1 1 1 1 1 1	0.0313
LR	1 2 2 2 2 2 2 2 2 1 2 2 2 1 2 1 1 1 2 1 2 2 2 1 2 2 1 1 1 1 1 1	0.5625
Multi	2 2 2 2 2 2 2 1 2 1 2 2 1 1 2 1 1 1 2 2 2 2 2 1 2 2 1 1 1 1 2 2	0.6250

This method was tested on *Test 0* that features the complete dataset and 4 classes of tissues. The results for classes I and II are shown in Tables 3 and 4 respectively. As seen in the case of class I an improvement is noted from 0.94 to 0.97 accurately classified samples. In the case of class II there was no noticeable improvement. The classification error for the fusion of classifiers is 0.62 while for the best classifier in the batch it is 0.66. This approach can be improved by excluding some of the more error-prone classifiers out of the voting process or ascribing weights to those votes according to their accuracy.

5   Conclusions

In the paper we presented an interesting approach to recognition and classification of histological images. The proposed method used vectors of accumulated Zernike moments as a means of image description. These descriptors served as image identifiers. While every image descriptor was of a different value, the descriptors within the same class were in the similar value range. Because of that, it was possible to identify and classify images from the same tissue class. To be certain that the measurements covered the widest range we used six different classifiers provided by Mathematics software and performed a diversified test suite.

As the results show in the majority of test cases the approach provides a satisfactory outcome that puts the results in the upper 90% range of correctly classified samples. The method is also easily scalable and can be applied in more complex classification methods as shown in the experiments with majority voting. This approach allowed also for boosting the overall effectiveness of Zernike-based image descriptors.

References

1. Athilakshm, R., Wahi, A.: Improving object classification using Zernike moment, radial cheybyshev moment based on square transform features: a comparative study. World Appl. Sci. J. **32**(7), 1226–1234 (2014). https://doi.org/10.5829/idosi. wasj.2014.32.07.21861
2. Sonka, M., Fitzpatrick, J.M.: Handbook of medical imaging, volume 2: medical image processing and analysis. In: SPIE-The International Society for Optical Engineering (2000)
3. Flusser, J., Suk, T., Zitova, B.: 2D and 3D Image Analysis by Moments. Wiley, New York (2017)
4. Górniak, A., Skubalska-Rafajłowicz, E.: Object classification using sequences of Zernike moments. In: Saeed, K., Homenda, W., Chaki, R. (eds.) CISIM 2017. LNCS, vol. 10244, pp. 99–109. Springer, Cham (2017). https://doi.org/10.1007/978-3-319-59105-6_9
5. Hew, P., Alder, M.: Zernike or Orthogonal Fourier-Mellon moments for representing and recognising printed digits. University of Western Australia, Department of Mathematics (1998)
6. Hill, D.L.G., Batchelor, P.G., Holden, M., Hawkes, D.J.: Medical image registration. Phys. Med. Biol. **46**(3), R1 (2001). https://doi.org/10.1088/0031-9155/46/3/201
7. Khotanzad, A., Hong, Y.H.: Invariant image recognition by Zernike moments. IEEE Trans. Pattern Anal. Mach. Intell. **12**(5), 489–497 (1990). https://doi.org/10.1109/34.55109
8. Ourselin, S., Roche, A., Subsol, G., Pennec, X., Ayache, N.: Reconstructing a 3D structure from serial histological sections. Image Vis. Comput. **19**(1–2), 25–31 (2001). https://doi.org/10.1016/S0262-8856(00)00052-4
9. Pawlak, M.: Image Analysis by Moments: Reconstruction and Computational Aspects. Oficyna Wydawnicza Politechniki Wrocławskiej, Wrocław (2006)
10. Wang, L., Healey, G.: Using Zernike moments for the illumination and geometry invariant classification of multispectral texture. IEEE Trans. Image Process. **7**(2), 196–203 (1998). https://doi.org/10.1109/83.660996
11. Zitova, B., Flusser, J.: Image registration methods: a survey. Image Vis. Comput. **21**(11), 977–1000 (2003). https://doi.org/10.1016/S0262-8856(03)00137-9

A Study of Friction Ridge Distortion Effect on Automated Fingerprint Identification System – Database Evaluation

Łukasz Hamera🆔 and Łukasz Więcław(✉)🆔

University of Bielsko-Biala, 2 Willowa Street, 43-309 Bielsko-Biala, Poland
lucas.hamera@gmail.com, lwieclaw@ath.bielsko.pl

Abstract. Fingerprint identification is an important part of forensic science (e.g. criminal investigations or identity verification). Friction ridge impressions left at the crime scene can be affected by the nonlinear distortion due to elasticity of the skin, pressure changes or finger movement during deposition. These deformations affect relative distances between fingerprint features such as minutiae point, ridge frequency and orientation, which eventually leads to difficulties in establishing a positive match between impressions of the same finger.

In this study we present preliminary results of the impact of fingerprint friction ridge distortion on NBIS Bozorth3 fingerprint matching algorithm. For this purpose special fingerprint database was developed. The database contained 5175 prints obtained from 40 volunteers. Experimental results reveal that the some types of fingerprint distortion (especially movement to right and left) impacts the recognition performance. The results of our studies can be used in future work on statistical friction ridge analysis and fingerprint algorithms robust to distortions.

Keywords: Fingerprint · Friction ridge · Deformation · Distortion
Database · AFIS · NBIS · Biometrics

1 Introduction

Fingerprint recognition is one of the most common used commercial biometric techniques and also play an important role in forensic science (criminal investigations). Like every other biometric techniques, fingerprint recognition system can work as verification or identification system. Typical automated fingerprint recognition process consists of three main steps [1]. First step is preprocessing, where fingerprint image is enhanced to reduce the background noise and improve clarity of ridge and furrow structures [2]. In the next step, fingerprint local features (typically minutiae) are extracted from the enhanced image [3]. Feature extraction methods are usually based on either: skeletonization and minutiae detection [4] or ridge following [5]. The last step is matching feature templates and calculating similarity score by analyzing relationships between features [6].

© Springer Nature Switzerland AG 2018
K. Saeed and W. Homenda (Eds.): CISIM 2018, LNCS 11127, pp. 27–36, 2018.
https://doi.org/10.1007/978-3-319-99954-8_3

Despite the advanced development of automatic fingerprint algorithms during the last two decades, there still exists demanding research problems, for instance, low quality fingerprints, partially overlapped images and plastic distortions or deformations [7].

Since fingerprint image enhancement is essential in fingerprint preprocess, the algorithms for detecting low quality fingerprints is also important. Most known fingerprint quality control software is NIST NFIQ package [8]. However, skin distortion, which is a very important factor, is not measured by NFIQ and only differences between plain, rolled and latent fingerprint matching were observed in technology evaluations conducted by NIST in studies on latent fingerprints [9].

Nonlinear distortions of fingerprint are introduced in contact-based fingerprint acquisition procedure where pressure is applied by flexible fingertip to flat surface. Since fingertips have an elastic nature and are also not flat, those distortions are unavoidable. Moreover, any finger movement during acquisition increase those distortions. As the direction of movement, pressure and friction with contact area can vary, the distortion is always different. Inconsistent distortion increases the intra-class variations (difference among fingerprints from the same finger) and thus leads to false non-matches [10]. To reduce the impact of inconsistent distortion, the finger should be always pressed in the same manner, with press force vertical to the contact area. Such comfortable conditions are typical for commercial areas, but forensic applications are characterized by diverse conditions. Therefore, deformations problem is more visible in latent prints. For reliable latent print identification, these non-linear distortions must be considered.

To handle the distortion most popular method is to use a proper tolerance threshold. For example, the following three types of strategies have been adopted [10]: (*i*) assume a global rigid transformation and use a tolerant box of fixed size [11] to compensate for distortion; (*ii*); describe elastic distortions by models and uses that to normalize the shape of the fingerprint [6]; (*iii*) only enforce constraint on distortion locally [12].

Ross et al. [13] developed an average deformation model based on minutia point correspondences [14] and ridge curves [15], which is utilized to distort the template fingerprint prior to matching step with an input fingerprint. Similar method was proposed by: Chen et al. [17] where also TPS model based on minutiae locations with orientation values was used, and Cappelli et al. [18] where plastic distortion model was introduced to simulate how fingerprint images are deformed. Cao et al. [16] proposed using finger placement direction and ridge compatibility, which is determined by the singular values of the affine matrix estimated by some matched minutiae and their associated ridges, to handle fingerprint distortions. Uz et al. [19] developed approach to account for within-class variations by template synthesis algorithm based on Delaunay triangulation. It constructs a super-template by combining minutiae from multiple impressions of the same finger in order to increase coverage area, restore missing and eliminate spurious minutiae. Singh [20] et al. developed an image correction method which uses deformation model. The algorithm is based on phase congruency information and locally minimizes the variations between two images. Jain and Watson et al. [21] proposed to use distortion-tolerant filters to build a composite filter of the finger, which significantly improve the performance of fingerprint correlation matching. Senior and Bolle [22] handle distortion by normalizing friction ridge density in the whole image to consistently map the fingerprint image into a new canonical representation. Finally, Dabouei et al. [23] proposed a approach to estimate distortion parameters from raw fingerprint images without computing the ridge frequency and orientation maps. A deep convolutional neural network is utilized to estimate distortion parameters of input samples.

In order to validate the methods mentioned above, researchers used sets of fingerprint images from NIST Special DB24 [24], FVC2000 [25], FVC2002 DB1 [26] and FVC2004 [27] databases. None of these databases was specially prepared for friction ridge distortion analysis and consequently images contained in them doesn't hold meta-information about type of distortion. Therefore, some researchers proposed to simulate distortion [28] by: (*i*) randomly remove certain number of minutiae; (ii) randomly replace certain number of minutiae; (*iii*) randomly disturb the locations and orientations of the minutiae; (*iv*) deform the images by use of templates. More recently, Si et al. [29] prepared Tsinghua Distorted Fingerprint database, which contains 640 images distorted in 10 different ways, grouped in pairs: plain and distorted fingerprint. Hence, it contains only 320 images of deformed fingerprints. In spite of all these databases, it remains a challenging problem to analyze distorted fingerprint with such insufficiency of research data.

The future aim of our work is to introduce new distorted fingerprint database. In this paper we conduct a study on preliminary version of fingerprint distortion database. The second goal was to evaluate this database on NBIS MINDTCT/Bozorth3 fingerprint matching algorithm [30].

The rest of the paper is structured as follows. In Sect. 2, we describe methods used to build database and types of distortions captured in the images. The details of the evaluation of this database with Bozorth3 algorithm are given in Sect. 3. Finally, we summarize the paper in Sects. 4 and 5.

2 Distorted Fingerprint Database

In this paper we present a preliminary study on building distorted fingerprint database. Final version of this database will be publicly available for researchers to develop and test new AFIS algorithms robust to friction ridge distortion effect.

2.1 Data Collection Methodology

The preliminary version of database is composed of 5175 images collected from 40 volunteers. All volunteers participating in the data acquisition have been provided with acquaintance regarding this research and an acceptance note has been obtained.

Every person were asked to submit a 10 fingerprint from each finger, where 2 imprints were plain (see Fig. 1a) and 8 were purposely distorted as shown below (see Fig. 1b-i). Plain fingerprints were created, by perpendicularly pressing the finger to the sensor surface, at the same time trying not to make any additional moves. Therefore, it was important that volunteer were in comfortable position. For the rest of images, the procedure assumed that the person which submits fingerprint purposely adds distortion, by graduated movement of finger, to achieve maximum degree of deformation. It was ascertained that each image has apparent fingerprint core. The sensor surface was consistently cleaned between acquisition of each imprint.

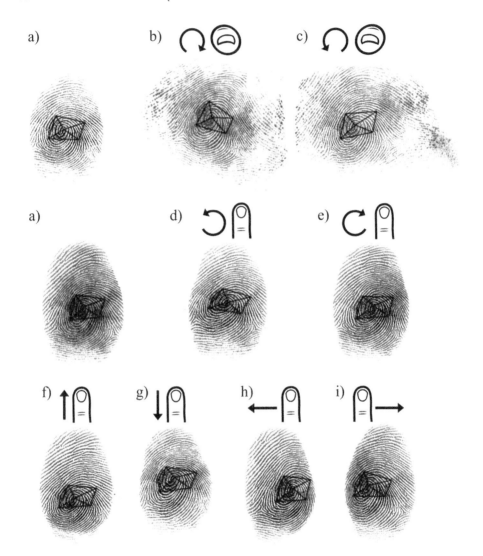

Fig. 1. Examples distorted fingerprints: (a) plain, (b) rolled to right, (c) rolled to left, (d) moved counterclockwise, (e) moved clockwise, (f) moved to top, (g) moved to bottom, (h) moved to left, (i) moved to right. To show a scale of deformation, five of the same feature points were connected by red line.

The fingerprints were collected from 40 volunteers aged 7 to 72 years old (68% male), where:

- half of the volunteers were between 13–50 years old;
- one-third of the volunteers were over 50 years old;
- one-six of the volunteers were under 13 years old;

2.2   Image Parameters

The database size is approximately 4,3 Gbytes and images are not compressed. Each image size is 800 × 750 pixels and has been scanned at 500ppi resolution, quantized to 256 levels of gray. All images were captured by Futronic FS60 fingerprint scanner, which is compliant with IQS IAFIS Appendix F [31].

All files have been saved preserving the following naming scheme: XXXX_YY_DT, where:

- XXXX – sequentially numbered ID of volunteer;
- YY – sequentially numbered ID of finger [thumb - little finger]: [01–05] – right hand, [06–10] – left hand;
- DT – type of distortion: *N* – plain, *RR* - rolled to right, *RL* - rolled to left, *CCW* - counterclockwise, *ACW* - clockwise, *TT* - moved to top, *TB* - moved to bottom, *TL* - moved to left, *TR* - moved to right;

The database is available on: http://fingerprint-recognition.org/.

3   Experimental Results

In this section, we evaluate the proposed distorted fingerprint database by performing matching with popular fingerprint software NBIS published by NIST [30]. To compute the performance values we have conducted the feature extraction process for all files using MINDTCT minutiae detector. Next, to compute the characteristics, we have compared every *xyt* minutiae template file with the others in database, using Bozorth3 matching algorithm.

Our results can be classified in four categories: (*i*) true positive: the query fingerprint template has been correctly matched to other fingerprint template from the same person; (*ii*) true negative: the query fingerprint template has been correctly rejected in comparison to fingerprint template from the other person; (*iii*) false positive: the query fingerprint template has been incorrectly matched to fingerprints from the other person; (*iv*) false negative: the query fingerprint template has been incorrectly rejected to fingerprint from the same person.

To compare the performance of matching algorithm for different distortion types the FAR, FRR and ROC curves were computed (see. Figs. 2 and 3). The results of EER levels were shown in Table 1.

Table 1. EERs estimated for different types of fingerprint distortion.

Distortion type	RL/RR	CCW	ACW	TT	TB	TL	TR
EER level	0,134	0,189	0,204	0,271	0,135	0,226	0,224

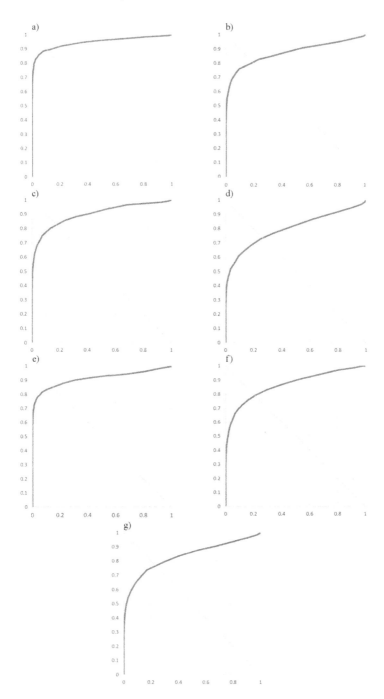

Fig. 2. The ROC curves computed for each distortion types, respectively: (a) *RL/RR*, (b) *CCW*, (c) *ACW*, (d) *TT*, (e) *TB*, (f) *TL*, (g) *TR*. (x-axis: FAR, y-axis: 1-FRR).

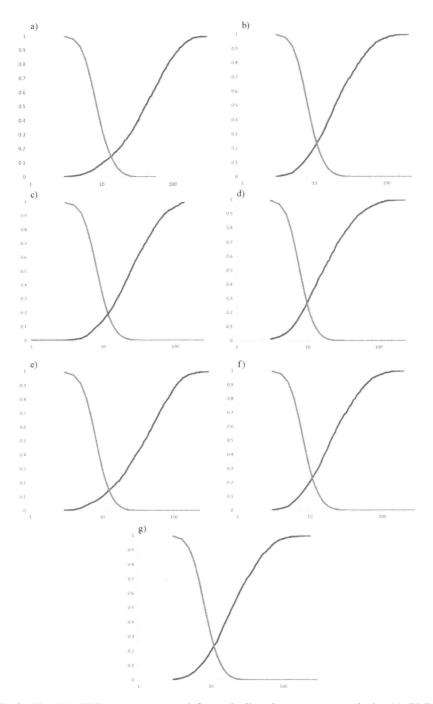

Fig. 3. The FAR/FRR curves computed for each distortion types, respectively: (a) *RL/RR*, (b) *CCW*, (c) *ACW*, (d) *TT*, (e) *TB*, (f) *TL*, (g) *TR*. (x-axis: threshold, y-axis: error rate).

As shown in the figures and Table 1, we can see that rolled prints provide the least EER level. This does not necessarily mean that it induces the least distortions level, because the large area of friction ridge allows to localize much higher number of minutiae points. It is also not possible that the entire surface of the rolled imprint is deformed. Therefore, there is a possibility that numerous minutiae points lies on a non-deformed part of image, what finally allows for effective identification.

Similar level of EER to the rolling imprints have the fingerprints deformed by moving to bottom (See Table 1 – *TB* column). This fact has not been noticed in any aforementioned publications. Such a low EER value may result from the lower elasticity of the finger skin during movement to bottom. Due to the fact that the fingers evolved to have a strong grip. Also during acquisition process it has been seen that skin is less elastic in that direction.

4   Conclusions

This paper described a preliminary study on building distorted fingerprint database. A major limitation of the existing database is lack of distortion type information or to small dataset which not allows to measure recognition accuracy with high confidence. The presented database can be used by other scientists to develop new, more robust to distortion, fingerprint matching algorithms.

We also investigated the distortion effects on fingerprint matching algorithm, which is conducted with openly available and popular NBIS software published by NIST [30]. The experimental results show that rolled and moved to bottom fingerprints has the least distortion influence on recognition rate.

From these results, it can be learned that the performance of fingerprint recognition system greatly depends on fingerprint distortion type.

5   Future Work

The most of future work is expected to be focused on final version of distorted friction ridge fingerprint database, where we want to:

- extend the number of distortion types by 8 new combined deformations (e.g. move to left and then to top);
- extend the number of plain fingerprint images, especially by images submitted with different pressure values;
- increase the number of volunteers to 120 persons;
- break down volunteer fingerprinting session to two distant in time session;
- separately evaluate the *rolled to left* and *rolled to right* distortion types;
- extract and verify fingerprint features on each image, including most minutiae types (not only simple bifurcation and ridge ending) and 3 level features;
- propose a new measurement and test metric to evaluate the amount of deformation of the friction ridge area.

As points mentioned above require a new acquisition procedure, we also plan to add to database:

- rotated plain images – to test the matching algorithms to robustness on image rotation;
- images of friction ridges located on tip of finger – which to date have not been included in the available fingerprint databases.

References

1. Porwik, P.: The modern techniques of latent fingerprint imaging. In: 2010 International Conference on Computer Information Systems and Industrial Management Applications (CISIM), Krackow, pp. 29–33 (2010)
2. Hong, L., Wan, Y., Jain, A.K.: Fingerprint image enhancement: algorithm and performance evaluation. IEEE Trans. Pattern Anal. Mach. Intell. **20**(8), 777–789 (1998)
3. Doroz, R., Wrobel, K., Porwik, P.: An accurate fingerprint reference point determination method based on curvature estimation of separated ridges. Int. J. Appl. Math. Comput. Sci. **28**(1), 209–225 (2018)
4. Surmacz, K., Saeed, K., Rapta, P.: An improved algorithm for feature extraction from a fingerprint fuzzy image. Opt. Appl. **43**(3), 515–527 (2013)
5. Maio, D., Maltoni, D.: Direct gray-scale minutiae detection in fingerprints. IEEE Trans. Pattern Anal. Mach. Intell. **19**(1), 27–40 (1997)
6. Chen, X., Tian, J., Yang, X., Zhang, Y.: An algorithm for distorted fingerprint matching based on local triangle feature set. IEEE Trans. Inf. Forensics Secur. **1**, 169–177 (2006)
7. Bazen, A., Gerez, S.: Fingerprint matching by thin-plate spline modelling of elastic deformations. Pattern Recogn. **36**, 1859–1867 (2003)
8. Tabassi, E., Wilson, C., Watson, C.: Fingerprint Image Quality. NISTIR 7151 (2004)
9. Dvornychenko, V.N., Garris, M.D.: Summary of NIST Latent Fingerprint Testing Workshop. NISTIR 7377 (2006)
10. Si, X., Feng, J., Zhou, J.: Detecting fingerprint distortion from a single image. In: Proceedings IEEE International Workshop Information Forensics Security, pp. 1–6 (2012)
11. Ratha, N.K., Karu, K., Chen, S., Jain, A.K.: A real-time matching system for large fingerprint databases. IEEE TPAMI **18**(8), 799–813 (1996)
12. Kovacs-Vajna, Z.M.: A fingerprint verification system based on triangular matching and dynamic time warping. IEEE TPAMI **22**(11), 1266–1276 (2000)
13. Ross, A., Shah, S., Shah, J.: Image versus feature mosaicking: a case study in fingerprints. In: Proceedings SPIE, pp. 620208-1– 620208-12 (2006)
14. Ross, A., Dass, S., Jain, A.K.: A deformable model for fingerprint matching. Pattern Recogn. **38**, 95–103 (2005)
15. Ross, A., Dass, S., Jain, A.K.: Fingerprint warping using ridge curve correspondences. IEEE Trans. Pattern Anal. Mach. Intell. **28**(1), 19–30 (2006)
16. Cao, K., Yang, X., Tao, X., Li, P., Zang, Y., Tian, J.: Combining features for distorted fingerprint matching. J. Netw. Comput. Appl. **33**, 258–267 (2010)
17. Chen, Y., Dass, D., Ross, A., Jain, A.K.: Fingerprint deformation models using minutiae locations and orientations. In: Proceedings IEEE Workshop on Applications of Computer Vision, pp. 150–155 (2005)

18. Cappelli, R., Maio, D., Maltoni, D.: Modelling plastic distortion in fingerprint images. In: Singh, S., Murshed, N., Kropatsch, W. (eds.) ICAPR 2001. LNCS, vol. 2013, pp. 371–378. Springer, Heidelberg (2001). https://doi.org/10.1007/3-540-44732-6_38

19. Uz, T., Bebis, G., Erol, A., Prabhakar, S.: Minutiae-based template synthesis and matching for fingerprint authentication. Comput. Vis. Image Underst., 979–992 (2009)

20. Singh, R., Vatsa, M., Noore, A.: Improving verification accuracy by synthesis of locally enhanced biometric images and deformable model. Sig. Process. **87**, 2746–2764 (2007)

21. Watson, C., Grother, P., Cassasent, D.: Distortion-tolerant filter for elastic-distorted fingerprint matching. In: Proceedings SPIE Optical Pattern Recognition, pp. 166–174 (2000)

22. Senior, A., Bolle, R.: Improved fingerprint matching by distortion removal. IEICE Trans. Inf. Syst. **84**(7), 825–831 (2001)

23. Dabouei, A., Kazemi, H., Iranmanesh, S.M., Dawson, J., Nasrabadi, N.M.: Fingerprint distortion rectification using deep convolutional neural networks. In: The 11th IAPR International Conference on Biometrics, CoRR abs/1801.01198 (2018)

24. Watson, C.I.: NIST Special Database 24 Digital Video of Live-Scan Fingerprint Data, U.S. National Institute of Standards and Technology (1998)

25. Maio, D., Maltoni, D., Cappelli, R., Wayman, J.L., Jain, A.K.: FVC2000: fingerprint verification competition. IEEE Trans. Pattern Anal. Mach. Intell. **24**(3), 402–412 (2002)

26. Maio, D., Maltoni, D., Cappelli, R., Wayman, J.L., Jain, A.K.: FVC2002: second fingerprint verification competition. In: Object Recognition Supported by User Interaction for Service Robots, vol. 3, pp. 811–814 (2002)

27. Maio, D., Maltoni, D., Cappelli, R., Wayman, J.L., Jain, A.K.: FVC2004: third fingerprint verification competition. In: Zhang, D., Jain, A.K. (eds.) ICBA 2004. LNCS, vol. 3072, pp. 1–7. Springer, Heidelberg (2004). https://doi.org/10.1007/978-3-540-25948-0_1

28. Gao, Q., Zhang, X.: A study of distortion effects on fingerprint matching. Comput. Sci. Eng. **2**(3), 37–42 (2012)

29. Si, X., Feng, J., Zhou, J., Luo, Y.: Detection and rectification of distorted fingerprints. IEEE Trans. Pattern Anal. Mach. Intell. **37**(3), 555–568 (2015)

30. Ko, K., Salamon, W.J.: NIST Biometric Image Software (NBIS) https://www.nist.gov/services-resources/software/nist-biometric-image-software-nbis. Accessed 29 Mar 2018

31. http://www.neurotechnology.com/fingerprint-scanner-futronic-fs60.html. Accessed 29 Mar 2018

Pattern Recognition Framework for Histological Slide Segmentation

Łukasz Jeleń[1]([envelope]), Michał Kulus[2], and Tomasz Jurek[3]

[1] Department of Computer Engineering, Wrocław University of Science and Technology, Wybrzeże Wyspiańskiego 27, 50-370 Wrocław, Poland
lukasz.jelen@pwr.edu.pl
[2] Histology and Embryology Division, Department of Human Morphology and Embryology, Wrocław Medical University, ul. Chałubińskiego 6a, 50-368 Wrocław, Poland
mkulus@gmail.com
[3] Department of Forensic Medicine, Wrocław Medical University, ul. J. Mikulicza–Radeckiego 4, 50-345 Wrocław, Poland
tomasz.jurek@umed.wroc.pl

Abstract. The venous system is similar in all people, but there are some individual variations. The system is well described and compared in the literature but it seems that there is a lack of comparison on the microscopic level. In this paper we present a segmentation framework for histological image segmentation that uses a clustering approach. The described framework can be used for further comparison of the venous system at the microscopic level. For that purpose we adopted a k–means and fuzzy c–means algorithms to classify image pixels to obtain vein segmentation. The presented results are promising and achieved partitioning can further be utilized for quantitative vein comparison.

Keywords: Movat · FCM Segmentation · KNN segmentation
Fuzzy c-means · k-means · Image processing
Computer aided diagnosis · Pattern Recognition · Histological slide

1 Introduction

The venous system is similar in all people, but there are some individual variations. In particular, the system of the cephalic and the basilic veins of the forearm show significant variations [3]. Three most common venous systems can be distinguished: M, N, Y, which dependent on the relative size of v. basilica and v. Cephalica. Type Y is considered the most efficient and most frequent among physically active people [8].

In literature we can find numerous thorough descriptions and comparisons of the venous systems [4,7,8], however to the best of our knowledge, there are no comparisons at the microscopic level.

© Springer Nature Switzerland AG 2018
K. Saeed and W. Homenda (Eds.): CISIM 2018, LNCS 11127, pp. 37–45, 2018.
https://doi.org/10.1007/978-3-319-99954-8_4

Basic histological observations and tools allow to determine only the thickness, volume and diameter of veins, although they can also differ in other parameters, impossible to measure by traditional methods. For better explanation of this issue, it is necessary to briefly determine the histological structure of blood vessels (see Sect. 1.1). To address this problem, in this paper, a pattern recognition approach to vein structure segmentation is described. The information about a color is used with an unsupervised clustering algorithms to provide segmentation that can be further used in analysis of individual variations of the venous system.

1.1 Histological Structure of Blood Vessels

The veins consist of three layers described as [10]:

– **tunica intima** – inner layer – consists of one layer of epithelial cells, a thin layer of connective tissue and elastic lamina (made of elastic fibers), which forms also the borders of the layer. Its total thickness is usually a few micrometers (which may drastically increase in pathologies such us varicose veins),
– **tunica media** – middle layer – consists of smooth muscle, collagen fibers and usually a small amount of elastic fibers. Its thickness changes strongly depending on the place of collection and on the individual. The external boundary of t. media is determined by a cluster of elastic fibers,
– **tunica adventitia** – outer layer – it is a connective tissue rich in collagen and elastic fibers.

It can be hypothesized that the percentage content of collagen fibers and muscles in t. media can vary in particular venous types. This can be well visualized with Movat staining, in which collagen fibers are stained in yellow, muscles in red, elastic fibers and cell nuclei in black [11].
Unfortunately, it is not possible to precisely define differences between percentage of these components by classical methods used today. For this reason, it was necessary to create framework that would allow the separation of individual vein layers and allowed to estimate the approximate content of muscles and collagen fibers.

2   Materials and Method

In this paper the focus is put on two pattern recognition clustering approaches for vein structure segmentation. This section describes a dataset, proposed framework and algorithms that were applied for the segmentation. That includes a fuzzy c-means and k-means clustering and segmentation based on entropy filter that was used for performance comparison.

2.1   Dataset

The dataset used in this study consists of 125 color images that where extracted form a Whole slide image of the Movat satined vein tissue. In Fig. 1 we provide a sample image from the database. The images were taken with the resolution of 2576×1932 pixels which corresponds to the viewing field under the 200x magnification on the light microscope. The images where saved in the RGB colorspace with DPI of 200 pixels per inch in analySIS 5.0 software provided by Olympus Soft Imaging Solutions.

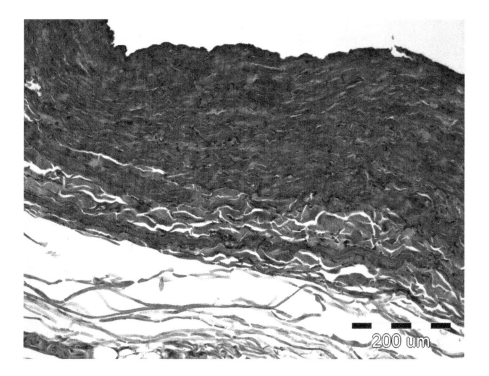

Fig. 1. Original Movat stained vein image.

The slides were prepared in the Department of Forensic Medicine in Wroclaw, where fragments of v. basilica and v. cephalica were taken from the deceased. Veins were fixed in 4% formaldehyde solution and prepared with standard histology methods [10]. Briefly, the fragments of fixed veins were dehydrated with several ethanol solutions with rising concentration, then immersed in xylene and embedded in paraffin. The paraffin block was cut into $6 \, \mu m$ sections, which were put on a basic slide and stained with a modified Movat method [12]. A histological cross–sections through the vein with stained connective tissue elements were obtained in this way.

2.2   The Proposed Framework

To perform segmentation of Movat stained vein slides we have implemented three segmentation frameworks according to the diagram in Fig. 2.

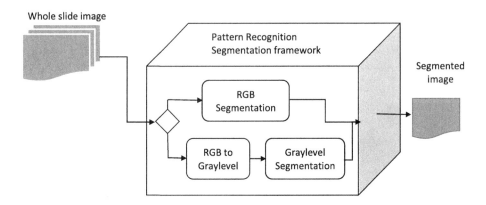

Fig. 2. Diagram of a proposed framework.

In the first step, a region from the histological whole slide scan was selected by an expert. The selected region was then provided as an entry point to a segmentation framework. For the color segmentation we have applied clustering methods and for the grayscale segmentation we have used an entropy-based segmentation, which required an image to be previously converted. After segmentation, the results are presented as an output image to a user.

2.3   K–means Segmentation

K–means is one of the simplest unsupervised learning algorithms that solves clustering problem. The algorithm's input parameter is only a number of input clusters k which needs to be known before clustering process can begin. The main idea is to define k centroids, one for each cluster, which should be placed in cunning way since k means is a heuristic algorithm and there is no guarantee that it will converge to global optimum. Next step is to take each point belonging to a given data set and associate it to the nearest centroid. When all of the points are assigned, the first step of the algorithm is completed and an initial grouping is done. Following procedure is to re-calculate k new centroids as centers of the groups calculated initially. After that we have new k centroids and the association procedure for all of the data needs to be repeated [9]. The consecutive steps of a generated loop make the k centroids change their location until convergence is reached. The aim of this algorithm is to minimize an objective function which is a squared error function (see Eq. 1).

$$J = \sum_{j=1}^{k}\sum_{i=1}^{n} ||x_i^j - c_j||^2, \tag{1}$$

where $||x_i^j - c_j||^2$ is a chosen distance measure between a data point x_i^j and the cluster centre, c_j is an indicator of the distance of the n data points from their respective cluster centers.

Here we use the RGB color distance between pixel and a mean cluster RGB color as a measure of distance. The initial clusters centroids are picked in random fashion. The segmentation result is picked as a cluster whose mean RGB value is the highest. After empirically testing different setting of clusters the conclusion was reached that the optimal number of clusters is 3. Higher value of k resulted in dispatching of a meaningful data, sometimes even creating holes inside nuclei or jagged groups. When using only 2 clusters, too much meaningless data was introduced into a segmented image and the result was not satisfactory. Three clusters are a trade-off between processing meaningless data and discarding potentially important information.

2.4   Fuzzy c–means Segmentation

Similarly, to k-means, a fuzzy c-means is a method of clustering but it allows one piece of data to belong to two or more clusters in a fuzzy logic fashion. In this algorithm each point has a degree of cluster membership rather than completely belonging to just one cluster as in the k-means segmentation. Because of that, it is possible that the points on the edge of the cluster belongs to the cluster in a lesser degree than those in the centre of it [1]. The method was developed by Dunn [5] and improved by Bezdek [2] and frequently used in pattern recognition. The objective of this algorithm is to minimize objective function given by Eq. 2.

$$J = \sum_{i=1}^{N}\sum_{j=1}^{C} u_{ij}^{m}||x_i - c_j||^2, \tag{2}$$

where m is any real number greater than 1, u_{ij} is the degree of membership of x_i in cluster j, x_i is the i–th dimension of the d–dimensional measured data, c_j is the d–dimension centre of the cluster and $|| * ||$ is any norm expressing the similarity between any measured data and the centre.

Fuzzy partitioning is carried out by iterative optimization of the objective function with update of membership u_{ij} and the cluster centers c_j. The iterations stops when the error of the result is lower than set accuracy, or the number of iterations already computed is higher than maximum number of iterations set. The parameters of the algorithm are: desired accuracy, maximum number of iterations, number of clusters, and m fuzzy parameter which controls how much weight is given to the closest centre and must be greater or equal to 1.

2.5   Entropy Based Segmentation

This segmentation method uses an entropy filter that measures relative changes of entropy within an image. We can define entropy to describe texture of the image as a measure of intensity randomness [6]. For a gray–scale image we can

define the intensity probability as a histogram of grey levels and the entropy
with Eq. 3, below.

$$E = - \sum_{k=0}^{255} P(h_k) \log(P(h_k)),$$ (3)

where $P(h_k)$ is a histogram count for intensity k.

Here we calculate entropy in a 9×9 neighborhood of a pixel to obtain entropy for
the entire input image (see Fig. 3). Based on the entropy filtered image we can
now discriminate between textures obtaining a desired segmentation as shown
in the result section.

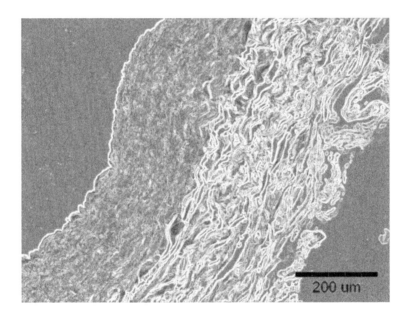

Fig. 3. Entropy filter output.

3   Results and Discussion

In this section segmentation results of the methods described in Sect. 2 are presented. The results consist of a set of images that are obtained after segmentation
and their correctness was visually compared.

Evaluation of segmentation's quality is very important. In literature one can
find numerous metrics used for that purpose. Unfortunately in most of the cases
they use a ground truth image for evaluation [13]. In medical imaging, obtaining
such an image is very difficult and therefore the segmentation results were verified
by an expert.

Fig. 4. K-means segmentation results, (a) algorithm output, (b) out superimposed on the original image.

In Fig. 4 one can see partition achieved with k–means algorithm. It can be noticed that the internal structures of a vain are correctly segmented providing a lot of details. Figure 4(a) shows a sample output of the algorithm while Fig. 4(b) shows the output superimposed on the original input image.

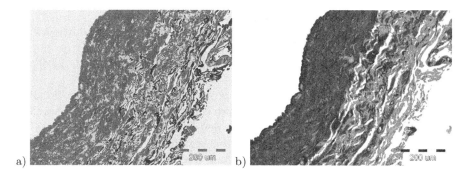

Fig. 5. Fuzzy c-means segmentation results, (a) algorithm output, (b) out superimposed on the original image

In Fig. 5 we have presented results of the c–means algorithm. Here, it is easy to see that these results are similar to those obtain with k–means. Here we can notice that fuzzy approach gave only a slightly better results providing a little more details. For this segmentation we present an output of the algorithm in Fig. 5(a) and in Fig. 5(b) this output was superimposed on the original image. Since the clustering segmentations are very precise and give similar results we have compared their running time. We have noticed that k–means was roughly 3 times faster than the fuzzy approach. Figure 6 presents results of the entropy-based segmentation. From this result we can see that the partitioning with entropy does not resemble all of the details, just roughly segmenting inner and outer parts of a vain. Same as previously Fig. 6(a) presents a segmentation output and Fig. 6(b) presents superposition of the output on the input image.

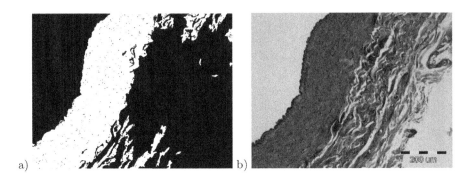

Fig. 6. Entropy based segmentation results, (a) algorithm output, (b) out superimposed on the original image

4   Conclusions and Final Remarks

In this work, we have compared three segmentation methods that can be used for the proposed Movat stained vein structure segmentation framework. The two clustering algorithms take a color information to perform a desired image partitioning and an entropy filter uses grayscale images.

As presented in Sect. 3, clustering methods outperformed segmentation with entropy filter. The latter could be used for rapid segmentation of the tunica media – the middle layer, but will not provide enough details for its in-depth analysis.

Better results where obtained with clustering algorithms, where more detailed segmentations were achieved. Out of the two compared methods fuzzy approach provided more details than popular k–means. Obtained results show that the difference between these methods are not that significant. In this case it is worth to look at the running time of each method. The processing time for a single image with k–means was about 20 s and fuzzy c–means took roughly 3 times as much time. Therefore, it is easy to draw a conclusion that a faster algorithm should be used for further research.

Furthermore, the presented results are promising and will allow for further investigation of the problem on a larger scale when taking into consideration the entire slide scan. In this paper we described a preliminary segmentation results and in the future we plan to modify the proposed framework to be able to quantify the ratio between layers of a vein in the Movat stained images.

References

1. Ahmed, M.N., Yamany, S.M., Mohamed, N., Faraga, A.A., Moriarty, T.: A modified fuzzy c-means algorithm for bias field estimation and segmentation of MRI data. IEEE Trans. Med. Imaging **21**, 193–199 (2002)
2. Bezdek, J.C.: Pattern Recognition with Fuzzy Objective Function Algorithms. Plenum Press, New York (1981)

3. Bochenek, A., Reicher, M.: Anatomia czowieka. Wydawnictwo Lekarskie PZWL, Warszawa (2012)
4. Bożiłow, W., Jarosińska, A., Kaźmierczak, L.: Z badań nad zróżnicowaniem połączeń powierzchownych żył przedniej okolicy łokciowej u osobników żywych. Rozpr Nauk AWF We Wrocławiu, vol. 13, pp. 109–124 (1977)
5. Dunn, J.C.: A fuzzy relative of the isodata process and its use in detecting compact well-separated clusters. J. Cybern. **3**, 32–57 (1973)
6. Gonzalez, R.C., Woods, R.E., Eddins, S.L.: Digital Image Processing Using MAT-LAB. Prentice Hall, Upper Saddle River (2003)
7. Gościcka, D., Flisiński, P.: żyły powierzchowne przedniej okolicy łokciowej u dzieci wiejskich. Przegląd Antropol, pp. 119–123 (1992)
8. Jasiński, R.: Morfofunkcjonalne czynniki różnicujące obraz zespoleń powierz-chownych żył kończyny górnej u człowieka. Studia i Monografie Akademii Wychowania Fizycznego we Wrocławiu z. 71. AWF, Wrocław (2004)
9. Kanungo, T., Mount, D.M., Netanyahu, N., Piatko, C., Silverman, R., Wu, A.Y.: An efficient k-means clustering algorithm: analysis and implementation. In: IEEE Conference on Computer Vision and Pattern Recognition, pp. 881–892 (2002)
10. Mescher, A.: Junqueira's Basic Histology: Text and Atlas, 13th edn. McGraw-Hill Education, New York (2013)
11. Movat, H.: Demonstration of all connective tissue elements in a single section; pentachrome stains. AMA Arch. Pathol. **60**, 289–295 (1955)
12. Russell, H.K.: A modification of Movat's pentachrome stain. Arch. Pathol. **94**, 187–191 (1972)
13. Taha, A.A., Hanbury, A., del Toro, O.A.J.: A formal method for selecting evalu-ation metrics for image segmentation. In: 2014 IEEE International Conference on Image Processing (ICIP), pp. 932–936, October 2014

Information System of Arterial Oscillography for Primary Diagnostics of Cardiovascular Diseases

Vasyl Martsenyuk[1](✉) ⓘ, Dmytro Vakulenko[2] ⓘ,
Ludmyla Vakulenko[3] ⓘ, Aleksandra Kłos-Witkowska[1] ⓘ,
and Oksana Kutakova[4] ⓘ

[1] Department of Computer Science and Automatics, University of Bielsko-Biala,
Bielsko-Biala, Poland
{vmartsenyuk,awitkowska}@ath.bielsko.pl
[2] Department of Medical Informatics, I.Horbachevsky Ternopil State
Medical University, Ternopil 46001, Ukraine
dmitro_v@ukr.net
[3] Ternopil Volodymyr Hnatiuk National Pedagogical University,
Ternopil, Ukraine
vakulenko3@ukr.net
[4] P. Shupyk National Medical Academy of Postgraduate Education,
Kiev, Ukraine
oksana.poshtackaya@gmail.com

Abstract. According to the World Health Organization, each year cardiovascular diseases (CVD) cause the death of 17.5 million people. Equipment used for oscillograms has great inertia and low sensitivity.

The authors have suggested morphological, temporal, spectral methods of analysis of arterial oscillograms. These methods were used to study the adaptive capacity of cardiovascular system to compression of blood vessels in arm during rest and application of 26 kinds of external influences.

Application of these ICT methods for arterial oscillogram analysis allows the physician expand information on: the state of the autonomic nervous and cardiovascular systems and centralization level of their activities management; activity and interaction of various parts of nervous system, heart and brain rhythms. They increase the information content on functional reserves and body adaptive ability to resist external influences, mechanisms and quality process of homeostasis maintaining, speed and quality of recovery processes herewith, pathological process dynamics and effectiveness of rehabilitation methods application. The suggested methods will be useful for general physicians, pediatricians, cardiologists, neurologists, researchers, in sports medicine.

Keywords: Arterial oscillogram · Functional state · Shoulder vessels
Heart · Level of regulation · Cardiovascular system · Circulatory system
Hilbert-Huang transform · Fourier transform

K. Saeed and W. Homenda (Eds.): CISIM 2018, LNCS 11127, pp. 46–56, 2018.
https://doi.org/10.1007/978-3-319-99954-8_5

1 Introduction

The implementation of modern ICT in health care practice makes it possible to improve prevention, diagnosis, early rehabilitation and treatment of cardiovascular system (CVS) [7]. According to the World Health Organization each year cardiovascular diseases (CVD) cause the death of 17.5 million persons; it is 31% of all deaths worldwide). High blood pressure is a major risk factor for heart attacks. The current instrumental diagnostics of CVS disorders by ultrasonic Doppler examination, ultrasound scanning and digital optical capillaroscopy, MR angiography, mathematical analysis of cardiac rhythm, Holter monitoring (and other methods) contribute to improving the diagnosis and treatment of CVS diseases. However, "rejuvenating" of vascular disorders that lead to profound disability, indicates that today there is an urgent need in fundamental studies on cardiovascular system, changes in cases of pathological conditions, effective technologies for early detection and treatment of vascular pathology [3].

Peripheral circulation factor was thoroughly studied by Yanovsky [9]. He has formulated the hypothesis of the existence of "peripheral heart" – active hemodynamic factor that helps the heart in its propulsive work. Saving the elasticity of arterial wall is an important element of harmonious functioning of heart and vessels [3, 11]. Without elastic tonetic characteristics of arterial wall response, heart as a pump would be 80 times bigger [12].

Peripheral blood flow has highly interindividual heterogeneity [10]. It may be different in the same person in the same vessel on both limbs in different states of a body [3]. Arterial oscillography is one of the most common and affordable methods of investigation of peripheral arterial system. If oscillogram reflects changes in the volume area of tissue under a compression sleeve, it will be a volume oscillometry [5]. The first oscilloscope was designed by Uskov (1934). This method consists of registering by an oscilloscope the pulse value fluctuations of arterial wall at different cuff pressure; the obtained curve reflects the amplitude of the artery wall stretching. The fundamental tool of this and following devices was a sensor that ensures the proportionality of the pressure output on both sides of recording membrane. Oscillogram recording was carried out by a recorder on a graded (mm Hg) paper [15].

The equipment that was used for oscillograms has a great inertia and low sensitivity. The complexity of traditional processing of oscillatory signals and lack of theoretical issues on the accuracy and reliability of blood pressure measurement, metrology hardware and software prevented the widespread implementation of oscillatory techniques in clinical practice. The use of electronic sphygmomanometer provides an opportunity to remove defects, extend the information on the process of blood pressure measurement [8, 15, 18]. The topical issue of the study is the need to improve existing [2, 4] and creating new information technologies of visualization and monitoring cardiovascular system functions (and peripheral vessels in particular) for physicians' temporal diagnostics and appropriate decisions making [19–21].

The aim of the research is to suggest new approach to cardiovascular system monitoring by analyzing arterial oscillogram by means of information computer technology (ICT); to substantiate the methods and criteria of morphological, temporal, spectral, cluster analysis of arterial oscillograms which are registered in the process of blood pressure measurement by electronic tonometer; to develop a structural scheme and web-based software environment.

2   Methods

Arterial oscillogram obtained using monitor of blood pressure and heart rate, which records the value of pressure pulse changes in cuff when measuring blood pressure and export information through an external interface of data exchange to personal computer. Further analysis of the obtained data and creating of arterial oscillogram was conducted by computer programs developed by the authors.

To analyze oscillograms the use of ICT for morphological, temporal, spectral, correlation and cluster analysis of oscillograms was offered [13]. Due to the absence of any researches on this subject, for temporal and spectral analysis of arterial oscillograms the information used in electrocardiography and electroencephalography was prepared; for morphological analysis they are in plethysmography and reography. Due to the lack of the necessary terminology we have used the terms that are used in the above mentioned methods.

For spectral analysis we used Fourier and Hilbert-Huang transform.

The results of our research are based on assessment during 2012–2017. 626 people which are volunteers were divided into 2 groups. The first group consisted of 580 healthy males (27%) and females (73%), aged 18–22 years, who study in the medical and pedagogical universities of Ternopil, Ukraine. Also from list of students, arterial oscillograms were recorded at rest and after Ruffier test at 68 healthy males (63%) and females (47%), aged 18–22 years.

The second group consisted of 46 patients with neurological syndrome of the cervical spine osteochondrosis (remission), who had undergone the rehabilitation at the Sanatorium of V. Hnatiuk Ternopi National Pedagogical University. Age was 43–70 years old. 79% were females, 21% were males. Disease duration was 3–10 years. Oscillograms were recorded before and after the procedure of massage of the back and neck area.

2680 oscillograms were registered and analyzed, including 2584 for the healthy individuals, 580 for the patients and 46 (92 oscillograms) patients with neurological syndrome of the cervical spine osteochondrosis (remission) [15]. The research was approved by the local Commission on Bioethics and performed due to the Patients' consent from each. The study protocol confirms to the ethical guidelines of the 1975 Declaration of Helsinki as reflected in a priori approval by the institution's human research committee. The obtained data was analyzed using standard statistical functions of the program Statistica 11. The degree of statistical significance of the studied indicators difference was determined by Student's T-test; in data analysis that was different from normal distribution law, Wilcoxon method was applied ($p < 0.05$ was considered statistically significant, 95%).

3   Results

The essence of oscillometric method is to register the values of pressure pulse of arterial wall in cuff, and the obtained curve reflects the process of air pumping in cuff and the effect of the vascular artery wall on cuff. The recorded oscillator signals thus, reflect the regulations of the processes occurring in the formation of blood vessels oscillograms under the influence of growing pressure in the cuff. The sequence of registration of arterial oscillograms is presented in Fig. 1 [15].

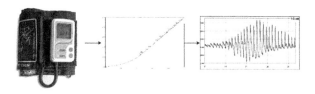

Fig. 1. Schematic sequence of arterial oscillograms registration: sphygmomanometer VAT 41-2 → interface window where the pressure curve reflects after being exported from the sphygmomanometer → arterial oscillogram.

Arterial oscillogram obtained without any constant increasing pressure component in cuff under compressor, is presented in Fig. 2.

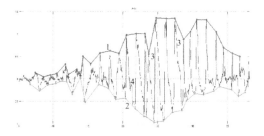

Fig. 2. Arterial vascular shoulder oscillogram obtained from pressure curve. 1 – the envelope of the oscillogram top, 2 – the envelope of the oscillogram bottom, 3 – oscillation that deviates from the top of the envelope oscillogram. 4 – dicrotic wave.

Note. This and the following figures of oscillograms on X axis shows the time of oscillogram registration (s) on the axis Y – value of pressure oscillations in cuff under the influence of artery vessel wall (mm Hg).

After an arterial oscillogram is selects we detects positive and negative extrema of pressure curve. Further extremes are manually adjusted.

The methods of analysis of oscillograms, we is offered here, are presented in Fig. 3.

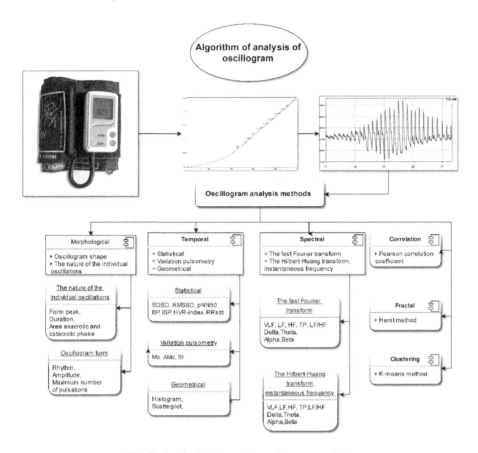

Fig. 3. Methods of arterial oscillogram analysis.

3.1   Morphological Analysis of Oscillograms

Morphological analysis of oscillograms enables visually assessing the oscillatory ability of shoulder vessels to counteract the increased compression of cuff when measuring blood pressure. The nature of pulsation makes it possible to evaluate vascular tone, heart activity, the state of the autonomic nervous system, blood pressure, neuro-reflex effects on the vessels state.

For the analysis of 1680 oscillograms the features, which are mentioned above, were combined in 8 groups according to the following criteria [15]: 1. The analysis of increase and decrease of ripple amplitude dynamic. 2. Quantitative evaluation of pulsations rhythm disturbances. 3. Quantitative evaluation of small pulsations at the beginning of compression (to achieve diastolic pressure) 4. The number of pulsations with irregular ripple amplitude increase. 5. The number of maximum ripple amplitude. 6. Visual analysis of forms of the upper pulsation extremes at the beginning of compression. 7. Evaluation of the dynamics of changes in the area of ascending pulsations. 8. Evaluation of the dynamics of changes in the area of descending part of pulsations [1, 2].

We suggested morphological criteria of oscillograms evaluation, defined standards of normal findings; developed the ICT methods of value oscillogram evaluation, differentiated 5 levels of deviations from the norm, which are compared with 5 types of health level gradation established in electrocardiography.

Morphological oscillogram analysis enables visual evaluation of vessels condition before compression and their oscillatory ability to counteract compression increase by the cuff when measuring blood pressure. The nature of pulsation will help the doctor to examine pulsation rhythm, cardiac function, and condition of the autonomic nervous system, blood pressure and neuro-reflex effects on the blood vessels state, differentiate functional and organic causes of changes in them. The use of the suggested morphological criteria of value oscillogram evaluation to estimate health condition will help the doctor make appropriate decisions both during primary examination, and for monitoring the effectiveness of treatment.

3.2   Analysis of Temporal Oscillograms

Temporal analysis was implemented by identifying and analyzing the length of intervals between peaks of pulsations in the process of growth of shoulder compression due to (pos) and minimum (neg) extremes. Evaluation of pulsations duration variability by the methods and indicators of statistical, geometric analysis and variation pulsometry adopted for assessment of electrocardio signals were used [5].

The following indicators were used: SDSD – standard deviation of the differences between adjacent normal extremes (ms); NN50 – the number of successive intervals (separately maximum and minimum), the difference between them is greater than 50 ms; pNN50 – the percentage of the number of R-R intervals pairs that differ by more than 50 ms, Mo (moda) – the range of the oscillations duration meanings that occur the most frequently (s); AMo (moda amplitude) – the number of intervals that correspond to the moda value (%); VS (variation scope) – the difference between maximum and minimum values of the duration of intervals between adjacent oscillations (c); Si – stress index (index of regulatory systems tension); ABI – autonomic balance index (conventional unit) VIR – vegetative index rate (conventional unit) VI – index of regulatory systems voltage (conventional unit) HRV-index – triangular index (conventional unit); RMSSD – square root of mean squares difference between adjacent extremes (ms), RR std – standard deviation between extremes (ms), power_osc_stdev – mean square deviation of amplitudes [17].

For temporal analysis and assessment of oscillograms indicators we managed to adapt the criteria and methods of ECG. They have determined their average value for healthy people. The congruence of some oscillogram indicators (Mo, AMo, RMSSD, pNN50, $p < 0.05$) and other research on heart rate variability (HRV) indicates their objectivity and confirms their informative value not only in heart work, in vessels as well; it also proves the same degree of participation of ANS in heart and peripheral vessels work. The absence of such links between other indicators makes it possible to predict their dependence on the resilient-elastic features of vascular wall and various neuro-reflex effects on vessels activity.

To study the condition of shoulder vessels the definition of standard deviation amplitude, area of anacrotic and catacrotic ripple phases, the ratio of length of anacrotic phase to the duration of the entire wave is justified. To evaluate the state of autonomic nervous system the use of histo-, scatter- and chaosgram has an informative value.

Temporal analysis of oscillograms allows to evaluate the condition of the autonomic nervous and cardiovascular systems and the level of centralization management of their activities, the state of peripheral vessels and their role in the hemodynamic disturbances, ways and quality of adaptation to external factors influence that help the doctor to diagnose timely and make appropriate decisions.

3.3   Spectral Analysis of Oscillogram

Spectral analysis of oscillograms allows evaluating the activity and interaction of various parts of the nervous system, heart and brain rhythms, peripheral vessels state, adaptive ability of the body to external factors in healthy and sick people. Their study and evaluation can provide reliable information about the dynamics of pathological process and effectiveness of rehabilitation methods.

To study and evaluate the spectrum power (the signal, but not intervals) of arterial oscillogram due to spectral analysis criteria of ECG [1, 5] the rapid Fourier transform from 0 Hz to 60 Hz was applied. The mentioned range was divided into 2 intervals ranges. The first range is 0.003 Hz–0.4 Hz (used in ECG): high (HF, 0.15–0.40 Hz); low (LF, 0.04–0.15 Hz), extremely low rate (VLF, 0.003–0.04 Hz), Total (TP < 0.40 Hz) and $k = LF /HF$. The second range is 0.4–60 Hz (used in electroencephalograph): 0.4 to 4 Hz (Delta), 4–8 Hz (Theta), 8–13 (Alpha), 13 Hz and more (beta waves) [6, 12, 14]. To study the mechanical activity of arterial wall in various phases of shoulder compression, except the fast Fourier transform, the instantaneous frequency from 0 Hz to 3 kHz and instantaneous phase (according to Hilbert-Huang transform) were evaluated.

To evaluate the power of arterial oscillogram spectrum except spectral analysis criteria of ECG (power in the range of 0.003–0.4 Hz). Also range from 0.4 to 50 Hz (used in EEG) were justified: 0.4 to 4 Hz (Delta), 4–8 (Theta), 8–13 Hz (Alpha), 13 Hz or more (beta waves). To determine the mechanical activity of the arterial wall in various phases of shoulder compression except fast Fourier transform, the use of the instantaneous frequency indicators (from 0 Hz to 3 kHz) and instantaneous phase obtained by Hilbert-Huang transform was suggested. Their objectivity was confirmed by correlation analysis method and conducted experiments [6, 14].

Information on temporal and spectral analysis of oscillograms obtained in the blood pressure measurement will help the doctor to diagnose peripheral vessels disorders. Depending on the gradation level of health it allows to plan preventive measures, to conduct early rehabilitation and to prevent progression of the pathological process. Using electronic sphygmomanometer and the software general practitioner (or any other user) can monitor the CVS state and peripheral vessels according to the suggested signs [1].

3.4   Application for Arterial Oscillograms Analysis

To improve methods of arterial oscillography a web-based software environment has been developed (see a structural scheme on Fig. 4).

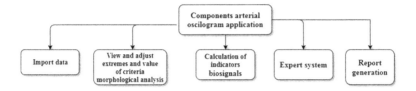

Fig. 4. Flowchart of the application for analysis of arterial oscillogram.

In Fig. 4 we present flowchart of the application for arterial oscillogram analysis. Data import provides the ability to download biosignals from the blood pressure monitor or from PC. The algorithm for calculation of positive and negative extrema of arterial oscillogram and value of criteria of morphological analysis with option of adjustment of result is developed. After adjustment of extremum temporal indicators are calculated and methods of spectral analysis are applied. In expert system there is analysed the value of indicator and the conclusion about state of patient is proposed. Report can include all necessary result for analysis of arterial oscilography in *.pdf or *.html format.

Web-based software environment for analysis of arterial oscillogram developed in Javascript language. It is presented at the url-addresses http://projects.tdmu.edu.ua/ InfSysPhyReh/ and http://projects.tdmu.edu.ua/ariada/#/login. Main page of interface is presented in Fig. 5.

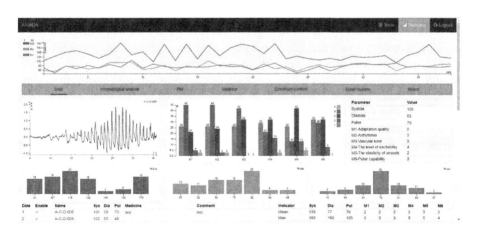

Fig. 5. Main page of interface of software for analysis of arterial oscillogram.

4 Discussion

So, the research results obtained by means of information technology analysis of arterial oscillogram coincide with the results obtained in the above mentioned studies that prove the reliability and informational content of the applied methods. They allow us estimating the state of cardiovascular and nervous systems, the role of autonomic nervous system and vascular state in neurological symptoms. The dynamics of these criteria allow to estimate efficiency of prescription and quality of the massage in order to correct them during the next procedures.

ICT of morphological, temporal, spectral, correlation and cluster analysis of oscillograms has been developed. An informative analysis of oscillograms criteria, criteria norms and averages and graded scales of deviations have been suggested. The studies, biological interpretation, methods of application and evaluation of the suggested methods are presented.

Unlike other, the suggested approach allows to get cheap, simple, rapid, objective, dynamic information during the procedure of blood pressure measurement. This refers primarily to the peripheral vessels state. Informational content and objectivity of the suggested technologies were approved by the detailed analysis of vessels of left and right shoulder, simultaneously registered electorcardio- and oscillogram; oscillograms recorded before and after exercise, massage and influence of others (26 kinds) factors.

Application of these ICT methods for arterial oscillogram analysis allows the physician expand information on: the state of the autonomic nervous and cardiovascular systems and centralization level of their activities management; activity and interaction of various parts of nervous system, heart and brain rhythms. They increase the information content on functional reserves and body adaptive ability to resist external influences, mechanisms and quality process of homeostasis maintaining, speed and quality of recovery processes herewith, pathological process dynamics [16] and effectiveness of rehabilitation methods application.

In addition, physicians will be able to expand information about the state of peripheral vessels, their role in preserving or violating of hemodynamics, neuro-reflex effects on blood vessels; differentiate organic and functional causes of changes in their condition, diagnose timely the state of pre-existing diseases. Physicians will get of new information to evaluate the ability of blood vessels pulsating dynamics: their adaptive capacity to estimate the increase in shoulder compression by cuff during the entire procedure of blood pressure measurement and its individual phases at rest after impact of external factors and rehabilitation.

This research made it possible to define that due to morphological analysis of 110 oscillograms of healthy persons only $8.9 \pm 0.2\%$ meets the norm criteria. Due to the health level gradation only $32.4 \pm 0.3\%$ oscillograms (coinciding with other researches) were evaluated as healthy and almost healthy, all other participants of the study need further examination, rehabilitation or treatment. According to blood vessels in healthy individuals after exercise, stress (Ruffier test) only in $21.2 \pm 1.4\%$ high adaptive capacity was registered, in $17.2 \pm 0.3\%$ functional nature of their disturbance was defined. Temporal, spectral, correlation analysis of oscillograms of 68 people registered before, after exercise stress and in 2 min of rest provided an opportunity to define ways to adapt to stress and homeostasis restoration. Use of ICT methods in patients with neurological syndromes of cervical spine osteochondrosis allows proving increased activity of sympathetic link of ANS and its significant decrease after massage.

So, the suggested information technology enables medical professionals to expand information on cardiovascular system of patients, promote early revealing of premorbid and donozological state and help to plan diagnostics and therapy. They will be useful for general practitioners, paediatricians, cardiologists, neurologists, researchers, in sports medicine.

References

1. Baevskyi, R.M., Berseneva, A.P.: Estimation of Adaptation Capabilities of the Organism, and the Risk of Disease. Meditsyna, Moscow (1997)
2. Baevskyi, R.M., Ivanov, G.G.: Variability of cardiac rhythm: theoretical aspects of application Clinical and Opportunity. Ultrason. Funct. Diagn. **3**, 106–127 (2001)
3. Caro, C.G.: The Mechanics of the Circulation. Cambridge University Press, London (2012). https://doi.org/10.1017/CBO9781139013406
4. Chashchin, A.B.: Use of biofeedback modern management methods of blood pressure (BP) and its control. News of SPbGETU «LETY», vol. 1, pp. 82–84 (2005)
5. Heart rate variability: standards of measurement, physiological interpretation and clinical use. Task Force of the European Society of Cardiology and the North American Society of Pacing and Electrophysiology. Circulation **93**(5), 1043–1065 (1996). https://doi.org/10.1161/01.CIR.93.5.1043
6. Rodgers, J., Lee, W.A.: Nicewander, Thirteen ways to look at the correlation coefficient. Am. Stat. **42**(1), 59–66 (1988). https://doi.org/10.1080/00031305.1988.10475524
7. Lushhyk, U.B., Novytsky, V.V.: Background of innovative medical requirements of modern information technology program media technologies on the example of diagnosis and correction of cardiovascular disease. Zaporozhye Med. J. **1**(76), 97–100 (2013)
8. Myhajlov, V.M.: Heart Rate Variability: The Experience of the Practical Application of the Method, Ivanovo, Ivan. gos. med. akademyia (2002)
9. Obrezan, A.G., Shunkevych, T.N.: The theory of "peripheral heart" Professor MV Yanovsky: classic and modern ideas. Vestn Sankt-Peterb un-ta **11**, 4–23 (2008)
10. Pedley, T.J.: The Fluid Mechanics of Large Blood Vessels. Cambridge University Press, London (1980). https://doi.org/10.1017/CBO9780511896996
11. Rogoza, A.N., Oshchepkova, E.V., Tsagareishvili, E.V., Gorieva, S.B.: Modern Non-Invasive Blood Pressure Measurement for the Diagnosis of Hypertension and Evaluating the Effectiveness of Antihypertensive Therapy: A Guide for Physicians. Medica, Moscow (2007)
12. Smyrnov, K.Y., Smyrnov, Y.A.: Development and research of methods of mathematical modeling and analysis of bioelectric signals, Research laboratory "Dynamics", Saint Petersburg (2001)
13. Martsenyuk, V.P., Vakulenko, D.V., Vakulenko, L.O.: Information technologies of studying of cardio-vascular system adaptation ability to physical loading according to morphological, temporal and spectral analysis of oscillograms. Med. Inf. Eng. 4, 36–43 (2015). ISSN: 1996-1960. https://doi.org/10.11603/mie.1996-1960.2015.4.5506. https://ojs.tdmu.edu.ua/index.php/here/article/view/5506/5059

14. Mintser, O.P., Vakulenko, D.V., Sirant, H.O., Misula, I.R., Bakalyuk, T.G.: Information technologies in the implementation of rehabilitation programs in elderly patients with primary gonarthrosis. Med. Inf. Eng. 4, 71–76 (2017). ISSN: 1996-1960. https://doi.org/10.11603/mie.1996-1960.2017.4.8468.   https://ojs.tdmu.edu.ua/index.php/here/article/view/8468/8009

15. Martsenyuk, V.P., Vakulenko, D.V., Selskyi, P.R.: Information system for physical (medical) rehabilitation. Med. Inf. Eng. 1, 90–91 (2016). ISSN: 1996-1960. https://doi.org/10.11603/mie.1996-1960.2016.1.5934.   https://ojs.tdmu.edu.ua/index.php/here/article/view/5934/5433

16. Marzeniuk, V.: Taking into account delay in the problem of immune protection of organism. Nonlinear Anal. Real World Appl. 2, 483–496 (2001). https://doi.org/10.1016/S1468-1218(01)00005-0

17. Martsenyuk, V.P., Vakulenko, D.V.: On model of interaction of cell elements at bone tissue remodeling. J. Autom. Inf. Sci. 39(3), 68–80 (2007). https://doi.org/10.1615/JAutomatInfScien.v39.i3.70

18. Vakulenko, D.V.: The use of information technology time method analysis of artery oscillograms for the study of adaptive mechanisms of the organism. J. Educ. Heal. Sport 5(9), 621–632 (2015). https://doi.org/10.5281/zenodo.31730

19. Martsenyuk, V.P.: On the problem of chemotherapy scheme search based on control theory. J. Autom. Inf. Sci. 35(1–4), 46–56 + 64 (2003)

20. Nakonechny, A.G., Marzeniuk, V.P.: Uncertainties in medical processes control. In: Lecture Notes in Economics and Mathematical Systems, vol. 581, pp. 185–192 (2006). https://doi.org/10.1007/3-540-35262-7_11

21. Martsenyu, V.P., Andrushchak, I.Y., Gvozdetska, I.S.: Qualitative analysis of the antineoplastic immunity system on the basis of a decision tree. Cybern. Syst. Anal. 51(3), 461–470 (2015). art. no. A013. https://doi.org/10.1007/s10559-015-9737-6

Deep Neural Network for Whole Slide Vein Segmentation

Bartosz Miselis[1], Michał Kulus[2], Tomasz Jurek[3], Andrzej Rusiecki[1],
and Łukasz Jeleń[1(✉)]

[1] Department of Computer Engineering, Wrocław University of Science
and Technology, Wybrzeże Wyspiańskiego 27, 50-370 Wrocław, Poland
bartosz.miselis@gmail.com,{andrzej.rusiecki,lukasz.jelen}@pwr.edu.pl
[2] Histology and Embryology Division, Department of Human Morphology
and Embryology, Wrocław Medical University, ul. Chałubińskiego 6a,
50-368 Wrocław, Poland
mkulus@gmail.com
[3] Department of Forensic Medicine, Wrocław Medical University, ul. J.
Mikulicza–Radeckiego 4, 50-345 Wrocław, Poland
tomasz.jurek@umed.wroc.pl

Abstract. Semantic segmentation of medical images is an area of active
research all over the world. It can dramatically improve accuracy and efficiency of diagnosis if used properly. High reliability of potential solutions
is required to support specialists. In this work we introduce a novel solution to perform pixelwise segmentation of vein preparations dyed with
movat stain. Our proposed deep convolutional neural network achieves
the accuracy of 89%.

Keywords: Movat · Deep neural networks · Deep learning
Whole slide segmentation · Image processing
Computer aided diagnosis

1 Introduction

Recent years have brought completely new, previously unreachable quality in
deep learning, especially in the field of computer vision [7,15]. Not only does
it allow to perform human-level classification of objects in the scene (like cars,
trees, pedestrians, animals), but also to split the image into semantically coherent
fragments (see [3,6]) Such action is called *segmentation*. Exploiting its potential
in medicine is the aim of numerous researchers all over the world, mainly for the
analysis of histological preparations, scans from magnetic resonance imaging,
X-rays and ultrasonography.

In the field of patomorphology, opportunities are being explored to improve
on activities that are very time-consuming for humans (like examining fragments
of tissues under the microscope) by supporting the analysis with learning algorithms. It is worth noting that the aim is not to replace the human factor, but

© Springer Nature Switzerland AG 2018
K. Saeed and W. Homenda (Eds.): CISIM 2018, LNCS 11127, pp. 57–67, 2018.
https://doi.org/10.1007/978-3-319-99954-8_6

rather to create cooperation between a specialist and an algorithm, carried out in such a way that it is possible to perform high quality analysis of more histological preparations, which would have a measurable impact on patients' benefit. [4] presented the idea of systems supporting doctors in faster and more effective diagnosis, providing better response to detected abnormalities.

Another application of this type of algorithms in medicine is, bringing a more specific example, segmentation of microscopic scans containing veins' cross-sections. The target is the identification of specific layers from which they are built. Such segmentation is the subject of this paper. We created a deep convolutional encoder-decoder network to check its potential in performing pixelwise tissue segmentation.

2   Related Work

Classical segmentation approaches based on deep neural networks were presented by [5, 10] and [16]. In [5] authors used ten-layer convolutional network, which classifies an individual pixel as a neuronal membrane, or a non-neuronal membrane, based on pure probabilities. Wang *et al.* in [16] used a deep neural network to segment medical slides, firstly by dividing them into 256×256 tiles, then assigning a healthy/tumor label to each. Such fragments enter the network, which outputs probability of specific tile being a tumor. Next, single results are merged to produce global probability heat map. As described in [10], Liu *et al.* build upon that solution. In order to balance the data in the training set, a number of dataset expansion methods were introduced (such as 90° rotation, reflection, multiple rotation and color distortion). Expansion was necessary due to the fact that tumors constituted only a small percentage of all analyzed slide samples (median was 2% content).

Another approach to the problem of pixel-wise segmentation is to use fully convolutional networks (FCNs). In [11], Long *et al.* presented the architecture that is able to combine general, high layer information with detailed, low layer information. This way network produces pixel-wise segmentation maps without the necessity to use dense layers. Resulting architecture contains far less parameters, thus having dramatically lower memory footprint.

After the introduction of FCNs multiple ideas emerged, one of them particularly interesting in the area of semantic segmentation — encoder-decoder architecture. The concept standing behind it is that the network is built from two paths: first one is called *contracting* and the second one *expansive*. Contraction of the image generates features that are then upsampled in an expansive path to produce multi-class segmentation map.

Decoders described by Badrinarayanan *et al.* use pooling indices computed in the max-pooling step of the corresponding encoder to perform upsampling [2]. This simplifies training by not requiring learning how to upsample.

According to the description in [12] authors based their solution on an idea that one should not assume that pooling indices are the best way to perform upsampling. The network could learn how to upsample by itself, hence the requirement to create *transposed convolution* layer that could do it.

Ronneberger *et al.* [13] have built FCN based on the concept presented by Long *et al.* in [11]. The main difference, however, is that the network does not produce a single output value of probability that the pixel belongs to a class — the result is a multi-channel image. Each channel is a separate grayscale –image, containing values representing the probability with which a specific pixel belongs to a given class.

We decided to adapt a solution presented by [13] with modifications described in Sect. 4.1.

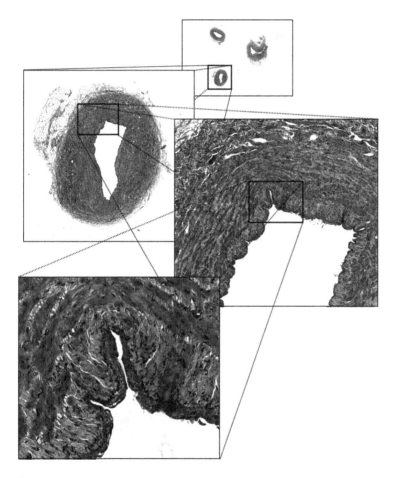

Fig. 1. Illustration of a MIRAX format. From the top down a subsequent fragments of the whole slide zoom levels are presented.

3   Dataset

Dataset consists of training examples (high resolution slide cut-outs) and ground-truth labels (output segmentation maps). Sample pair is shown in Fig. 2. Raw data are MIRAX slides (see Fig. 1) with resolution of 40000 × 50000 pixels. To pass these data into the network it is necessary to divide it into smaller tiles (e.g. 512 × 512) that can be processed.

3.1   MIRAX Format

MIRAX slide is built from multiple layers. This fact makes it possible to preview it in a very efficient way. First layer contains raw data from the microscope. To compute second layer, fragments from first layer are upsampled and merged, forming single tile that contains more general view of raw data. Multiple layers with details of different resolution results in smooth preview, allowing for quick zooming in and out without any delays.

3.2   Dataset Augmentation

Tiling resulted in 17677 image-label pairs. The analysis of what exactly is in the dataset revealed that the fraction of fragments containing relevant data (such as parts of a preparation) is relatively low when compared to tiles completely covered with background. To perform such analysis we generated features for each label, which contained the information what the coverage of a specific class in this specific tile is. Sample result is shown in Fig. 3.

There are at least several methods that one can choose to artificially balance the dataset (i.e. to make classes' distributions closer to each other by ensuring that each class has sufficient amount of samples):

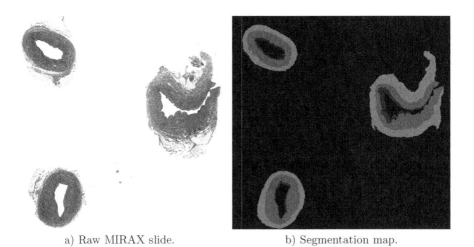

a) Raw MIRAX slide.   b) Segmentation map.

Fig. 2. Raw image with corresponding labels.

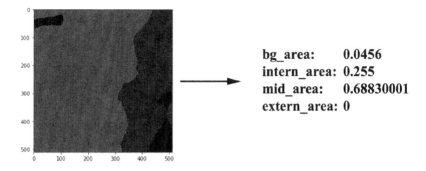

bg_area: 0.0456
intern_area: 0.255
mid_area: 0.68830001
extern_area: 0

Fig. 3. Sample results of color coverage calculation.

- removal of the redundant samples that make specific class too numerous,
- increase number of samples from under-represented class by using simple affine transformations like rotations or mirroring,
- dataset augmentation with elastic distortions.

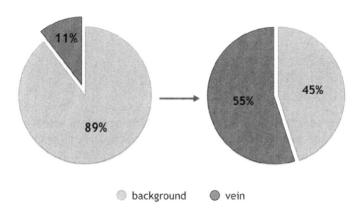

Fig. 4. Dataset before and after augmentation.

First method is very primitive, which of course balances classes' distributions, but reduces number of available information. Hence, it is not recommended.

Second method is applied relatively frequently mainly due to its simplicity and effectiveness.

The third one is the most sophisticated method and can provide valuable output, especially when working with biological data. Main fact that makes it suitable for tissues' images is that elastic distortions mimic, in some way, the organic nature of the content. Elastically distorting slide produces new data that models cell's alternative position. As a result, one can artificially increase number of the information without causing the network to overfit (distorted images are not just a rotated version of the same slide but are rather treated by the network as entirely new ones).

Since our work involves biological data, we have decided to use elastic distortions method.

3.3   Elastic Distortions

A distorting method was applied to increase the amount of valuable information in the dataset. Elastic distortions idea comes from [14]. It is worth highlighting that pairs have to be deformed by exactly the same transformation, otherwise the network would learn from false information (pixels from the distorted image would not correspond to the ones from the label). Strength of distortions can be regulated using random seed, which in our implementation serves as a base for transformation map generation. Such approach is very convenient since, when the necessity emerges, one can replicate previously applied distortion just by looking at random seed value.

We have chosen all the tiles, that contained less than or equal to 50% of background (in our dataset there were 1291 of them) and applied 15 various distortions to each of the images. Augmentation resulted in 18074 new images. To distort each tile, it took 1.6 s, so the overall process lasted approximately 8.5 h. Content in the dataset from semantic perspective can be seen in Fig. 4.

4   Methods

4.1   Base: U-Net

The inspiration for creating a deep neural network capable of achieving satisfactory results in the segmentation of medical images is U-net, presented by [13]. Looking at the schema of it (Fig. 5) one can easily separate it into two halves: left one is called *contracting* path, while the right one is called *expansive* path. It is build out of simple blocks. To contract, successive convolution → convolution → max-pooling is done. To expand, successive transposed convolution → concatenation → convolution → convolution is done. Concatenation's task is to merge corresponding information from contracting and expansive paths to form unique features that can be used to perform effective semantic segmentation.

4.2   Architectural Improvements

To concatenate the information from encoding and decoding paths, original U-net requires cropping of several layers in order to make the dimensions match. The requirement origins from the fact, that correct calculation of the convolutions for pixels on the edges of the image results in losing one pixel along each side. We propose a better solution: each convolutional layer should use zero-padding to keep the dimensions of the image between convolutions constant.

There are several advantages of such approach:

- the image dimensions change only during max-pooling and upsampling operations,
- it is easier to integrate the results from the encoding and decoding parts – the corresponding layers have identical dimensions,
- information on the edges is not lost.

Second improvement (not mentioned in [13]) was to the usage of batch normalization layer after convolutional layer and before activation. Resulting blocks are as follows: convolution → batch normalization → ReLU activation. Thanks to this layer it is possible to use higher learning rates without the risk that training process will diverge. Batch normalization reduces internal covariate shift, understood as the gradual degeneration of internal inputs' distributions (see [8] for explanation).

The most important fact we had to consider was that our dataset was relatively small (below 100000 samples). In TensorFlow's implementation of batch normalization layer, there is a parameter called *decay* (interpreted as momentum responsible for adding inertia to moments' convergence). By default its value is set to 0.999 that is not suitable for small datasets. Thus, we decided to reduce it to 0.9 that worked well with the dataset's size of the order of 10000.

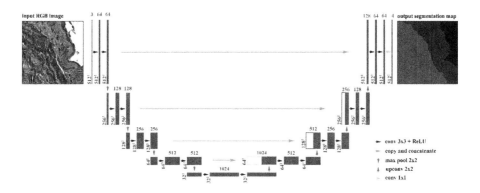

Fig. 5. Modified U-net network structure.

4.3 Dataset Generation

To generate the dataset from raw MIRAX data, several steps had to be performed:

1. Convert MIRAX slide to TIFF format.
2. Load TIFF into Python environment.
3. Divide the image into 512 × 512 tiles.
4. Calculate color coverage features to have an insight into the data.
5. Analyze the data using color features.

6. Augment the data with elastic distortions to balance classes (there was a problem that only 10% of the tiles contained valuable content that wasn't pure background).
7. Analyze the data once more to ensure that everything is ready to be divided into subsets.
8. Divide tiles into train, validation and test subsets (keeping in mind that each and every one of them should be a representative subset of the whole dataset by containing not only the tiles with pure background, but also with parts of the vein's layers).
9. Shuffle tiles inside train, validation and test subsets to provide randomness and learning time.
10. Write the data into TFRecord file (TensorFlow alternative for HDF files that works very efficiently).

After all these steps have been carefully taken, network could be fed with the data stored in TFRecord files.

4.4   Training Process

Training process was done using TensorFlow framework [1]. To get the results presented in this article, we let the network learn for 42 epochs (approximately 60 h of continuous learning on GTX 1080Ti GPU). The decision was made not to use pre-trained U-net network — we wanted it to learn from scratch. Several details were essential to carry out the learning process in an effective way. The first one was the choice of optimizer. We used Adam [9] with the learning rate empirically found to be 0.016. Second most important fact was the usage of batch normalization and ReLU activations both with standard convolutions and transposed convolutions. The order of layers was as follows: convolution $\rightarrow$ batch normalization $\rightarrow$ ReLU. Batch of size 8 was used.

4.5   Error Measurement

Ronneberger *et al.* in [13] propose to apply softmax layer at the end of the network, which produces normalized probabilities. After softmax, in order to find error for the entire output, pixelwise cross-entropy (xent) is calculated. These operations can be written as a single formula:

$$L_{ij} = -\log\left(\frac{e^{f_{y_{ij}}}}{\sum_j e^{f_j}}\right), \tag{1}$$

where L_i indicates an error resulting from xent, $f_{y_{ij}}$ is an element from the output array of the network for which xent is currently calculated, and $\frac{e^{f_{y_{ij}}}}{\sum_j e^{f_j}}$ is the value of the softmax function for that element.

5   Results

Metric used to measure network's accuracy is relatively simple: how many pixels were correctly classified with regard to the overall amount of pixels in segmented image. The overall accuracy is understood as an average accuracy on a test set of 7400 images. Our best solution achieves the accuracy of 89% (see Fig. 6 for details).

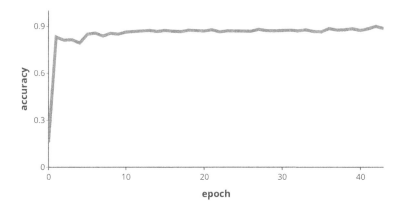

Fig. 6. Validation accuracy curve.

Looking at Fig. 7 several facts are worth noticing: network is able to learn what should be treated as a background (even when it is vein's epithelium), although there is some space for further improvements. Both outer and middle layers (light and dark pink color on a segmentation map) are segmented relatively well, compared with the inner layer (purple one, closest to the vein's interior). Output was created by merging multiple tiles. Segmentation of the image with a resolution of 15184 × 15184 pixels took 2 min (on GTX 1080Ti GPU).

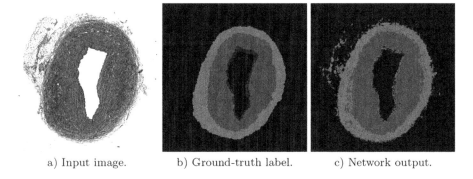

a) Input image.   b) Ground-truth label.   c) Network output.

Fig. 7. Comparison of the output result with the ground-truth label. (Color figure online)

6   Conclusions and Future Work

The main goal of the research was to create a deep neural network that would be able to segment histological images, marking specific layers of veins in microscopic images. Building upon U-net network architecture, a couple of modifications (zero-padding, batch normalization) were performed to increase model's precision.

Zero-padding prevented the loss of information on the edges of the segmented slide. Batch normalization made the model more resistant to the diversity of input data through normalization of the data inside the network.

6.1   Future Research

Proposed solution is highly flexible – network is not strictly bounded to the problem from this article. It would be possible to parametrize its structure to achieve higher generality level and work e.g. in varied situations.

In order to check further potential, we plan to increase size of the dataset by annotating more data with the support of specialist.

Here we focused mainly on the design and implementation of the algorithm itself. In the future we plan to create an application that would guide the specialist through the whole pipeline – from loading MIRAX slide, tiling, segmentation and displaying results. Such application would make proposed solution more intuitive and useful in practice by possibility to really affect specialist's day-to-day work.

Acknowledgements. Images used in this study are a courtesy of the Histology and Embryology Division, Department of Human Morphology and Embryology, Wroclaw Medical University, Wroclaw, Poland.

References

1. Abadi, M., et al.: TensorFlow: large-scale machine learning on heterogeneous systems (2015). www.tensorflow.org
2. Badrinarayanan, V., Kendall, A., Cipolla, R.: Segnet: a deep convolutional encoder-decoder architecture for image segmentation. arXiv preprint arXiv:1511.00561 (2015)
3. Chen, H., Qi, X., Yu, L., Heng, P.-A.: DCAN: deep contour-aware networks for accurate gland segmentation. In: Proceedings of the IEEE Conference on Computer Vision and Pattern Recognition, pp. 2487–2496 (2016)
4. Ying Chen, J.D., Argentinis, E., Weber, G.: IBM Watson: how cognitive computing can be applied to big data challenges in life sciences research. Clin. Ther. **38**(4), 688–701 (2016)
5. Ciresan, D., Giusti, A., Gambardella, L.M., Schmidhuber, J.: Deep neural networks segment neuronal membranes in electron microscopy images. In: Advances in Neural Information Processing Systems, pp. 2843–2851 (2012)
6. He, K., Gkioxari, G., Dollár, P., Girshick, R.: Mask R-CNN. In: 2017 IEEE International Conference on Computer Vision (ICCV), pp. 2980–2988. IEEE (2017)

7. He, K., Zhang, X., Ren, S., Sun, J.: Deep residual learning for image recognition. In: Proceedings of the IEEE Conference on Computer Vision and Pattern Recognition, pp. 770–778 (2016)

8. Ioffe, S., Szegedy, C.: Batch normalization: accelerating deep network training by reducing internal covariate shift. In: International Conference on Machine Learning, pp. 448–456 (2015)

9. Kingma, D., Adam, J.B.: A method for stochastic optimization. arXiv preprint arXiv:1412.6980 (2014)

10. Liu, Y., et al.: Detecting cancer metastases on gigapixel pathology images. arXiv preprint arXiv:1703.02442 (2017)

11. Long, J., Shelhamer, E., Darrell, T.: Fully convolutional networks for semantic segmentation. In: Proceedings of the IEEE Conference on Computer Vision and Pattern Recognition, pp. 3431–3440 (2015)

12. Noh, H., Hong, S., Han, B.: Learning deconvolution network for semantic segmentation. In: Proceedings of the IEEE International Conference on Computer Vision, pp. 1520–1528 (2015)

13. Ronneberger, O., Fischer, P., Brox, T.: U-Net: convolutional networks for biomedical image segmentation. In: Navab, N., Hornegger, J., Wells, W.M., Frangi, A.F. (eds.) MICCAI 2015. LNCS, vol. 9351, pp. 234–241. Springer, Cham (2015). https://doi.org/10.1007/978-3-319-24574-4_28

14. Simard, P.Y., Steinkraus, D., Platt, J.C., et al.: Best practices for convolutional neural networks applied to visual document analysis. ICDAR **3**, 958–962 (2003)

15. Szegedy, C., Vanhoucke, V., Ioffe, S., Shlens, J., Wojna, Z.: Rethinking the inception architecture for computer vision. In: Proceedings of the IEEE Conference on Computer Vision and Pattern Recognition, pp. 2818–2826 (2016)

16. Wang, D., Khosla, A., Gargeya, R., Irshad, H., Beck, A.H.: Deep learning for identifying metastatic breast cancer. arXiv preprint arXiv:1606.05718 (2016)

Automated Immunohistochemical Stains Analysis for Computer-Aided Diagnosis of Parathyroid Disease

Bartłomiej Płaczek[1]([envelope]), Marcin Lewandowski[1], Rafał Bułdak[2,3], and Marek Michalski[4]

[1] Institute of Computer Science, University of Silesia, Sosnowiec, Poland
placzek.bartlomiej@gmail.com, marcin.lewandowski@us.edu.pl
[2] Department of Physiology, School of Medicine with the Division of Dentistry,
University of Silesia, Zabrze, Poland
rbuldak@gmail.com
[3] Department of Human Nutrition, School of Public Health,
Medical University of Silesia, Zabrze, Poland
[4] Department of Histology and Embryology, School of Medicine with the Division
of Dentistry, Medical University of Silesia, Zabrze, Poland
mmichalski@gmail.com

Abstract. Parathyroid disease has a huge impact on overall health and quality of life. Immunohistochemistry (IHC) is a biological technique, which is useful in diagnosis and prognosis of the parathyroid disorders. The use of IHC as a diagnostic tool brings a substantial methodological problem related to evaluation of stain intensity in micrographs. This paper introduces an image processing approach for automatic IHC stain analysis in micrographs of parathyroid tissue. The introduced approach can be used for computer-aided diagnosis of parathyroid disease as well as for medical research studies in this field. The main novelty of this approach lays in the combination of color deconvolution procedure with a parathyroid cell nuclei localization algorithm, which is based on custom image filtering and circular objects recognition. Accuracy of the proposed approach was verified by comparison with results of experts' evaluation in experiments conducted on micrographs of healthy tissue, adenomas, and hyperplasias with various IHC markers.

Keywords: Image processing · Immunohistochemistry
Hyperparathyroidism · Light microscopy

1 Introduction

Immunohistochemistry (IHC) is a powerful technique based on antigen-antibody interaction, which uses selected antibodies as markers for localization of target antigens in tissues. IHC staining enables visual analysis of the localization and distribution of specific cellular components within cells in proper tissue context.

© Springer Nature Switzerland AG 2018
K. Saeed and W. Homenda (Eds.): CISIM 2018, LNCS 11127, pp. 68–79, 2018.
https://doi.org/10.1007/978-3-319-99954-8_7

When using the IHC method, the antigen-antibody complexes are visualized in a color image by means of light microscopy. Morphology visualization of the tissue around the specific stained antigen is obtained by counterstaining. Results of stained IHC markers have important implications for various disease diagnosis, drug development and biological research [1]. They are especially useful for the diagnosis of abnormal cells such as those found in tumors [2].

IHC methods are widely used in current studies on disorders of parathyroid glands. The use of IHC as a diagnostic tool brings a substantial methodological problem related to evaluation of the amount and intensity of stain in selected regions of micrographs [3]. The common practice is visual scoring of the immunostains by expert observers. However, visual scoring is biased, poorly reproducible, time-consuming and subjective. The interpretation of visual scoring causes inconsistencies upon the evaluation process.

Digital image processing techniques [4,5,16] can be used to overcome the issues of visual scoring. Computer-aided analysis of IHC stains enables faster diagnosis and reduces inter-observer variation when the stain concentration levels are evaluated [6]. Currently, several image processing methods have been proposed for the computer-aided extraction of stained regions and evaluation of the IHC stain intensity. Some methods perform color classification for the quantitative analysis of IHC stain by using components of the RGB color space [6], their normalization (nRGB) [7], HSL model [3], and YUV color space [8]. Advantages of CMYK color space for reproducible and unbiased evaluation of IHC stain intensity were discussed in [9].

Recently, a considerable attention has been paid to color deconvolution approach [10]. According to this approach, the RGB matrix of the input image is multiplied by the inverse of a color spread matrix (color deconvolution matrix) to separate the stain, counterstain and background in IHC micrographs [11]. This method can effectively solve staining overlap and better separate stain than the color classification methods. A disadvantage of this approach is that it requires determination of pure stain color [12].

This paper introduces a new image processing approach for automatic quantitative IHC stain analysis in micrographs of parathyroid tissue. This approach combines the algorithms of stain intensity evaluation with custom image filtering and localization of parathyroid cell nuclei. It allows the IHC stain concentration to be evaluated for image regions that correspond to individual parathyroid cells. As a result, detailed information can be obtained regarding the amount of cells with low, medium and high stain concentration. Moreover spatial density of these cells can be analyzed. Accuracy of the introduced approach was verified in experiments on IHC stained parathyroid tissue sections that were obtained from patients undertaking surgery due to primary hyperparathyroidism. Experimental results show that the proposed approach effectively extracts precise information, which can be useful for diagnosis of the parathyroid disorders.

The paper is organized as follows. Details of the methods that support the proposed automatic approach are presented in Sect. 2. Section 2.3 includes results of the experiments on cell staining analysis in IHC micrographs of parathyroid tissue. Discussion of the results is provided in Sect. 3. Finally, summary and conclusions are given in Sect. 4.

2   Proposed Approach

In this section the new approach is presented which enables automatic analysis of cell staining in IHC micrographs of parathyroid tissue. An overview of the proposed approach is depicted in Fig. 1. According to this approach, cell regions are determined in input image on the basis of cell nuclei localization. Circle detection algorithms are used to localize the cell nuclei. Accuracy of this localization is improved by introducing a custom image filtering procedure, which enables extracting a grayscale image of the nuclei. The color deconvolution method is applied in order to obtain a grayscale image that shows staining intensity in the analyzed micrograph. This image is further used for classification of the stain concentration in particular parathyroid cells as low, medium or high. As a result, statistics are computed that describe amounts of cells for each category of stain concentration as well as spatial density of the stained cells.

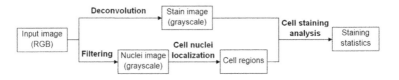

Fig. 1. Block diagram of the proposed image analysis approach.

2.1   Image Filtering

The proposed image filtering operation enables extracting a grayscale nuclei image (Fig. 2b) from the input RGB micrograph of parathyroid tissue (Fig. 2a). This operation was designed to achieve high pixel intensity values in image regions that correspond to the locations of the parathyroid cell nuclei, In input RGB image, the cell nuclei are visible as circular objects of low luminance. After decomposing the input image into red, green and blue color channels, it can be observed that the cell nuclei are especially apparent in the red channel (Fig. 2c). In green and blue channels (Fig. 2d and e), the nuclei are obscured by the stain and their contrast is significantly lower than in red channel. To take into account the fact that locations of cell nuclei correspond to image regions of low luminance and low red intensity, the filtering operation is performed by multiplying complement of luminance values and complement of red values:

$$N(x, y) = (1 - L(x, y)) \times (1 - R(x, y)), \tag{1}$$

where $N(x, y)$ denotes intensity of pixel (x, y) in the filtered nuclei image and $L(x, y)$ is the luminance of pixel (x, y) in input image. According to the standard NTSC conversion, the luminance is calculated as weighted sum of the intensities for R, G, and B color channels:

$$L(x, y) = 0.2989 \times R(x, y) + 0.5870 \times G(x, y) + 0.1140 \times B(x, y). \tag{2}$$

It should be also noted here that the intensity values belong to the unit interval $[0, 1]$.

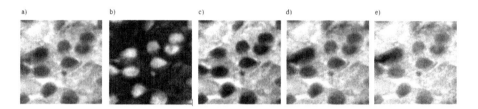

Fig. 2. Filtering of IHC stained parathyroid tissue (a) input image (RGB), (b) filtered cell nuclei image (grayscale), (c) red channel of input image, (d) green channel of input image, (e) blue channel of input image (Color figure online)

2.2 Cell Nuclei Localization

After filtering operation, locations of individual cell nuclei are recognized in the filtered nuclei image ($\mathbf{N}$) by using a circle detection method. In this study, application of two different circle detection methods is considered. The first method (DoG) is based on Difference of Gaussian filtering, while the second method (CHT) utilizes Circle Hough Transform.

The DoG method [13] uses a scale-space representation of image $\mathbf{N}$. This representation ($\mathbf{F}$) is a family of images, where each image corresponds to a particular scale. Let $\mathbf{F}(\sigma)$ denote an image in scale-space representation $\mathbf{F}$ at scale level σ. The scale parameter σ corresponds to variance of a Gaussian kernel, which is used to compute image $\mathbf{F}(\sigma)$:

$$\mathbf{F}(\sigma) = \mathbf{N} * \mathbf{G}(\sigma) - \mathbf{N} * \mathbf{G}(\sqrt{2}\sigma), \tag{3}$$

where $\mathbf{G}(\sigma)$ is the Gaussian kernel with variance σ and symbol $*$ denotes convolution operation.

Initially, centers of circles with radius r are recognized as local maxima in the image representation $\mathbf{F}$ at a scale level $\sigma = 0.6r$. Selection of the scale level σ is justified by the fact that for a circle centered at pixel (x, y) whose radius equals r, the maximum value in $\mathbf{F}$ is obtained for the element $F(0.6r, x, y)$ [14]. An element $F(\sigma, x, y)$ of the scale-space image representation $\mathbf{F}$, i.e. pixel (x, y)

in image $\mathbf{F}(\sigma)$, is recognized as a local maximum if its value is higher than the values of eight neighboring elements at the same scale level (σ) and higher than the values of two elements with the same location (x, y) at scale levels $\sigma + 0.6, \sigma 0.6$. A local maximum found at (σ, x, y) is taken into consideration if the value of $F(\sigma, x, y)$ is above threshold τ_{DoG}.

At the next step, a local Hessian analysis is performed to eliminate false detections. The Hessian matrix for pixel (x, y) in scale-space representation $\mathbf{F}$ at scale level σ is defined as follows:

$$\mathbf{H} = \begin{bmatrix} \mathbf{F}(\sigma)_{xx} & \mathbf{F}(\sigma)_{xy} \\ \mathbf{F}(\sigma)_{xy} & \mathbf{F}(\sigma)_{yy} \end{bmatrix} \tag{4}$$

The derivatives in matrix $\mathbf{H}$ are estimated by taking differences of neighboring pixels. Let 1 and 2 denote eigenvalues of $\mathbf{H}$ such that $\lambda_1 \geqslant \lambda_2$. For ideally circular (radially symmetric) shapes, the ratio of eigenvalues λ_1/λ_2 equals 1, whereas larger values of this ratio are obtained in case of irregular, elongated structures [14]. In order to verify that the ratio λ_1/λ_2 is below a threshold value ρ, the following test is used:

$$\frac{Tr^2(\mathbf{H})}{Det(\mathbf{H})} < \frac{(\rho + 1)^2}{\rho} \tag{5}$$

Nucleus detection at pixel (x, y) is discarded, if condition (5) is not satisfied. The threshold ρ is a parameter of this algorithm.

Figure 3 shows an example of nuclei localization results that were obtained by using the DoG method.

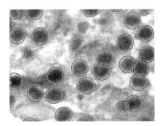

Fig. 3. Localization of cell nuclei in IHC stained parathyroid tissue micrograph.

According to the CHT method, the circle detection starts by determining edge points in the filtered nuclei image $\mathbf{N}$. At the next step, a two-dimensional accumulator array is used to find centers of the circles. One cell in the accumulator array (a, b) corresponds to one pixel. Initially these cells are set to 0. For each edge point, candidate centers of circles (a, b) can be determined by using the equation

$$(x - a)^2 + (y - b)^2 = r^2. \tag{6}$$

where r is radius of the circle. If pixel (a, b) is found to be a candidate circle center then the corresponding cell in accumulator array is incremented.

In order to limit the number of false detections and increase the processing speed, only the edge points with gradient magnitude above a threshold τ_{CHT} are considered. Moreover, the fact is taken into account that the circle center lies on the line passing through the edge point along the gradient direction. Finally, centers of circles are recognized as local maxima in the accumulator array. To identify the radius of circle, the distance of each edge point from a candidate centre is determined and a radius histogram is calculated [15].

2.3   Stain Deconvolution

The objective of stain deconvolution is to provide a grayscale stain image with pixel intensity values proportional to stain concentration in the examined tissue sample. The applied color deconvolution method was originally proposed by Ruifrok and Johnston [11]. This method is based on the Beer-Lambert law, which describes intensity I of light after passing through the sample:

$$I = I_0 e^{-\alpha st}, \tag{7}$$

where I_0 is the incident intensity, α denotes absorbance of the stain, s is the concentration of the stain, and t is thickness of the sample. The product αst is referred to as optical density d:

$$d = \alpha st = -ln(I/I_0), \tag{8}$$

The input image is composed of three color channels (R, G, and B), thus three optical densities of the stain (d_R, d_G, d_B) can be determined for each pixel on the basis of Eq. (8). In the discussed method, it is assumed that there are three stains in the sample that contribute linearly to light absorption. Therefore, Eq. (8) is reformulated as follows:

$$d = \begin{bmatrix} d_R \\ d_G \\ d_B \end{bmatrix} = \begin{bmatrix} \alpha_{R1}t & \alpha_{R2}t & \alpha_{R3}t \\ \alpha_{G1}t & \alpha_{G2}t & \alpha_{G3}t \\ \alpha_{B1}t & \alpha_{B2}t & \alpha_{B3}t \end{bmatrix} \begin{bmatrix} s_1 \\ s_2 \\ s_3 \end{bmatrix} = \mathbf{Ms} \tag{9}$$

where d denotes the registered optical density vector, $\mathbf{M}$ is convolution matrix (characteristic for given stains) and $\mathbf{s}$ is stain concentration of i-th stain).

In order to simplify the calculations, optical density vector $\mathbf{d}$ and concentration vector $\mathbf{s}$ are normalized:

$$\hat{\mathbf{d}} = \mathbf{d}/|\mathbf{d}|, \hat{\mathbf{s}} = \mathbf{s}/|\mathbf{s}|, \tag{10}$$

thus

$$\hat{\mathbf{d}} = \begin{bmatrix} \hat{d_R} \\ \hat{d_G} \\ \hat{d_B} \end{bmatrix} = \begin{bmatrix} m_{11} & m_{12} & m_{13} \\ m_{21} & m_{22} & m_{23} \\ m_{31} & m_{32} & m_{33} \end{bmatrix} = \hat{\mathbf{M}}\hat{\mathbf{s}} \tag{11}$$

and the stain concentration can be found by using the following formula:

$$\hat{\mathbf{s}} = \hat{\mathbf{M}}^{-1}\hat{\mathbf{d}}. \tag{12}$$

The resultant normalized stain concentration vector $\hat{\mathbf{s}}$ describes relative contribution of three stains to the corresponding pixel of the input image.

In an IHC stained sample, there are only two stains, i.e., stain and counterstain. Since the color deconvolution method requires three stains to be considered, a background color of the micrograph is used as the third "stain". An example of the stain image obtained by color deconvolution is presented in Fig. 4.

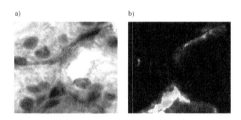

Fig. 4. Color deconvolution of IHC stained parathyroid tissue micrograph: (a) input image (RGB), (b) stain image (grayscale).

2.4   Analysis of Cell Staining

Quantitative analysis of parathyroid cell staining is performed on the basis of the extracted stain image and the recognized locations of cell nuclei. The results of this analysis are the statistics related to amount and spatial density of stained cells in the examined sample.

Since membranes of the parathyroid cells are not visible in the IHC stained micrographs, the image regions that correspond to particular cells cannot be precisely determined. According to the proposed approach, Voronoi diagrams are used to obtain a rough estimate of the cell regions in the analyzed image. The Voronoi diagram is created by partitioning pixels into regions based on distance to centers of the detected nuclei. Each region in the Voronoi diagram consists of pixels that are located closer to center of a given nucleus than to centers of other nuclei. Figure 5 shows a Voronoi diagram for centers of the cell nuclei that were detected by using DoG method as illustrated in Fig. 3.

Concentration of the stain can be categorized for each pixel (x, y) based on the pixel intensity value $S(x, y)$ in the stain image obtained by color deconvolution. In this study four categories of the stain concentration are considered: no stain $(S(x, y) \leq 0.25)$, low stain concentration $(0.25 < S(x, y) \leq 0.50)$, medium stain concentration $(0.50 < S(x, y) \leq 0.75)$, and high stain concentration $(S(x, y) > 0.75)$. The above threshold values were selected experimentally.

Cell staining level is determined as no stain, low, medium or high by taking into account the stain concentration categories assigned to pixels that belong to

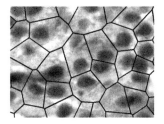

Fig. 5. Voronoi diagram for recognized centers of parathyroid cell nuclei

the Voronoi region of that cell. To this end, a set of n pixels with highest stain concentration categories is selected form the Voronoi region of the given cell. The cell staining level corresponds to the minimum stain concentration category of the selected pixels. The number of selected pixels is calculated as $n = m/100$, where m is average pixel number of Voronoi regions in the analyzed image. Local spatial density i of stained cells is calculated for each detected nucleus (i) by counting the nuclei (j) of highly stained cells, whose centers are located closer to the center of nucleus i than τ_{dist}:

$$\varphi_i = |\{(x_j, y_j) : (x_j, y_j) \in C \wedge level(x_j, y_j) = high \wedge dist((x_j, y_j), (x_i, y_i)) \leq \tau_{dist}\}|, \tag{13}$$

where $|.|$ denotes cardinality of the set, (x_i, y_i) are coordinates of i-th nucleus center, C is set of all detected nucleus centers, $level(x_j, y_j)$ is the stain concentration level of a cell, which has nucleus center localized at pixel (x_j, y_j), and $dist$ is the Euclidean distance. It means that the local density φ_i is calculated by counting the cell nuclei in circular regions of radius τ_{dist}. Global spatial density of stained cells for the examined sample is defined as average of the local densities φ_i.

3   Results

The proposed approach was applied to analysis of IHC stained parathyroid tissue sections that were obtained from patients undertaking surgery due to primary hyperparathyroidism caused by adenoma and primary hyperplasia. The aim of the IHC staining procedure was to assess the expression of angiogenesis markers, i.e., VEGF, CD31 and CD106. Frozen tissue sections were incubated with purified mouse monoclonal antihuman antibodies: anti-VEGF (clone SP28), anti-CD31 (clone JC/70A) and anti-CD106 (clone 1.4C3). Dilution of the primary antibodies was 1:500 and was verified in a series of pilot experiments. The IHC labeling procedure was performed by using the BrightVision technology from Immunologic. The sections were counterstained with Mayer's haematoxylin. Micrographs of parathyroid tissue sections were captured by using a light microscope equipped with Nicon DS-Fi1-L2 color camera head at 100x magnification. The RGB color format with 24-bit depth was used for the acquisition of digital images.

First set of experiments was conducted in order to examine accuracy of the proposed parathyroid cell nuclei localization method and compare it with other methods. During these experiments the cell nuclei were localized in 20 micrographs of IHC stained parathyroid tissue sections. The total number of the parathyroid cells in the analyzed images is above 7500. Reference locations of the cell nuclei in the test images were determined manually by an expert.

Accuracy of cell nuclei localization was evaluated by using two metrics: percent of false negative locations (FNL) and percent of false positive locations (FPD). The accuracy metrics are defined as follows:

$$FNL = \frac{|\{c_T : c_T \in C_T \land dist(c_T, c_D) > r \forall c_D \in C_D\}|}{|C_T|} \cdot 100\% \qquad (14)$$

$$FPL = \frac{|\{c_D : c_D \in C_D \land dist(c_T, c_D) > r \forall c_T \in C_T\}|}{|C_T|} \cdot 100\% \qquad (15)$$

where $C_T = c_T$ is a set of true nuclei centers (localized by an expert), $C_D = c_D$ is a set of detected nuclei centers, and $dist(c_T, c_D)$ denotes the Euclidean distance between a true center c_T and a detected center c_D. The centers of nuclei are determined as points in the image space. Localization is considered as correct if the distance between the center of the detected nucleus and center of true nucleus is less than its radius r. Additionally, the localization error LE is analyzed, which aggregates the two above accuracy metrics:

$$LE = \sqrt{FNL^2 + FPL^2}. \qquad (16)$$

In this study, four different nucleus localization algorithms were compared. DoG and CHT algorithms apply the standard Difference of Gaussian method and Circle Hough Transform to detect the immunogold particles directly in input images. F-DoG and F-CHT algorithms are based on the new introduced approach, which combines the standard circle detection methods with the proposed filtering procedure, as discussed in Sect. 2.1. It means that these algorithms localize the nuclei in the filtered image.

Figure 6a shows the FNL and FPL values obtained while localizing the parathyroid cell nuclei in all test images. During this experiment the threshold parameters of the compared algorithms (τ_{DoG}, and τ_{CHT}) were gradually changed from 0 to 1. At each step, the same threshold value was used for all images. Based on preliminary results, the ρ parameter of DoG was set to 5. The lowest percentages of false locations were obtained by using F-DoG algorithm. For optimal parameter settings, F-DoG algorithm enables achieving high localization accuracy with FNL and FPL metrics below 5%. In case of the F-CHT algorithm with optimized settings, the localization accuracy metrics are close to 10%. Considerably worse nuclei localization results were achieved by using the state-of-the-art algorithms (DoG and CHT). Figure 6b shows the dependency between thresholds value and localization error for the analyzed algorithms. For F-DoG algorithm the best results (minimum error LE = 5.2%) were achieved for $\tau_{DoG} = 0.50$. When using F-CHT algorithm, the lowest value of LE (14.7%) was obtained for $\tau_{CHT} = 0.07$. In case of standard DoG and Hough algorithms, the minimum localization error values were equal to 17.6% and 21.1%, respectively. Based on the results presented in Fig. 7 it can be observed that the proposed F-CHT algorithm ensure a low detection error in a relatively wide range of the threshold value. In case of the algorithms that utilize Hough transform, a minimum localization error can be achieved by using threshold values from a very narrow interval. Thus, an advantage of the DoG approach is the fact that it is less sensitive to threshold selection.

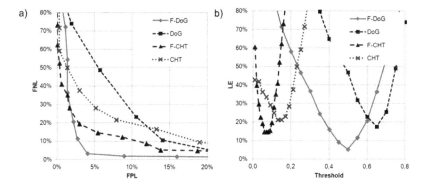

Fig. 6. (a) Percentages of false negative locations and false positive locations for compared nuclei localization algorithms (b) Dependency between threshold parameters and nuclei localization error

The second part of the experiments was devoted to quantitative analysis of parathyroid cell staining in the test micrographs. During these experiments the amount of stained cells and their spatial density were determined by using the automatic image processing approach that was presented in Sect. 2. Localization of the cell nuclei was performed by using the with F-DoG algorithm. The experimental results obtained for micrographs of healthy parathyroid tissue were compared with those obtained from adenomas and hyperplasias.

Figure 8 shows percentages of cells with low, medium, and high stain concentration in micrographs of parathyroid tissue sections for which the IHC staining process was performed to assess the expression of different angiogenesis markers (VEGF, CD31 and CD106). The results presented in Fig. 8 were obtained by using the introduced automatic approach for image analysis. These results were compared with the percentages evaluated manually by experts. The differences are below 1%. In Fig. 8 it can be observed that for healthy parathyroid tissue the count of cells with high stain concentration is negligibly low. In contrast, the percentage of such cells is close to 10% for parathyroid adenomas and 5% for parathyroid hyperplasias. The percentage of highly stained cells in case of adenoma is significantly higher than in case of hyperplasia. When considering the cells with medium and low concentration of the stain, it can be noticed that the percentage of such cells is considerably higher for the healthy parathyroid tissue than for the diseased one. These findings are similar for all three IHC markers considered in this study.

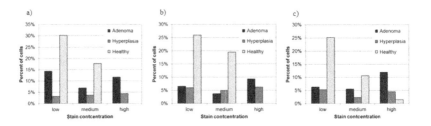

Fig. 7. Percentages of stained cells for different IHC markers: (a) CD31, (b) CD106, (c) VEGF

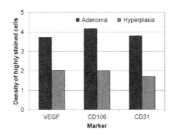

Fig. 8. Global spatial density of highly stained cells for different IHC markers

4   Conclusion

In this paper an approach was introduced which enables automatic analysis of IHC micrographs of parathyroid glands. The proposed approach can be used for computer-aided diagnosis of parathyroid disease as well as for medical research studies in this field. Usefulness of this approach was demonstrated in experiments conducted on micrographs of healthy tissue, adenomas, and hyperplasias with various IHC markers. Accuracy of the proposed method was verified by comparing the obtained results with results of experts' evaluation.

The main novelty of this approach lays in the combination of color deconvolution procedure with a parathyroid cell nuclei localization algorithm, which is based on custom image filtering and circle recognition. Results of the experiments show that the proposed nuclei localization algorithm significantly reduces the error rates of the standard DoG and CHT algorithms. Moreover, the new algorithm is less sensitive to parameter selection.

The proposed approach is capable of automatically analyzing IHC micrographs related to parathyroid disease to develop prediction/diagnostic models with a high degree of accuracy in a relatively short time. Moreover, this approach has the potential to help medical professionals in the diagnostic related decision processes for different diseases. In future research, the introduced approach will be extended to enable applications in decision support for diagnosis of autoimmune skin diseases, such as scleroderma and psoriasis.

References

1. Pathak, S., Joshi, S.R.: Basics of immunohistochemistry. J. Investig. Dermatol. **135**, e30 (2015). https://doi.org/10.1038/jid.2014.541
2. Dabbs, D.J.: Diagnostic Immunohistochemistry: Theranostic and Genomic Applications, 4th edn. Saunders, Philadelphia (2013)
3. Kaczmarek, E., Górna, A., Majewski, P.: Techniques of image analysis for quantitative immunohistochemistry. Ann. Acad. Medicae Bialostoc. **49**, 155–158 (2004)
4. Wesołowski, T., Wróbel, K.: A computational assessment of a blood vessel's roughness. In: Burdu, R., Jackowski, K., Kurzynski, M., Wozniak, M., Zolnierek, A. (eds.) Proceedings of the 8th International Conference on Computer Recognition Systems CORES 2013. AISC, vol. 226, pp. 227–236. Springer, Heidelberg (2013). https://doi.org/10.1007/978-3-319-00969-8_22
5. Wrobel, K., Doroz, R., Palys, M.: A method of lip print recognition based on sections comparison. In: Proceedings of International Conference on Biometrics and Kansei Engineering ICBAKE 2013, pp. 47–52. IEEE Computer Society, Tokyo (2013)
6. Prasad, K., Prabhu, G.K.: Image analysis tools for evaluation of microscopic views of immunohistochemically stained specimen in medical research-a review. J. Med. Syst. **36**(4), 2621–2631 (2012)
7. Brey, E.M., et al.: Automated selection of DAB-labeled tissue for immunohistochemical quantification. J. Histochem. Cytochem. **51**(5), 575–584 (2003)
8. Dong, J., Li, J., Fu, A., Lv, H.: Automatic segmentation for Ovarian Cancer immunohistochemical image based on YUV color space. In: Muchin, V.E., Hu, Z. (eds.) International Conference on Biomedical Engineering and Computer Science ICBECS 2010, pp. 750–753. IEEE, New York (2010)
9. Pham, N.A., et al.: Quantitative image analysis of immunohistochemical stains using a CMYK color model. Diagn. Pathol. **2**(1), 8 (2007)
10. Varghese, F., Bukhari, A.B., Malhotra, R., De, A.: IHC profiler: an open source plugin for the quantitative evaluation and automated scoring of immunohistochemistry images of human tissue samples. PloS ONE **9**(5), e96801 (2014)
11. Ruifrok, A.C., Johnston, D.A.: Quantification of histochemical staining by color deconvolution. Anal. Quant. Cytol. Histol. **23**(4), 291–299 (2001)
12. Tadrous, P.J.: Digital stain separation for histological images. J. Microsc. **240**(2), 164–172 (2010)
13. Lowe, D.G.: Distinctive image features from scale-invariant keypoints. Int. J. Comput. Vis. **60**(2), 91–110 (2004)
14. Wang, R., Pokhariya, H., McKenna, S.J., Lucocq, J.: Recognition of immunogold markers in electron micrographs. J. Struct. Biol. **176**(2), 151–158 (2011)
15. Atherton, T.J., Kerbyson, D.J.: Size invariant circle detection. Image Vis. Comput. **17**(11), 795–803 (1999)
16. Kłos-Witkowska, A.: The phenomenon of fluorescence in immunosensors. Acta Biochimica Polonica **63**(2), 215 (2016)

Finger Veins Feature Extraction Algorithm Based on Image Processing Methods

Maciej Szymkowski[(✉)] and Khalid Saeed

Faculty of Computer Science,
Bialystok University of Technology, Bialystok, Poland
szymkowskimack@gmail.com, k.saeed@pb.edu.pl

Abstract. Recently more interest in the recognition algorithms based on human veins is observable. In the literature we can find results confirm that this trait provide huge accuracy level. This feature is used for instance in cash machines. In the last years, more financial institutions took into consideration vein-based identification technology. Its popularity is connected with ease of use and analyzed trait uniqueness. A method to extract finger veins features with image processing algorithms is presented in this paper. In the preliminary stage of the research, the device to collect finger veins images was created. The second part of the work is implementation of the algorithm to process input images. The authors used soft computing algorithm that is artificial neural network to find specific structures on the image. The last stage of the work is connected with confirmation of the results obtained with artificial neural network.

Keywords: Biometrics · Image processing · Finger vein · Feature extraction
Artificial neural networks

1 Introduction

In the last few years we can observe that huge amount of identification algorithms based on measurable human traits were developed. One of the main reasons why we take biometrics and its methods into consideration for human recognition are: measurable traits uniqueness and simplicity of its retrieval.

Sometimes people write significant passwords in their notes or even on their credit cards. It helps them to provide correct codeword when it is needed. Nonetheless it can also cause loss of access to the data if their memos will be stolen. Regarding this problem, biometrics ensures different algorithms and methods that can prevent steal of the data. When it comes to this technology advantages, it can be easily pointed out that the user is the password. It is connected with the fact that his measurable traits represent him in the security system. What is more it is not possible to steal these "passwords". One of the safest traits is veins pattern. It can be obtained from our eyes (retina) or hands (especially fingers). In the literature one can easily find different approaches to show that biometrics systems based on veins pattern are not safe. Despite multiple tries no one provided significant proof that veins pattern can be spoofed. Recently financial institutions begin bringing on them to the cash machines. It shows that veins pattern can assure high accuracy human identification.

K. Saeed and W. Homenda (Eds.): CISIM 2018, LNCS 11127, pp. 80–91, 2018.
https://doi.org/10.1007/978-3-319-99954-8_8

There are many diversified approaches to process veins pattern from hands and a few that are connected with the fingers. It can be claimed that human finger can provide multiple different traits which can be used for human recognition. Technology development enables usage of different devices to collect veins image although it is still the challenge to process them and extract their features.

In this paper the processing algorithm for fingers veins pattern is described. As the first step of the authors approach, hardware to collect samples was set up. The second stage is creation of the image processing algorithm for image preparation to feature extraction that is the third step. At the end significant features are extracted by the artificial neural networks and Crossing Number (CN) algorithm. One of the main aims of this research is to check whether it is possible to effectively extract finger veins features and whether artificial neural network can provide satisfactory results in the case of minutiae detection.

This work is organized as follows: in the first section the authors describe known approaches to process finger veins images. In the second one the proposed solution is presented with the processing algorithm and the device scheme. The third section contains information about performed experiments, especially about different hardware configurations. Finally, the conclusions and future work are given.

2 Literature Review

In the literature we can easily find multiple approaches to veins processing and extraction of their features. Most of the works are based on simple image processing algorithms. Novelty of the algorithm presented in this paper lies in the use of artificial neural network combined with Crossing Number (CN) algorithm for the finger veins features extraction.

An approach using Convolutional Neural Networks (CNN) for the finger-vein based identification was presented in [1]. The Authors' solution consists of two steps: image preprocessing and CNN stage. In the article the way in which image acquisition was done is not referred. At the beginning original image that is in 240×320 resolution is captured. Then it is cropped to 70×130 size. Before that its origin is set at the center pixel of the finger image. As the next step, the image is resized to 55×67 size. The Authors claimed that these stages are needed to easily train neural network. The last step of image preprocessing procedure is image binarization with local thresholding. By this step finger veins are separated from background. The second stage of the approach is human identification with Convolutional Neural Networks. CNN was created with 5 layers where four of them are convolutional. Each of the hidden layers has 5, 13 and 50 neurons respectively. The Authors claimed that their solution has 100% of identification rate when 80% of their database is the training set.

In the article [2] the Authors presented the algorithm for finger vein recognition using Local Line Binary Pattern (LLBP) technique. The image preprocessing algorithm consists of four steps. The first of them is Region of Interest (ROI) extraction. The goal of the stage is to separate the finger from the background. It is obtained with Otsu binarization and cropping image to 480×160 size. The second step of the approach relies on reducing the image resolution to 192×64 pixels with the resize ratio equal 0.4.

The goal of the another algorithm stage is image enhancement. The Authors have claimed that it was done with a symmetrical modified Gaussian high-pass filter. After this operation contrast of finger vein image was enhanced. The last preprocessing step is translation alignment that is done with the phase only correlation function calculated between two enhanced images. The most interesting part of the algorithm is feature extraction. In this stage a new texture descriptor called Local Line Binary Pattern (LLBP) was used. LLBP consists of two components: horizontal and vertical. The LLBP magnitude can be obtained by calculating the line binary codes for both components. The comparison between two samples is done with calculation of the similarity between two extracted binary codes. The Authors used Hamming Distance as a similarity function.

In [3] an interesting approach to finger veins detection was presented. The Authors split their algorithm into four subsequent steps. The first stage is connected with cropping image so that it contains only finger. Then the sequence of the filters is applied on the image. In the paper there is information that this step consists of median filtering, image smoothing, convolution with "special" kernel, thinning and at last "special median" filtering. The third step relies on the top of a finger detection. It is performed with Sobel filtering. As the last stage the finger contour detection is done. The Authors claimed that in the finger contour additional significant information can be included. In this step erase of falsely detected veins is performed.

Finger vein recognition system that relies on image processing was described in [4]. The system consists of two main stages: enrollment and verification. Both of them have four steps. The first of them is image acquisition. In the paper is no information about the scheme of the used device. The second stage is image preprocessing. At the beginning image is converted from RGB to Grayscale. Then image enhancement is used to improve quality of the analyzed sample, nonetheless there is also no information about specific operations that were used to deal with that goal. Another step is image normalization into smaller size. By this operation high accuracy finger vein image is obtained. The last step of the second stage is image resize. The third step is image segmentation with Canny operator. In this operation finger veins are separated from its background and also a noise is eliminated. As the last step matching between two samples is done. In this step Euclidean distance is calculated between two images. The Authors claimed that their system achieves FRR of 20% and FAR of 0% for database consists of 150 images.

In the literature one may easily find other articles that refer to finger-vein based identification and to finger-vein image processing. It should be pointed out that most of them base on simple image processing procedures. A significant example of the processing algorithm is presented in [5]. In this work the authors introduced complete veins pattern recognition system. Its innovative part is a binarization method used in image processing stage. Proposed solution main points are: lower time consuming comparing to the methods selected by the Authors and working with low contrast images.

Another group of papers that refers to finger-veins are review articles. Each of them presents current state of the art and makes a comparison between known solutions [6]. One of the most attractive reviews is shown in [7]. This article mainly focuses on three aspects: general information about finger veins in biometrics solutions, a review of the existing works connected with image acquisition and feature extraction. A consideration of the key problems and future directions is also given in order to provide better results in finger vein recognition algorithms. The paper presents not only information from different articles but also gives summaries and conclusions about each analyzed approach.

The image of the veins can be obtained not only from the finger or hand but also from the retina. In the literature there are multiple approaches to extract veins features. An interesting algorithm was presented in [8]. The Authors prepared a solution that basis on a simple image processing methods. The first step of the proposed procedure is image conversion to grayscale and then its enhancement on the basis of its histogram. Another operation is segmentation with Canny operator and morphological operations. After these stages image is represented by two colors: black background and white veins. Thereafter the veins were thinned to 1-pixel width. At the end of the algorithm information about ridges and bifurcations on an image were obtained with Scanning Window Analysis (SWA).

Artificial neural network can also be used in the case of the retina processing and classification. Example of its usage was presented in [9]. This solution consists of four main blocks: Preprocessing of a color retinal image, Locating anatomic structures and detecting lesions, Feature extraction, Classification of retinal disease using artificial neural network. At the beginning an image was changed to grayscale and then it was enhanced with histogram equalization and median filtering. In the second step Gaussian-like linear patterns profiles were improved. Feature extraction was based on location of the optic disk and then pattern recognition for diseases detection was performed. The last block of the algorithm was used to classify found diseases with artificial neural network.

3 Methodology

The authors have already published articles in the field of the image processing. The main point of [10] was connected with fingerprint processing and novel method to feature vector creation while [11] was dealing with pathological changes in Optical Coherence Tomography images..

In this chapter the authors present the complete algorithm that was worked out. The proposed approach is based on experiences obtained during previous works.

The significant part of the work was creation of the device that was used to obtain finger-vein images. The authors used three 840–870 nm IR LEDs placed below the finger and the camera Tracer Prospecto Cam that was located above the finger. The scheme of the system is presented in Fig. 1.

The second, noteworthy, part is connected with image processing and feature extraction algorithms. Both of them were implemented with Java Programming Language and authors' image processing mathematical framework. The most important part of the solution is gradient filter by which all of the veins are extracted. In Fig. 2 block diagram of the algorithm is presented.

The first algorithm step is image cropping. This stage enabled region of interest (ROI) separation. In the case of the study described in this work, finger-veins are the main point of the acquired image. Another step is connected with noise removal. The authors used median filter to deal with the noise visible in the image. The original sample and its shape after both described steps are presented in Fig. 3.

The next two operations that is conversion to grayscale and histogram equalization are connected with image enhancement. By these steps veins are clearly visible and can be extracted in the next steps. It should be pointed out that conversion was done with the green channel. It is a kind of a standard in the veins processing algorithms [12–15]. Images obtained after these two steps are presented in the Fig. 4.

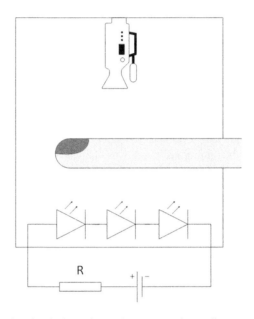

Fig. 1. The device scheme that was used to collect samples

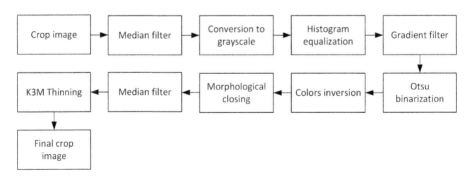

Fig. 2. Block diagram of the image processing algorithm

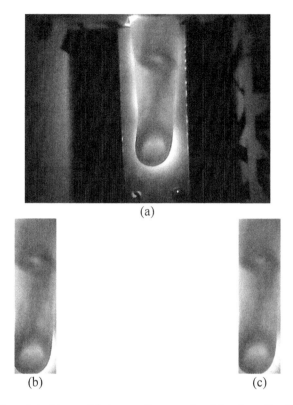

(a)

(b)   (c)

Fig. 3. The original image (a), image after cropping (b) and median filtering (c)

(a)   (b)

Fig. 4. Image in the grayscale (a) and after histogram equalization (b)

The another operations used in the algorithm are gradient filtering and Otsu binarization. In this approach only 0° gradient mask is used to get information about vertical veins from the finger. The size of the mask is 13×13. By binarization the significant data about the veins is obtained. During the experiments different binarization techniques were used, nonetheless Otsu algorithm returned the best result. In this case the best means that the veins were clearly visible and can be easily used in the next processing steps. The images after both of these operations are presented in Fig. 5.

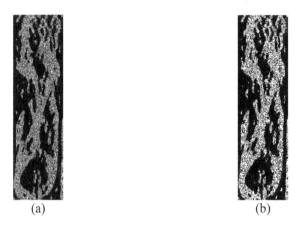

Fig. 5. Gradient filtered image (a) and binarized with Otsu algorithm (b)

Thereafter the colors on the image are inverted. It means that black pixels change their value to white and white pixels are shown in black. This step is needed to have possibility to use morphological operations for veins enhancement. Next operation applied to the image in the preprocessing section is morphological closing of black pixels. Closing means morphological dilation applied on previously eroded image. This stage leaves us with the most important part of the image – the finger-veins. In Fig. 6 images after both of the operations are presented.

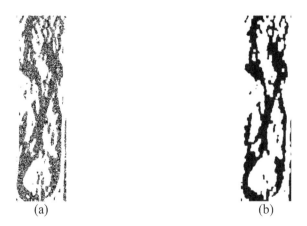

Fig. 6. Image after color inversion (a) and morphological closing (b)

The three last steps are connected with veins quality enhancement and preparation to the feature extraction. At the beginning of this stage median filter is multiply applied on the image. This filter allows to improve veins shapes. Next, the thinning algorithm K3M [16] is applied to the image. It is used to obtain 1-pixel width veins skeleton. The authors also tested KMM [17] algorithm for this aim although K3M provided better, clearer results. The last step was final image cropping for removing loose edges visible after thinning. In Fig. 7 final form of the processed image is presented.

Fig. 7. The final form of the processed image

3.1   Feature Extraction

The second part of the approach was connected with feature extraction. It was done on the basis of the image obtained after preprocessing stage. The authors focused on simple minutiae like ridge endings and ridge bifurcations. In this case two-step extractor was used to deal with this task. Soft computing method, artificial neural network is used to detect significant features. For this aim it is composed of one input layer, two hidden layers and one output layer. Each of them consists of 9, 25, 25 and 3 neurons respectively. Input and output layers activation function was (1) and hidden layers neurons were activated by (2). The scheme of the artificial neural network is presented in Fig. 8.

$$f(x) = \frac{1}{1 + e^{-x}} \tag{1}$$

$$g(x) = \frac{e^x - e^{-x}}{e^x + e^{-x}} \tag{2}$$

The second stage of the feature extraction was applied on the results obtained with previously created neural network. This step was based on CN (Crossing Number) algorithm. Each of the points classified by the neural network as a minutiae was once again studied by CN algorithm. The final decision was undertaken on the basis of CN number. This value was calculated as in (3).

$$CN = \frac{1}{2} \cdot \sum_{i=1}^{8} |P_i - P_{i-1}|$$ (3)

The computed CN number enables easy classification of each pixel. When it equals 0, the analyzed pixel belongs to the background, CN = 1 means that pixel is a ridge terminal, CN = 2 points out that the analyzed element represents ridge continuation and when CN = 3 the pixel is a ridge bifurcation. In Fig. 9 all ridge endings are pointed with the circle whilst the ridge bifurcations with a triangle.

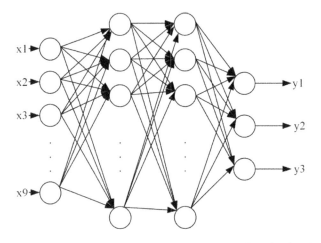

Fig. 8. The scheme of the artificial neural network used for minutiae detection

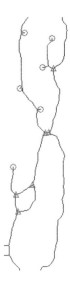

Fig. 9. The features extracted from the thinned veins image

4   Experiments

The significant part of the work is connected with the performed experiments. The authors' database consists of 20 users, each of them is represented by 3 samples. Due to the fact that the database is small, the authors do not measure the identification accuracy level of the proposed feature extraction algorithm. The experiments were mostly connected with the created device configuration. We took into consideration different wavelengths like 450 nm, 620 nm and 840 nm. The first of them represents white diode, the second one is connected with red diodes and 840 nm represents infrared light. The most informative was the last of them, most of the veins were clearly visible and can be processed in the proposed algorithm. In Fig. 10 comparison between three light types is presented.

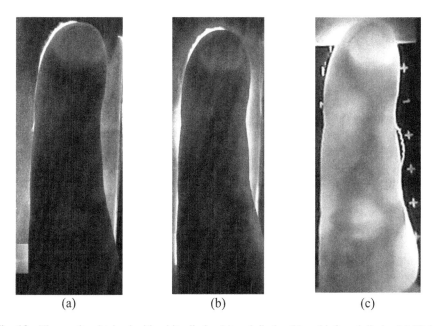

(a)   (b)   (c)

Fig. 10. The results obtained with white diodes (a), red diodes (b) and infrared diodes (c) (Color figure online)

Another discussed algorithm step is conversion to the grayscale. The authors have tested different configurations for this operation: green channel, red channel, blue channel and average value of all RGB channels. On the basis of our observations it has to be claimed that the most informative is green channel. Next multiply tested configuration was the one connected with artificial neural network. Different number of hidden layers and neurons in each of them were taken into consideration although the most precise results were obtained with the configuration presented in Fig. 8. It has to be pointed out that when hidden layers number was lower than two, too much points were accepted as minutiae, in the case of more hidden layers than boundary value only a part of the real minutiae were selected. Also the authors took into consideration different number of input neurons. The experiments were performed for 9 and 25 neurons. Nonetheless when the artificial neural network has 25 inputs the results were not precise, it means that too much of false minutiae were selected.

5   Conclusions and Future Work

In the last few years it can be observed that human veins became one of the most precise and popular identification features. As it was formerly indicated, veins from fingers, hands or eyes can be used in the recognition process. Nonetheless the finger-veins can be obtained in the easiest way and they provide the same recognition accuracy level as retina or hand-veins.

The approach presented in this paper was implemented in real development environment and was tested on more than 50 samples. Each stage of image processing can be displayed by the software user. The final result of the algorithm is an image with selected minutiae. The feature vector can be easily created from information presented in an obtained image.

In the work the authors do not present any results connected with accuracy level of the proposed algorithm. This stage will be prepared in the future with convolutional neural networks. The soft computing methods used in the presented solution can provide the satisfactory results although two-step extractor used in this approach gives more precise results because it eliminates false minutiae.

As a future work the authors would like to provide significant changes in the processing part and the device. These modifications will aim to improve the image quality. On the other hand convolutional neural networks will be used to get identification results and to extract minutiae. What is more the authors will work under different feature vectors that can be used in the recognition step.

Acknowledgment. This work was supported by grant S/WI/3/2018 from Białystok University of Technology and funded with resources for research by the Ministry of Science and Higher Education in Poland.

References

1. Ahmad Radzi, S., Khalil-Hani, M., Bakhteri, R.: Finger-vein biometric identification using convolutional neural networks. Turk. J. Electr. Eng. Comput. Sci. **24**, 1863–1878 (2016)
2. Affendi Rosdi, B., Wuh Shing, C., Azmin Suandi, S.: Finger vein recognition using local line binary pattern. Sensors **11**, 11357–11371 (2011). https://doi.org/10.3390/s111211357
3. Hejtmankova, D., Dvorak, R., Drahansky, M., Orsag, F.: A new method of finger veins detection. Int. J. Bio-Sci. Bio-Technol. **1**(1), 11–16 (2009)
4. Tallam, R., Temgire, S., Zirange, R.: Finger vein recognition system using image processing. Int. J. Electr. Electron. Data Commun. **2**(5), 65–68 (2014)
5. Waluś, M., Kosmala, J., Saeed, K.: Finger vein pattern extraction algorithm. In: HAIS 2011 – Hybrid Artificial Intelligent Systems, Wroclaw, Poland, 23–25 May 2011, Proceedings, pp. 404–411 (2011)

6. Nakamaru, Y., Oshina, M., Murakami, S., Edgington, B., Ahluwalia, R.: Trends in finger vein authentication and deployment in Europe. Hitachi Rev. **64**(5), 275–279 (2015)
7. Yang, L., Yang, G., Yin, Y., Zhou, L: A survey of finger vein recognition. In: 9th Chinese Conference on Biometric Recognition, CCBR 2014, Shenyang, China, 7–9 November 2014, Proceedings, pp. 234–243 (2014)
8. Panchal, P., Bhojani, R., Panchal, T.: An algorithm for retinal feature extraction using hybrid approach. Procedia Comput. Sci. **79**, 61–68 (2016)
9. Jayanthi, D., Devi, N., SwarnaParvathi, S.: Automatic diagnosis of retinal diseases from color retinal images. Int. J. Comput. Sci. Inf. Secur. **7**(1), 234–238 (2010)
10. Szymkowski, M., Saeed, K.: A novel approach to fingerprint identification using method of sectoralization. In: ICBAKE 2017 – International Conference on Biometrics and Kansei Engineering, Kyoto, Japan, 15–17 September 2017, IEEE Proceedings (2017)
11. Szymkowski, M., Saeed, E.: A novel approach of retinal disorder diagnosing using optical coherence tomography scanners. In: Gavrilova, M.L., Tan, C.J.K., Chaki, N., Saeed, K. (eds.) Transactions on Computational Science XXXI. LNCS, vol. 10730, pp. 31–40. Springer, Heidelberg (2018). https://doi.org/10.1007/978-3-662-56499-8_3
12. Xu, L., Luo, S.: A novel method for blood vessel detection from retinal images. Biomed. Eng. Online **9**(14) (2010)
13. Siva Sundhara Raja, D., Vasuki, S.: Automatic detection of blood vessels in retinal images for diabetic retinopathy diagnosis. Comput. Math. Methods Med. (2015)
14. Zhang, J., Cui, Y., Jiang, W., Wang, L.: Blood vessel segmentation of retinal images based on neural network. In: Zhang, Y.-J. (ed.) ICIG 2015. LNCS, vol. 9218, pp. 11–17. Springer, Cham (2015). https://doi.org/10.1007/978-3-319-21963-9_2
15. Szymkowski, M., Saeed, E., Saeed, K.: Retina tomography and optical coherence tomography in eye diagnostic system. In: Chaki, R., Cortesi, A., Saeed, K., Chaki, N. (eds.) Advanced Computing and Systems for Security. AISC, vol. 666, pp. 31–42. Springer, Singapore (2018). https://doi.org/10.1007/978-981-10-8180-4_3
16. Tabędzki, M., Saeed, K., Szczepański, A.: A modified K3M thinning algorithm. Int. J. Appl. Math. Comput. Sci. **26**(2), 439–450 (2016)
17. Saeed, K., Rybnik, M., Tabedzki, M.: Implementation and advanced results on the non-interrupted skeletonization algorithm. In: Skarbek, W. (ed.) CAIP 2001. LNCS, vol. 2124, pp. 601–609. Springer, Heidelberg (2001). https://doi.org/10.1007/3-540-44692-3_72

On Modeling Objects Using Sequence of Moment Invariants

Magdalena Wiercioch[1,2(✉)]

[1] Faculty of Physics, Astronomy and Applied Computer Science,
Jagiellonian University, Lojasiewicza 11, 30-348 Krakow, Poland
magdalena.wiercioch@uj.edu.pl
[2] Faculty of Mathematics and Computer Science, Jagiellonian University,
Lojasiewicza 6, 30-348 Krakow, Poland

Abstract. The paper addresses the problem of rotation and translation invariant recognition of objects described by many features. A new set of rotation invariants features are introduced. Numerical experiments are performed to test the invariance for coloured images and chemical compounds. A comparisons with the other methods are made. The obtained results suggest it is worth to explore the proposed method.

1 Introduction

This paper explores the problem of rotational invariance of objects. Undoubtedly, moment functions have a broad spectrum of applications in image processing fields, such as object classification, invariant pattern recognition, pose estimation, image coding [6,7,14]. From practical point of view set of moments provides global characteristics of the image shape and gives information about different types of geometrical features of the image. The first of these functions are regular moments which find applications since they are both algorithmically and computationally simple.

Generally, the earliest significant work on the application of moments was published by Hu [4] in 1962. His classic paper on pattern recognition has been cited in almost all moment related publications and has received wide attention during the past few decades [11,13]. His approach was based on the paper about the theory of algebraic forms by Boole, Cayley and Sylvester [10]. He used regular moments theory to introduce a set of non-linear functions called moment-invariants that are invariant to translation, scale and rotation. Then, he applied the concept to a simple character recognition problem. Hu proposed two different methods for obtaining invariance to rotation. The first technique is based on combinations of regular moments using algebraic invariants, which he called as the absolute moment invariants. The other method was derived using the principal axis method. In this paper, we shall refer to both these concepts collectively as Hu's moments. Subsequently, this method was used for pattern recognition by Alt [1] in 1962, ship identification by Smith and Wright in 1971, aircraft identification by Dudani et al. in 1977, pattern matching by Dirilten

© Springer Nature Switzerland AG 2018
K. Saeed and W. Homenda (Eds.): CISIM 2018, LNCS 11127, pp. 92–102, 2018.
https://doi.org/10.1007/978-3-319-99954-8_9

in 1977 and scene matching by Wong and Hall in 1978 [10]. In 2002 Flusser [3] derived an extended version of Hu's concept. He developed a method to generate invariants of any orders and they are independent. But there is a problem with using these moments for objects which can be described by many features. Some examples are like coloured images where each RGB channels are expected to be considered.

In this paper, that problem is addressed and a simple solution is proposed. It involves in obtaining a set of new features, which are computed by concatenation of moment features. The experimental analysis are performed on either coloured images Fig. 1 or chemical compounds Fig. 2.

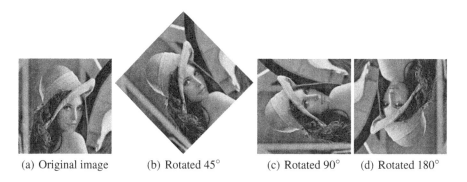

(a) Original image   (b) Rotated 45°   (c) Rotated 90°   (d) Rotated 180°

Fig. 1. The four images of Lena used in the experiments.

| 1 | 0 | 0 | 0 | 0 | 0 | 0 | 0 | 0 | 0 | 0 | 0 | 0 | 0 | 0 | 0 | 0 | 0 | 0 | 0 | 1 | 0 | 0 | 0 | 0 | 0 | 1 | 0 | 0 | 0 | 0 | 0 | ...

(a) An example of known fingerprint representation of chemical compound (4860 features).

| 1 | 1.2 | 0.4 | 0.27 | -0.38 | 0.15 | -0.07 | 1 | 1 | -0.74 | 0.27 | -0.38 | 0.18 | -0.1 | | | | | ...

N

(b) Our model of a molecule presented in Figure 2(a).

Fig. 2. Two representations of a molecule - commonly known (a) and our model (b).

In Sect. 2, we describe the basic theory of moment invariant along with a description on the multidimensionality problem. Section 3 presents the algorithm to construct a novel representation for exemplary objects. Section 4 deals with invariance of rotated images using the new moments. The next section treats the application of the new moments for chemical compounds. Section 6 provides the conclusion.

2   Theory

This section builds on the idea of a novel data model construction. For the reader's convenience, we recall Hu's [4] and Flusser's [2] derivations (see Subsect. 2.1). Then, our method is introduced (see Sect. 3).

2.1   Fundamentals of Moments

In [4] Hu introduced seven nonlinear functions defined on regular moments which are translation, scale, and rotation invariant. These seven so called moment invariants were used in a number of pattern recognition problems [2]. The definition of regular moments has the form of projection of $g(x, y)$ function onto the monomial $x^p y^q$.

The geometric two-dimensional (p+q)-th order moments of an image g(x, y) are defined as

$$m_{pq} = \int_{-\infty}^{\infty} \int_{-\infty}^{\infty} x^p y^q g(x, y) dx dy$$

where $p, q = 0, 1, 2, \ldots$

Invariance to translation can be provided by using central moments. They are defined as

$$\mu_{pq} = \int_{-\infty}^{\infty} \int_{-\infty}^{\infty} (x - x_t)^p (y - y_t)^q g(x, y) dx dy$$

where $p, q = 0, 1, 2, \ldots$, and $x_t = \frac{m_{10}}{m_{00}}$, $y_t = \frac{m_{01}}{m_{00}}$ are the coordinates of the centroid. If one uses quotients:

$$v_{pq} = \frac{\mu_{pq}}{\mu_{00}^{\frac{(p+q+2)}{2}}}$$

then their function is invariant under scaling, too. The moments mentioned previously are normalized to translation and scaling.

Nevertheless, the major weakness of Hu's theory is that it does not provide for the possibility of any generalization. Using it, we could not derive invariants from higher-order moments and invariants to more general transformations. To overcome this problem Flusser [3] proposed a general theory of constructing rotation moment invariants of any orders.

It is advantageous to use complex moments for the normalization to the rotation. According to Flusser, the complex moment c_{pq} of order $(p + q)$ is defined as

$$c_{pq}^g = \int_{-\infty}^{\infty} \int_{-\infty}^{\infty} (x + iy)^p (x - iy)^q g(x, y) dx dy.$$

The theorem below allows constructing invariants:

Theorem 1 *[2]. Let $n \geq 1$ and let k_i, p_i, and q_i and be a set of be nonnegative integers such that*

$$\sum_{i=1}^{n} k_i(p_i - q_i) = 0$$

Then

$$I = \prod_{i=1}^{n} c_{p_i q_i}^{k_i}$$

is invariant to rotation.

Note that Theorem 1 allows us to construct an infinite number of the invariants for any order of moments, but only few of them are mutually independent. Fortunately, there exist relatively small complete and independent subset of invariant which are defined by Theorem 2.

Theorem 2 *[2]. Let us consider complex moments up to the order $r \geq 2$. Let a set of rotation invariants B be constructed as follows:*

$$B = \{\phi(p,q) \equiv c_{p,q} c_{q_0,p_0}^{p-q} | p \geq q \wedge p + q \leq r\}$$

where p_0 and q_0 are arbitrary indices such that $p_0 + q_0 \leq r$, $p_0 - q_0 = 1$ and $c_{p_0 q_0} \neq 0$ for all admissible one dimensional objects. Then B is a basis of all rotation invariants created from the moments of any kind up to the order r.

We now consider the desirable properties of a descriptor based on moments.

Independence. The independence of B follows from the mutual independence of the complex moments themselves.

Completeness. It is sufficient to resolve so-called inverse problem, which means recovering all complex moments (and, consequently, all geometric moments) up to the order r when knowing the elements of B. The system of equations must be resolved:

$$\phi^g(0,0) = c_{00}^g;$$
$$\phi^g(1,1) = c_{11}^g;$$
$$\phi^g(2,0) = c_{20}^g(c_{12}^g)^2;$$
$$\phi^g(2,1) = c_{21}^g c_{12}^{(g)};$$
$$\phi^g(3,0) = c_{30}^g(c_{12}^{(g)})^3;$$
$$\dots;$$
$$\phi^g(r,0) = c_{r0}^g(c_{q_0 p_0}^{(g)})^r;$$
$$\phi^g(r,1) = c_{r-1,1}^g(c_{q_0 p_0}^{(g)})^{r-2}.$$

3   Generalized Hu Invariants

3.1   Problem Explanation

Generally, Hu and Flusser applied their methods to objects described by one attribute, i.e. grayscale images, where only the information about pixel intensity is given and the other is lost. The problem appears if more features are taken into account. In our approach we suggest to concatenate representation build for each considered attribute.

For instance, in our experiments we consider two types of objects: color images and chemical compounds.

Example 1. A color image consists of pixels, and pixels are made of combinations of primary colors represented by a series of code. So called channel refers to the grayscale image of the same size as a color image, made of just one of these primary colors. A typical color will have a red, green and blue channel. A grayscale image has just one channel. So, for color image we take three attributes into consideration: each one connected with its separate channel (R, G, B).

Example 2. A molecule consists of atoms. For chemical compounds we consider each type of a compound as an attribute. The molecule's coordinates are complex. For chemical compounds it is natural to associate atomic mass given in Table 1 for instance.

Table 1. Atoms weights represented with atomic mass.

Symbol	Standard atomic weight	Symbol	Standard atomic weight
B	10.811	Br	79.904
C	12.0107	Cl	35.453
F	18.998403	I	126.90447
O	15.9994	P	30.973762
N	14.0067	Na	22.989769
S	32.065	Si	28.0855
Li	6.941	H	1.00794

3.2   Methodology

The above observations lead to the following algorithm to compute the novel features. The values r, p_0 and q_0 have to be determined before starting the algorithm. Note that this step is independent of a particular object and may be done offline.

```
                         3D
Structure written by MMmdl.

 4   3   0   0   0   0   0   0   0  0999 V2000
   -6.6000      2.7500      0.0000 C    0  0   0  0  0  0  0  0  0  0  0  0
   -6.6000      4.2500      0.0000 O    0  0   0  0  0  0  0  0  0  0  0  0
   -7.8990      2.0000      0.0000 C    0  0   0  0  0  0  0  0  0  0  0  0
   -5.3010      2.0000      0.0000 C    0  0   0  0  0  0  0  0  0  0  0  0
 1   2   2   0   0   0   0
 1   3   1   0   0   0   0
 1   4   1   0   0   0   0
M   END
```

Fig. 3. A simple example of a molecule - aceton.

Example 3. Let us show how to compute features with Hu_{Rc} for a simple molecule in SDF-file format presented in Fig. 3.

As it can be seen, there are 2 types of objects here: the first one is connected with oxygen and the second with carbon. We express the positions of atoms as a vector of complex numbers: $[(-6.6 + 2.75j), (-7.899 + 2j), (-5.301 + 2j)]$ and $[(-6.6 + 4.25j)]$. Next, r is set to 2, p_0 to 0 and q_0 equals 2. After that one may calculate coefficients. According to Table 1, the w_i for carbon and oxygen is: 12.0107 and 15.9994. Since we work on complex values, the obtained coefficients has to be split into a real and imaginary part.

4   New Moments for Coloured Images

In this section, the experimental setup to evaluate $Hu2D$ descriptor for image representation is outlined and results are discussed.

Since the purpose of this paper is to analyze the quality of Hu_{Rc} model in context of improvement in performance of machine learning techniques, let us show its properties compared with the following models:

– Hu is the classical Hu's approach, the features vector is computed on binary image;
– $CBIR$ uses the visual contents of an image to retrieve a feature vector [9].

In further experiments we take moment invariants of 2 order into consideration.

Rotations Case Study. Undoubtedly, the most vital property of moment invariants is invariance to rotation. Table 2 shows the sample values of the new moments for different types of rotated images with a different angle of rotation Fig. 1. To be comparable, the numerical values obtained with Hu are considered as well (Table 3). It can be seen that the new moments are invariant to rotation. Note the exact values are not obtained within a class since the images are digital.

Table 2. Moments calculated for each of four images presented in Fig. 1.

Angle	ϕ_0	ϕ_1	ϕ_2	ϕ_3	ϕ_4
0°	[2.73, 2.25, 4.12]	[1.72, 4.32, 6.19]	[5.82, 2.43, 9.44]	[11.95, 8.38, 3.12]	[7.13, 3.64, 6.32]
45°	[2.73, 2.25, 4.12]	[1.72, 4.32, 6.19]	[5.82, 2.43, 9.44]	[11.95, 8.38, 3.12]	[7.13, 3.64, 6.32]
90°	[2.73, 2.25, 4.12]	[1.72, 4.32, 6.19]	[5.82, 2.43, 9.44]	[11.95, 8.38, 3.12]	[7.13, 3.64, 6.32]
180°	[2.73, 2.25, 4.12]	[1.72, 4.32, 6.19]	[5.82, 2.43, 9.44]	[11.95, 8.38, 3.12]	[7.13, 3.64, 6.32]

Table 3. Moments calculated employing Hu model for grayscale versions of images presented in Fig. 1.

Angle	ϕ_1	ϕ_2	ϕ_3	ϕ_4
0°	2.439	6.318	5.185	8.602
45°	2.439	6.318	5.185	8.602
90°	2.439	6.318	5.185	8.602
180°	2.439	6.318	5.185	8.602

Usablility Exploration. Another experiment checks how good classification outcomes can be obtained for different types of representation. We uses here pictogram database - PASCAL Visual Object Classes Challenge (PASCAL VOCC) [1]. The benchmark contains nearly 10,000 images of 20 different object categories such as: car, bird. The conducted experiments were performed for four sets of images: animal, sailing, people and tree. 50 images from each category were selected manually and divided into test set and train set in ratio 1:5. Some of images are shown in Fig. 4. For the classification task, Scikit-learn implementation of Support Vector Machine (SVM) for the case of a linear kernel is applied and F-score is calculated. As Table 4 yields our approach (Hu_{Rc}) provides the best results. It suggests that Hu_{Rc} concept could be further investigated since it improves the quality of representation of image although it is not directly intended for image processing tasks (as opposed to CBIR).

Table 4. Summary of SVM results (F-score) for classification of diverse categories of images shown in Fig. 4.

Representation	Animal	Tree	Sailing	People
Hu	0.74	0.8	0.85	0.78
Hu_{Rc}	**0.76**	**0.81**	**0.87**	**0.8**
CBIR	0.66	0.75	0.87	0.77

Fig. 4. The sample classes of animal, tree, sailing and people selected manually to inspect the classification performance of our representation Hu_{Rc} compared with Hu and CBIR.

5   New Moments for Molecules

After observing the results when images are applied, the attention has to be paid on another kind of objects: molecules.

In order to understand importance of the problem, some of chemistry knowledge has to be provided. Obviously, there are a lot of methods of representation of molecules [8]. Chemical compounds are usually represented by fingerprints, i.e. high dimensional binary strings where a given bit indicates the absence or presence of particular feature of compound. Since many features can be taken considered, various fingerprint representations were constructed. The length of popular representations varies from 166 (MACCS) to 4860 bits (Klekota-Roth [5]). Nevertheless, although the fingerprint representations can be very long, they do not provide the uniqueness of representation. In other words, in every representation there exist chemical compounds which have identical fingerprints. Clearly, the concatenation of fingerprints allows for a better (but not ideal) distinction of compounds. One of the basic problems of cheminformatics is to find compounds which are active on particular biological target. This allows for construction drugs for various diseases, e.g. 5-HT_{1A} receptor ligands is responsible for basic functions of central nervous system. The active compounds are the source of medicines. Therefore, clustering and classification of chemical

compounds with respect to their chemical activities is of basic importance. There
are two problem chemists face here. First of all, fingerprints are long strings and
it extends computational time. Secondly, they do not include all information
connected with a molecule. According to experts, all valuable chemical information connected with molecules is contained in SDF-format files. To be more
precise, the files in the SD format file (called Structure data file) contain structural information and additional data associated directly with the molecule, e.g.
physical-chemical properties, or the results of calculations made. It is a widely
used format for the exchange of information between database systems or computing packages. Each of the molecules contained in the SDF is represented by
a single block. The examplary fragment of SDF file is shown in Fig. 5.

```
   -CPSS-   0804941117

 13 14  0  0  0  0  0  0  0  0  0
      0.8400   -0.1600    0.0000 N    0  0      0  0  0  0  0  0
      1.4800    0.4300    0.0000 N    0  0      0  0  0  0  0  0
      0.0900    0.2700    0.0000 N    0  0      0  0  0  0  0  0
      1.1100    1.2100    0.0000 C    0  0      0  0  0  0  0  0
      0.2700    1.1200    0.0000 C    0  0      0  0  0  0  0  0
      0.8400   -1.0300    0.0000 C    0  0      0  0  0  0  0  0
      1.5300    1.9900    0.0000 C    0  0      0  0  0  0  0  0
      1.0700    2.7400    0.0000 C1   0  0      0  0  0  0  0  0
      1.5900   -1.4600    0.0000 C    0  0      0  0  0  0  0  0
      0.0800   -1.4600    0.0000 C    0  0      0  0  0  0  0  0
      1.5900   -2.3300    0.0000 C    0  0      0  0  0  0  0  0
      0.0700   -2.3200    0.0000 C    0  0      0  0  0  0  0  0
      0.8400   -2.7600    0.0000 C    0  0      0  0  0  0  0  0
  2  1  1  0  2  0  0
  3  1  1  0  2  0  0
  4  2  2  0  2  0  0
  5  3  2  0  2  0  0
  6  1  1  0  2  0  0
  7  4  1  0  2  0  0
  8  7  1  0  2  0  0
  9  6  1  0  1  0  0
 10  6  2  0  1  0  0
 11  9  2  0  1  0  0
 12 10  1  0  1  0  0
```

Fig. 5. SDF file.

As explained, the available representations are lengthy and do not describe
all important features of molecules. Furthermore, the suffer from limitations such
as not concerning geometrical properties. Thus, we want to determine how Hu_{Rc}
model may be helpful to overcome this problem.

In case of chemical compounds the moment invariants are calculated in the
following way:

– each molecule is considered as one object;
– for each object we consider different attributes and concatenate the final
  representations.

The aim of this experiment is to examine the power of Hu_{Rc} model by
classification quality assessment - SVM (both linear and gaussian) with 5-fold
cross-validation (C = 1). For the experiments chemical information contained in
SDF of M1 target is applied. The predictive power is measured by MCC, Recall,
F-score [12]. We compare our method with Hu, Hu_{Rc} method and commonly-
known representation of fingerprint (Klekota Roth) (Table 5).

Table 5. Values after applying classification methods for M1 target (SVM with gaussian kernel and linear kernel).

Representation	Kernel	MCC	F-score	Recall
Hu	Gaussian	0.5 ± 0.08	0.63 ± 0.06	0.58 ± 0.07
Hu_{Rc}	Gaussian	0.55 ± 0.02	0.67 ± 0.03	0.61 ± 0.03
KR	Gaussian	0.74 ± 0.09	$\mathbf{0.76 \pm 0.06}$	0.77 ± 0.08
Hu	Linear	0.56 ± 0.05	0.65 ± 0.07	0.64 ± 0.11
Hu_{Rc}	Linear	0.6 ± 0.01	0.68 ± 0.05	0.69 ± 0.4
KR	Linear	0.8 ± 0.09	0.85 ± 0.06	0.85 ± 0.08

The results yield that for specific type of data our representation outperforms Hu techniques. Interestingly, the Hu_{Rc} model of molecule for M1 receptor works only on more than 100 features vector. Note, typically for Klekota Roth the length is 4860. Although our model does not improve the known approach, it shows this kind of methodology should be further investigated.

6   Conclusion

This paper proposes new moment invariants that solves 2-dimensionality problem faced with previously known moment functions. The solution involves in obtaining a set of new features, which are computed by concatenation of features obtained for each analysed attribute. This technique produces satisfactory values for all tested data (images and molecules) taking into consideration the fact that the new model provides much less dimensions of retrieved vector.

Acknowledgments. This research was partially supported by National Centre of Science (Poland) Grants No. 2016/21/N/ST6/01019.

References

1. Everingham, M., Van Gool, L., Williams, C.K.I., Winn, J., Zisserman, A.: The PASCAL visual object classes challenge 2007 (VOC2007) results. http://www.pascal-network.org/challenges/VOC/voc2007/workshop/index.html
2. Flusser, J.: Moment invariants in image analysis (2005)
3. Flusser, J., Zitova, B., Suk, T.: Moments and Moment Invariants in Pattern Recognition. Wiley Publishing, New York (2009)
4. Hu, M.K.: Visual pattern recognition by moment invariants. IRE Trans. Inf. Theory **8**(2), 179–187 (1962). https://doi.org/10.1109/TIT.1962.1057692
5. Klekota, J., Roth, F.P.: Chemical substructures that enrich for biological activity. Bioinformatics **24**(21), 2518–2525 (2008). https://doi.org/10.1093/bioinformatics/btn479

6. Li, D.: Analysis of moment invariants on image scaling and rotation. In: Sobh, T., Elleithy, K. (eds.) Innovations in Computing Sciences and Software Engineering, pp. 415–419. Springer, Netherlands (2010). https://doi.org/10.1007/978-90-481-9112-3_70

7. Mukundan, R., Ramakrishnan, K.: Moment Functions in Image Analysis: Theory and Applications. World Scientific, Singapore, New Jersey, London (1998)

8. Murray-Rust, P., Rzepa, H.: XML and Its Application in Chemistry, vol. 2, pp. 466–490. Wiley-VCH, New York (2003)

9. Chaudhari, A.M.P.R.: Content based image retrieval using color and shape features. Int. J. Adv. Res. Electr. Electron. Instrum. Eng. 1(5), 386–392 (2012)

10. Rodrigues, M.A. (ed.): Invariants for Pattern Recognition and Classification. World Scientific, Singapore (2000)

11. Rodríguez-Damián, M., Cernadas, E., Formella, A., de Sá-Otero, P.: Pollen classification using brightness-based and shape-based descriptors. In: 17th International Conference on Pattern Recognition, ICPR 2004, Cambridge, UK, 23–26 August 2004, pp. 212–215 (2004). https://doi.org/10.1109/ICPR.2004.1334098

12. Singh, S., Jokhan, A., Sharma, B., Lal, S.: An innovative approach of progressive feedback via artificial neural networks. J. Mach. Learn. Technol. 2(1), 64–71 (2011). http://bioinfopublication.org/viewhtml.php?artid=BIA0001170

13. Tangelder, J.W.H., Veltkamp, R.C.: A survey of content based 3d shape retrieval methods. Multimed. Tools Appl. 39(3), 441–471 (2007). https://doi.org/10.1007/s11042-007-0181-0

14. Xiao, B., Cui, J., Qin, H., Li, W., Wang, G.: Moments and moment invariants in the radon space. Pattern Recognit. 48(9), 2772–2784 (2015). https://doi.org/10.1016/j.patcog.2015.04.007

Computer Information Systems

Light Sensor Based Vehicle
and Pedestrian Detection Method
for Wireless Sensor Network

Marcin Bernas[1]([✉])(iD) and Jarosław Smyła[2](iD)

[1] Faculty of Mechanical Engineering and Computer Science,
University of Bielsko-Biala, Bielsko-Biala, Poland
marcin.bernas@gmail.com
[2] Institute of Innovative Technologies EMAG, Katowice, Poland
jaroslaw.smyla@ibemag.pl

Abstract. The paper proposes a method, which utilizes light sensors from wireless nodes, to detect moving objects like vehicles or pedestrians. The method is analyzing light intensity of the general red, green, and blue spectrums of visible light from nodes that are placed on a roadside. The proposed aggregation algorithm, based on justified granulation paradigm, adapts exponential forgetting mechanism to descriptive statistic functions (features). This approach allows to reduce memory utilization of wireless node. The aggregated values are used by lightweight state-of-the-art machine learning methods to build profile of moving objects. The method is tuned using heuristic-based genetic algorithm. Advantages of the introduced method were demonstrated in real-world scenarios. Broad experiments were conducted to test various classification approaches and feature subsets. The experimental results confirm that the introduced method can be adopted for sensor node, which can detect objects independently or in cooperation with other nodes (working as classifier ensemble).

Keywords: Sensor network · Light sensor · Object detection
Machine learning · Data granulation

1 Introduction

The population in cities and surrounding areas are growing rapidly. The cities, to be able to grow even further, require efficient road infrastructure management to meet current and future needs. The road infrastructure is controlled by Intelligent Transportation Systems (ITS). The ITS optimizes road networks utilization using predefined rules (trained based on historical data or engineering experience) or by adapting to a current traffic. Both approaches are demanding, due to a spatio-temporal characteristic [1] of the traffic flow. Therefore, they require precise traffic data (historical and present ones), which can be obtained by traffic monitoring system or dedicated Wireless Sensor Networks (WSN).

© Springer Nature Switzerland AG 2018
K. Saeed and W. Homenda (Eds.): CISIM 2018, LNCS 11127, pp. 105–116, 2018.
https://doi.org/10.1007/978-3-319-99954-8_10

Until recently, the main source of traffic data was obtained by inductive loops, magnetometers, visual sensing technologies or microwave radars. Each of these technologies has advantages in terms of sensing distance, detection accuracy or vulnerability to weather conditions. Among vast technologies, image processing and intelligent video analytics based on cameras proved to have great possibilities and was widely investigated in many papers [2]. Despite potential of light based detection, the direct utilization of light sensor for WSN was not investigated [12]. Therefore, in this paper sensor network based on light intensity measure was proposed to obtain precise data considering vehicle or pedestrian crossing a detection area. Transmitting raw time series (TS) data can consume significant energy resources of WSN device, thus for proposed sensor node the edge mining technique [3] was implemented. In contrast to the traditional data mining, edge mining takes place on the wireless, battery-powered, and smart sensing devices that sit at the edge points of the network. The mining technique was based on a justified granular computing paradigm [4]. The exponential forgetting is used to aggregate the TS data into information granules describing given time period. The approach allows to describe short term and medium term events as well as background changes. The proposed method doesn't store a raw TS data in memory, but only granule representation. The light measurements are processed by the sensor node, which detects object (vehicle or pedestrian) using lightweight machine learning method. Both the granules and the machine learning method are tuned using genetic algorithm. The capabilities of the proposed method were verified in various weather condition scenarios. The paper is organized as follows. Section 2 includes a survey of related literature and describes contribution of this work. Details of the proposed light based sensor network are discussed in Sect. 3. Obtained results during experiments are described in Sect. 4. Finally, conclusions and further work are given in Sect. 5.

2   Related Works

Road traffic monitoring via various sensors is a research topic of current interest. Various sensor technologies were researched. Several efforts have been made to investigate the possibility of vehicles detection and classification using data from wireless communication as channel state information (CSI), the received signal strength indicator (RSSI), a link quality indicator (LQI), or a packet loss rate [5]. Detection of passing vehicles using a magnetometer has been described in [6]. It should be noted that high detection accuracy was achieved when placing the sensors in the lane axis. The combination of two sensor readings for classifying vehicles using machine learning was described in [7,8]. The use of radar to detect vehicles and its configuration is presented in [9]. Such solutions are also used in vehicles for detecting obstacles [10]. Infrared light waves [11] have been used to detect shadows of moving objects. The solution is used in video-detection systems. However, a relatively low interest was placed on light sensors. The first tests carried out in [12] indicate that the light sensor can be used to detect moving objects. The changes in lighting intensity that occur during the movement of people or vehicles have been used by the sensor wake-up system [13]. In this work, light sensors for detection of vehicles and pedestrians in a sensor network will be further examined for application of WSN. As already stated, sending a raw data can consume significant energy resources of WSN devices [14], thus several surveys were performed, which focused on data mining techniques for the end devices (edge mining) [16]. The edge mining does not take under consideration the simplified construction of devices (especially nano sensors [15]) thus previous research [17] was focused on the segmentation methods that are characterized by linear computation complexity and low memory consumption. The segmentation problem of time series is widely researched by authors. In this paper justified granulation paradigms [18] was proposed to aggregate data. Using this paradigm and exponential forgetting method the sensor data can be aggregated into many formal representations of information granules [4]. There are several works that prove the usefulness of this concept [19,20] in various applications. Vehicle classification has been investigated using various machine learning methods, which after training can be used in real time by sensor node: k-Nearest Neighbor (k-NN) [21], linear kernel based support vector machine (SVM) [22] and decision tree (DT) [23]. In this paper lightweight implementation of learning methods was proposed for node based real time processing.

3   Proposed Method

The proposed method is designed for WSN networks, where nodes are placed on the roadside (road curbs and poles) as presented in Fig. 1.

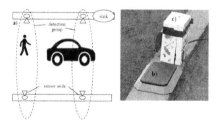

Fig. 1. The researched sensor network: (a) nodes distribution, (b) WSN node implementation, (c) reference Lidar device

Each WSN node is equipped with light sensor, processing unit and wireless communication module (Fig. 1b). The node, during initialization, obtains unique identifier (id), type of operation $(op = 0, 1, 2)$ and detection group (gid). The detection group is formed from nodes monitoring the same area. To reduce energy resources the decision making procedure is performed by single node $(op = 0)$ or in cooperation with nodes within the same group $(op = 1$ or $op = 2)$. The overview of proposed method is presented in Fig. 2.

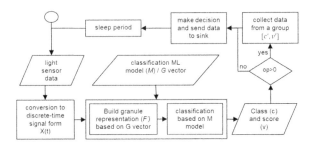

Fig. 2. The light sensor object detection algorithm

The method allows the node to make a decision and send it to a sink. Firstly, the data from sensors are preprocessed to a form, which is acceptable for the proposed granulation method. The method converts the sensor readings to a set of predefined features (F) using vector of parameters G. Then the classification is performed using a trained classifier based on features set. The class (detected $c = 1$ or not detected $c = 0$ object) together with score value, representing posterior probability of class c, are also used as quality measure to tune the method (parameters G and M) using genetic algorithm [24]. All novel method elements will be described in following subsections.

3.1 Preprocessing Light Sensor Data

The sensor readings can have various representations depending on a sensor type. In case of color sensors three value representation like RGB (red, green, blue) or HSL (Hue, Saturation, Lightness) can be read. In case of simple light intensity sensors only one value can be registered. After initial research the color representation (RGB) was selected for further analysis as it contains more useful information than simple light intensity sensor. The data obtained by light sensor, to be processed by WSN node, has to be converted to discrete time signal form. In this case the readings can be represented as time series (TS) with predefined sampling rate (dt). To register moving object at least one reading should be made, while object is passing the sensor. Thus, for object moving at maximum velocity (v in m/s) and for its length (l in meters) the minimum required frequency (in Hz) can be calculated as follows:

$$c_{min} = v/l. \tag{1}$$

Thus, in case of vehicle ($v = 28$ m/s $= 100$ km/h and $l = 2.8$ m) the minimum frequency equals 9.25 Hz. In case of moving person ($v = 1.1$ m/s $= 4$ km/h and $l = 0{,}2$ m) minimum frequency equals 5.5 Hz. Thus, in this study the minimal sensor time between each reading should not be lower than dt value (Eq. 2).

$$dt = \left\lceil \frac{1}{c_{min}} \right\rceil \tag{2}$$

Based on performed calculation the $dt = 0.1$ s was selected. In this research, for simplicity, an intensity for each R, G, B channel is described as ordered set of integer values $X(t) = x_1, x_2, ..., x_t, ..., x_m$ registered in equal time periods (dt). Figure 3 presents the light sensor readings for both moving vehicle and pedestrian collected using network presented in Fig. 1.

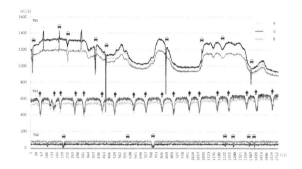

Fig. 3. The light sensor TS example

The Fig. 3 presents the sensor readings registered during passing of vehicle in various weather conditions (TS1 and TS2) and passing of pedestrian in a good weather conditions (TS3). The object passing was marked as a symbol. In case of these TS the changes and their magnitude are not constant. The registered value can be on relatively low level and changes can be small (TS2). On the other hand changes can be more rapid and irregular (TS1). Finally, for small period of time the TS can witness some false periodicity. Therefore, classic TS analysis could not be applied as well as simple detection methods on raw data (e.g. simple thresholding or local minimum detection) are not applicable. Initial analysis allows to notice several relations. The moving objects decreases value of light intensity for each RGB channel. Time of passing is characteristic for a given road spot. Furthermore, the background value of light sensor changes with the time of a day. Finally, despite the placement of a sensor the light reflexes can influence the readings. The observations allowed to propose a granulation method, which describes changes generated by a moving object.

3.2   Granulation Mechanism and Object Profiles

The proposed granulation algorithm eliminates the need to store previous sensor readings in the device memory. The algorithm was based on statistic estimators (e) and exponential forgetting function. The proposed features representing average (f_1), standard deviation (f_2), minimum (f_3), maximum (f_4) and asymmetry (f_5) are calculated based on current sensor value and previous feature value. The features $F = (f_1, f_2, f_3, f_4, f_5)$ are calculated based on current sensor reading $X(t)$, level of granularity $g_i \in [1, 0), i = 1, ..., n$ representing characteristic time period. The vector $G = [g_1, ..., g_i, ..., g_n]$, defines method parameters. The features f_j, $j = 1, ..., 5$ can be calculated using function based on exponential forgetting (Eq. 3) for each g_i value.

$$f_j(t,i) = \begin{cases} g_i e_j(t,i) + (1 - g_i) f_j(t-1,i) : 1 \leq i \leq n, t > 1 \\ e_j(t,i) \qquad\qquad\qquad\qquad : 1 \leq i \leq n, t = 1 \end{cases} \qquad (3)$$

The values $e_j(t,i)$ are calculated using standard measures. Their definition was presented in Eqs. 4–8.

$$e_1(t,i) = X(t) \qquad\qquad\qquad\qquad\qquad\qquad\qquad\qquad (4)$$

$$e_2(t,i) = |X(t) - f_1(t,i)| \qquad\qquad\qquad\qquad\qquad\qquad (5)$$

$$e_3(t,i) = \begin{cases} X(t) & : X(t) < f_1(t,i) - f_2(t,i) \\ f_3(t-1,i) & : \qquad else \end{cases} \qquad (6)$$

$$e_4(t,i) = \begin{cases} X(t) & : X(t) > f_1(t,i) + f_2(t,i) \\ f_4(t-1,i) & : \qquad else \end{cases} \qquad (7)$$

$$e_5(t,i) = X(t) - f_1(t,i) \qquad\qquad\qquad\qquad\qquad\qquad (8)$$

Modification of g_i value allows to change the level of details described by features and in consequence describe short (g_i values closer to 1) and long (g_i values closer to 0) TS characteristics. The example of features $F = f_1, f_2, f_3, f_4, f_5$ was presented in Fig. 4.

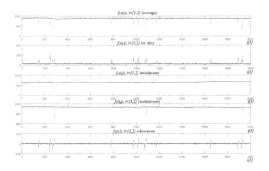

Fig. 4. F function values for defined G vector [$g_1 = 0.8$ (gray line), $g_2 = 0.008$ (black line)]

The features F for value 0.8 represent short term changes that are generated by moving object, while granule with value equal 0.008 represents a changing of light during a day (background).

To extract features ($F' = f'_1, f'_2, f'_3, f'_4, f'_5$) unaffected by background and normalized to interval $[-1, 1]$ the values of two f features for different granularity i and n are used. The conversion procedure is described by Eq. 9.

$$f'_j(t,i) = \begin{cases} \frac{f_j(t,i) - f_j(t,n)}{max(f_j(t,i), f_j(t,n))} & : |f_j(t,n) - f_j(t,i)| > f_2(t,n) \wedge j \in \{1,3,4\} \\ \frac{f_j(t,i) - f_j(t,n)}{max(f_j(t,i), f_j(t,n))} & : \quad |f_j(t,i)| > f_2(t,n) \wedge j \in \{2,5\} \\ 0 & : \qquad else \end{cases} \qquad (9)$$

The normalized values f'_j , $j = 1, ..., 5$ are calculated for $i = 1..n-1$. The function f' values are representing the characteristic features for G vector.

3.3 Machine Learning Method and Decision Making

The values F' calculated using proposed granulation mechanism for defined granularity G and light spectrum R, G, B type creates feature vector denoted as F''. Vector F'' is used by trained machine learning algorithm (M) to perform classification (Eq. 10).

$$(c, v) = M(F''), \tag{10}$$

where: M - machine learning model, c - class label, v - posterior probability.

The classes represent passing objects or their absence. In this research the three models (M) based on machine learning methods were researched (k-NN, LS-SVM and DT) which could be applied within a sensor node. The node can perform classification independently or with cooperation within detection group (sensors detecting the same object). Each sensor has defined sensor read time (dt), type of operation op (1-cooperation node, 2-cooperation coordinator or 0-independent) and detection group id (gid). Then the decision is performed according to algorithm 1:

1. $t0 = $ current time,
2. Read sensor data $X(t)$,
3. Evaluate c, v using Eq. 10,
4. If $op = 0$ then goto 12.
5. Create empty table tab=[],
6. Add to tab vector $[v, c]$,
7. $rand = $ random number within interval $[current\_time - t0, dt/4]$,
8. While $(current\_time\text{-}t0) <= 0.25dt + rand$ do
    (a) Read frame $[gid', v', c']$ and if gid' equal device gid store vector $[v', c']$ in tab,
    (b) If $(currenttime - t0) > rand$ and $op = 1$ broadcast once frame =[id,v,c],
9. Create $tab2$ with size equal to number of classes with zeros,
10. For each vector $[v'', c'']$ in tab do $tab2[c'']+ = v''$,
11. Select class as $c = arg_x max(tab2[x])$, $v = tab2[x]/sizeof(tab)$,
12. If $c > 0$ and op in $\{0,2\}$ send frame $= [id, v, c]$ to a sink, sleep for $dt -$ $(current\_time - t0)$, and goto 1.

The algorithm is based on the classification method (lines 2–3). In case on independent solution the classification result is send directly to the sink. In case of classification via cooperation the nodes exchange their results (line 8). The added random value (line 7) minimizes the frame collision probability during transmission both to neighbors and to the sink. Based on highest joined posteriori probability the final class is selected and send to sink by coordinator ($op = 2$) (line 11–12), but only if object is detected ($c > 0$).

3.4   Tuning Using Granular Algorithm

The method parameters are tuned using genetic algorithm (GA) described in [24]. The tuning parameters constrains are $G = [g_1, ..., g_i, ..., g_n], g_i = [1, 0), g_1 > g_2 > ... > g_n, i = 1, ..., n$ vector. Initially, n equals 2. M model is constructed based on feature representation F'', class labels C obtained using reference device and methods parameters. The following parameters are tuned for particular classification methods: $k = 3, 5, 7, 9$ (k-NN), $nu = (0.3, 0.7)$ (LS-SVM) and no parameter (DT - C4.5 algorithm). The number of population equals i_{po} in each iteration. The populations are generated using uniform distribution. For each individual feature representation (based on G^*) is created in form of vector F''^*. Then the model M^* is created using vector value F''^* and reference class value C. The fitness function of individual is measured by overall accuracy measure (r). If accuracy $r > r_{th}$ (defined as parameter) then the individual is selected. Otherwise the mutation and crossover is performed [24]. The best population individual always passes to next iteration. If the model obtained in i_{th} iteration did not fulfill estimated r_{th} accuracy, the vector G length is extended by 1 (up to $n = 5$). In this case the best individual is moved to next iteration by adding random number to existing vector (in the middle). The rest of the implementation is consistent with the classical GA.

4   Experiments

The proposed method was verified using ZigBee communication based sensor network. The nodes are using ILS29125 RGB light sensor with an infrared filter and a built-in 16-bit transmitter and measuring range up to 10000 lx. The advantage of this sensor is low power consumption, which equals 0,18 mW. The network presented in Fig. 1 was implemented in three scenarios using the proposed algorithm. First two scenarios measured road traffic in single lane. The sensors were distributed 4 m from each other. The first scenario presents sunny day, while the second scenario presents bad weather conditions: cloudy and rainy day. The third scenario illustrates the network installed on sidewalk (2 by 2 m), where the network was used to detect pedestrians passing. The Light Detection and Ranging (Lidar) device was used as the source of reference data for training stage. The collected time series was divided into training subsequence and verification sub-sequence in rate 60% to 40%. The tuning was performed for various set of features and three lightweight state-of-the-art classification methods. The GA parameters were set: $i_{op} = 10$, $i_{th} = 50$ and $r_{th} = 0.95$. The further increase of population number did not increase the accuracy value. The results, for scenario 1 are presented in Table 1A.

The results show that with the increase of features number the accuracy of the proposed method is raising in case of kNN and SVM classifier. However, in case of decision trees, the additional features are causing overestimation, that reduces detection precision. What is worth to note the background is stable, thus the last value of G vector is relatively small. The results of a scenario for changing weather conditions (scenario 2) were presented in Table 1B. Due to

Table 1. The vehicle detection under good weather conditions

Scen.		Features (F)	Training accuracy	G vector	Class. params	Verification accuracy
(A)	kNN (k)	1–2	98.0%	[1, 0.09, 0.003125]	3	93.9%
		1–4	98.8%	[1, 0.1, 0.00625]	5	94.3%
		1–5	99.4%	[1, 0.0.08, 0.0002]	3	95.5%
	SVM (nu)	1–2	97.1%	[1, 0.09, 0.0015]	0.49	92.7%
		1–4	97.6%	[1, 0.1, 0.003]	0.51	92.9%
		1–5	97.2%	[1, 0.09, 0.003]	0.5	93.1%
	DT (-)	1–2	100.0%	[1,0.09,0.025]	–	93.4%
		1–4	100.0%	[1, 0.08, 0.003]	–	89.0%
		1–5	100.0%	[0.9, 0.07, 0.0004]	–	90.1%
(B)	kNN (k)	1–2	96.9%	[1, 0.05, 0.08]	5	86.5%
		1–4	97.9%	[1, 0.05, 0.08]	5	86.5%
		1–5	98.4%	[1, 0.05, 0.003]	7	86.8%
	SVM (nu)	1–2	96.8%	[1, 0.05, 0.08]	0.4	85.8%
		1–4	97.5%	[1, 0.05, 0.08]	0.45	86.1%
		1–5	97.3%	[1, 0.05, 0.08]	0.47	86.5%
	DT (-)	1–2	99.5%	[1, 0.08]	–	84.1%
		1–4	99.8%	[1, 0.04, 0.003]	–	79.2%
		1–5	99.8%	[1, 0.04, 0.003]	–	79.2%
(C)	kNN (k)	1–2	99.1%	[0.6, 0.08, 0.00078]	3	92.1%
		1–4	99.6%	[0.6, 0.1, 0.00078]	3	91.2%
		1–5	99.6%	[0.6, 0.1, 0.00078]	3	93.9%
	SVM (nu)	1–2	98.7%	[0.7, 0.07, 0.003]	0.51	92.5%
		1–4	99.3%	[0.7, 0.09, 0.0015]	0.49	94.2%
		1–5	99.6%	[0.8, 0.08, 0.0015]	0.5	95.6%
	DT (-)	1–2	100.0%	[0.8, 0.05]	–	94.7%
		1–4	100.0%	[0.8, 0.05]	–	93.9%
		1–5	100.0%	[0.8, 0.05]	–	94.2%

rapid changes of the light conditions the long term granulation is not present. However, two G vector values remain unchanged. They are 1 and 0.08. Thus for next research, those values were selected as most reliable representation of TS. In case of kNN and SVM algorithm all 5 features were used. In case of DT algorithm only 2 features average and standard deviation were selected. The detection of pedestrians was also researched. The results were presented in Table 1C.

Comparing the results with values obtained for vehicles, it can be noticed that first value is not equal to 1. That means that pedestrians are moving slower and precise value at given time is not required to detect a pedestrian. The tuned method was compared against machine learning methods, using methods on raw data, defined features without granulation mechanism and two version of operation: independent and evaluation for a group containing 2 sensors. The results are presented in Table 2.

Table 2. Detection accuracy of proposed method

Method	Classifier	Accuracy vehicles	Accuracy pedestrians
Granule based + independent	kNN	90.40%	93.90%
	SVM	89.70%	95.60%
	DT	88.90%	94.70%
Granule based + cooperation	kNN	92.40%	95.80%
	SVM	91.30%	96.40%
	DT	89.90%	95.10%
Features + window	kNN	90.30%	93.70%
	SVM	89.80%	94.90%
	DT	89.10%	94.60%
Raw data + window	kNN	83.30%	86.40%
	SVM	79.70%	83.30%
	DT	67.80%	78.10%

The results firmly show that raw data are inferior to feature approach due to a changing background. The proposed granulation method using exponential forgetting allows to save memory utilization of sensors, while retaining high detection accuracy comparable to features values extracted directly from TS. All tested machine learning algorithms were able to detect both pedestrians and vehicles with accuracy above 90%, however in case of vehicles the kNN method proves superior over SVM method. On the other hand SVM method better detects pedestrians. The proposed cooperation algorithm allows to increase the accuracy from single detection group. This approach is vital, if object is moving close to one sensor. The proposed cooperation algorithm increase detection accuracy up to 5.9%. Additionally, only information about detected passing are sent to the sink, thus data transfer if reduced by 78% on average.

5　Conclusion

The paper proposes to use a light based sensor network to detect object like moving pedestrians or vehicles. The research results show that passive sensors as light sensor are able to detect objects with accuracy above 90% in good weather condition and above 85% in case of rainy weather. The proposed method of cooperation of sensor network allowed to further increase detection accuracy up to 92.4% and 96.4% for vehicles and pedestrians respectively. The proposed granulation mechanism allows reducing memory utilization by updating features values each time new values are read from sensor. What is worth to note that proposed mechanism generate repeatable results. Additionally, the cooperation mode allows the group of sensors to act as one by exchanging classification results. The obtained results are promising. The next step is to verify method during day and night conditions. Additionally, the data from sensor network group can be further optimized by suppression algorithm to further save resources. Furthermore, the light sensor can be connected with other sensor to further improve accuracy.

Acknowledgement. The research was supported by The National Centre for Research and Development (NCBR) grant number LIDER/18/0064/L-7/15/NCBR/2016.

References

1. Van Ommeren, J.N., Wentink, D., Rietveld, P.: Empirical evidence on cruising for parking. Transp. Res. Part A Policy Pract. **46**, 123–130 (2012)
2. Liu, H., Chen, S., Kubota, N.: Intelligent video systems and analytics: a survey. IEEE Trans. Ind. Inform. **9**, 1222–1233 (2013)
3. Gaura, E., Brusey, J., Allen, M., Wilkins, R., Goldsmith, D., Red, R.: Edge mining the Internet of Things. IEEE Sensors J. **13**(10), 3816–3825 (2013)
4. Zhang, Y., Zhang, L., Xu, C.: The property of different granule and granular methods based on quotient space. In: Pedrycz, W., Chen, S.-M. (eds.) Information Granularity, Big Data, and Computational Intelligence. SBD, vol. 8, pp. 171–190. Springer, Cham (2015). https://doi.org/10.1007/978-3-319-08254-7_8
5. Roy, S., Sen, R., Kulkarni, S., Kulkarni, P., Raman, B., Singh, L.K.: Wireless across road: RF based road traffic congestion detection. In: Third International Conference on IEEE Communication Systems and Networks (COMSNETS), pp. 1–6 (2011)
6. He, H., Jiang, T., Zhao, H., Li, J., Qiu T., Hu, Y.: An energy-efficient vehicle detection algorithm for a complex urban traffic environment. In: CICTP (2015)
7. Ma, W., Xing, D., Mckee, A., Bajwa, R., Flores, C.: A wireless accelerometer-based automatic vehicle classification prototype system. IEEE Trans. Intell. Transp. Syst. **15**, 1 (2014)
8. Hostettler, R., Djuric, P.: Vehicle tracking based on fusion of magnetometer and accelerometer sensor measurements with particle filtering. IEEE Trans. Veh. Technol. **64**(11), 4917–4928 (2015)
9. Youngtae, J.: Analysis of vehicle detection with WSN-based ultrasonic sensors. Sensors **14**, 14050–14069 (2014)
10. Liu, J., Han, J., Lv, H., Li, B.: An ultrasonic sensor system based on a two-dimensional state method for highway vehicle violation detection applications. Sensors **15**, 9000–9021 (2015)
11. Fredembach, D.C., Susstrunk, S.: Automatic and accurate shadow detection using near-infrared information. IEEE Trans. Pattern Anal. Mach. Intell. **36**(8), 1672–1678 (2014)
12. Mao, X., Tang, S., Li, X.: Multiple objects device-free passive tracking using wireless sensor networks. In: IEEE ICC 2011 Proceedings, pp. 1–6 (2011)
13. Scientific description. https://www.Scientific.Net/AMR.457-458.690
14. Płaczek, B.: Uncertainty-dependent data collection in vehicular sensor networks. In: KwiecieÅD, A., Gaj, P., Stera, P. (eds.) Computer Networks. Communications in Computer and Information Science, vol. 291, pp. 430–439. Springer, Heidelberg (2012). https://doi.org/10.1007/978-3-642-31217-5_45
15. Balasubramaniam, S., Kangasharju, J.: Realizing the internet of nano things: challenges, solutions, and applications. Computer **46**(2), 62–68 (2013)

16. Starner, T.: The challenges of wearable computing: part 1. IEEE Micro **21**(4), 44–52 (2001)
17. Bernas, M., Płaczek, B., Sapek, A.: Edge real-time medical data segmentation for iot devices with computational and memory constrains. In: Nguyen, N.T., Papadopoulos, G.A., Jędrzejowicz, P., Trawiński, B., Vossen, G. (eds.) ICCCI 2017. LNCS (LNAI), vol. 10449, pp. 119–128. Springer, Cham (2017). https://doi.org/10.1007/978-3-319-67077-5_12
18. Pedrycz, W., Homenda, W.: Building the fundamentals of granular computing: a principle of justifiable granularity. Appl. Soft Comput. **13**(10), 4209–4218 (2013)
19. Song, M., Wang, Y.: Human centricity and information granularity in the agenda of theories and applications of soft computing. Appl. Soft Comput. **27**, 610–613 (2015)
20. Bernas, M., Orczyk, T., Porwik, P.: Fusion of granular computing and k–NN classifiers for medical data support system. In: Nguyen, N.T., Trawiński, B., Kosala, R. (eds.) ACIIDS 2015. LNCS (LNAI), vol. 9012, pp. 62–71. Springer, Cham (2015). https://doi.org/10.1007/978-3-319-15705-4_7
21. Porwik, P., Doroz, R., Orczyk, T.: The k-NN classifier and self-adaptive Hotelling data reduction technique in handwritten signatures recognition. Pattern Anal. Appl. **18**(4), 983–1001 (2015)
22. Haferkamp, M., et al.: Radio-based Traffic flow detection and vehicle classification for future smart cities. In: 2017 IEEE 85th Vehicular Technology Conference (VTC Spring), Sydney, NSW, pp. 1–5 (2017)
23. Martsenyuk, V., et al.: On multivariate method of qualitative analysis of Hodgkin-Huxley model with decision tree induction. In: 16th International Conference on Control, Automation and Systems (ICCAS), Gyeongju, pp. 489–494 (2016)
24. Goldberg, D.: Genetic Algorithms in Search, Optimization & Machine Learning. Addison-Wesley, Boston (1989)

Behavioral Analysis of Service Oriented Systems Using Event-B

Anasuya Chaudhuri, Shreya Banerjee, and Anirban Sarkar[(✉)]

Department of Computer Science and Engineering,
National Institute of Technology, Durgapur, India
anasuyachaudhury@gmail.com,
shreya.banerjee85@gmail.com, sarkar.anirban@gmail.com

Abstract. Service Oriented Architecture (SOA) is a widely used architectural style for constructing Service Oriented Systems (SOS). SOS incorporates several crucial features such as, service composition, service discovery; those are related with different behavioral aspects of SOS. Further, effective analysis of these behavioral characteristics depends on suitable specification of events and constraints in SOA. Thus, to achieve precise and correct specification for SOS, there is a serious need of formal conceptualization of SOA and its associated behavioral characteristics. In this context, this paper proposes a conceptual model for SOA using set theoretic approach and its behavioral aspects using Event-B language [2]. Further, correctness of the model is proved through Rodin platform [2]. A case study is also specified for exhibiting the practical usability of the proposed concepts. The novelty of the proposed work is to model SOA, its behavioral characteristics, related phenomenon and constraints in a way that is more feasible, effective and suitable for service-oriented system.

Keywords: Service oriented architecture · Service composition
Service discovery · Service Oriented System · Event-B · Rodin
Proof of correctness

1 Introduction

Service oriented architecture (SOA) is an architectural paradigm that provides the vocabulary for Service Oriented Systems (SOS). A service is a distributed software application accessed over the network through its interface [11]. However, modelling SOA possess several challenges. *Firstly*, in existing literature, different characteristics of SOA are described with graphical and textual notations, which result in ambiguous and different level of usage. *Secondly*, SOS is loosely coupled, distributed and reactive systems. These features facilitate services to be discovered and composed with each other dynamically in SOS. However, effective specification of these features depends on precise representation of behavior characteristics of SOS. Thus, formal specification for SOA needs to exhibit such characteristics and relationships with structural characteristics of SOS. *Thirdly*, there is need of suitable semantics representation of distinct events and constraints. Events impose different constraints on several behavioral phenomenon including service composition, service discovery etc. and it is an

© Springer Nature Switzerland AG 2018
K. Saeed and W. Homenda (Eds.): CISIM 2018, LNCS 11127, pp. 117–129, 2018.
https://doi.org/10.1007/978-3-319-99954-8_11

important construct for analyzing behavioral characteristics of SOS. *Fourthly*, checking consistency of behavioral characteristics of SOA is a prime requisite.

In the related literature, most described conceptual models for SOA are represented in a combination of textual description and a graphical presentation [3]. Proprietary notations [4] based on SOA design patterns are also used to make SOA easy to interpret. However, graphical or proprietary descriptions do not facilitate formal specifications. Thus, these make the model ambiguous and may lack details. Several research works have applied formal object-oriented design patterns known as Gang of Four (GoF) defined in [3]. Authors in [5], specify 23 GoF patterns formally in First-Order Logic (FOL) and in the Graphic Extension of BNF (GEBNF) to define both structural and behavioral features of design patterns. Authors in [8], extends design patterns of GoF based on concepts of role, which is transferred to Object-Z for specifying only structural features of patterns. Authors in [9] describe methodologies for pattern specifications and reuse of them in B method through several examples only for structural characteristics. In [6, 14], message-oriented SOA design patterns are modelled in a semi-formal language SoaML [7] and further are transformed into Event-B specifications using XSLT (eX-tensible Stylesheet Language Transformations) language. Yet, authors have not addressed different constraints, those may exist in a service. Authors in [5], carried out a functional validation based approach using Petri Net to check the seamless connectivity between individual services to be composed. Thus, major approaches represent only structural characteristics of SOS. Further, very few have proved correctness of their described specifications.

In this paper, SOA is formally specified and correctness is proved of overall specification using Event B method [2]. Event-B is a widely used formal language, built on first-order logic and set theory. It is supported by the Rodin platform [2], which offers a range of simulation and verification technologies. In this paper, Event B language is chosen for several reasons. Event-B specification is executable and can be used as a prototype. Event-B facilitates to construct a model from high-level of abstraction to more detailed level specification in the context of SOA. The proposed work defines the behavior of system directly by constructing a model of system, uses in reactive and distributed system [12] such as SOS. Besides this, the relationships between the structural and behavioral elements are specified using Event-B. Moreover, Event-B method support decomposition of proof and thus specification represented in Event-B is consistent throughout its refinements. Major approaches SOA modelling existing in literature do not have these capabilities of formal specification, refinement and proofing their correctness simultaneously in reactive and distributed systems like SOS. The benefits of the proposed approach are manifolds. *Firstly*, it formalizes and proves correctness and consistency of both structural and behavioral features of SOA. *Secondly*, different behavioral aspects of SOA including service discovery and composition are formally specified and correctness of specifications are proved using Event B language. *Thirdly*, different constraints and events are formalized to analyses behavioral aspect of SOA.

2   The Event-B Modelling Notation

The key construct of Event-B is model. A model in Event-B is made of two parts - contexts and machines. Static elements of the model are described by context part. Dynamic behavior of a model is specified by machine part [2]. One or several contexts can be "Seen" by one or several machines. A context can "Extend" another one. On the other hand, a machine can "Refine" another machine. Table 1 describes distinct components and their elements of an Event B language.

Table 1. Distinct components of Event-B

Components of Event-b Model	Elements of a component	Description
Context	Extends	A context can extend another context using this element
	Sets	Introduce list of distinct sets
	Constants	Define distinct constants in the context
	Axioms	Represents predicates that the constant must obey and type of constants
Machine	Refines	A machine can refine another machine optionally using this element
	Sees	When a machine "Sees" a context, then all sets and constants defined in the context can be used in that machine
	Variables	Represented as a list that constitutes the state of the machine
	Invariants	Invariants should be true for every reachable state
	Events	Lists of transitions that can occur under certain circumstances
	Guard	Represents the necessary conditions so that an event can occur
	Action	Describes the way so that certain state variables are modified as a consequence of an event occurrence

3   Proposed Conceptual Model of Service Oriented Architecture (SOA)

SOA consists of several concepts such as Service, Service Description, Service Interface, Real World Effect, Interaction, Contract & Policy, Execution Context and Visibility [1]. In this section, a conceptual model for SOA is proposed. The proposed conceptual model is represented in set logic that can be directly mapped towards Event-B language. In proposed model, concepts of SOS are specified into four parts: *Information Model* (*IM*), *Action Model* (*AM*), *Behavioral Model* (*BM*) and *Artefacts Model* (*AFEM*). Thus, SOA can be represented as a tuple, *SOA* = {*IM, AM, BM, AFEM*}.

(a) **Information** **Model** (*IM*): *Information Model* (*IM*) represents all the structural concepts of SOA such as *Service* (*S*), *Service Interface* (*SI*), *Actor* (*AC*), *Service Description* (*SD*), *Registry* (*REG*), *Data* (*DA*), and *System* (*SYS*). Thus, *Information Model* can be represented as a tuple, *IM* = {*S, DA, SI, AC, SD, REG, SYS*}.

 (i) *Service (S):* Service is a package of closely related business functionalities and may have distinct properties such as Service Version, Service Identification Number etc. [1]. *Service* can be specified as a set *S* = {(*Service_ID, Version_No.*)}.

 (ii) *Data (D):* Data represents input and output parameters for service capabilities. It has a property - Data Type. Thus, *Data* can be represented as a set, *D* = {(*Data_Type*}.

(iii) *Actor (AC):* Actor plays the roles of consumer, provider or performer. Actor can be represented as a set, *AC* = {(*Actor_Role*)}.

(iv) *Service Description (SD):* A service description includes functional and non-functional properties of services, service interfaces, the legal and technical constraints or rules for its usage. It can be represented as a set, *SD* = {(*Functional_Description, Non_Functional_Description*)}.

 (v) *Registry (REG):* The registry is an information catalogue that is constantly updated with information about the different services. Registry allows service consumer to discover and communicate with provider efficiently. A registry can be represented as a set, *REG* = {(*registry_implementation, Registry_User*)}.

(vi) *Service_Interface (SI):* Service Interface defines the way in which other elements may interact and exchange information with a service [10]. In this section, *SI* is classified in two types – *Interface_in_General* and *Interface_Orchestrator*. A *service interface* can be represented as a set, *SI* = {(*Interaction_Type, Protocol*)}.

(vii) *System (SYS):* A system is an organized collection of services. In this section, *SYS* is classified in two types - *Choreography System* (*SYSCHG*) and *Orchestration System* (*SYSORC*). It can be represented as a set, *SYS* = {(*System_ID*)}.

(b) **Action Model (AM):** It specifies all the functionality in SOA offered by different services. Functionalities are represented as *Activity Elements* (*AE*).

 (i) *Action (ACN):* Action has represented the activities or operations through which functionality of a service is accomplished. Action can be of two types – *Composite Action* (*CACN*) and *Simple Action* (*SACN*). It can be represented as, *ACN* = {(*Action_Type, Ordering Number*)}. *Ordering Number* denotes precedence number of participations of different services and actions in compositions.

 (ii) *Simple Action (SACN):* It represents an atomic activity that has several decomposable tasks and can be expressed as, *SACN* = {(*Service, task, Ordering Number*)}.

(iii) *Composite Action (CACN):* This comprises of several simple actions performed by services and can be expressed as, *CACN* = {(*Service, task, Ordering Number*)}.

(c) **Behavioral Model (BM):** It represents all the real world effect achieved from triggering of different *Event Elements* (*EE*) and can be represented as, *BM* = {*EE*}.

(i) *Effect (EFF)*: *Effect* has denoted the outcome after invoking a service. It can be represented as, *EFF* = {*(Constraints)*}.

(d) **Artefacts Model (AFEM):** It includes all the artefact elements those are synthesized in service domain such as *Constraint (CO)*, *Task (task)*, *Flag (FLG)*, *Ordering Number (ORD)* etc. It can be represented as, *AFEM* = {*CO*, *task*, *FLG*, *ORD*}.

(a) *Constraint (CO):* Constraint denotes conditions based on which effects can be achieved. It can be represented as a set *CO* = {*(Condition)*}. Constraint can be of two types – *Visibility* and *Ordering*. *Ordering Constraint* specifies both ordered and unordered arrangement of services in an orchestrator or choreography system. *Visibility Constraint* can be considered as the pre requirements for a service to be visible. This constraint can be of three types - *Awareness*, *Reachability* and *Willingness*.

(b) *Ordering Number (ORD):* It specifies precedence number of participations of different services and actions in compositions. It can be represented as a variable *ORD*.

(d) *Flag (FLG):* It denotes the state of visibility constraints. If all of visibility constraints are true, then value of *Flag* will be true. It can be represented as a variable *FLG*.

4 Event B Specification of Proposed Conceptual Model for SOA

In this section, proposed conceptual model of SOA are realized in Event-B language. All constructs of *Information Model* and *Action Model* are specified through "Context" construct. On the other hand, all constructs of *Behavioral Model* and *Artefact Model* are represented through "Machine" construct. Moreover, action level composition, service level composition and discovery of services are realized through "Machine" construct. Tables 2 and 3 summarize the "Context" part and the "Machine" part of proposed conceptual model respectively.

4.1 Specification of Incremented Machine Approach of Proposed Conceptual Model of SOA

Event B method is based on Refinement concept. In the proposed work, conceptual model specification for SOA is done in four refinement steps. Proposed conceptual model is composed of total five machines named *Consumer-Provider Communication (SOA_M_1)*, *Reachability and Willingness (SOA_M_2)*, *Awareness, Publish and Discover Service (SOA_M_3)*, *Action Composition (SOA_M_4)*, *Orchestration Choreography (SOA_M_5)* and only one context (*SOAC*). In each refinement step, all constructs in abstract machine can be used in the refined machine. Additionally, other constructs are also introduced in refined machine. Thus, refinement techniques are used to introduce details and complexity into proposed conceptual model of SOA in an incremented way. All machines are related with only one context part - *SOAC*. Thus, all machines "See" the Context part *SOAC*. Figure 1 illustrates the refinement technique.

Table 2. Realization of proposed conceptual model through "Context" in Event-B language

Conceptualizations	Concepts	"Context" in Event-B
Information Model	Service	Defined as a set of "Services"
	Actor	Defined as a set, "Actor"
	Data	Defined as a set, "Message_Type"
	Service Description	Defined as set, "Service_Description"
	Registry	Defined as a constant related to set "Actor"
	System	Defined as a set named "System"
	Choreography System	Defined as a constant related to set "System" inside axiom clause of Context
	Orchestration System	Defined as a constant related to set "System" inside axiom clause of Context
	Service Interface	Defined as set, "Interface" inside Context
	Interface_in_General	Defined as a constant related to set "Interface" inside axiom clause of Context
	Interface_Orchestrator	Defined as a constant related to "Interface" inside axiom clause of Context
Action Model	Action	Define as a set named "Action" inside context
	Simple Action	Define as a constant related to set "Action" inside axiom clause of Context
	Composite Action	as a constant related to set "Action" inside axiom clause of Context

Table 3. Realization of proposed conceptual model through "Machine" in Event-B language

Conceptualizations	Concepts	"Machine" in Event-B
Behavioural Model	Effect	Effect is the result, that is recognized in the action part (then clause) of every event of every Machine
Artefact Model	Visibility Constraint	Implemented through *Awareness event, Willingness event, Reachability event* and *Activating_Flag event*
	Ordering Constraint	Implemented through *Execute_is_next_to, Execute_is_last_to, Execute_AND* and *Execute_OR* events
	Flag	Define as a variable of Boolean type
	Ordering Number	Define as a variable *ORD*
	Service Composition	Implemented using *Choreography* and *Orchestration* events
	Service Discovery	Implemented using *Has_published* and *Has_found* events

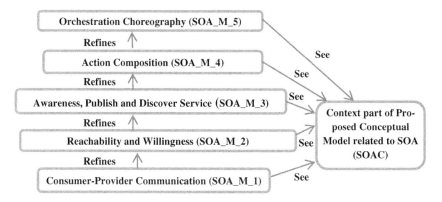

Fig. 1. Illustration of refinement technique in Event-B for proposed conceptual model

(a) **Description of first machine - *Consumer-Provider Communication Machine* (*SOA_M_1*):** First machine specifies the communication between Provider and Consumer. The *SOAC* context related with this machine is consisting of two sets. Set *Actor*is related with three constants – *Provider, Consumer* and *Registry*; Set *Mesaage_Type* is related with two constants - *request_service* and *response_service*; Beside this, three variables are used to represent the state of the machine - *Flag, send* and *Reply.* invariants that are used to specify these variables. In addition, this machine consists of total five events. First event is *Initialisation*, which is used to initialise all the variables. Second event *Sending_request* is used to trigger a *Consumer* to send a *request_service* message to *Provider* when variable *Flag* is true. Third event *Reply_response* triggers *Provider* to reply to the *Consumer* with the *response_service* message when variable *Flag* is true. *Request_service* message is in the range of *send* and *response_service* yet not replied by the *provider*. Fourth event *Receiving_Response* triggers *Consumer* to receive the *response_service* message and set the *Flag* false, when *response_service* is presented in the range of *Reply* relation, Fifth event *Activating_flag* is used to activate the *Flag* whenever it is deactivated. Figure 2 illustrates the first machine.

(b) **Description of second machine - *Reachability and Willingness Machine* (*SOA_M_2*):** Second machine, *SOA_M_2* refines the first machine *SOA_M_1*. This machine specifies *Reachability* and *Willingness* of *Consumer* and *Provider* to communicate. A new set named *Interface* introduced in the context *SOAC* with four constants - *provider_interface, consumer_interface, Interface_in_General* and *Interface_Orchestrator*. Four invariants are used to specify four new variables – *Reachability_Flag, Willingness_Flag, process* and *receive*. New three events are introduced in second Machine. Event *Reachability* sets the value of variable *Reachability_Flag,* which is of Boolean type to true only when consumer sends a message to the provider and provider receive a same message. Event *Willingness* sets the status of the variable *Willingness_Flag* to true if consumer is willing to request for a service and provider is willing to service that request, and event *Processing_req* triggers *provider_interface* to process the requested service,

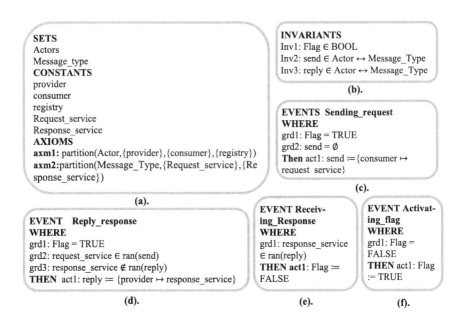

Fig. 2. Description of First Machine *Consumer-Provider Communication* (*SOA_M_1*): Illustration of (a). Context; (b). Invariants; (c). event *Sending_request*; (d). event *Reply_response*; (e). event *Receiving_response*; (f). event *Activating_flag*

when the *request_Service* message is received and yet not processed. Event *Activity_flag* is refined by adding two new guard that when both value of variables *Reachability_Flag* and *Willingness_Flag* will be true. Event *Reply_response* is also refined here by adding two more guards to apply the condition that when requested service has been received and processed. Event *Processing_Resp* is refined form of event *Receiving_response* in first machine. This event triggers *consumerconsumer_interface* to process *response_service*, when the consumer has received *response_service* but the *consumer_ interface* yet not process it. Figure 3 illustrates the second machine.

(c) **Description of third machine - *Awareness, Discover and Publish Service Machine* (*SOA_M_3*):** The third machine (*SOA_M_3*) refines the second machine (*SOA_M_2*). In this machine, another visibility constraint *Awareness* is formalized. Besides this, the machine also specifies publishing and discovery of services. Two new sets named *Service_Description* and *Actions* with two constants named as *Simple* denoting simple action and *Composite* denoting composite action respectively are added into the context *SOAC*. Five new variables are introduced in the third machine. Those are *publishing, searching, send_description, Has_new_service*, and *Awarness_Flag*. Further, three new events are added. Event *Has_published* is triggered whenever a producer has a new service and need to publish its service description into the registry. The event *Has_found* is triggered when consumer search for a service description into the registry that provider has published and the registry not yet send the service description to the consumer.

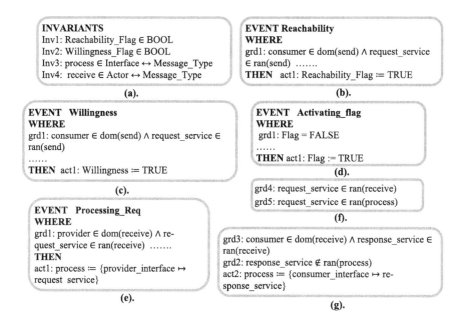

INVARIANTS
Inv1: Reachability_Flag ∈ BOOL
Inv2: Willingness_Flag ∈ BOOL
Inv3: process ∈ Interface ↔ Message_Type
Inv4: receive ∈ Actor ↔ Message_Type

(a).

EVENT Reachability
WHERE
grd1: consumer ∈ dom(send) ∧ request_service
∈ ran(send) ....
THEN   act1: Reachability_Flag ≔ TRUE

(b).

EVENT Willingness
WHERE
grd1: consumer ∈ dom(send) ∧ request_service ∈
ran(send)
......
THEN act1: Willingness ≔ TRUE

(c).

EVENT Activating_flag
WHERE
 grd1: Flag = FALSE
......
THEN act1: Flag ≔ TRUE

(d).

grd4: request_service ∈ ran(receive)
grd5: request_service ∈ ran(process)

(f).

EVENT   Processing_Req
WHERE
grd1: provider ∈ dom(receive) ∧ re-
quest_service ∈ ran(receive) ....
THEN
act1: process ≔ {provider_interface ↦
request service}

(e).

grd3: consumer ∈ dom(receive) ∧ response_service ∈
ran(receive)
grd2: response_service ∉ ran(process)
act2: process ≔ {consumer_interface ↦ re-
sponse_service}

(g).

Fig. 3. Description of second Machine (*SOA_M_2*): Illustration of (a) Invariants; (b) event *Reachability*; (c) event *Willingness*; (d) event *Activating_flag;* (e) event *Processing_Req* (f) additional guards and actions in event *Reply_response*; (g) additional guards and action in event *Receiving_response*

Event *Awareness* set the value of variable *Awarness_Flag* true only when consumer is aware of the provider and it will happen if the service description searched by the consumer is found into the registry and registry has sent it to the consumer. Beside this, event *Activating_flag* is again refined in this machine by adding one more guard to apply the condition, when the value of the variables *Awarness_Flag* is true.

(d) **Description of fourth machine - *Action Composition Machine* (*SOA_M_4*):** The fourth machine (*SOA_M_4*) refines the third machine (*SOA_M_3*). This machine formalizes different kinds of action compositions. A new set named as *Service* and two constants *List_of_Service,* which lists all the simple services of a composite service, and *n*, which is a natural number, are defined in the context *SOAC*. Six new variables are introduced. Those are contain_action_of_type, Contain_action, Order_of_act, Has_interface, composed_with, and process_simple. Besides these six variables, there are ten more variables are added to specify different composition patterns. The fourth machine consists of total five events. Those are *Execute_is_next_to*, *Execute_is_last_to*, *Execute_AND*, *Execute_OR* and *Processing_Simple_Service*. These events specify different ordered constraints that may be applied at the action composition level. As an example, event *Execute_is_next_to*, which specifies one ordering constraint is triggered when the service under consideration consists of composite action, which is formed by the simple actions *a1*, *a2* and *a3* with their respective interfaces *I1*, *I2*, *I3*. The action *a1* and *a2* have order *ORD1* and *ORD2* to composed with action *a3* such that *ORD2* = *ORD1* + 1. Then in the action part union of the pairs {{*I3* ↦ *I1*} ↦ *ORD1*} and {{*I3* ↦ *I2*} ↦ *ORD2*} is add to the relation *Composed_with* to define that interface *I1* will be composed with interface *I3* before interface *I2* is composed with *I3*.

(e) **Description of fifth machine - Orchestration Choreography (SOA_M_5):** The fifth machine (*SOA_M_5*) refines the fourth machine (*SOA_M_4*). The fifth machine (*SOA_M_5*) specifies two types of system: *Choreography System* and *Orchestration System*. A new set named *System* and two new constants *Choreography_System* and *Orchestration_System* related with the set *System* are introduces into the context *SOAC*. Six new variables are introduced in the fifth machine - *System_has_interface*, *Serivce_has_interface*, *Invoke*, *Reply*, *Order_of_Service* and *I_Co*. Two events are introduced in the fifth machine – Event *Choreography* formalizes *Choreography_System* and event *Orchestration* specifies how the service composition happens between service interfaces through a coordinator interface. Figure 4 demonstrates this machine.

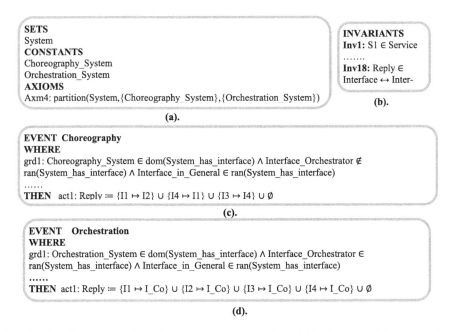

SETS
System
CONSTANTS
Choreography_System
Orchestration_System
AXIOMS
Axm4: partition(System,{Choreography_System},{Orchestration_System})

(a).

INVARIANTS
Inv1: S1 ∈ Service
……..
Inv18: Reply ∈ Interface ↔ Inter-

(b).

EVENT Choreography
WHERE
grd1: Choreography_System ∈ dom(System_has_interface) ∧ Interface_Orchestrator ∉ ran(System_has_interface) ∧ Interface_in_General ∈ ran(System_has_interface)
……
THEN act1: Reply := {I1 ↦ I2} ∪ {I4 ↦ I1} ∪ {I3 ↦ I4} ∪ ∅

(c).

EVENT Orchestration
WHERE
grd1: Orchestration_System ∈ dom(System_has_interface) ∧ Interface_Orchestrator ∈ ran(System_has_interface) ∧ Interface_in_General ∈ ran(System_has_interface)
……
THEN act1: Reply := {I1 ↦ I_Co} ∪ {I2 ↦ I_Co} ∪ {I3 ↦ I_Co} ∪ {I4 ↦ I_Co} ∪ ∅

(d).

Fig. 4. Description of fifth Machine (*SOA_M_5*): Illustration of (a). Context; (b). Invariants; (c). Event *Choreography*; (d). Event *Orchestration*

4.2   Proof of Correctness of the Proposed Conceptual Model

In this section, correctness of the proposed formal specification of SOA presented in Event B is proved using Rodin tool. The proof obligations in Rodin tool define what is to be proved to show the consistency and correctness of an Event-B specification.

These proof obligations are automatically generated by the Rodin Platform. Theorem Prover of Rodin platform discharge all the proofs of every machine described in Sect. 4.1. Hence, every machine is correct by construction.

Each proof obligation is identified by its label. The proof statistics belonging to proposed specification is specified in Table 4. A statement of the form $H \mid - > G$, called as sequent, is used to express proof obligation rule. Meaning of such a statement is that the goal G is provable under the set of assumptions H. Next, two proof obligation rules are specified related to the proposed conceptual model.

Table 4. Numbers of different proof Obligations generated for the proposed specification

Proof Obligations	Numbers
Invariant preservation proof Obligation rules	20
Well defindness of guard proof Obligation rules	18
Feasibility proof Obligation rules	13

Fig. 5. Illustration of Proof Obligation for preservation of "Execute_is_next_to/inv15/INV" invariant in fourth machine

(a) ***Proof obligation rule for Invariant preservation:*** This proof obligation rule ensures that each invariant in a machine is preserved whenever values of variables change by each event. Figure 5 gives a screenshot of *"Execute_is_next_to/ inv15/INV"* invariant preservation proof obligation of fourth machine. Rodin theorem prover automatically discharges this proof using different rules of inference.

This proof can be illustrated manually. Hence, the sequent mentioned in the screenshot is simplified here by applying the inference rule *MON* and get a sequent of the form ($r \in N \mid -> r + 1 \in N$). After this, another rule of inference named *second Peano Axiom* is applied for natural numbers.

(b) **Well-definedness of a guard:** This proof obligation rule ensures that a guard is well-defined. For example rules such as function applications, may not be defined everywhere. As an instance, *List_of_Service*(r) is an function application which is only defined if r is in the domain of *List_of_Service* - $r \in dom$ (*List_of_Service*).

(c) **Feasibility proof obligation rule:** The purpose of this proof obligation is to ensure that a non-deterministic action is feasible. As an instance non-deterministic action *a1:*$\in$ *Actions* will be feasible only when *Action* $\neq \varnothing$. In proposed specification, there are 13 feasibility rules.

5 Evaluation of the Proposed Model Based Specification Using Case Study

This section illustrates the proposed conceptual model using a case study based on Clinical Decision Support System (CDSS) specified in [13]. The CDSS consists of two services *Patient_Information_Service* and *Consultation_Service*. These two services make CDSS a Choreography system. *Patient_information_Service* is consisting of three composite actions. *Problem_Listing_Act* lists problems of a patient; *Finding_Past_Records_Act* finds out past health records of the patient and *Making_Health_record_Act* makes a current health status of the patient. *Consultation_Service* is consisting of three composite actions. *Diagnosis_test_Act* performs diagnosis test; *Medication_Act* prescribes medicines and *Care_Plan_Guideline_Act* prescribes care plan and guideline.

According to the case study, the first machine represents the interaction between a *patient* and *Clinical_Decision_Service_Provider*. The three visibility constraints *Reachability, Willingness and Awareness* related to the case study are implemented in the second and third machine. Two events *Execute_is_next_to* and *Execute_OR* in fourth machine specify the compositions between six actions of the case study. Fifth machine specify the *Choreography* composition between the two services *Patient_Information_Service* and *Consultation_Service*.

6 Conclusion

In this paper, a conceptual model of SOA is proposed in Event-B specification language. Correctness of this proposed specification is also proved in Rodin platform. It facilitates a suitable formalization of several behavioral aspect of SOA like service discovery, service invocation, distinct constraints, and events and prove their correctness. The novelty of this work is that it formalizes different constraints and events to analyses behavioral aspect of SOA. The proposed work further facilitates delivering an executable specification. Prime objective of the future work is implementation of automatic transformation from the proposed conceptual model of SOA to the specification represented in Event-B.

References

1. Reference Architecture Foundation for Service Oriented Architecture Version 1.0, OASIS, December 2012. https://docs.oasis-open.org/soarm/soa-ra/v1.0/soa-ra-cd-02.pdf. Accessed 20 Feb 2018
2. Abrial, J.R.: Modeling in Event-B: System and Software Engineering, 1st edn. Cambridge University Press, New York (2010)
3. Gamma, E., Helm, R., Johnson, R.E., Vlissides, J.: Design Patterns: Elements of Reusable Object-Oriented Software. Addison-Wesley Longman Publishing Co., Inc., Boston (1995)
4. Rischbeck, T., Erl, T.: SOA Design Patterns (The Prentice Hall Service-Oriented Computing Series from Thomas Erl), 1st edn. Prentice Hall PTR, Upper Saddle River (2009)
5. Zhu, H., Bayley, I.: Laws of pattern composition. In: Dong, J.S., Zhu, H. (eds.) ICFEM 2010. LNCS, vol. 6447, pp. 630–645. Springer, Heidelberg (2010). https://doi.org/10.1007/978-3-642-16901-4_41
6. Tounsi, I., Zied, H., Kacem, M.H., Kacem, A.H., Drira, K.: Using SoaML models and event-B specifications for modeling SOA design patterns. In: 15th International Conference on Enterprise Information Systems (ICEIS), Angers, France, pp. 1–11 (2013)
7. OMG: Service Oriented Architecture Modeling Language (SoaML) Specification, Version 1.0.1 (2012). https://www.omg.org/spec/SoaML/1.0.1. Accessed 15 Mar 2018
8. Kim, S.K., Carrington, D.A.: A formalism to describe design patterns based on role concepts. Formal Aspects Comput. 21(5), 397–420 (2009)
9. Blazy, S., Gervais, F., Laleau, R.: Reuse of specification patterns with the B method. In: Bert, D., Bowen, J.P., King, S., Waldén, M. (eds.) ZB 2003. LNCS, vol. 2651, pp. 40–57. Springer, Heidelberg (2003). https://doi.org/10.1007/3-540-44880-2_4
10. Todoran, I., Hussain, Z., Gromov, N.: SOA integration modeling: an evaluation of how SoaML completes UML modeling. In: 15th International Enterprise Distributed Object Computing Conference Workshops, pp. 57–66. IEEE, Helsinki (2011)
11. Ren, H., Liu, J.: Service substitutability analysis based on behavior automata. Innov. Syst. Softw. Eng. 8(4), 301–308 (2012)
12. Kaur, A., Gulati, S., Singh, S.: A comparative study of two formal specification languages: Z-notation & B-method. In: Proceedings of the 2nd International Conference on Computational Science, Engineering and Information Technology (CCSEIT), pp. 524–531. ACM (2012)
13. Mandal Kr., A., Sarkar, A.: Service oriented system design: domain specific model based approach. In: Proceedings of the 3rd International Conference on Computer and Information Sciences (ICCOINS), pp. 489–494. IEEE, Kuala Lumpur (2016)
14. Tounsi, I., Kacem, M.H., Kacem, A.H., Drira, K.: Transformation of compound SOA Design Patterns. Proc. Comput. Sci. 109(C), 408–4015 (2017)

Pattern Recognition Solutions for Fake News Detection

Michał Choraś[1], Agata Giełczyk[1(✉)], Konstantinos Demestichas[2],
Damian Puchalski[3], and Rafał Kozik[1]

[1] UTP University of Science and Technology, Bydgoszcz, Poland
agata.gielczyk@utp.edu.pl
[2] Institute of Communication and Computer Systems - ICCS National Technical
University of Athens, Athens, Greece
[3] ITTI Sp. z o.o., Poznan, Poland

Abstract. Information is a crucial value nowadays in network digital
societies. Therefore, the phenomenon of "fake news" is a serious problem
in modern media and communication, e.g. with respect to information
spreading within the society about current events and incidents. Fake
news are currently a problem for media and broadcasting sector, for
citizens, but also for homeland security. In this paper we present and
overview the problem of fake news, we show the ideas and solutions for
fake news detection, and we present our initial results for one of such
approaches based on forged images detection.

Keywords: Fake news detection · Pattern recognition
Image processing

1 Introduction and Problem Statement

The classification of fake news is challenging due to its vague definition and
tensions related to freedom of speech. Even trusted sources, such as news agencies
that are readily available in content production systems, e.g. Associated Press
ENPS, are not easy to verify. In practice, verification relies upon a second source
or an implicit editorial trust for specific agencies or journalists developed by
Editors from experience regarding the trustworthiness of specific sources. In the
majority of cases, information that is completely un-sourced or misleading for
various purposes is described with the "fake news"? term. Fake news is referred to
non-satirical news stories, published online (via social media or news websites),
or in the traditional news media (newspapers, radio, television), presented as to
be factually accurate but published with no confirmation in facts [1].

Serious concerns about the growing fake news problem have been raised in
the EU Parliament [2], whereas various organizations (including social media
such as Facebook [3]) are starting to fight with a mass of fake news and are
taking steps to reduce the number of fake news spreading and re-posted in the
web. For example, Google is launching the Perspective API for troll-fighting and

© Springer Nature Switzerland AG 2018
K. Saeed and W. Homenda (Eds.): CISIM 2018, LNCS 11127, pp. 130–139, 2018.
https://doi.org/10.1007/978-3-319-99954-8_12

toxic comments detection based on machine learning algorithms [4], and the Wikipedia portal is starting to consider some sources as doubtfully reliable (e.g. Daily Mail tabloid) and to ban/change those sources in articles [5].

Moreover, in December 2016, the German Interior Ministry announced plans for creating the Center of Defence Against Misinformation, to detect and eliminate fake news (or false information in general) from online news feeds [6]. In light of the next German Parliament elections, the ministry instructed political parties to disable bots automatically sharing news and social media posts, due to the fact that they can be easily compromised and exploited to sharing propaganda on the web. Also, the German government proposed fines (up to 50M€) for the online publishers and media in case of not removing illegal content (including fake news and "hate speech" reported by the media users). The law called Netzwerkdurchsetzungsgesetz (NetzDG) law was agreed at the end of June 2017 and came into force in October 2017. Social media have to prepare themselves for the adoption of rules provided by the NetzDG until the end of 2017 [7].

This paper is structured as follows: in Sect. 2 we provide the overview of current state of the art. In Sect. 3 we present our ideas and possible solutions to counter fake news problem. In Sect. 4 we focus on one of the approaches, namely photo analysis. In Sect. 5 we present our solution vased on image analysis techniques and we present the initial results. Conclusions are given thereafter.

2   Related Work

Recently, also scientists started to pay growing attention to automated methods for the detection of fake news, particularly circulating through social media. Some research efforts [8] focus on a fake news detection system assisting users in detecting and filtering potentially deceptive news, where three main groups of fake news are differentiated: serious fabrications (uncovered in the mainstream), large-scale hoaxes, and humorous fakes (news satire, parody, etc.).

Accordingly, each of these fake news types requires individual methods for the assessment of their credibility. For example, large scale multi-platform hoaxes are possible to detect, but using means beyond static text analysis, e.g. involving network analysis. One of examples of automated detection of fake news is so called CSI model [9], where detection of fake news is based on combination of three characteristics: temporal activity of posting user, article (source) characteristics and a news propagation schema.

The detection of satire fakes [10] has also been investigated. The researchers translated theories of humour, irony, and satire into a predictive method for satire detection by integrating word-level, scmantic features (e.g. headlines, slang, profanity) supported by Support Vector Machines (SVM) in text classification to derive empirical cues indicative to deception.

The combination of two groups of methods to classify fake news [11] has also been proposed: linguistic approaches (such as deep syntax analysis, semantic analysis, rhetorical structure and discourse analysis, automated numerical analysis, based on SVM or Bayesian models), and network analysis approaches, including analysis of poster's network behaviour, and analysis of data linked to the original news/content. SVM has been also used to detect paid posters on social media [12] to classify online users by semantic analysis and user behaviour features such as ration of newly created posts to replies on comments/other posts, intervals between online activities, time that a user remains active online (paid posters often use "shared"? accounts and log out after the activity) and distribution of commented news.

One of limitations related to employing statistical methods or machine learning in automated detection of fake news is lack of accordingly labelled benchmark datasets. One of the most promising and possibly helpful in deep learning for purposes of fake news detection is the LIAR dataset [13]. The open-source dataset includes almost 13000 short, real-life (authentic) statements labelled with such features as: truthfulness, subject, context/venue, speaker, state, party, and prior history. The dataset includes statements collected for 10-year time-span and with its volume, LIAR is significantly larger than the other currently available resources.

A methodology for detection of tweets from false Twitter profiles [14] has also been presented. Authors state that, in the majority of cases, behind each fake account, there is a real person and another real Twitter account, and that those accounts can be associated through the machine learning algorithms and by analysing different features fingerprinted in these accounts. These features include data connection, tweet semantic characteristics, geo-position of the Twitter client, correlation of logging/tweets publication time, etc. For the experiments, authors have used supervised machine learning algorithms of the Waikato Environment for Knowledge Analysis (WEKA) framework.

Also several R&D EU projects recently addressed some aspects of trustworthiness of the social media content. FP7 iSAR+ (http://isar.i112.eu) aimed at research and development of the platform and guidelines enabling citizens using new mobile and online technologies (including social media) in case of emergency or crisis. As the citizens are the first sensors in crisis situation, the project focuses on text messaging and internet-based applications connected to social media platforms. For example, the consortium worked on verification of trustworthiness of the social media content based on textual messages related to crisis situation. FP7 SOTERIA (http://soteria.i112.eu) aimed at providing guidelines and courses of action for PSOs (Public Safety Organisations) and citizens in order to create an effective and efficient use of social media in emergencies, and integrating emergency-related ICT tools and functionality (e.g., social media tools and mobile applications) that offer additional (bi-directional) communication channels between PSOs and citizens. FP7 SocialSensor (http://www.socialsensor.eu) project was focused on collecting, processing, and aggregation of big streams of social media data and multimedia to discover trends, events, influencers, and interesting media content. The output of the project is a set of software applications automatically transforming social media data into content for the informative and news providing purposes. One of the characteristics of SocialSensor application is trust (content verification) and contextualization (e.g. including location, time and sentiment features). FP7 Reveal (https://revealproject.eu) project had ambitions to enable Internet users to reveal characteristics of social media content/channels such as reputation, influence or credibility of information. Two out of three use cases considered in the project concerned journalism, namely event coverage and content production. The project objectives included analysis of social media communities (e.g. discovering relationships), context-based analysis of information and organization of information based on event recognition and entity extraction techniques, allowing for clustering relevant information. H2020 InVID Project (http://www.invid-project.eu) is an ongoing initiative with the objective to provide innovative platform able to verify and assess reliability of video content shared via social media in order to help the journalist to evaluate the originality and trustworthiness of a user-generated video. The services integrated into the InVID Verification Application use such techniques as: context aggregation and analysis (detection of locations, tweet mentions and the collection of metadata) and video analysis (e.g. logo/watermarks detection, near duplicate searching, forensic analysis such as video filtering).

3   Fake News Detection Approaches and Possible Solutions

The analyzed news can contain variety of data types such as unstructured text, images/videos, references to other sources, etc.

Therefore, we can consider the following ideas to address fake news detection:

– Indexation and gathering of information published in the Internet in order to cross-reference current news with previous ones (e.g. to detect duplicates or pictures/photos used in different context). We can consider:
  • Image processing techniques for content analysis and images comparison
  • Text analysis techniques (e.g. document term matrices, etc.).
– Reputation scoring – to identify reliability of person and/or information source providing the news. We can consider reputation evaluation of:
  • Webpage providing/forwarding news
  • Person publishing information/news via social network, etc.
  • Reputation of the content.
– Comparison, of the similar news published by different information sources – in that case we can use common data mining techniques for text analysis
– Machine learning techniques for content features analysis
– Analysis of semantics by means of applied ontologies.

The problem of machine learning in such a complex and dynamic environment as fake news detection, requires efficient and effective techniques. In the future, our ambition is to adapt Lifelong Machine Learning techniques in order to gradually improve detection models and incrementally update the knowledge,

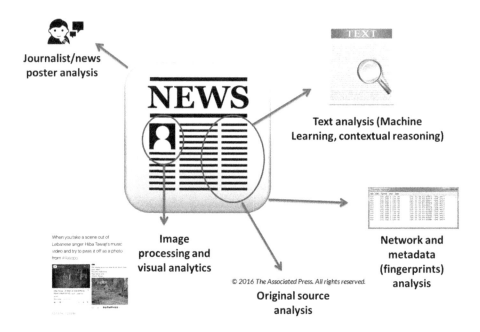

Fig. 1. Suggested approaches to fake news detection

so that the system can learn faster (reusing historical knowledge) e.g. by transferring the knowledge (e.g. from different news topics and tasks) [15].

Hereby, in this paper we focus on image processing techniques for photo content verification, as presented in the next sections (Fig. 1).

4   Image Processing Techniques for Verification of the Photo Content and Detection of Fake Images

Nowadays, the photo and video content is essential part of media coverage, often more attracting a content consumer's attraction than information provided as a text. Image processing has become easier due to rising popularity and development of specific software tools. They are enough sophisticated to unable us confirmation whether an image is manipulated by "naked eyes" [16]. Thus, image and video can be powerful tool used to create untruthful information or to unreasonably strengthen a message provided to recipient. Therefore, fake photos illustrating the textual content can be considered as common elements of fake news.

Fake photos can be linked to both factual (true) news and to totally fake information shared online. Fabricated photos might be posted due to propaganda reasons, but also for strengthening the intended message and for inducing emotions. Often publishers exemplify the textual content of news by means of a random photo stored in the publisher's archives that is contextually related to an ongoing situation, however not taken at the time and place of the presented or analyzed event.

The other indicators of possibly fake photos are: excessively drastic scenes, emotional messages, unrealistic scenes, and short time passed from the described event to the photo publication (sometimes seconds). Also, doubtful quality of image/video content in relation to the context (e.g. excessively low or excessively high quality) can indicate that the photo/video could not be captured during given situation.

Probably the most common image forgery method is cloning (often called copy-paste), where some portion of the image is copied and pasted in other place inside the image. When it is performed carefully, it can be hard to detect cloning visually [17].

To verify the trustworthiness of photos, the following approaches can be employed and combined:

- Reverse image searching – finding the same or slightly modified photos in relation to the searched photo, including photos with changed ratio and resolution, colours, horizontally flipped, trimmed, etc. Reverse image search engines allow also for ordering the search results depending on the time of online publication, therefore it is possible to find that the photo illustrating the current events is shared on the web for a number of months or years. The most popular online tools include: google.images.com and tineye.com.
- Verification of the publisher – examining the history of posts/news and other online activities can be helpful, since a fake piece of news or photo is, often the first piece of content published by a malevolent user, or even his/her first online activity ever.
- Context analysis – inconsistencies in such elements as actual weather or season, architecture of depicted place, indicators of the time in which the photo was taken (e.g. clocks) can be helpful to verify that the presented photo was taken at another place or at another time than it pretends.
- Analysis of image features – services such as http://fotoforensics.com allow for online analysis of modifications done in a given photo, using Error Level Analysis (ELA) of submitted .jpeg files. In general, such an algorithm detects modified regions of a photo, due to the fact that in these regions .jpeg (lossy) compression generates more errors during re-savings of the photo.

On the other hand, there is a limited number of online tools for analysis of video similarities, and thus for detection of modified, fake video content. One such example is the YouTube Data Viewer developed by the Amnesty International [18], allowing for detection of identical video frames in different material.

5   Proposed Method and Obtained Results

Our proposed method is based on the image assessment. The assumption is that if the image is corrupted, the whole news may be fake. In the algorithm we have

Fig. 2. Samples from the CASIA database (first row contains original photos, second row contains modified photos, the lowest row contains images modified with the copy-paste method) [19]

three factors evaluated: ELA analysis, copycat searching and meta data of file analysis.

In our research we used the image manipulation database which is available online [19]. It consists of 800 unmodified images (original) and 921 images with additional elements added. 25 images were classified as modified by cloning. Some samples from the database are presented in Fig. 2.

To detect pasted elements, the analyzed image is saved on the disc and read again. Then, the absolute value of difference between corresponding pixel is calculated and multiplied by the scale factor. In order to detect cloning, the image is divided into overlapping blocks. Then, to extract features from blocks, the SURF [20] algorithm was performed and FLANN algorithm for matching.

Meta data analysis may be performed using various libraries. They can give the information about modification done by any image processing tool. However, not all modified images by means of Photoshop are fake images. That is why, the final decision is based on the result of logic function F expressed with Eq. 1, where x – ELA decision, y – copycat decision, z – meta data decision and $x, y, z \in \{true, false\}$. Values of F, x, y and z are $false$, when the image is assessed as modified and $true$ otherwise.

$$F(x, y, z) = x \cdot y + y \cdot z + z \cdot x \tag{1}$$

For the research assessment, the accuracy and FAR, FRR measures were used. Accuracy is expressed with Eq. 2, where TP – modified images assessed as modified and FP – not modified images assessed as unmodified, N – number of samples.

FAR (False Acceptance Rate) gives the information about the number of defrauded images classified as unmodified and is expressed with Eq. 3, where FP – number of incorrectly classified unmodified images and NP – total number of unmodified images.

FRR (False Rejection Rate) tells about the number of unmodified images classified as defrauded and is expressed with Eq. 4, where FN – number of incorrectly classified modified images and NN – total number of modified images.

When FRR and FAR are equal, the other measure may be introduced, namely EER (Equal Error Rate), which is equal to $FAR = FRR$.

$$Acc = \frac{TP + TN}{N} \cdot 100\% \tag{2}$$

$$FAR = \frac{FP}{NP} \tag{3}$$

$$FRR = \frac{FN}{NN} \tag{4}$$

Table 1 shows the accuracy of the SURF-based part of the system. The accuracy depends on the Hessian threshold value, which was set experimentally.

Figure 2 presents the EER measure of the ELA part of the system. The ELA analysis was performed for different scale parameters (20 and 40) and two quality parameters (75 and 100). By combining the most promising results it was possible to obtain the 64% accuracy of image forgery detection (Fig. 3).

Table 1. Accuracy of SURF-based part of the system

Hessian threshold	Accuracy
100	76%
400	74%
1500	64%

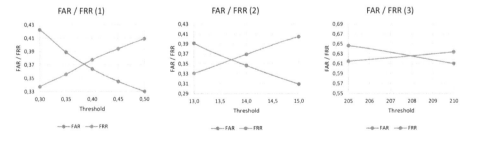

Fig. 3. FAR/FRR results of ELA part of the system for various scale and quality parameters

6   Conclusions

The major contributions of this paper are twofold: firstly, we address the problem of fake news and we present several ideas and approaches to counter this problem and build "fake news detectors". Secondly, we present the method to detect forged/fake images. We show how image processing techniques can be used to achieve this goal and we present initial results. In the future, we plan to work on holistic system based on correlation of various approaches, e.g. those based on image processing, fingerprinting, reputation and text analysis. Moreover, we also work on advanced machine learning solutions.

References

1. Allcott, H., Gentzkow, M.: Social media and fake news in the 2016 election. J. Econ. Perspect. **31**(2), 211–236 (2017). https://doi.org/10.3386/w23089
2. Euobserver's Article. https://euobserver.com/foreign/136503. Accessed 24 Mar 2018
3. Bloomberg's   Article.   https://www.livemint.com/Consumer/LKK03QAnhO05 wWdT6qCl8O/Facebooks-Journalism-Project-pledges-stronger-media-ties.html. Accessed 06 Apr 2018
4. Business   Insider's   Article.   http://www.businessinsider.com/google-jigsaw-perspective-tool-exposes-online-harassment-trolling-2017-2?IR=T.   Accessed   28 Mar 2018
5. The Guardian's Article. https://www.theguardian.com/technology/2017/feb/08/ wikipedia-bans-daily-mail-as-unreliable-source-for-website. Accessed 06 Apr 2018
6. DW's   Article.   http://www.dw.com/en/germany-plans-creation-of-center-of-defense-against-fake-news-report-says/a-36887455. Accessed 25 Mar 2018
7. BBC's Article. http://www.bbc.com/news/technology-42510868. Accessed 02 Apr 2018
8. Rubin, V.L., Chen, Y., Conroy, N.J.: Deception detection for news: three types of fakes. Proc. Assoc. Inf. Sci. Technol. **52**(1), 1–4 (2015)
9. Ruchansky, N., Seo, S., Liu, Y.: CSI: a hybrid deep model for fake news detection. In: Proceedings of the 2017 ACM on Conference on Information and Knowledge Management Journal, pp. 797–806 (2017)
10. Rubin, V.L., Conroy, N.J., Chen, Y., Cornwell, S.: Fake news or truth? Using satirical cues to detect potentially misleading news. In: Proceedings of the Second Workshop on Computational Approaches to Deception Detection, pp. 7–17 (2016)
11. Conroy, N.J., Rubin, V.L., Chen, Y.: Automatic deception detection: methods for finding fake news. Proc. Assoc. Inf. Sci. Technol. **52**(1), 1–4 (2015)
12. Chen, C., Wu, K., Srinivasan, V., Zhang, X.: Battling the internet water army: detection of hidden paid posters. In: Proceedings of 2013 IEEE/ACM International Conference on Advances in Social Networks Analysis and Mining (ASONAM), pp. 116–120. IEEE (2013)
13. Wang, W.Y.: Liar, Liar Pants on Fire: A New Benchmark Dataset for Fake News Detection. arXiv preprint arXiv:1705.00648 (2017)
14. Galán-García, P., Puerta, J.G.D.L., Gómez, C.L., Santos, I., Bringas, P.G.: Supervised machine learning for the detection of troll profiles in twitter social network: application to a real case of cyberbullying. Logic J. IGPL **24**(1), 42–53 (2016)

15. Choraś, M., Kozik, R., Renk, R., Hołubowicz, W.: The concept of applying life-long learning paradigm to cybersecurity. In: Huang, D.-S., Hussain, A., Han, K., Gromiha, M.M. (eds.) ICIC 2017. LNCS, vol. 10363, pp. 663–671. Springer, Cham (2017). https://doi.org/10.1007/978-3-319-63315-2_58
16. Huynh, T.K., Huynh, K.V., Le-Tien, T., Nguyen S.C.: A survey on image forgery detection techniques. In: Proceedings of 2015 IEEE RIVF International Conference on Computing & Communication Technologies-Research, Innovation, and Vision for the Future (RIVF), pp. 71–76. IEEE (2015)
17. Farid, H.: Image forgery detection. IEEE Signal Process. Mag. **26**(2), 16–25 (2009)
18. Amnesty International's Report. http://www.amnestyusa.org/sites/default/custom-scripts/citizenevidence/. Accessed 12 Mar 2018
19. CASIA Database. http://forensics.idealtest.org/casiav1/. Accessed 02 Apr 2018
20. Bay, H., Ess, A., Tuytelaars, T., Van Gool, L.: SURF: Speeded Up Robust Features. Comput. Vis. Image Underst. (CVIU) **110**(3), 346–359 (2008)

Development of Visibility Expectation System Based on Machine Learning

Akmaljon Palvanov, Andrey Giyenko, and Young Im Cho[✉]

Gachon University, Seongnam-si, Gyeonggi-do, Korea
akmaljon.palvanov@gmail.com,
andrey.giyenko@gmail.com, yicho@gachon.ac.kr

Abstract. Visibility impairment is maximum definitely defined because the formation of haze that obscures the clarity, shade, texture, and form of what's visible through the atmosphere. It's far a complex phenomenon inspired via some of the emissions and air pollutants and tormented by some of the herbal factors which include temperature, humidity, meteorology, time and sunlight. The aim of the research is that to estimate weather visibility using machine learning techniques. We use images taken from CCTV cameras as inputs and deep convolutional neural network model to predict results. We implemented Java based GUI application that can flexibly operate all operations in real-time. Users are also able to use a specially built web page to estimate visibility that a built-in machine learning (ML) model gives an opportunity to the user to get results. In this paper, we will detail explain regarding an architecture of the ML model, System Structure, and other essential details.

Keywords: Machine learning · Visibility · CNN · GUI

1 Introduction

Visibility is a degree of ways nicely an observer can view a scene. This consists of how some distance you can see within the surroundings as well as the ability to see the textures and colors of the scene. Haze is the inverse of visibility that is the measure of the inability to view a scene [1]. Visibility is reduced, or haze expanded, by means of the absorption and scattering of gases and aerosols (debris) in the atmosphere [2]. The focus of this study is visibility impairment precipitated mainly by way of tiny particles suspended inside the air, and by gases. These particles and gases scatter or absorb light, thereby reducing visibility and inflicting haze. The pollution chargeable for reducing visibility are emitted from a ramification of resources, each herbal and human. Different factors that cause terrible visibility encompass evidently happening atmospheric situations which includes fog and occasional cloud. Where such atmospheric situations arise on the identical time as excessive pollution incidents, their effects on visibility may be considered, however simplest by the way.

Nobody would intentionally agree that poor air great is acceptable. The advantages of correct visibility are apparent. Visibility is a primary and enormously apparent indicator of preferred air excellent. Visibility is distinctly easy to recognize via public.

© Springer Nature Switzerland AG 2018
K. Saeed and W. Homenda (Eds.): CISIM 2018, LNCS 11127, pp. 140–153, 2018.
https://doi.org/10.1007/978-3-319-99954-8_13

Many humans regard suitable visibility as a figuring out thing for the satisfactory of out of doors existence. As an end result, the community can also decide the effectiveness of environmental control policies to improve air satisfactory by means of visibility.

So visibility cannot constantly be without difficulty quantified or described. In reality monitoring one indicator, including visual range, might not be enough to apprehend the impact of degraded visibility. One objective of visibility monitoring is to apprehend the effect that diverse types of particles and lighting fixtures situations have on the advent of a scene. Another is to understand the causes of visibility impairment, which can be complicated and not constantly apparent from simple monitoring. Due to the fact its miles hard to extract quantitative data from images, instruments to record optical traits of the atmosphere and the composition of visibility-lowering debris also are used. Shortly, we can say that visibility is a measure of atmosphere's transparency which in turn essential aspect for several cases such as air, road and of course water transport systems safety. Many factors affect during measuring visibility say, dust, haze and fog. Also, the pollution is one of vital factor that reduces the accuracy of visibility measure.

Experts use special equipment to provide measurement of visibility. These tools themselves and their installation processes are ample expensive and measuring range is also limited. Additionally, the factors mentioned above strongly affects the outcomes. Hereby, we propose camera and ML based technique to estimate visibility since combinations of these methods gives strong superiorities. On the one hand, comparing to tools like visibility meter camera-based visibility measuring is more close to visual method. Also, the technique does not cost expensive, weather conditions like dust and fog etc. can be artificial removed while measuring and can be achieved very accurately results. Therefore, we built ML model that can evaluate visibility based on CCTV camera images. Similar approached have been done but with dissimilar ML models and all have its advantages and disadvantages. Concerning approaches that provide on the topic we discuss in next section.

2   Related Studies

Research at visibility variation of Korea was accomplished since the 1990s. Park et al. (1994) examine the trend of visibility variation of Seoul at some stage in 1980–1993. It became found out that annual common visibility has been reduced during the 1980s besides 1988 and 1989 however no longer decreasing during the early nineteen nineties and the variety of motors and the attention of criteria air pollution on the fashion of visibility variation of Seoul could not be without delay associated with the version of visibility [4]. Authors of [5] proposed visibility estimation based on meteorological laws using digital images. They used deep learning model to artificially extract features from input images. Another approaches for estimating visibility proposed by [6, 7] and essential properties of these studies are using single camera and evaluate visibility on a basis of daytime light from the input images. In the field of meteorology, one of the main law is Koschmieder's law and many researchers used this function to estimate visibility in both cases, using digital images and also using special equipment for visibility estimation, these works have been done in [8–10]. Since all these methods use images as an input quality of the images is vital to get better results, means that degradation of images strongly restricts accurately estimation. This requires essential extra step prior estimate visibility the step is enhancement of the quality of input images. For this situation Dark Channel Prior (DCP) method is widely used. For instance, in poor visibility conditions enhancement of color images proposed by [11], in this study, several visibility conditions tested using synthetic images taken via airborne camera. Another effective use of DCP can be seen in [12] they used a haze imaging model to estimate the thickness of the haze then recover quality of the image. Additionally, haze removing from the image using deep fully convolutional regression network (DFCRN) in [13] and rain detection and removing from the single image proposed in [14]. Convolutional neural network based dehazing method [15] relies on the re-formulated atmospheric scattering model. In next section we will detailed explain our approach and our techniques.

3 Methods and Techniques

3.1 The Dataset

In order to estimate visibility using CCTV camera we first collected dataset of images taken by the cameras which were located in different regions. Afterwards we balanced dataset since some ranges of visibility were significantly more than the other one so we firstly fulfilled this task prior to feed our network. To be more accurate, an initial dataset included images that visibility distance of 20000 m, and these kind of images overlapped approximately 70% of the dataset. However, we need to more allocate our focus on shorter distances. Thus, we randomly doubled images belong to short visibility range and with this way we re-created balanced dataset.

3.2 The System and Its Working Principle

As we already mentioned in the final structure access to the system is performed though a web interface. Also any computer or smartphone can be used for this goal. Figure 1 shows interaction of clients and server. Clients upload input image server receives request sends respond as a predicted results. Also, Fig. 2 elaborates on how the system works in detail.

In this scenario several processes are occurring at the same time:

1. The user terminals (PC/Tablet/Smartphone) receives the live video feed, takes image screenshots and sends them to the AI enabled server
2. The server receives the screenshots and performs on demand visibility estimations
3. The server generates a web page with the estimated visibility and sends the resulting web page to the client.

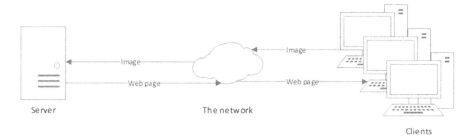

Fig. 1. Client and server relationship via network

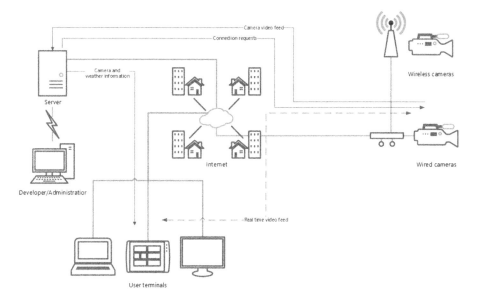

Fig. 2. The working principle of the system

Another way this service can be implemented is described below. In this scenario the clients do not connect to the cameras directly, instead:

1. The cameras constantly send new images in a stream to the server
2. The server stores images for each camera in storage and keeps an index in the database
3. At the same time the AI service performs the estimation of the visibility in the stored images and saves it in the database
4. When the user requests the visibility for some camera, the server just sends them the last stored image with its computed visibility.

Illustrated figure below informs working principles of the server and its in-built ML model. Owing to this architecture lets the user to use the app in real-time. Data collection in both cases is performed by using frame capture on CCTV cameras, IP cameras or other capture devices. The only camera specifications are:

5. Images in color RGB format;
6. Saved in JPEG, PNG or BMP compression;
7. For direct access from the server the camera must provide remote IP access (Fig. 3).

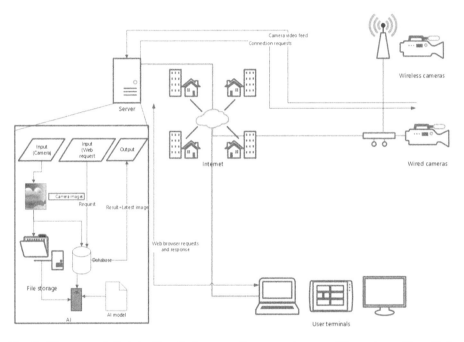

Fig. 3. The approach that significantly improves the responsiveness of the system with multiple connected clients.

For the prototype the dataset was provided on a portable hard drive. Specifications for user terminals:

- Operation system: Windows, Linux, Mac OS, iOS or Android
- HTML 4+ compatible web browser
- Screen resolution: 800 × 600 or higher.

Specifications for the server:

- Operation system: Windows or Linux
- Minimum 4 GB RAM, Recommended 8 GB RAM or higher
- For Linux based server a NVIDIA based GPU that supports Compute 3.5 or higher
- At least 3 GB of file storage space for model + software (images not included).

There have been several software pieces developed. The following diagrams describe the structure of each of them (Fig. 4).

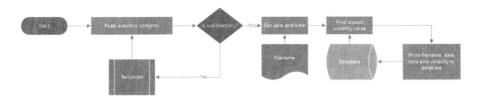

Fig. 4. Image filename to database parser

According to this diagram, program reads the list of files from disk, parses metadata, finds the closest visibility value and saves the resulting data set to the database table (Fig. 5).

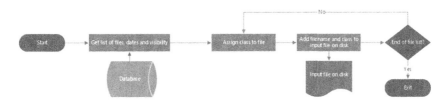

Fig. 5. Input file generator software

This software performs an SQL query to the database to retrieve a list of files that can be used as input. After that it assigns each file a class and saves them in a text file that the python software can use. Each line of that file consists of "filename class" pairs.

3.3 AI Model

Algorithm illustrated in Fig. 6. It starts with preprocessing inputs before feeding the network. First stage input images are transformed black and white images right before resizing. Next stage inputs are normalized and feed the network. The diagram below represents the visual web interface of the application. The web interface is used to upload an image to the server for evaluation. This is done in a servlet (java program) that loads the AI model from disk, transforms the image into a byte array, performs the estimation and generates a simple HTML page containing the result. This page is displayed in the client's browser.

Following software implements the CNN model and is used to train it with the training set images.

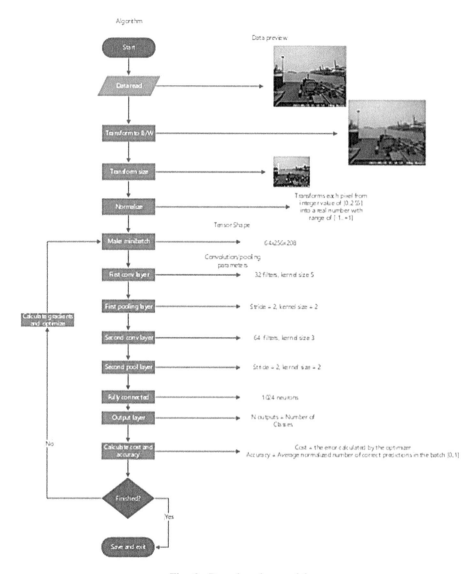

Fig. 6. Deep learning model

The representation given in Fig. 7. depicts the visual web interface of the application. The web interface is used to upload an image to the server for evaluation. This is done in a servlet (java program) that loads the AI model from disk, transforms the image into a byte array, performs the estimation and generates a simple HTML page containing the result. This page is displayed in the client's browser.

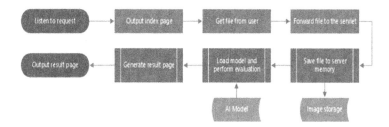

Fig. 7. Web based software structure

Fig. 8. Batch evaluation software structure

This software loads the saved model from disk, connects to the database and performs correctness checks on each image, one image at a time. After getting the results it saves the predicted class to the database Fig. 8.

A logical structure of the convolutional neural network (CNN) used to develop the software can be seen below:

The Fig. 9 shows the structure of the Convolutional Neural Network:

- The convolution layers are used to extract features from the images
- The pooling layers are used to reduce the dimensions of the data

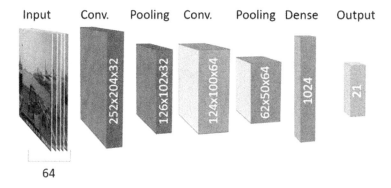

Fig. 9. CNN structure diagram

- The densely connected layer is used to implement classification of features into classes
- The output layer contains the 21 outputs containing probabilities of correct answer – one for each class.

4   Experiments Results

The program is a convolutional neural network. It reads the images form disk, shuffles the whole set and then choses random batches. The training process is computationally expensive. The evolutions of the loss (cost function) and accuracy functions over the course of training can be seen in the following figure. While training, 4 epochs perform per second, which means the graph covers total of 20000s.

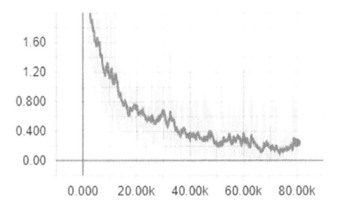

Fig. 10. The evolutions of the loss. The horizontal axis represents training epochs; The vertical axis is the Loss

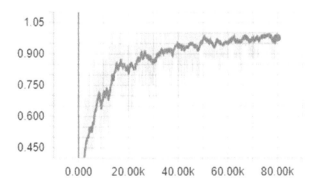

Fig. 11. The accuracy functions over the course of training. The horizontal axis represents training epochs; the vertical axis is the Training accuracy functions

As we can see the loss function is successfully reduced to approximately 20% and as we can see below during training our accuracy on random batches approaches 90% of successful visibility classification based in image similarity.

Next step is to perform a random data evaluation. To perform the evaluation, we developed a java application that selects images from the reference image database and performs an evaluation on each of them separately (Fig. 10).

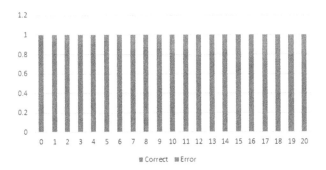

Fig. 12. The testing results on random samples of original data

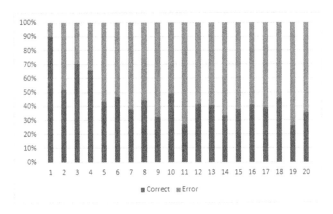

Fig. 13. The testing results on separate testing set

Fig. 14. Web interface

Figure 11 shows the result of the accuracy estimation test based on the random sample of 10000 images from the dataset. Due to the original dataset bias towards 20 km visibility, the random selection of images was heavily skewed to contain mostly long range visibility images. This can explain the anomaly in accuracy drop when evaluating randomly selected low visibility images. Further research is required (Figs. 12 and 13).

After training the model, we exported the model into a compressed file for deployment. This is performed at the end of the training stage. We decided to train for 80000 epochs as after that there is almost no progress and the system stabilizes.

For the deployment of the model we chose to develop a Java EE based web application. This application is designed to run on a remote server accessible over a TCP/IP network such as LAN or the Internet. The prototype interface is simple but can be easily upgraded according to the requirements of the final system. The application takes a .jpeg or .png image as input, uploads it to the server, loads the trained neural network model and returns the inference result to the clients' web browser (Figs. 14 and 15).

3000m file

7000m file

13000m file

20000m file

Fig. 15. Some image examples from the dataset which was taken by CCTV cameras and prediction results

We also developed a simple offline GUI for testing the model, which can be seen in Fig. 16.

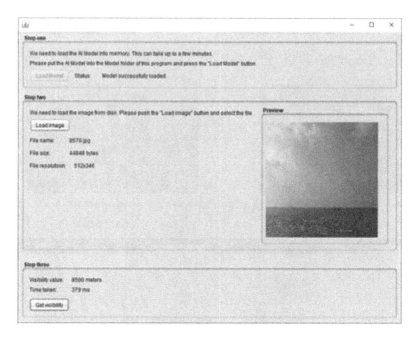

Fig. 16. Offline GUI testing program

5 Conclusion

To sum up, our studies showed that one of methods to estimate visibility can be done by deep CNN model. However, sometimes the models might predict wrong outcomes since some images have many features to be learnt whereas others have only sky and sea. Additionally we need to take into account that the original training set images suffer from multiple noise factors:

- image labeling anomalies
- different lighting conditions for the same visibility will result in drastically different pictures
- JPEG artifacts
- objects close to the camera obstructing view
- generally low visual difference between close visibility values.

This makes difficult to the network to make correct predictions. Even though during training the accuracy reached high levels, when we tested the solution on an isolated training set, the results were not as impressive.

At the same time, night time images were excluded from being classified using CNN as there is usually not enough information conveyed by the camera to evaluate the distance. Notwithstanding some difficulties our team achieved good results. In our feature works we will try different algorithms so we can classify all images without any issues given earlier.

Our future research will focus on evolving the AI model beyond applying CNN along with the use of additional image processing techniques to extract atmospheric visibility values.

Acknowledgement. This research was supported by the MSIT (Ministry of Science and ICT), Korea, under the ITRC (Information Technology Research Center) support program (IITP-2018-2017-0-01630) supervised by the IITP (Institute for Information & communications Technology Promotion) and NRF project "Intelligent Smart City Convergence Platform". Project number is 20151D1A1A01061271.

References

1. Dickson, D.R., Hales, J.V.: Computation of visual range in fog and low clouds. J. Appl. Meteorol. **2**(2), 281–285 (1963)
2. Adams, R.M., et al.: Global climate change and US agriculture. Nature **345**(6272), 219 (1990)
3. Kim, K.W.: Development of Remote Digital Vision Visibility Monitor (RDVVM). Kwangju Institute of Science and Technology (K-JIST)
4. Kim, K.W., Kim, Y.J.: Feasibility of forecasting visibility impairment in an urban area. In: The 35th Meeting of KOSAE, Korea, pp. 197–198 (2003)
5. Li, S., Fu, H., Lo, W.-L.: Meteorological visibility evaluation on webcam weather image using deep learning features. Int. J. Comput. Theory Eng. **9**(6) (2017)
6. Varjo, S., Hannuksela, J.: Image based visibility estimation during day and night. In: Computer Vision - ACCV 2014 Workshops, pp. 277–289 (2015)
7. Wauben, W., Roth, M.: Exploration of fog detection and visibility estimation from camera images. R&D Observations and Data Technology Royal Netherlands Meteorological Institute (KNMI), 3730 AE De Bilt, Netherlands (2016)
8. Sutter, T., Nater, F., Sigg, C.: Camera based visibility estimation (2014)
9. Du, K., Wang, K., Shi, P., Wang, Y.: Quantification of atmospheric visibility with dual digital cameras during daytime and nighttime. Atmos. Meas. Tech. **6**(8), 2121–2130 (2013)
10. Jeevan, S., Usha, L.: Estimation of visibility distance in images under foggy weather condition. Int. J. Adv. Comput. Electron. Technol. (IJACET) **3**, 2394–3416 (2016)
11. Tan, K.K., Oakley, J.P.: Enhancement of color images in poor visibility conditions. In: Proceedings 2000 International Conference on Image Processing (Cat. No. 00CH37101), Vancouver, BC, Canada, Canada (2002)
12. He, K., Sun, J., Tang, X.: Single image haze removal using dark channel prior. IEEE Trans. Pattern Anal. Mach. Intell. **33**, 2341–2353 (2011)
13. Zhao, X., Wang, K., Li, Y., Li, J.: Deep fully convolutional regression networks for single image haze removal. IEEE Vis. Commun. Image Process. (VCIP) (2017). https://doi.org/10.1109/vcip.2017.8305035
14. Yang, W., Tan, R.T., Feng, J., Liu, J., Guo, Z., Yan, S.: Deep joint rain detection and removal from a single image. In: Conference on Computer Vision and Pattern Recognition (CVPR), Honolulu, HI, USA (2017)
15. Li, B., Peng, X., Wang, Z., Xu, J., Feng, D.: AOD-Net: all-in-one dehazing network. In: IEEE International Conference on Computer Vision (ICCV), Venice, Italy (2017)

Robustness of Raw Images Classifiers Against the Class Imbalance – A Case Study

Ewaryst Rafajłowicz[(⊠)]

Faculty of Electronics, Wrocław University of Science and Technology,
Wrocław, Poland
ewaryst.rafajlowicz@pwr.edu.pl

Abstract. Our aim is to investigate the robustness of classifiers against the class imbalance. From this point of view, we compare several most widely used classifiers as well as the one recently proposed, which is based on the assumption that the probability densities in classes have the matrix normal distribution. As the base for comparison we take a sequence of images from that laser based additive manufacturing process. It is important that the classifiers are fed by raw images. The classifiers are compared according to several criterions and the methodology of all pair-wise comparisons is used to rank them.

Keywords: Matrix normal distribution · Bayesian classifier
Robustness of classifiers · Class imbalance

1 Introduction

The class imbalance phenomenon, i.e., a largely different fractions of examples from different classes in the learning and in the testing sequences, is known to cause troubles when learning and assessing the quality of classifiers. The reason is in that most of the known classifiers tend to give the priority to the largest class in the learning sequence. This, in turn, leads to a poor generalization properties. On the other hand, the class imbalance is unavoidable when classifiers are used for detecting rare events (e.g., faults in production processes or diagnosis of rare diseases).

Many attempts were proposed in order to circumvent this difficulty. They can be, roughly, clustered as follows.

1. Data editing strategies that attempt to artificially increase the fraction of the minority class (classes) examples in the learning and in the testing sequences. Typically, it is achieved by either the re-sampling from the minority class or by the under-sampling from the majority class or by combining them. These ways, although useful in many cases, have one common drawback, namely, they distort a priori class probabilities, which – in turn – may lead to undesirable preference voting for the minority class.

K. Saeed and W. Homenda (Eds.): CISIM 2018, LNCS 11127, pp. 154–165, 2018.
https://doi.org/10.1007/978-3-319-99954-8_14

2. Attaching a high cost for a minority class misclassification, in particular, by using a dedicated metrics.
3. Designing classifiers dedicated to cope with the class imbalance phenomenon.

Our approach differs from the above. Namely, we take several popular classifiers and we propose to rank them from the view point of their robustness against the class imbalance in the data. In addition to the popular classifiers, we consider also the classifier for matrix normal distributions (see [5,8,9]).

The second challenge in comparing the robustness of classifiers against the class imbalance is the choice of criterions for their comparisons. Again, a number of criterions is advocated in the literature. For this reason, we propose to use a pair-wise comparisons of classifiers, for which several criterions are calculated. This approach was originated by Slowinski [11] and its applicability is still growing (see [4]).

As an empirical material for case studies we take raw images of the laser additive manufacturing process (see [8] for more detailed description why this process is important).

An important issue in our case study is that we put raw images as the inputs of classifiers. This approach seems to be of importance at least for two reasons, namely,

- it demonstrates that easily available PC computers can be successful in a cheap way of classifying images, since the process of features extraction is time-consuming (expensive)
- the results of comparisons of classifiers are not biased by a human-dependent way of feature extraction.

The paper is organized as follows.

- In Sect. 2 we provide the description of a modified classifier for matrix normal distributions.
- The well known classifiers that are selected for comparisons are listed and briefly commented in Sect. 3.
- In Sect. 4 we describe the methodology of testing and comparisons as well as their results.
- Section 5 contains conclusions, while in the Appendix we summarize the known properties of matrix normal distributions.

2   A Modified Classifier for Matrix Normal Distributions

2.1   MND as Class Densities and Their Estimation

We assume that probability distributions of gray-level images from class $j = 1, 2, \ldots, J$ have MND with probability density functions (p.d.f.'s) $f_j(\mathbf{X})$ defined in Appendix.

MND densities have special covariance structure in comparison to a general multivariate Gaussian densities. Namely, their covariance matrices do not have inter rows-columns covariances, which makes them much easier to estimate (see Appendix).

Further on, we assume that we have J learning sequences of the following form: $\mathbf{X}_i^{(j)}$, $i = 1, 2, \ldots N_j$, $j = 1, 2, \ldots, J$.

Denote by $p_j > 0$, $j = 1, 2, \ldots, J$, $\sum p_j = 1$, a priori class probabilities. It is well known that in a general case the MAP classifier assigns $\mathbf{X}$ to class j^* such that

$$j^* = \arg \max_j [p_j \, f_j(\mathbf{X})], \tag{1}$$

where $\arg \max_j [\,]$ stands for the argument for which the maximum is attained. It is also well known that this rule is the optimal one when the 0-1 loss function is used (see, e.g., [2]).

For symmetric and positive definite matrix A define the following function: $\kappa(A) = \frac{\lambda_{max}(A)}{\lambda_{min}(A)}$, which indicates how large numerical errors can be committed when the inverse of A is calculated. Select $0 < \kappa_{max} < 100$.

A Modified Matrix Normal Distribution Classifier (MMNDCL)
I. The Learning Phase

Step (L1) Collect J learning sequences (for each class) of the following form: $\mathbf{X}_i^{(j)}$, $i = 1, 2, \ldots N_j$, $j = 1, 2, \ldots, J$.

Step (L2) Estimate the class mean matrices and a priori class probabilities as follows

$$\hat{M}_j = N_j^{-1} \sum_{i=1}^{N_j} \mathbf{X}_i^{(j)}, \quad \hat{p}_j = N_j/N, \quad j = 1, 2, \ldots, J. \tag{2}$$

Step (L3) Calculate the maximum likelihood estimates (MLE) of the inter-row and inter-column covariance matrices by solving the following set of equations:

$$\hat{U}_j = \frac{1}{N_j \, m} \sum_{i=1}^{N_j} (\mathbf{X}_i - \hat{\mathbf{M}}_j) \, \hat{V}_j^{-1} \, (\mathbf{X}_i - \hat{\mathbf{M}}_j)^T, \tag{3}$$

$$\hat{V}_j = \frac{1}{N_j \, n} \sum_{i=1}^{N_j} (\mathbf{X}_i - \hat{\mathbf{M}}_j)^T \, \hat{U}_j^{-1} \, (\mathbf{X}_i - \hat{\mathbf{M}}_j) \tag{4}$$

for $j = 1, 2, \ldots, J$. Equations (3) and (4) can be solved by the flip-flop method.

Step (L4) Estimate the normalization constants of class densities as follows:

$$\hat{c}_j = (2\,\pi)^{0.5\,n\,m} \det[\hat{U}_j]^{0.5\,n} \det[\hat{V}_j]^{0.5\,m}. \tag{5}$$

II. The recognition Phase

Step 1 Acquire $\mathbf{X}$ to be classified.

Step 2 Check whether all the inequalities:

$$\kappa(\hat{U}_j) < \kappa_{max}, \; j = 1, 2, \ldots, J \tag{6}$$

as well as

$$\kappa(\hat{V}_j) < \kappa_{max}, \; j = 1, 2, \ldots, J \tag{7}$$

are fulfilled. If so, go to Step 3, otherwise, go to Step 4.

Step 3 Classify new image (matrix) $\mathbf{X}$ according to the following rule:

$$\hat{j} = \arg \min_{1 \leq j \leq J} \left[\frac{1}{2} \text{tr}[\hat{U}_j^{-1}(\mathbf{X} - \hat{\mathbf{M}}_j) V_j^{-1} (\mathbf{X} - \hat{\mathbf{M}}_j)^T] \right] - \log(\hat{p}_j/\hat{c}_j), \qquad (8)$$

where $\hat{j}$ is the predicted class for $\mathbf{X}$.

Acquire the next image (matrix) $\mathbf{X}$ for classification and repeat (8).

Step 4 Classify new image (matrix) $\mathbf{X}$ according to the nearest mean rule, i.e., classify it to the class

$$\tilde{j} = \arg \min_j ||\mathbf{X} - \hat{M}_j||^2, \qquad (9)$$

where the squared distance $||\mathbf{X} - \hat{M}_j||^2$ is defined as follows:

$$||\mathbf{X} - \hat{M}_j||^2 = \text{tr}[(\mathbf{X} - \hat{\mathbf{M}}_j)(\mathbf{X} - \hat{\mathbf{M}}_j)^T]. \qquad (10)$$

If the class $\tilde{j}$ in (9) is selected in a sufficiently sure way, e.g., if the following condition holds for a pre-specified $\zeta > 0$

$$(1 + \zeta) ||\mathbf{X} - \hat{M}_{\tilde{j}}||^2 < ||\mathbf{X} - \hat{M}_j||^2, \quad j \neq \tilde{j}, \qquad (11)$$

then update the estimates of $\hat{U}_{\tilde{j}}$ and $\hat{V}_{\tilde{j}}$ by adding current $\mathbf{X}$ to the learning sequence as $(\mathbf{X}, \tilde{j})$. Independently whether condition (11) is fulfilled or not, go to Step 1.

It was proved in [14] that it suffices to perform only one flip-flop operation in Step (L3) in order to obtain the efficient estimates of U_j and V_j.

2.2   The Methodology of Cross-Validation Testing

In order to test MMNDCL algorithm and to verify its robustness against the class imbalance, we used the cross-validation (CV) methodology in the following extensive version.

Step 1 Select from the set of images of the length 900 (at random with the same probabilities) a learning sequence of the length 450 and denote it as L_{450}. The rest of the sequence, denoted as T_{450}, use it for testing.

Step 2 Learn MMNDCL, using the L_{450} sequence.

Step 3 Test the classifier from Step 2, applying it to T_{450}, calculate and store the accuracy and other quality criterions (recall, precision, etc., see the next subsection).

Step 4 Repeat Steps 1–3 1000 times.

Step 5 Provide the averages of the quality indicators, obtained in Step 3, as the outputs.

Notice that this is an intensive testing procedure, because we have to estimate two matrices of the means and four covariance matrices, each of them 1000 times when learning MMNDCL.

3   Classifiers Selected for Verifying Their Robustness Against the Class Imbalance

The following classifiers are selected for comparisons.

(a) The MMND classifier in the version that was described in the previous section.

(b) The logistic regression classifier with L2 regularization coefficient equal 1. We refer the reader to [12] for a contemporary description of this classifier.

(c) The naive Bayes classifier. Despite of its simplicity, this classifier works quite well in many applications. It is of interest to check its robustness against the class imbalance.

(d) The feed forward, sigmoidal neural network classifier with the following parameters: two hidden layers, each containing 900 nodes with tanh activation functions. L2 regularization coefficient equal 0.1 was used (see [3]).

(e) The random forest (RF) classifier was proposed in the famous paper of Breiman [1] in which also the proof of consistency is provided. The popularity of the RF classifiers is still growing. In our experiments, the number of generated trees was 200.

(f) The support vector machine (SVM) classifier is currently considered as the classifier of the first choice in most of applications. In our experiments, the Gaussian radial basis functions were used. The soft margin parameter was selected to be 8.

(g) The nearest neighbors classifier is the golden classic. Its consistency and other properties are investigated in [2]. In the experiments reported in the next section, the version with 10 nearest neighbors (referred to as 10-NN) is reported.

We refer the reader to [2] for a wide and deep discussions concerning classifiers and their properties.

4   The Results of Testing Classifiers by Cross-Validation

Before providing the results of testing classifiers, we briefly discuss criterions that are selected for comparisons. We also provide a short description of the methodology of comparing classifiers when multiple criterions are used.

4.1   Criterions Selected for Comparisons

When testing a two class classifier on a large number of examples, we collect the following data:

- TP – the number true positive examples,
- TN – the number of true negative cases,
- FP – the number of false positive examples,
- FN – the number of of false negative cases.

Thus, the total number of test cases is $FP + FN + TP + TN$.

The following, widely used, measures of classifiers quality are selected for further comparisons.

Accuracy. The accuracy (Acc) is defined as the ratio of all properly classified patterns to all the patterns in the testing sequence:

$$Acc = \frac{TP + TN}{FP + FN + TP + TN}. \tag{12}$$

It is well known that Acc is not quite adequate, especially when we are faced with a large class imbalance, since it can provide a seemingly high accuracy just by classifying improperly all (or most) items from the minority class.

Recall. The recall (Rec), also known as the sensitivity, is defined as

$$Rec = TP/(TP + FN), \tag{13}$$

i.e., it is the proportion of positive patterns that are correctly classified. It does not take into account TN and FP cases.

Precision. The precision (Prec), also called (specificity), defined as

$$Prec = TP/(TP + FP) \tag{14}$$

is – in fact – the true positive accuracy. It does not take into account TN and FN cases.

F1 Score. The F1 score (F1sc) attempts to reduce the drawbacks of Rec and Prec measures by calculating their harmonic mean:

$$F1sc = 2.0\, Prec\, Rec/(Prec + Rec). \tag{15}$$

Although F1sc is more informative than Prec and Rec separately, it still neglects TN cases, which are of importance in class imbalance cases.

Matthews Correlation Coefficient. A widely accepted alternative to F1sc is the Matthews Correlation Coefficient (MCC) that is defined as follows:

$$MCC = \frac{(TP\,TN - FP\,FN)}{\sqrt{(TP + FP)\,(TP + FN)\,(TN + FP)\,(TN + FN)}}. \tag{16}$$

MCC takes into account all the entries of a classifier confusion matrix. MCC is easy to interpret. Namely, if MCC is close to $+1$, then a classifier at hand provides a good prediction. Conversely, MCC being about -1 indicates that a classifier works properly, but it is advisable to exchange the roles of "true" and "false" classes. Finally, when MCC is near zero, then a classifier is not a good predictor at all, i.e., the tossing of the fair coin would provide comparable results.

4.2   Multiple Criteria Sorting for Assessing Classifiers Quality

The above discussion of the quality measures of classifiers indicates that all of them, although widely used, have also their drawbacks. For this reason, we propose to apply all of them in our case study. This leads to the need of selecting a method for multiple criteria sorting.

Problems of multiple criteria sorting (ranking) of objects have a long history that is documented in a large number of papers. For our purpose of sorting the classifiers according to the above criterions, we use a simplified version of the approach proposed in [4] (see also [11] for the discussion of the fundamental notion of the pair-wise comparisons).

Denote by $a_1, a_2, \ldots, a_7$ the set of algorithms (classifiers) to be compared. Let $g_1, g_2, \ldots, g_5$ stands for the set of criterions defined in the previous subsection. Then,

$$\bar{g}(a_i) \stackrel{def}{=} [g_1(a_i), g_2(a_i), \ldots, g_5(a_i)], \quad i = 1, 2, \ldots, 7 \tag{17}$$

is the vector of criterions that are evaluated for algorithm a_i.

Select $\epsilon_k > 0$ as the level of uncertainty of k-th criterion, i.e., if $|g_k(a_i) - g_k(a_j)| < \epsilon_k$, then a_i and a_j are considered to be equivalent with respect to k-th criterion, $k = 1, 2, \ldots, 5$. When algorithms (classifiers) a_i and a_j, $i \neq j$ are compared as one pair, then the following rules of adding scores to their total scores (denoted as S_i and S_j, respectively) are applied.

Scoring the comparison of a_i and a_j
For $k = 1, 2, \ldots, 5$ perform the following steps.

Step (C1) If $|g_k(a_i) - g_k(a_j)| < \epsilon_k$, do not change S_i and S_j and set k to $k+1$ (Step (C2) is not performed).
Step (C2) If $g_k(a_i) > g_k(a_j)$, then set $S_i := S_i + 1$ and $S_j := S_j - 1$. Set k to $k + 1$ and go to Step (C1), unless $k > 5$, otherwise, finish the comparison of a_i and a_j.

Overall Comparison. Initialize the all pairs comparison approach by setting $S_i = 0$, $i = 1, 2, \ldots, 7$. Perform Step (C1) and (C2) for all pairs of algorithms $i \neq j$, $i, j = 1, 2, \ldots, 7$. Sort S_i's as the output of the all pairs comparisons and consider the one with the largest S_i as the winner.
Remarks.

(1) In the next subsection $\epsilon_k = 0.01$ for $k = 1, 2, \ldots, 5$ was selected.
(2) An easy generalization of the above approach to multi-criteria comparisons is to attach nonnegative weights to criterions and to use them in Step (C2), instead of ± 1, but we skip this generalization in the next subsection.

4.3   The Empirical Material

As an empirical material for comparisons we selected 900 images of the laser based additive manufacturing process. In [8] it was explained in details why it is important to distinguish cases when the laser head is in the middle of a wall to be constructed (class 1) versus the cases when it is near endpoints of the wall (class 2). Roughly speaking, when it is recognized that the laser head is near endpoints of the wall, it is desirable to reduce the laser power in order to prevent the endpoints to be too thick.

Clearly, one can expect that the empirical material contains a smaller number of examples of Class 2 than that of Class 1 since the laser head moves much longer along the middle of the wall than near its endpoints. Indeed, in the testing sequence of images we had 29 images from Class 2 out of all 450 images and a similar fraction in the learning sequence.

Typical examples of images from Class 1 and 2 are shown in Fig. 1 (upper row). These original images have the size of 111×241. Down-sampled images of the size 10×22 were supplied as inputs of the classifiers (see Fig. 1 – lower row). Notice that such images as in Fig. 1 (lower row) were inputs of the tested classifiers, without applying any features extraction.

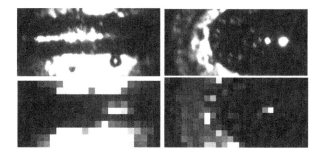

Fig. 1. Examples of images: Classes 1 and 2 (from the left). Original images – upper row and down-sampled images – lower row.

Table 1. The confusion matrix obtained when the MMNDCL (as described in Sect. 1) is applied to 450 long testing sequence.

	Pred. Cl. 1	Pred. Cl. 2	Sum
Act. Cl. 1	416	4	420
Act. Cl. 2	2	28	30
Sum	418	32	450

4.4 The Robustness Against the Class Imbalance – The Results of CV Testing

In this subsection we provide the comparisons of the classifiers that are important from the view-point of their robustness against the class imbalance. Conclusions

Table 2. The confusion matrix obtained when the logistic regression classifier (left panel) and the naive Bayes classifier (right panel) are applied to 450 long testing sequence.

	Pred. Cl. 1	Pred. Cl. 2	sum
Act. Cl. 1	415	6	421
Act. Cl. 2	0	29	29
sum	415	35	450

	Pred. Cl. 1	Pred. Cl. 2	sum
Act. Cl. 1	397	24	421
Act. Cl. 2	0	29	29
sum	397	53	450

Table 3. The confusion matrix obtained when the artificial neural network classifier (left panel) – with two hidden layers and 900 nodes, having tanh activation function – and the random forest classifier (right panel) are applied to 450 long testing sequence.

	Pred. Cl. 1	Pred. Cl. 2	sum
Act. Cl. 1	406	15	421
Act. Cl. 2	0	29	29
sum	406	44	450

	Pred. Cl. 1	Pred. Cl. 2	sum
Act. Cl. 1	420	1	421
Act. Cl. 2	0	29	29
sum	420	30	450

Table 4. The confusion matrix obtained when the SVM classifier (left panel) and 10-NN classifier (right panel) are applied to 450 long testing sequence.

	Pred. Cl. 1	Pred. Cl. 2	sum
Act. Cl. 1	418	3	421
Act. Cl. 2	0	29	29
sum	418	32	450

	Pred. Cl. 1	Pred. Cl. 2	sum
Act. Cl. 1	421	0	421
Act. Cl. 2	4	25	29
sum	425	25	450

Table 5. The summary of the tests of the classifiers for robustness against the class imbalance. In columns 3–5 the values of criterions for each classifier are displayed. Column 6 contains the scores collected by each classifier according to all the pairs comparisons (see Sect. 4.2). In column 7 the classifiers are ranked according to the scores gained in column 6.

nr	ind./meth.	Acc.	MCC	Rec.	Prec.	F1sc.	Comp.	Rank
a	MMNDCL	0.987	0.896	0.990	0.995	0.993	4	**1**
a	Log.-Reg.	0.987	0.904	0.986	1.000	0.993	2	**2≡ 3**
c	n.-Bayes.	0.947	0.718	0.943	1.000	0.971	−16	**7**
d	Neural n.	0.967	0.797	0.964	1.000	0.982	−12	**6**
e	Rand-for.	0.998	0.982	0.997	1.000	0.999	2	**2≡3**
f	SVM	0.993	0.948	0.993	1.000	0.996	1	**4**
g	10-NN	0.991	0.924	1.000	0.991	0.995	0	**5**

are based on the values of criterions and on the multiple criteria sorting of classifiers that were discussed in the previous subsections. Firstly, we display the confusion matrix for each classifier. Then, in Table 5 we provide the comparison of the classifiers and their sorting, according to the methodology of all the pairs comparisons that is described in Subsect. 4.2.

As expected in the class imbalance case, the confusion matrices in Tables 1, 2, 3 and 4 and the Acc. column in Table 5 display very high accuracies of all the classifiers. However, according to the rest of the criterions (columns 4–7 in Table 5), these classifiers are essentially different. In particular, when the methodology of all the pairs comparisons (see Subsect. 4.2) is applied, then they collect largely different scores (see column 8 in Table 5). In the analysis of this column, notice that a classifiers which is essentially the dominant over all the other classifiers, with respect of all the criterions, would be able to collect at most plus 30 scores. Conversely, a classifier that is dominated by all the other six classifiers would gain minus 30 scores.

From this point of view, the classifiers: MMNDCL, Logistic Regression, Random forests, SVM and 10-NN collected non-negative scores, which means that they are – to some extent – robust against the class imbalance. On the other hand, and somewhat unexpectedly, the naive Bayes the neural networks classifiers gained high negative scores for the comparisons.

In column 9 of Table 5 the ranking of the classifiers is presented, which is based on the scores that are shown in column 8. Formally, the winner is the MMND classifier, when the methodology of Subsect. 4.2 is used. Its success can be explained by the fact that it is essentially based on the rule of the nearest mean (in the Mahalonobis or the Euclidean distances). Notice however, that the winner MMNDCL is only slightly better than the last non-negatively tested 10-NN classifier. Notice also that both the MMNDCL and the 10-NN classifiers require only 10–30 images for a proper functioning. This is in contrast to all the others competing methods. On the other hand, the losers, i.e., the naive Bayes and the neural networks classifiers, are more global and they require relatively more longer learning sequences than they are usually in our disposal.

On the other hand, when only the MCC criterion is considered, the winner is the Random Forest method, while the MMNDCL is ranked at the 4-5 position.

5   Conclusions

A modified MAP classifier for images (matrices) having matrix normal distribution was extensively tested on down-sampled images of the laser additive manufacturing process. In parallel, the well known classifiers are tested using the same sequence of images. The main aim of the tests was to check the robustness of all these classifiers against the class imbalance troubles.

The conclusions are the following:

(I) There is the group of classifiers with positive scores in column 8 of Table 5. They can be considered as more robust against the class imbalance than others classifiers, i.e., the neural network and the naive Bayes one.

(2) The highest overall scores in column 8 of Table 5 was collected by the MMNDCL method.

(3) The above conclusions are based on extensive comparisons, but they are restricted to only one learning-testing sequence of images. These conclusions are – to some extend – confirmed by tests for another sequence of real-life images, namely, by the attempts to classify images of an industrial gas burner (see [10, 13]).

Summarizing, although our attempts of selecting a group of classifiers that are robust against the class imbalance seems to be promising, it is highly desirable to verify these findings on other sets of real-life data.

A   Appendix

The densities of the matrix normal distribution are defined as follows:

$$f_j(\mathbf{X}) = \frac{1}{c_j} \exp\left[-\frac{1}{2} \operatorname{tr}[U_j^{-1}(\mathbf{X} - \mathbf{M}_j) V_j^{-1} (\mathbf{X} - \mathbf{M}_j)^T]\right], \tag{18}$$

where the normalization constants are given by:

$$c_j \stackrel{def}{=} (2\pi)^{0.5\,n\,m} \det[U_j]^{0.5\,n} \det[V_j]^{0.5\,m}, \tag{19}$$

where $n \times m$ matrices M_j's denote the class means matrices. The covariance structure of MND class densities is as follows

1. $n \times n$ matrix U_j denotes the covariance matrix between rows of an image from j-th class,
2. $m \times m$ matrix V_j stands for the covariance matrix between columns of an image from j-th class.

The above definitions are meaningful only when $\det[U_j] > 0$, $\det[V_j] > 0$.

The equivalent description of MND is the following:

$$\operatorname{vec}(\mathbf{X}) \sim \mathcal{N}_{n\,m}(\operatorname{vec}(\mathbf{M}_j), \Sigma_j), \text{ for } j = 1, 2, \ldots, J, \tag{20}$$

where $\mathcal{N}_K$ stands for the classic (vector valued) normal distribution with K componentnts. In (20), $\operatorname{vec}(\mathbf{X})$ is the operation of stacking columns of matrix $\mathbf{X}$, while Σ_j is a $n\,m \times n\,m$ covariance matrix of j-th class, which is the Kronecker product (denoted as $\otimes$) of U_j and V_j, i.e.,

$$\Sigma_j \stackrel{def}{=} U_j \otimes V_j, \quad j = 1, 2, \ldots, J. \tag{21}$$

Formulas (20) and (21) show clearly that MND's form a subclass of all normal distributions. Namely, MND's have the special structure of the covariance matrix given by (21) (see [7]). Thus, in practice, it suffices to estimate two much smaller matrices U_j and V_j instead of a general covariance matrix which is $n\,m \times n\,m$. As the consequence, it suffices to have:

$$N_j \geq \max\left\{\frac{n}{m}, \frac{m}{n}\right\} + 1, \quad j = 1, 2, \ldots, J. \tag{22}$$

(see [6] for the proof).

References

1. Breiman, L.: Random forests. Mach. Learn. **45**, 5–32 (2001)
2. Devroye, L., Gyorfi, L., Lugosi, G.: A Probabilistic Theory of Pattern Recognition. Springer, Berlin (2013). https://doi.org/10.1007/978-1-4612-0711-5
3. Haykin, S.S.: Neural Networks and Learning Machines. Pearson, Upper Saddle River (2009)
4. Kadziński, M., Słowiński, R.: Parametric evaluation of research units with respect to reference profiles. Decis. Support. Syst. **72**, 33–43 (2015)
5. Krzysko, M., Skorzybut, M., Wolynski, W.: Classifiers for doubly multivariate data. Discuss. Math Probab. Stat., 31 (2011)
6. Manceur, A.M., Dutilleul, P.: Maximum likelihood estimation for the tensor normal distribution: algorithm, minimum sample size, and empirical bias and dispersion. J. Comput. Appl. Math. **239**, 37–49 (2013)
7. Ohlson, M., Ahmad, M.R., Von Rosen, D.: The multi-linear normal distribution: introduction and some basic properties. J. Multivar. Anal. **113**, 37–47 (2013)
8. Rafajłowicz, E.: Data structures for pattern and image recognition with application to quality control. Acta Polytechnica Hungarica, Informatics (accepted for publication)
9. Rafajłowicz, E.: Classifiers for matrix normal images: derivation and testing. In: Rutkowski, L., Scherer, R., Korytkowski, M., Pedrycz, W., Tadeusiewicz, R., Zurada, J.M. (eds.) ICAISC 2018. LNCS (LNAI), vol. 10841, pp. 668–679. Springer, Cham (2018). https://doi.org/10.1007/978-3-319-91253-0_62
10. Rafajłowicz, E., Rafajłowicz, W.: Image-driven decision making with application to control gas burners. In: Saeed, K., Homenda, W., Chaki, R. (eds.) CISIM 2017. LNCS, vol. 10244, pp. 436–446. Springer, Cham (2017). https://doi.org/10.1007/978-3-319-59105-6_37
11. Salvatore, G., Matarazzo, B., Slowinski, R.: Rough approximation of a preference relation by dominance relations. Eur. J. Oper. Res. **117**(1), 63–83 (1999)
12. Schein, A.I., Ungar, L.H.: Active learning for logistic regression: an evaluation. Mach. Learn. **68**(3), 235–265 (2007)
13. Skubalska-Rafajłowicz, E.: Sparse random projections of camera images for monitoring of a combustion process in a gas burner. In: Saeed, K., Homenda, W., Chaki, R. (eds.) CISIM 2017. LNCS, vol. 10244, pp. 447–456. Springer, Cham (2017). https://doi.org/10.1007/978-3-319-59105-6_38
14. Werner, K., Jansson, M., Stoica, P.: On estimation of covariance matrices with Kronecker product structure. IEEE Trans. Signal Process. **56**(2), 478–491 (2008)

Open-Set Face Classification for Access Monitoring Using Spatially-Organized Random Projections

Ewa Skubalska-Rafajłowicz(✉)🆔

Faculty of Electronics, Department of Computer Engineering,
Wrocław University of Science and Technology,
Wrocław, Poland
ewa.rafajlowicz@pwr.edu.pl

Abstract. In this paper, we present an easy method of open-set face classification problem with application to access control and an identity verification. We use normal random projections as a method of feature extraction from face images. The image transformation consists of local projections of spatially-organized rectangular blocks of an image. Two classification algorithms are analyzed: the nearest neighbor method with scalar product similarity measure and individual acceptance/rejection thresholds and multinomial logistic regression. The computational complexity of designing the transformation is linear with respect to the size of images and does not depend on the form of image partition. Experiments performed on the ORL Database demonstrate that the proposed technique is simple and suitable not only for an access monitoring system but also for face verification. The contents of an image after RP-based transformation is hidden and will not be stably recoverable. So, this approach can be used in systems where the privacy-preserving property is important.

Keywords: Random projections · Access control
Person identification · Person authentication · Face classification
Open set classification · Privacy preserving

1 Introduction

Biometric technology [12–14,27] allows us digitally manage the identity of people. Methods based on the physical or behavioral attributes of the individual such as face, fingerprints, voice and iris are applied to human recognition techniques in secure access control, security systems, searching for potential criminals, biometric authentication for various computing platforms and devices and also for workforce management. Face recognition has been around for many years, and is a problem that has been paid a lot of attention [8,16,18,22,26,30,33]. This technique plays ever greater roles in surveillance and access control applications [4,5,11]. The face as a biometrics factor is gaining increasing acceptance. It may

© Springer Nature Switzerland AG 2018
K. Saeed and W. Homenda (Eds.): CISIM 2018, LNCS 11127, pp. 166–177, 2018.
https://doi.org/10.1007/978-3-319-99954-8_15

not be most reliable and efficient but could work without the co-operation of the test subject. Passers-by could even not be aware of the system. In most instances, the images were not taken in a controlled environment. Illumination, facial expression, pose and noise during face capture can affect the performance of facial recognition systems. A very accurate recognition system, not requiring the activity of users, should probably combine face recognition with other biometrics, such as gait, skin, or hair color [18].

In this paper, we propose an easy to implement approach to a facial biometric recognition system. It can be used as a part of surveillance and access control system. We apply a dimensionality reduction method based on random projections (RP), i.e., a randomly generated image transformation. The transformation consists of local projections spatially-organized, rectangular, blocks of an image. Usually, the images under consideration are treated as vectors and these vectors are randomly projected onto lower-dimensional space [2,3]. Here we develop a method proposed in [32] to partition every image into many blocks of the same size. We concentrate on two classification algorithms: the nearest neighbor method with scalar product similarity measure and individual acceptance/ rejection thresholds and multinomial logistic regression with application to access control and identity verification.

Due to the very high dimensionality of image data the dimensionality reduction is rather necessary. Random projections seem to be a good choice in the case of face images monitoring. Random projections (RP) based approaches have been widely used as a powerful method for dimensionality reduction in computer science and machine learning applications and in image processing [1,3,25,31,32,34,35]. RP outperform principal component analysis (PCA) in many applications [16,33]. RP are one of the methods used for obtaining a privacy-preserving data transformation [21,32].

It should be stressed that the computational complexity of designing the RP based transformation is linear with respect to the size of images and does not depend on the form of image partition. Experiments performed on the ORL database demonstrate that the proposed technique is simple and suitable not only for an access monitoring system but also for face verification.

In the next section, we provide some information about access control systems based on a database of face digital images. Section 3 presents a method of image feature extraction and dimensionality reduction using RP. Open-set face classification methods, i.e., the nearest neighbor classifier with scalar product measure of similarity and multinomial logistic with regression acceptance/ rejection thresholds are described. Section 5 shows results of simulation studies implemented on data from the ORL database (http://www.cam-orl.co.uk). They concerned both access control and identity verification. The results of the closed set classification are also presented. Finally, in Sect. 6 some brief conclusions are presented.

2   Access Control Systems Based on a Database of Face Digital Images

The considered access control problem belongs to the class of problems sometimes called novelty detection or open-set classification problems. Regardless of the terminology we deal with the collection (database) of well-known, positive examples and our task is to build a decision function that will assign a label (allowed/denied) to each new subject: - a subject is similar to elements from the database (access granted) or - a subject is unlike any of them (access denied). This requires building a model (set of models) of objects from the database and determining the measure of the similarity of the object to the model and acceptance threshold. Another approach is to determine the probability of belonging to the class of accepted objects or to test the appropriate hypothesis (outlier detection). Statistical methods based on data distributions generally require a large amount of data in the database.

False alarm rate (FAR) and false permission rate (FPR) are used as measures of errors. FAR (can be also termed as the false rejection rate) corresponds to I type error α in statistical hypothesis tests. FPR (can be also termed as a false acceptance rate) corresponds to II type error β in statistics. Both FPR and FAR are functions of a threshold used in the classification method that can control the tradeoff between the two error rates.

3   Image Feature Extraction and Dimensionality Reduction Using RP

Random projections are closely related to the Johnson-Lindenstrauss lemma [17], which states that any set of N points in a Euclidean space can be embedded in a Euclidean space of lower dimension ($\sim O(\log N)$) with relatively small distortion of the distances between any pair of points from the set of points. The Johnson-Lindenstrauss-lemma has been shown to be useful in many applications in computer science [1, 25, 35], among many others.

The main idea of a random linear projection is that we can estimate the distance between two points (two vectors), say u and z, in a d-dimensional Euclidean space $D^2(u, z) = ||u - z||^2 = (u - z)^T (u - z)$, $u, z \in \mathcal{R}^d$ from the sample squared distances as follows:

$$\hat{D}^2(u, z) = \frac{1}{k} \sum_{j=1}^{k} (s_j(u - z))^2 = \frac{1}{k} ||Su - Sz||^2, \tag{1}$$

where s_j is the j-th row of S, i.e., individual projection.

We will use normal random projections as a method of feature extraction from face images. Usually, images under consideration are treated as vectors and these vectors are randomly projected onto lower-dimensional space [2, 3]. In [32] we have proposed to partition every image into M blocks of the same size. So, each image block is considered as a separate image and it is projected independently from other image blocks, forming only an adequate part of a new feature vector. As a consequence, the dimension of the feature vector is kM, where k stands for the dimensionality of the projection. For the sake of simplicity, we have assumed that the size of each image is $m \times n$ pixels, where $m = 0 \ mod \ m_b$ $n = 0 \ mod \ n_b$, and $m_b \times n_b$ is the size of the each image block. Denote by XB_i, $i = 1, \ldots, M$ the subsequent image blocks.

Let $S \in R^{k \times mn}$ stand for a projection matrix, where k denotes the dimension of each image and each image block after projection. Each entry of projection matrix S is generated independently from the standard normal distribution $\mathcal{N}(0, 1)$. Linear transformation $S \, vec(X)$ is a non-orthogonal projection of X into k dimensional space. Symbol vec stands for vectorization. Let $S = [S_1, S_2, \ldots, S_M]$ consists of M sub-matrices of the same size: $S_i \in R^{k \times d}$, $i = 1, \ldots, M$, $d = \frac{mn}{M}$. Notice, that the number of random numbers that we have to generate is equal to the number of image pixels $m \ n$, independently of the number of blocks.

$y_i = S_i vec(XB_i) \in R^k$ is a projection of block XB_i into k dimensions. Let $T(X)$ stands for the obtained feature vector for image $X \in R^{m \times n}$. $[y_1, \ldots, y_M] = T(X) \in R^{k \times M}$ forms a feature vector. It is called a block projection of X.

Further, the feature vectors are normalized since we want to accept images taken under different illumination conditions. Thus, endpoints of normalized feature vectors lie on an $M \times k$-dimensional unit sphere. It is important to notice, that random projections do not depend on data, so adding or removing an image from the database does not require changing the projection.

4   Open-Set Classification

Problems of face classification with possible intruders, face verification or access control using face recognition belong to open-set classification problems [28, 29]. Problems of this type are also sometimes termed as novelty detection [6, 23, 24] or outliers detection in statistics or data mining [15]. Outliers may indicate a variability in observations, gross errors or a novelty. It is also well known that the reject option can improve the reliability of classification even when all observed objects belong to one of the defined classes (closed set classification) [10]. All these terms indicate little different aspects of decision problems connected to face recognition.

4.1   Nearest Neighbor Classifier Using Scalar Products

After normalization, feature vectors lie on an $M \times k$-dimensional unit sphere. It is convenient to use a scalar product of two vectors as a measure of vicinity of corresponding images instead of the Euclidean distance. First, computing the scalar product of two vectors needs only $2/3$ of elementary operations in comparison to the number of such operations necessary for obtaining the Euclidean distance. Second, the scalar product of two unit vectors is nonlinear with respect to the Euclidean distance of their end-points. It is easy to see, that

$$x^T y = <x, y> = 1 - 0.5||x - y||^2, \quad ||x|| = ||y|| = 1,$$

where $|| \cdot ||$ denotes the Euclidean norm. So, the scalar product is a little less sensitive to small changes in the position of vectors than the Euclidean distance, and even the squared Euclidean distance, between these vectors.

We assume that each class is represented by a small set of face images $\{X_1(c), \ldots, X_r(c)\}$, where c is the class label, $c = 1, 2, \ldots, C$, and C is the number of classes (number of subjects in the face base). After projection, one has only $r \times C$ vectors of dimensionality Mk to memorize.

If there exists $c \in \{1, \ldots, C\}$ such that

$$T_c(X) = \max_i < T(X), T(X_i(c)) > \geq \lambda L(c), \tag{2}$$

then the subject visualized on image X is accepted as a person belonging to the database.

This means that a query subject is sufficiently similar to the person labeled by index c. Otherwise, if there is no such label, he/she is treated as an unknown person. In general, if there is more than one label that meets condition (2) then

$$c^\star \in arg \max_c T_c(X)$$

indicates the class-membership of the query subject. In practice, condition (2) should be verified only for $c^\star$. $\lambda \geq 0$ in (2) is the parameter allowing to control the relationship between FPR and FAR errors. $L(c)$ will be defined as follows.

$$L(c) = \min\{R_{ij}(c) : i \neq j, \ i, j = 1, \ldots, r\},$$

where $R_{ij}(c) =< T(X_i(c)), T(X_j(c)) >$. We assume that the face database consists of Cr images, where r - the number of images of the same subject - is rather small. $L(c)$ is the smallest value of the scalar product of feature vectors of two different images belonging the same person. Thus, if $\lambda = 1$, no image from the database could be rejected. Furthermore, each image will be verified as belonging to the right person. Nevertheless, it may happen that the image will be classified as an image more similar to the images of another person in the base. The proposed approach is very easy to implement even if the training data set is rather small. When the larger number of images is available it will be possible to use statistical methods for $L(c)$ and/or $\lambda L(c)$ estimation.

4.2   Multinomial Logistic Regression for Face Classification

Another method of classification we propose to use for face images classification is the multinomial logistic regression (known also as the log-linear model, softmax regression, or maximum-entropy classifier) [15,19,36]. The logistic regression classifier provides models of class probabilities as logistic functions of linear combinations of features. A symmetric formulation for multi-class logistic regression is given as:

$$Pr\{Y = c | T(X) = x\} = \frac{\exp(\beta_{0c} + x^T \beta_c)}{\sum_{l=1}^{C} \exp(\beta_{0l} + x^T \beta_l)}, \ c = 1, \ldots, C, \tag{3}$$

where β_l is the weight vector corresponding to class l and β_{0l} is a corresponding bias parameter. The unknown parameters in each vector β are typically jointly estimated by maximum a posteriori (MAP) estimation using regularization of the weights (usually L_2 regularization term). In our case, it suffices to minimize with respect to β's the following regularized negative log-likelihood function:

$$-\sum_{c=1}^{C}[\sum_{j=1}^{r}(\beta_{0c} + \beta_c^T T(X_j(c))) - \sum_{j=1}^{r} \log \sum_{i=1}^{C} \exp(\beta_{0i} + \beta_i^T T(X_j(c)))]$$
$$+\rho(\sum_{c=1}^{C}(\beta_{0c}^2 + \beta_c^T \beta_c)), \tag{4}$$

where ρ is the regularization parameter.

5   Experiments on the ORL Database

The ORL database (http://www.cam-orl.co.uk) contains 400 images from 40 persons, each subject represented by 10 different images. For some subjects, the images were taken at different times with different facial expressions and illumination conditions. Images in the ORL database also vary in facial details (with or without glasses) and head pose.

All images are gray-scale and normalized to a resolution of 92×112 pixels. In our experiments, the images were additionally cropped to a size of 90×108 pixels. The images of the two subjects from the ORL face database are presented in Fig. 1.

Fig. 1. Sample images of the ORL database (two different subjects).

5.1   Closed Set Classification

In the first part of the experiments, we concentrate on recognition possibilities of the system based on Gaussian random projections of the images. It is assumed that all images belong to one of the defined classes. Multinomial logistic regression (LR) was applied as a classification method. In every case, we used 5 images of each subject as a part of the training set. The remaining images form testing sets. In the experiments, we have used images of the first 10, then the first 20 subjects taken from the ORL base, and finally, images of all 40 subjects from this database. The process of the learning set selection and the projection matrix generation were performed many times. Usually, it was 100 repetitions used for the Monte Carlo cross-validation. The same procedure for error (or accuracy) estimation was performed in all subsequent experiments. First, the classification results for the first 10 persons based on projections of the whole images were averaged over 10 randomly selected learning sets and 10 projection matrices, i.e., over 100 elementary results. Each learning set consisted of 50 examples, i.e., 5 learning examples were randomly chosen for each class. The remaining images, i.e., the last 50 formed a test set. The random projections dimension was set to $k = 50$, $k = 70$, $k = 100$, $k = 200$, and $k = 300$. Obtained mean classification accuracy, estimated by Monte Carlo cross-validation, was 96.6%, 98.2%, 98.6%, 98.2%, and 98.8%, respectively, with ranges of the accuracy results equal to $[0.94 - 0.98]\%$ for $k = 50$, and to $[0.94 - 1.0]\%$ for $k = 70$, $k = 100$, $k = 200$ and $k = 300$. In the last case, i.e., for $k = 300$, 51 from all 100 experiments provided no classification errors.

The subsequent experiments were conducted for 20 classes (20 subjects). Each training set contains 100 images. The remaining 100 images formed a test sequence. This time, each image is divided into 30 blocks of the size 18×18 pixels. The projection dimensions were set to $k = 10, 20, 40, 50$ and 100. Thus, each image represented feature vector consists of 300, 600, 1200, 1500, and 3000 elements, respectively. Mean classification accuracy averaged, as previously, over 100 repetitions (10 randomly selected learning sets times 10 randomly generated projection matrices) was equal to 94.6, 96.8, 96.6, 96.7, and 96.6, respectively. The similar average results provided projections of the whole images with dimensionality of projections $k = 300$ or even $k = 500$, but this approach is more time consuming. In both cases, the feature extraction time linearly depend on k and the size of an image. Thus, the block-based approach provides good features being about 10 times faster.

When the number of subjects increased to 40, with 200 images used for learning and another 200 images used for testing, and $k = 70 \times 30$ blocks, the LR method gives a mean accuracy of 94.7% (and standard deviation 0.6%). As usually, the accuracy was estimated by the Monte-Carlo cross-validation performed on a hundred experiments. The larger values of k provide less accurate classification results. Notice that our results for the ORL data are definitely better than those recently reported in [26].

5.2   Novelty Detection

In this part of the experiments, the classification system provides an answer to the question: does the image under consideration belong to any of the known persons collection (being in the database) or it is a photo of a stranger (an attacker)? Thus, the system produces only one of the two labels - yes (1) or no (0).

Experiments were conducted for the first 20 subjects from the ORL database. A training set contains 100 images (5 images per subject). The remaining

Table 1. Median of false alarm rates (FAR) and median of false acceptance rates (FPR) calculated on the basis of 100 experiments with different randomly generated projections and randomly selected training set for the 1-NN method and the LR method (the last column). Dimension of the random projections was: $k = 20$, $k = 30$, $k = 50$; $\lambda = 1$. Ranges of the error rates are given in brackets.

k	20	30	50	50 (LR)
FAR	0.055 (0.0–0.11)	0.065 (0.0–0.17)	0.065 (0.05–0.11)	0.08 (0.01–0.11)
FPR	0.5 (0.35–0.83)	0.413 (0.225–0.625)	0.453 (0.41–0.66)	0.30 (0.22–0.895)

Table 2. Median of false alarm rates (FAR) and median of false permission rates (FPR) calculated on the basis of 100 experiments for 1-NN method and for different rejection/acceptance levels. Dimension of projections was set to $k = 50$. Ranges of the error rates are given in brackets.

λ	1.0	1.005	1.01	1.15
FAR	0.065 (0.05–0.11)	0.13 (0.08–0.26)	0.285 (0.15–0.47)	0.48 (0.34–0.58)
FPR	0.453 (0.41–0.66)	0.298 (0.24–0.515)	0.165 (0.105–0.355)	0.0475 (0.025–0.195)

100 images are collected as a part of the test sequence. The second part of the test sequence consists of 200 images of the other persons from the ORL who do not belong to the current face database.

We use two classification algorithms: a 1-NN classifier with individual acceptance levels and different values of the λ parameter, and the LR method with the probability acceptance level h treated as a parameter. Table 1 gives the median of false alarm rates (FAR) and the median of false acceptance rates (FPR) for 1-NN method with $\lambda = 1$. Table 2 contains similar results for $k = 50$ and different λ values. Due to the relatively small number of training data, individual selection of the λ parameter was abandoned This would require the separation of a validation set. As a consequence, the spread of results was quite large (see ranges of results given in brackets). Nevertheless, the results based on determining the medians form a coherent, easy to approximate the curve of FPR dependence on FPR. The error defined by FAR=FPR, i.e., the equal error rate (EER) is about 22%. The ERR is calculated on the basis of the ROC curve obtained by LMS fitting of pairs FAR and FPR values from Table 2 to a quadratic function.

Table 3 gives the median of false alarm rates (FAR) and the median of false acceptance rates (FPR) for the LR method with the probability acceptance level $h = 0.5$, 0.75, 0.9. The experiments were repeated 10 with randomly chosen the projection matrix and the training set.

5.3   Identity Verification

In person identity verification, an image is matched to only one set of images in the database. This set is indicated by the subject's possible identity. An attacker

Table 3. Median of false alarm rates (FAR) and false permission rates (FPR) averaged over 10 experiments with different randomly generated projections and randomly selected training set, $k = 50$, for different rejection/acceptance levels in the LR classification method. Ranges of the error rates are given in brackets.

h	0.5	0.75	0.9
FAR	0.08 (0.01–0.11)	0.245 (0.07–0.28)	0.35 (0.13–0.53)
FPR	0.3 (0.22–0.895)	0.08 (0.05–0.755)	0.04 (0.0–0.565)

Table 4. Median of false alarm rates (FAR) and false permission rates (FPR) averaged over 10 experiments with different randomly generated projections and randomly selected training set, $k = 50$, for different rejection/acceptance levels. The subject is claiming his/her identity. Ranges of the error rates are given in brackets.

λ	0.99	0.995	1.0	1.01
FAR	0.045 (0.0–0.09)	0.075 (0.01–0.11)	0.14 (0.09–0.23)	0.41 (0.29–0.46)
FPR	0.115 (0.097–0.125)	0.0716 (0.0645–0.0945)	0.043 (0.071–0.135)	0.0122 (0.0065–0.0273)

is a person outside the database or also a person indicated to be someone other than his/her own identity. Thus, we have additional information about subject's class-membership and this information should be verified by the face recognition system. If the person in the database gives his or her real identity, then he should get permission to have access. In a case where he/she indicates another person from the database as his own identity, access should be denied. Thus, the facial recognition system is used to verify whether a given person uses his or her individual identifier (password) or he/she is an intruder who impersonates the identity of the person authorized to access. Summarizing, the access should be denied to any person whose image has not been placed in the database. Similarly, access should be denied to any person whose image is in the database, but he/she uses the identity of other person who belongs to the database (identity negative verification).

Table 4 gives the median of false alarm rates (FAR) and the median of false acceptance rates (FPR) for the 1-NN classification method and for different rejection/acceptance levels $\lambda = 0.99$, 0.995, 1.0 and 1.01. Table 5 gives the median of false alarm rates (FAR) and the median of false acceptance rates (FPR) for the LR classification method and for different rejection/acceptance levels $h = 05$, 0.75, 0.9. For both methods, the experiments were repeated 10 with randomly chosen the projection matrix and the training set (100 images). Projection dimension was set to 50.

Notice, that no recognition errors are observed for $h = 0.75$ and $h = 0.9$. The approximate EER for this system is about 10% (using LMS fitting to a quadratic function). In real systems, the observed errors depend on many factors. Probability of unauthorized attack carried out by unknown subjects is one of the most important pieces of information which should be taken into account during

Table 5. Median of false alarm rates (FAR) and median of false permission rates (FPR) averaged over 10 experiments with different randomly generated projections and randomly selected training set, $k = 50$ (in %). Three different rejection/acceptance levels in the LR classification method are assumed: 0.5, 0.75, and 0.9. Ranges of the error rates are given in brackets.

h	0.5	0.75	0.9
FAR	9. (5–12)	24.5 (3–28)	35. (13–53)
FPR	15. (11–44.8)	4. (0.25–37.8)	2. (0.0–28.3)

the process of designing the control system. It is clear that formula

$$(1 - p_a)FAR + p_aFPR,$$

where p_a is the probability of unauthorized attack, estimates the expected error of the classification system in a sufficiently long period of time. The choice of FAR and FPR values should depend not only on the expected value of p_a, but also on the costs of making wrong decisions of both types.

6   Comments and Conclusion

The methods of open-set face classification developed in the paper are based on spatially-organized Gaussian RP of face images. This method of dimensionality reduction and feature extraction is easy to implement, fast and additionally it protects the privacy of image data. The contents of an image after RP based transformation is hidden and will not be stably recoverable. So this approach can be used in systems where privacy-preserving property is important.

In addition, the user is able to easily change the parameters of the classification system.

Furthermore, the transformed image provides good features for correct classification. The proposed approach is independent of the data. Thus, adding or removing images from the classification system does not require a change of the transformation.

It should be stressed that in open systems, outliers (intruders) are not precisely defined. Thus, RP-based features work as additional regularizers and they prevent overfitting learning data.

Acknowledgments. This research was supported by grant 041/0145/17 at the Faculty of Electronics, Wrocław University of Science and Technology.

References

1. Achlioptas, D.: Database-friendly random projections: Johnson-Lindenstrauss with binary coins. J. Comput. Syst. Sci. **66**, 671–687 (2003)
2. Amador, J.J.: Random projection and orthonormality for lossy image compression. Image Vis. Comput. **25**, 754–766 (2007)
3. Brigham, E., Maninila, H.: Random projection in dimensionality reduction: applications to image and text data. Proc. Conf. Knowl. Discov. Data Min. **16**, 245–250 (2001)
4. Brigham, E., Maninila, H.: News: facial recognition tech secures enterprise access control. Biom. Technol. Today **2017**(10), 2–3 (2017). https://doi.org/10.1016/S0969-4765(17)30145-5
5. Buolamwini, J., Gebru, T.: Gender shades: intersectional accuracy disparities in commercial gender classification. Proc. Mach. Learn. Res. **81**, 1–15 (2018)
6. Bishop, C.M.: Novelty detection and Neural Network validation. Proc. IEE Conf. Vis. Image Signal Process. **141**(4), 217–222 (1994)
7. Bishop, C.M.: Pattern Recognition and Machine Learning, pp. 206–209. Springer, New York (2006)
8. Brunelli, R., Poggio, T.: Face recognition: features versus templates. IEEE Trans. PAMI **10**(15), 1042–1052 (1993)
9. Brunelli, R.: Template Matching Techniques in Computer Vision. Theory and Practice. Wiley, Chichester (2009)
10. Fukunaga, K.: Introduction to Statistical Pattern Recognition, 2nd edn. Academic Press, New York (1990)
11. Haghighat, M., Abdel-Mottaleb, M.: Low resolution face recognition in surveillance systems using discriminant correlation analysis. In: 12th IEEE International Conference on Automatic Face & Gesture Recognition (FG 2017), pp. 912–917 (2017)
12. Jain, A.K., Arun Ross, A., Pankanti, S.: An introduction to biometric recognition. IEEE Trans. Circ. Syst. Video Technol. **14**(1), 4–20 (2004)
13. Jain, A.K., Ross, A.A., Pankanti, S.: Biometrics: a tool for information security. IEEE Trans. Inf. Forensics Secur. **1**(2), 125–144 (2006)
14. Jain, A.K., Patrick Flynn, P., Ross, A.A. (eds.): Handbook of Biometrics. Springer, Heidelberg (2007). https://doi.org/10.1007/978-0-387-71041-9
15. James, G., Witten, D., Hastie, T., Tibshirani, R.: An Introduction to Statistical Learning. Springer, New York (2013). https://doi.org/10.1007/978-1-4614-7138-7
16. Jeong, K., Principe, J.C.: Enhancing the correntropy MACE filter with random projections. Neurocomputing **72**(1–2), 102–111 (2008)
17. Johnson, W.B., Lindenstrauss, J.: Extensions of Lipshitz mapping into Hilbert space. Contemp. Math. **26**, 189–206 (1984)
18. Kimmel, R., Sapiro, G.: The Mathematics of face recognition. SIAM News **36**(3) (2003)
19. Krishnapuram, B., Carin, L., Figueiredo, M.A.T., Hartemink, A.J.: Sparse multinomial logistic regression: fast algorithms and generalization bounds. IEEE Trans. Pattern Anal. Mach. Intell. **27**(6), 957–968 (2005)
20. Learned-Miller, E., Huang, G.B., RoyChowdhury, A., Li, H., Hua, G.: Labeled faces in the wild: a survey. In: Kawulok, M., Celebi, M.E., Smolka, B. (eds.) Advances in Face Detection and Facial Image Analysis, pp. 189–248. Springer, Cham (2016). https://doi.org/10.1007/978-3-319-25958-1_8

21. Liu, K., Kargupta, H., Ryan, J.: Random projection-based multiplicative data perturbation for privacy preserving distributed data mining. IEEE Trans. Knowl. Data Eng. **18**, 92–106 (2006)
22. Mandal, B., Lim, R.Y., Dai, P., Sayed, M.R., Li, L., Lim, J.H.: Trends in machine and human face recognition. In: Kawulok, M., Celebi, M.E., Smolka, B. (eds.) Advances in Face Detection and Facial Image Analysis, pp. 145–187. Springer, Cham (2016). https://doi.org/10.1007/978-3-319-25958-1_7
23. Markou, M., Singh, S.: Novelty detection: a review, part 1: statistical approaches. Signal Process. **83**, 2481–2497 (2003)
24. Markou, M., Singh, S.: Novelty detection: a review, part 2: neural network based approaches. Signal Process. **83**, 2499–2521 (2003)
25. Matousek, J.: On variants of the Johnson-Lindenstrauss lemma. Random Struct. Algorithms **33**(2), 142–156 (2008)
26. Ning, X., Li, W., Tang, B., He, H.: BULDP: biomimetic uncorrelated locality discriminant projection for feature extraction in face recognition. IEEE Trans. Image Process. **27**(5) (2018). https://doi.org/10.1109/TIP.2018.2806229
27. Reid, D., Samangooei, S., Chen, C., Nixon, M., Ross, A.: Soft biometrics for surveillance: an overview. Mach. Learn. Theory Appl. **31**, 327–352 (2013)
28. Rudd, E.M., Jain, L.P., Scheirer, W.J., Boult, T.E.: The extreme value machine. IEEE Trans. PAMI **40**(3), 762–768 (2018)
29. Scheirer, W.J., Rocha, A., Sapkota, A., Boult, T.E.: Towards open set recognition. IEEE Trans. PAMI **35**(7), 1757–1772 (2013)
30. Szymkowski, M., Saeed, K.: A multimodal face and fingerprint recognition biometrics system. In: Saeed, K., Homenda, W., Chaki, R. (eds.) CISIM 2017. LNCS, vol. 10244, pp. 131–140. Springer, Cham (2017). https://doi.org/10.1007/978-3-319-59105-6_12
31. Skubalska-Rafajłowicz, E.: Random projections and Hotelling's T^2 statistics for change detection in high-dimensional data stream. Int. J. Appl. Math. Comput. Sci. **23**(2), 447–461 (2013)
32. Skubalska-Rafajłowicz, E.: Spatially-organized random projections of images for dimensionality reduction and privacy-preserving classification. In: Proceedings of 10th International Workshop on Multidimensional (nD) Systems (nDS), pp. 1–5 (2017)
33. Skubalska-Rafajłowicz, E.: Relative stability of random projection-based image classification. In: Rutkowski, L., Scherer, R., Korytkowski, M., Pedrycz, W., Tadeusiewicz, R., Zurada, J.M. (eds.) ICAISC 2018, part I. LNCS, vol. 10841, pp. 702–713. Springer, Cham (2018). https://doi.org/10.1007/978-3-319-91253-0_65
34. Tsagkatakis, G., Savakis, A.: A random projections model for object tracking under variable pose and multi-camera views. In: Proceedings of the Third ACM/IEEE International Conference on Distributed Smart Cameras, ICDSC, pp. 1–7 (2009)
35. Vempala, S.: The Random Projection Method. American Mathematical Society, Providence (2004)
36. Yu, H.-F., Huang, F.-L., Lin, C.-J.: Dual coordinate descent methods for logistic regression and maximum entropy models. Mach. Learn. **85**, 4–75 (2011)

Industrial Management and Other Applications

Cooperation in Clusters: A Study Case in the Furniture Industry in Colombia

Daniela Landinez Lamadrid[1], Diana Ramirez Rios[1,2],
Dionicio Neira Rodado[3(✉)], Fernando Crespo[4], Luis Ramirez[1],
Miguel Jimenez[3], and William Manjarres[5]

[1] Fundación Centro de Investigación en Modelación Empresarial del Caribe,
Barranquilla, Colombia
{dlandinez,dramirez,lramirez}@fcimec.org
[2] Rensselaer Polytechnic Institute, Troy, USA
ramird2@rpi.edu
[3] Universidad de la Costa CUC, Barranquilla, Colombia
{dneira1,mjimenez7}@cuc.edu.co
[4] Universidad Mayor, Santiago, Chile
facrespo@gmail.com
[5] Universidad del Atlántico, Barranquilla, Colombia
wmanjarres4@gmail.com

Abstract. Cooperation is increasingly been used in the industrial sector because of its benefits. This have motivated companies to establish alliances and agreements with others in order to reduce cost or access new markets, for example. In the literature, we could find many works aimed at cooperation in supply chains. A smaller amount was focused at cluster cooperation and few of them propose methodologies or models to facilitate the development and implementation of cooperation in industrial clusters. This paper provides a methodology for cooperation in clusters, which was applied to the furniture industry of Atlántico region in Colombia. Shapley value was used in order to evaluate the different coalitions and to split the benefits obtained with these coalitions. The methodology is useful for cluster members in order to encourage the formation of alliances within the cluster in order to overcome the prevailing mistrust, strengthening the cluster and gaining competitiveness.

Keywords: Game theory · Supply chain · Shapley value · Clusters
Cooperation

1 Introduction

Currently companies all over the world strive to gain a bigger market share in the existing globalized and competitive markets [1, 2]. In order to deal with this scenario, the concept of cluster has emerged and gained interest among the different regions and industry sectors. A cluster is known as a group of interconnected companies that share geographical boundaries or perform common practices, as they are related to the same supply chain. According to Porter [3], clusters dominate today's economic world map,

© Springer Nature Switzerland AG 2018
K. Saeed and W. Homenda (Eds.): CISIM 2018, LNCS 11127, pp. 181–192, 2018.
https://doi.org/10.1007/978-3-319-99954-8_16

and this is a relevant feature of virtually every national, regional, state, and even metropolitan economy, especially in more developed nations.

Clusters are based on cooperation activities. Nevertheless Patti [4] states that, clusters benefit from both competition and cooperation. Specifically, in the case of cooperation, much of this has been evidenced at a vertical level of the supply chain and at a horizontal level if there is no direct competition or any external threat to the cluster existence. Yet, as this author highlights, trust among companies and the face-to-face interactions are key factors for cluster success.

The importance of clusters can also be highlighted in developing countries. For example, in Colombia the government has implemented a state policy in order to encourage the cluster formation, aiming to give an impulse to innovation, and competitiveness. By this way the government looks for the consolidation of a long term sustainable national manufacturing sector. In the particular case of the Atlántico region in Colombia, the furniture industry is grouped in a cluster called AMOBLAR-C which is of great importance for the region since by 2014, it was made up of 200 companies that registered annual sales around US$ 160 million and generated more than 10 thousand direct and indirect jobs.

The government has established different strategies with the companies associations with the aim of strengthening the furniture cluster with faint success, therefore it is trying to promote trust and real linkage within the cluster members with the implementation of cooperative game theory and in particular Shapley Value.

The paper is organized as follows, Sect. 2 contains a literature review of cooperation in supply chains, and cooperative game theory applied to clusters, Sect. 3 describes a cooperation scheme, Sect. 4 shows cooperation scenarios applied to furniture industry, and finally conclusions of the study are exposed.

2   A Methodology for Cooperation in Clusters

After analyzing the cluster concept and the possible ways to cooperate inside of them, a methodology for cluster cooperation has been developed. This methodology consists of six main steps which facilitate the implementation of cooperative activities in any cluster. Steps are described as follows:

a. Establishment of cooperation strategy: it is necessary to establish a cooperation strategy by which the cluster is expected to obtain better results. It may be in terms of profits, costs, effectiveness, productivity, times, etc.
b. Players definition: the type of player who can participate in the game must be established and identified.
c. Coalition formation: it refers to all possible combinations of players that can form an alliance.
d. Determination and calculation of the characteristic function of the game: corresponds to a function or equation with which the resulting values of each coalition will be obtained.
e. Calculation of Shapley value: the Shapley value is calculated with the next equation:

$$\emptyset_i(v) = \sum_{S \in N : i \in S} \frac{(S-1)!(n-S)!}{n!}(S) - v(S - \{i\}) \tag{1}$$

f. Evaluation of results: the results are analyzed by comparing the Shapley value with the initial state of each player in order to determine if it is profitable to cooperate, otherwise Shapley's value should be recalculated without including players whose participation is not feasible.

3   Case Study: Furniture Cluster in Atlántico Region in Colombia

Atlántico is a Colombian region located in the Caribbean coast. It limits to the north and northeast with the Caribbean Sea, to the east, with the Magdalena River, to the south, southwest and west with the Bolivar department. The Atlantic department covers an area of 3,386 km^2 and represents 0.29% of the total area of the country.

The Atlántico furniture cluster is composed by companies that develop, design, produce, distribute, and trade goods and services activities, whose objective is to contribute to the improvement of productivity through the articulation of the sector and the competitive development of products and processes (Board of Trade of Barranquilla). The main players in the chain of the furniture cluster can be grouped as: suppliers, furniture manufacturers, marketers, educative and research centers, and government and support entities, as shown in Fig. 1.

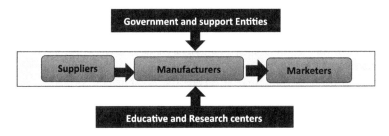

Fig. 1. Supply Chain of furniture companies. Source: Own elaboration.

3.1   Application of Methodology for Cluster Cooperation

According to Capó-Vicedo et al. [5], an important issue for the development of the sector is related to business cooperation, in fact, the success of the most dynamic clusters is associated with the way of managing the knowledge among its main economic agents, and for this to be possible, proactive attitudes of business and institutional cooperation are required. It also highlights the Government role as a strengthening entity of the conditions that facilitate cooperation between companies.

To evaluate the cooperation in Atlántico furniture cluster, a study was carried out with sample of 35 companies. In this research, Landinez Lamadrid et al. [6] developed four hypothetical scenarios with the purpose that companies express their position regarding different cooperation strategies, described by Guo [7]. The results obtained of each scenario with a coalition of six particular companies are shown below:

– **Scenario 1**

Hypothetical scenario: The government has a call for proposals for R + D + I projects to improve different aspects of the cluster. The government will contribute 50% of the total cost of the benefited project, by which the cluster must place the other 50%. With what amount (cash or money in kind) would you be willing to collaborate to be able to execute the benefited project? Table 1 presents the answer of six companies to this scenario.

Table 1. Contribution of each player. Source: Authors

Contribution of each player	
P1	$30.000.000
P2	$5.000.000
P3	$10.000.000
P4	$20.000.000
P5	$500.000
P6	$2.000.000

Applying the developed methodology:

a. Establishment of cooperation strategy: Participation in a call for R + D + I project.
b. Players definition: The strategy is intended for cluster companies, which means that players are defined as Suppliers, Manufacturers and Marketers who are willing to participate in the call for projects.
c. Coalition formation: Corresponds to all possible combinations of players that can be allied, as shown in the Table 2 through a 3 players example. The number of coalitions is given by $2^n - 1$, where n is the total number of players.

Table 2. Coalitions with three players. Source: Authors

Possible coalitions with 3 players		
1- member coalitions	2 - members coalitions	3 - members coalitions
1	1-2	-------
2	1-3	1-2-3
3	2-3	-------

d. Determination and calculation of the characteristic function of the game: At this point, an equation to calculate the values of each coalition must be established. In the hypothetical scenario, government provides 50% of the Project value and cluster the remaining 50%, according to this, the value of each coalition can be calculated through the following expression:

$$\begin{cases} v_i, & if \ s = 1 \\ 2 \sum_i^s v_i, & if \ s \geq 2 \end{cases} \tag{2}$$

Where,

$i = set\ to\ players$
$s = number\ of\ players\ in\ coalitions$
$v_i = amount\ that\ player\ i\ is\ willing\ to\ contribute\ with\ in\ order\ to\ participate.$

Following these equations, Table 3 presents the results for each coalition. Through Eq. 2, the value of the game when there is only player 1 in the coalition, can be calculated ($v(\{P1\})$). In the case of a coalition between players 1, 2 and 3, then s = 3 (three players would be in the coalition and the value of the game will be twice the sum of the value of the game for each individual player coalition ($v(\{P1, P2, P3\})$).

Table 3. Examples of game characteristic function results. Source: Authors

Game characteristic function results (n1, v)

v({P1})	$30.000.000	v({P1, P2, P3})	$90.000.000	v({P1, P2, P3, P5})	$45.500.000
v({P2})	$5.000.000	v({P1, P2, P4})	$110.000.000	v({P1, P2, P3, P6})	$94.000.000
v({P3})	$10.000.000	v({P1, P2, P5})	$71.000.000	v({P1, P2, P4, P5})	$111.000.000
v({P4})	$20.000.000	v({P1, P2, P6})	$74.000.000	v({P1, P2, P4, P6})	$114.000.000
v({P5})	$500.000	v({P1, P3, P4})	$120.000.000	v({P1, P2, P5, P6})	$75.000.000
v({P6})	$2.000.000	v({P1, P3, P5})	$81.000.000	v({P1, P3, P4, P5})	$121.000.000

e. Shapley value calculation: Considering the values found above, the Shapley value was calculated, obtaining the results presented in Table 4.

Table 4. Shapley Value for the simulated scenario. Source: Authors

Player i in each coalition	Contribution to j players coalitions						
	1	2	3	4	5	6	ji(v)
1	$30.000.000	$337.500.000	$600.000.000	$554.500.000	$300.000.000	$60.000.000	$ 55.491.667
2	$ 5.000.000	$112.500.000	$100.000.000	$ 54.500.000	$ 50.000.000	$10.000.000	$ 10.491.667
3	$10.000.000	$157.500.000	$200.000.000	$154.500.000	$100.000.000	$20.000.000	$ 19.491.667
4	$20.000.000	$247.500.000	$400.000.000	$400.000.000	$245.500.000	$40.000.000	$ 39.766.667
5	$ 500.000	$ 72.000.000	$ 10.000.000	-$ 35.500.000	$ 5.000.000	$ 1.000.000	$ 2.391.667
6	$ 2.000.000	$ 85.500.000	$ 40.000.000	$ 40.000.000	$ 65.500.000	$ 4.000.000	$ 7.366.667
P(j)	0,166666667	0,033333333	0,016666667	0,016666667	0,033333333	0,166666667	$135.000.000
$\frac{(s-1)!(n-s)!}{n!}$	$\phi_i(v) = \sum_{\{S \bullet N : i \in S\}} \frac{(S-1)!(n-S)!}{n!}(v(S) - v(S - \{i\}))$						

f. Evaluation of results: Once obtained the results, it must be verified that Shapley value is better than the initial value of each player, only thus, the player would be willing to cooperate. In this case, the Shapley value must be greater than the initial value.

Thus, player 1 before cooperating had $30,000,000 for the project execution, and after cooperating, this value is expected to increase to approximately $55,491,667, having an expected extra benefit of $25,491,667 from the government support; Player 2 before cooperating had $5,000,000, after cooperating, this amount is expected to increase to $10,491,667, earning a profit of $5,491,667. The information related with the other players can be found on Table 5.

Table 5. Comparission between initial values and Shapley value for scenario 1. Source: Own Elaboration

Initial investment	Shapley value
$30.000.000	$55.491.666,67
$5.000.000	$10.491.666,67
$10.000.000	$19.491.666,67
$20.000.000	$39.766.666,67
$500.000	$2.391.666,67
$2.000.000	$7.366.666,67

Resources for the project execution, are formed by initial contributions of each player and government contribution. The purpose of Shapley value is to distribute those resources considering the contribution of each player, obtaining a fair allocation. In our example, Shapley value is greater than initial contributions of all player, so it is assumed that all of them would be willing to cooperate. However, if one of them were not profitable to participate in cooperation, then the Shapley value would have to be recalculated, not including that player, and this procedure is repeated until it is feasible for all to cooperate.

The other three scenarios were developed similarly. Therefore each of them will be described only form the coalition calculations.

– **Scenario 2**

Hypothetical scenario: In order to access a new high volume market it is desired to work together with other cluster members in such a way that it is necessary to reduce prices. At what maximum rate would you be willing to reduce your prices in order to gain access to this new market?

In order to deal with this scenario, it has to be considered that it proposes a strategy at the level of marketers and producers-marketers, therefore, these will be the links that will be taken into account. The percentage of price reduction will be taken into account, in order to find a maximum reduction in each possible coalition and calculate the Shapley value based on this coalition maximum reduction.

In this case, the individual values correspond to the current net profits of the companies. In order to calculate the values associated to each coalition in which 2 or more players participate, these current profits are taken and reduced in the maximum coalition percentage. This implies that if a coalition involves companies with different percentages of price reduction, then the maximum coalition price reduction percentage will be the lowest percentage of companies in the coalition. This assumption is made under the criterion that if a company is willing to reduce their prices by a high percentage, it would not have any problem to do so in a lower percentage. This would not happen in the opposite way. As coalitions are formed, these perceived "profits" of each of the participants are added together. Finally, the Shapley value is compared to the original profits that each company had. Cooperation will be feasible if the Shapley value is greater than the original profits. The entering values for this scenario are shown in Table 6.

Table 6. Scenario 2 entering values. Source: Own Elaboration

Player	Net profit	% of Price reduction	Expected additional profit
Company 1	$25.000	3%	$10.000
Company 2	$15.000	10%	$5.000
Company 3	$20.000	20%	$8.000
Company 4	$14.000	5%	$5.000
Company 5	$22.000	10%	$7.000
Company 6	$24.000	10%	$9.000

The scenario operates as follows:

- Companies that will be included in the coalition are selected.
- Companies indicate their current profit, the price reduction that they can grant, and the additional profit related with the gain of a new market associated with the granted price reduction.
- Coalition values are calculated. For example coalition $v(\{P1, P2\})$ gives a value of $53.800. This value is obtained in first place by noticing which company has the lower price reduction in the coalition. In this particular case, between P1 and P2, it happens to be company P1 with a value of 3%. This means that their profit will be 97% of their current profit plus the additional expected profit. The same logic applies to company P2. So the calculations are: $v(\{P1, P2\}) = (25.000 \times 0,97) + 10.000 + (15.000 \times 0,97) + 5.000$. This calculations give the value of $53.800 that can be found on Table 7.
- Similarly the values for the other coalitions and the Shapley value are calculated (Tables. 8 and 10).

From Table 9 it can be noticed that the Shapley value is greater than the current profit for all the companies. This makes scenario 2 as a viable cooperation scenario, considering this particular companies, and its associated data. In this case Company 1 had an initial profit of $25.000 and with the coalition its expected profit is $35.173.

Table 7. Sample of coalitions values for scenario 2. Source: Own Elaboration

Game characteristic function results (n1, v)					
v({P1})	$25.000	v({P1, P2, P3})	$81.200	v({P1, P2, P3, P5})	$109.540
v({P2})	$15.000	v({P1, P2, P4})	$72.380	v({P1, P2, P3, P6})	$113.480
v({P3})	$20.000	v({P1, P2, P5})	$82.140	v({P1, P2, P4, P5})	$100.720
v({P4})	$14.000	v({P1, P2, P6})	$86.080	v({P1, P2, P4, P6})	$104.660
v({P5})	$22.000	v({P1, P3, P4})	$80.230	v({P1, P2, P5, P6})	$114.420
v({P6})	$24.000	v({P1, P3, P5})	$89.990	v({P1, P3, P4, P5})	$108.570

Table 8. Shapley Values for scenario 2. Source: Own Elaboration

Player i in each coalition	Contribution to j players coalitions						
	1	2	3	4	5	6	$j_i(v)$
1	$ 25.000	$ 202.400	$ 362.250	$ 366.050	$ 182.900	$ 36.150	$ 35.173
2	$ 15.000	$ 125.250	$ 191.450	$ 193.550	$ 97.450	$ 19.550	$ 19.598
3	$ 20.000	$ 160.850	$ 268.600	$ 271.400	$ 136.600	$ 27.400	$ 26.815
4	$ 14.000	$ 125.980	$ 196.270	$ 196.830	$ 96.670	$ 18.580	$ 19.403
5	$ 22.000	$ 166.290	$ 277.460	$ 280.540	$ 141.260	$ 28.340	$ 27.942
6	$ 24.000	$ 183.730	$ 316.320	$ 319.680	$ 160.920	$ 32.280	$ 31.468
P(j)	0,16666667	0,03333333	0,01666667	0,01666667	0,03333333	0,16666667	$160.400
$\frac{(s-1)!(n-s)!}{n!}$	$\phi_i(v) = \sum_{(S \in N, i \in S)} \frac{(S-1)!(n-S)!}{n!}(v(S) - v(S - \{i\}))$						

Table 9. Comparison between current profits and Shapley value for scenario 2. Source: Own Elaboration

Current profit	Shapley value
$25.000	$35.173
$15.000	$19.595
$20.000	$26.815
$14.000	$19.103
$22.000	$27.941
$24.000	$31.468

– **Scenario 3**

"In order to reduce inventory levels and inventory costs, it is necessary to implement collaborative strategies such as VMI type in which it is necessary to share information on levels and references in inventory. What percentage of your inventory would you be willing to share with your supplier or customer in order to achieve these goals?"

This scenario refers to collaborative strategies related to inventory management; Although the VMI or Vendor Managed Inventory is an example, it was decided that the scenario should not necessarily be limited to that methodology. Since the question

Table 10. Input values for scenario 3. Source: Own Elaboration

Company	Warehouse used space m^3	Warehouse space that the company is willing to share m^3	Warehousing cost per m^3
1	20	10	$6
2	80	30	$3
3	42	38	$7
4	73	49	$8
5	89	46	$4
6	34	13	$5

posed refers to the inventory that they would be willing to share and it is considered that the company can share it with Suppliers, customers and even with companies from the same link.

Considering that the collaboration strategy to be developed in this scenario will be focused on sharing inventory between different companies in the cluster, then if a company is interested in evaluating this strategy, it should provide the following data:

- Average cost of inventory per m^3
- Used storage capacity (m^3)
- Capacity in m^3 that the company is willing to share with other companies in the cluster.

The possibility of sharing inventory was represented by moving product units from one warehouse to another and taking into account two important aspects: cost and capacity. If units are going to be moved from one company to another, as a rule of the game you will be given priority to move units of the company with higher cost to the warehouse of the company with lower cost, considering space constraints. Given that there is no precise information about the products stored and considering that these can be very variable, their movement from one warehouse to another was made by transferring cubic meters that are in use in a warehouse, to another in which space is available and has lower warehousing costs. By this way it would free up space in the first warehouse that has a higher cost and in the end this will translate into savings for the company with higher cost, and additional income for the company with lower warehouse cost.

The current inventory cost of each company is calculated considering the used space and the warehousing cost. At the moment when multi-player coalitions are being formed, the total inventory cost is calculated for those coalitions. In order to make this calculations it was necessary to make the process of inventory sharing following the rule of the specified game and thus to be able to obtain the inventory cost considering the changes made in the companies' warehouses. By this way, there will be an inventory cost associated with each coalition. This value was used to calculate the Shapley value. Shapley value determines how to distribute costs among cooperating companies that are willing to share their inventory. Finally, the proposed strategy will be feasible for a company if the Shapley value is less than its current inventory cost.

The scenario operates as follows:

- Companies that will be included in the coalition are selected.
- Companies indicate their warehouse used space, the space in (m^3) that they are willing to share with other members of the cluster, and the warehousing cost per m^3.
- Coalition values are calculated. For example coalition v({P1, P2}) gives a value of $300. This value is obtained in first place by noticing that company 2 has a lower warehousing cost per m^3, than company 1. So company 1 will rent the space of company 2 and pay for it at a rate of $3 per rented m^3. In this case company 1 need 20 m^3 to stock and company 2 has 30 m^3 to share. Therefore company 1 can send all its inventory to companies 2 warehouse and pay the agreed rate. In this case the agreed rate is supposed to be company 2 warehousing cost per m^3. So the calculations are: v({P1, P2}) = $(80 \times 3) + (20 \times 3)$. This calculations give the value of $300 that can be found on Table 11.
- Similarly the values for the other coalitions and the Shapley value are calculated.

Table 11. Sample of coalition values of scenario 3. Source: Own Elaboration

Game characteristic function results (n1, v)

v({P1})	$120	v({P1, P2, P3})	$524	v({P1, P2, P3, P5})	$814
v({P2})	$240	v({P1, P2, P4})	$774	v({P1, P2, P3, P6})	$679
v({P3})	$294	v({P1, P2, P5})	$646	v({P1, P2, P4, P5})	$972
v({P4})	$584	v({P1, P2, P6})	$450	v({P1, P2, P4, P6})	$905
v({P5})	$356	v({P1, P3, P4})	$940	v({P1, P2, P5, P6})	$782
v({P6})	$170	v({P1, P3, P5})	$636	v({P1, P3, P4, P5})	$1.133

Comparing the initial values with the value of Shapley of each company, it becomes clear that there are savings in the inventory cost after implementing the cooperation strategy that poses the Scenario 3. It is also important to note that in some scenarios for some players their particular cost after cooperation may be negative. This happens because in these cases the cost of these companies is very low in relation to the rest of the players and they also have plenty space to share in their warehouse.

Table 12. Shapley Values for scenario 3. Source: Own Elaboration

Player i in each coalition	Contribution to j players coalitions						$j_i(v)$
	1	2	3	4	5	6	
1	$ 120	$ 457	$ 1.000	$ 1.011	$ 534	$ 110	$ 105
2	$ 240	$ 780	$ 1.417	$ 1.348	$ 667	$ 120	$ 154
3	$ 294	$ 1.150	$ 2.306	$ 2.401	$ 1.295	$ 268	$ 254
4	$ 584	$ 2.489	$ 4.658	$ 4.437	$ 2.187	$ 427	$ 476
5	$ 356	$ 1.366	$ 2.516	$ 2.369	$ 1.157	$ 218	$ 261
6	$ 170	$ 678	$ 1.410	$ 1.427	$ 745	$ 144	$ 147
P(j)	0,16666667	0,03333333	0,01666667	0,01666667	0,03333333	0,16666667	$ 1.397
$\frac{(s-1)!(n-s)!}{n!}$	$\phi_i(v) = \sum_{\{S \in N : i \in S\}} \frac{(S-1)!(n-S)!}{n!}(v(S) - v(S - \{i\}))$						

Table 13. Comparison between initial warehousing cost and Shapley value for scenario 3. Source: Own Elaboration

Current (initial) cost	Shapley value
$120	$104.88
$240	$154.32
$294	$253.62
$584	$475.95
$336	$261.18
$170	$147.05

This generates that these companies end up making money by renting their warehouse, which is represented by a negative cost.

4 Conclusions and Future Research

There is a global concern about the importance that clusters have in the gain of competitiveness of companies, regions and nations. This gain of competitiveness will help nations to guarantee a wellbeing to the nation´s population. The effectiveness of clusters in the gain of competitiveness is well documented by several studies throughout the world, but it is relevant to point out that it does not limit only to industry clusters, but also to health care clusters, construction clusters, among others (Tables 12 and 13).

One of the key success factors of clusters is the fact that they encourage the integration of all the supply chain. This alignment helps companies forming this supply chain to establish common aims and targets, which ease the decision making process in the companies. Unfortunately there is still big mistrust on sharing information with others members of the cluster. One of the major causes of this lack of trust is the fact the companies in the coalition (cluster) worry about the fairness of benefits splitting. This is one of the major benefits of using cooperative game theory, and in particular Shapley value. It helps to make a fair split of benefits obtained with the implementation of a particular cooperation strategy.

In the case described for the furniture cluster in Colombia the companies considered in the study expressed its intention of cooperation, now that they know this tool. The project additionally developed a software that can measure the competitiveness of the companies, and the coalitions that the company wants to establish. On the other hand it gives the opportunity to predict the benefits and fair splits in four particular cooperation scenarios.

This software allows companies to test different coalitions in order to make a decision to joint or not a particular coalition depending on the benefits associated with joining the coalition. Additionally the company can identify if the coalition will be stable, by checking that there are benefits for all the members of the coalition.

Another important contribution of clusters is the fact that they gives a strong impulse to innovation and in general to the implementation of best managerial practices in all the key success factor of companies such as quality, personnel, production process, design, service, and organization. It is important to point out that there are still important areas to explore the application of cooperative games, such as healthcare, agriculture, and green logistics. Finally it is necessary to continue working on the developing of software aids that can be integrated to different cluster and are flexible enough to consider tens of scenarios in order to increase the speed of the integration process along the supply chain.

Acknowledgments. This research was funded by COLCIENCIAS, through the project 2333-6694-6964. This work was developed by Universidad de la Costa (CUC) and Fundación Centro de Investigación en Modelación Empresarial del Caribe (FCIMEC).

References

1. Atencio, F.N., Rodado, D.N.: A Sule's Method initiated genetic algorithm for solving QAP formulation in facility layout design: a real world application. J. Theoret. Appl. Inf. Technol. **84**(2) (2016)
2. Neira Rodado, D., Escobar, J.W., García-Cáceres, R.G., Niebles Atencio, F.A.: A mathematical model for the product mixing and lot-sizing problem by considering stochastic demand. Int. J. Ind. Eng. Comput. **8**(2), 237–250 (2016). http://doi.org/10.5267/j.ijiec.2016.9.003
3. Porter, M.E.: Location, competition, and economic development: local clusters in a global economy. Econ. Dev. Q. **14**(1), 15–34 (2000)
4. Patti, A.L.: Economic clusters and the supply chain: a case study. Supply Chain Manag. Int. J. **11**(3), 266–270 (2006)
5. Capó-Vicedo, J., Expósito-Langa, M., Masiá-Buades, E.: La importancia de los clusters para la competitividad de las PYME en una economía global. EURE (Santiago) **33**(98), 119–133 (2007)
6. Landinez-Lamadrid, D.C., Ramirez-Rios, D.G., Neira Rodado, D., Parra Negrete, K., Combita Nino, J.P.: Shapley value: its algorithms and application to supply chains. INGE CUC **13**(1), 61–69 (2017)
7. Guo, Y.: A game analysis of cooperative relationship between enterprises on supply chain. Res. Pract. Issues Enterp. Inf. Syst. **II**, 1319–1323 (2008)

Workflow Petri Nets with Time Stamps and Their Using in Project Management

Ivo Martiník[(⊠)] [iD]

VŠB-Technical University of Ostrava, Sokolská třída 33, 702 00 Ostrava 1,
Czech Republic
ivo.martinik@vsb.cz

Abstract. Workflow Petri nets with time stamps (WPNTS) are the newly introduced class of low-level Petri nets, whose definition and the properties are the main topic of this article; they generalize the properties of Petri net processes in the area of design, modeling and verification of generally parallel systems with the discrete time. Property-preserving Petri net process algebras (PPPA) does not need to verify composition of Petri net processes because all their algebraic operators preserve the specified set of the properties. These original PPPA are generalized for the class of the WPNTS in this article. The new **JOIN**, **EBPS**, **COMP** and **SYNC** algebraic operators are defined for the class of WPNTS and their chosen properties are proved. With the support of these operators the WPNTSs can be extended also to the area of the project management and the determination of the project generalized critical path with the support of the principles of the critical path method (CPM). The new CPWPNTS subclass of WPNTS class is specially designed for the generalization of the CPM activities charts, its properties are proved and then demonstrated on the generalized critical path specification of simple project example in this article.

Keywords: Workflow Petri nets with time stamps
Property-preserving Petri net process algebras · Critical path method
Discrete time · Process management

1 Introduction

There are currently a number of formally defined classes of *Petri nets* [2] available for modeling of generally parallel systems. When studying distributed parallel programming systems, real-time systems, economic systems and many other types of systems, it plays a role modeling of the time variables associated with individual system events, the duration of the studied activities, the time history of the modeled system, and many other time characteristics. *Time Petri nets* and *timed Petri nets* [2, 8] are currently the two most important classes of low-level Petri nets that use the concept of discrete time in their definition. Other classes of low-level Petri nets with discrete time are introduced and discussed for instance in [3, 4, 6] and it can be stated that most of them use only the relative time variables usually related to the specific marking of the given Petri net. This fact can then cause difficulties, for example, in modeling complex time-synchronized

© Springer Nature Switzerland AG 2018
K. Saeed and W. Homenda (Eds.): CISIM 2018, LNCS 11127, pp. 193–206, 2018.
https://doi.org/10.1007/978-3-319-99954-8_17

distributed systems in which individual components of this system must be synchronized with the given external time source.

Workflow Petri nets (WPN) [1] were primarily introduced as the special subclass of classic low-level process Petri nets [5] for their using in the area of workflow management. WPN is a continuous Petri net that includes within the set of all its places the unique input place and the unique output place. *Workflow Petri nets with time stamps* (WPNTS) are the newly introduced class of low-level Petri nets whose definition and the properties are the main topics of this article. WPNTS generalize the properties of WPN in the area of modeling of generally parallel systems with the discrete time.

Property-preserving Petri net process algebras (PPPA) [5] does not need to verify composition of Petri net processes represented by WPN because all their algebraic operators preserve the specified set of the properties. Hence, if the source WPNs satisfy the desirable properties, each of the composite WPN, including the WPN that models the resulting system itself, also satisfies these properties. These original PPPA are generalized for the class of the WPNTS in this article and their property of properformed WPNTS is then newly introduced. The new **JOIN**, **EBPS**, **COMP** and **SYNC** algebraic operators are defined for the class of WPNTS and their chosen properties are proved.

With the support of these operators the WPNTS can be extended also to the areas of the project management and the determination of the generalized project critical path with the support of the critical path method (CPM) [7]. The new CPWPNTS subclass of WPNTS class is then defined in this article to represent proper-formed time-dependent processes and it is specially designed for the generalization of the CPM activities charts and their properties. This fact is then demonstrated on the simple project example and its generalized critical path and other properties specification.

2   Workflow Petri Nets with Time Stamps and Their Properties

Let N denotes the set of all natural numbers, $N := \{1, 2, \ldots\}$; N_0 denotes the set of all non-negative integer numbers, $N_0 := \{0, 1, 2, \ldots\}$; $\varnothing$ denotes the empty set; $|A|$ denotes the cardinality of the given set A; $\mathscr{P}(A)$ denotes the family of all the subsets of the given set A; $A \times B := \{(x, y) \mid (x \in A) \wedge (y \in B)\}$ denotes the cartesian product of the sets A and B; $\ulcorner$ denotes the logical negation operator; $f : A \to B$ denotes the function f with the domain A and the codomain B. Let $(A \subset N_0) \wedge (\exists n \in N : |A| = n) \wedge (A \neq \varnothing)$; then $max(A) := x$, where $(x \in A) \wedge (\forall y \in A : x \geq y)$.

Let A be the non-empty set. By the (non-empty finite) *sequence* σ over the set A we understand the function $\sigma : \{1, 2, \ldots, n\} \to A$, where $n \in N$, that is denoted by $\sigma := <a_1, a_2, \ldots, a_n>$, where $a_i = \sigma(i)$ for $1 \leq i \leq n$. Function $\varepsilon : \varnothing \to A$ is called the *empty sequence* over the set A. We denote the set of all finite sequences over the set A by the notation A_{SQ}. If $\sigma \in A_{SQ}$, $\sigma := <a_1, a_2, \ldots, a_n>$, the function *elems*: $A_{SQ} \to \mathscr{P}(A)$ is defined as follows: $elems(\sigma) := \{a \mid \exists i, 1 \leq i \leq n : a = \sigma(i)\}$.

Multiset M over the non-empty set S is a function $M : S \to N_0$. The non-negative integer number $M(a) \in N_0$, where $a \in S$, denotes the number of occurrences of the element a in the multiset M and we will say that $a \in M$ if $M(a) > 0$. The non-empty multiset M over a non-empty set S will be represented by the notation $M := \left[a^{M(a)}, b^{M(b)}, c^{M(c)}, \ldots\right]$, where $S := \{a, b, c \ldots,\}$, empty multiset M will be represented by the notation $M := \varnothing$. Notation S_{MS} then denotes the class of all the multisets over the set S.

Let $K, M \in S_{MS}$ be the multisets. Then the following is defined:

- addition of multisets: $K \oplus M := \left[s^{K(s) + M(s)} | s \in S\right]$,
- comparison of multisets: $K \leq M \Leftrightarrow \forall s \in S : K(s) \leq M(s)$,
- cardinality of multiset: $|M| := \sum_{s \in S} M(s)$,
- subtraction of multisets: if $K \leq M$ then $M \backslash K := \left[s^{M(s) - K(s)} | s \in S\right]$.

Definition 1. *Net NET* is an ordered triple $NET := (P, T, A)$, where P is finite non-empty set of the *places*, T is finite set of the *transitions*, $P \cap T = \varnothing$, and A is finite set of the *arcs*, $A \subseteq (P \times T) \cup (T \times P)$. $\qquad\square$

Some commonly used notations for the nets are $\bullet y = \{x | (x, y) \in A\}$ for the *preset* and $y\bullet = \{x | (y, x) \in A\}$ for the *postset* of the net node y (i.e., place or transition). A *path* leading from the node x_1 to the node x_k of a net is a non-empty sequence $<x_1, x_2, \ldots, x_k>$ of net nodes, where $k \in N$, which satisfies $(x_1, x_2), (x_2, x_3), \ldots, (x_{k-1}, x_k) \in A$. We will denote the set of all such paths of the given net *NET* by $\boldsymbol{PATHS}_{NET}(x_1, x_k)$. A path of the net leading from its node x to its node y is the *circuit* if $(y, x) \in A$. We will denote the set of all circuits of the given net *NET* by $\boldsymbol{CIRCUITS}_{NET}$.

Definition 2. *Workflow net with time stamps* (WNTS) *WNTS* is an ordered tuple $WNTS := (P, T, A, AF, TP, TI, IP, OP)$, where:

- (P, T, A) is the *net*,
- $AF : (P \times T) \cup (T \times P) \rightarrow N_0$ is the *arc function*,
  $AF(x, y) > 0 \Leftrightarrow (x, y) \in A$, $AF(x, y) = 0 \Leftrightarrow (x, y) \notin A$, where $x, y \in P \cup T$,
- *TP* is the *transition priority function*, $TP : T \rightarrow N$,
- $TI : (T \times P) \rightarrow N_0$ is the *time interval function*,
- *IP* is the *input place*, $(IP \in P) \wedge (\bullet IP = \varnothing) \wedge (\forall p \in (P \backslash \{IP\}) : \bullet p \neq \varnothing)$,
- *OP* is the *output place*, $(OP \in P) \wedge (OP\bullet = \varnothing) \wedge (\forall p \in (P \backslash \{OP\}) : p\bullet \neq \varnothing)$;
- $\forall x \in P \cup T \exists \sigma \in \boldsymbol{PATHS}_{WNTS}(IP, OP) : x \in elems(\sigma)$.

The class of all the WNTSs will be denoted by **WNTS**. $\qquad\square$

The net (P, T, A) contains the finite non-empty set P of the *places* that expresses the conditions of the modeled process and that are represented by the circles; the finite set T of the *transitions* that describes the changes in the modeled process and that are drawn by rectangles; the finite set A of the oriented *arcs* connecting the chosen place with the chosen transition or the chosen transition with the chosen place; the *arc function AF* that assigns with each arc the natural number (with the default value of 1, if not explicitly indicated in the WNTS diagram) that expresses the number of removed or added tokens from or to the place associated with that arc when firing the given transition; *transition priority function TP* that assigns with each transition the natural number that expresses its priority (with the default value of 1); the *time interval function TI* that assigns with each arc of the type *(transition, place)* the non-negative integer number d that expresses the minimum time interval during which the token has to remain in the *place* instead of being able to participate in the next firing of some transition (the value d associated with the respective arc is given in the format $+d$ in the WNTS diagram); the *input place IP* that is the only one place of WNTS *WNTS* with no input arc(s); the *output place OP* that is the only one place of WNTS *WNTS* with no output arc(s). It must be fulfilled that every node x of WNTS *WNTS* is the element of some path from its input place *IP* to its output place *OP* (i.e., every WNTS is the connected net).

Definition 3. Let $WNTS := (P, T, A, AF, TP, TI, IP, OP)$ be the WNTS. Then:

1. *marking M* of the WNTS *WNTS* is the function $M : P \to (N_0)_{MS}$,
2. variable $\tau \in N_0$ is the *net time* of the WNTS *WNTS*,
3. *state S* of the WNTS *WNTS* is an ordered pair $S := (M, \tau)$,
4. transition $t \in T$ is *enabled* in the state $S := (M, \tau)$ of the WNTS *WNTS* that is denoted by t *en* S, if $\forall p \in \bullet t \, \exists K \le M(p) : (|K| = AF(p, t)) \wedge (\forall n \in K : n \le \tau))$,
5. *firing of the transition* $t \in T$ results in changing the state $S := (M, \tau)$ of the WNTS *WNTS* into its state $S' := (M', \tau)$ that is denoted by $S[t\rangle S'$, where

$$\forall p \in P : M'(p) := (M(p) \backslash K) \oplus [(\tau + TI(t, p))^{AF(t,p)}],$$

6. *elapsing of time interval* $\delta \in N$ results in changing the state $S := (M, \tau)$ of the WNTS *WNTS* into its state $S' := (M, \tau + \delta)$, where $\forall t \in T : \neg(t \, en \, (M, \tau))$, that is denoted by $S[\delta\rangle S'$, so that:
   $(\forall t \in T \, \forall n \in N, 1 \le n < \delta : \neg(t \, en \, (M, \tau + n))) \wedge (\exists t \in T : t \, en \, (M, \tau + \delta))$,

7. if the transitions $t_1, t_2, \ldots, t_n \in T$ are enabled in the state $S := (M, \tau)$ of the WNTS *WNTS* (i.e., $(t_1 \, en \, S) \wedge (t_2 \, en \, S) \wedge \ldots \wedge (t_n \, en \, S)$) we say that these transitions are *enabled in parallel* in the state S that is denoted by $\{t_1, t_2, \ldots, t_n\} \, en \, S$,
8. finite non-empty sequence $\sigma := \, <t_1, t_2, \ldots, t_n> $ of the transitions $t_1, t_2, \ldots, t_n \in T$ for which the following is valid in the state $S_1 := (M_1, \tau_1)$ of the WNTS *WNTS*:

   • $(M_1, \tau_1) [t_1\rangle (M_2, \tau_1) [t_2\rangle \ldots [t_2\rangle (M_{n+1}, \tau_1)$,
   • $\forall t \in T : \neg(t \, en \, (M_{n+1}, \tau_1))$,
   is called *step* σ in the given state S_1 of the WNTS *WNTS* and it is denoted by

$$(M_1, \tau_1) [\sigma\rangle (M_{n+1}, \tau_1),$$

9. finite non-empty sequence ρ of steps and time intervals elapsing that represents the following state changes

$$(M_1, \tau_1) [\sigma_1\rangle (M_2, \tau_1) [\delta_1\rangle \ldots (M_{n+1}, \tau_n) [\delta_n\rangle (M_{n+1}, \tau_{n+1}),$$

   of the WNTS *WNTS* is the sequence $\rho := \, <\sigma_1, \delta_1, \sigma_2, \delta_2, \ldots, \sigma_n, \delta_n> $ of the steps $\sigma_1, \sigma_2, \ldots, \sigma_n$ and the time intervals elapsing $\delta_1, \delta_2, \ldots, \delta_n$,
10. we say that the state S' of the WNTS *WNTS* is reachable from its state S if there exists the finite sequence $\rho := \, <\sigma_1, \delta_1, \sigma_2, \delta_2, \ldots, \sigma_n, \delta_n> $ of the steps $\sigma_1, \sigma_2, \ldots, \sigma_n$ and the time intervals elapsing $\delta_1, \delta_2, \ldots, \delta_n$ such that $S[\sigma_1 \delta_1 \sigma_2 \delta_2 \ldots \sigma_n \delta_n\rangle S'$; the set of all

the reachable states of the WNTS *WNTS* from its state S is denoted by $[S\rangle$; the set of all the finite sequences $\rho := <\sigma_1, \delta_1, \sigma_2, \delta_2, \ldots, \sigma_n, \delta_n >$ associated with all the reachable states $S' \in [S\rangle$ is denoted by $[S\rangle\rangle$, i.e.,

$$[S\rangle\rangle := \{ <\sigma_1, \delta_1, \sigma_2, \delta_2, \ldots, \sigma_n, \delta_n > | \exists S' \in [S\rangle: S[\sigma_1\delta_1\sigma_2\delta_2\ldots\sigma_n\delta_n\rangle S', n \in N\},$$

11. the set of all the states $S := (M, \tau)$ of the WNTS *WNTS* is denoted by S,
12. the set of all the markings M associated with the set S of all the states of the WNTS *WNTS* is denoted by M, i.e., $M := \{M \mid (S = (M, \tau)) \wedge (S \in S)\}$,
13. *entry state* $S_e := (M_e, \tau_e)$ of the WNTS *WNTS* is every of its states where $(M_e(IP) \neq \varnothing) \wedge (\forall p \in (P \backslash \{IP\}) : M_e(p) = \varnothing)$,
14. the set of all the entry states $S_e := (M_e, \tau_e)$ of the WNTS *WNTS* is denoted by S_e,
15. *exit state* $S_x := (M_x, \tau_x)$ of the WNTS *WNTS* that is reachable from its entry state $S_e := (M_e, \tau_e)$ is every of its states where $(S_x \in [S_e\rangle) \wedge (|M_x(OP)| = |M_e(IP)|) \wedge (\forall p \in (P \backslash \{OP\}) : (M_x(p) = \varnothing))$,
16. the set of all the exit states $S_x := (M_x, \tau_x)$ of the WNTS *WNTS* that are reachable from its entry state $S_e := (M_e, \tau_e)$ is denoted by $[S_e\rangle_x$,
17. the set of all the exit states S_x of the WNTS *WNTS* that are reachable from all its entry states $S_e \in S_e$ is denoted by S_x. ☐

The above established concepts will be demonstrated in the simple example of the WNTS *WNTS1* := $(P, T, A, AF, TP, TI, IP, OP)$ that is shown in Fig. 1, where P := $\{$IP, P1, P2, P3, OP$\}$; T := $\{$T1, T2, T3, T4$\}$; A := $\{$(IP, T1), (IP, T2), (T1, P1), (T1, P2), (T2, P2), (T2, P3), (P1, T3), (P2, T3), (P3, T4), (T4, P2), (T3, OP)$\}$; AF := $\{$((IP, P1), 2), ((IP, T2), 1), ((T1, P1), 1), ((T1, P2), 1), ((T2, P2), 1), ((T2, P3), 1), ((P1, T3), 1), ((P2, T3), 1), ((P3, T4), 3), ((T4, P2), 1), ((T3, OP), 1)$\}$; TP := $\{$(T1, 2), (T2, 1), (T3, 1), (T4, 1)$\}$; TI := $\{$((T1, P1), 3), ((T1, P2), 4), ((T2, P2), 5), ((T2, P3), 0), ((T4, P2), 1), ((T3, OP), 2)$\}$; IP := IP; OP := OP.

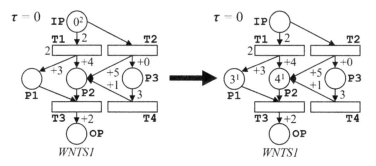

Fig. 1. Firing of transition T1 in WNTS *WNTS1*

WNTS *WNTS1* is in its entry state $S_e := (M_e, \tau_e)$, where marking $M_e := (M_e(\text{IP}),$ $M_e(\text{P1}), M_e(\text{P2}), M_e(\text{P3}), M_e(\text{OP})) = ([0^2], \varnothing, \varnothing, \varnothing, \varnothing)$, net time $\tau_e = 0$ (i.e., $\tau_e = \tau$). Marking M of any WNTS expresses the current time state of the modeled system using the time stamp associated with each of its anonymous token that occurs in any of its places in its state S. Individual values of the time stamps associated with the anonymous tokens, informally said, represent the values of the net time τ at which the respective token can first participate in the firing of selected enabled transition t of the WNTS.

The transitions T1 and T2 are enabled in the entry state S_e of the WNTS *WNTS1* because (see 4 of Definition 3):

- $\forall p \in \bullet\text{T1}\ \exists K = [0^2] \leq [0^2] = M(\text{IP}): ([[0^2]] = 2 = AF(\text{IP}, \text{T1})) \wedge ((\forall n \in [0^2]: n = 0 \leq 0 = \tau)$,
- $\forall p \in \bullet\text{T2}\ \exists K = [0^1] \leq [0^2] = M(\text{IP}): ([[0^1]] = 1 = AF(\text{IP}, \text{T2})) \wedge ((\forall n \in [0^1]: n = 0 \leq 0 = \tau)$.

At the enabling of the transitions t_1 and t_2 of the given WNTS in its state S so called *conflict* occurs, if both transitions t_1 and t_2 have at least one common place in their presets, each of the transitions t_1 and t_2 is individually enabled in the state S, but the transitions t_1 and t_2 are not enabled in parallel in the state S (see 7 of Definition 3) and enabling of one of them will prevent enabling of the other (i.e., $(\bullet t_1 \cap \bullet t_2 \neq \varnothing) \wedge (t_1\ \textit{en}\ S) \wedge (t_2\ \textit{en}\ S) \wedge \neg(\{t_1, t_2\}\ \textit{en}\ S))$. The term of conflict can be obviously generalized for the case of the finite set $t_1, t_2, \ldots, t_n, n \in N$, of the transitions of the given WNTS.

The transitions T1 and T2 in the entry state S_e of the WNTS *WNTS1* are in conflict. When solving such conflict we will therefore follow the rule which determines, informally said, that from the set of transitions in conflict the one will be enabled whose value of the transition priority function *TP* is the highest. If such transition from the set of the transitions in conflict does not exist, the given conflict would have to be solved by other means. The transition T1 is then enabled in the entry state S_e on the basis of that rule in our studied example (because $TP(\text{T1}) = 2$ and $TP(\text{T2}) = 1$).

Firing of the transition T1 changes the entry state $S_e := (M_e, \tau_e)$ of the WNTS *WNTS1* into its state $S_1 := (M_1, \tau_e) = ((\varnothing, [3^1], [4^1], \varnothing, \varnothing), 0)$ (i.e., $S_e\ [\text{T1}\rangle\ S_1$ - see Fig. 1), where (see 5 of Definition 3):

- $M_1(\text{IP}) = M_e(\text{IP}) \setminus K = [0^2] \setminus [0^2] = \varnothing$,
- $M_1(\text{P1}) = M_e(\text{P1}) \oplus [(\tau_e + TI(\text{T1}, \text{P1}))^{AF(\text{T1, P1})}] = \varnothing \oplus [(0 + 3)^1] = [3^1]$,
- $M_1(\text{P2}) = M_e(\text{P2}) \oplus [(\tau_e + TI(\text{T1}, \text{P2}))^{AF(\text{T1, P2})}] = \varnothing \oplus [(0 + 4)^1] = [4^1]$.

There is no enabled transition in the state $S_1 := (M_1, \tau_1)$ because the token in the place P1 can first participate in firing of the transition T3 if the net time $\tau = 3$ and the token in the place P2 can first participate in firing of the transition T3 if the net time $\tau = 4$. So it is necessary to perform the time interval elapsing with the value of $\delta = 4$. This will change the state $S_1 := (M_1, \tau_e)$ into the state $S_2 := (M_1, \tau_1)$, where $\tau_1 := \tau_e + \delta = 4$ (i.e., $S_1[4\rangle S_2)$. It can be easily verified that $S_2\ [\text{T3}\rangle\ S_x$ where $S_x := (M_x, \tau_1) = ((\varnothing, \varnothing, \varnothing, \varnothing, [6^1]), 4)$. There are no enabled transitions in the exit state $S_x := (M_x, \tau_1)$ of the

WNTS *WNTS1* that is reachable from its entry state $S_e := (M_e, \tau_e)$ (see 15 of Definition 3) and there is also no time interval elapsing value δ in the state S_x that enables any of the transitions.

Definition 4. Let *WNTS* := $(P, T, A, AF, TP, TI, IP, OP)$ be the WNTS, S_e be the set of all of its entry states. Then:

- *WNTS* is *k-bounded* WNTS if

$$\forall S_e \in S_e \exists k \in N_0 \, \forall p \in P \forall S \in [S_e\rangle, S := (M, \tau) : M(p) \leq k,$$

- *WNTS* is *proper-formed* WNTS if

$$\forall S_e \in S_e : (\forall S \in [S_e\rangle \exists S_x \in [S_e\rangle_x : S_x \in [S\rangle) \wedge (\exists n \in N : |[S_e\rangle\rangle| = n). \qquad \square$$

Definition 5. *Workflow Petri net with time stamps* (WPNTS) *WPNTS* is the ordered couple *WPNTS* := $(WNTS, S_e)$, where *WNTS* := $(P, T, A, AF, TP, TI, IP, OP)$ is the WNTS and $S_e \in S_e$ is the entry state of the WNTS *WNTS*. The class of all WPNTSs will be denoted by **WPNTS**. $\qquad \square$

3 Algebraic Operators JOIN, EBPS, COMP and SYNC

We will study the issue of transforming WNTSs through precisely defined unary operators **JOIN** and **EBPS**, binary operator **COMP** and *n*-ary operator **SYNC** over the class **WNTS** and we will also examine the preservation of proper-formed property of the WNTSs when applying each of these operators. Formal enrollment of an application of generally *n*-ary operator **OP** whose operands are the WNTSs $WNTS_1$, $WNTS_2$, ..., $WNTS_n$ $(n \in N)$ and whose application requires the specification of the values of k formal parameters $(k \in N)$ par_1, par_2, ..., par_k, will be denoted by the expression

$$WNTS := [WNTS_1, WNTS_2, \ldots, WNTS_n].\mathbf{OP}(par_1, par_2, \ldots, par_k),$$

where *WNTS* is the resulting WNTS.

Premise 1. Let $WNTS_1 := (P_1, T_1, A_1, AF_1, TP_1, TI_1, IP_1, OP_1)$, $WNTS_2 := (P_2, T_2, A_2, AF_2, TP_2, TI_2, IP_2, OP_2)$, ..., $WNTS_n := (P_n, T_n, A_n, AF_n, TP_n, TI_n, IP_n, OP_n)$, be the arbitrary WNTSs, $\forall i, 1 \leq i \leq n, \forall j, 1 \leq j \leq n : i \neq j \Rightarrow (P_i \cap P_j = \varnothing) \wedge (T_i \cap T_j = \varnothing)$, where $n \in N$; p, pi and po be the arbitrary places, $(p \notin P_1 \cup P_2 \cup \ldots \cup P_n) \wedge (pi \notin P_1 \cup P_2 \cup \ldots \cup P_n) \wedge (po \notin P_1 \cup P_2 \cup \ldots \cup P_n) \wedge (pi \neq po)$; ti and to be the arbitrary transitions, $(ti \notin T_1 \cup T_2 \cup \ldots \cup T_n) \wedge (to \notin T_1 \cup T_2 \cup \ldots \cup T_n) \wedge (ti \neq to)$; $t1$ and $t2$ be the arbitrary transitions, $(t1 \neq t2) \wedge (t1 \in T_1) \wedge (t2 \in T_1)$; $af1 \in N, af2 \in N, \ldots, afn \in N, ti1 \in N_0, ti2 \in N_0, \ldots, tin \in N_0, tio \in N_0, ti \in N_0$. Let $BASE_p \in$ **WNTS**, $BASE_p := (\{p\}, \varnothing, \varnothing, \varnothing, \varnothing, \varnothing, p, p)$.

Definition 6. Let Premise 1 be fulfilled. The function **EPBS**: $WNTS \rightarrow WNTS$ of *extended bypass* is defined as follows: $EWNTS := WNTS_1.\textbf{EBPS}(pi, ti, to)$, if WNTS $EWNTS := (P, T, A, AF, TP, TI, IP, OP)$ fulfills the following: $P := P_1 \cup \{pi\}; T := T_1 \cup \{ti, to\}; A := A_1 \cup \{(pi, ti), (ti, IP_1), (pi, to), (to, OP_1)\}; AF := AF_1 \cup \{((pi, ti), 1), ((ti, IP_1), 1), ((pi, to), 1), ((to, OP_1), 1)\}; TP := TP_1 \cup \{(ti, 1), (to, 1)\}; TI := TI_1 \cup \{(ti, IP_1), 1), ((to, OP_1), 1)\}; IP := pi; OP := OP_1.$

Let $DELAY_{p,k} \in \textbf{WNTS}$, $DELAY_{p,k} := (P, T, A, AF, TP, TI, IP, OP) = BASE_p.$ $\textbf{EBPS}(p_1, ti_1, to_1).\textbf{EBPS}(p_2, ti_2, to_2). \dots .\textbf{EBPS}(p_k, ti_k, to_k)$, where $P := \{p, p_1, p_2, \dots, p_k\}, T := \{ti_1, to_1, ti_2, to_2, \dots, ti_k, to_k\}, IP := p_k, OP := p, k \in N_0$, $DELAY_{p,0} := BASE_p$. The class of all WNTSs $DELAY_{p,k}$, where $k \in N_0$, will be denoted by **DELAY**.

The function **JOIN**: $WNTS \times DELAY \rightarrow WNTS$ of *net transition joining* is defined as follows: $JWNTS := [WNTS_1, DELAY_{p,k}].\textbf{JOIN}(t1, t2, ti)$ where $DELAY_{p,k} := (\underline{P}, \underline{T}, \underline{A}, \underline{AF}, \underline{TP}, \underline{TI}, \underline{IP}, \underline{OP})$, if WNTS $JWNTS := (P, T, A, AF, TP, TI, IP, OP)$ fulfills the following: $P := P_1 \cup \underline{P}; T := T_1 \cup \underline{T}; A := A_1 \cup \underline{A} \cup \{(t1, \underline{IP}), (\underline{OP}, t2)\}; AF := AF_1 \cup \underline{AF} \cup \{((t1, \underline{IP}), 1), ((\underline{OP}, t2), 1)\}; TP := TP_1 \cup \underline{TP}; TI := TI_1 \cup \underline{TI} \cup \{(t1, \underline{IP}), ti)\}; IP := IP_1; OP := OP_1.$

The function **COMP**: $WNTS \times WNTS \rightarrow WNTS$ of *nets composition* is defined as follows: $CWNTS := [WNTS_1, WNTS_2].\textbf{COMP}(t, ti)$, if WNTS $CWNTS := (P, T, A, AF, TP, TI, IP, OP)$ fulfills the following: $P := P_1 \cup P_2; T := T_1 \cup T_2 \cup \{t\}; A := A_1 \cup A_2 \cup \{(OP_1, t), (t, IP_2)\}; AF := AF_1 \cup AF_2 \cup \{((OP_1, t), 1), ((t, IP_2), 1)\}; TP := TP_1 \cup TP_2 \cup \{(t, 1)\}, TI := TI_1 \cup TI_2 \cup \{(t, IP_2), ti)\}; IP := IP_1; OP := OP_2.$

The function **SYNC**: $WNTS \times WNTS \times \dots \times WNTS \rightarrow WNTS$ of *synchronous nets composition* is defined as follows: $SWNTS := [WNTS_1, WNTS_2, \dots, WNTS_n].\textbf{SYNC}(pi, po, ti, to, af1, \dots, afn, ti1, \dots, tin, tio)$, if WNTS $SWNTS := (P, T, A, AF, TP, TI, IP, OP)$ fulfills the following: $P := P_1 \cup \dots \cup P_n \cup \{pi, po\}; T := T_1 \cup \dots \cup T_n \cup \{ti, to\}; A := A_1 \cup \dots \cup A_n \cup \{(pi, ti), (ti, IP_1), \dots, (ti, IP_n), (OP_1, to), \dots, (OP_n, to), (to, po)\}; AF := AF_1 \cup \dots \cup AF_n \cup \{((pi, ti), 1), ((ti, IP_1), af1), \dots, ((ti, IP_n), afn), ((OP_1, to), af1), \dots, ((OP_n, to), afn), ((to, po), 1)\}; TP := TP_1 \cup \dots \cup TP_n \cup \{(ti, 1), (to, 1)\}; TI := TI_1 \cup \dots \cup TI_n \cup \{((ti, IP_1), ti1), \dots, ((ti, IP_n), tin), ((to, po), tio)\}; IP := pi; OP := po.$ ☐

Symbolic representation of the **JOIN**, **EBPS**, **COMP** a **SYNC** algebraic operators applications can be seen in Fig. 2.

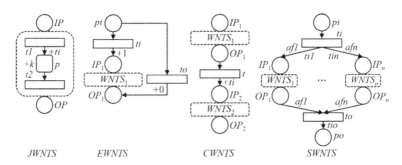

JWNTS   EWNTS   CWNTS   SWNTS

Fig. 2. Symbolic representation of the **JOIN**, **EBPS**, **COMP** and **SYNC** operators applications

WNTS $DELAY_{p,k}$ (where $k \in N_0$, $DELAY_{p,0} := BASE_p$) represents by its meaning a special place that will be drawn in the WNTS diagram by the square with rounded edges with an associated numeric value k (see Fig. 3). Each token located in this special place in a certain state S of the given WNTS may be then generally placed in it for the next k time units beside the current value of its actual time stamp before it will participate in the firing of the next transition (each such token is therefore associated with the lower and upper net time τ values for participating in the firing of the next transition).

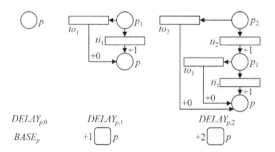

Fig. 3. WNTSs $DELAY_{p,0}$, $DELAY_{p,1}$ and $DELAY_{p,2}$ and their symbolic representations

The function dl: **DELAY** $\rightarrow N_0$ is defined such that

$$\forall DELAY_{p,k} \in \mathbf{DELAY} : dl\big(DELAY_{p,k}\big) := k$$
$$\big(\text{i.e.,} \, dl\big(DELAY_{p,0}\big) := dl\big(BASE_p\big) := 0\big).$$

Lemma 1. Let Premise 1 be fulfilled. If $WNTS_1, WNTS_2, \ldots, WNTS_n$ are proper-formed WNTSs then:

- $\forall k \in N_0 : DELAY_{p,k}$ is proper-formed WNTS,
- $[WNTS_1, WNTS_2].\mathbf{COMP}(t, ti)$ is proper-formed WNTS,
- $[WNTS_1, WNTS_2, \ldots, WNTS_n].\mathbf{SYNC}(pi, po, ti, to, af1, \ldots, afn, ti1, \ldots, tin, tio)$ is proper-formed WNTS.

Proof. Clear, it directly follows from Definitions 3, 4 and 6. □

Definition 7. Let Premise 1 be fulfilled, $k \in N_0$. The class **CPWN** $\subset$ **WNTS** contains the following WNTSs:

1. $\forall k \in N_0 : DELAY_{p,k} \in \mathbf{CPWN}$,
2. if $WNTS_1 \in \mathbf{CPWN}$, $WNTS_2 \in \mathbf{CPWN}$, then also

$$[WNTS_1, WNTS_2].\mathbf{COMP}(t, ti) \in \mathbf{CPWN},$$

3. if $WNTS_1 \in CPWN$, $WNTS_2 \in CPWN$, ..., $WNTS_n \in CPWN$, then also

   $[WNTS_1, ..., WNTS_n].\mathbf{SYNC}(pi, po, ti, to, 1, ..., 1, ti_1, ti_2, ..., ti_n, tio) \in CPWN$,

4. if $WNTS_1 \in CPWN$ and $JWNTS := [WNTS_1, DELAY_{p,k}].\mathbf{JOIN}(t1, t2, ti)$ then $JWNTS \in CPWN$ only if $\mathbf{CIRCUITS}_{JWNTS} = \varnothing$.   □

   Simple example of WNTS $CPWN1 \in CPWN$ can be seen in Fig. 4 where

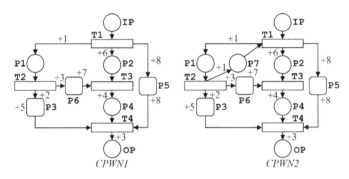

Fig. 4. WNTSs *CPWN1* and *CPWN2*

Simple example of WNTS $CPWN1 \in CPWN$ can be seen in Fig. 4 where
$CPWN1 := [[[BASE_{P1}, DELAY_{P3,5}].\mathbf{COMP}(T2, 2),$
$\qquad [BASE_{P2}, BASE_{P4}].\mathbf{COMP}(T3, 4), DELAY_{P5,8}]$
$\qquad .\mathbf{SYNC}(\text{IP}, \text{OP}, T1, T4, 1, 1, 1, 1, 6, 8, 3), DELAY_{P6,7}].\mathbf{JOIN}(T2, T3,$
3).

Remark 1. It si clear from the previous Definitions and Lemma that every WNTS $WNTS \in CPWN$ is k-bounded and proper-formed WNTS. If we allow the application of the operator **JOIN** leads to create any circuit in the resulting WNTS (i.e., Definition 7 does not allow this option) it can be proved that the proper-formed property is no longer retained for the resulting WNTS as it can be seen in the example of WNTS $CPWN2 := CPWN1.\mathbf{JOIN}(T2, T1, 1)$ in Fig. 4, where $<T1, P1, T2, P7> \in \mathbf{CIRCUITS}_{CPWN2}$ and the transition T1 is not enabled in any of its entry state $S_e \in \mathbf{S}_e$.

Definition 8. *CP workflow Petri net with time stamps* (CPWPNTS) *CPWPNTS is an ordered couple* $CPWPNTS := (WNTS, S_e)$, *where* $WNTS \in CPWN$ *and* $S_e := (([0^1], \varnothing, ..., \varnothing), 0)$. *The class of all CPWPNTSs will be denoted by* **CPWPNTS**. □

Lemma 2. *Let* $CPWPNTS \in \mathbf{CPWPNTS}$, $CPWNTS := (P, T, A, AF, TP, TI, IP, OP, S_e)$. *Then CPWPNTS is 1-bounded and proper-formed CPWPNTS.*

Proof. Clear, it directly follows from the Definitions 3, 4, 6, Lemma 1 and the fact, that $\forall a \in A: AF(a) = 1$. □

4 Workflow Petri Nets with Time Stamps and Their Applications in Project Management Area

Critical Path Method (CPM) is a method commonly used in project management for all the types of projects and it was developed at the end of 1950's [7]. The CPM is designed to analyze the time-consuming of only projects where the duration of each of their activities including all their sub-activities is known (including the cases when it is uncertain). The basis for using CPM is to create a project model that includes the list of all its activities, the time duration of each activity that is constant and the dependencies between the project activities. A critical path is then a designation for a sequence of activities whose time duration directly affects the time duration of the entire project. There may be several critical paths in the project. The critical path can be then used to determine the shortest time required to complete the project. The application of the CPM method can therefore determine which activities within the studied project are "critical" and which activities may be delayed in the execution of the project without increasing its total time.

The theory of CPWPNTSs can be successfully applied especially to modeling processes and determining their critical paths. It is even possible to associate with each activity of the studied process its lower and upper time duration for the purpose of determining the whole critical path and thereby generalize the standard CPM. An example of a simple process will be presented in the following paragraphs the characteristics of which will be studied with using of the theory of CPWPNTSs. The above mentioned process is described in the following table of its activities (see Table 1):

Table 1. Table of activities and their time durations and dependencies of studied process

Activity	Lower time duration	Upper time duration	Previous activities
A	5	7	-
B	2	2	-
C	3	3	-
D	3	4	C
E	5	5	A
F	6	7	A
G	2	2	B, D
H	4	4	C
I	3	3	F, G, H

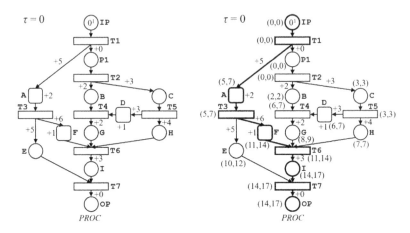

Fig. 5. CPWPNTS *PROC* and its marked critical path

The 1-bounded and proper-formed CPWPNTS *PROC* that represents the process comprising the activities listed in Table 1 can be seen in Fig. 5, where

$PROC := [[[[DELAY_{A,2}, BASE_E].\textbf{COMP}(\text{T3}, 5),$
$[[BASE_B, BASE_G].\textbf{COMP}(\text{T4}, 2), [BASE_C, BASE_H].\textbf{COMP}(\text{T5}, 4)]$
$.\textbf{SYNC}(\text{P1}, \text{I}, \text{T2}, \text{T6}, 1, 1, 2, 3, 3)]$
$.\textbf{SYNC}(\text{IP}, \text{OP}, \text{T1}, \text{T7}, 1, 1, 5, 0, 0)], DELAY_{F,1}]$
$.\textbf{JOIN}(\text{T3}, \text{T6}, 6), DELAY_{D,3}].\textbf{JOIN}(\text{T5}, \text{T4}, 1).$

The places A, B, C, D, E, F, G, H and I of CPWPNTS *PROC* represent individual activities of the studied process, the appropriate values of the time interval function *TI* then express the lower time durations of relevant activities and the values k of the places of the type $DELAY_{p,k}$ then serve to determine the upper time durations of these activities (i.e., for instance, the activity A is represented by the place $DELAY_{A,2}$, its lower time duration is represented by the value of $TI(\text{T1}, \text{A}) = 5$ and its upper time duration by the value $TI(\text{T1}, \text{A}) + dl(DELAY_{A,2}) = 5 + 2 = 7$, etc.).

In order to find the critical path of the process represented by CPWPNTS *PROC*, we first perform the association of each node of the CPWPNTS *PROC* with the value $<cp_1, cp_2>$ of the critical path function *CP* that was introduced in the Definition 9.

Definition 9. Let *CPWPNTS* $\in$ **CPWPNTS**, *CPWNTS* := $(P, T, A, AF, TP, TI, IP, OP, S_e)$. The *critical path function CP* : $(P \cup T) \to N_0 \times N_0$ is defined as follows:

1. $CP(IP) := (0, 0)$,
2. $\forall p \in \textbf{DELAY} : CP(p) := (CP(t)_1 + TI(t,p), CP(t)_2 + TI(t,p) + dl(p))$, where $t = \bullet p$,
3. $\forall t \in T : CP(t) := (max(\{CP(p_1)_1, CP(p_2)_1, ..., CP(p_n)_1\}),$
   $max(\{CP(p_1)_2, CP(p_2)_2, ..., CP(p_n)_2\}))$, where $\bullet t = \{p_1, p_2, ..., p_n\}, n \in N.$ □

It follows directly from the Definition 3 that the first element cp_1 of the critical path function CP value (cp_1, cp_2) associated with any transition $t \in T$ of the arbitrary CPWPNTS *CPWPNTS* represents the lower net time τ value and the second element cp_2 then represents the upper net time τ value when the given transition t can be fired. The value of the critical path function CP associated with the output place OP (i.e., CP (OP)) then immediately indicates the total lower and upper time duration of the process critical path (i.e., the net time τ value when the transition $t = \bullet OP$ can be first and last fired). The algorithm for finding the set of nodes of the given CPWPNTS that forms the project critical path is then obvious and it is expressed by the following pseudocode in PASCAL (the set of nodes forming the critical path of the project is then contained in the **CriticalPath** variable). The critical path of CPWPNTS *PROC* is after applying of this algorithm represented by the sequence **CriticalPath** := <IP, T1, A, T3, F, T6, I, T7, OP> (see Fig. 5). It is also clear that the given CPWPNTS may contain two or more critical paths with the same total time duration.

Node := OP; **CriticalPath** :=<OP>;
WHILE (**Node** <> IP) DO
BEGIN
  MaxValue := $max(\{CP(X_1)_1, ..., CP(X_n)_1\})$, where •**Node** = $\{X_1, ..., X_n\}$, $n \in N$;
  Node := X_i, where $(X_i \in \{X_1, X_2, ..., X_n\}) \wedge (CP(X_i)_1 = $ **MaxValue**$)$;
  CriticalPath := **CriticalPath** $\cup$ <**Node**>;
END;

5 Conclusions

Further research in the field of WPNTSs is mainly focused on the definition of additional unary, binary and n-ary PPPA operators preserving their specified properties, for instance the binary **SUBST** operator that performs the substitution of the given WPNTS for the selected place of another WPNTS, etc. In the field of the project management the research is focused on modeling complex processes, which individual activities can additionally share in parallel a selected set of the resources. These resources are then represented in the given WPNTS by individual tokens located in the resource places of its selected net marking. Finding the time-optimal critical path of such a process as well as verifying the properties of the given WPNTS that models such a process is generally non-trivial problem and the use of PPPAs plays a crucial role here.

Acknowledgement. This paper has been elaborated in the framework of the projects SP2018/146 and CZ.1.07/2.3.00/20.0296 supported by the European Social Fund.

References

1. van der Alst, W., van Hee, K.: Workflow Management: Models, Methods and Systems, 1st edn. MIT Press, Massachusetts (2004)
2. Diaz, M.: Petri Nets: Fundamental Models, Verification and Applications, 1st edn. Willey, London (2009)
3. Furia, C.A., Mandrioli, D., Morzenti, A., Rossi, M.: Modeling Time in Computing, 1st edn. Springer, Heidelberg (2012)
4. van Hee, K., Sidorova, N.: The right timing: reflections on the modeling and analysis of time. In: Colom, J., Desel, J. (eds.) Application and Theory of Petri Nets and Concurrency. LNCS, vol. 7927, pp. 1–20. Springer, Heidelberg (2013)
5. Huang, H., Jiao, L., Cheung, T., Mak, W.M.: Property-Preserving Petri Net Process Algebra in Software Engineering, 1st edn. World Scientific Publishing, Singapore (2012)
6. Martos-Salgado, M., Rosa-Velardo, F.: Dynamic networks of timed petri nets. In: Ciardo, G., Kindler, E. (eds.) Application and Theory of Petri Nets and Concurrency. LNCS, vol. 8489, pp. 294–313. Springer, Heidelberg (2014)
7. O'Brien, J.J., Plotnick, F.L.: CPM in Construction Management, 8th edn. McGraw-Hill, New York (2016)
8. Popova-Zeugmann, L.: Time and Petri Nets, 1st edn. Springer, Heidelberg (2013)

Accident Simulation for Extended eCall System Without Integration in Existing Car Onboard Systems

Miroslaw Omieljanowicz[1], Adam Klimowicz[1(✉)],
Grzegorz Rubin[2], Marek Gruszewski[1], Lukasz Zienkiewicz[1],
Anna Lupinska-Dubicka[1], Marek Tabedzki[1], Marcin Adamski[1],
Mariusz Rybnik[3], and Maciej Szymkowski[1]

[1] Faculty of Computer Science,
Bialystok University of Technology, Bialystok, Poland
{m.omieljanowicz,a.klimowicz}@pb.edu.pl
[2] Faculty of Computer Science and Food Science,
Lomza State University of Applied Sciences, Lomza, Poland
grubin@pwsip.edu.pl
[3] Faculty of Mathematics and Informatics,
University of Bialystok, Bialystok, Poland

Abstract. New passenger cars and light commercial vehicles manufactured after March 31st, 2018 should be obligatorily equipped with an eCall system that automatically calls for assistance in the event of an accident. The idea of our research was to develop a system, that will be possible to integrate into older that date vehicles without modification and connection to existing onboard car systems. The system will be able to detect a road accident and beyond standard calls recognize number of vehicle's travelers and report their vital functions. This paper focuses on a road accident detection part of the whole system. We need to know if an accident took place actually or not, i.e. it might be just a car shock, not collision. In the beginning the state of the art was briefly presented and our direction regarded to the approach was taken based on the worked out model, sensors, equipment and the way of simulation. The second part was focused on the created physical model of test set lab with the designed machine for collision simulation with impact force analysis using selected sensors. At this stage of the project we have built the machine with pendulum and trolley on which we put three-axial accelerometers. We have done some controlled collision with data gathering and the first data analysis of the results.

Keywords: eCall · Accident detection · Safety · Vehicle

1 Introduction

The Regulation (EU) 2015/758 of The European Parliament and of The Council stands that new cars category M1 and N1 (passenger cars and light commercial vehicles) manufactured after March 31, 2018 should be obligatorily equipped with an eCall system that automatically calls for assistance in the event of an accident. It is expected

© Springer Nature Switzerland AG 2018
K. Saeed and W. Homenda (Eds.): CISIM 2018, LNCS 11127, pp. 207–219, 2018.
https://doi.org/10.1007/978-3-319-99954-8_18

that eCall system will speed up emergency response time by 60% in urban areas and by 50% in the countryside [1] and reduce number of fatalities and the number of severe injuries. In practice only passengers of newer cars can benefit from the system. The idea of our research and development is to build a in-vehicle system (IVS) in accordance to the eCall, it will allow to install the system in used cars without connection to existing onboard car systems. Moreover, the system that we work on will go beyond standard specification and will send additional field in MSD message [2] about number of passengers and their vital functions after the accident. The aim of such function is to help organize the rescue operation more efficiently by allowing PSAP (Public Safety Answering Point) operator exactly decide what kind of rescue team should be sent to the place of the event.

First needed information is to know if accident took place or not, i.e. it was just car bump and not a collision. This paper focuses mainly on a road accident detection part of the whole system. In the beginning, the state of the art will be briefly presented and then our approach onto model, sensors, equipment and the way of simulation. The second part will be focused on the creation of physical model for tests in laboratory with the experimental stand for collision simulation, impact force analysis with a use of selected sensors. Results of the experiments and conclusion are presented.

2 Related Works

During related works analysis, the main focus was on systems which apply the accelerometer as the main sensor used for collision detection. In [3] the device accelerometers with a range of ± 16 g were used, and these data were limited to the threshold of 3 g, to check whether the proposed algorithm will work correctly in the process of detecting car accidents using a smartphone. Data was taken from the sensors in the phone to construct a dynamic time warping algorithm (DTW) for accident detection. DTW is a time series comparison algorithm originally developed for speech recognition. Two sequences of feature vectors are compared by warping the time axis until an optimal fit (depending on the relevant markers) is found between the two sequences. The formulas were given in the paper and the assessment of the method's effectiveness was shown.

In the accident detection method discussed in [4], the front bumper sensor and the position sensor together with the accelerometer sensor were used to increase the effectiveness of collision detection. The bumper sensor informs the microcontroller what force affects the bumper. Of course, it is significantly greater in the collision event comparing to a parking event. The position sensor is used to determine the occurrence of a drastic change in speed. The information is additionally supplemented with data from the accelerometer (the appearance of sudden acceleration changes).

The paper [5] proposes the use of an IMU (Inertial Measurement Unit) low-cost sensor. An AHRS (Attitude Heading Reference System) sensor was also used to determine the orientation of the vehicle. To analyze the accelerometer, gyroscope and magnetometer data, DCM (Direction Cosine Matrix) was used. After detection of the deceleration above 5 g, the system proposed in [5] checks the vehicle speed. Confirmation of the accident occurs if the speed is less than 5 kph.

The detection method described in [6] uses the ADXL335 module. It is a small, complete, 3-axis accelerometer with voltage outputs. Accelerations in the range of ± 3 g were checked. The X axis is connected to the controller and continuous verification was carried out whether the value of acceleration changes. In addition, the LM35 temperature sensor was used to continuously monitor the temperature of the surface on which it is attached, e.g. the engine and the bodywork. The IR infrared sensor module was also used to detect a fire inside the vehicle. The final information was created on the basis of a combination of signals from the above mentioned sensors.

In paper [7], to detect the accident, a 3-axis MMA7660FC sensor was used, which allows detecting various changes such as tilt, tap, shock, etc. The combination of information triggers a signal informing about the occurrence of a collision. In work [8] a tilt sensor was used to detect the accident. The detection method was based on the fact that during a collision a "jump" of the car usually occurs (for a moment some of the wheels loses contact with the surface) or even rollover. The angle of rotation relative to the ground was detected and its value indicates the occurrence of an accident.

Paper [9] concerns the development of an accident detection sensor in situations difficult to clear assessment. The described sensor was adapted to detect frontal and side impact. In addition, the sensor allows to determine the strength and intensity of the collision. An integral part of the structure was a microprocessor with advanced software analyzing and processing in real time all measured parameters and generating a final information of the accident occurrence.

The detection system presented in [10] uses a combination of an accelerometer with a GPS (Global Positioning System). The Kalman filter, the HI-204III GPS receiver and the ADXL345 accelerometer were used. The accident detection scenario is triggered when the vehicle speed exceeds 23 kph. In case of a frontal collision, any negative acceleration greater than 5 g was considered an accident. After detecting a deceleration less than 5 g, the system checks the speed. If the speed drops below 5 kph, the system confirms the accident detection.

In [11], the collision detection module consists of an accelerometer with a large measuring range - MMA621010EG and a small measuring range - MMA7260QT. MMA621010EG is a special car accident detector that is an integrated XY accelerometer. It has a self-test and advanced calibration functionalities. MMA621010EG automatically detects the collision rate (e.g. parking event, serious collision) and rollover, while the MMA7260QT accelerometer detects inclination, changes in orientation in space, shocks and vibrations. An accident was detected on the basis of signals' processing from both sensors.

In road collision detection systems, sensors of mobile devices such as smartphones are also increasingly used. Work [12] presents the WreckWatch system which uses an accelerometer built into the mobile phone. The acceleration filter prevents false calls from being triggered. Filtering alone does not eliminate all false alarms, such as a fall of the phone inside the vehicle or sudden stop. WreckWatch eliminates this type of problems by ignoring all events with deceleration below 4 g. This value is intended to detect even minor accidents but excludes a fall or sudden stop and it was based on empirical analysis. It is also interesting that authors add information known as acoustic events (noise) as an aid to the detection criterion.

The work [13] presents a system called CADANS in which the following sensors were used: accelerometer, GPS - for speed testing, microphone – for noise detection (threshold is 140 dB), camera - for taking pictures or movie. The most important factor used by CADAN to detect car accidents is exceeding the acceleration value above 4 g. Authors claim that the delay threshold of 4 g is not sufficient evidence to conclude that there was a car accident, therefore additional parameters were introduced. Two types of accidents were distinguished: at speeds above and below 24 kph. An interesting idea is to add the "speed variation period" parameter, which measures the value of speed fluctuations in a given time interval.

The analysis of available studies showed that there is no complex systems integrated with the eCall system where not only the accident detection information is sent to emergency services but also the number and life activity of vehicle passengers. In the research process using the hardware platform it is planned to select the target sensor (or group of sensors - in accordance with the Data Fusion approach), ensuring the correct operation of the hardware model.

3   Collision Detection System

3.1   System Structure and Requirements

The detailed description of the compact system that could be installed in any vehicle is presented in wok [17] where device's operating concept and design are shown. The authors' concept of mentioned paper assumes that this would allow every car user to rely on the extra security that it provides, for a relatively small price. The scheme of the system and where is the focus of research (the collision sensors and accident detection) is depicted in Fig. 1.

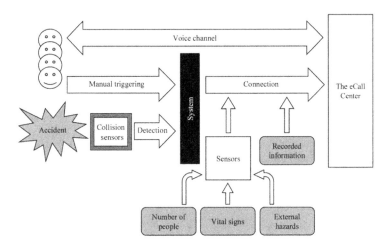

Fig. 1. System block diagram – based on [17]

The mechanism which determines whether an accident has occurred or not is the key element of collision detection system. It should not generate alarms like "false positives" because it turns on other components of eCall system and also initializes the rescue operation.

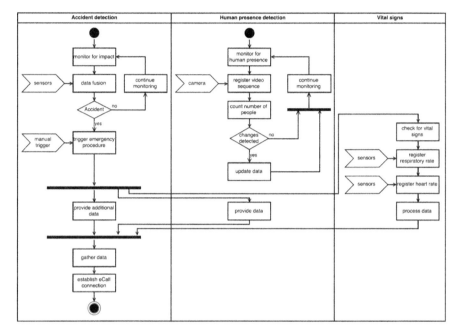

Fig. 2. The activity diagram of the system [17]

Activity diagram of the whole system is presented in Fig. 2. For the accident detection the authors decided to consider using a vast range of sensors and data fusion algorithms. Selected devices and sensors such as accelerometers, gyroscopes, pressure sensors, temperature sensors and sound detectors are used as a source of the information. In this paper the authors focused on accelerometers apply, first of simulation experiments and try to define when accident occurs.

3.2   Choice of Sensors and Collision Detection Criteria

The methods and algorithms of accident detection known from the literature discussed in Sect. 2 refer mainly to the use of the accelerometer as a measuring sensor. An accelerometer can measure acceleration in relation to earth acceleration in three axes X, Y, Z. For applications in automotive systems, mainly biaxial accelerometers are used, but the use of the third axis with the use of a gyroscope can help to determine the scale of the accident.

The basic parameter discriminating against the occurrence of an accident is the value of acceleration (deceleration). In most works, a threshold of 5 g [5, 9] (sometimes 4 g [11, 12]) was given.

In addition to the acceleration (a), the following parameters are used to detect the accident [13, 14]:

- Velocity $v = \int a \, dt$ - one of the most commonly used methods in Airbag SRS (Supplemental Restraint System),
- Displacement $x = \int v \, dt = \int \int a \, dt$,
- Jerk (a change of acceleration) $j = \frac{da}{dt}$,
- Energy density $E = \frac{1}{2} m(v^2 - v_0^2)$, where m – mass,
- Power $\bar{p} = \frac{dE}{dt} = mva$,
- Density of power $p = \frac{\bar{p}}{m} = va$,
- A change of density of power $p' = \frac{dp}{dt} = vj + a^2$ (when collisions occurs at low speed and at an angle).

An acceleration signal from the accelerometer should be filtered with a low-pass filter. For example a data from the crash tests are usually prefiltered with a 4 kHz low-pass filter. Then, the data is sampled at 12500 S/s (0.08 ms per sample). In addition, the digital filtering can be applied, where four filter classes are used [13]:

- class 1000 (f = 1000 Hz),
- class 600 (f = 600 Hz),
- class 180 (f = 180 Hz),
- class 60 (f = 60 Hz).

For the first two classes, any filtration algorithm (e.g. Chebyshev or Butterworth) is recommended, but the Butterworth filter is recommended for the last two classes.

A simple technique of low pass filtering is also the moving window (Moving Averaging Window), where filtering frequency f can be determined as:

$$f = \frac{f_s}{2(M+1)} \tag{1}$$

where f_s - sampling frequency, M - window length in samples.

To determine the criterion of accident occurrence, the threshold estimators for SRS systems can be used [14, 15]. In [16], the time necessary for a collision with a rigid barrier to reduce the speed by 10 kph was experimentally determined - this time was 36 ms (for the Dodge Intrepid car and the initial speed from range 40–120 kph).

The final algorithm should set the threshold based on the additional configuration of the collision, including various vehicle models, lateral impacts, vehicle to vehicle impacts and the impact of the vehicle with the rigid barrier. The following models for implementation and testing on the hardware platform were selected:

- a model based on the measurement of acceleration in a given time window,
- a model based on the measurement of speed in a given time window,
- a model based on displacement measurement in a given time window,
- a model based on measurement of jerks in a given time window,
- a composite model that includes several models selected from the above.

In each of the above models, the method of digital signal filtration (low-pass filter) using the Butterworth filter and Moving Window Averaging will be applied.

4 The Test Lab

Gathering real data from collision detection sensors requires accident environment reproduction. Ideal situation is if we use real vehicle and proceed an accident several times, but such scenario is very expensive. For the early stage of collision detection data gathering and trying to identify proper sensors to apply is enough to build a machine for collision simulation. Presented approach is similar to method which can be found in the work [18] where the value of acceleration (deceleration) measurement was done during impact after free fall of sensors. The fall was amortized by interchangeable elastic elements of varying thickness and stiffness. The adjustment of the duration of the collision and its occurring overloads were made using replaceable sleepers, using materials with different mechanical characteristics and thickness.

In our test set lab, at this stage of research, we have built a machine with pendulum and carriage containing sensors (see Fig. 3). Pendulum position can be regulated what allows for modifying force level of impact in rear side of carriage where accelerometers are placed. Such prepared test set machine allows for impact simulation the stopped car, but it's enough for that early stage of our research. For the further simulation and measurement, we need to build a machine for free fall consisting carriage fixed with 3 axis handle to simulate side/angle impact occurrence not only straight.

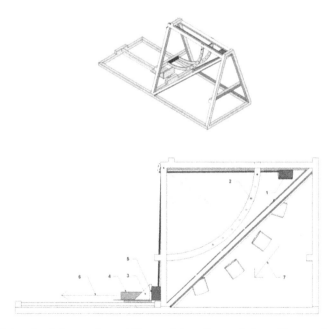

Fig. 3. Collision simulation equipment (1 - pendulum, 2 - regulation of impact, 3 - carriage, 4 - electronic circuits (accelerometers) in the carriage, 5 - point of impact, 6 - direction in which the carriage moves at the stroke of the pendulum, 7 - direction of pendulum movement)

5 Experimental Results

Gathering data for analysis and define the alarm threshold of vehicle accident requires accurate sensors apply. For our experiments two accelerometers were used:

- LIS35DE from ST Microelectronics (± 2 g/± 8 g dynamically selectable full-scale, I^{2}C/SPI digital output interface, 10000 g high shock survivability),
- MMA7455 from NXP Freescale Semiconductor (± 2 g/± 8 g full scale with sensitivity 64 LSB/g in 10-Bit Mode, I^{2}C/SPI digital output interface, 5000 g high shock survivability),

We have proceeded three sets series of pendulum impacts to not moving carrier with accelerometers. Elastic elements of 5 mm thickness were applied just for acoustic noise lowering not for collision time extending. Each set was performed with eight pendulum start position what means eight impact values. The results of recorded values of accelerometers are depicted on Figs. 4 and 5 for inclinations accordingly 10 and 30 degrees. The sampling frequency was 196.5 Hz.

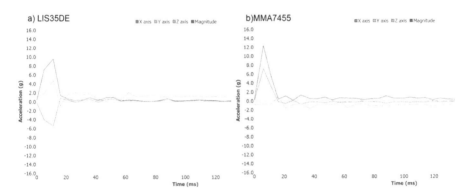

Fig. 4. Acceleration measurement for pendulum inclination 10° (a – LIS35DE, b – MMA7455)

The analysis of the graphs shows that the acceleration measurement is able to determine if an impact has occurred. The value of acceleration in most cases depends on the degree of pendulum inclination. In some cases (MMA7455 sensor) the values measured at 10° are higher than for higher pendulum inclinations. It can be noticed that the values obtained from the LIS35DE sensor are generally larger than the values from the MMA7455 sensor and the X axis of the LIS35DE accelerometer was placed in the opposite direction than the X axis of the MMA7455 accelerometer.

Tables 1 and 2 present minimum and maximum values of acceleration for all 3 measurement series obtained from LIS35DE and MMA7455 sensors for inclinations 10, 20, 30 and 40 degrees.

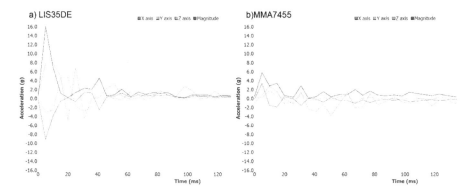

Fig. 5. Acceleration measurement for pendulum inclination 30° (a – LIS35DE, b – MMA7455)

Table 1. Values of acceleration obtained from LIS35DE sensor

Inclination	Series	X min	Y min	Z min	X max	Y max	Z max	Magnitude
10°	1	−5.472	−0.216	−0.936	0.792	0.432	4.68	9.47778
	2	−8.208	−0.288	−1.44	0.792	0.504	3.24	14.2167
	3	−9.216	−0.504	−1.8	0.72	0.576	3.312	15.9626
20°	1	−9.216	−1.44	−5.184	6.12	1.224	9.144	15.9626
	2	−6.696	−1.08	−9.144	1.584	2.736	5.4	11.5978
	3	−9.216	−1.08	−3.168	4.392	1.944	6.552	15.9626
30°	1	−9.216	−3.024	−4.824	1.296	4.608	7.704	15.9626
	2	−9.216	−6.552	−9.144	5.616	4.752	6.624	15.9626
	3	−2.304	−1.224	−9.144	4.752	3.816	5.832	8.23071
40°	1	−9.216	−6.48	−9.144	8.856	4.248	8.208	15.9626
	2	−9.216	−3.816	−5.976	2.952	9.144	9.144	15.9626
	3	−3.6	−1.728	−9.144	6.048	4.968	9.144	10.4754

Table 2. Values of acceleration obtained from MMA7455 sensor

Inclination	Series	X min	Y min	Z min	X max	Y max	Z max	Magnitude
10°	1	−0.725	−0.33906	−1.7328	7.10313	0.317187	0.829687	12.303
	2	−0.65625	−0.51406	−2.6672	5.34375	0.485938	1.56719	9.25565
	3	−0.73125	−0.3125	−2.0875	5.28438	0.5625	1.45938	9.15281
20°	1	−1.36094	−0.70312	−3.3	2.87344	1.35938	0.934375	4.97694
	2	−1.15937	−0.92656	−3.4844	5.95	1.30781	3.40625	10.3057
	3	−0.95781	−1.17969	−3.2469	5.1047	1.67969	2.09687	8.84158
30°	1	−1.93438	−1.25781	−3.8297	3.3	1.69531	2.68594	5.71577
	2	−1.46094	−0.98281	−3.1719	4.52344	1.25156	3.70312	7.83483
	3	−0.975	−0.70156	−2.6484	2.04063	1.90781	2.47656	3.53447
40°	1	−1.14844	−1.22031	−3.4891	4.02344	3.45156	1.82344	6.9688
	2	−3.22969	−0.78281	−3.6078	5.36406	3.10781	2.06406	9.29082
	3	−4.14687	−1.65781	−3.1484	3.3375	2.77969	2.42969	7.18259

The analysis of Table 1 shows that the greatest influence on the acceleration result for the LIS35DE sensor has values from the X and Y axes. The values of the Y axis increase significantly for larger pendulum movements. This is consistent with the predictions, because the X axis is consistent with the direction of the impact, and the values from the other axes are mainly the result of secondary vibrations.

The analysis of Table 2 shows that the greatest influence on the acceleration result for the MMA7455 sensor has values from the X axis. It can be noticed that the obtained values often exceed the measuring range of both accelerometers (especially LIS35DE sensor). Therefore there is a need to use accelerometers with a larger measuring range, in order to obtain more reliable results for higher accelerations, although the value of 4–5 g is often used in literature as detection threshold. This will be used in the future to determine the scale of the accident together with the data received from the gyroscope.

As a preliminary threshold of an accident occurrence a value of 4.5 g of acceleration magnitude was set (implemented as LED indicator in tested device). It corresponds to first mentioned model at the end of paragraph 3.2. Based on above criterion, the ratio of impact detection was 100% for LIS3DE and 91.7% for MMA7455 sensor.

Table 3 presents minimum and maximum values of acceleration for test driving a real car with detection system mounted onboard. The results was taken only from LIS3DE accelerometer because it had higher ratio of impact detection than MMA7455 sensor. Each series corresponds to driving in different road conditions and at different speeds: stop, slow drive through residential streets (30 kph), normal city driving (50 kph), driving out of town at higher speed (up to 90 kph), driving on uneven surface and emergency braking (from 60 kph to 0).

Table 3. Values of acceleration obtained from LIS3DE sensor during car driving

Series	X max	X min	Y max	Y min	Z max	Z min	Magnitude
1	0.144	−0.144	0.144	−0.144	1.152	0.864	0.161
2	0.504	−0.432	0.648	−0.648	1.800	0.360	0.709
3	0.576	−0.504	0.576	−0.504	1.440	0.576	0.664
4	0.504	−0.504	0.792	−0.720	1.728	0.288	0.805
5	0.432	−0.360	0.504	−0.504	1.656	0.504	0.519
6	0.576	−0.648	0.576	−1.224	2.232	0.000	1.224
7	1.152	−0.144	0.864	−1.008	1.368	0.504	1.207
8	1.152	−0.144	1.080	−1.080	1.368	0.576	1.163
9	0.936	−0.144	1.152	−1.152	1.512	0.288	1.207
10	0.648	−0.648	0.864	−1.080	2.160	−0.144	1.163
11	1.224	−0.504	0.792	−1.008	2.016	0.000	1.239
12	0.864	−0.432	1.800	−0.720	1.800	0.144	1.806

The sample results of recorded values are depicted on Fig. 6. These measurements were obtained during driving on an uneven surface and then on the express way with speed up to 80 kph and with emergency breaking. Original data from accelerometer is presented on upper chart and the filtered results – on lower chart. The sampling frequency was increased in relation to previously presented results and it was 406.5 Hz. A fourth order Butterworth low pass filter with a limit frequency of 60 Hz (class 60) was used for filtering. The analysis of Table 3 and Fig. 6 shows that for none of test cases during test drive the 4.5 g threshold value was exceeded, even in the case of sudden braking and driving on uneven surfaces, so the false positive rate was 0%.

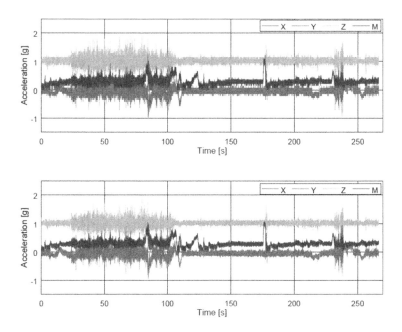

Fig. 6. Acceleration measurement for sample test drive

6 Conclusion

Performed analysis and experimental work have shown that, accident detection is possible with a use of accelerometers not associated with the airbag system in vehicles. Used sensors were placed on additional IVS module. The results of the work indicate also the need for further experiments. The sensors used so far, initially were selected on the basis of a literature review, however they have limited measurement range to show a full picture of the changes of accelerations/decelerations occurring in the collision of mechanical objects. In decelerations too often there were extreme values, which also indicates the possibility of misrepresenting their changes over time. Performed work has shown that it is necessary to use accelerometers that will allow to gather readings with a frequency more than 1 kHz and the required measurement range above 80 g.

In the experiments carried out so far, the fast moving object hits the standing measuring platform. It maps the scenario of an accident when a stationary vehicle is hit by a moving vehicle. In further work, it is planned to carry out tests in a situation when the moving measuring platform hits a standing obstacle and simulate the situation of the overturning vehicle and to detect this fact. Moreover the use of additional gyroscopes and the determination of the accident force on the basis of the classification of the values and direction of decelerations are foreseen.

Acknowledgements. The research has been done in the framework of the grant S/WI/3/2018 and financed from the funds for science by MNiSW.

References

1. European Telecommunications Standards Institute. http://www.etsi.org/news-events/news/960-2015-05-european-parliament-makes-ecall-mandatory-from-2018. Accessed Apr 2018
2. Standard: CEN - EN 15722 Intelligent Transport Systems - ESAFETY - ECALL Minimum Set of Data, 01 April 2015
3. Aloul, F., Zualkernan, I., Abu-Salma, R., Al-Ali, H., Al-Merri, M.: iBump: smartphone application to detect car accidents. In: IAICT 2014, Bali, 28–30 August 2014
4. Kushwaha, V.S., et al.: Car accident detection system using GPS and GSM. Int. J. Eng. Res. Gen. Sci. **3**(3), 1025–1033 (2015)
5. Amin, S., et al.: Low cost GPS/IMU integrated accident detection and location system. Indian J. Sci. Technol. **9**(10), 1–9 (2016)
6. Sulochana, B., Sarath, B.A., Babu, M.: Monitoring and detecting vehicle based on accelerometer and MEMS using GSM and GPS technologies. Int. J. Comput. Sci. Trends Technol. (IJCST) **2**(4), 55–59 (2014)
7. Reddy, M.R., Tulasi, J.: Accident detection depending on the vehicle position and vehicle theft tracking, reporting systems. Int. J. Sci. Eng. Technol. Res. **3**(9), 2359–2362 (2014)
8. Islam, M., et al.: Internet of car: accident sensing, indication and safety with alert system. Am. J. Eng. Res. (AJER) **02**(10), 92–99. e-ISSN 2320-0847, p-ISSN 2320-0936
9. Rich, D., Kosiak, W., Manlove, G., Potti, S.V., Schwarz, D.: A Sensor for Crash Severity and Side Impact Detection, Delphi Delco Electronics Systems, Kokomo, IN 46901, USA
10. Amin, S., et al.: Kalman filtered GPS accelerometer based accident detection and location system: a low-cost approach. Curr. Sci. **106**(11), 10 (2014)
11. Vidya Lakshmi, C., Balakrishnan, J.R.: Automatic Accident Detection via Embedded GSM message interface with Sensor Technology. Int. J. Sci. Res. Publ. **2**(4), 1 (2012)
12. White, J., et al.: WreckWatch: automatic traffic accident detection and notification with smartphones. Mob. Netw. Appl. **16**, 285–303 (2011)
13. Ali, H.M., Alwan, Z.S.: Car accident detection and notification system using smartphone. IJCSMC **4**(4), 620–635 (2015)
14. Kaminski, T., Niezgoda, M., Kruszewski, M.: Collision detection algorithms in the eCall system. J. KONES Powertrain Transp. **19**(4), 267–274 (2012)
15. Kendall, J., Solomon, K.A.: Air bag deployment criteria, The Forensic Examiner (2014)

16. Huang, M.: Vehicle Crash Mechanics. CRC Press, New York (2002)
17. Adamski, M., et al.: The conceptual approach of system for automatic vehicle accident detection and searching for life signs of casualties. In: 5th International Doctoral Symposium on Applied Computation and Security Systems (ACSS) (2018)
18. Kamiński, T.: Selected aspects of running the development project entitled. Developing methodology of evaluating automatic system of notification about the road accidents - eCall, ITS, vol. 2, pp. 61–83 (2012). (in Polish)

Integrated Risk Management in Production Systems

Dominika Rysińska-Wojtasik$^{(\boxtimes)}$ and Anna Burduk

Faculty of Mechanical Engineering, Wroclaw University of Science and
Technology, Wybrzeze Wyspianskiego 27, 50-370 Wroclaw, Poland
{dominika.rysinska-wojtasik,anna.burduk}@pwr.edu.pl

Abstract. The article focuses on the issue of risk management in productive systems through risk assessment and analysis. Different approaches of risk management have been presented. The use of integrated methodology of risk assessment and analysis in productive systems have been discussed. The author describes the matter of performing identification of possible risks from 4M group (machine, material, method, man), their continuous analysis, assessment and mitigation method. This article features a case study by which production efficiency disturbing factors have been identified. Additionally the risk levels have been assessed and process improving actions indicated.

Keywords: Risk management · Risk assessment · FMEA analysis
4M method · Production system · Production process

1 Introduction

Risk is inevitable and it accompanies the activities of every organization. It is defined as *the impact of the unknown upon the goals* or the combination of probability of the unwanted occurrence and its effect [11]. Risk cannot be fully eliminated. However, it can be effectively managed in order to reduce its negative impact on the achievement of organization's goals. It ultimately means determining the possibility of constant improvement.

Risk in productive system described in this article relates to the changing production processes effectiveness. It can be disturbed by randomly occurring hazards causing disorder (risk factors) such as: equipment breakdown, insufficient quality of materials used in production process, lack of material from suppliers, decreased productivity or error of the operator. In such cases, production levels will be lower than planned.

In order to minimize the impact of factors disturbing the activities of production systems, organization's risk management has to be handled fairly and properly [8]. The aim of risk management is to avoid or minimize company's losses, such as material losses, production breaks, loss of *know-how* or negative impact on the company image. In order to reduce the level of risk in a production system, a series of action must be taken.

The final goal of this article is to present an integrated risk management methodology related to the analysis and assessment of risk factors from 4M categories

© Springer Nature Switzerland AG 2018
K. Saeed and W. Homenda (Eds.): CISIM 2018, LNCS 11127, pp. 220–229, 2018.
https://doi.org/10.1007/978-3-319-99954-8_19

(machine, material, method and man) in the production system. The proposed method is to give the company management the necessary information for their decision making processes to support control of the risk in integrated and dynamic.

2 Literature Review

There are many different views on what risk management is, how to define it [11, 12, 14], how to describe it and how to proceed with it [6, 7, 11, 12, 14]. With regard to this overview, it can be stated that risk management should be a logical, ordered and continuous process [7]. Risk factors and their levels can change unexpectedly, for this reason they require constant identification and assessment. During the identification, it is important to search for the answers to the following questions: in which area of the production system the risk occurs and which area is affected by the highest risk. The process of risks identification and assessment should also include their potential impact on intended goals. This should determine prioritization of their elimination, mitigation and damage control [13]. While analyzing the risk to support production control, proper areas have to be evaluated comprehensively and in detail. Risks should be constantly monitored and the existing system updated and improved.

Methods of risk assessment and analysis are designed for these purposes and several dozen of them can be distinguished [9]. They can be divided into qualitative, quantitative and mixed methods [11]. Qualitative methods are meant to identify the risk and alert of its existence. Quantitative methods assess the risk level. Mixed methods are the combination of both quantitative and qualitative method.

Production system management is operational in its nature and its control requires reliance on numerical values. Therefore only quantitative methods should be used in risk assessment of production systems. One of the most advanced of such methods is FMEA analysis [1]. It aims to identify areas of the highest risks in the process and eliminate or mitigate the threat they pose. It can be accomplished by identifying cause-effect relationships of the pain points in the process. It allows for continuous improvement through analysis and application of preventative measures eliminating the source of risk [2, 4].

Due to the complexity of system, developing an effective method of risk management requires long period of time. It is advised to develop a method applicable to the whole organization and for each and every process as well as have it managed at the highest level [15].

3 Process Assessment of Risk in the Production Company

Despite the fact that risk assessment and analysis are a significant endeavor in the decision-making process, they are not always applied by organizations. This can be justified by the methods suggested by literature which might be inadequate to the requirements of businesses nowadays [3]. That is mostly related to challenges around the fulfillment of all stakeholders' expectations defined with operational goals. Such expectations may be mutually exclusive, therefore it is crucial to have a wide and comprehensive view on the organization and processes as well as to integrate all the areas likely to cause any disturbances.

Risk management creates the possibility of production process risk assessment through identification and categorization of risk factors. The proposed methodology of risk assessment is based on the assumption according to which the main risk factors have been divided to 4M categories. The 4M approach takes into account all the most important aspect involved in risk generation [5, 10]:

- *Machine* – risk related to all devices and their work,
- *Material* – risk related to the components and their quality,
- *Method* – risk related to the procedures and standards of work,
- *Man* – risk related to the workers.

Mentioned factors impact the realization of productive processes which are directly related to executing established production plan, that is fulfilling planned production efficiency. The described methodology resembles the FMEA analysis in its application - it allows to identify pain points in organization and creates the space for improvement.

The methodology divides assessment of risk associated with the presence of risk factors into following stages:

STAGE 1: Identification of risk factors in the process - use of standardized data gathering tools to identify risk factors.

STAGE 2: Categorization of risk factors - division of risk factors into 4M categories: machine, material, method, man. The occurring disturbance should be assigned to proper category.

STAGE 3: Analysis of risk factors from each category based on the frequency of occurrence (O), severity of their impact (S) and probability of their detection (D) – in accordance with the suggested criteria of assessment.

STAGE 4: Assessment of risk level based on:

- value of single risk indicator regarding 4M categories - machine, material, method, man (SRIM, SRI2M, SRI3M, SRI4M),
- value of risk level indicator regarding 4M categories - machine, material, method, man (RLI1M, RLI2M, RLI3M, RLI4M),
- value of total risk indicator in production systems (TRI).

Structure of mentioned risk indicators is presented in Fig. 1.

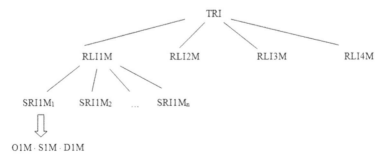

Fig. 1. Assessment of risk's scheme.

STAGE 5: Introduction of appropriate improvement actions in order to eliminate or minimize risk occurrence. According to the Pareto principle, roughly 80% of results can be achieved with 20% of possible actions. That is why implementing appropriate improvement actions for the top 20% of risk level indicators should minimize the risk of occurring system disturbances.

4 Risk Assessment for the Production Company from Automotive Sector – Case Study

The case study was conducted in February 2017 in an automotive industry business in lower Silesian voivodship. It focused on risk management which was to ensure the continuity of production process. The study lasted 20 working days. The assembly line chosen for the study produces safety valves for truck semi-trailers. The analyzed assembly line works in a three shift system. Maximum number of staff on production line is 2 people. Average production efficiency is 82 pieces/person/shift.

The aim of the conducted analysis was to assess process risks by identifying and categorizing risk factors occurring during production process. Additional objective was to establish improvement activities in the described process.

Within the identification of risk factors, the analyzed organization was offered monitoring and registration of the amount of pieces meeting the acceptance criteria per shift. Every day, at the end of production shift, each assembly line employee filled in a number of these pieces in the form. The introduction of such forms enabled continuous monitoring of the daily production plan realization. As a result of using this simple tool, the production supervisors were able to determine what is the status of the monthly production plan realization and if their daily goals are being achieved. Next stage included the implementation of hours forms used for detailed registration of produced pieces per every hour of the process. Production line employees were evidencing the amount of produced pieces after each hour and the number was compared with the calculated efficiency target per hour. If the target was not reached, the assembly line employee was obliged to provide the rationale on why and how long did the production break last. Such information enabled to establish the reason of failure in reaching production efficiency target – that is the identification of disturbance. Hours form prepared this way became the base to risk factors identification. Based on the information provided in forms, the amount of pieces produced in February 2017 on the analyzed assembly line was 2991 (Table 1). The planned efficiency was 4806. 1815 pieces were not produced due to occurring disturbances - risk factors in the production process.

Only 44 out of 59 planned one-person production shifts were operating due to the absence of employees or missing parts from the vendor. Only 8 out of 44 operating shifts reached the efficiency target. The failure in fulfilling the production plan during

Table 1. Summary of information from hours forms.

Number of filled hours forms [pcs]	44
Planned efficiency [pcs]	4806
Efficiency reached - pieces meeting the acceptance criteria [pcs]	2991
Number of defected produced pieces (for disassembly) [pcs]	316
Number of available production shifts	60
Number of operating production shifts	44
Number of planned productive shifts with 1-person staff	59
Number of planned productive shifts with 2-person staff	29,5
Number of operating productive shifts with 1-person staff	23
Number of operating productive shifts with 2-people staff	15
Number of operating productive shifts with incomplete staff	6
Number of shifts that reached the efficiency target	8
Number of shifts that failed to reach the efficiency target	36
Average efficiency utilization [%]	65

operating shifts was caused by the occurrence of risk factors. After analyzing the information provided in the hours forms, the following factors resulted in line stoppages in fulfilling the planned efficiency within the analyzed month:

- training of employees - the disturbance of production process by training of employees in the available production time, the training should be planned outside the production time,
- visits on assembly line - employees were not able to perform the operations due to vendors visiting the assembly line,
- lack of components due to logistic/quality issues,
- equipment breakdown,
- tester breakdown,
- settings/adjustment of the tester after changeover - equipment requires manual settings performed by mechanic after the changeover,
- excessive changeovers - unconsidered planning forces the necessity of excessive changeovers between product variants,
- assembly line occupied by engineer – engineer's interference in production process disturbs the regular operations,
- error analysis by assembly operator - in case of any error occurring, the operator is forced to stop the operation and perform an analysis of a faulty piece,
- adding components (supplying the line) - operator has to supply the production line with components.

The above mentioned risk factors were grouped into categories - Table 2.

After grouping the presented risk factors into categories, it can be observed that the greatest impact on process realization was related to risk associated with the method of process realization (Fig. 2).

Table 2. Causes of disturbances in the production process based on 4M categories.

Machine	Equipment breakdown Tester breakdown Settings/adjustment of the tester after changeover
Material	Lack of components due to logistics issues Lack of components due to quality issues
Method	Excessive changeovers Assembly line occupied by engineer Error analysis by assembly operator Adding components
Man	Training of employees Visits on assembly line

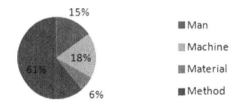

Fig. 2. Division of risk factors into 4M categories.

In the further stages, the identified risk factors were analyzed according to the frequency of their occurrence, severity of the impact and probability of their detection. The analysis was conducted in accordance with the suggested assessment criteria and its results are presented in Table 3.

There were two risk factors unregistered in hours forms – lack of components from the vendors and absence of employees. However, their impact on the process realization was so significant that they could not be omitted in the analysis (severity of the effect higher than 10 units).

Next stage of the research included risk assessment of analyzed process based on established formulas. Value of single risk indicators for each category were calculated as first.

Value of single risk indicator for first factor in the machine category ($1M_1$) - that is equipment breakdown – equals:

$$SRI1M_1 = O1M_1 \cdot S1M_1 \cdot D1M_1 \tag{1}$$

hence

$$SRI1M_1 = 4 \cdot 3 \cdot 2 = 24 \tag{2}$$

Value of single risk indicator for equipment breakdown equals 24 units. Values of single risk indicators for factors second and third correspondingly equal:

Table 3. Analysis of risk factors

Cat.	No.	Risk factor	Frequency of occurrence		Severity of the effect		Probability of detection	
				O1M		S1M		D1M
1M	$1M_1$	Equipment breakdown	1/ month	4	Equipment breakdown = 45 min	3	V. high probability of detection	2
	$1M_2$	Tester breakdown	The same breakdown occurred 3/month	5	Total breakdown time = 178 min	4	Medium probability of detection via current controls. The detection of the cause of risk is likely	5
	$1M_3$	Settings of tester after changeover	Frequent, weekly occurrence 13 instances/month	7	Assembly line offline for 147 min/mth. Risk factor 1 hr/day, not exceeding 1 hr/week	4	Current controls will certainly detect the risk factor as well as its cause	1
				O2M		S2M		D2M
2M	$2M_1$	Parts unavailable due to logistic issue	1 occurrence in a month	3	Assembly offline for 10min.	2	V. high probability of detection.	2
	$2M_2$	Components unavailable due to quality issues	Few occurrences in a month	4	Few breaks of assembly line (for 113 minutes total)	4	V. high probability of detection.	2
	$2M_3$	Component unavailable from the vendors	4 cases/mth. of supply running behind the schedule	6	Failure in starting production on 6 shifts	10	Certain probability of detection via current controls	1
				O3M		S3M		D3M
3M	$3M_1$	Excessive changeovers	Frequent reorientations – few times in a week	5	154 offline minutes noted due to assembly line changeover	3	Certain detection based on the suggested production plan	1
	$3M_2$	Assembly line occupied by engineer	Likely cases of assembly line occupied by engineer to solve the problem – 10 cases (2/week)	6	Breaks occurring few times in a week. Total offline time was 308 min.	4	Medium probability of detection through current controls. The detection of the cause of risk is likely	5
	$3M_3$	Error analysis by assembly operator	Very frequent fault analysis daily occurrence; 29 on 44 operating shifts	7	Breaks of assembly line for 670 min in a month. On average, 23 min/day	4	Medium probability of detection through current controls. Likely detection of the cause of risk	6
	$3M4$	Adding components (supplying the line)	5 cases of risk factor occurrence in a month	4	Breaks of production for 88 min. due to adding components by the operator	3	Risk factor will certainly be detected	1
				O4M		S4M		D4M
4M	$4M_1$	Employee Training	Training of employees in every week	3	Assembly offline for 30 min 10 min/shift	2	Probability of risk factor detection and its cause is v. high	2
	$4M_2$	Visits on assembly line	Probability of risk factor occurring is low	3	Assembly offline for 262 min in total; preparations & client visit = 198 min	4	Probability of risk factor detection and its cause is v. high	2
	$4M_3$	Absence of employees	Likely occurrence - 9 cases/month	6	Lack of staff caused the breaks of assembly line for 9 production shifts	10	Probability detection is v. low. Minimal supervision of HR	7

$$\text{SRI1M}_2 = 5 \cdot 4 \cdot 5 = 100 \tag{3}$$

$$\text{SRI1M}_3 = 7 \cdot 4 \cdot 1 = 28 \tag{4}$$

Having the values of all risk factors from each category, value of risk level indicator for the machine category RLI1M could be calculated:

$$\text{RLI1M} = \sum_{i=1}^{n} \text{RLI1M}_i \tag{5}$$

that is

$$\text{RLI1M} = \text{RLI1M}_1 + \text{RLI1M}_2 + \text{RLI1M}_3 \tag{6}$$

hence

$$\text{RLI1M} = 24 + 100 + 28 = 152 \tag{7}$$

According to the established formula, value of risk level indicator for the machine category RLI1M is 152 units.

The calculations have been made for remaining categories similarly. The summary of calculations is presented in Table 4.

Table 4. Assessment of risk level

1M		O1M	S1M	D1M	SRI1M	RLI1M	TRI
	$1M_1$	4	3	2	24	152	1027
	$1M_2$	5	4	5	100		
	$1M_3$	7	4	1	28		
2M		O2M	S2M	D2M	SRI2M	RLI2M	
	$2M_1$	3	2	2	12	104	
	$2M_2$	4	4	2	32		
	$2M_3$	6	10	1	60		
3M		O3M	S3M	D3M	SRI3M	RLI3M	
	$3M_1$	5	3	1	15	315	
	$3M_2$	6	4	5	120		
	$3M_3$	7	4	6	168		
	$3M_4$	4	3	1	12		
4M		O4M	S4M	D4M	SRI4M	RLI4M	
	$4M_1$	3	2	2	12	456	
	$4M_2$	3	4	2	24		
	$4M_3$	6	10	7	420		

Value of total risk indicator in production system TRI for analyzed system is 1027 units. The factors from men category of 4M prove to have the largest impact on the total risk value as they sum up to 44% of the whole. The smallest share relates to the risk factors for material category (10%).

The last stage was the introduction of improvement actions in order to eliminate or minimize risk occurrence. According to Pareto principle, the threshold of 80% was established. The factor that required immediate improvement was related to employees' absences ($4M_3$) – Fig. 3.

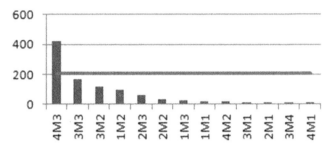

Fig. 3. Application of Pareto principle.

The analyzed organization introduced following actions:

- continuous system of human resources monitoring - a database with vacation, presences, possible replacements. The database allows to plan the vacation of all employees and increases the possibility of reaction in case of assembly operator's absence,
- assembly employees qualification development in order to provide the possibility of replacement on assembly line,
- monthly bonus for lack of absences of an employee.

5   Conclusion

Despite many procedural methods described in literature, risk management is fairly difficult. In many systems, risk management is improper or disregarded at all. This article endeavors to present the issue of risk management in production systems. It has been done through presenting the integrated methodology of risk assessment and analysis with regards to the main categories of factors disturbing the proper production process.

Suggested method of risk assessment and analysis in production systems should be an integral part of management process on every level of the organization. In order to know which area requires improving the most, it is crucial to identify, categorize and establish the probability of occurrence, the severity and detection rate of each risk. This way, proper action can be applied to certain areas as an endeavor to improve them.

It should be taken into consideration that conducting the analysis one time will not bring any results. Risk levels are constantly changing, depending on circumstances. The risk factors decrease, disappear or new risks emerge. However, efficient risk management drives the organizations towards improving operational activities and increasing organization value.

References

1. Bobik, D.: Myślenie oparte na zarządzaniu ryzykiem – wywiad z wykładowcą Jerzy Zgierskim-Strumiłłą. ABC Jakości. Badania. Certyfikacja. Notyfikacja. Qual. Rev. **8**(83), 55 (2015)
2. Burduk, A.: Modelowanie systemów narzędziem oceny stabilności procesów produkcyjnych. Oficyna Wydawnicza Politechniki Wrocławskiej, Wrocław (2013)
3. Burduk, A., Chlebus, E.: Evaluation of the risk in production systems with a parallel reliability structure. Eksploatacja i Niezawodność – Maint. Reliab. **2**(42), 84–86 (2009)
4. Burduk, A., Jagodziński, M.: Assessment of production system stability with the use of the FMEA analysis and simulation models. In: Jackowski, K., Burduk, R., Walkowiak, K., Wozniak, M., Yin, H. (eds.) IDEAL 2015. LNCS, vol. 9375, pp. 216–220. Springer, Cham (2015). https://doi.org/10.1007/978-3-319-24834-9_26
5. Favi, C., Germani, M., Marconi, M.: A 4M approach for a comprehensive analysis and improvement of manual assembly lines. Proc. Manuf. **11**, 1510–1511 (2017)
6. Gaschi-Uciecha, A.: Istota ryzyka w procesach logistycznych. In: Zeszyty Naukowe Politechniki Śląskiej. Organizacja i Zarządzanie, vol. 70, p. 121. Wydawnictwo Politechniki Śląskiej, Gliwice (2014)
7. Jonek-Kowalska, I., Turek, M.: Zarządzanie ryzykiem operacyjnym przedsiębiorstwie górniczym. PWN, Warszawa (2011)
8. Kulińska, E.: Selected tools for risk analysis in logistics process. Arch. Transp. **XXIV**(1), 27–41(2012)
9. Łuczak, J.: Risk assessment methods – ISO/IEC 27001 information security management system's key element. Sci. J. Marit. Univ. Szczecin **19**(91), 65 (2009)
10. Pacaiova, H., Sinay, J., Nagyova, A.: Development of GRAM – a risk measurement tool using risk based thinking principles. Measurement **100**, 288–289 (2017)
11. PN-ISO 31000:2012: Zarządzanie ryzykiem – Zasady i wytyczne
12. Pritchard, C.L.: Zarządzanie ryzykiem w projektach. Teoria i praktyka. WIG-Press, Warszawa (2001)
13. Stasiuk, A.K., Werner-Lewandowska, K.: Rola ryzyka w zarządzaniu produkcją. In: Konferencja Innowacje w Zarządzaniu i Inżynierii Produkcji - IZIP Zakopane, p. 519. Polskie Towarzystwo Zarządzania Produkcją, Zakopane (2013)
14. Whitman, M.E., Mattord, H.J.: Readings and Cases in the Management of Information Security. Thomson Course Technology, Boston (2006)
15. Zapłata, S.: Zarządzanie ryzykiem: ciągłość działania, znormalizowane systemy zarządzania. Problemy Jakości **45**(3), 30–35 (2013)

Machine Learning and High Performance Computing

Granular Computing and Parameters Tuning in Imbalanced Data Preprocessing

Katarzyna Borowska and Jarosław Stepaniuk[(✉)]

Faculty of Computer Science, Bialystok University of Technology, Wiejska 45A,
15-351 Bialystok, Poland
{k.borowska,j.stepaniuk}@pb.edu.pl
http://www.wi.pb.edu.pl

Abstract. Selective preprocessing, representing data–level approach to the imbalanced data problem, is one of the most successful methods. This paper introduces novel algorithm combining this kind of technique with the filtering phase. The information granules are formed to distinguish specific types of positive examples that should be adequately treated. Three modes of oversampling, dedicated to minority class instances placed in specific areas of the feature space, are available. The rough set theory is applied to filter and remove inconsistencies from the generated positive samples. The experimental study shows that proposed method in most cases obtains better or similar performance of standard classifiers, such as C4.5 decision tree, in comparison with other techniques. Additionally, multiple values of algorithm's parameters are evaluated. It is experimentally proven that two of the examined parameters values are the most appropriate to various applications. However, the automatic parameters tuning, based on the specific requirements of different data distributions, is recommended.

Keywords: Data preprocessing · Imbalanced data · Rough sets
Information granules · Oversampling · Parameters tuning

1 Introduction

Nowadays, in the century of Big Data revolution, more and more companies are able to collect large volumes of data. It is obvious that simply storing information is not enough to make a profit. The most valuable is uncovering hidden patterns, correlations and generating recommendations for the future based on these insights. Benefits of advanced data analytics, involving creation of models that predict some important outcomes, are inestimable. Hence, the researchers attempt to not defeat the hopes of business and adjust the existing solutions or develop new ones to meet the requirements of real–life domains. Since these domains are very differential and inconsistent, the expectations are also very high and challenging. One of the most common problems occurring in practical applications is disproportion of classes cardinalities (namely imbalanced data). It is usual that the underrepresented class is the one of great importance.

© Springer Nature Switzerland AG 2018
K. Saeed and W. Homenda (Eds.): CISIM 2018, LNCS 11127, pp. 233–245, 2018.
https://doi.org/10.1007/978-3-319-99954-8_20

In other words, these rare data which could not be gathered in sufficient amount, is crucial to properly handle examined issue. Moreover, recent studies revealed that the class imbalance is not the problem itself, though the complex data distribution should be considered as the most inhibitive. Standard classifiers tend to overgeneralize, thus additional difficulties such as small disjuncts, class overlapping or presence of noise (as well as outliers - real positive examples different from all other available positive examples) are very problematic - they have adverse impact on the classification results [7,15].

Naturally, over recent decades multiple methods were developed to address these difficulties in machine learning [11]. However, they usually encompass only specific aspects of the problem. Even if they are considered as flexible, they often have some parameters that need to be manually tuned. We believe that comprehensive analysis involving evaluation of multiple parameters values is crucial to easily and effectively handle new datasets in the future. Hence, we propose new preprocessing method that not only improves the classification results for the imbalanced data, but also helps with recognizing most suitable values of k nearest neighbours and *complexity_threshold* parameters.

In this paper we focus only on the data preprocessing as the most versatile technique of imbalanced learning. There are also two other approaches, namely algorithm-level and cost-sensitive methods. Their main disadvantage is the need of modifications in base classifiers. Therefore, they are incompatible with our assumption to devise flexible algorithm, independent from classifier.

Data-level techniques is the group of methods including oversampling and undersampling. First of these subcategories involves generating new instances of the minority (underrepresented) class. The second one is based on removing examples from the majority (predominant) class. There are also some combinations of both approaches. Since eliminating some of the instances representing majority class is equivalent to information loss, we assumed that the oversampling would be safer choice. Therefore, the aim of our novel technique, presented in this paper, is to create synthetic examples from the minority class and improve classification results reducing the complexity. In other words, our method assures that new samples are created only in certain regions of the feature space to not introduce undesirable inconsistencies. It is achieved by formation of information granules of various types that are handled independently. Any improperly generated sample is removed by applying rough set approach. The details are described in next sections.

2   Related Works

Considering only preprocessing approach, we are still able to distinguish multiple available algorithms in this overview. Since imbalanced data is one of the major classification problems of the last years, researchers work intensively to provide more and more effective solutions. One of the most groundbreaking methods is undoubtedly Synthetic Minority Oversampling Technique (SMOTE) [6]. The author of this algorithm proved that it is profitable to create minority class examples similar, but not identical to the existing ones. In spite of the indisputable advantages of applying this technique, some drawbacks were pointed out by the data science community [7]. Main objection was the fact that algorithm does not take into account the local neighbourhood of minority class instances. Therefore, new examples may be potentially created in the regions occupied by the representatives of majority class. To avoid this undesirable effect, many improvements of this method were proposed. Among them there are popular techniques like Borderline-SMOTE [9] that oversamples only minority examples belonging to the class boundaries and Modified Synthetic Minority Oversampling Technique (MSMOTE) [10] that creates new samples only for safe and border minority class instances. The Safe–Level SMOTE [5] assumes that the most profitable is creating synthetic samples only in safe regions. On the other hand, some group of solutions combines oversampling with additional filtering step. Selective Preprocessing of Imbalanced Data (SPIDER) [12] is an example of sophisticated algorithm belonging to this category. It has two phases, namely identification of safe and noisy instances. Three options of processing are provided. They differ in types of minority class examples that are amplified and the approach to deal with noise in majority class - it can be relabelled or removed. SMOTE–RSB$_*$ [14] is the method that combines SMOTE algorithm with rough set theory. It introduces additional filtering phase to remove synthetic examples that do not belong to the lower approximation. SMOTE-ENN [2] and SMOTE + Tomek links [2] are hybrids of oversampling and undersampling: SMOTE method and Edited Nearest Neighbours Rule (ENN) or Tomek links respectively. Granular undersampling [19] is an novel approach assuming elimination of information granules characterized by insufficient specificity. These information granules consist of majority class instances. Finally, VIS_RST [3] and VISROT [4] are methods that involve generating new samples in specific areas of the input space based on the minority data categorization and selected automatically mode of processing. These algorithms remove inconsistencies from the synthetic samples by applying rough set methods (e.g., based on lower approximation). The last method improves VIS_RST algorithm by considering both qualitative and quantitative attributes values.

Each of these methods requires proper parameters tuning. Since most of them are based on the SMOTE method, they at least need to have k parameter specified. Other parameters are the similarity threshold, the number of data forming information granule and percentile of removed noise instances.

3 Proposed Method: RGAL

In this section the proposed Rough–Granular Algorithm (RGAL) technique is described. The introduced preprocessing method applies granular computing to the imbalanced data problem. It also enables comparison of different parameters values. Both the number of nearest neighbours and complexity threshold can be modified and examined. Therefore, the proposed technique becomes more flexible than techniques with fixed parameters' values. The selective oversampling was combined with the additional filtering phase to provide consistent data distribution in the result set. The Fig. 1 shows main steps of the presented algorithm.

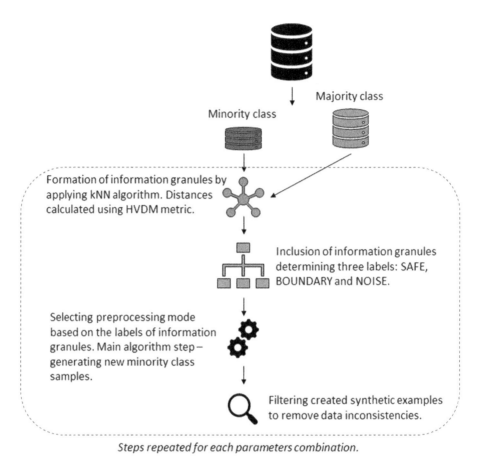

Fig. 1. The flowchart of the RGAL algorithm.

Firstly, information granules are formed (for more details on information granules see e.g. [16]). Information granules, among other things, represent clumps of similar examples. Since the similarity can be identified with proximity in feature space (distance function), we decided to apply the kNN algorithm. It is used to create information granules. Minority class objects with k nearest neighbours form information granules. To properly recognise the neighbourhood of individual instances, described by both numeric and symbolic features, the Heterogeneous Value Distance Metric (HVDM) is utilized [18].

Second step involves categorizing identified granules. The inclusion degrees are verified. In other words, it is investigated to what extent each information granule is included in minority class $X_{d=+}$. This verification is needed to properly handle each kind of positive data when generating synthetic samples. The local neighbourhood of instances is thereby taking into consideration and method can be more fitted to the specific dataset. Three categories are available: $SAFE$, $BOUNDARY$ and $NOISE$. Details are described in the following Definitions 1, 2 and 3.

Definition 1. *Etiquette $Label(x) = SAFE$ for $x \in X_{d=+}$*
More than a half of minority class instances and the nearest neighbour belonging to the positive class implies that x should be labelled as $SAFE$. High inclusion degree corresponds to the safe, homogeneous area in the feature space. There are information granules characterized by the features typical of the positive class.

Definition 2. *Etiquette $Label(x) = BOUNDARY$ for $x \in X_{d=+}$*
Half or more than a half of instances belonging to the negative class or the nearest neighbour representing the majority class implies that x should be labelled as $BOUNDARY$. Low inclusion degree represents regions occupied mainly by the instances from the majority class. Information granule belongs to the borderline area, close to the negative examples.

Definition 3. *Etiquette $Label(x) = NOISE$ for $x \in X_{d=+}$*
The lack of instances from the minority class between the neighbours of x example implies that the information granule should be labelled as $NOISE$. Noninclusion in the $X_{d=+}$ set reflects the special case when all surrounding examples represent majority class, thus the anchor point of the information granule has features specific to the negative class.

Next, the mode of preprocessing is chosen. It is strictly related to the previous step. Based on the number of information granules labelled as $BOUNDARY$ and the *complexity_threshold*, the following assumptions are made.
Having less $BOUNDARY$ entities, i.e.

$$\frac{card(\{x \in X_{d=+} : Label(x) = BOUNDARY\})}{card(X_{d=+})} < complexity\_threshold$$

means that the problem is not complex and the following method of creating new instances can be applied:

Definition 4. *LowComplexity mode for obtaining $DT_{balanced}$ table from DT table: $DT \longmapsto^{LowComplexity} DT_{balanced}$*

– *$Label(x) = SAFE$: there is no need to increase significantly the number of instances in these safe areas. Only one new instance per existing minority SAFE instance is generated. Numeric attributes are handled by the interpolation with one of the k nearest neighbours. For the nominal features, new sample has the same values of attributes as the instance under consideration.*
– *$Label(x) = BOUNDARY$: the most of synthetic samples are generated in these borderline areas, since numerous majority class representatives may have greater impact on the classifier learning, when there are not enough*

minority examples. Hence, many new examples are created closer to the instance x under consideration. One of the k nearest neighbour is chosen for each new sample when determining the value of numeric feature. Values of nominal attributes are obtained by the majority vote of k nearest neighbours' features.

On the other hand, prevalence of $BOUNDARY$ information granules, i.e.

$$\frac{card(\{x \in X_{d=+} : Label(x) = BOUNDARY\})}{card(X_{d=+})} \geq complexity\_threshold$$

involves more complications during learning process. Therefore, dedicated approach (described below) is chosen:

Definition 5. *HighComplexity mode for obtaining $DT_{balanced}$ table from DT table: $DT \longmapsto^{HighComplexity} DT_{balanced}$*

- *Label(x) = SAFE: assuming that these concentrated instances provide specific and easy to learn patterns that enable proper recognition of minority samples, a plenty of new data is created by interpolation between SAFE instance and one of its k nearest neighbours. Nominal attributes are determined by majority vote of k nearest neighbours' features.*
- *Label(x) = BOUNDARY: the number of instances is doubled by creating one new example along the line segment between half of the distance from BOUNDARY instance and one of its k nearest neighbours. For nominal attributes values describing the instance under consideration are replicated.*

The last option is the special case, when no SAFE information granule is recognized i.e. $\{x \in X_{d=+} : Label(x) = SAFE\} = \emptyset$. Hence, the following method is applied:

Definition 6. *noSAFE mode: $DT \longmapsto^{noSAFE} DT_{balanced}$*

- *Label(x) = BOUNDARY: all of the synthetic instances are created in the area surrounding class boundaries. This particular solution is selected in case especially complex data distribution, which do not include any SAFE samples. Missing SAFE elements indicates that most of the examples are labelled as BOUNDARY (there are no homogeneous regions). Since only BOUNDARY and NOISE examples are available, only generating new instances in neighbourhood of BOUNDARY instances would provide sufficient number of minority samples.*

No new instances are created when $Label(x) = NOISE$, since it could potentially introduce additional inconsistencies to the data distribution.

The final step involves filtering inconsistencies. Each generated minority example that do not belong to the lower approximation (defined by the rough set notions [13,16]) is considered as noise and removed. Since both qualitative and quantitative attributes are permitted, tolerance relation [16] is applied instead of standard indiscernibility relation. The *distance_threshold* enables establishing the level of similarity between synthetic members of minority class and examples from majority class that means strong resemblance. Similar instances representing both classes form the boundary region, that in ideal scenario should be empty to minimize the data distribution complexity. The smallest acceptable distance between synthetic samples and majority class representatives is specified by the percentage of average distance (namely *distance_threshold*). In order to eliminate inconsistent samples, each newly generated minority class example being placed too close to any of its neighbours from majority class is removed. This phase ensures that newly added positive instances have only features specific to the minority class.

Traditionally, the number of generated synthetic samples is assorted to even the cardinalities of both classes. Algorithm described in this paper requires some redundancy reflecting the need of more examples than usual. It results from the filtering some of the improperly generated instances.

4   Experiments

There are two aims of the experiments described in this section. One of them involves the comprehensive analysis of the impact that algorithm's parameters have on the classification results. Two parameters were examined, namely k and *complexity_threshold*. The second aim is to evaluate proposed algorithm in comparison with five other methods, being representatives of distinct approaches. The results of classification without preprocessing step are presented for reference. The C4.5 decision tree was used as the classifier due to its simplicity, effectiveness and efficiency [7].

The experimental study was performed on five imbalanced data sets. They are described in Table 1. They were downloaded from the KEEL repository [1]. Originally they were published in the popular UCI machine learning database [17]. Since researchers all over the world use these datasets, one could easily compare our results with other similar methods. Moreover, these data is gathered from real–life domains, being perfect representation of important and complex problems. Datasets were previously prepared by dividing into separate training and test partitions. The 5-folds stratified cross validation was applied. *IR* (imbalance ratio) values indicate the level of class imbalance. Another important column in Table 1 is the one that presents information about boundary region prevalence. Datasets that have nonempty boundary region may be considered as more complex.

4.1   RGAL Parameters Tuning - Analysis

Two main parameters of the algorithm were analysed. The k value was chosen, since it has significant impact on the preliminary step of preprocessing, namely forming information granules, as well as generating synthetic samples with proper features (selecting nearest neighbours). Due to the space limit, four values were examined: from very low number like 3, through 5, 7 up to 11. The second parameter is the *complexity_threshold* indicating to what extent the dataset is complex. This value implicitly designates processing mode. Relatively wide spectrum of values was validated, from 0.1 to 0.6, giving 6 different options. The *distance_threshold* was set to 25%. Three tables below (Tables 2, 3 and 4)

Table 1. Characteristics of evaluated datasets

Dataset	Instances	Attributes	IR	Boundary region
ecoli-0-1_vs_5	240	6	11	Nonempty
ecoli-0-1-4-6_vs_5	280	6	13	Nonempty
glass-0-1-6_vs_5	184	9	19.44	Empty
glass5	214	9	22.78	Empty
led7digit-0-2-4-5-6-7-8-9_vs_1	443	7	10.97	Nonempty

Table 2. Detailed classification results for ecoli-0-1_vs_5 dataset depending on the two parameters values (k and *complexity_threshold*). Mode: HighComplexity.

k	Complexity threshold	Generated samples	Added	Improperly generated	Accuracy	TP rate	TN rate	F measure	AUC
3	0.1	208	160	0	0.9583	0.7500	0.9773	0.7600	0.8636
	0.2	208	160	0	0.9583	0.7500	0.9773	0.7600	0.8636
	0.3	208	160	0	0.9542	0.7500	0.9727	0.7400	0.8614
	0.4	208	160	0	0.9583	0.7500	0.9773	0.7600	0.8636
	0.5	208	160	0	0.9542	0.7500	0.9727	0.7400	0.8614
	0.6	208	160	0	0.9583	0.7500	0.9773	0.7600	0.8636
5	0.1	208	160	0	0.9583	0.7500	0.9773	0.7500	0.8636
	0.2	208	160	0	0.9625	0.8000	0.9773	0.7800	**0.8886**
	0.3	208	160	0	0.9625	0.8000	0.9773	0.7800	**0.8886**
	0.4	208	160	0	0.9583	0.8000	0.9727	0.7600	0.8864
	0.5	208	160	0	0.9583	0.7500	0.9773	0.7500	0.8636
	0.6	208	160	0	0.9583	0.8000	0.9727	0.7600	0.8864
7	0.1	208	160	0	0.9542	0.8000	0.9682	0.7500	0.8841
	0.2	208	160	0	0.9542	0.8000	0.9682	0.7500	0.8841
	0.3	208	160	0	0.9542	0.8000	0.9682	0.7500	0.8841
	0.4	208	160	0	0.9500	0.8000	0.9636	0.7300	0.8818
	0.5	208	160	0	0.9542	0.8000	0.9682	0.7500	0.8841
	0.6	208	160	0	0.9625	0.8000	0.9773	0.7900	**0.8886**
11	0.1	208	160	0	0.9625	0.7000	0.9864	0.7600	0.8432
	0.2	208	160	0	0.9583	0.6500	0.9864	0.7000	0.8182
	0.3	208	160	0	0.9542	0.7000	0.9773	0.7200	0.8386
	0.4	208	160	0	0.9583	0.7000	0.9818	0.7400	0.8409
	0.5	208	160	0	0.9542	0.7000	0.9773	0.7100	0.8386
	0.6	208	160	0	0.9625	0.7000	0.9864	0.7600	0.8432

Table 3. Detailed classification results for ecoli-0-1-4-6_vs_5 dataset depending on the two parameters values (k and *complexity_threshold*). Mode: LowComplexity.

k	Complexity threshold	Generated samples	Added	Improperly generated	Accuracy	TP rate	TN rate	F measure	AUC
3	0.1	249	172	77	0.9571	0.7000	0.9769	0.6900	0.8385
	0.2	249	172	77	0.9571	0.7000	0.9769	0.6900	0.8385
	0.3	249	172	77	0.9571	0.7000	0.9769	0.6900	0.8385
	0.4	249	172	77	0.9500	0.7000	0.9692	0.6700	0.8346
	0.5	249	172	77	0.9571	0.7000	0.9769	0.6900	0.8385
	0.6	249	172	77	0.9571	0.7000	0.9769	0.6900	0.8385
5	0.1	249	191	58	0.9607	0.7000	0.9808	0.6800	**0.8404**
	0.2	249	191	58	0.9428	0.6000	0.9692	0.5700	0.7846
	0.3	249	191	58	0.9607	0.7000	0.9808	0.6800	**0.8404**
	0.4	249	191	58	0.9607	0.7000	0.9808	0.6800	**0.8404**
	0.5	249	191	58	0.9535	0.7000	0.9731	0.6600	0.8366
	0.6	249	191	58	0.9607	0.7000	0.9808	0.6800	**0.8404**
7	0.1	249	192	46	0.9536	0.6500	0.9769	0.6600	0.8135
	0.2	249	192	46	0.9428	0.6000	0.9692	0.5800	0.7846
	0.3	249	192	46	0.9500	0.6000	0.9769	0.6100	0.7885
	0.4	249	192	46	0.9428	0.6000	0.9692	0.5800	0.7846
	0.5	249	192	46	0.9500	0.6000	0.9769	0.6100	0.7885
	0.6	249	192	46	0.9357	0.5000	0.9692	0.5100	0.7346
11	0.1	249	192	46	0.9250	0.7000	0.9423	0.5700	0.8212
	0.2	249	192	46	0.9357	0.7000	0.9538	0.5800	0.8269
	0.3	249	192	46	0.9286	0.7000	0.9462	0.5600	0.8231
	0.4	249	192	46	0.9321	0.7000	0.9500	0.5700	0.8250
	0.5	249	192	46	0.9357	0.5500	0.9654	0.5500	0.7577
	0.6	249	192	46	0.9286	0.5500	0.9577	0.5200	0.7538

show selected detailed results of classification preceded by applying proposed RGAL algorithm with Cartesian of specified parameters values. Each dataset was examined separately. The columns show number of synthetic minority class samples with redundancy of 30%, number of new examples actually added to the original dataset and number of generated instances recognized as noise (inconsistencies) that were removed. There are also four measures, commonly used in this kind of experimental studies involving classification of imbalanced data. Especially the AUC measure is recommended to be applied, since it combines the trade-offs between benefits (true positives) and costs (false positives).

Investigating various k parameter values, it revealed, that almost all datasets (except the last one) had the best results (measured by the AUC) for 5 nearest neighbours. Hence, it is confirmed that selecting this value can be profitable in most cases (for reference see [8]). Nevertheless, the last dataset obtained better results for 3 nearest neighbours. Moreover, three datasets had best AUC results

Table 4. Detailed classification results for glass-0-1-6_vs_5 dataset depending on the two parameters values (k and *complexity_threshold*). Mode: LowComplexity.

k	Complexity threshold	Generated samples	Added	Improperly generated	Accuracy	TP rate	TN rate	F measure	AUC
3	0.1	171	132	0	0.9784	0.8000	0.9886	0.7200	**0.8943**
	0.2	171	132	0	0.9784	0.8000	0.9886	0.7200	**0.8943**
	0.3	171	132	0	0.9784	0.8000	0.9886	0.7200	**0.8943**
	0.4	171	132	0	0.9784	0.8000	0.9886	0.7200	**0.8943**
	0.5	171	132	0	0.9784	0.8000	0.9886	0.7200	**0.8943**
	0.6	171	132	0	0.9784	0.8000	0.9886	0.7200	**0.8943**
5	0.1	171	132	0	0.9730	0.8000	0.9828	0.6800	0.8914
	0.2	171	132	0	0.9730	0.8000	0.9828	0.6800	0.8914
	0.3	171	132	0	0.9730	0.8000	0.9828	0.6800	0.8914
	0.4	171	132	0	0.9730	0.8000	0.9828	0.6800	0.8914
	0.5	171	132	0	0.9784	0.8000	0.9886	0.7200	**0.8943**
	0.6	171	132	0	0.9730	0.8000	0.9828	0.6800	0.8914
7	0.1	171	132	0	0.9730	0.8000	0.9828	0.6800	0.8914
	0.2	171	132	0	0.9730	0.8000	0.9828	0.6800	0.8914
	0.3	171	132	0	0.9730	0.8000	0.9828	0.6800	0.8914
	0.4	171	132	0	0.9730	0.8000	0.9828	0.6800	0.8914
	0.5	171	132	0	0.9730	0.8000	0.9828	0.6800	0.8914
	0.6	171	132	0	0.9730	0.8000	0.9828	0.6800	0.8914
11	0.1	171	132	0	0.9730	0.8000	0.9828	0.6800	0.8914
	0.2	171	132	0	0.9784	0.8000	0.9886	0.7200	**0.8943**
	0.3	171	132	0	0.9730	0.8000	0.9828	0.6800	0.8914
	0.4	171	132	0	0.9784	0.8000	0.9886	0.7200	**0.8943**
	0.5	171	132	0	0.9730	0.8000	0.9828	0.6800	0.8914
	0.6	171	132	0	0.9730	0.8000	0.9828	0.6800	0.8914

also with k values different than 5. For example, glass-0-1-6_vs_5 dataset achieved the maximum AUC value 0.8943 having 3, 5 and 11 nearest neighbours. Only value equal to 7 gave slightly worse result. However, the TP_{rate} value was the same for all parameters combinations in case of this dataset. The best AUC result for glass5 dataset was achieved when the k parameter was set to 5, 7 and 11. In case of ecoli-0-1_vs_5 dataset maximum AUC value was obtained for 5 and 7 nearest neighbours. Only ecoli-0-1-4-6_vs_5 dataset appointed 5 as the best k value resulting in the highest AUC for this number of nearest neighbours. It is also worth mentioning that in case of glass5 dataset number of nearest neighbours equal to 5 and 7 contributed to 100% correctness in recognizing members of the minority class (TP_{rate}) despite of the *complexity_threshold* value.

Very interesting may be also analysis of the correlation between k value and the number of improperly generated synthetic samples (introducing inconsistencies that should be removed). Only the second and the last dataset had some noise in newly created minority class instances. Surprisingly, each of these datasets showed completely different tendency: while ecoli-0-1-4-6_vs_5 had less improper samples for higher k values, the led7digit had more and more inconsistencies when the number of nearest neighbours was increased.

Focusing on the *complexity_threshold* parameter, we can observe that it had slightly less impact on the classification results than its predecessor. All datasets obtained the highest AUC result for the 0.3 value of *complexity_threshold* for at least one value of the nearest neighbours. The best values for ecoli-0-1_vs_5 dataset are 0.2, 0.3 ($k = 5$) and 0.6 ($k = 7$). For ecoli-0-1-4-6_vs_5 dataset three values emerged as the most appropriate: 0.1, 0.3, 0.4 and 0.6 ($k = 5$). However, in case of three last datasets all values of the *complexity_threshold* parameter could be considered as correct, since they were not as significant as the k value.

To sum up, even if we can try to distinguish some preferred values of the k and *complexity_threshold*, like 5 and 0.3 respectively, it should be emphasised that their values are strictly dependent on the data distribution and problem complexity. Moreover, they should always be tuned collectively.

4.2   RGAL in Comparison with Other Approaches

Table 5 presents the results of experimental study. The classifiers' performance was evaluated by applying the AUC measure. Approach introduced in this paper was compared with five other methods. Also the results of classification without preprocessing step are presented. Results for the RGAL algorithm are maximum AUC values achieved for the specific parameters values. The proposed algorithm outperformed all other methods in case of two datasets (namely ecoli01_vs_5 and glass5). For one dataset (glass016_vs_5) it had the same result as VISROT technique and classification without preprocessing step - the remaining methods had worse results. For two remaining datasets the proposed solution had better performance than VISROT algorithm, however, SMOTE-RSB$_*$ was subtly more effective.

Table 5. Classification results for the selected UCI datasets - comparison of proposed algorithm RGAL (maximum AUC values) with five other techniques and classification without preprocessing step (noPRE).

Dataset	noPRE	SMOTE	S–ENN	Border–S	S–RSB$_*$	VISROT	RGAL
ecoli01_vs_5	0.8159	0.7977	0.8250	0.8318	0.7818	0.8636	**0.8886**
ecoli0146_vs_5	0.7885	**0.8981**	**0.8981**	0.7558	0.8231	0.8366	0.8404
glass016_vs_5	0.8943	0.8129	0.8743	0.8386	0.8800	**0.8943**	**0.8943**
glass5	0.8976	0.8829	0.7756	0.8854	0.9232	0.9951	**0.9976**
led7digit02456789_vs_1	0.8788	0.8908	0.8379	0.8908	**0.9019**	0.8918	0.8931

5 Conclusions

Novel preprocessing algorithm applying information granules and rough set notions to imbalanced data problem was presented in this paper. The positive synergy of the selective oversampling and additional filtering phase was proven. Based on the performed experimental study, we claim that introduced method is able to effectively handle various real–life problems. Its versatility is attained by several parameters. Indeed, proper tuning of these parameters is crucial for expected classification results. Therefore, we presented detailed analysis of multiple parameters values. Both k and *complexity_threshold* were examined. It revealed that the most appropriate values of these parameters are dependent on the dataset. Hence, it is recommended to develop algorithm adjusting all available parameters to the particular data distributions automatically.

Acknowledgements. This research was supported by the grant S/WI/1/2018 of the Polish Ministry of Science and Higher Education.

References

1. Alcala-Fdez, J., et al.: KEEL data-mining software tool: data set repository, integration of algorithms and experimental analysis framework. J. Mult. Valued Log. Soft Comput. **17**(2–3), 255–287 (2011)
2. Batista, G.E.A.P.A., Prati, R.C., Monard, M.C.: A study of the behavior of several methods for balancing machine learning training data. SIGKDD Explor. Newsl. **6**(1), 20–29 (2004)
3. Borowska, K., Stepaniuk, J.: Imbalanced data classification: a novel re-sampling approach combining versatile improved SMOTE and rough sets. In: Saeed, K., Homenda, W. (eds.) CISIM 2016. LNCS, vol. 9842, pp. 31–42. Springer, Cham (2016). https://doi.org/10.1007/978-3-319-45378-1_4
4. Borowska, K., Stepaniuk, J.: Rough sets in imbalanced data problem: improving re–sampling process. In: Saeed, K., Homenda, W., Chaki, R. (eds.) CISIM 2017. LNCS, vol. 10244, pp. 459–469. Springer, Cham (2017). https://doi.org/10.1007/978-3-319-59105-6_39
5. Bunkhumpornpat, C., Sinapiromsaran, K., Lursinsap, C.: Safe-Level-SMOTE: Safe-Level-Synthetic Minority Over-Sampling TEchnique for handling the class imbalanced problem. In: Theeramunkong, T., Kijsirikul, B., Cercone, N., Ho, T.-B. (eds.) PAKDD 2009. LNCS (LNAI), vol. 5476, pp. 475–482. Springer, Heidelberg (2009). https://doi.org/10.1007/978-3-642-01307-2_43
6. Chawla, N.V., Bowyer, K.W., Hall, L.O., Kegelmeyer, W.P.: SMOTE: synthetic minority over-sampling technique. J. Artif. Int. Res. **16**(1), 321–357 (2002)
7. Galar, M., Fernandez, A., Barrenechea, E., Bustince, H., Herrera, F.: A review on ensembles for the class imbalance problem: bagging-, boosting-, and hybrid-based approaches. IEEE Trans. Syst. Man Cybern. Part C (Appl. Rev.) **42**(4), 463–484 (2012)
8. Garcia, V., Mollineda, R.A., Sanchez, J.S.: On the k-NN performance in a challenging scenario of imbalance and overlapping. Pattern Anal. Appl. **11**(3–4), 269–280 (2008)

9. Han, H., Wang, W.-Y., Mao, B.-H.: Borderline-SMOTE: a new over-sampling method in imbalanced data sets learning. In: Huang, D.-S., Zhang, X.-P., Huang, G.-B. (eds.) ICIC 2005. LNCS, vol. 3644, pp. 878–887. Springer, Heidelberg (2005). https://doi.org/10.1007/11538059_91

10. Hu, S., Liang, Y., Ma, L., He, Y.: MSMOTE: improving classification performance when training data is imbalanced. In: Second International Workshop on Computer Science and Engineering, WCSE 2009, Qingdao, pp. 13–17 (2009)

11. López, V., Fernández, A., García, S., Palade, V., Herrera, F.: An insight into classification with imbalanced data: empirical results and current trends on using data intrinsic characteristics. Inf. Sci. **250**, 113–141 (2013)

12. Napierała, K., Stefanowski, J., Wilk, S.: Learning from imbalanced data in presence of noisy and borderline examples. In: Szczuka, M., Kryszkiewicz, M., Ramanna, S., Jensen, R., Hu, Q. (eds.) RSCTC 2010. LNCS (LNAI), vol. 6086, pp. 158–167. Springer, Heidelberg (2010). https://doi.org/10.1007/978-3-642-13529-3_18

13. Pawlak, Z., Skowron, A.: Rudiments of rough sets. Inf. Sci. **177**(1), 3–27 (2007)

14. Ramentol, E., Caballero, Y., Bello, R., Herrera, F.: SMOTE-RSB$_*$: a hybrid pre-processing approach based on oversampling and undersampling for high imbalanced data-sets using SMOTE and rough sets theory. Knowl. Inf. Syst. **33**(2), 245–265 (2011)

15. Stefanowski, J.: Dealing with data difficulty factors while learning from imbalanced data. In: Matwin, S., Mielniczuk, J. (eds.) Challenges in Computational Statistics and Data Mining. SCI, vol. 605, pp. 333–363. Springer, Cham (2016). https://doi.org/10.1007/978-3-319-18781-5_17

16. Stepaniuk, J.: Rough-Granular Computing in Knowledge Discovery and Data Mining, vol. 152. Springer, Heidelberg (2008). https://doi.org/10.1007/978-3-540-70801-8

17. UC Irvine Machine Learning Repository. http://archive.ics.uci.edu/ml/. Accessed 28 Apr 2018

18. Wilson, D.R., Martinez, T.R.: Improved heterogeneous distance functions. J. Artif. Intell. Res. **6**, 1–34 (1997)

19. Zhu X., Pedrycz W.: Granular under-sampling for processing imbalanced data. IEEE (2018, in Print)

The Use of Geometric Mean
in the Process of Integration
of Three Base Classifiers

Robert Burduk$^{(\boxtimes)}$ and Andrzej Kasprzak$^{(\boxtimes)}$

Department of Systems and Computer Networks, Wroclaw University of Science
and Technology, Wybrzeze Wyspianskiego 27, 50-370 Wroclaw, Poland
{robert.burduk,andrzej.kasprzak}@pwr.edu.pl

Abstract. One of the most important steps in the formation of multiple
classifier systems is the integration process also called the base classifiers
fusion. The fusion process may be applied either to class labels or confidence levels (discriminant functions). These are the two main methods
for combining base classifiers. In this paper, we propose an integration
process which takes place in the geometry space. It means that the fusion
of base classifiers is done using decision boundaries. In our approach, the
final decision boundary is calculated by using the geometric mean. The
algorithm presented in the paper concerns the case of 3 basic classifiers
and two-dimensional features space. The results of the experiment based
on several data sets show that the proposed integration algorithm is
a promising method for the development of multiple classifiers systems.

Keywords: Ensemble selection · Multiple classifier system
Decision boundary

1 Introduction

Ensembles of classifiers (EoC) [5,8,17] are meta-algorithms that combine several base classifiers into one model in order to improve classification accuracy
or decrease variance and bias of the single base classifier. These methods for
fuse classifiers have been discussed for over twenty years [7,18]. EoC methods
can use homogeneous base classifiers, i.e. learners of the same type, or heterogeneous classifiers, i.e. learners of different types, leading to build one model.
Additionally, the task of constructing EoC can be generally divided into three
steps: generation, selection and integration [1]. In the first step a set of base classifiers is trained. There are two ways, in which base classifiers can be trained.
In the case of the homogeneous base classifiers randomness is introduced to the
learning algorithms by initializing training objects with different weights, manip-
ulating the training objects or using different features subspaces. While in the
case of the heterogeneous base classifiers the base learners are trained on the
same data set.

© Springer Nature Switzerland AG 2018
K. Saeed and W. Homenda (Eds.): CISIM 2018, LNCS 11127, pp. 246–253, 2018.
https://doi.org/10.1007/978-3-319-99954-8_21

The second phase of building EoC is related to the choice of a set of classifiers or one classifier from the whole available pool of base classifiers. If we choose one classifier, this process will be called the classifier selection. But if we choose a subset of base classifiers from the pool, it will be called the ensemble selection. Generally, in the ensemble selection, there are two approaches: the static ensemble selection and the dynamic ensemble selection [1]. In the static classifier selection one set of classifiers is selected to create EoC during the training phase. This EoC is used in the classification of all the objects from the test set. The main problem in this case is to find a pertinent objective function for selecting the classifiers. Usually, the feature space in this selection method is divided into different disjunctive regions of competence and for each of them a different classifier selected from the pool is determined. In the dynamic classifier selection, also called instance-based, a specific subset of classifiers is selected for each unknown sample [4]. It means that we are selecting different EoCs for different objects from the testing set. In this type of the classifier selection, the classifier is chosen and assigned to the sample based on different features or different decision regions [6]. The existing methods of the ensemble selection use the validation data set to create the so-called competence region or level of competence. These competencies can be computed by K nearest neighbours from the validation data set. In this paper, we will use the static classifier selection and regions of competence will be designated by the decision boundary of the base classifiers.

The integration process is widely discussed in the pattern recognition literature [12,16]. One of the existing ways to categorize the integration process is using the outputs of the base classifiers selected in the previous step. Generally, the output of a base classifier can be divided into three types [10].

- The abstract level – the classifier ψ assigns the unique label j to a given input x.
- The rank level – in this case for each input (object) x, each classifier produces an integer rank array. Each element within this array corresponds to one of the defined class labels. The array is usually sorted and the label at the top is the first choice.
- The measurement level – the output of a classifier is represented by a confidence value (CV) that addresses the degree of assigning the class label to the given input x. An example of such a representation of the output is a posteriori probability returned by Bayes classifier. Generally, this level can provide richer information than the abstract and rank levels.

For example, when considering the abstract level, voting techniques [15] are most popular. As majority voting usually works well for classifiers with a similar accuracy, we will use this method as a baseline.

In this paper we propose the concept of the classifier integration process which takes place in the geometry space. It means that we use the decision boundary in the integration process. In other words, the fusion of base classifiers is done using decision boundaries instead of using the class labels or confidence values. In our approach, the final decision boundary is calculated by using the harmonic mean. The algorithm presented in the paper concerns the case of 3 basic classifiers and a two-dimensional features space.

The geometric approach discussed in [11] is applied to find characteristic points in the geometric space. These points are then used to determine the decision boundaries. Thus, the results presented in [13] do not concern the process of integration of base classifiers, but a method for creating decision boundaries.

The remainder of this paper is organized as follows. Section 2 presents the basic concept of the classification problem and EoC. Section 3 describes the proposed method for the integration base classifiers in the geometry space in which the harmonic mean is used to determine the decision boundary. The experimental evaluation is presented in Sect. 4. The discussion and conclusions from the experiments are presented in Sect. 5.

2   Basic Concept

Let us consider the binary classification task. It means that we have two class labels $\Omega = \{0, 1\}$. Each pattern is characterized by the feature vector x. The recognition algorithm Ψ maps the feature space x to the set of class labels Ω according to the general formula:

$$\Psi(x) \in \Omega. \tag{1}$$

Let us assume that $k \in \{1, 2, ..., K\}$ different classifiers $\Psi_1, \Psi_2, \ldots, \Psi_K$ are available to solve the classification task. In MCSs these classifiers are called base classifiers. In the binary classification task, K is assumed to be an odd number. As a result of all the classifiers' actions, their K responses are obtained. Usually all K base classifiers are applied to make the final decision of MCSs. Some methods select just one base classifier from the ensemble. The output of only this base classifier is used in the class label prediction for all objects. Another option is to select a subset of the base classifiers. Then, the combining method is needed to make the final decision of EoC.

The majority vote is a combining method that works at the abstract level. This voting method allows counting the base classifiers outputs as a vote for a class and assigns the input pattern to the class with the majority vote. The majority voting algorithm is as follows:

$$\Psi_{MV}(x) = \arg\max_{\omega} \sum_{k=1}^{K} I(\Psi_k(x), \omega), \tag{2}$$

where $I(\cdot)$ is the indicator function with the value 1 in the case of the correct classification of the object described by the feature vector x, i.e. when $\Psi_k(x) = \omega$. In the majority vote method each of the individual classifiers takes an equal part in building EoC.

3   Proposed Method

Conventional fusion methods fuse the class labels or confidence values produced by the base classifiers to produce the class labels of the ensemble classifier. Assuming that the decision boundary for each base classifier is known we present the integration process that is performed in the geometric space. Therefore in proposed method we don't use in fusion the class labels or confidence values. The calculation of one decision boundary for three base classifiers is performed as follows.

Algorithm 1. Algorithm for finding decision boundary of combining classifier Ψ_{GM}

    Input   : Decision boundaries for the 3 basic classifiers Ψ_1, Ψ_2, Ψ_3
    Output: Decision boundary of combining classifier Ψ_{HM}

1 **for** $x \in \mathbb{R}^1$ **do**
2      $g_{min}(x) = min(g_{\Psi_1}(x), g_{\Psi_2}(x), g_{\Psi_3}(x))$;
3      $g_{max}(x) = max(g_{\Psi_1}(x), g_{\Psi_2}(x), g_{\Psi_3}(x))$;
4      $g_{med}(x) = median(g_{\Psi_1}(x), g_{\Psi_2}(x), g_{\Psi_3}(x))$;
5      $h_1 = g_{max}(x) - g_{med}(x)$;
6      $h_2 = g_{med}(x) - g_{min}(x)$;
7      $gm = $ geometric mean(h_1, h_2);
8   **if** $g_{med}(x) > (g_{max}(x) + g_{min}(x))/2$ **then**
9 | $g_{\Psi_{GM}}(x) = g_{max}(x) - gm$;
10   **else**
11 | $g_{\Psi_{GM}}(x) = g_{min}(x) + gm$;
12   **end**
13 **end**

The graphical interpretation of the proposed method for the two-dimensional data set and three base classifiers is shown in Figs. 1 and 2. Decision boundaries defined by 3 linear classifiers are presented in Fig. 1. In addition, there are also marked values of h_1, h_2 which are distances between the decision boundaries $g_{\Psi_1}(x), g_{\Psi_2}(x), g_{\Psi_3}(x))$ in point x. From these distances the geometric mean is calculated. The decision boundaries defined by the majority vote method (for the base classifier presented in Fig. 1) and the method of integration base classifiers in the geometry space by using the geometric mean are presented in Fig. 2. The decision boundary defined by the majority vote method is the piecewise linear function (green line) when the decision boundary defined by the proposed method is a polynomial function (red line).

The earlier work [3] presents results of the integration base classifier in the geometric space in which the harmonic mean is used. In the paper [2] the fusion of classifiers is preceded by the selection process and the average is used during integration of base classifiers.

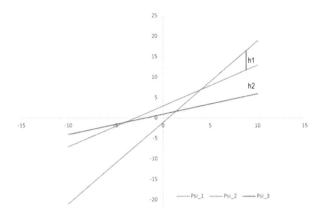

Fig. 1. Decision boundaries defined by 3 linear classifiers (Color figure online)

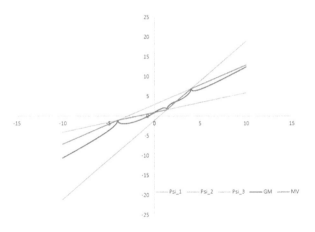

Fig. 2. Decision boundaries defined by the majority vote method (MV) and the method of integration of base classifiers in the geometry space by using the geometric mean (GM) (Color figure online)

4   Experimental Studies

The main aim of the experiments was to compare the quality of classifications of the proposed base classifiers integration algorithm Ψ_{GM} with majority voting rule Ψ_{MV} and all base classifiers $\Psi_1, ..., \Psi_3$.

In the experiment as base classifiers we used: Fisher linear discriminant rule, the Logistic regression model and the nearest mean rule. In the experimental research we use 10 real world problems from UCI machine learning repository and the KEEL Project. We used binary data sets and the feature selection process [9,14] was performed to indicate two most informative features. In Table 1 the numbers of attributes and available examples are presented. All experiments were repeated 10 times and averages were computed as the final results.

Table 1. Description of data sets selected for the experiments

Data set	Examples	Attributes
Blood Transfusion	748	5
Bupa	345	6
Haberman's Survival	306	3
Magic Gamma Telescope	19020	11
Phoneme	5404	5
Pima Indians Diabetes	768	8
Sonar	208	60
Spambase	4597	57
Twonorm	7400	20
Wdbc	569	30

Table 2 shows the classification accuracy (ACC) while Table 3 shows the Matthews correlation coefficient (MCC). Additionally, the mean ranks obtained by the Friedman test are presented. Lower average rank values indicate better classification results. In the case of ACC measure, the proposed method Ψ_{GM} proved to be more effective than all base classifiers Ψ_1, Ψ_2, Ψ_3 and the MV method Ψ_{MV}. Using the post-hoc Nemenyi test at 0.05 significance level (critical difference equal 1.92), we conclude that the proposed method Ψ_{GM} is significantly better than the nearest mean approach. However, the MV method is statistically equivalent to all base classifiers. It should be noted that the post-hoc

Table 2. Classification accuracy and mean rank positions for the base classifiers Ψ_1, Ψ_2, Ψ_3, the majority voting method Ψ_{MV} and the proposed method Ψ_{GM} produced by the Friedman test

Data set	Ψ_1	Ψ_2	Ψ_3	Ψ_{MV}	Ψ_{GM}
Blood	0.767	0.767	0.675	0.766	0.775
Bupa	0.583	0.583	0.568	0.583	0.583
Haberman	0.745	0.742	0.719	0.745	0.745
Magic	0.780	0.790	0.749	0.790	0.793
Phoneme	0.748	0.742	0.711	0.748	0.748
Pima	0.767	0.764	0.727	0.767	0.770
Sonar	0.755	0.760	0.702	0.755	0.760
Spambase	0.748	0.768	0.757	0.755	0.763
Twonorm	0.721	0.721	0.721	0.721	0.721
Wdbc	0.851	0.896	0.840	0.882	0.859
Mean rank	3.10	2.60	4.60	2.80	1.90

Table 3. Matthews correlation coefficient and mean rank positions for the base classifiers Ψ_1, Ψ_2, Ψ_3, the majority voting method Ψ_{MV} and the proposed method Ψ_{GM} produced by the Friedman test

Data set	Ψ_1	Ψ_2	Ψ_3	Ψ_{MV}	Ψ_{GM}
Blood	0.154	0.154	0.165	0.148	0.210
Bupa	0.046	0.046	0.149	0.046	0.045
Haberman	0.194	0.165	0.306	0.194	0.194
Magic	0.498	0.523	0.438	0.523	0.526
Phoneme	0.345	0.319	0.420	0.346	0.351
Pima	0.464	0.457	0.411	0.464	0.471
Sonar	0.511	0.518	0.407	0.509	0.508
Spambase	0.461	0.507	0.483	0.477	0.493
Twonorm	0.442	0.442	0.441	0.442	0.445
Wdbc	0.682	0.776	0.664	0.747	0.747
Mean rank	3.40	2.90	3.30	3.15	2.25

Nemenyi test at $p = 0.05$, $p = 0.1$ significance level, is not powerful enough to detect any significant differences between the proposed algorithm and the MV method. In case of MCC measure, no statistical difference between classifiers was found. However, the proposed method has the lowest average rank.

5   Conclusion

In this paper we propose the fusion method that uses decision boundary of the base classifiers to calculate the decision boundary of EoC. The algorithm presented in the paper concerns the case of 3 basic classifiers and two-dimensional features space. Additionally, in the proposed method we use geometric mean calculated between the decision boundary.

The aim of the experiments was to compare the proposed algorithm Ψ_{GM} with base classifiers and the majority voting method Ψ_{MV}. Two measures were used to determine the quality of the classification: accuracy and Matthews correlation coefficient. The results of the experiment show that the proposed integration algorithm is better than MV method because the proposed method has the lowest average rank obtained by Friedman test.

Acknowledgments.. This work was supported in part by the National Science Centre, Poland under the grant no. 2017/25/B/ST6/01750.

References

1. Britto, A.S., Sabourin, R., Oliveira, L.E.: Dynamic selection of classifiersa comprehensive review. Pattern Recognit. **47**(11), 3665–3680 (2014)
2. Burduk, R.: Integration base classifiers based on their decision boundary. In: Rutkowski, L., Korytkowski, M., Scherer, R., Tadeusiewicz, R., Zadeh, L.A., Zurada, J.M. (eds.) ICAISC 2017. LNCS (LNAI), vol. 10246, pp. 13–20. Springer, Cham (2017). https://doi.org/10.1007/978-3-319-59060-8_2
3. Burduk, R.: Integration base classifiers in geometry space by harmonic mean. In: Rutkowski, L., Scherer, R., Korytkowski, M., Pedrycz, W., Tadeusiewicz, R., Zurada, J.M. (eds.) ICAISC 2018. LNCS (LNAI), vol. 10841, pp. 585–592. Springer, Cham (2018). https://doi.org/10.1007/978-3-319-91253-0_54
4. Cavalin, P.R., Sabourin, R., Suen, C.Y.: Dynamic selection approaches for multiple classifier systems. Neural Comput. Appl. **22**(3–4), 673–688 (2013)
5. Cyganek, B.: One-class support vector ensembles for image segmentation and classification. J. Math. Imaging Vis. **42**(2–3), 103–117 (2012)
6. Didaci, L., Giacinto, G., Roli, F., Marcialis, G.L.: A study on the performances of dynamic classifier selection based on local accuracy estimation. Pattern Recognit. **38**, 2188–2191 (2005)
7. Drucker, H., Cortes, C., Jackel, L.D., LeCun, Y., Vapnik, V.: Boosting and other ensemble methods. Neural Comput. **6**(6), 1289–1301 (1994)
8. Giacinto, G., Roli, F.: An approach to the automatic design of multiple classifier systems. Pattern Recognit. Lett. **22**, 25–33 (2001)
9. Guyon, I., Elisseeff, A.: An introduction to variable and feature selection. J. Mach. Learn. Res. **3**, 1157–1182 (2003)
10. Kuncheva, L.I.: Combining Pattern Classifiers: Methods and Algorithms. Wiley, New York (2004)
11. Li, Y., Meng, D., Gui, Z.: Random optimized geometric ensembles. Neurocomputing **94**, 159–163 (2012)
12. Ponti, Jr., M.P.: Combining classifiers: from the creation of ensembles to the decision fusion. In: 2011 24th SIBGRAPI Conference on Graphics, Patterns and Images Tutorials (SIBGRAPI-T), pp. 1–10. IEEE (2011)
13. Pujol, O., Masip, D.: Geometry-based ensembles: toward a structural characterization of the classification boundary. IEEE Trans. Pattern Anal. Mach. Intell. **31**(6), 1140–1146 (2009)
14. Rejer, I.: Genetic algorithms for feature selection for brain computer interface. Int. J. Pattern Recogn. Artif. Intell. **29**(5), 1559008 (2015)
15. Ruta, D., Gabrys, B.: Classifier selection for majority voting. Inf. Fusion **6**(1), 63–81 (2005)
16. Tulyakov, S., Jaeger, S., Govindaraju, V., Doermann, D.: Review of classifier combination methods. In: Marinai, S., Fujisawa, H. (eds.) Machine Learning in Document Analysis and Recognition, vol. 90, pp. 361–386. Springer, Heidelberg (2008). https://doi.org/10.1007/978-3-540-76280-5_14
17. Woźniak, M., Graña, M., Corchado, E.: A survey of multiple classifier systems as hybrid systems. Inf. Fusion **16**, 3–17 (2014)
18. Xu, L., Krzyzak, A., Suen, C.Y.: Methods of combining multiple classifiers and their applications to handwriting recognition. IEEE Trans. Syst. Man Cybern. **22**(3), 418–435 (1992)

Parallel C–Fuzzy Random Forest

Łukasz Gadomer$^{(\boxtimes)}$ and Zenon A. Sosnowski$^{(\boxtimes)}$

Faculty of Computer Science, Bialystok University of Technology,
Wiejska 45A, 15-351 Bialystok, Poland
{l.gadomer,z.sosnowski}@pb.edu.pl
http://www.wi.pb.edu.pl

Abstract. The C–fuzzy random forest is a novel ensemble classifier which uses C-fuzzy decision trees as unit classifiers. The main problem connected with this classifier is a relatively long learning process time. In this paper the method of reducing the C–fuzzy random forest's learning time is proposed. Authors proposed and described the method of parallelization of this classifier's learning process by generating trees which are the parts of the forest in separate threads. The experiments which were designed to check the effectiveness of the proposed method were performed and the results were presented and discussed.

Keywords: C–fuzzy decision tree · C–fuzzy random forest
Parallel computing

1 Introduction

C–fuzzy random forest is our ensemble classifier. It combines the reliability of a forest — a classifier which consist of many trees — with the strength of randomness. This kind of forest uses C–fuzzy decision trees as a unit classifier. The final decision made by the forest bases on the decisions of C–fuzzy decision trees. The main problem connected with C–fuzzy random forest is its working time, especially for relatively big datasets. C–fuzzy decision trees by their nature are relatively large and for datasets consisting of many attributes and objects their learning time can be quite long. This problem multiplies for an ensemble classifier which consists of many such trees — every tree must be constructed separately. The same issue concerns the decision–making process. The idea of resolving this problem and the main topic of this paper is using parallel computing to reduce C–fuzzy random forest learning time.

In the first part of this paper the basic issues connected with the created classifier are presented. The ideas of Fuzzy random forest and C–fuzzy decision trees are described shortly. Then, the C–fuzzy random forest classifier is presented. After that, the meaning of parallel computing is presented. In the main part of this paper, the idea of using parallel computing to improve C–fuzzy random forest working time is presented. Performed experiments are described and explained, then achieved results are presented and discussed.

© Springer Nature Switzerland AG 2018
K. Saeed and W. Homenda (Eds.): CISIM 2018, LNCS 11127, pp. 254–265, 2018.
https://doi.org/10.1007/978-3-319-99954-8_22

2   Related Work

The idea of C–fuzzy random forest is based on the Fuzzy Random Forest. Before presenting this issue it is worth to take a look at two classifiers which are the fundaments of the mentioned forest. The first one is the Fuzzy Tree, the second one is the Random Forest. Both of these issues are described in following paragraphs.

2.1   Fuzzy Random Forests

Fuzzy random forest [1–3] is a classifier which joins Fuzzy decision trees [8] with Random forest [4]. This classifier's construction process is similar to Forest–RI [4]. When the forest is constructed, the algorithm begins from the root of each tree. At first, a random set of attributes is chosen. For each of these attributes information gain is computed, using all of the objects from training set. Attribute with the highest information gain is chosen to node split. After splitting, the selected attribute is removed from the set of attributes possible to select in order to divide the following nodes. Then, for all of the following tree nodes, this operation is repeated using a new set of randomly selected attributes (excluding attributes used before) and the same training set.

During the tree's construction process, when the node is being divided, the object's membership degree to the node is being computed. Before the division, for each node the membership degree is 1. When the division is completed, each object can belong to any number of created leaves (at least one). If the object belongs to one leaf, its membership degree to this leaf achieves 1 (for the other leaves it is equal to 0). If it belongs to more leaves, the membership degree to each leaf take values between 0 and 1 and it sums to 1 in the set of all children of the node. If the division is performed using attribute with missing value, the object is assigned to each split node with the same membership degree.

According to described algorithm trees are constructed. Each tree is created using randomly selected set of attributes, different for each tree. It makes each tree in the forest a bit different.

2.2   C–Fuzzy Decision Trees

In [15] Pedrycz and Sosnowski proposed the new kind of decision trees, called C–Fuzzy Decision Trees. This class of trees was a response to the main problems of traditional trees. They usually operate on a relatively small set of discrete attributes. To split the node in the tree construction process, the single attribute which brings the most information gain is chosen. In their traditional form such trees are designed to operate on discrete class problems (regression trees deal with continuous decision attribute problems). These assumptions bring some problems. To handle continuous values it is necessary to perform the discretization, which can impact on the overall performance of the tree. What is more, information brought by the nodes which were not selected to split the given node forfeits as it is not used in the tree construction process.

C–Fuzzy Decision Trees were developed to resolve these problems. The idea of such trees assumes treating data as collection of information granules (analogous to fuzzy clusters). Authors decided to span the proposed tree over these granules. The data is grouped in such clusters characterized by high homogenity (low variablity), which are the generic building blocks of the tree.

The construction of C–Fuzzy Decision Tree starts from grouping the data set into c clusters. It is performed in the way that the similar objects are placed in the same cluster. Each cluster is characterized by its prototype (centroid), which is randomly selected first and then improved iteratively during the tree construction process. When objects are grouped into clusters, the diversity of the each of these clusters is computed using the given heterogenity criterion. From all of the nodes the most heterogenous is chosen to split. The selected node is divided into c clusters using fuzzy clustering. Then, for the newly created nodes, the diversity is computed and the selection to split is performed. This algorithm works until it achieves the given stop criterion.

When the tree is constructed it can be used for classification. Each object which has to be classified starts from the root node. The membership degrees of this object to the children of the given node are computed. These membership degrees are the numbers between 0 and 1 and they sum to 1. The node where the object belongs with the highest membership is chosen and the object is getting there. The same operation is repeated as long as the object achieves to the node which has no children. The classification result is the class assigned to achieved node.

3   C–Fuzzy Random Forest

To describe created classifier we used the following notations (based on [2, 15]):

- T is the number of trees in the C–fuzzy random forest ensemble,
- t is the particular tree,
- N_t is the number of nodes in the tree t,
- n is a particular leaf reached in a tree,
- I is the number of classes,
- i is a particular class,
- C_FRF is a matrix with size $(T \times MAX_{N_t})$ with $MAX_{N_t} = max\{N_1, N_2, ..., N_t\}$, where each element of the matrix is a vector of size I containing the support for every class provided by every activated leaf n on each tree t; this matrix represents C–Fuzzy Forest or C–fuzzy random forest,
- c is the number of clusters,
- E is a training dataset,
- e is a data instance,
- $V = [V_1, V_2, ..., V_b]$ is the variability vector.
- $U = [U_1, U_2, ..., U_{|E|}]$ is the tree's partition matrix of the training objects,
- $U_i = [u_1, u_2, ..., u_c]$ are memberships of the ith object to the c cluster,
- b is the number of unsplitted nodes,
- $B = \{B_1, B_2, ..., B_b\}$ are the unsplitted nodes,

In [6] we proposed the new kind of classifiers: Fuzzy random forest with C–fuzzy decision trees, which we called C–fuzzy random forest. It bases on the idea of Fuzzy random forest and consists of C–Fuzzy Decision Trees. Combination these two structures was expected and proved to give promising results.

The randomness in C–fuzzy random forest is ensured by two main aspects. The first of them refers to the Random forest. During the tree's construction process, node to split is selected randomly. The second aspect refers to the C–fuzzy decision trees and it concerns the creation of partition matrix. At first, the centroid (prototype) of the each cluster selection is fully random. Objects which belong to the parent node are divided into clusters grouped around these centroids using the shortest distance criterion. Then the prototypes and the partition matrix are being corrected as long as they achieve the stop criterion. Each tree in the forest, created the described way, can be selected from the set of created trees. To create the single tree which will be chosen to the forest there can be build the set of trees. Each tree from such set is tested and the best of these trees (the one which achieved the best classification accuracy for the training set) is being chosen as the part of forest. The size of the set is given and the same for the each tree in the forest.

The split selection idea is similar to the one used in Fuzzy random forest. The difference is about the nature of tree used in the classifier. In Fuzzy Random Forest, the random attribute was being chosen to split. The node which was chosen to split was specified by tree growth strategy. In C–fuzzy random forest for each of the splits all of the attributes are considered. The choice concerns the node to split selection which means some nodes does not have to be split (when the stop criterion is achieved). The same idea is expressed in two different ways of building trees. Each C–fuzzy decision tree in the forest can be completely different or very similar — it depends on the stop criterion and the number of clusters. The influence of randomness can be set using algorithm parameters which allows classifier to fit the given problem in a flexible way.

Prototypes of each cluster are selected randomly and then corrected iteratively, which means some of created trees can work better than others. Diversity of trees created that way depends on the number of the iterations of the correction process. It is possible to build many trees and choose only the best of them to the forest in order to achieve better results. The diversity of the trees in the forest can be modified by changing the size of the set from which the best tree is chosen and the number of iterations. These parameters specifiy the strength of randomness in the classifier. Operating on these values also allow to fit to the given problem to improve the classification quality.

3.1   C–Fuzzy Random Forest Learning

The process of C–fuzzy random forest learning is analogous to the learning of Fuzzy Random Forest, proposed in [2]. The differences concern two aspects. First is about the kind of trees used in the forest. The proposed classifier uses C–Fuzzy Decision Trees instead of Janikow's Fuzzy Trees. The second aspect refers to the way of random selection of the node to split, which was described before.

C–fuzzy random forest is created using Algorithm 1.

Algorithm 1. C–fuzzy random forest learning

1: **procedure** FRFwC–FDTLEARNING
2:     **for** 1 to T **do**
3:         1. Take a random sample of $|E|$ examples with replacement from the dataset E
4:         2. Apply Algorithm 2 to the subset of examples obtained in the previous step to construct C–Fuzzy Decision Tree
5:     **end for**
6: **end procedure**

Each tree in C–fuzzy random forest is created using Algorithm 2.

Algorithm 2. C–Fuzzy Decision Tree learning

1: **procedure** C–FDTLEARNING
2:     1. Start with the examples in E
3:     2. Create the partition matrix U randomly
4:     3. Perform FCM
5:     **while** Stop criterion is not satisfied **do**
6:         4. Divide the samples belonging to the splitted node into its children
7:         5. Make a random selection of nodes from the set of unsplitted nodes B
8:         6. Compute the variability matrix V
9:         7. Choose the node with maximum variability to split nodes
10:         8. Perform FCM
11:     **end while**
12: **end procedure**

3.2   C–Fuzzy Random Forest Classification

After the C–fuzzy random forest is constructed it can be used for new object's classification. The decision–making strategy used in the proposed sollution assumes making decision by forest after each tree's decisions are made.[1] It is performed according to the Algorithm 3. It can be described by equation, similar to the one presented in [2]:

$$
D_F RF(t, i, C\_FRF) = \begin{cases} 1 \text{ if } i = arg \max_{j, j=1,2,...,I} \left\{ \sum_{n=1}^{N_t} C\_FRF_{t,n,j} \right\} \\ 0 \text{ otherwise} \end{cases}
$$

---

[1] There is also another decision–making strategy which assumes making the single decision by the whole forest. It is described in [2].

Algorithm 3. C–fuzzy random forest classification

1: **procedure** FRFwC–FDTCLASSIFICATION
2:     DecisionOfTrees
3:     DecisionOfForest
4: **end procedure**
5: **procedure** DECISIONOFTREES
6:     **for** 1 to T **do**
7:         1. Run the example e to obtain the tree's partition matrix U_i
8:         2. Choose the class c where $c = arg \max_{i,i=1,2,...,I} D\_FRF_{t,i,C\_FRF}$
9:     **end for**
10: **end procedure**
11: **procedure** DECISIONOFFOREST
12:     Assign to class according to the simple majority vote of trees decisions
13: **end procedure**

3.3   Parallel Computing

The idea of parallel computing is to perform the computations, which are independent of each other, at the same time. In theory, the typical algorithm is executed sequentially. Let's assume that hypothetical algorithm consists of p iterations of the similar and completely independent sequences of operations. It means that this algorithm could be successfully divided into p or less parts, which could be computed separately. Each such part is computed by different processing element. Let the execution time of sequential algorithm be $T(1)$ and the execution time of parallel algorithm consisting of p processing elements be $T(p)$ (we assume that each part is computed at the same time). The speedup $S(p)$ can be defined as [11]:

$$S(p) = \frac{T(1)}{T(p)} \tag{1}$$

If the parallelization was performed in a perfect way, in theory it should be possible to achieve the perfect speedup, which is $S(p) = p$. This kind of speedup is called linear. Sometimes it happens that $S(p) > p$, which makes the speedup superlinear — however, such situation happens hardly ever. In a typical situation it is not possible to achieve perfect (linear) speedup — $S(p) < p$. It is caused by many factors, but the most important are:

– the time markup connected with the necessity of dividing algorithm into parts, sending them to processing elements and collecting results achieved in a parallel way,
– the delays caused by the communication between parallely executed parts of algorithm (in practical situations, these parts are hardly ever completely separated).

The measure of the fraction of time for which a processing element is usefully employed is called Efficiency — E(p). It is the ratio of speedup to the number of processing elements [11]:

$$E(p) = \frac{S(p)}{p} = \frac{T(1)}{p \times T(p)} \tag{2}$$

In a ideal parallel system, the $E(p) = 1$. For a superlinear speedup, the $E(p) > 1$. In practice, most parallel systems are slower than linear: $0 < E(p) < 1$. [11]

Parallel systems can be realized in many different ways. It is performed on machines (or group of machines), which can be called parallel computers. The examples parallel computing ways with such computers (classification based on a distance between computing nodes) are [14]:

– Multi–core computing – single processor with multiple cores,
– Symmetric multiprocessing – single computer with multiple processors,
– Cluster computing – multiple computers connected by a network,
– Grid computing – multiple computers communicating over the Internet.

There are also many other ways of performing parallel computing than using processors. The most popular are [14]:

– Graphics processing unit (GPU) – using many simple units, created to deal with processing graphics, to perform operations not typical for graphics,
– Vector processors – using the processor to perform the same instructions on large sets of data.

No matter which parallel computing structure is used, the aim is the same: to make the computation times faster by computing some parts of the algorithm in a parallel way. The selection of the parallel computing structure should be adjusted to the given problem. For a typical and quite simple algorithms which operate on a relatively small dataset, the multi–core computing or symmetric multiprocessing should be enough. For a bigger problems operating on a big data it is more suitable to choose cluster computing or grid computing. Algorithms with multiple simple operations can be successfully parallelized on graphics processing units.

Many authors widely use parallel computing in their research. There were also multiple researches which performed parallelization of forests. The example parallel optimization of Random Forest algorithm was presented in [13]. Authors performed their parallelization on IPython - an interactive Python with parallelization functionalities. They tested the implementation on 107 samples dataset, using EC2 cluster with 32 cores and it showed 80% of CPU utilization. In [5] authors presented the Parallel Random Forest (PRF) algorithm, implemented on the Apache Spark platform. Their algorithm was dedicated to operate on big data. The Parallel Random Forest algorithm's optimization is based on a hybrid approach, which combines data–parallel and task-parallel optimization.

The another popular way of using parallel computing is using graphics units. In [10] authors use graphics processing units for fast simulations of magnetic resonance imaging (MRI). They accelerate MRI simulations with general purpose computation on GPU (GPGPU). The another example of using GPGPU to accelerate computations is [9]. Authors propose GPGPU parallelization of evolutionary induction of decision trees. They show that this process can be accelerated even up to 800 times with GPGPU. Using this method of parallelization also allowed them for processing much larger datasets.

4   Parallelization of C–Fuzzy Random Forest

One of the greatest problems connected with C–fuzzy random forest classifier is its learning time, especially for large classifiers. This problem is connected with C–fuzzy decision tree's nature. This kind of tree has tendency to overgrowth, especially for large datasets, large number of assumed clusters and not restrictive stop criteria. As a result, C–fuzzy decision tree's learning process may take some time. This problem's size is multiplied if C–fuzzy decision trees are used in an ensemble classifier, which takes place for C–fuzzy random forest.

The C–fuzzy random forest's learning algorithm idea is about learn all of the trees which are the part of an ensemble classifier separately and then use all of them to make the final decision. It means each tree can be learn independent of the other ones. It means that the whole C–fuzzy random forest learning algorithm, which is definitely the most time consuming part of this classifier's working cycle, can be fully parallelized. Each tree can be learned separately in its own thread at the same time as the other trees.

Parallelizing C–fuzzy random forest's learning process means that in the most optimistic situation it is expected to learn the whole forest in the same time as a single tree (or at least in a similar time). To prove this and to make our classifier more attractive, the experiments which allow to rate the algorithm's parallelization potential were preformed. These experiments are described in Sect. 5, their results are presented in Sect. 6.

5   Experimental Studies

In order to check the C–fuzzy random forest parallelization potential several experiments were performed. To make the research process continuous, the same datasets which were used in [6] were also used for the current experiments. These datasets were downloaded from UCI Machine Learning Repository [12]. The mentioned are Hepatitis, Dermatology, Pima Indians Diabetes and Ionosphere. The choice of the datasets was motivated by several aspects. They are popular and widely known which gives an opportunity to compare results with another solutions. They represent different real life problems and they differ between each other. All of them were used in our previous researches, which allow to compare achieved results with the results obtained before.

Each dataset was divided into five parts with equal size (or as close to the equal as it's possible) randomly. Each of these parts had the same proportions of objects representing each decision class as it is in the whole dataset (or as close to the same as it's possible). There were no situations when in some of parts there weren't any objects representing some of decision classes. This random and proportional division was saved and used for each experiment.

Each experiment was performed using 5–fold crossvalidation. Four of five parts were used to train the classifier, one to test the learned forest. This operation was repeated five times, each time the other part was excluded from training and used for testing the classifier. After that, classification accuracy of all five out of bag parts were averaged.

Experiments were performed on the same machine which was used for experiments presented in [6]. It was a single personal computer with four core CPU, 3.5 GHz each. Each of these cores has two threads, which allows to perform computations using eight different threads at the same time.

For each dataset the parallelized forest was constructed using 256 trees. Each tree was built using 5 clusters. Parallelization levels from 1 to 16 were tested. As the processor which was used to perform computations has 8 threads, it is expected to achieve the benefits from parallelization with maximum 8 threads. The further increasing of parallelization level using this machine should not improve (cut) the computation time.

The objective of the research is to prove the possibility of successful parallelization of C–fuzzy random forest learning process, which should allow to achieve similar C–fuzzy random forest learning times to single C–fuzzy decision time learning time.

Achieved results are presented in paragraph Sect. 6.

6   Results and Discussion

The results for tested datasets are presented in Tables 1 (Hepatitis), Table 2 (Dermatology), Table 3 (Pima Indians Diabetes) and Table 4 (Ionosphere).

The results from table are visualized on Fig. 1 (speedup) and Fig. 2 (efficiency).

The results show that for each dataset the tendencies were similar. The greatest speedup and the best efficiency (close to linear or, form Pima Indians Diabetes, even slightly superlinear) were achieved with increasing the number of

Table 1. Results – Hepatitis

Number of threads	Computation time	Speedup	Efficiency
1	00:11:14.28	1	1
2	00:05:41.68	1.973425427	0.986712714
3	00:04:03.47	2.769458249	0.92315275
4	00:03:07.51	3.595968215	0.898992054
5	00:02:54.48	3.864511692	0.772902338
6	00:02:46.41	4.051919957	0.675319993
7	00:02:37.95	4.268945869	0.60984941
8	00:02:30.02	4.49460072	0.56182509
9	00:02:37.65	4.277069458	0.47522994
10	00:02:34.45	4.365684688	0.436568469
11	00:02:37.19	4.289585852	0.38996235
12	00:02:36.12	4.318985396	0.35991545
13	00:02:39.62	4.224282671	0.324944821
14	00:02:37.91	4.270027231	0.305001945
15	00:02:38.48	4.254669359	0.283644624
16	00:02:37.68	4.276255708	0.267265982

Table 2. Results – Dermatology

Number of threads	Computation time	Speedup	Efficiency
1	00:15:28.54	1	1
2	00:08:04.52	1.916412119	0.95820606
3	00:05:34.54	2.775572428	0.925190809
4	00:04:27.18	3.47533498	0.868833745
5	00:03:57.98	3.90175645	0.78035129
6	00:03:58.23	3.897661923	0.649610321
7	00:03:35.51	4.308570368	0.615510053
8	00:03:26.57	4.495038002	0.56187975
9	00:03:25.26	4.523726006	0.502636223
10	00:03:35.86	4.30158436	0.430158436
11	00:03:35.66	4.305573588	0.391415781
12	00:03:27.62	4.472305173	0.372692098
13	00:03:35.22	4.314375987	0.331875076
14	00:03:25.01	4.529242476	0.32351732
15	00:03:35.67	4.305373951	0.28702493
16	00:03:36.97	4.279577822	0.267473614

Table 3. Results – Pima Indians Diabetes

Number of threads	Computation time	Speedup	Efficiency
1	00:29:58.08	1	1
2	00:14:56.55	2.005554626	1.002777313
3	00:10:39.48	2.811784575	0.937261525
4	00:08:15.21	3.630944448	0.907736112
5	00:07:40.91	3.901152069	0.780230414
6	00:07:15.89	4.125077428	0.687512905
7	00:06:50.86	4.376381249	0.625197321
8	00:06:30.21	4.607980318	0.57599754
9	00:06:44.16	4.448931116	0.49432568
10	00:06:47.90	4.40813925	0.440813925
11	00:06:47.05	4.417344307	0.401576755
12	00:06:37.57	4.522675252	0.376889604
13	00:06:55.53	4.327196592	0.332861276
14	00:06:35.30	4.548646598	0.324903328
15	00:06:46.82	4.419841699	0.294656113
16	00:06:38.85	4.508160963	0.28176006

Table 4. Results – Ionosphere

Number of threads	Computation time	Speedup	Efficiency
1	00:27:14.67	1	1
2	00:13:43.95	1.9839432	0.9919716
3	00:09:36.47	2.835654934	0.945218311
4	00:07:24.90	3.674241403	0.918560351
5	00:06:50.86	3.97865453	0.795730906
6	00:06:34.73	4.141235781	0.690205964
7	00:06:18.44	4.319495825	0.617070832
8	00:05:59.62	4.545548079	0.56819351
9	00:06:21.00	4.290472441	0.47671916
10	00:06:16.60	4.340600106	0.434060011
11	00:06:10.42	4.413017656	0.401183423
12	00:06:05.37	4.474012645	0.372834387
13	00:06:26.94	4.224608466	0.324969882
14	00:06:22.08	4.278344849	0.305596061
15	00:06:04.56	4.483953259	0.298930217
16	00:06:07.14	4.45244321	0.278277701

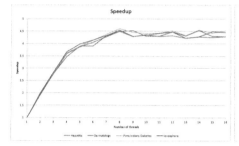

Fig. 1. Speedup

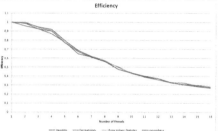

Fig. 2. Efficiency

threads from 1 to 2. While increasing the number of threads from 2 to 4, the benefits from parallelizm were also significant. The further increasing of the number of threads from 4 to 8 still caused the improvement of the speedup and efficiency, but it was a bit smaller than before. The number of threads larger than 8 did not cause the further improvement of the computation time — it was even slower than before.

These observations cleary correspond with the assumptions, theory and expectations. The processor used for the research has four physical cores, so parallelizing computations into four threads gave the best results. Another four threads was utilized by using the second thread on each physical core. Using those threads also allowed to improve computation time, but the improvement was a bit less significant than using only physical threads. The further increasing of the number of threads did not improve achieved results, as the used machine had not more free processing units which could parallelize these threads successfully. What is more, the further increasing of the number of threads slowed up computations a bit, which is connected with the cost of communication between useless threads.

Although the results for all of the datasets were similar, it is possible observe that some datasets could be parallelized more successfully than others. The greatest speedup and efficiency were achieved for Pima Indians Diabetes and

Ionosphere datasets. Noticeably worse improvements were observed for Dermatology and Hepatitis datasets.

7   Conclusion

The idea of parallelizing computations with C–fuzzy random forest was presented in this paper. The most time–consuming part of C–fuzzy random forest working algorithm — the learning process — was parallelized the way trees were being trained in separate threads.

The experiments showed that the proposed way of parallelizing C–fuzzy random forest learning process can significantly reduce the algorithm's working time. Even using the single processor with 4 cores (8 threads) showed that this way of parallelizing, using efficient parallel computer, can reduce the forest learning time almost to the single tree learning time. Of course such perfect parallelization is not possible because of the necessity of the communication between threads, but omitting this limit the parallelization would be close to linear. C-fuzzy random forest's nature and the way of its construction makes this classifier susceptible to parallelization.

Of course the proposed way of parallelization is not the only possible way of improving C-fuzzy random forest working time. Even a single tree learning process can be parallelized, as there are many operations within this process which can be performed separately. Such parts which are possible to parallelization can be divided into even smaller parts, which also gives opportunity to use other parallelization methods, for example using GPU. Another algorithm parts which can be parallelized are connected with the extensions of C–fuzzy random forest, for example using OWA operators [7]. This way of deeper parallelization of C–fuzzy random forest working algorithm can be the object of the further studies.

Acknowledgment. This work was supported by the grant S/WI/3/2018 from Bialystok University of Technology founded by Ministry of Science and Higher Education.

References

1. Bonissone, P.P., Cadenas, J.M., Garrido, M.C., Diaz-Valladares, R.A.: A fuzzy random forest: Fundamental for design and construction. In: Proceedings of the 12th International Conference on Information Processing and Management of Uncertainty in Knowledge- Based Systems (IPMU 2008), pp. 1231–1238 (2008)
2. Bonissone, P., Cadenas, J.M., Carmen Garrido, M., Andres Diaz-Valladares, R.: A fuzzy random forest. Int. J. Approx. Reason. **51**(7), 729–747 (2010)
3. Bonissone, P.P., Cadenas, J.M., Garrido, M.C., Diaz-Valladares, R.A.: Combination methods in a Fuzzy Random Forest. In: IEEE International Conference on Systems, Man and Cybernetics, SMC 2008, pp. 1794–1799, October 2008
4. Breiman, L.: Random forests. Mach. Learn. **45**(1), 5–32 (2001)
5. Chen, J., et al.: A parallel random forest algorithm for big data in a spark cloud computing environment. IEEE Trans. Parallel Distrib. Syst. **28**(4), 919–933 (2017)

6. Gadomer, Ł., Sosnowski, Z.A.: Fuzzy random forest with c–fuzzy decision trees. In: Saeed, K., Homenda, W. (eds.) CISIM 2016. LNCS, vol. 9842, pp. 481–492. Springer, Cham (2016). https://doi.org/10.1007/978-3-319-45378-1_43

7. Gadomer, Ł., Sosnowski, Z.A.: Knowledge aggregation in decision-making process with c-fuzzy random forest using OWA operators. Soft Comput., 1–15 (2018)

8. Janikow, C.Z.: Fuzzy decision trees: issues and methods. IEEE Trans. Syst. Man Cybern. Part B Cybern. **28**(1), 1–14 (1998)

9. Jurczuk, K., Czajkowski, M., Kretowski, M.: Evolutionary induction of a decision tree for large-scale data: a GPU-based approach. Soft Comput. **21**(24), 7363–7379 (2017)

10. Jurczuk, K., Kretowski, M., Bezy-Wendling, J.: GPU-based computational modeling of magnetic resonance imaging of vascular structures. Int. J. High Perform. Comput. Appl

11. Kumar, V.: Introduction to Parallel Computing, 2nd edn. Addison-Wesley Longman Publishing Co. Inc., Boston (2002)

12. Lichman, M.: UCI machine learning repository (2013)

13. Limprasert, W.: Parallel random forest with IPython cluster. In: 2015 International Computer Science and Engineering Conference (ICSEC), pp. 1–6, November 2015

14. Patterson, D.A., Hennessy, J.L.: Computer Organization and Design. The Hardware/Software Interface, 5th edn. Morgan Kaufmann Publishers Inc., San Francisco (2013)

15. Pedrycz, W., Sosnowski, Z.A.: C-fuzzy decision trees. IEEE Trans. Syst. Man Cybern. Part C Appl. Rev. **35**(4), 498–511 (2005)

Waste Collection Vehicle Routing Problem on HPC Infrastructure

Ekaterina Grakova$^{(\boxtimes)}$, Kateřina Slaninová$^{(\boxtimes)}$, Jan Martinovič, Jan Křenek,
Jiří Hanzelka, and Václav Svatoň

IT4Innovations, VŠB - Technical University of Ostrava,
17. listopadu 15/2172, 708 33 Ostrava, Czech Republic
{ekaterina.grakova,katerina.slaninova,jan.martinovic,jan.krenek,
jiri.hanzelka,vaclav.svaton}@vsb.cz

Abstract. Waste companies need to reduce the cost of collection of
the municipal waste, to increase the separation rate of different types
of waste, or site of waste source. The collection of waste is an important logistic activity within any city. In this paper, we mainly focus on
the daily commercial waste collection problem. One of the approaches for
how to resolve this problem is to use optimization algorithms. Ant colony
optimisation metaheuristic algorithm (ACO) was used to solve the problem in this paper. This algorithm was adapted for a real data set (Waste
Collection). The aim of this paper is to adapt the ACO algorithm and
run it on HPC infrastructure to resolve the waste collection problem.
We used High-End Application Execution Middleware (HEAppE), that
provides smart access to the supercomputing infrastructure (in our case
Salomon cluster operated by IT4Innovations National Supercomputing
Centre in the Czech Republic). The results showed that the paralelisation
of the algorithm is beneficial and brings together with the supercomputing power the possibility to solve larger problems of this type.

Keywords: Waste collection · Vehicle routing problem · Recycling
Trash cans

1 Introduction

Nowadays, people produce large amounts of waste. With the increase of waste
volume, it is necessary to transport it and ecologically dispose, or in better
cases, to recycle. There are several options for waste treatment: (a) landfilling of
waste, (b) waste incineration, (c) higher level of waste sorting, i.e. the collection
of separated waste and its further material and energy utilization. The waste
itself is very diverse, so it is desirable to separate some of its components from
the total amount of waste. Depending on its nature, the components can be
further processed. At the beginning of the last century, the municipal waste was
the ash from stove. Today municipal waste consists mainly of food packaging
and from consumer goods. Nevertheless, the amount of waste is still growing.

© Springer Nature Switzerland AG 2018
K. Saeed and W. Homenda (Eds.): CISIM 2018, LNCS 11127, pp. 266–278, 2018.
https://doi.org/10.1007/978-3-319-99954-8_23

It is about $531\,kg$ per year per resident in the Czech Republic [1]. The most often waste is classified according to the following types: paper, plastics, glass, bio waste, municipal solid waste, combustible waste.

Waste companies need to reduce the cost of the municipal waste collection, to increase the rate of the separation of the different types of waste, site of the waste source, and to increase the waste sorting (pricing of waste collection, motivation of residents and companies, support for the concept of the waste management). One of the approaches to resolve this problem is to use optimization algorithms. The aim of this paper is to adapt and connect the ACO algorithm on HPC infrastructure to resolve the waste collection problem. We used a vehicle routing problem (VRP) to solve the problem of waste collection.

The waste collection problem is very difficult to calculate. In large cities, the optimization of waste collection is a very important task. The tasks are broad and very computationally demanding. To solve the problem, we used the meta-heuristics algorithm for the Capacitated VRP. The quality of results from the metaheuristic algorithms depends on settings of input parameters. It is required to run the algorithm with different settings to get the best results. These are the reasons, why we needed to use high performance computing (HPC) to solve the large tasks. In this paper, we used High-End Application Execution Middleware (HEAppE)[1], that provides smart access to the supercomputing infrastructure (in own case Salomon cluster operated by IT4Innovations National Supercomputing Centre in the Czech Republic). HEAppE is able to transfer files between a client application and an HPC infrastructure, and provides necessary functions for job management, monitoring and reporting, user authentication and authorization, file transfer, encryption, and various notification mechanisms. The following Sect. 2 provides a brief state of the art focused on the the waste collection problem and its solutions. A detailed problem formulation is described in Sect. 3, while the metaheuristic ACO algorithm is described in Sect. 4. Section 5 then provides a detailed description of automatic computation on the supercomputing infrastructure. Finally, Sect. 6 concludes the paper.

2   Literature Review

There are several approaches, which address the optimization of the waste collection routes. These are Traveling salesman problem (TSP), Vehicle routing problem (VRP) and Arc routing problem (ARP). TSP represents a business traveler, who has to visit M customers from surrounding K cities just once and then returns to the point of origin. The time required to travel from town i to j town is t_{ij}. The aim is to find the best way in which these cities should be visited, so that the route is as short as possible. Extending TSP is VRP.

VRP is formally defined as a weighted oriented graph $G = (V; H)$ where the nodes are represented by $V = (v_1, \ldots, v_n)$ and the arcs are represented by $H = ((v_i, v_j) : i \neq j)$. A central depot is a special node where every vehicle starts and ends its route. The central depot is denoted by v_0 and the rest of the

---

[1] HEAppE middleware: http://heappe.eu.

nodes are the customers. Each customer has demand q_i, each arc has distance d_i and each vehicle has its capacity c_i [7]. The following constraints have to be complied with:

- Each customer is visited only once by a single vehicle;
- Each vehicle must start and end its route at the depot v_0;
- Total demand of customers served by vehicle cannot exceed capacity c_i.

Arc routing problem (ARP) is a generalization of a Chinese postman problem and many other problems involved. The study of arc routing problems began on August 26, 1735 when Leonhard Euler presented his solution to the Konigsberg bridge problem [9]. Given a connected graph $G = (N, E)$ find a closest tour that visits every edge in E exactly once, or determine that no such tour exists. Euler proved that the Euler Tour exists if and only if every node in G has an even degree. Many years later, Fleury presented an algorithm for constructing an Euler Tour [9]. Chinese postman problem (CPP) is the problem, which searches for the best passage given by the graph, provided that we have to go each edge of the graph at least once. For the first time, this problem was solved by Mei-Ko Kwan, a Chinese mathematician in 1962 [8]. CPP is defined by undirected graph $G = (V, H)$, where the nodes are represented by $V = (1, \ldots, n)$ and the set of undirected edges, which are represented by $H = ((i, j) : i, i \neq j, j \in V)$. The traversal cost t_{ij} of an edge (i, j) in H is supposed to be non-negative and is also called cost or distance of (i, j). For edge, it is usually assumed that $t_{ij} = t_{ji}$.

Another CPP modification is the rural postman problem (RPP), where there are the edges, which do not need to go through, and are therefore only for crossing. This problem belongs among the most common ARP applications.

Windy postman problem (WPP), which was first introduced in 1979 (Minieka) [9], is another problem falling under ARP. WPP depends on the direction from which we come to the edge, which is reflected in the cost of crossing. All of these ARPs can be used on both the oriented and non-oriented graphs.

In this article, we used VRP for waste collection solutions. A large number of authors used VRP to optimize waste collection problem. Authors in [11] used a real life waste collection vehicle routing problem with time windows (VRPTW) with the consideration for multiple disposal trips and drivers lunch breaks. For this type of problem, the authors used Solomon's well-known insertion algorithm, which has been extended. In [10], the authors represented the following type of the problem: waste collection vehicle routing problem with time windows (WCVRPTW). The vehicles must be empty when returning to the depot. Multiple trips to disposal sites are allowed for the vehicles. To resolve the WCVRPTW, the authors used an adaptive large neighborhood search (ALNS). The authors of [12] studied rollon-rolloff vehicle routing problem with time windows (RR-VRPTW). They proposed a large neighborhood search (LNS) based on interactive heuristic approach to solve the problem. In [13], the authors represented a multi-objective genetic algorithm for VRPTW, which used a crossover procedure (Best Cost Route Crossover). The authors in [14] adapted two metaheuristic algorithms: Tabu search (TS) and variable neighborhood search (VNS) to solve the VRPTW problem.

3   Problem Formulation

The problem of routing and planning of the waste collection by the vehicle falls within the classic Capacitated vehicle routing problem (CVRP). The problem is represented by a single depot per town, an operational area (such as a town or villages around the town), a finite number of homogeneous vehicles, and a set of trash cans and dump sites. In the town, there are 10 dump sites, while each site is designed for its type of the waste. When a vehicle is full, it needs to go to the closest available disposal dump site. Each vehicle can make (and typically does) multiple disposal trips per day.

Each stop contains one or more trash cans for emptying. The set of trash cans are served once every two weeks. Each vehicle has a limited capacity. The capacity is determined by the type of the waste and by vehicle types. There are several types of the vehicles, the first type is a vehicle with linear press and the other is a vehicle with an hydraulic arm. Vehicles start from the depot, pick-up the waste from the stops until they are full, dump them at one of the dump sites, repeat pick-up and dumping, and finally return to the depot. The working time is eight hours per day.

The waste trash cans are placed in a group, which is called 'line'. Each 'line' is assigned to the vehicle. The size of the 'line' depends on the type of the trash cans. In the 'line', there may be trash cans of different weights. The frequency of collection of the 'lines' depends on the type of the waste.

Capacity constraints are considered when creating a route: a vehicle capacity. Vehicle capacity is the maximum volume and weight that each vehicle can hold. Each vehicle is assumed to start from a depot and finish at the depot with zero volume. Representation of the problem can be summarized as follows:

– Objectives:
   1. Balance workload among the vehicles;
   2. Minimize the global transportation cost based on the global distance traveled.
– Constraints:
   1. Vehicle capacity (i.e., volume, weight);
   2. Driver working time;
   3. The beginning and the end of the route is in the depot;
   4. All trash cans must be serviced;
   5. Waste must be transported to the closest dump.

There are a lot of algorithms that resolve this type of the problem. In this article, metaheuristics ACO algorithm was adapted.

4   Algorithm for Waste Collection VRP

Ant colony optimization (ACO) is a metaheuristics algorithm, which uses artificial ants to find the solution of the optimization problem. The algorithm represents a behavior of real ants, which always find the shortest path between their nest and a food source thanks to their local message exchange via the deposition of pheromone trails. The ants are blind, so they communicate with each other by means of a pheromone. The ants fundamentally move after the pheromone trails, which the previous ants left. Pheromones on the way constantly evaporate accordingly to the path length. Pheromones on shorter paths evaporate more slowly than pheromones on longer paths. On a shorter path, pheromone increases its concentration, while on a longer path it decreases. After a certain amount of passage, most ants are already on a shorter path, but once in a while, an ant will appear on a longer route. Dorigo [19] represented the ACO model from the biologic phenomenon and used the simulation of ant behavior to solve the TSP problems. The ACO is still being improved and many approaches have been proposed since then. We present an overview of the most popular extensions int he following text, namely Ant System (AS), Ant Colony System (ACS), Max-Min Ant System (MMAS) and Elite Ant System (EAS). The extensions are, in practice, often combined together to provide the best result.

In [15], the authors used ACO algorithm for a real live waste collection problem, which was adapted for a variant of the VRPTW. The aim of the paper [15] was to solve the problem using a minimum number of vehicles and minimizing the total distance crossed by the vehicles. Authors in [16] proposed a model for waste collection arc vehicle routing problem with turn constraints (WCAVRPTC) with the aim of minimizing the length of municipal solid waste (MSW) collection routes, which presents several characteristics derived from traffic regulations. The ACS algorithm in paper [16] is based on a clustering-based multiple strategy. In paper [17], the authors used ACO algorithm for solving solid waste collection problem as a VRP scheduling problem. A set of data modified from the well known 50 customers problems were used to find the route, so that the expected traveling cost was minimized. The authors of paper [18] focused on designing collection routes for urban wastes for the Capacitated ARP (CARP). The authors implemented an ACO algorithm for this type of the problem.

In this article, we implemented the ACO algorithm for CVRP. The original implementation of the algorithm was represented by the authors in paper [19,20]. The implementation from [21] has been adapted to the waste collection problem. We introduce an extended version of the ACO algorithm in Algorithm 1. The basic version of the algorithm has been extended to the task with one central depot and multiple dump sites on which the vehicle carries the waste. For each set of the trash cans is defined by one vehicle.

Table 1 describes meaning of the parameters in the code, its equivalent name in the theory, the default value, and a short description [19]. When the input data and configuration parameters are loaded, they are passed into the *Solve method*. This method returns a collection of the solutions. The first solution is the initial one and then it is compared against the best solution and the iteration of the best solution at the end of every iteration. The *SetInitialPheromone method* just iterates through all the arcs and sets the pheromone value to the initial pheromone from the configuration instance. That we call a *ConstructSolutions method*. This method is responsible for constructing solutions. We have constructed the solutions and the *LocalSearch method* so it is executed. We pass all solutions on and the $2 - Opt$ *algorithm* is performed.

Algorithm 1. Ant Colony Optimization

Input: trash cans, vehicle, distance matrix
Output: order of trash cans, landfills and depots

1. Set initial pheromone for the graph.
2. Generate a new population ants.
   2.1. Generate route for ant.
   2.2. If this is the first route then add depo to the route else add final landfill from the previous route.
   2.3. Add random unassigned trash cans to route until sum of trash cans weights is less or equal to vehicle capacity or all the trash cans are assigned.
   2.4. Add a random landfill to route.
   2.5. If all trash cans are not assigned, continue adding routes to ant by going to Step 2.1, else add depot to this route and continue generate other ants in Step 2.
3. Use *LocalSearch algorithm* for the new population ants. We pass all solutions in and the $2 - Opt$ *method* is performed.
4. Perform local pheromone trail update of the graph.
   4.1. Reduce the pheromone for the graph.
   4.2. Update pheromones in all arcs from distance matrix.
5. Find the best solution in an iteration and If the best solution of iteration is better than global solution than the global solution = the best solution of the iteration.
6. Repeat Steps 2-5 until maximum generation step is not reached, otherwise go to Step 7.
7. Return the best ant.

4.1   Identification of Optimal Number of Threads

We carried out to check the optimal number of threads of the proposed ACO algorithm on one node, which has 128 GB RAM, two processors Intel Xeon E5-2680v3, 2.5 GHz and operating system CentOS 6.9. We used one set of size 300 trash cans for the testing. The algorithm is programmed using $C\#$ 6 and used threads from .NET framework 4.6.2. For running on CentOS we used Mono 5.0.0 platform[2].

Speedup can be defined as [22]:

$$S = \frac{T_s}{T_p} \qquad (1)$$

---

[2] Mono platform: https://www.mono-project.com/.

Table 1. Configuration parameters description

Code name	Theory name	Brief description
AntCount	p	Number of ants
Iterations	it	Number of iterations
Alpha	α	Importance of pheromone
Beta	β	Importance of heuristic information
P	r	Evaporation rate
Q	Q	Constant to adjust laid pheromone
Min	τ_{min}	Minimum pheromone
Max	τ_{max}	Maximum pheromone
InitialPheromone	τ_0	Initial pheromone value
CandidateFraction	cf	Candidate fraction
Q_0	q_0	Exploitation versus exploration

Table 2. Average speedup of optimization algorithm

Number of ants a	Number of the used threads n						
	2	4	8	12	16	20	24
24	1.90	3.25	4.86	5.58	5.74	6.05	6.32
48	1.94	3.40	5.06	5.96	6.25	6.03	6.81
96	1.95	3.41	5.08	6.00	6.23	6.24	6.81
192	1.98	3.45	5.17	6.03	6.39	6.13	6.79

where T_s is execution time of serial algorithm and T_p of parallel algorithm respectively.

The following Table 2 shows average speedup values from 10 measurements for different number of the used threads n and ants a. Table 3 shows number of ants per thread and for visualization we used speedup values for which number of ants is divisible by number of threads without remainder, see Fig. 1, where a is number of ants. That was becasuse it would otherwise make spikes in logarithmic speedup.

From our experiments, we can see that from eight threads the speedup is not increasing dramatically similarly as in studies [24, 25]. In future work, this can help us to choose range of parameters for hyperparameter search.

5 Automatic Computation on Supercomputing Infrastructure

We used one set of 280 trash cans for the speedup testing (see Fig. 2). The set of the trash cans serves once every two weeks. The 'line' means transport of municipal waste with one vehicle. The vehicle takes the waste to two dump

Table 3. Ants per threads of optimization algorithm

Number of ants a	Number of the used threads n						
	2	4	8	12	16	20	24
24	12	6	3	2	1.5	1.2	1
48	24	12	6	4	3	2.4	2
96	48	24	12	8	6	4.8	4
192	96	48	24	16	12	9.6	8

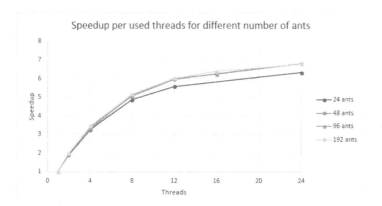

Fig. 1. Speedup of optimization algorithm

sites. We can see a form to run the ACO algorithm on the right side of Fig. 2. The input parameters 'line' code - *IT4L1* and Number plate - *1SPZ1234* are filled.

The quality of results from the metaheuristic algorithms depends on settings of input parameters. Because of that, it is required to run the algorithm with different settings to get the best results. Repeating runs causes the increasing of total time for solving the problem, if we require solution close to the optimal one. Various configuration parameters have been used to achieve the optimal results. Configuration parameters for the ACO algorithm and their constraints are described in Table 4. For example, the parameter α directly influences the concentration of the pheromone and β influences the global distance. The tested parameters α and β were set from 0 to 5. If $\beta = 0$ then the solutions for α in any adjustment are wrong. It is clear from the experiments that if $\alpha = 0$ and β had the growing character, the results of the experiment were improved. If $\alpha = 0$ and $\beta = 0$ then there was missing information about the pheromone (which ants were used to navigate). It means that if the pheromone route is created, all the ants will use the same route, even though it is a wrong route.

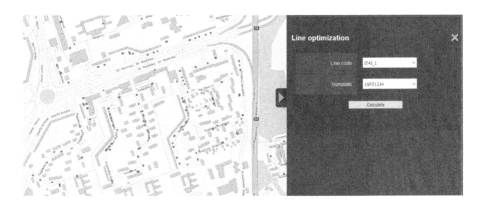

Fig. 2. Visualization of trash cans

Table 4. Configuration parameters constraints

Code name	Theory name	Default value	Constraints
AntCount	p	128	$p \in \mathbb{Z}^+$
Iterations	it	500	$it \in \mathbb{Z}^+$
Alpha	α	1	$\alpha \in \mathbb{R}^+$
Beta	β	2	$\beta \in \mathbb{R}^+$
P	r	0.001	$r \in (0,1)$
Q	Q	5000	$Q \in \mathbb{R}^+$
Min	τ_{min}	0.0001	$\tau_{min} < \tau_{max} \in \mathbb{R}^+$
Max	τ_{max}	1	$\tau_{min} < \tau_{max} \in \mathbb{R}^+$
InitialPheromone	τ_0	0.001	$\tau_{min} \le \tau_0 \le \tau_{max}$
CandidateFraction	cf	3	$cf \in \mathbb{Z}^+$
Q_0	q_0	0.2	$q_0 \in \langle 0,1 \rangle$

5.1 Automatization and Data Processing

The automatic computation of the waste optimization problem was performed by High-End Application Execution Middleware (HEAppE). HEAppE is developed as middleware framework for managing and providing information about submitted and running jobs and their data between the client application and the HPC infrastructure. HEAppE framework developed by IT4Innovations allows the enhancement of HPC capabilities and the supercomputing infrastructure usability. The architecture of HEAppE middleware framework adopted for ACO algorithm is shown in Fig. 3.

Data processing. Before the execution, a user must specify parameters ('line', vehicles) for the calculation of the optimal waste collection route in the Front-end part of the system.

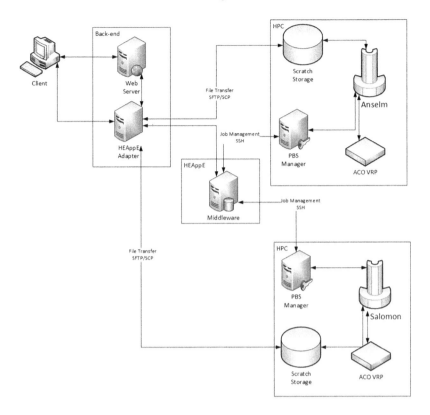

Fig. 3. Architecture scheme

The Back-end part is then responsible for the generation of the input files from the parameters specified by a user and calculates a distance matrix for each waste container in the selected line.

The generated input files are sent to the cluster via the HEAppE middleware for the calculation. After successfully sending files to the cluster, HEAppE middleware allocates computing resources and runs the ACO algorithm over the input files.

When the calculation is completed, data is transferred from the cluster back to the Back-end part of the system, and then the result data are mapped to enumeration tables and imported into a Geospatial database. Then imported data are provided to the Front-end side of the system via the services of the map server. We could divide provided data into two separate parts in the client. The first part contains the geographic data (points and lines) of the optimization and optimization routes displayed on the map component and the second one provides detailed information of displayed routes and different optimized length.

6 Conclusion

The paper presents a parallel version of the ACO optimization problem for the waste disposal. The work was focused on the adaptation and parallelization of the metaheuristic algorithm using HPC. We tested different settings of input parameters of the metaheuristics algorithm, which improve the quality of results. In the future, we would like to increase the size of the problems which can be solved in reasonable time/price by using HPC computational power by HPC optimization techniques. Furthermore, we will intend to search for optimal parameter setting for the ACO algorithm, where we want to use HyperLoom platform for the definition of our hyperparameter search pipeline [23]. From the experiments in the Sect. 4.1 is evident that the identification of an appropriate number of threads is important for proper cluster utilisation for hyperparameter search pipeline where the significant amount of ACO runs is needed.

We extended a possibility to use VRP computations on HPC clusters by the special remote execution middleware. In this paper, we used the High-End Application Execution Middleware middleware (HEAppE), that provides smart access to the supercomputing infrastructure. The ACO algorithm has been tested on real data set from the waste collection area for daily planning of the collection route.

Acknowledgments. This work was supported by The Ministry of Education, Youth and Sports from the National Programme of Sustainability (NPS II) project 'IT4Innovations excellence in science - LQ1602' and by the IT4Innovations infrastructure which is supported from the Large Infrastructures for Research, Experimental Development and Innovations project 'IT4Innovations National Supercomputing Center LM2015070', partially supported by the SGS grant No. SP2018/173 'Dynamic Systems Problems and their Implementation on HPC', VŠB - Technical University of Ostrava, Czech Republic.This work was partially supported by the TAČR GAMA PP1 No. G PP1 20 'Raising the Waste Recycling Rate with Lowering the Costs of Waste Collection', VŠB - Technical University of Ostrava, Czech Republic.

References

1. Ministry of the Environment of the Czech Republic (2017). https://www.mzp.cz/cz/news/. Accessed 17 Oct
2. Kulcar, T.: Optimizing solid waste collection in Brussels. Eur. J. Oper. Res. **90**(1), 71–77 (1996)
3. Tung, V.D., Pinnoi, A.: Vehicle routing-scheduling for waste collection in Hanoi. Eur. J. Oper. Res. **125**(3), 449–468 (2000)
4. Faccio, M., Persona, A., Zanin, G.: Waste collection multi objective model with real time traceability data. Waste Manag. **31**(12), 2391–2405 (2011)
5. Bautista, J., Pereira, J.: Modeling the problem of locating collection areas for urban waste management. An application to the metropolitan area of Barcelona. Omega **34**(6), 617–629 (2006)
6. Son, L.H.: Optimizing Municipal Solid Waste collection using Chaotic Particle Swarm Optimization in GIS based environments: a case study at Danang city. Expert. Syst. Appl. **41**(18), 8062–8074 (2014)

7. Dantzig, G., Ramser, R.: The truck dispatching problem. Manag. Sci. **6**, 80–91 (1959)
8. Kuan, M.K.: Graphic programming using odd or even points. Chin. Math., 237–277 (1962)
9. Corbern, Á., Laporte, G.: Arc Routing Problem, Methods and Applications. MOS-SIAM Series on Optimization. SIAM, Philadelphia (2014)
10. Buhrkal, K., Larsen, A., Popke, S.: The waste collection vehicle routing problem with time windows in a city logistics context. Procedia Soc. Behav. Sci. **39**, 241254 (2012)
11. Kim, B.-I., Kim, S., Sahoo, S.: Waste collection vehicle routing problem with time windows. J. Comput. Oper. Res. **33**(12), 3624–3642 (2006)
12. Wy, J., Kinm, B.-I., Kim, S., Sahoo, S.: Rollon-rolloff vehicle routing problem in the waste collection industry. In: The 11th Asia Pacific Industrial Engineering and Management Systems Conference, Melaka (2010)
13. Ombuki-Berman, B.M., Runka, A., Hanshar, F.T.: Waste collection vehicle routing problem with time windows using multi-objective genetic algorithms. In: Andonie, B.R. (ed.) Presented at Computational Intelligence, Proceedings of Computational Intelligence, Calgary, Canada, pp. 91–97. Acta Press (2007)
14. Benjamin, A.M., Beasley, J.E.: Meta heuristics for the waste collection vehicle routing problem with time windows, driver rest period and multiple disposal facilities. Comput. Oper. Res. **37**, 2270–2280 (2010)
15. Islam, R., Rahman, M.: An ant colony optimization algorithm for waste collection vehicle routing with time windows, driver rest period and multiple disposal facilities. In: Conference: Informatics, Electronics and Vision (ICIEV) (2012)
16. Liu, J., He, Y.: Ant Colony Algorithm for waste collection vehicle arc routing with turn constraints. IEEE (2013)
17. Ismail, Z., Loh, S.L.: Ant colony optimization for solving solid waste collection scheduling problem. J. Math. Stat. **5**(3), 199–205 (2009)
18. Bautista, J., Pereira, J.: Ant algorithms for urban waste collection routing. In: Dorigo, M., Birattari, M., Blum, C., Gambardella, L.M., Mondada, F., Stützle, T. (eds.) ANTS 2004. LNCS, vol. 3172, pp. 302–309. Springer, Heidelberg (2004). https://doi.org/10.1007/978-3-540-28646-2_28
19. Dorigo, M., Maniezzo, V., Colorni, A.: The ant system: an autocatalytic optimizing process. Technical report, 91–016 (1991)
20. Colorni, A., Dorigo, M., Maniezzo, V.: Distributed optimization by ant colonies. In: Toward a Practice of Autonomous Systems: Proceedings of the First European Conference on Artificial Life, p. 134. MIT Press (1992)
21. Vargovský, J.: Ant Colony Optimization algorithm for vehicle routing problem (2017). http://hdl.handle.net/10084/118964
22. Hanzelka, J., Dvorský, J.: Flexible neural trees—parallel learning on HPC. In: Chaki, R., Saeed, K., Cortesi, A., Chaki, N. (eds.) Advanced Computing and Systems for Security. AISC, vol. 568, pp. 67–77. Springer, Singapore (2017). https://doi.org/10.1007/978-981-10-3391-9_4
23. Cima, V., et al.: HyperLoom: a platform for defining and executing scientific pipelines in distributed environments. In: Proceedings of the 9th Workshop and 7th Workshop on Parallel Programming and RunTime Management Techniques for Manycore Architectures and Design Tools and Architectures for Multicore Embedded Computing Platforms, pp. 1–6 (2018)

24. Abouelfarag, A.A., Aly, W.M., Elbialy, A.G.: Performance analysis and tuning for parallelization of ant colony optimization by using OpenMP. In: Saeed, K., Homenda, W. (eds.) CISIM 2015. LNCS, vol. 9339, pp. 73–85. Springer, Cham (2015). https://doi.org/10.1007/978-3-319-24369-6_6
25. Zhou, Y., He, F., Hou, N., Qiu, Y.: Parallel ant colony optimization on multi-core SIMD CPUs. Futur. Gener. Comput. Syst. **79**(2), 473–487 (2018)

Betweenness Propagation

Jiří Hanzelka$^{(\boxtimes)}$, Michal Běloch$^{(\boxtimes)}$, Jan Křenek$^{(\boxtimes)}$, Jan Martinovič$^{(\boxtimes)}$,
and Kateřina Slaninová$^{(\boxtimes)}$

IT4Innovations, VŠB-Technical University of Ostrava, 17. listopadu 15,
708 33 Ostrava, Poruba, Czech Republic
{jiri.hanzelka,michal.beloch,jan.krenek,jan.martinovic,
katerina.slaninova}@vsb.cz

Abstract. In the traffic network, the betweenness centrality helps in identification of the most occupied roads and crossroads. Usually, the main roads have the highest betweenness centrality score, given their importance in the traffic flow. The side roads' score is generally lower and it never takes into account what is happening on the main road. In a case of unusual event happening in the city, the betweenness score of the main road can increase multiplicatively, while the score of the side road is increased only slightly. Thus, we propose an extension to the original betweenness centrality score algorithm that enables the propagation of the betweenness centrality score from the main road to the side roads, allowing us better description of the current traffic situation. This is the continuation of our work on better refinement of the BC score for the purpose of the traffic modelling and the traffic flow control.

Keywords: Betweenness centrality · HPC · MPI · OpenMP
Traffic network

1 Introduction

Accurate description of the traffic network is usually very difficult. The network of crossroads and roads that connect them can be complicated even for small cities. An understanding of the traffic network can be gained when the graph theory is applied. This interpretation comes naturally, as there is clear resemblance between the printed map and a typical graph used in the graph theory. It is not a stretch to imagine that the vertices of the graph can be interpreted as the crossings and crossroads, and the edges are roads between them. This is not very novel idea, similar approach was adopted in other areas where such simplification is possible. Complicated structures like human brain and protein network can be better understood and studied when replaced with a graph [1–3], the same applies to the vast and intricate social networks [4–6], or immense world wide web [7,8].

The world population is still growing and is likely to grow further. The number of vehicles on the road is probably to grow as well, because of their decreasing

© Springer Nature Switzerland AG 2018
K. Saeed and W. Homenda (Eds.): CISIM 2018, LNCS 11127, pp. 279–287, 2018.
https://doi.org/10.1007/978-3-319-99954-8_24

cost and wider availability. The city infrastructure must be carefully expanded with the road network in mind. Therefore, the research must also focus on better understanding of the traffic behaviour. There are various strategies how to tackle the traffic flow. Some authors focus on the trend pattern of the traffic flow and approach it as time series [9,10]. Others are associating the problem with known physical phenomena, like an author in [11], where he applies his knowledge of the hydrodynamics to the traffic flow, noting their similarities, and uses the differential equations to solve it. While those approaches certainly have their merits, the traffic flow is tied to the transportation network and it is desirable to keep those two together. Introducing the concept of the oriented weighted graph provides a very accurate estimate of the real situation.

When dealing with a graph of such a magnitude, since the transportation network's graph is enormous especially for greater cities, the set of tools to extract the needed information must be developed. Fortunately, such tools exist in the form of centrality scores. While many types can be used (closeness, degree, eigenvector) [12], it is the betweenness centrality score that is the most popular. Its use has been researched by various authors [13–15] and although the authors comment on some limiting factors of the betweenness centrality, it is still very useful starting point.

This paper is the continuation of our work on the traffic flow analysis and modelling. In our previous work [16] we modified the original algorithm for betweenness computation with the concept of the vertex importance. This allowed us to dynamically change the values of the betweenness based on the various events that can happen in a city, from something unexpected like a car crash to planned events like sport matches. We soon realised this was not enough to accurately model the day-to-day life of the city traffic. Therefore, we provide an extension to the original betweenness algorithm that allows us to better refine the behaviour of the traffic network by the betweenness propagation in the graph.

The paper is organised as follows. Section 2 describes the computation of the betweenness centrality score. Section 3 gives a brief overview of our previous modification, the vertex importance. Section 4 talks about the key points of our new modification. Section 5 shows our modification in action. And Sect. 6 concludes the paper.

2   Betweenness Centrality

Betweenness centrality or in full form Shortest path betweenness centrality first appeared in sociology [17]. Its main purpose was to quantify the individual's influence over the information flow in the social network. It has been generalised and adopted since as one of the centrality measures in the network. The higher value of betweenness centrality means greater importance within the network. Specifically, within the context of the traffic network it usually represents a problematic section of the traffic flow.

Betweenness centrality of a vertex is defined as the ratio of the number of the shortest paths between origin and destination that pass through the vertex and the number of all the shortest paths between origin and destination. Let us describe the traffic network with the graph $G = (V, E)$, where V is the set of vertices pair-wise connected by edges forming the set E. We define a path from $s \in V$ to $t \in V$ as an alternating sequence of vertices and edges, beginning with s and ending with t, such that each edge connects its preceding vertex with its succeeding vertex. The symbol $\sigma_{st} = \sigma_{ts}$ denotes the number of the shortest paths between vertex $s \in V$ and $t \in V$, and $\sigma_{st}(v)$ is the number of the shortest paths between s and t that goes through $v \in V$. Betweenness centrality BC for the vertex $v \in V$ is then defined as:

$$BC(v) = \sum_{s \neq v \neq t \in V} \frac{\sigma_{st}(v)}{\sigma_{st}} \tag{1}$$

To get the shortest paths we use standard Dijkstra algorithm [18]. Betweenness centrality is computed using Brandes algorithm [19].

3   Vertex Importance Modification

In an attempt to better model the traffic behaviour, we implemented the concept of the vertex importance to the original Brandes algorithm. This implementation is discussed in greater detail in [16].

In short, we consider two important events that can occur in the network. The first event occurs when the vertex becomes an important origin point. In this case, the shortest paths originating here leading away from this point are influenced. To increase the importance of this vertex, we set the parameter α.

The other case is when the vertex is an important destination. This influences all the shortest paths leading toward this point, although the betweenness centrality in this case has decaying quality i.e. it gradually decreases away from this spot. We set the parameter β when we want to increase the destination importance.

The values of α and β are chosen from the interval $(0, \infty)$. Naturally, the values from the interval $(0, 1)$ are used to apply the decrease in origin or destination importance, while the values from the interval $(1, \infty)$ apply the increase in the importance. Value of α and β equal to 1 means no change.

4   Betweenness Propagation

Let us consider a situation illustrated in Fig. 1. We consider the road between vertex A and B to be the main road. Now suppose that the vertex A is the source of an event (people are leaving a concert or sport event). In this case, we significantly increase the value of α for the vertex A. Therefore, every shortest path leading away from the vertex A has an increased betweenness centrality score. In practical sense, we might expect traffic jams on road leading from the vertex A to vertex B. Then a new car wants to move from vertex C to vertex A. This orientation does not lead away from the vertex A, therefore it is not influenced by the increase in α. But the density of the traffic leading away from the vertex A certainly influences the car moving from vertex C. It might manifest as increased waiting times on crossroads, or increased likeliness of the traffic accident can slow down the traffic in both directions, not just the one leading away from A. The car coming from vertex C can just be passing the main road between vertices A and B, but he will be influenced by the increase on it nonetheless.

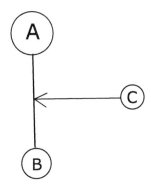

Fig. 1. A situation that arises when α is big and a car coming from vertex C wants to join the road between vertex A and B.

This line of thinking means we need to further adjust the betweenness centrality score of the roads with low values when they are near to the roads with significantly higher values. Such adjustment makes the road 'aware of what is happening further down the road.

How our extension works can be best described with the help of Fig. 2. The vertices M form the main road with the high value of betweenness B. Vertices with label s are side roads leading towards the main road. Their betweenness score is denoted as b_n, where $n \in \{1, 2, 3, 4\}$ is the identifier of the side roads. We see there are three side roads leading towards the main road. Since we expect their $b_{1..3}$ scores are lower than B score, we increase their value according to formula 2.

$$b_i = B * \xi \tag{2}$$

and $\xi \in (0; 1)$. In the equation, value b_i is the betweenness centrality score of the road we are adjusting. Value B is the betweenness centrality score of the referential road towards the adjusted road leads. Parameter ξ is the regulation value that allows us to control the increase. It is bounded so that the betweenness score of the side road cannot surpass the value of the referential road. For discussed example, the index i is set $\{1, 2, 3\}$, but in general $i \in \mathbb{N}$. So in the first step, we increased the values $b_{1..3}$. In the next step, we look if there are roads connected to the adjusted side roads. We see there is one road with betweenness score b_4. We adjust its value according to Eq. 2 and obtain a new value of $b_4 = b_3 * \xi$, or $b_4 = B * \xi^2$. Going further away from the original main road will lead to an increase of the power of the regulation parameter ξ causing gradual decrease in the betweenness score gain. This means that closer roads are influenced more than distant ones. The value of regulation parameter ξ does not have to be fixed. It can even be a function that can better regulate the propagation of the main road's betweenness score.

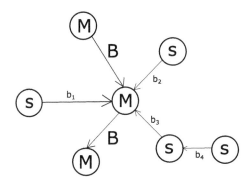

Fig. 2. Description of the betweenness propagation algorithm.

Formally, our algorithm works as follows:

1. Find the edges where the change in betweenness score occurred (due to the change of α or due to other input restrictions).
2. Order the betweenness score in descending order then take top P percent of the edges with the highest score. This allows us to identify the main roads in new graph.
3. Find the beginning vertex of one of the chosen edges. Then take all the other edges leading to this vertex with lower betweenness score and change it to a new value according to Eq. 2, but only if the new value would be higher than the current.
4. Repeat the third step until you get through all the chosen edges from step 2.
5. Perform the step 3 to 4 as many times as defined in the depth parameter d, although next time take all the changed edges so the betweenness correctly propagates away from the main road.

As we can see, there are two more parameters in our algorithm. Parameter P is used to define the amount of the changed routes we start with. It takes top P percent of the roads with the highest betweenness score. This means we really work only with the roads that changed significantly. Another parameter is the depth d. This parameter tells us how far from the original road we want to spread the betweenness score. In the example above, the value $d = 1$ means that only the values $b_{1..3}$ are changed. To further propagate and change the value of b_4, we have to set $d = 2$.

This algorithm requires only the map and computed values of the betweenness. Therefore, it is independent of the Brandes algorithm and in general, any method to compute the betweenness centrality of the graph can be used.

5   Visualisation

To test the result of our algorithm, we used the Floreon+ system[1] operated by IT4Innovations National Supercomputing Centre[2]. The objectives of the Floreon+ system are monitoring, modelling and prediction of crisis situations. We chose the part of Ostrava city to illustrate the results. We can see the chosen area of the dimensions 20×15 km in Fig. 3. The full lines refer to the value of the betweenness centrality score. The wider lines mean the higher values. Figure 3 also shows the removed area (red). This area is vulnerable to floods, so it might even be useful in the future. We can see how the traffic behaviour changes and the increase in betweenness score of previously not fully utilised roads. Now we can run our algorithm. It first compares the situation in Fig. 3 and then it stores the edges where betweenness changed. The values of betweenness are ordered and the top P % of values are chosen. We set $P = 10$ and $\xi = 0.85$. The first and second run is shown in Fig. 4. There is noticeable increase in betweenness score of the side roads along the main roads (green areas). We can see how it branches further away from the main road. It is much more evident in Fig. 5, where we can see the situation after four runs and also after eight runs.

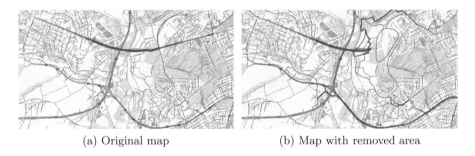

(a) Original map   (b) Map with removed area

Fig. 3. Map of the traffic network of Ostrava city before and after the removal of the red area. (Color figure online)

The changes in output for each iteration are also shown in Table 1. The first column shows the current iteration of the algorithm. The second column is the number of the edges whose betweenness score was changed in previous iteration, or in the case of the first iteration, the number of edges that had their betweenness score changed when we removed the red area in Fig. 3. The original

---

[1] https://floreon.it4i.cz.
[2] http://www.it4i.cz/?lang=en.

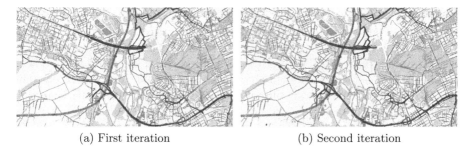

(a) First iteration   (b) Second iteration

Fig. 4. Result of the algorithm after the first and second run with $P = 10\%$ and $\xi = 0.85$. The green areas on the left picture show the increased betweenness values for the roads connected to the road with significantly high increase in betweenness score. (Color figure online)

(a) Fourth iteration   (b) Eighth iteration

Fig. 5. Result of the algorithm after four and eight runs with $P = 10\%$ and $\xi = 0.85$.

Table 1. Number of changed edges and their average betweenness for each iteration.

Iteration	Number of changed edges	Changed edges taken	Number of updated edges	Average betweenness of edges before update	Average betweenness of edges after update
1	6269	626	324	1,784,493	7,354,781
2	324	324	439	1,395,744	6,126,729
3	439	439	518	1,205,731	5,239,808
4	518	518	600	946,891	4,436,458
5	600	600	707	836,521	3,795,078
6	707	707	771	710,053	3,256,629
7	771	771	808	706,034	2,829,600
8	808	808	843	624,909	2,425,605

graph has 31,874 edges and 14,224 vertices. The removal of the red area changed the number of edges to 31,832 and the number of vertices to 14,205. The third column is the number of the edges that enters the algorithm. In the case of the first iteration, it takes top P percent of the changed edges, where P is 10%. Then it takes all the other edges leading to each of those changed edges separately and changes their betweenness score only if the new value would be higher than the current. The number of these newly updated edges is in the fourth column. The fifth and sixth column show the average betweenness score of the changed edges before and after they were changed.

6   Conclusion

In this paper, we described a new algorithm to better adjust the value of betweenness centrality score in the network where important change occurred. The main objective of this change is to better anticipate the behaviour of the network in unexpected situations. Using the results from this algorithm, we can also better recommend the optimal way in the network.

Provided visualisation of Ostrava city traffic network clearly demonstrates how the algorithm works. It is also noticeable how the value of the depth parameter d influences the result.

Generally, higher values of ξ allow us to choose higher values of d, because it takes longer for the powers of ξ to converge to zero. As for the value of P, it should be chosen so that sufficient number of the changed routes is obtained.

So far, the algorithm works only with the increase. We would like to implement the propagation when the betweenness score decreases on the main road in the next version. Future work will be done on the three parameters as well. We would like to test the behaviour of the network based on the set values of the parameters. We also want to implement this algorithm to Floreon+ system. These results will also be useful when they are implemented to the project ANTAREX[3]. Its goal is the development of the self-sustaining system capable of auto adjustment depending on the current situation and its use case is focused on self-adapted server side/client navigation system.

Acknowledgments. This work was supported by The Ministry of Education, Youth and Sports from the National Programme of Sustainability (NPS II) project 'IT4Innovations excellence in science - LQ1602', partially supported by the SGC grant No. SP2018/142 'Optimization of machine learning algorithms for HPC platform II', VŠB - Technical University of Ostrava, Czech Republic, and by the IT4Innovations infrastructure which is supported from the Large Infrastructures for Research, Experimental Development and Innovations project 'IT4Innovations National Supercomputing Center – LM2015070'.

---

[3] http://www.antarex-project.eu.

References

1. Xia, J., Sun, J., Jia, P., Zhao, Z.: Do cancer proteins really interact strongly in the human protein-protein interaction network? Comput. Biol. Chem. **35**, 121–125 (2011)
2. Li, M., Wang, J., Chen, X., Wang, H., Pan, Y.: A local average connectivity-based method for identifying essential proteins from the network level. Comput. Biol. Chem. **35**, 143–150 (2011)
3. Hagmann, P., et al.: Mapping the structural core of human cerebral cortex. PLoS Biol. **6**, 1479–1493 (2008)
4. Szell, M., Thurner, S.: Measuring social dynamics in a massive multiplayer online game. Soc. Netw. **32**, 313–329 (2010)
5. Wasserman, S., Faust, K.: Social Network Analysis: Methods and Application. Cambridge University Press, Cambridge (1994)
6. Clifton, A., Turkheimer, E., Oltmanns, T.F.: Personality disorder in social networks: Network position as a marker of interpersonal dysfuction. Soc. Netw. **31**, 26–32 (2009)
7. Zhou, S., Mondragón, R.J.: Accurately modeling the internet topology. Phys. Rev. **E70**, 066108 (2004)
8. Kawamoto, H., Igarashi, A.: Efficient packet routing strategy in complex networks. Phys. A Stat. Mech. Appl. **391**, 895–904 (2012)
9. Shang, P., Li, X., Kamae, S.: Chaotic analysis of traffic time series. Chaos Solitons Fractals **25**, 121–128 (2005)
10. Hong, W.C., Dong, Y., Zheng, F., Lai, C.Y.: Forecasting urban traffic flow by SVR with continuous ACO. Appl. Math. Model. **35**, 1282–1291 (2011)
11. Daganzo, C.F.: The cell transmission model: a dynamic representation of highway traffic consistent with the hydrodynamic theory. Transp. Res. Part B Methodol. **28**, 269–287 (1994)
12. Klein, D.J.: Centrality measure in graphs. J. Math. Chem. **47**, 1209–1223 (2010)
13. Galafassi, C., Bazzan, A.L.C.: Analysis of traffic behavior in regular grid and real world networks (2013)
14. Gao, S., Wang, Y., Gao, Y., Liu, Y.: Understanding urban traffic flow characteristics: a rethinking of betweenness centrality. Environ. Plan. B Plan. Des. **40**, 135 (2012)
15. Zhao, P.X., Zhao, S.M.: Understanding urban traffic flow characteristics from the network centrality perspective at different granularities. Int. Arch. Photogramm. Remote. Sens. Spat. Inf. Sci. **41**, 263–268 (2016)
16. Hanzelka, J., Běloch, M., Martinovič, J., Slaninová, K.: Vertex importance extension of betweenness centrality algorithm. In: International Conference on Data Management, Analytics and Innovation - ICDMAI, Pune, India (2018)
17. Freeman, L.C.: A set of measures of centrality based on betweenness. Sociometry **40**, 35–41 (1977)
18. Dijkstra, E.W.: A note on two problems in connexion with graphs. Numerische Mathematik **1**, 269–271 (1959)
19. Brandes, U.: A faster algorithm for betweenness centrality. J. Math. Sociol. **25**, 163–177 (2001)

SciJava Interface for Parallel Execution in the ImageJ Ecosystem

Michal Krumnikl[1,2]([⊠]), Petr Bainar[2], Jana Klímová[2], Jan Kožusznik[1,2],
Pavel Moravec[1,2], Václav Svatoň[2], and Pavel Tomančák[2,3]

[1] Department of Computer Science, FEECS, VŠB – Technical University of Ostrava,
17. listopadu 15, 708 33 Ostrava, Poruba, Czech Republic
{michal.krumnikl,jan.kozusznik,pavel.moravec}@vsb.cz
[2] IT4Innovations, VŠB – Technical University of Ostrava, 17. listopadu 15, 708 33
Ostrava, Poruba, Czech Republic
{petr.bainar,jana.klimova,vaclav.svaton,pavel.tomancak}@vsb.cz
[3] Max Planck Institute of Molecular Cell Biology and Genetics, Pfotenhauerstrasse
108, 01307 Dresden, Germany

Abstract. ImageJ has become a popular software platform for image processing and its community has developed and made available numerous plugins for scientific audiences. Nevertheless, no platform-wide solution for parallel processing of big data has been created so far. As ImageJ is a part of the SciJava collaboration project, we propose the concept of seamlessly integrating parallelization-providing capability into one of the SciJava libraries. Specifically, this approach strives to make high-performance infrastructure accessible to ImageJ plugin developers whilst remaining extensible and technology-agnostic. Two parallelization approaches were created and experimentally evaluated on an HPC infrastructure. The results indicate good scalability and are promising for prospective integration of the created functionality into the SciJava Common library.

Keywords: Big data · High-performance computing (HPC)
ImageJ · Fiji · SciJava · ImageJ server · Parallel computing
Remote execution

1 Introduction

The open-source software platform ImageJ has become a renowned tool for image processing, analysis, and visualization, particularly due to its accessibility and extensibility [19, 22, 25]. End users benefit from easy installation, online Wiki documentation and tutorials as well as convenient plugins, which can be downloaded from multiple update sites. Advanced users can make use of an embedded editor which provides the capability to write scripts in multiple programming languages and immediately execute them. Lastly, software developers appreciate being able to leverage SciJava components which provide the foundations for

© Springer Nature Switzerland AG 2018
K. Saeed and W. Homenda (Eds.): CISIM 2018, LNCS 11127, pp. 288–299, 2018.
https://doi.org/10.1007/978-3-319-99954-8_25

efficient development of sophisticated plugins [18]. Fiji ("Fiji Is Just ImageJ"), is a distribution of ImageJ tailored for life sciences, bundling numerous selected plugins for biomedical research [21].

Imaging techniques have emerged as a crucial means of understanding the structure and function of living organisms in primary research, as well as medical diagnostics. In order to maximize information gain, achieving as high spatial and temporal resolution as practically possible is desired. However, long-term time-lapse recordings at the single-cell level produce vast amounts of multidimensional image data, which cannot be processed on a personal computer in a timely manner, therefore requiring utilization of high-performance computing (HPC) clusters. For example, processing a 2.2 TB dataset of drosophila embryonic development, taking a week on a single computer, was brought down to 13 h by employing an HPC cluster supporting parallel execution of individual tasks [23,24]. Unfortunately, life scientists often lack access to such infrastructure.

Addressing this issue is particularly challenging as Fiji is an extraordinarily extensible platform and new plugins emerge incessantly. So far, plugin developers have typically implemented task parallelization within a particular plugin, but no universal approach has yet been incorporated into the SciJava architecture. In this paper we propose the concept of integrating parallelization support into one of the SciJava libraries, thereby enabling developers to access remote resources (e.g., remote HPC infrastructure) and delegate plugin-specific tasks to its compute nodes. As the cluster-specific details are hidden in respective interface implementations, the plugins can remain extensible and technology-agnostic. In addition, the proposed solution is highly scalable, meaning that any additional resources can be efficiently utilized.

2   ImageJ Ecosystem

ImageJ (or Fiji, its popular distribution tailored for research audiences) greatly benefits from the community which has built up around it throughout its more than 20-year existence [19,20,22,25]. Close collaboration between scientists and software developers has yielded numerous plugins, which are available to end users at ImageJ update sites. Moreover, the ImageJ community participates in multiple activities which further extend the universality and interoperability of ImageJ.

2.1   SciJava

SciJava is a collaboration of projects committed to integrating with each other in order to create seamless workflows available for scientific computing [18]. The involved software tools and applications are prevailingly focused on image processing, visualization, workflow execution, and machine learning. Furthermore, the cooperating projects strive to reuse code where practicable, often by utilizing general libraries.

ImageJ is built upon the SciJava Common library, leveraging its plugin discovery mechanism. Provided that a created plugin (e.g., `DoubleParser` in Listing 1) has been properly annotated, a corresponding metafile is generated at compile time, making the plugin available to other components.

Moreover, annotated plugin inputs (`textInput` and `opService`) and outputs (`numericOutput`) are analyzed at run time by Java reflection. If possible, the input parameters are automatically resolved, typically from the application context (e.g., singleton SciJava services, such as `opService`) or from user input (usually plugin-specific values, such as `textInput`).

```java
@Plugin(type = Command.class)
public class DoubleParser implements Command {

  @Parameter
  private String textInput;

  @Parameter(type = ItemIO.OUTPUT)
  private double numericOutput;

  @Parameter
  private OpService opService;

  @Override
  public void run() {
    double val = Double.parseDouble(textInput);
    numericOutput = opService.math().abs(val);
  }
}
```

Listing 1. Fragment of source code within a SciJava plugin

2.2   ImageJ Server

ImageJ functionalities can be accessed from various programming languages, as well as through diverse graphical user interfaces. However, there are still several cross-language and cross-machine integration issues to be tackled[1]. To solve some of those challenges and further enhance ImageJ versatility, a network wrapper called ImageJ Server[2] exposing its modules through RESTful services has been introduced. The first implementation was introduced in 2013 and it is now a working prototype with multiple use cases such as CellProfiler [12]. An initial release of ImageJ Server contained a JavaScript/HTML web client and Python bindings.

ImageJ Server can be used not only as a web backend but also as a computational component on nodes of larger configurations, typically HPC clusters.

---

[1] https://github.com/imagej/imagej-server/wiki/Rationale.
[2] https://github.com/imagej/imagej-server.

One of the parallelization approaches proposed in this paper is based precisely on remote utilization of ImageJ Server nodes.

3 Parallelization Approaches in the ImageJ Ecosystem

As ImageJ is a Java-based application, it can benefit from both low-level parallelization techniques as well as approaches implemented on higher levels of the software architecture.

3.1 Massive Parallelization in Java

There are numerous parallelization approaches in the Java ecosystem, ranging from single-purpose libraries to complex cluster-computing frameworks, typically based on standard concurrent approaches with shared, distributed shared or distributed memory models. The following paragraphs give a brief overview of communication tools in distributed computing as well as libraries and frameworks for parallelization in the Java ecosystem. For a more comprehensive review of different methods, see [26].

Message Passing Interface (MPI) has become a de facto standard for inter-process communication in systems based on distributed memory models. Java has no official binding for MPI, however several convenient third-party libraries have been implemented. As a part of the HPJava [15] project, mpiJava was developed, and should be portable to any platform that provides a JDK-compatible and native MPI environment. However, the last version was released in 2003 and it is no longer maintained. FastMPJ [9] is currently a maintained project, providing support for shared memory models running on high-speed networks among cluster nodes (e.g., InfiniBand).

Furthermore, there are many providers implementing the Java Message Service (JMS) in the Java ecosystem, such as ActiveMQ [1] or RabbitMQ [3], for example. These libraries can be employed for managing communication among cluster nodes.

One of the first distributed shared memory approaches was introduced in Jackal [27], providing a modified compiler that implements a Java memory model, and allows multithreaded Java programs to run unmodified on distributed memory systems. The research project JOMP [7] defined and implemented an OpenMP-like set of directives and runtime routines. Moreover, akka [6], a state-of-the-art library for concurrent and distributed JVM computing, has been incorporated into the Scala standard library.

Parallel Java 2 Library [13] provides parallel programming primitives such as parallel loop and reductions, and supports the shared memory model, kernel GPUs, and the Map-Reduce model.

Hadoop [4] is a widely used framework in distributed computing, comprising a distributed file system solution as well as an implementation of the MapReduce programming model for data processing. Hadoop is often used together with

Spark [2], which supersedes its data processing part. Spark facilitates implementation of iterative methods such as training algorithms for machine learning systems.

Due to the immense variety of parallelization approaches, one of the key requirements for the library API needs to be universality and adaptability to various parallel computing environments.

3.2 ImageJ and HPC-Aware Plugins

The urgent need for employment of high-performance computing in image data processing has led to the development of numerous parallelization approaches on the plugin level, yet a platform-wide solution for ImageJ has still not been implemented [11, 24].

Many processing and analysis techniques in scientific imaging could be classified as embarrassingly parallel. Specifically, the input dataset can often be easily separated into multiple chunks. Each of them is then simultaneously processed and results are eventually combined. A basic example of such a pipeline is depicted in Fig. 1.

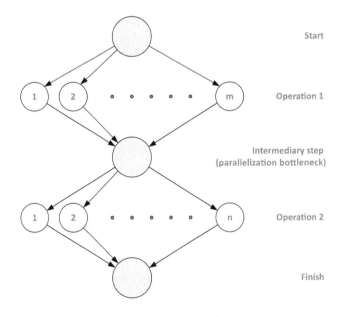

Fig. 1. Pipeline comprising embarrassingly parallel operations and a bottleneck

Schmied introduced an analogous SPIM data processing pipeline, based on parallel processing of individual time points and data sets. The pipeline utilizes Snakemake, a workflow engine capable of resolving dependencies between subsequent processing steps [14, 23, 24]. Consequently, any pipeline tasks appearing to be independent can be executed in parallel. This approach has cleared the way to significantly decreasing the processing time.

Grunzke proposed a new HPC integration method in data-intensive KNIME (Konstanz Information Miner [5,10]) workflows making use of the UNICORE (Uniform Interface to Computing Resources) middleware [16,17,28]. This approach could potentially be applicable for SciJava plugins as any SciJava plugin can be converted into a KNIME node and then added to a workflow [28]. However, the community of biology users capable of exploiting ImageJ/KNIME interoperability is relatively small compared to the ImageJ community. Therefore, it is beneficial to develop a standalone parallelization solution for the ImageJ ecosystem.

4   Design Proposal

To provide universal and extensible foundations for hardware-agnostic parallelization of image processing tasks in the ImageJ software ecosystem, we decided to utilize SciJava services. They are reusable classes, tracking application-wide parameters in ImageJ, and we decided to add one that governs parallelization-specific functionalities, which was deemed a favorable option. Consequently, an interface called `ParallelService` has been defined. Currently it only provides available parallelization paradigms upon request, however it is intended that in the future it would also allow end users to create and configure paradigms at runtime using the standardized ImageJ GUI. An overview of the library design is depicted in Fig. 2.

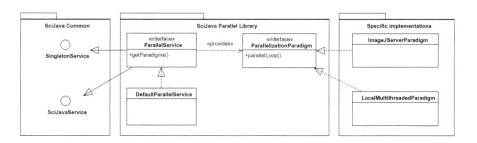

Fig. 2. Overall design of the SciJava Parallel library

Each parallelization paradigm is an object representing a unique parallelization approach, encapsulating both cluster access and task execution details. Multiple implementations of the `ParallelizationParadigm` interface can be installed independently in the ImageJ application environment. The interface provides a pivotal method called `parallelLoop` in this initial proposal, however support of other possible methods is currently under development. Usage of the method `parallelLoop` is demonstrated in a code snippet in Listing 2.

```
@Parameter
ParallelService parallelService;
public void run() {
  Collection<P_Input> inputs = prepareInputs();
  Collection<Path> outputs = new LinkedList<>();
  ParallelizationParadigm paradigm
    = parallelService.getParadigms().get(0);
  paradigm.parallelLoop(inputs, (input, task) -> {
    Dataset ds = task.importData(input.dataset);
    RotateImageXY<?> command
      = task.getRemoteModule(RotateImageXY.class);
    command.setAngle(input.angle);
    command.setDataset(ds);
    command.run();
    ds = command.getDataset();
    Path result = task.exportData(ds);
    outputs.add(result);
  });
}
```

Listing 2. Demonstration of the `parallelLoop` method executing a standard Fiji image-rotating plugin `RotateImageXY` and using a custom interface for data import/-export

Particularly, the `parallelLoop` method has got arguments structured as follows:

- a collection of values
- a block of code

Each value from the passed collection serves as an input argument to an individual execution of the specified block of code, where multiple executions can be run concurrently. The block of code can contain, among others, calls of SciJava Commands. Nonetheless, the outlined interface is designed for generality, to accommodate a wide range of prospective parallel paradigm implementations.

For concept exploration purposes, two different paradigms were implemented:

- the ImageJ Server Paradigm, which approaches task execution by distributing the calls to registered ImageJ Server instances running on different HPC cluster nodes
- the Local Multithreaded Paradigm, which calls SciJava Commands using the SciJava Command Service

The implemented paradigms are represented in the design overview (Fig. 2) by classes `ImageJServerParadigm` and `LocalMultithreadedParadigm`, respectively.

4.1 ImageJ Server Paradigm Overview

The proposed parallel execution environment is composed of multiple computational units running ImageJ Server (denoted as workers) and a worker manager, responsible for deploying individual tasks and acting as a task scheduler. Workers can be located in a cloud environment or cluster infrastructure. The only requirement is that HTTP connections for RESTful services must be enabled so the worker manager can connect to worker APIs. In most cases, the worker manager is running within an ImageJ instance on an end-user terminal, usually situated outside the cloud or cluster infrastructure.

Figure 3 depicts a typical configuration of computational clusters located in a data center and connected to the outside world through login or middleware nodes. All workers running on individual nodes are controlled by a worker manager, which is responsible for scheduling and deployment of individual tasks. Network connections can be established directly, via a proxy server or another form of middleware (this is essential in case incoming connections are blocked by security policies). The middleware provides additional functions for job submission and management, and its main purpose is to simplify access to large systems and to provide HPC capabilities to users without tedious and excessive administration steps.

In order to provide proof of applicability and to perform basic experiments, we created a simple scheduler for executing the paradigm benchmarks.

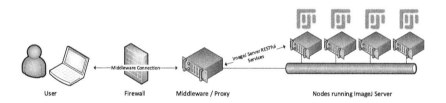

Fig. 3. Accessing ImageJ Server Nodes via middleware or a proxy server

4.2   Simple ImageJ Task Scheduler

The implementation of the simple high-level scheduler internally holds a pool of available workers and an interface through which the workers can be requested. Moreover, it provides a simple queue management system. For example, within the method named `parallelLoop`, the available workers are being allocated and the results are simultaneously being gathered until the computational task is finished. In cases of repetitious errors or timeouts, the worker is removed from the pool and the task is rescheduled to a different worker.

There are three distinct states a worker may be in: free, occupied and finished. Initially, the worker is in the free state, in which it awaits requests from the worker manager. Once a request is received (e.g., via a RESTful service), the worker is transitioned to the occupied state and starts performing the requested task (e.g., executing a SciJava Command). Should an error occur, an appropriate response (e.g., an HTTP error message) is returned. When in the occupied state, the worker does not accept any other requests until it finishes its current operation and returns the result back to the worker manager. The final state, denoted as "finished", is an indication that the worker is available again, however it still holds data from the previous assignment. The data must be downloaded by the worker manager before the worker can return back to the free state.

The scheduler was used as proof of concept for performing basic benchmark tasks. A more sophisticated approach shall be adopted for large tasks composed of hundreds or thousands of scheduled subtasks, e.g. [8,14].

4.3   Local Multithreaded Paradigm

To compare the ImageJ Server Paradigm with a standard SciJava Command execution, the Local Multithreaded Paradigm was created.

Likewise to the ImageJ Server Paradigm, it also utilizes the simple scheduler pattern described above. The only substantial difference is that the local Multithreaded Paradigm does not pass command calls to the ImageJ Server instances, but rather executes available commands via the SciJava Command Service locally. Essentially, this naive implementation approaches parallelization by delegating tasks to workers in separate threads.

5   Evaluation

To validate the developed parallelization paradigms, a set of tasks was performed on the Salomon HPC cluster at the IT4Innovations national supercomputing center[3]. Each task comprised rotating an image with a size of 2643×2048 pixels stored in the PNG format (3.8 MB occupied space)[4] by a defined number of degrees.

Experiments with the ImageJ Server Paradigm were carried out in multiple configurations, with the number of cluster nodes allocated for each task varying from 1 to 8. Each configuration was employed 10 times.

Similarly, validation of the Local Multithreaded Paradigm was performed in numerous configurations, which varied in the number of threads. Specifically, the set of tasks was carried out on a single cluster node utilizing from 1 to 24 threads. Likewise, each configuration was used 10 times.

The results are depicted in Fig. 4. For the ImageJ Server Paradigm (left), there is almost no deviation of execution times across multiple runs of the same configuration, as the nodes are exclusively dedicated for the respective job. Conversely, there are minor deviations among individual configuration runs when employing the Local Multithreaded Paradigm (right). These deviations are caused mainly by the Java Virtual Machine internal processes (cache, garbage collector, Just-In-Time compilation, etc.).

---

[3] https://docs.it4i.cz/salomon/hardware-overview/.

[4] Super-resolution microscopy frame, available at https://idr.openmicroscopy.org, ID 3138072.

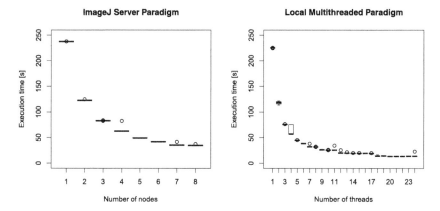

Fig. 4. Scalability of the predefined set of tasks when employing the ImageJ Server Paradigm (left) and the Local Multithreaded Paradigm (right). The horizontal axis denotes the number of processing nodes and threads, respectively, the vertical axis represents the required execution time.

6   Conclusion

The ever increasing amount of data produced by various sensors and imaging devices boosts the potential of parallelization techniques and approaches in image processing. Addressing the need for parallelization in ImageJ has been particularly challenging as the platform is extraordinarily extensible, and developers would typically implement parallelization support only within a specific plugin. No platform-wide solution has been adopted yet.

This paper describes the concept of integrating parallelization support into one of the SciJava libraries, enabling ImageJ plugin developers to conveniently distribute execution of individual tasks to multiple computational units, such as nodes of an HPC cluster. An interface providing parallelization functionality has been defined as a SciJava service, and serves as an access point for parallelization-specific functionalities. Particularly, the interface provides information about available parallelization paradigms, objects encapsulating details on cluster access, and task execution. For experimental purposes, two different paradigms were implemented and evaluated. The initial results indicate good scalability, and are promising in terms of prospective incorporation into the SciJava ecosystem. Nevertheless, additional work is needed in order to support parallelization of non-trivial tasks and to provide a more extensive interface for ImageJ plugin developers.

The advantage of the proposed approach is that cluster-specific details are hidden in respective interface implementations, so plugins remain technology-agnostic. The source codes of the implemented paradigms are available on GitHub[5] for further development by the SciJava community.

---

[5] https://github.com/PetrBainar/scijava-parallel.

Acknowledgement. This work was supported by the European Regional Development Fund in the IT4Innovations national supercomputing center – path to exascale project, project number CZ.02.1.01/0.0/0.0/16_013/0001791 within the Operational Programme Research, Development and Education.

We would like to thank Curtis Rueden from Laboratory for Optical and Computational Instrumentation, University of Wisconsin-Madison for his assistance and comments that greatly improved this work.

References

1. ActiveMQ - Apache ActiveMQ - index. http://activemq.apache.org/. Accessed 31 May 2018
2. Apache Spark - unified analytics engine for big data. https://spark.apache.org/. Accessed 31 May 2018
3. RabbitMQ - messaging that just works. https://www.rabbitmq.com/. Accessed 31 May 2018
4. Welcome to Apache Hadoop. https://hadoop.apache.org/. Accessed 31 May 2018
5. Berthold, M.R., et al.: KNIME - the Konstanz information miner: version 2.0 and beyond. ACM SIGKDD Explor. Newslett. **11**(1), 26–31 (2009)
6. Bonér, J.: Introducing Akka - simpler scalability, fault-tolerance, concurrency & remoting through actors. Technical report (2009)
7. Bull, J., Westhead, M.D., Kambites, M., Obdržálek, J.: Towards OpenMP for Java. In: European Workshop on OpenMP (EWOMP 2000), vol. 39, p. 40 (2000)
8. Cima, V., Böhm, S., Martinovič, J., Dvorský, J., Ashby, T.J., Chupakhin, V.: HyperLoom possibilities for executing scientific workflows on the cloud. In: Barolli, L., Terzo, O. (eds.) CISIS 2017. AISC, vol. 611, pp. 397–406. Springer, Cham (2018). https://doi.org/10.1007/978-3-319-61566-0_36
9. Expósito, R.R., Ramos, S., Taboada, G.L., Touriño, J., Doallo, R.: FastMPJ: a scalable and efficient Java message-passing library. Cluster Comput. **17**(3), 1031–1050 (2014)
10. Fillbrunn, A., Dietz, C., Pfeuffer, J., Rahn, R., Landrum, G.A., Berthold, M.R.: KNIME for reproducible cross-domain analysis of life science data. J. Biotechnol. **261**, 149–156 (2017)
11. Grunzke, R., Jug, F., Schuller, B., Jäkel, R., Myers, G., Nagel, W.E.: Seamless HPC Integration of data-intensive knime workflows via UNICORE. In: Desprez, F., et al. (eds.) Euro-Par 2016. LNCS, vol. 10104, pp. 480–491. Springer, Cham (2017). https://doi.org/10.1007/978-3-319-58943-5_39
12. Jones, T.R., et al.: Cellprofiler analyst: data exploration and analysis software for complex image-based screens. BMC Bioinform. **9**(1), 482 (2008). https://doi.org/10.1186/1471-2105-9-482
13. Kaminsky, A.: Big CPU, Big Data: Solving the World's Toughest Computational Problems with Parallel Computing, 1st edn. CreateSpace Independent Publishing Platform, North Charleston (2016)
14. Köster, J., Rahmann, S.: Snakemake - a scalable bioinformatics workflow engine. Bioinformatics **28**(19), 2520–2522 (2012)
15. Lee, H.K., Carpenter, B., Fox, G., Lim, S.B.: HP Java: programming support for high-performance grid-enabled applications. Parallel Algorithms Appl. **19**(2–3), 175–193 (2004)

16. Romberg, M.: The unicore architecture: seamless access to distributed resources. In: The Eighth International Symposium on High Performance Distributed Computing, Proceedings, pp. 287–293. IEEE (1999)
17. Romberg, M.: The unicore grid infrastructure. Sci. Program. **10**(2), 149–157 (2002)
18. Rueden, C., Schindelin, J., Hiner, M., Eliceiri, K.: SciJava Common [software]. http://scijava.org
19. Rueden, C.T., Eliceiri, K.W.: The ImageJ ecosystem: an open and extensible platform for biomedical image analysis. Microscopy Microanal. **23**(S1), 226–227 (2017)
20. Rueden, C.T., et al.: Image J2: ImageJ for the next generation of scientific image data. BMC Bioinform. **18**(1), 529 (2017)
21. Schindelin, J., et al.: Fiji: an open-source platform for biological-image analysis. Nature Methods **9**(7), 676 (2012)
22. Schindelin, J., Rueden, C.T., Hiner, M.C., Eliceiri, K.W.: The ImageJ ecosystem: an open platform for biomedical image analysis. Mol. Reprod. Dev. **82**(7–8), 518–529 (2015)
23. Schmied, C., Stamataki, E., Tomancak, P.: Open-source solutions for SPIMage processing. Methods Cell Biol. **123C**, 505–529 (2014)
24. Schmied, C., Steinbach, P., Pietzsch, T., Preibisch, S., Tomancak, P.: An automated workflow for parallel processing of large multiview SPIM recordings. Bioinformatics **32**(7), 1112–1114 (2016)
25. Schneider, C.A., Rasband, W.S., Eliceiri, K.W.: NIH Image to ImageJ: 25 years of image analysis. Nat. Meth. **9**(7), 671–675 (2012)
26. Taboada, G.L., Ramos, S., Expósito, R.R., Touriño, J., Doallo, R.: Java in the high performance computing arena: research, practice and experience. Sci. Comput. Program. **78**(5), 425–444 (2013)
27. Veldema, R., Bhoedjang, R., Bal, H.E.: Distributed shared memory management for Java. In: Proceedings of Sixth Annual Conference of the Advanced School for Computing and Imaging (ASCI 2000). Citeseer (1999)
28. Wollmann, T., Erfle, H., Eils, R., Rohr, K., Gunkel, M.: Workflows for microscopy image analysis and cellular phenotyping. J. Biotechnol. **261**, 70–75 (2017)

On Investigation of Stability and Bifurcation of Neural Network with Discrete and Distributed Delays

Vasyl Martsenyuk[1]([✉]) [iD], Igor Andrushchak[2][iD], Andrii Sverstiuk[3][iD], and Aleksandra Klos-Witkowska[4][iD]

[1] Department of Computer Science and Automatics, University of Bielsko-Biala, 43-309 Bielsko-Biala, Poland
vmartsenyuk@ath.bielsko.pl
[2] Department of Computer Technologies, Lutsk National Technical University, 43000 Lutsk, Ukraine
9000@lntu.edu.ua
[3] Department of Medical Informatics, Ternopil State Medical University, 46001 Ternopil, Ukraine
sverstyuk@tdmu.edu.ua
[4] Department of Computer Science and Automatics, University of Bielsko-Biala, 43-309 Bielsko-Biala, Poland
awitkowska@ath.bielsko.pl

Abstract. Paper presents our results dealing with qualitative investigation of neural network including discrete and distributed time delays. We use indirect method to get exponential decay rates of the model. Dynamic behavior is also investigated numerically when changing model parameters. As a result we get point attractors which transit to periodic ones when increasing absolute values of parameters.

Keywords: Neural network · Discrete delay · Distributed delay
Exponential stability · Bifurcation

1 Introduction

One of the most modern application of differential equations with delay is dealt with modeling artificial neural networks. Such models allow us to investigate convergence of recognition algorithms. This is the most significant feature of such models enabling constant interest to analysis of their qualitative behavior.

Hopfield [2] constructed a simplified neural network model, in which each neuron is represented by a linear circuit consisting of a resistor and a capacitor, and is connected to other neurons via nonlinear sigmoidal activation functions, called transfer functions. An survey of first works in area of neural network models based on differential equations with delay is presented in [11].

Supported by University of Bielsko-Biala.

K. Saeed and W. Homenda (Eds.): CISIM 2018, LNCS 11127, pp. 300–313, 2018.
https://doi.org/10.1007/978-3-319-99954-8_26

When analysing publications in field of models of artificial neural networks based on differential equations with delay nowadays we can differ two general approaches.

The first one studies local behavior of such systems with help of comparison with linearised system. Here we would like to mention work [11] applying general technique presented in [9,10] for two-neuron model including method based on Rouché's theorem. Linear stability of the model is investigated by analyzing the associated characteristic transcendental equation. The same method was implemented in [12] for four-neuron model.

The next very important problem included in qualitative behavior of these models is Hopf bifurcation. Here we again consider work [11] where for the case without self-connection, it was found that the Hopf bifurcation occurs when the sum of the two delays varies and passes a sequence of critical values. Similar results were obtained in [3,12]. The stability and direction of the Hopf bifurcation were determined by applying the normal form theory and the center manifold theorem.

The second approach is dealt with Lyapunov-Krasovkii functionals. The main advantage of this method is ability to obtain constructive stability conditions. As a rule these conditions are very flexible because include parameters of Lyapunov-Krasovskii functionals. That is they admit optimization also.

That's why the purpose of this work is to offer a method of investigation of dynamic behavior of neural network model with discrete and distributed delays.

In Sect. 2 we describe model of neural network with discrete and distributed delays studied in the paper.

In Sect. 4 we present method of exponential estimate construction and demonstrate its application when analysing dependence of exponential decay rate and time delay.

In Sect. 5 we investigate behavior of two-neuron model with four delays numerically.

Within this paper we use the following notation:

- the symbol $i = \overline{m,n}$ for some integer $i, m, n, m < n$ means $i = m, m+1, ..., n$;

- $\lambda_{\min}(M)$, $\lambda_{\max}(M)$ and $tr(M)$ for minimal, maximal eigenvalues and trace of matrix M respectively;

- Euclidean norm $\|x\|$ for vector $x \in \mathbb{R}^n$;

- the norm of a vector-function $|\phi(\bullet)|^\tau = \sup\limits_{\theta \in [-\tau,0], i=\overline{1,n}} |\phi_i(\theta)|$, where functions $\phi \in \mathbb{C}^1[-\tau,0]$;

- an arbitrary matrix norm $\|M\|$ and spectrum $\sigma(M)$ for matrix $M \in \mathbb{R}^{n \times n}$;

- let the space $C[-\tau,0] = C([-\tau,0], \mathbb{R}^n)$ be the Banach space of continuous functions mapping the interval $[-\tau,0]$ into $\mathbb{R}^n$ with the topology of uniform convergence;

– the space $\mathbb{C}^1[-\tau, 0]$ of continuously differentiable functions $\phi : [?\tau, 0] \to \mathbb{R}^n$, with the norm $|\phi(\bullet)|^\tau$.

2   Problem Statement

We consider neural network described by system with mixed delays

$$\dot{x}(t) = -Ax(t) + \sum_{m=1}^{r} W_{1,m} g(x(t - \tau_m(t))) + \sum_{m=1}^{r} W_{2,m} \int_{t-\tau_m(t)}^{t-h_m(t)} g(x(\theta))d\theta \ (1)$$

$x(t) \in \mathbb{R}^n$ is the state vector. $A = diag(a_1, a_2, ..., a_n)$ is a diagonal matrix with positive entries $a_i > 0$, $W_{1,m} = (w_{ij}^{1,m})_{n \times n}$, $W_{2,m} = (w_{ij}^{2,m})_{n \times n}$ $m = \overline{1,r}$ are the connection weight matrices, $g(x(t)) = [g_1(x(t)), g_2(x(t)), ..., g_n(x(t))]^\top \in \mathbb{R}^n$ denotes the neuron activation functions which are bounded monotonically non-decreasing with $g_j(0) = 0$ and satisfy the following condition

$$0 \le \frac{g_j(\xi_1) - g_j(\xi_2)}{\xi_1 - \xi_2} \le l_j \tag{2}$$

$\xi_1, \xi_2 \in \mathbb{R}$, $\xi_1 \ne \xi_2$, $j = 1, 2, ..., n$. [1]
According to the customary, in the system (1) we call the second term with discrete time-varying delays and the third term with distributed time-varying delays.

The bounded functions $\tau_m(t)$ represent mixed delays of system with $0 \le \tau_m(t) \le \tau_M$, $\dot{\tau}_m(t) \le \tau_D < 1$, $m = \overline{1,r}$.

The bounded functions $h_m(t)$ represent minimal threshold for distributed delays of system with $h_{\min} \le h_m(t) \le \tau_m(t)$, $m = \overline{1,r}$, $t > 0$. Delays $h_m(t)$ and $\tau_m(t)$ have physical meaning as "controllable memory" of the network if neurons effects on network output only during some time interval. Here we consider the case if we have discrete delays as "maximal" thresholds for distributed delays. Indeed reasonings of this work can be extended to the case if we have entirely other "maximal" thresholds.

The initial conditions associated with system (1) are of the form

$$x_i(s) = \phi_i(s), \quad s \in [-\tau_M, 0], \tag{3}$$

where $\phi_i(s)$ is a continuous real-valued function for $s \in [-\tau_M, 0]$. Then, the solution of system (1) exists for all $t \ge 0$ and is unique [1] under the Assumption (2)

---

[1] In (1) denotion $\int g(x(\theta))d\theta$ means $[\int g_1(x(\theta))d\theta, \int g_2(x(\theta))d\theta, ..., \int g_n(x(\theta))d\theta]^\top \in \mathbb{R}^n$.

3   Indirect Method of Stability Investigation

We consider the system

$$\dot{x}(t) = -Ax(t) + F[x_t(\theta)], \quad t \geq 0,$$
$$x_0(\theta) = \phi(\theta), \quad \theta \in [-\tau, 0], \tag{4}$$

$x(t) \in \mathbb{R}^n$ is the state vector, $x_t \in C^1[-\tau, 0]$, $A \in \mathbb{R}^{n \times n}$ is positive definite matrix, functional $F : C^1[-\tau, -\delta] \to \mathbb{R}^n$ for some constant $\delta > 0 : \delta < \tau$. Let $\alpha > 0$ be maximal eigenvalue of A.

The method offered to find exponential estimate $X(t, k, \lambda) = k|\phi(\theta)|^\tau e^{-\lambda t}$ includes the following steps

Remark 1. For the sake of simplicity we will use hereinafter the notations for exponential estimates $X(t, k, \lambda) = X(t, \lambda) = X(t)$, $Y(t, k, \lambda) = Y(t, \lambda) = Y(t)$.

Step 1. Write Cauchy formula for (4)

$$x(t) = e^{-At}\phi(0) + \int_0^t e^{-A(t-s)}y(s)ds$$

where $y(s) = F[x_s(\theta)]$. It follows that

$$\|x(t)\| \leq X(t, k, \alpha) + \int_0^t (|\phi(\theta)|^\tau)^{-1} X(t-s, k, \alpha)\|y(s)\|ds \tag{5}$$

Step 2. We choose $Y(s, \lambda)$ as exponential estimate for $y(s)$ satisfying to Cauchy-like formula

$$X(t, k, \lambda) = X(t, k, \alpha) + \int_0^t (|\phi(\theta)|^\tau)^{-1} X(t-s, k, \alpha)Y(s, k, \lambda)ds \tag{6}$$

Step 3. Consider distances

$$\rho_1(t, k, \lambda) = \|x(t)\| - X(t, k, \lambda), \quad \rho_2(t, k, \lambda) = \|y(t)\| - Y(t, k, \lambda)$$

Subtracting (6) from (5) we get

$$\rho_1(t, k, \lambda) \leq \int_0^t (|\phi(\theta)|^\tau)^{-1} X(t-s, k, \alpha)\rho_2(s, k, \lambda)ds$$

Assume that $\lambda > 0$ such that

$$\rho_2(s, k, \lambda) \leq \Phi[\rho_{1_s}(\bullet, k, \lambda)] \tag{7}$$

where $\Phi : C[-\tau, -\delta] \to \mathbb{R}^1$ for some $\delta > 0$ is some monotonically increasing functional [2]. We get

$$\rho_1(t, k, \lambda) \leq \int_0^t (|\phi(\theta)|^\tau)^{-1} X(t-s, k, \alpha)\Phi[\rho_{1_s}(\bullet, k, \lambda)]ds \tag{8}$$

---

[2] We mean that functional $\Phi : C[a, b] \to \mathbb{R}^1$ is "monotonically increasing" if $f(t) \leq g(t)$, $t \in [a, b]$ imlies $\Phi[f] \leq \Phi[g]$.

Step 4. Combining condition (7) and

$$\lambda > 0: \quad \|\phi(t)\| < X(t, \lambda), \quad t \in [-\tau, 0] \tag{9}$$

and taking into account (8) we can find parameter $\lambda > 0$ for exponential estimate $X(t, \lambda)$.

4   Exponential Stability for Neural Network Model with Discrete and Distributed Delays

Theorem 1. *Let system (1) be such that*

- *matrix A satisfies the inequality $\|e^{-At}\| \leq k e^{-\alpha t}$ for $t \geq 0$ and some $k \geq 1$, $\alpha > 0$; Note that in case of diagonal matrix A with positive entries α can be chosen as $\alpha := \min_{1 \leq i \leq n}\{a_i\}$*

- *there exists a solution $\lambda > 0$ of the quasipolynomial inequality*

$$\frac{e^{-\lambda \tau_M}}{k}(\alpha - \lambda) \geq \sup_{t \geq 0}\left(\sum_{m=0}^{r}(\|W_{1,m}\| + \|W_{2,m}\|(\tau_m(t) - h_m(t)))\, l_m\right). \tag{10}$$

Then the estimate $\|x(t)\| \leq k|\phi(\theta)|^{\tau_M} e^{-\lambda t}$ is true for the solution of system (1) for any $t \geq 0$, where $\lambda > 0$ is a number satisfying inequality (10).

Note 1. Assumption (10) for positive λ implies $\lambda < \alpha$ obviously.

Theorem 1 can be obtained as a result of application of general method presented in Sect. 3 and gives us a simple method of calculation of exponential decay rate dependent on delay.

Analysing inequality (10) we can see general relations between estimates of model characteristics.

Corollary 1. *In practice instead of (10) we may use "rougher" quasipolynomial inequality*

$$\frac{e^{-\lambda \tau_M}}{k}(\alpha - \lambda) \geq \sum_{m=0}^{r}(\|W_{1,m}\| + \|W_{2,m}\|(\tau_M - h_{\min}))\, l_m. \tag{11}$$

Remark 2. Positive solution λ of quasipolynomial inequalities (10) or (11) exists only if $\alpha > \lambda$.

Theorem 1 gives us a clear estimate for lower memory threshold allowing exponential convergence due to (11).

Corollary 2. *The value of $h_{\min}$ admitting local exponential stability with decay rate due to (11) can be estimated from inequality*

$$h_{\min} \geq \left(\sum_{m=0}^{r}\|W_{2,n}\|l_m\right)^{-1}\left(\sum_{m=0}^{r}(\|W_{1,m}\| + \|W_{2,m}\|\tau_M)l_m - \frac{e^{-\lambda \tau_M}}{k}(\alpha - \lambda)\right) \tag{12}$$

Proof. It directly follows from (11). $\qquad\square$

Corollary 3. *At assumption of Theorem 1 there exists direct dependency between $h_{\min}$ and λ. That is, when increasing in model (1) the value of $h_{\min}$ we increase the estimate of exponential decay rate λ and vice versa.*

Proof. It follows immediately when considering dependency

$$
h_{\min}(\lambda) := \left(\sum_{m=0}^{r} \|W_{2,n}\| l_m \right)^{-1}
$$
$$
\times \left(\sum_{m=0}^{r} (\|W_{1,m}\| + \|W_{2,m}\| \tau_M) l_m - \frac{e^{-\lambda \tau_M}}{k} (\alpha - \lambda) \right)
$$

and calculating its derivative

$$
\frac{dh_{\min}}{d\lambda} = \left(\sum_{m=0}^{r} \|W_{2,n}\| l_m \right)^{-1} \frac{e^{-\lambda \tau_M}}{k} [\tau_m(\alpha - \lambda) + 1] \geq 0
$$

$\qquad\square$

Corollary 4. *For arbitrary $m \in \overline{1,r}$ exponential decay rate estimate λ calculated based on the Theorem 1 is symmetric with respect to $W_{i,m}$, $i = 1, 2$, i.e.*

$$
\lambda(W_{i,m}) = \lambda(-W_{i,m})
$$

Moreover, the estimate depends exceptionally on matrix norm $\|W_{i,m}\|$, $i = 1, 2$.

Proof. It follows immediately from inequality (2) including matrix norms $\|W_{i,m}\|$. $\qquad\square$

5   Numerical Research of Dynamical Behavior

Further research is based on numerical experiments.

Example 1. The model comes from ([3], p.808) where they considered the following simple two-neuron network with four delays ($n = 2$, $r = 4$) for some constant rates b and c:

$$A = \begin{pmatrix} -1 & 0 \\ 0 & -1 \end{pmatrix}, \quad W_{1,1} = \begin{pmatrix} b & 0 \\ 0 & 0 \end{pmatrix}, \quad W_{1,2} = \begin{pmatrix} 0 & b \\ 0 & 0 \end{pmatrix}$$

$$W_{1,3} = \begin{pmatrix} 0 & 0 \\ b & 0 \end{pmatrix}, \quad W_{1,4} = \begin{pmatrix} 0 & 0 \\ 0 & b \end{pmatrix}$$

$$W_{2,1} = \begin{pmatrix} c & 0 \\ 0 & 0 \end{pmatrix}, \quad W_{2,2} = \begin{pmatrix} 0 & c \\ 0 & 0 \end{pmatrix}$$

$$W_{2,3} = \begin{pmatrix} 0 & 0 \\ c & 0 \end{pmatrix}, \quad W_{2,4} = \begin{pmatrix} 0 & 0 \\ 0 & c \end{pmatrix} \tag{13}$$

$$g_1(x) = g_2(x) = \tanh(x) \text{ at } x \in \mathbb{R}^2,$$

$$\tau_1 = \frac{13}{12}\pi, \tau_2 = \frac{11}{12}\pi, \tau_3 = \frac{7}{12}\pi, \tau_4 = \frac{5}{12}\pi,$$

$$h_1 = h_2 = h_3 = h_4 = \frac{1}{12}\pi$$

Considering initial conditions $x_1(t) \equiv 0.001$, $x_2(t) \equiv 0.004$, $t \in [-\tau_M, 0]$ and applying Theorem 1 we can calculate the value of exponential decay λ. It can be readily solved by using the numerically efficient R package.

Previously in the work [7] it was studied model (13) provided that we don't have distributed delays, i.e., $c = 0$. At this case is shown in the Table 1 the dependence of λ on the value of b.

Table 1. Dependence of value of b and $\lambda > 0$ calculated for Example 1 without distributed delays

b	−0.25	−0.2	−0.1	−0.05	0.1	0.2	0.25
λ	0	0.0503686	0.2026738	0.3474646	0.2026738	0.0503686	0

If we have distributed delays with parameter $c = 0.005$ then resulting values of λ are presented in the Table 2.

Table 2. Dependence of value of b and $\lambda > 0$ calculated from (11) for Example 1 at $c = 0.005$. Symbol "-" means absence of positive solutions of (11).

b	−0.25	−0.2	−0.1	−0.05	0.1	0.2	0.25
λ	-	0.03337481	0.171189	0.2914205	0.171189	0.03337481	-

For the reasons given we conclude that distributed delays combined with discrete delays narrow the interval of parameters b admitting exponential convergence.

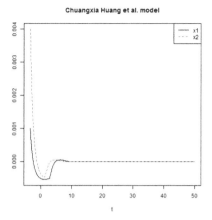

Fig. 1. State trajectories in Example 1 with $b = -0.1$ and $c = 0.005$

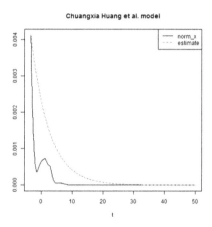

Fig. 2. Exponential estimate and norm of the solution of Example 1 with $b = -0.1$ and $c = 0.005$

As a supplement, Fig. 1 shows the time response of state variables $x_1(t)$, $x_2(t)$ in this example with $b = -0.1$ and initial vector $(0.001, 0.004)^\top$. Figure 2 shows exponential estimate constructed in this model at $b = -0.1$.

The dependence of $h_{\min}$ on λ due to (12) is presented on the Table 3.

As it was shown in the work [3] (Theorem 2.1) the equilibrium (0, 0) of system (13) with discrete delays only is delay-independently locally asymptotically stable if $b \in (-0.5, 0.5)$.

Here from Table 1 we can see that for network with both discrete and distributed delays, positive estimate of exponential decay rate based on Theorem 1 can be calculated for $b \in [-0.2, 0.2]$. That is in this case the equilibrium (0,0) of system (13) is delay-dependently locally exponentially stable.

Table 3. Dependence of value of h_{min} and $\lambda > 0$ calculated from (12) for Example 1 at $c = 0.005$.

$h_{\min}$	0.2616517	0.26168	0.2627265
λ	0.03337481	0.171189	0.2914205

This model approximates some most known nonlinear behaviors of nonlinear dynamic systems with delays. Further, some examples are given in which neural network converges to an attractor or limit cycle and oscillator. Problem of training trajectories by means of continuous recurrent neural networks with delay whose feedforward parts are as multilayer perceptron was currently studied. Given a set of parameters, initial conditions, and input trajectories, the set of equations (1) can be numerically integrated from $t = 0$ to final time $t = 500$. This will produce trajectories overtime for the state variables x_i. We have used Runge-Kutta with five-degree method in R package.

Here we can see that when changing the values of b and c we have changes of qualitative behavior of network. We considered the parameter value set given above and computed the long-time behavior of the system (1) for $b = 0.1$, 0.5, 2.3, 5.5, and $c = 0$, 0.5, 2.3, 5.5. The phase diagrams of the x_1 vs. x_2 for these values of b and c are shown in Figs. 3, 4, 5, 7, 7 and 8. For example, at $b \in [-0.5, 0.5]$ and $c = 0$ we can see trajectories corresponding to stable node for all pixels (see Fig. 3). At values $b = \sqrt{2}$, $c = 0$ Hopf bifurcation occurs and further trajectories correspond to stable limit cycles of "four-side" form for all pixels (see Fig. 5 for $b = 2.3$). We note that in order that the numerical solutions regarding Hopf bifurcation were in agreement with the theoretical results, we should look for a complex conjugate pair of purely imaginary solutions of the corresponding characteristic equation of the linearized system. For $b = 1.41$, $c = 1.41$, the phase diagrams in Fig. 4 show that the solution is a limit cycle with two local extrema (one local maximum and one local minimum) per cycle. Generally we can differ four kinds of periodic attractors for the neural network:

- "four-sided" form (see Figs. 4 and 5)
- "six-sided" form (see Fig. 6)
- ellipsoidal form (see Fig. 7)
- combining ellipsoidal and "four-sided" forms (see Fig. 8)

For the reasons given we can conclude that discrete delays correspond to "four-sided" forms whereas distributed delays correspond to ellipsoidal ones.

6   Conclusions

Indirect method offered here can be applied to other neural network models with delay. According to whether neuron states (the external states of neurons) or local fields states (the internal states of neurons) are taken as basic variables, neural networks can be classified as static neural networks or local field neural

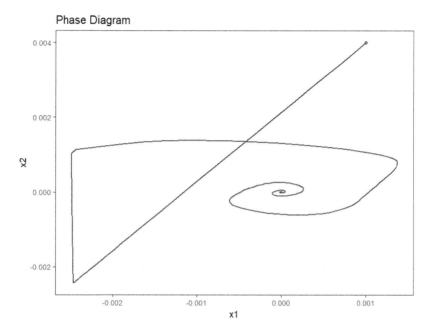

Fig. 3. State space trajectory at $b = -0.5$, $c = 0$ (point attractor).

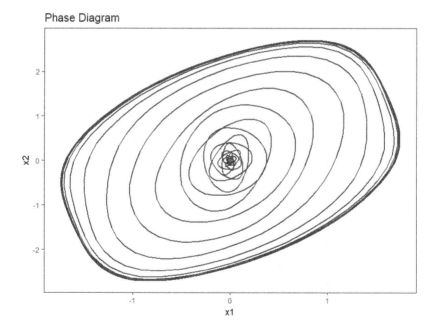

Fig. 4. State space trajectory at $b = -1.41$, $c = -1.41$ (periodic attractor 1).

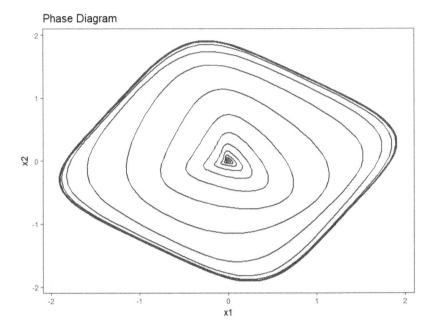

Fig. 5. State space trajectory at $b = -2.3$, $c = 0$ (periodic attractor 1).

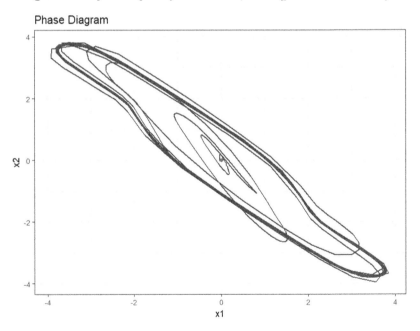

Fig. 6. State space trajectory at $b = -5.5$, $c = 0$ (periodic attractor 2).

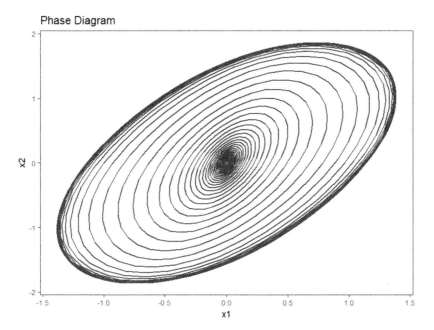

Fig. 7. State space trajectory at $b = 0.0$, $c = -2.3$ (periodic attractor 3).

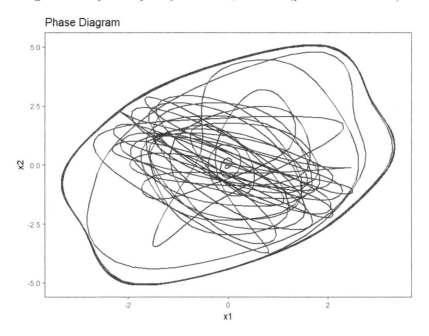

Fig. 8. State space trajectory at $b = -2.3$, $c = -2.3$ (periodic attractor 4).

networks [5]. For example, the recurrent back-propagation neural networks given below are static neural networks

$$\dot{x}(t) = -Ax(t) + \sum_{m=1}^{r} g(W_m x(t - \tau_m(t))) \tag{14}$$

where x_i is the state of neuron i with $\sum_{m=1}^{r} \sum_{j=1}^{n} w_{ij}^m x_j(t - \tau_m(t))$ as its local field state.

Systems (14) and (1) typically represent two fundamental modelling approaches in the present neural network research. Under the assumption that $r = 1$, $W_1 A = A W_1$ holds and W_1 is invertible, (14) can be easily transformed to network (1) by introducing the variable $v(t) = W_1 x(t)$. However, in many applications, it may not be reasonable to assume that the matrix W_1 is invertible. Many neural systems exhibiting short-term memory are modelled by non-invertible networks. Moreover in case of multiple delays, i.e. $r > 1$, we are also not able to transform local field neural network to static one.

Investigation of exponential stability for neural network models require decay estimates that can be obtained from clear dependencies (not LMIs). Earlier we have done some attempts to construct exponential estimates for linear systems with delay. In the works [4,6,8] such clear estimates are obtained for Lyapunov-Krasovskii functionals satisfying to some difference-differential inequalities. As a rule they try to apply such techniques for real application like neural networks models. Unfortunately, it requires decay rates that can be calculated as a result of clear dependencies between model parameters. It stimulated development of indirect method.

The term 'indirect method' is used in order to contrast with methods of obtaining exponential estimates based on application of Lyapunov functions (or 'direct' method)

As compared with Lyapunov-Krasovskii functional approach method offered here does not have such flexible possibilities for optimization of estimates and estimates obtained with help of developed approach are likely more rough and less accurate.

The 'price' of this inaccuracy and roughness is comparatively clear form of expression for decay rate (as compared with multidimensional LMIs). This expression is quasipolynomial inequality which is well-known in stability analysis of delay differential equations.

Such simplicity of expressions is of importance in practical application like neural networks for obtaining analytical results. Namely, it allows to study dependencies of neural network exponential stability and changes in model parameters.

Acknowledgments. The author would like to express his gratitude to the reviewer for the valuable comments.

References

1. Hale, J.K., Lunel, S.M.V.: Introduction to functional differential equations, vol. 99. Springer Science & Business Media (2013). https://doi.org/10.1007/978-1-4612-4342-7

2. Hopfield, J.J.: Neurons with graded response have collective computational properties like those of two-state neurons. Proc. Natl. Acad. Sci. **81**(10), 3088–3092 (1984)

3. Huang, C., Huang, L., Feng, J., Nai, M., He, Y.: Hopf bifurcation analysis for a two-neuron network with four delays. Chaos, Solitons and Fractals **34**(3), 795–812 (2007). https://doi.org/10.1016/j.chaos.2006.03.089

4. Khusainov, D., Marzeniuk, V.: Two-side estimates of solutions of linear systems with delay. Reports of Ukr. Nat. Acad. Sciences pp. 8–13 (1996)

5. Liang, J., Cao, J.: A based-on LMI stability criterion for delayed recurrent neural networks. Chaos, Solitons Fractals **28**(1), 154–160 (2006). https://doi.org/10.1016/j.chaos.2005.04.120

6. Marceniuk, V.: On construction of exponential estimates for linear systems with delay. In: Elaydi, S., Gyori, I., Ladas, G. (eds.) Advances in Difference Equations, pp. 439–444. Gordon and Breach Science Publishers (1997)

7. Martsenyuk, V.: On an indirect method of exponential estimation for a neural network model with discretely distributed delays. Electr. J. Qual. Theory Differ. Equs. (23), 1–16 (2017). https://doi.org/10.14232/ejqtde.2017.1.23

8. Marzeniuk, V., Nakonechny, A.: Investigation of delay system with piece-wise right side arising in radiotherapy. WSEAS Trans. Math. **3**(1), 181–187 (2004)

9. Ruan, S., Wei, J.: On the zeros of a third degree exponential polynomial with applications to a delayed model for the control of testosterone secretion. Math. Med. Biol. **18**(1), 41–52 (2001)

10. Ruan, S., Wei, J.: On the zeros of transcendental functions with applications to stability of delay differential equations with two delays. Dyn. Contin. Discret. Impuls. Syst. Ser. A **10**, 863–874 (2003)

11. Wei, J., Ruan, S.: Stability and bifurcation in a neural network model with two delays. Phys. D Nonlinear Phenom. **130**, 255–272 (1999). https://doi.org/10.1016/S0167-2789(99)00009-3

12. Yan, X.P., Li, W.T.: Stability and bifurcation in a simplified four-neuron bam neural network with multiple delays. Discret. Dyn. Nat. Soc. **2006** (2006)

Growing Neural Gas Based on Data Density

Lukáš Vojáček[1(✉)], Pavla Dráždilová[2], and Jiří Dvorský[1,2]

[1] IT4Innovations, VŠB - Technical University of Ostrava,
17. listopadu 15/2172, 708 33 Ostrava, Czech Republic
{lukas.vojacek,jiri.dvorsky}@vsb.cz

[2] Department of Computer Science, VŠB – Technical University of Ostrava,
17. listopadu 15/2172, 708 33 Ostrava, Czech Republic
pavla.drazdilova@vsb.cz

Abstract. The size, complexity and dimensionality of data collections are ever increasing from the beginning of the computer era. Clustering methods, such as Growing Neural Gas (GNG) [10] that is based on unsupervised learning, is used to reveal structures and to reduce large amounts of raw data. The growth of computational complexity of such clustering method, caused by growing data dimensionality and the specific similarity measurement in a high-dimensional space, reduces the effectiveness of clustering method in many real applications. The growth of computational complexity can be partially solved using the parallel computation facilities, such as High Performance Computing (HPC) cluster with MPI. An effective parallel implementation of GNG is discussed in this paper, while the main focus is on minimizing of inter-process communication which depends on the number of neurons and edges among neurons in the neural network. A new algorithm of adding neurons depending on data density is proposed in the paper.

Keywords: Growing neural gas · High-dimensional dataset
High performance computing · MPI · Data density

1 Introduction

The size and complexity of data collections are ever increasing from the beginning of the computer era, while the dimensionality of the data sets is rapidly increasing in recent years. Contemporary and especially future technologies allow us to acquire, store and process large high dimensional data collections that are commonly available in areas like medicine, biology, information retrieval, web analysis, social network analysis, image processing, financial transaction analysis and many others.

To have any chance to process such amount of the data we have to reduce amounts of raw data by categorizing them in smaller set of similar items, we have to identify groups that occurs in the data, we have to reveal structures hidden in

K. Saeed and W. Homenda (Eds.): CISIM 2018, LNCS 11127, pp. 314–323, 2018.
https://doi.org/10.1007/978-3-319-99954-8_27

the data. These tasks are precisely the purpose of methods known as *clustering*. There are many clustering methods, we will focus on clustering methods based on unsupervised learning in this paper.

Unfortunately, there are two major issues faced by clustering algorithms based on unsupervised learning, such as *Growing Neural Gas* (GNG) [10], that prevent them to be effective, in many real applications, on vast high dimensional data collection:

1. The fast growth of computational complexity with respect to growing data dimensionality, and
2. The specific similarity measurement in a high-dimensional space, where the expected distance, computed by Euclidean metrics to the closest and to the farthest point of any given point, shrinks with growing dimensionality [1].

The growth of computational complexity can be partially solved using the parallel computation facilities, such as *High Performance Computing* (HPC) cluster with MPI technology. Obviously, it is necessary to resolve technical and implementation issues specific to this computing platform, such as minimizing of interprocess communication, to provide effective parallel implementation of GNG.

The amount of interprocess increases with the growing number of neurons and edges connecting the neurons. The addition of a new neuron and edges to GNG is driven by condition given at the startup – neuron is added after predefined amount of time regardless the data collection properties. Respecting the data collection properties it is easy to see that some addition of a new neuron and edges is not necessary, for example the addition of a new neuron in dense data area caused just by precalculated condition. Similar approach can be used for outlying data. When a new neuron is created to cover this part of the data collection, there is no special need to attach a new neuron to more neurons than the nearest. In this way the future edge disposal is eliminated. A new neuron is attached to two nearest neurons only in the case that a new neuron would cover a part of the data collection located just nearby these two neurons. So, the sum of distances between a new neuron to these two neurons should be proportional to the distance between these two neurons themselves.

The proposed approach is based only on standard GNG learning algorithms, there is no need to apply space partitioning method to improve nearest neuron search. The performed experiments shows that our approach clearly adhere the structure of data collection, while quality of the GNG is preserved.

We will first introduce the terminology, the notation which we use in the article and related works to GNG. In the next section we describe a new approach how to add a new neuron to GNG. Section Experiments contains statistics and visualization of results. In conclusion, we discuss the advantages of our approach.

2   Growing Neural Gas

The principle of this neural network is an undirected graph which need not be connected. Generally, there are no restrictions on the topology. The graph is generated and continuously updated by competitive Hebbian Learning [9,13]. According to the pre-set conditions, new neurons are automatically added and connections between neurons are subject to time and can be removed. GNG can be used for vector quantization by finding the code-vectors in clusters [8], clustering data streams [7], biologically influenced [14] and 3D model reconstruction [12]. GNG works by modifying the graph, where the operations are the addition and removal of neurons and edges between neurons.

To understand the functioning of GNG, it is necessary to define the algorithm. The algorithm described in our previous article [16] is based on the original algorithm [6,8], but it is modified for better continuity in the SOM algorithm. Here is the Algorithm 1 which describes one iteration.

Remark. The notation used in the paper is briefly listed in Table 1.

2.1   Related Works

The methods based on Artificial Neural Networks (ANN) are computationally expensive. There are different approaches on how to improve effectivity of these methods – improve computation of the nearest neurons, reduce number of computation (batch), parallel implementation and other.

The authors of the paper [4] propose two optimization techniques that are aimed at an efficient implementation of the GNG algorithm internal structure. Their optimizations preserve all properties of the GNG algorithm. The technique enhances the nearest neighbor search using a space partitioning by a grid of rectangular cells and the second technique speeds up the handling of node errors using the lazy evaluation approach. The authors in [13] propose a algorithm for a GNG which can learn new input data (plasticity) without degrading the previously trained network and forgetting the old input data (stability). Online Incremental Supervised Growing Neural Gas in [3] is an algorithm whose features are zero nodes initialization, the original batch Supervised Growing Neural Gas node insertion mechanism and network size constraint. In [2] is proposed a batch variant of Neural gas (NG) which allows fast training for a priorly given data set and a transfer to proximity data. Author's algorithm optimizes the same cost function as NG with faster convergence than original algorithm. A paper [11] proposes a Growing Neural Gas based on density, which is useful for clustering. An algorithm creates new units based on the density of data, producing a better representation of the data space with a less computational cost for a comparable accuracy. Authors use access methods to reduce considerably the number of distance calculations during the training process.

In the paper [5] the authors combine the batch variant of the GNG algorithm with the MapReduce paradigm resulting in a GNG variant suitable for processing large data sets in scalable, general cluster environments. The paper [15] is focused on the actualizations of neurons weights in the learning phase of parallel implementation of SOM. Authors study update strategies between Batch SOM – updates are processed at the end of whole epoch – and immediately updating after processing one input vector.

Table 1. Notation used in the paper

Symbol	Description
M	Number of input vectors
n	Dimension of input vectors, number of input neurons, dimension of weight vectors in GNG output layer neurons
N	Current number of neurons in GNG output layer
N_{max}	Maximum allowed number of neurons in GNG output layer
N_i	i-th output neuron, $i = 1, 2, \ldots, N$
X	Set of input vectors, $X \subset \mathbb{R}^n$
$\boldsymbol{x}_i$	i-th input vector, $i = 1, 2, \ldots, M$
	$\boldsymbol{x}(t) \in X$, $\boldsymbol{x}(t) = (x_1, x_2, \ldots, x_n)$
$\boldsymbol{w}_k(t)$	Weight vector of neuron N_k, $k = 1, 2, \ldots, N$
	$\boldsymbol{w}_k(t) \in \mathbb{R}^n$, $\boldsymbol{w}_k(t) = (w_{1k}, w_{2k}, \ldots, w_{nk})$
N_{c_1}	The first Best Matching Unit (BMU_1), winner of learning competition
N_{c_2}	The second Best Matching Unit (BMU_2), the second best matching neuron in learning competition
$\boldsymbol{w}_{c_1}(t)$	Weight vector of BMU_1
$\boldsymbol{w}_{c_1}(t)$	Weight vector of BMU_2
l_{c_1}	Learning factor of BMU_1
l_{nc_1}	Learning factor of BMU_1 neighbours
e_i	Local error of output neuron N_i, $i = 1, 2, \ldots, N$
α	Error e_i reduction factor
β	Neuron error reduction factor
γ	Interval of input patterns to add a new neuron
a_{max}	Maximum edges age
p	Number of processes
k	Specify an area around BMU_1 without adding a new neuron; $0 < k \leq 1/2$

3   Optimization of Learning Phase

In our paper [16] we dealt with the parallelization of GNG. The main problem that reduces parallelization is communication between processes and threads. This communication increases with the number of neurons in the neural network. The goal of our optimization is to reduce the number of neurons and to manage the addition of new neurons.

By default, new neurons are added after the condition, which is determined at startup calculation - see Algorithm 1 step 8 (a neuron added after a certain period of time). We identified after analysing the GNG learning algorithm that the algorithm does not take into account the input data. The only limitation is the maximum number of neurons in the neural network. Our proposed solution

Algorithm 1. One iteration of the Growing Neural Gas algorithm

1. Find neurons BMUs neurons N_{c_1} and N_{c_2}.
2. Update the local error e_{c_1} of neuron N_{c_1}

$$e_{c_1} = e_{c_1} + \|w_{c_1} - x\|^2 \tag{1}$$

3. Update the weight vector w_{c_1} of neuron N_{c_1}

$$w_{c_1} = w_{c_1} + l_{c_1}(x - w_{c_1}) \tag{2}$$

4. For all neurons N_k where exists edge $e_{c_1 k}$ (N_{c_1} neighbourhood)
   (a) Update the weights w_k using l_{nc_1} learning factor

$$w_k = w_k + l_{nc_1}(x - w_k) \tag{3}$$

   (b) Increase age a_{kc_1} of edge $e_{c_1 k}$

$$a_{kc_1} = a_{kc_1} + 1 \tag{4}$$

5. If there is no edge between neurons N_{c_1} and N_{c_2}, then create such edge. If the edge exists, the age is set to 0.
6. If any edge has reached the age of a_{max}, it is removed.
7. If there is a neuron without connection to any edge, the neuron is then removed.
8. If the number of processed input vectors in the current iteration has reached the whole multiple of the value γ and the maximum allowed number of output neurons is not reached, add a new neuron N_{N+1}. The location and error of the new neuron is determined by the following rules:
   (a) Found neuron N_b(NBE) which has the biggest error e_b.
   (b) Found neuron N_c(NSE) among neighbours of neuron N_b and has the biggest error e_c among these neighbours.
   (c) Create a new neuron N_{N+1} and the value of w_n is set as:

$$w_{N+1} = \frac{1}{2}(w_b + w_c) \tag{5}$$

   (d) Creating edges between neurons N_b and N_{N+1}, and also between neurons N_c and N_{N+1}.
   (e) Removed edge between neurons N_b and N_c.
   (f) Reduction of error value in neurons N_b and N_c using the multiplying factor α. Error for neuron N_{N+1} is equal to the new error of neuron N_b.

consists of two parts. The first part is a change in the condition when inserting a new neuron and the second part is a change in the weight of this new neuron.

3.1   A New Approach How to Add a New Neuron

The goal is to change the current condition that adds a neuron (after a certain time) to a new condition that will take into account the data it is working on. We do not have to specify number of steps for which we add a new neuron. The basic principle of our approach for adding a new one is to evaluate the distance of the input vector from the neurons N_{c_1} and N_{c_2}. If the input vector is close to N_{c_1} then our algorithm does not add the new neuron. Standard approach allways add the new neuron in this situation.

The following inequalities determined when we add a new neuron. A new neuron is added to the neural network, if one of inequalities (6), (7), (8) is true.

$$||N_{c_2} - x(t)|| < ||N_{c_1} - N_{c_2}|| \quad \wedge \quad ||N_{c_1} - x(t)|| \geq k||N_{c_1} - N_{c_2}|| \qquad (6)$$

$$||N_{c_2} - x(t)|| \geq ||N_{c_1} - N_{c_2}|| \quad \wedge \quad ||N_{c_1} - x(t)|| \geq k||N_{c_1} - N_{c_2}|| \qquad (7)$$

$$||N_{c_2} - x(t)|| > ||N_{c_1} - N_{c_2}||, \qquad (8)$$

where $x(t)$ is input vector, parametr k specifies the size of area around N_{c_1} and $0 < k \leq 1/2$.

In Fig. 1, two neurons (N_1 and N_2) and four input vectors (x_1, x_2, x_3 and x_4) can be seen. Neurons N_1 and N_2 represent BMU N_{c_1} and second BMU N_{c_2} for all input vectors in the example. The input vector x_1 is too closed to N_1 ($||N_1 - x_1|| < k||N_{c_1} - N_{c_2}||$) and a new neuron is not added (Fig. 1(b)). If the input vectors x_2, x_3 and x_4 are selected then a new neuron is added. The input vector x_2 satisfies inequality (6) and it is in the standard situation (Fig. 1(a)). The new added neuron N_3 obtains weight which is calculated: $1/2(w_{c_1}(t) + w_{c_2}(t))$. The edge between N_1 and N_2 is deleted and new edges are created which connect a new neuron N_3 with neuron N_1 and N_2. The age of new edges is set to zerro.

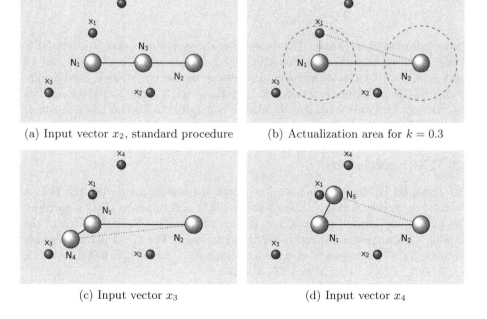

(a) Input vector x_2, standard procedure   (b) Actualization area for $k = 0.3$

(c) Input vector x_3 (d) Input vector x_4

Fig. 1. Addition of a new neuron based on given input vectors x_2, x_3 and x_4

The inequality (8) is true for the input vector x_3 (see Fig. 1(c)) and the inequality (7) is true for the input vector x_4 (see Fig. 1(d)). Only one edge connect the new added neuron N_4 (N_5) with BMU N_1 in both situations. The weight of new neuron and the age of the new edge is set in the standard way.

4   Experiments

4.1   Experimental Datasets and Hardware

One dataset was used in the experiments. The dataset was commonly used in benchmark – *Clustering dataset*.

Clustering Dataset. Three training data collections called TwoDiamonds, Lsun and Target from the Fundamental Clustering Problems Suite (FCPS) were used. A short description of the selected dataset used in our experiments is given in Table 2.

Table 2. Fundamental Clustering Problems Suite – selected datasets

Name	Cases	#Vars	#Clusters	Main clustering problem
Target	770	2	6	Outlying clusters
Lsun	400	2	3	Different variances in clusters
TwoDiamonds	800	2	2	Touching clusters

Experimental Hardware. The experiments were performed on a Linux HPC cluster, named Anselm, with 209 computing nodes, where each node had 16 processors with 64 GB of memory. Processors in the nodes were Intel Sandy Bridge E5-2665. Compute network is InfiniBand QDR, fully non-blocking, fat-tree. Detailed information about hardware is possible to find on the web site of Anselm HPC cluster[1].

4.2   The Experiments

The first part of the experiments was oriented towards comparing the results obtained in density versions (k = 0.3 and k = 0.5) and standard GNG algorithm. The Clustering dataset was used for the experiment. The parallel version of the learning algorithm was run using 16 MPI processes. The GNG parameters are the same for all experiments and are as follows $e_w = 0.05$, $e_n = 0.006$, $\alpha = 0.5$, $\beta = 0.0005$, $a_{max} = 100$, M = 1000, $\delta = 200$.

---

[1] https://support.it4i.cz/docs/anselm-cluster-documentation/hardware-overview.

Table 3. Graphical representations of data set layout and corresponding GNGs

| | Data Collection | | |
	Target	Lsun	TwoDiamonds
Input data			
Standard GNG			
Parallel GNG; k=0.3			
Parallel GNG; k=0.5			

The first row in the Table 3 shows a layout view of the input data, which are used for training GNG. The outputs of standard GNG algorithms are in the second row. In third and fourth rows are result of our proposal method, but each for different size areas that will not update.

In the Table 4, we can see number of neurons which have been used.

For data collection TwoDiamonds, the time computation of standard GNG is 6.05 s, parallel GNG with k = 0.3 is 3.9 s and parallel GNG with k = 0.5 is 2.2 s.

Table 4. Number of used neurons

Algorithm	Dataset		
	Target	Lsun	TwoDiamonds
Standard GNG	771	401	801
Parallel GNG; k = 0.3	583	187	231
Parallel GNG; k = 0.5	51	38	148

5   Conclusion

In this paper the parallel implementation of the GNG neural network algorithm based on data density is presented. The achieved speed-up was better than our previous approach. That's because there are only fewer neurons in the network. Therefore, it takes less time to locate the BMU. For parallelization, we generally try to keep communication as small as possible, which reduces this communication due to fewer neurons; this is most evident when adding and removing neurons.

In future work we intend to focus on the sparse date, use combinations of neural networks for improved result and improved acceleration.

Acknowledgments. This work was supported by The Ministry of Education, Youth and Sports from the Large Infrastructures for Research, Experimental Development and Innovations project "IT4Innovations National Supercomputing Center – LM2015070" and co-financed by SGS, VŠB – Technical University of Ostrava, Czech Republic, under the grant No. SP2018/126 "Parallel processing of Big Data V".

References

1. Beyer, K., Goldstein, J., Ramakrishnan, R., Shaft, U.: When is "Nearest Neighbor" meaningful? In: Beeri, C., Buneman, P. (eds.) ICDT 1999. LNCS, vol. 1540, pp. 217–235. Springer, Heidelberg (1999). https://doi.org/10.1007/3-540-49257-7_15
2. Cottrell, M., Hammer, B., Hasenfuß, A., Villmann, T.: Batch neural gas. In: 5th Workshop On Self-Organizing Maps, vol. 102, p. 130 (2005)
3. Duque-Belfort, F., Bassani, H.F., Araujo, A.F.: Online incremental supervised growing neural gas. In: 2017 International Joint Conference on Neural Networks (IJCNN), pp. 1034–1040. IEEE (2017)
4. Fišer, D., Faigl, J., Kulich, M.: Growing neural gas efficiently. Neurocomputing **104**, 72–82 (2013)

5. Fliege, J., Benn, W.: MapReduce-based growing neural gas for scalable cluster environments. Machine Learning and Data Mining in Pattern Recognition. LNCS (LNAI), vol. 9729, pp. 545–559. Springer, Cham (2016). https://doi.org/10.1007/978-3-319-41920-6_43

6. Fritzke, B.: A growing neural gas network learns topologies. In: Advances in Neural Information Processing Systems 7, pp. 625–632. MIT Press (1995)

7. Ghesmoune, M., Lebbah, M., Azzag, H.: A new growing neural gas for clustering data streams. Neural Netw. **78**, 36–50 (2016)

8. Holmström, J.: Growing Neural Gas Experiments with GNG, GNG with Utility and Supervised GNG. Master's thesis, Uppsala University (2002-08-30)

9. Martinetz, T.: Competitive hebbian learning rule forms perfectly topology preserving maps. In: Gielen, S., Kappen, B. (eds.) ICANN 1993, pp. 427–434. Springer, London (1993)

10. Martinetz, T., Schulten, K.: A "neural-gas" network learns topologies. Artif. Neural Netw. **1**, 397–402 (1991)

11. Ocsa, A., Bedregal, C., Guadros-Vargas, E.: DB-GNG: a constructive self-organizing map based on density. In: International Joint Conference on Neural Networks, 2007. IJCNN 2007, pp. 1953–1958. IEEE (2007)

12. Orts-Escolano, S., et al.: 3D model reconstruction using neural gas accelerated on GPU. Appl. Soft Comput. **32**, 87–100 (2015)

13. Prudent, Y., Ennaji, A.: An incremental growing neural gas learns topologies. In: Proceedings of the 2005 IEEE International Joint Conference on Neural Networks, 2005. IJCNN 2005, vol. 2, pp. 1211–1216 (2005)

14. Sledge, I., Keller, J.: Growing neural gas for temporal clustering. In: 19th International Conference on Pattern Recognition, 2008. ICPR 2008, pp. 1–4 (2008)

15. Vojáček, L., Dráždilová, P., Dvorský, J.: Self organizing maps with delay actualization. In: Saeed, K., Homenda, W. (eds.) CISIM 2015. LNCS, vol. 9339, pp. 154–165. Springer, Cham (2015). https://doi.org/10.1007/978-3-319-24369-6_13

16. Vojáček, L., Dvorský, J.: Growing neural gas – a parallel approach. In: Saeed, K., Chaki, R., Cortesi, A., Wierzchoń, S. (eds.) CISIM 2013. LNCS, vol. 8104, pp. 408–419. Springer, Heidelberg (2013). https://doi.org/10.1007/978-3-642-40925-7_38

Modelling and Optimization

Switching Policy Based Energy Aware Routing Algorithm for Maximizing Lifetime in Wireless Sensor Networks

Durba Chatterjee, Satrap Rathore, and Sanghita Bhattacharjee$^{(\boxtimes)}$

Department of Computer Science and Engineering,
National Institute of Technology, Durgapur 713209, India
durba.chatterjee94@gmail.com,
satraprathore@gmail.com, sanghita.b@gmail.com

Abstract. Data collection is one of the fundamental operations in Wireless Sensor Networks (WSNs). Sensor nodes can sense the data and forward the sensed data to the sink in multi hop communication. During the process of data collection, nodes consume a significant amount of energy by transmitting and receiving of data. Therefore, the key challenge is to minimize the energy dissipation of the nodes so as the network lifetime is maximized. In this paper, we propose a Switching Policy based Energy Aware Routing algorithm (SPEAR) for WSNs that aims to reduce energy usage of nodes and thus extends the network lifetime. In a data collection round, SPEAR constructs an energy balanced data collection tree considering the residual energy level of nodes. Furthermore, a switching policy is introduced to achieve energy balancing and longer lifetime. The proposed SPEAR directs some sensor nodes to switch to the new parents with higher energy when the energy level of the older parent is below some threshold value. The proposed method is loop less and dynamic in nature. Our algorithm is validated through simulation and compared with the existing routing protocol using some performance metrics. Simulation results demonstrate that SPEAR improves the network lifetime, alive nodes count and average residual energy significantly.

Keywords: Wireless sensor networks · Data collection · Energy consumption
Network lifetime · Parent switching

1 Introduction

Wireless Sensor Networks (WSNs) have attracted a substantial attention over the past few years for many applications such as remote sensing, environmental monitoring, agriculture and health care [1]. WSNs consist of a large number of tiny, cheap and resource constraint sensor nodes. These nodes are driven by the limited energy batteries and replacement or recharge of these batteries is impossible when they are deployed in harsh environments such as forest, sea and volcano. In WSNs, transmission and reception are two major concerns of sensor energy consumption. In multi hop data collection process, nodes near to the sink forward a large volume of data packets and expend their batteries quickly. This may cause imbalanced energy dissipation among

© Springer Nature Switzerland AG 2018
K. Saeed and W. Homenda (Eds.): CISIM 2018, LNCS 11127, pp. 327–340, 2018.
https://doi.org/10.1007/978-3-319-99954-8_28

the sensors and shortened network lifetime. There exist many definitions to define lifetime [4], but the commonly used definition is First Node Died Time (FNDT) i.e., the time when the first node drains out its energy completely and becomes non-functional. Therefore, balancing of sensor energy is a prime issue to improve the network lifetime and network performance. Several energy efficient algorithms [2] such as clustering [3, 4], data aggregation [5, 6], load balancing [10, 12, 13], have been developed in the literature to conserve the sensor energy. Among these, the energy efficient load balancing techniques are the most popular since they seek to maximize the network lifetime. In a load balancing approach, load balanced data collection routing tree is constructed. Such a tree topology should not be static all time, instead it can be formed dynamically based on the residual energy of node [10]. GSTEB proposed in [13] changes the root of the tree at each round and reconstructs the routing tree to reduce the energy expenditure of nodes. However, GSTEB improves the lifetime, but repeated formation of the routing tree increases substantially routing overhead.

In this paper, we propose a Switching Policy based Energy Aware Routing algorithm, which is called SPEAR, for WSNs, that aims to reduce energy consumption of the nodes so as the network lifetime is maximized. In SPEAR, data collection is performed in each round and sensor node sends the collected data to the sink using an energy optimized routing path. During the routing tree formation, each sender defines its potential parent set based on the average energy load and priorities the nodes in it according to energy consumption and residual energy level. These potential parents have positive progress towards the sink and have a higher energy value than the sender. Furthermore, a switching function is invoked to balance the energy usage of nodes. During switching, SPEAR directs some sensors to switch to new parents when the residual energy level of the older parent is lower than some threshold value. If switching is not possible at any stage, topology reconstruction is called to improve the network lifetime. The proposed algorithm is dynamic in nature and is loop free. We validate the performance of the proposed algorithm through simulations and compare with existing GSTEB [13] and Aggregation based method [5] with respect to some performance metrics. Simulation results demonstrate that SPEAR improves the network lifetime, alive nodes count and average residual energy than other algorithms.

The paper organization is as follows. Section 2 gives related work. In Sect. 3, we discuss various models and definitions. Section 4 describes the proposed work in details. We present the simulation results in Sect. 5. We conclude the paper in Sect. 6.

2   Related Work

In this section, some energy efficient routing algorithms studying lifetime maximization and energy consumption minimization have been discussed. Clustering is a promising solution to reduce the energy consumption of the nodes in WSNs. LEACH [3] is a popular example of distributed clustering. In LEACH, randomization is used to select cluster heads (CHs) and the role of CH is rotated among the nodes to minimize the energy usage. Although LEACH improves the energy efficiency, it causes imbalanced or uneven energy dissipation between the nodes. HEED [4] is also an example of distributed clustering, where the residual energy is considered for selecting CHs.

Aggregation is another effective approach to conserve the sensor energy so that the lifetime of the sensor network is extended. In [5], the authors introduced a shortest path aggregation tree based routing protocol to maximize the network lifetime. They used a constant value for transmission cost and reception cost, which is not realistic in WSNs. Another aggregation based routing protocol have been developed in [6]. Energy rich nodes aggregate the data of others and forward them to the sink. In each round, aggregator nodes are chosen for data forwarding and as a result, routing overhead increases.

Energy efficient load balancing algorithms are also broadly addressed in recent years to decrease the energy drain rate of the sensors. A distributed energy balanced routing (DEBR) was proposed in [7] to balance the traffic load of nodes and to increase the first node died time (FNDT). Authors in [8] introduced a data gathering sequence based data transmission technique for WSNs. This data sequence not only mutual transmission, but also ensures freedom from loop. In [9], a min-max weight spanning tree is constructed for data gathering with low energy nodes with less number of e less number of descendants. In this protocol, aggregation or data fusion was not taken into consideration. The work presented in [10] addressed dynamic energy efficient routing scheme that takes into account the residual energy of the node as well as energy efficiency to find the next hop forwarder in data routing. The scheme [10] improves improves the network lifetime, but it increases latency additionally. Furthermore, it does not consider parent switching to minimize the energy consumption of nodes.

Forwarding area based energy balanced routing methods are widely discussed in the literature [11, 12, 14]. In [12], the authors present forward factor based energy balanced routing scheme, where the forwarder of a node is chosen according to link weight metric and forward energy density. Authors in [15] proposed a randomized switching algorithm for WSNs to increase the network lifetime. Path load was taken into account to switch the nodes to the new parents when the load difference between the paths is greater than some threshold value. A prediction based switching algorithm was developed in [16]. The authors claimed that their algorithm has faster convergence than [15]. Markov decision based switching technique for sustainable WSNs was proposed in [17]. In this routing technique, the authors consider different energy levels of sensor nodes and balancing is done based on the residual energy.

3   Models and Definitions

In this section, we have discussed various models, definitions and notations that are used throughout the paper.

3.1   System Model

We consider a WSN which consists of N number of homogeneous sensor nodes randomly distributed in a $M \times M$ square area for monitoring objects. These nodes are static after deployment. The sink is also stationary and it is placed at the corner of the network. To get the sink position, we sort the nodes based on their y-coordinates followed by x-coordinates and then select the largest one. Let $v_1, v_2, v_3, \ldots \ldots, v_N$ are the sensor nodes and v_0 is the sink. Each node has a unique identifier, has sensing rang r and transmission range R where $r \leq R$. Nodes communicate with each other using wireless communication. A communication link $e(v_i, v_j)$ is established between two nodes v_i and v_j if they are 1-hop neighbors of each other. Moreover, two nodes are neighbors of each other if they are within the transmission range of each other. We assume that each sensor node has limited energy, while the sink has unlimited energy. Let E_0 is initial energy level and $RE(v_i)$ is residual energy of each node v_i. Since nodes are homogeneous, every node has the same range and the same initial energy (E_0). It is considered that each node has the capability to adjust its transmission power while communicating with the neighbor nodes.

3.2   Energy Model

We know that sensor nodes mainly consume energy for transmission (E_{tx}), reception (E_{rx}), sensing (E_s) and processing [3]. Since the processing energy is very small, we ignore it in our study. If energy consumption for sensing is e_s per bit and L is the length of the generated data packet in bits, then the amount of energy consumed by node v_i in sensing is given by

$$E_s(v_i) = e_s Lx \tag{1}$$

where x is the transmission time. Similar to [13], we have set the energy parameters. Let E_{elec} be the energy dissipation for running electronics circuitry and E_{amp} be the energy dissipation to amplify the signal. If d_{ij}^2 is the path loss due to free space propagation, then the energy consumed by node v_i for transmitting/receiving L bits data over the distance d_{ij} (where d_{ij} = distance between v_i and v_j) is

$$E_{tx}(v_i) = (E_{elec} + E_{amp}d_{ij}^2)Lx \tag{2}$$

$$E_{rx}(v_i) = E_{elec}Lx \tag{3}$$

Therefore, the total energy consumed by node v_i is

$$E_{tot}(v_i) = E_s(v_i) + E_{tx}(v_i) + E_{rx}(v_i) \tag{4}$$

3.3   Definitions

Definition 1: A round of data transmission [9] is defined as a process of transferring the data from the sensors to the sink without considering transmission latency.

Definition 2: Let $T(v_0, t)$ be the routing tree rooted at v_0 at round t. If $v_i \in T(v_0, t)$ and v_i has $Ch(v_i)$ children, then the traffic load at v_i at round t is $2(Ch(v_i) + 1)L$.

Definition 3: Energy required by a node v_i to transmit the collected data to v_j in $T(v_0, t)$ at each round is:

Case 1: when v_i is the non-leaf node

$$E_{tot}(v_i, T) = e_s Lx + Ch(v_i)E_{elec}Lx\rho + (Ch(v_i) + 1)Lx\rho(E_{elec} + E_{amp}d_{ij}^2) \quad (5)$$

where ρ is the compression factor.

Case 2: when v_i is the leaf node

$$E_{tot}(v_i, T) = e_s Lx + Lx\rho(E_{elec} + E_{amp}d_{ij}^2) \quad (6)$$

Definition 4: If residual energy of node v_i is $RE(v_i)$, the lifetime of v_i will be

$$L(v_i) = \left\lfloor \frac{RE(v_i)}{E_{tot}(v_i, T)} \right\rfloor \quad (7)$$

When $L(v_i) \leq 1$ in a round, the node v_i is the *"bottleneck node"*.

Definition 5: The lifetime of the network, denoted by $L(Network)$, is the time when the first node becomes non-functional due to the deficiency of energy.

$$L(Network) = \min_{T \in TS(T)} \min_{v_i \in T} L(v_i) \quad (8)$$

where $TS(T)$ is the set of possible trees formed before the first node death.

Definition 6: The forwarding region of a node v_i is the common section of two circles, C_i and C_0 where C_i is a circle centered at v_i with radius R and C_0 is a circle with v_0 as the centered and d_i is the radius (d_i: the distance between v_i and the sink v_0) [12, 14]. This area basically contains a set of potential parents of node v_i in our work. We use $FR(i)$ notation to define such region.

Remark 1: The area size of the $FR(i)$ is

$$Area(FR(i)) = Section\ 1 + Section\ 2 - (\frac{1}{2}R\sqrt{(4d_i^2 - R^2)}) \quad (9)$$

$$Section\ 1 = d_i^2 acos\left(\frac{R^2}{2Rd_i}\right)180/\pi \quad (10)$$

$$Section\ 2 = R^2 acos((2d_i^2 - R^2)/2d_i^2)180/\pi \quad (11)$$

If v_0 resides in $FR(i)$, v_i directly sends data to v_0. In this case, Area $(FR(i))$ will be

$$Area(FR(i)) = (2\frac{\pi}{3} - \sqrt{3}/2)d_i^2 \quad (12)$$

4 The Proposed Algorithm

In multi hop data collection, uneven energy depletion between nodes is an important issue, which radically reduces the network lifetime and may cause early network segmentation. In order to obtain balanced energy consumption in the network, we introduce a Switching Policy based Energy Aware Routing (SPEAR) algorithm for WSNs. The algorithm works in rounds. Firstly, based on the energy load of the nodes, an energy aware data collection tree $T(v_0, t)$ rooted at v_0 is constructed. In each data collection round, the bottleneck node is identified and marked. If no such node exists, the former tree is used to forward the data packets of the nodes to the sink. Otherwise, the algorithm directs the children of the bottleneck node to switch to the new parents, which have the smallest weight value detailed subsequently. If switching is not possible, a new data collection tree rooted at v_0 is constructed once again. In SPEAR, the routing tree is reconstructed less frequently in the initial rounds, but formation of the tree occurs with shorter delay as the simulation round increases. Moreover, tree formation and parent switching continue until no node dies. The details of the SPEAR are given below.

4.1 Energy Balanced Tree Formation (EBTF)

In this section, we describe the tree formation procedure that takes as input the nodes in the network and their residual energy level and returns an energy balanced data collection tree. Let, V is the set of sensor nodes in the network. Firstly, the proposed method SPEAR finds the forwarding region $FR(i)$ of each node $v_i \in V$. Factors such as transmission range and distance from the sink are considered while determining $FR(i)$. Next, SPEAR computes the average energy load of each node v_i. The average energy load of v_i is denoted by $AVE(i)$ and is calculated as

$$AVE(i) = \frac{\sum_{j \in FR(i)} RE(j)}{K} \tag{13}$$

where K is the number of nodes in $FR(i)$. After calculating the average energy load for all nodes, SPEAR selects the node that has the minimum weight $AVE(i)$ and calls a function *potential_parent_selection()* to choose the parent of the node. Selecting the minimum energy load value, energy consumption at the node can be minimized. Function *potential_parent_selection()* in SPEAR finds the potential parent set of the node and the selects the suitable parent among them. Algorithm 2 describes function *potential_parent_selection()*. Let $PPS(i)$ be the potential parent set of v_i. In order to get $PPS(i)$, SPEAR finds the average energy load of the sensor nodes in $FR(i)$ and then compares each value with $AVE(i)$. Any node $v_j \in FR(i)$ will be added in $PPS(i)$ if (i) $RE(j) > 0$ and (ii) $AVE(j) \geq AVE(i)$. After that, each node v_j in $PPS(i)$ is assigned a weight based on the residual energy of the node and transmission energy consumption of v_i as

$$P(j) = \frac{E_{tx}(v_i)}{RE(j)}, \qquad \forall v_j \in PPS(i) \tag{14}$$

Only the node with the smallest weight in $PPS(i)$ is selected as the parent node of v_i for data transmission. After selecting the parent, node v_i is removed from V and added into $T(v_0, t)$ and we update the value of $E_{tx}(v_i)$, $E_{rx}(v_j)$, $RE(i)$ and $RE(j)$ accordingly. For each node $v_j \notin T(v_0, t)$, we also update $FR(j)$ and $AVE(j)$. The whole process is repeated until all nodes (except the sink) choose their parent nodes. If $PPS(i)$ is empty and/or, the sink v_0 resides in $FR(i)$, node v_i sends directly data to v_0 and sets the flag value to true. The EBTF is described in Algorithm 1.

Algorithm 1. $EBTF(V, t, RE(v_i) \, \forall v_i \in V)$

```
T(v₀,t) = {}, N=|V|;
∀vᵢ ∈ V, vᵢ.Visited='false' and Find FR(i)
while (V!=0)
        ∀vᵢ ∈ V, if vᵢ.visited='false'
        Determine AVE(i) using Eq. (13)
        Select the node vᵢ which has the smallest AVE(i)
        vⱼ = potential_parent_selection(vᵢ)
        vᵢ.parent=vⱼ
        vᵢ.visited='true'
        Update Eₜₓ(vᵢ), Eᵣₓ(vⱼ), RE(i) and RE(j)
        Add vᵢ in T(v₀,t)
        Delete vᵢ from V
end while
Return (T(v₀,t))
```

Algorithm 2. $potential\_parent\_selection(v_i)$

```
Let K is the number of nodes in the forwarding region of
each node vᵢ
∀vⱼ ∈ K, Find AVE(j) using Eq. (13)
if RE(j) > 0 & AVE(j) ≥ AVE(i), add vⱼ into PPS(i)
if PPS(i) is empty or v₀ resides in PPS(i), node vᵢ sends
data directly to v₀
∀vⱼ ∈ PPS(i), Find P(j) using Eq. (14) and select the node
having the smallest weight value
Return (vⱼ)
```

4.2   Parent Switching

In each round, the data collection tree $T(v_0, t)$ as discussed earlier is updated by invoking a new function *parent switching*(). Algorithm 3 shows *parent switching*() in details. SPEAR calls function *parent_switching*() if $T(v_0, t)$ has bottleneck nodes (see Definition 4). If $T(v_0, t)$ has no such node, the routing tree remains unchanged. In *parent_switching*(), the bottleneck node with the smallest lifetime is selected. Next, function *potential_parent_selection*() is invoked by the children of the selected node to find their potential parents. Each child node chooses the minimum weight node among them as its new parent using Eq. (14). It is obvious that the lifetime of all nodes in the parent set should be greater than 1. We call function *parent_switching*() repeatedly until the smallest lifetime of a node in the tree is less than equal to 1. If switching is successful, the tree is updated. If any child node fails to switch, then function *parent_switching*() terminates and *EBTF* algorithm is invoked to construct a new routing tree. The proposed SPEAR not only improves the network lifetime by minimizing the energy consumption of the bottleneck nodes, but also reduces the routing overhead during tree formation. Moreover, by defining forwarding region, the proposed method ensures loop less routing.

4.3 Discussions

Lemma 1: The proposed algorithm ensures freedom from loops.

Proof: The proposed algorithm avoids the loop formation as follows. Firstly, when a node chooses its parent, the node will not be considered as the parent for other nodes until new parent selection is invoked. Secondly, the node can select its parent from its forward region. If the region is empty, then it sends the data directly to the sink. When a node becomes a bottleneck node, it will not be considered as the parent for other nodes for several rounds of data transmission and a new parent node is selected instead.

Lemma 2: The overall complexity of the proposed algorithm in worse case is $O(N^3 + r(N.h + N^5))$ where h = height of the tree and r = number of rounds.

Proof: We omit the proof due to the space limitation.

Algorithm 3.   *parent_switching*()

Let, $T(v_0, t)$ is an energy balanced data collection tree
formed using Algorithm 1 at round t
t=t+1
$\forall v_i \in T(v_0, t)$, Calculate $L(v_i)$
if $L(v_i) \leq 1$, v_i.type='bottleneck'
Select the bottleneck node v_i which has minimum lifetime
Set v_i.switching='true'
  while(true)
      Queue Q=$Ch(v_i)$
      while(Q!=empty)
          Remove node v_j from the head of Q
          v_j.visited='true'
          $v_k = potential\_parent\_selection(v_j)$
          if no such v_k exists
              v_i.switching='false'
              Call Algorithm *EBTF*
              Break;
          else
              v_j.parent=v_k
              v_j.visited='true'
              v_i.switching='true'
              Update $T(v_0, t)$
          end if
      end while
  end while
if switching of $Ch(v_i)$ is true,then select next bottleneck
node and repeat above steps

5 Performance Evaluation

In this section, we validate the performance of the proposed algorithm using extensive
simulations. For evaluation, we compare our protocol with GSTEB [13] and Aggregation based routing [5] in terms of several performance metrics. Performance metrics
include (a) network lifetime, (b) alive nodes count (c) average residual energy,
(d) average number of switching, and (e) energy balanced factor (EBF). To quantify
energy balancing between sensor nodes, we use EBF, which is the standard deviation
of all sensor nodes residual energy. Higher value of EBF implies unbalanced energy
consumption between nodes and hence, lower value is desirable for the energy aware
routing.

All simulations were done in CodeBlocks. We have carried out 10 runs for every experiment and then take the average. In this simulation study, we consider that 100 sensors are randomly deployed in a square area of 100×100 m^2. Nodes generate the data packet of size 1024 bytes and send that to the sink node. The sink can only receive the packets. It is not an energy constraint. The transmission range of each node is 30 m and the initial energy level of each node is set to 0.5 J. Communication parameters used in the simulations are as follows: $E_{elec} = 50$ nJ/bit and $E_{amp} = 100$ pJ/bit/m^2 [3, 13].

5.1 Results and Discussions

Figure 1 describes the performance of network lifetime for different routing algorithms for varying number of nodes. Here, the number of nodes is varied from 90 to 150 and the compression factor is fixed to 0.4. We notice that the network lifetime decreases as the number of nodes increases. In the dense network, nodes lying closer to the sink become overloaded by transmitting high volume traffic and deplete their energy faster than other nodes farther away from the sink. As a result, the network lifetime decreases. As shown in the figure, the performance of SPEAR is better than the other two algorithms. SPEAR saves the low energy nodes and minimizes their energy consumption by switching their children to high energy nodes. Moreover, in SPEAR, energy is more balanced in comparison to GSTEB and Aggregation based routing. Figure 2 depicts alive nodes count of SPEAR in comparison with other two algorithms as a function of rounds. We see that the number of alive nodes is high in the initial rounds, but it starts decreasing when round proceeds. This happens because energy expenditure at nodes increases when the round goes on. It is observed that SPEAR performs better than GSTEB and Aggregation based routing and its first node dies much later than that of other two algorithms.

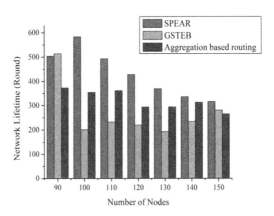

Fig. 1. Network lifetime

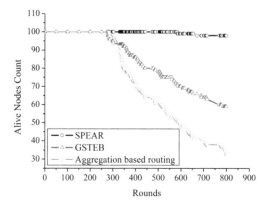

Fig. 2. Alive nodes count

From Fig. 3, we observe that SPEAR has lower EBF value than GSTEB. However, the performance gap between SPEAR and Aggregation tree based routing is not high. Since SPEAR uses energy saving strategy, both in data collection tree formation and parent switching, it has achieved a better energy balancing among the nodes. As a result, the EBF value in SPEAR is improved. Figure 4 shows the average residual energy of the network as a function of rounds. The network has higher energy effectiveness if it has higher average residual energy. As we can see, the total residual energy decreases as the round increases. SPEAR has better performance compared with GSTEB and Aggregation tree based routing. SPEAR constructs an energy balanced tree and performs parent switching periodically to keep the energy consumption of bottleneck nodes at the lower level. Since SPEAR has higher average residual energy, the network lifetime of SPEAR is much longer.

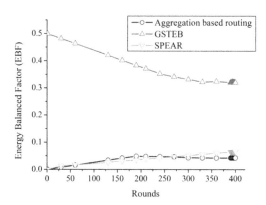

Fig. 3. Energy balanced factor

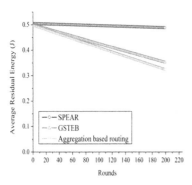 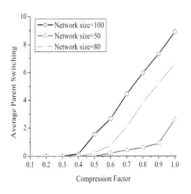

Fig. 4. Average residual energy   **Fig. 5.** Average parent switching

Figure 5 describes the average parent switching in SPEAR for varying compression factor and different network size. As shown in the figure, the average parent switching increases with the network size and compression factor value. When compression factor is low, SPEAR performs high compression. This not only reduces the energy cost at a node, but also minimizes the number of parent switching and energy expenditure associated with it. However, we notice an opposite trend when compression factor is high. The performance of SPEAR in terms of average parent switching is shown in Fig. 6. In this simulation, the average parent switching grows up when round proceeds. According to Fig. 4, the energy consumption at nodes increases as the round increases. This increased energy consumption directs more nodes to switch their parents frequently.

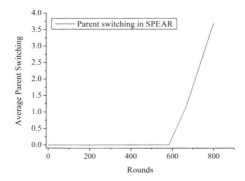

Fig. 6. Average parent switching in various rounds

6 Conclusions

In this paper, we have presented a switching policy based energy aware routing algorithm for WSNs, which improves the network lifetime by minimizing energy consumption between the nodes. The proposed method constructs an energy balanced data collection tree. In each data collection round, the switching decision is invoked to minimize the energy expenditure of low energy nodes. If switching is unsuccessful, a new energy balanced tree is reconstructed for data collection so that the lifetime is improved. Simulations are done to validate the performance of the proposed algorithm. Results show that the proposed method performs better in comparison to existing routing algorithms and extends the network lifetime significantly.

References

1. Akyildiz, I.F., Su, W., Sankarasubramaniam, Y., Cayirci, E.: A survey on sensor networks. IEEE Commun. Mag. **40**(8), 102–114 (2002)
2. Anastasi, G., Conti, M., Fransco, M.D., Passarella, A.: Energy conservation in wireless sensor networks: a survey. Ad Hoc Netw. **7**(3), 537–568 (2009)
3. Heinzelman, W.R., Chandrakasan, A., Balakrishnan, H.: Energy efficient communication protocol for wireless microsensor networks. In: Proceedings of the 33rd Hawaii International Conference on System Sciences (2000)
4. Younis, O., Fahmy, S.: HEED: a hybrid, energy-efficient, distributed clustering approach for ad hoc sensor networks. IEEE Trans. Mob. Comput. **3**(4), 366–379 (2004)
5. Luo, D., Zhu, X, Wu, X., Chen, G.: Maximizing lifetime for the shortest path aggregation tree in wireless sensor networks. In: Proceedings of IEEE INFOCOM (2011)
6. Misra, S., Thomasinous, P.D.: A simple, least-time and energy efficient routing protocol with one level data aggregation for wireless sensor networks. J. Syst. Softw. **83**(5), 852–860 (2010)
7. Ok, C.S., Lee, S., Mitra, P., Kumara, S.: Distributed energy balanced routing for wireless sensor networks. Comput. Ind. Eng. **57**(1), 125–135 (2009)
8. Zhu, Y., Wu, W.D., Pan, J., Tang, Y.: An energy-efficient data gathering algorithm to prolong lifetime of wireless sensor networks. Comput. Commun. **33**(5), 639–647 (2010)
9. Liang, L., Wang, J., Cao, J., Chen, J., Lu, M.: An efficient algorithm for constructing maximum lifetime tree for data gathering without aggregation in wireless sensor networks. In: Proceedings of IEEE INFOCOM, pp. 1–5 (2010)
10. Bhattacharjee, S., Bandyopadhyay, S.: Lifetime maximizing dynamic energy efficient routing protocol for multi hop wireless networks. Simul. Model. Pract. Theory **32**, 15–29 (2013)
11. Ren, F., Zhang, J., He, T., Lin, C., Das, S.K.: EBRP: energy balanced routing protocol for data gathering in wireless sensor networks. IEEE Trans. Parallel Distrib. Syst. **22**(12), 2108–2125 (2011)
12. Zhang, D., Li, G., Zheng, K., Ming, X.: An energy balanced routing method based on forward-aware factor for wireless sensor networks. IEEE Trans. Industr. Inf. **10**(1), 766–773 (2014)
13. Han, Z., Wu, J., Zhang, J., Liu, L., Tian, K.: A general self-organized tree-based energy-balance routing protocol for wireless sensor network. IEEE Trans. Nucl. Sci. **61**(2), 732–740 (2014)

14. Chen, D., Deng, J., Varshney, P.K.: Selection of a forwarding area for contention based geographic forwarding in wireless multi hop networks. IEEE Trans. Veh. Technol. **56**(5), 3111–3122 (2007)
15. Imon, S.K., Khan, A., Francesco, M.D., Das, S.K.: Energy efficient randomized switching for maximizing lifetime in tree based wireless sensor networks. IEEE/ACM Trans. Networking **23**(5), 1401–1415 (2015)
16. Yi, C.J., Yang, G., Dai, H., Liu, L., Li, N.: Switching algorithm with prediction strategy for maximizing lifetime in wireless sensor networks. Int. J. Distrib. Sens. Netw. **11**(11), 1–12 (2015)
17. Rout, R.R., Krishna, M.S., Gupta, S.: Markov decision process based switching algorithm for sustainable rechargeable wireless sensor networks. IEEE Sens. J. **16**(8), 2788–2797 (2016)

Multiple Codes State Assignment and Code Length Reduction for Power Minimization of Finite State Machines

Tomasz Grzes[✉]

Bialystok University of Technology, Bialystok, Poland
t.grzes@pb.edu.pl
http://www.wi.pb.edu.pl

Abstract. The method of a minimization of the power consumed by the finite state machine (FSM) is discussed in the presented paper. The proposed algorithm uses two performed sequentially methods of equivalent transformations of the FSM, which do not change the function, but the structure of an FSM.

One method assigns multiple codes to the internal states of an FSM. Using more than one code gives more opportunities to assign to the neighbor states the codes with lower Hamming distance, which in result lead to decrease a power consumption. The other method reduces the length of the internal state's code using a special model of an FSM, in which the orthogonal state codes are obtained from a concatenation of the parts of the input and output vectors, and the subcode stored in a memory. This approach gives the possibility to reduce the size of the memory used for storing the internal state's code, which leads to reducing the power consumption.

Proposed algorithm executes methods starting from the state splitting, followed by the implementation the common architectural model. The experimental results show that the proposed method reduces the power consumption compared to NOVA, JEDI, column based and sequential algorithms.

Keywords: Finite state machine · Power minimization
Architectural models of FSM · Multiple codes state assignment
Internal state splitting

1 Introduction

There are many different approaches to reduce the power consumption of FSM, including:

- assigning the codes to the internal states that have a minimal Hamming distance [7, 10, 15, 19, 20, 22, 26],
- a decomposition of an FSM [10],
- disabling the unused parts of an FSM and power gating [10, 17],

© Springer Nature Switzerland AG 2018
K. Saeed and W. Homenda (Eds.): CISIM 2018, LNCS 11127, pp. 341–353, 2018.
https://doi.org/10.1007/978-3-319-99954-8_29

- the timing control [6],
- selecting the type of flip-flop used for memory elements [5],
- using embedded blocks of the programmable logic device [14],
- applying the artificial intelligence algorithms [13,20,25,26],
- modifying the number of bits in the codes of internal states [21],
- splitting the internal states [24] etc.

The presented paper introduces the algorithm of a dynamic power minimization that uses two performed sequentially methods of equivalent transformations of the FSM, which do not change the function, but the structure of an FSM. One method assigns multiple codes to the internal states of an FSM what can be the result of the state splitting. The operation of splitting the internal states is widely used in a variety of algorithms for logic synthesis of an FSM, for examples: to reduce the number of function arguments [8], to improve the parameters (power consumption and cost) of the synthesized FSM [12], to transform the FSM to a specific class [16], etc.

The other method used in an algorithm reduces the length of the code using a special model of an FSM, in which the orthogonal state codes are obtained from a concatenation of the parts of the input and output vectors, and the subcode stored in a memory. Therefore, this approach gives the possibility to reduce the size of the memory used for storing the internal state's code, which leads to reducing the power consumption. This method was previously used i.e. to improve results of synthesis of the FSMs [9].

Note that the operations of splitting and merging of internal states, as well as the converting to the desired architectural model, are the equivalent transformations of the FSM, and do not alter the algorithm of its operation [2].

Previous author's work was related to the state assignment algorithms oriented on the power minimization [15,22–24]. The impact on this work was also from the selected papers that were not related to the FSM synthesis, one on the iterative antirandom tests [18], and one on the rough sets [11].

This paper is organized as follows. In Sect. 2 the general information related to the power dissipation estimation are provided. Section 3 focuses on the transformations on the FSM used in the algorithm. In Sect. 4.3 the algorithm is described, while Sect. 5 is devoted to the experimental results.

2   Power Dissipation in Finite State Machine

Let's define finite state machine (FSM) as a tuple $F = \{A, X, Y, \varphi, \psi, a_1\}$ where $A = \{a_1, \ldots, a_M\}$ – set of the internal states of FSM (M – amount of states); $X = \{x_1, \ldots, x_L\}$ – set of the input variables (L – amount of input variables); $Y = \{y_1, \ldots, y_N\}$ – set of the output variables (N – amount of output variables); φ – state transition function, $\varphi : A \times X \rightarrow A$; ψ – output function, $\psi : A \times X \rightarrow Y$ for Mealy model or $\psi : A \rightarrow Y$ for Moore model; a_1 – reset (initial) state. When FSM is implemented as a sequential circuit, every FSM's internal state should be assigned the code from the set $C = \{c_1, \ldots, c_M\}$, such $c_i = Enc(a_i)$, where Enc – encoding function, $Enc \rightarrow A : C$. To distinguish each one state, all the codes must be mutually orthogonal (unique), i.e. satisfies the formula $\forall i \neq j, i, j \in \langle 1, M \rangle, c_i \neq c_j$. This condition defines the lower limit of the binary code length, which is equal to $R = \lceil log_2 M \rceil$.

In general, the power consumption in the digital circuits consists of the two parts: static power – connected with the sustaining the circuit in the particular state (eg. high level on the outputs) and the dynamic power – connected with changing the state of the circuit.

To determine the dynamic power consumption of an FSM one can use the method described in [3], that is based on the internal states' encoding and the probability that the value on the input of FSM is equal to "1" (or "0"). The power consumption of an FSM describes the expression:

$$P = \sum_{r=1}^{R} P_r = \frac{1}{2} \times V_{DD}^2 \times f \times C \times \sum_{r=1}^{R} N_r, \tag{1}$$

where P_r – power dissipated by flip-flop r; V_{DD} – power supply voltage; f – FSM operating frequency; C – capacitance of output of each flip-flop; N_r – switching activity of r-th flip-flop, $r \in \langle 1, R \rangle$.

Let c_i – some binary code of state a_i. Let c_i^r denote the value of r-th bit of code c_i of state a_i, $r \in \langle 1, R \rangle$. Consequently the switching activity N_r of flip-flop r of FSM memory can be expressed by the following equation:

$$N_r = \sum_{i=1}^{M} \sum_{j=1}^{M} P(a_i \rightarrow a_j) \times (c_i^r \oplus c_j^r), \tag{2}$$

where $P(a_i \rightarrow a_j)$ – transition probability from state a_i to state a_j $(a_i, a_j \in A)$; $\oplus$ – logic operation "exclusive or".

Transition probability $P(a_i \rightarrow a_j)$ from state a_i to state a_j $(a_i, a_j \in A)$ can be obtained from:

$$P(a_i \rightarrow a_j) = P(a_i) \times P(X(a_i, a_j)), \tag{3}$$

where $P(a_i)$ – probability that the state of the FSM is a_i; $P(X(a_i, a_j))$ – probability that the input vector on the inputs of the FSM is equal to the value $X(a_i, a_j)$ that initiates transition from the state a_i to the state a_j.

Let $V^b(X)$ denotes the value of the b-th variable of vector X. Then the probability $P(X(a_i, a_j))$ that input vector of the FSM is equal to the $X(a_i, a_j)$ is defined by the formula:

$$P(X(a_i, a_j)) = \prod_{b=1}^{L} P(V^b(X(a_i, a_j)) = d), \tag{4}$$

where $d \in \{'1','0','-'\}$; $P(x_b = d)$ – probability that input variable x_b of input vector $X(a_i, a_j)$ is equal to d. In this paper it was assumed that probabilities of either 0 or 1 on any FSM input are equal, thus $P(x_b = 0) = P(x_b = 1) = \frac{1}{2}$ and $P(x_b = '-') = 1$.

The probability $P(a_i)$ that a present state of an FSM is $a_i, i = \langle 1, M \rangle$, can be evaluated from the following system of equations:

$$P(a_i) = \sum_{m=1}^{M} P(a_m) \times P(X(a_m, a_i)), i = \langle 1, M \rangle. \tag{5}$$

When there are not any transition between states a_m and a_i we assume $P(X(a_m, a_i)) = 0$. Consequently when there are several transitions from the state a_m to state a_i the value $P(X(a_m, a_i))$ is defined as a sum of the probabilities for each input vector, which initiates a transition from state a_m to state a_i.

The system of Eq. (5) represents the linear system of M equations in M variables $P(a_1), \ldots, P(a_M)$. Since the state machine is always in one of its internal states, the following equation is true:

$$\sum_{i=1}^{M} P(a_i) = 1. \tag{6}$$

To solve the system of Eq. (5) one of the equations in (5) is replaced by Eq. (6).

3   Equivalent Transformations Used in Proposed Algorithm

This section describes the equivalent transformations of FSM that were used in the proposed solution. The first transformation is the state splitting, in which the states are divided to a number of the new states. The amount of the states increase but the functionality of the FSM is preserved.

The second transformation is based on the structural models of FSM, in which parts of the code are stored in the input and the output registers. Using this transformation decreases the size of the code of the internal state.

3.1   State Splitting

The classic approach to the state assignment requires that for every state $a_i, i \in \langle 1, M \rangle$ is assigned exactly one code which is orthogonal to all other codes. But it is impossible to ensure that the Hamming distance $H = 1$ for every pair of the codes. Hence one of the solutions can be the assigning more than one code to the particular state. Increasing the amount of the codes gives more options for selecting the codes with the Hamming distance $H = 1$. Consequently, this should lead to the power minimization in an FSM [24].

Let $X_P(a_i) = \{z \in Z : \varphi(a_j, z) = a_i, a_i \in A, a_j \in A\}$ denotes the set of all input vectors, that initiate the transition to the state a_i. Let $X_F(a_i) = \{z \in z : \varphi(a_i, z) = a_k, a_i \in A, a_k \in A\}$ denotes the set of all input vectors, that initiate the transition from the state a_i. Let $|S|$ denotes the cardinality of the set S (number of elements of the set S).

Any state a_i of an FSM for which $|X_P(a_i)| > 1$ can be split to two new states $a_i^{(1)}$ and $a_i^{(2)}$. After this operation the state a_i is replaced with states $a_i^{(1)}$ and $a_i^{(2)}$ such that:

- X_F for the new states are identical to the set for original state – $X_F(a_i^{(1)}) = X_F(a_i^{(1)}) = X_F(a_i)$,
- X_P of the original state is divided to two separate parts – $X_P(a_i^{(1)}) \cup X_F(a_i^{(1)}) = X_F(a_i)$, $X_P(a_i^{(1)}) \cap X_F(a_i^{(1)}) = \emptyset$.

Operation of splitting the internal states is reversible, hence the FSM can be restored to its original structure by the simple merging the states $a_i^{(1)}$ and $a_i^{(2)}$ into one state a_i.

Resulting FSM has more internal states, but the mean amount of the input vectors that causes the transition to the particular state is lower. Furthermore, it is more probable to assign the codes with a lower Hamming distance, causing the lower power dissipation in an FSM.

3.2 FSM Structural Models

Nowadays for FSM synthesis there are used two models of the FSMs: Mealy model and Moore model. However in practical applications in the programmable logic devices such as the field programmable gate arrays (FPGAs) it is possible to use the architectural features of those circuits. Among them is the possibility to use the input and output registers as the memory elements storing the code of the internal state.

The new architectural models of a FSM were introduced in [4], where FSM models were divided into the six classes from "A" to "F" and the common models of the classes "AD", "AE", "BF" and "ADE" – the only permissible common classes. In the proposed solution the ADE class was used. As it was stated in [4] the common model of class ADE uses input and output buffer registers as the memory elements that store the internal states' code of the FSM.

4   Proposed Algorithm

In this section, one can find the proposed solution of the power minimizing in an FSM through the reducing the code length and assigning the multiple codes to one internal state.

4.1 State Splitting

The first step towards the final outline of the algorithm is to deal with the problem of assigning multiple codes to one internal state by the splitting this state. One of the solutions to this problem is to split an internal state into the new states and assign the resulting states the codes.

To find the encoded FSM with optimal state splitting in the terms of the power dissipation one can use the Algorithm 1.

Algorithm 1 for encoding the internal states with multiple codes using the state splitting operation.

INPUT: Finite state machine FSM
OUTPUT: FSM after state splitting
     with minimum power
1: $Encode(FSM)$
2: $P \leftarrow Power(FSM)$
3: $P_{best} \leftarrow P$
4: $A^* \leftarrow A$
5: **while** $A^* \neq \emptyset$ **do**
6:     $a_i \leftarrow a \in A^*$
7:     **if** $|X_P(a_i)| > 1$ **then**
8:         $A = A \setminus a_i$
9:         $D \leftarrow Splits(a_i)$
10:        $P^* \leftarrow P_{best}$
11:        **while** $D \neq \emptyset$ **do**
12:            $d_i \leftarrow d \in D$
13:            $A = A \cup d_i$
14:            $Encode(FSM)$
15:            **if** $Power(FSM) < P^*$ **then**
16:                $P^* \leftarrow Power(FSM)$
17:                $d_{best} \leftarrow d_i$
18:            **end if**
19:            $D = D \setminus d_i$
20:        **end while**
21:        **if** $P^* < P_{best}$ **then**
22:            $P_{best} = P^*$
23:            $A \leftarrow A \cup d_{best}$
24:        **else**
25:            $A = A \cup a_i$
26:        **end if**
27:    **end if**
28:    $A^* = A^* \setminus a_i$
29: **end while**

In presented algorithm lines 1–2 provide the initial value of the power dissipation P. Also, in line 3 value P is stored as the "current best" P_best, and in line 4 the set A^* is assigned the initial set of states A. As the encoding $Encode(FSM)$ can be used any low-power state assignment algorithm, i.e. the sequential algorithm [23].

Loop in lines 5–29 is for generating the splits for all the states from the set A, and line 7 restricts the splitting for the states that satisfy the condition $|X_P(a_i)| > 1$. The state is removed from the set A in line 8.

In line 9 state a_i is split in all possible ways, and every split $d = \{a_i^{(1)}, \ldots, a_i^{(s)}\}$, where $s \in \langle 2, X_P(a_i) \rangle$ is the amount of states in the split, is stored in the set D. For every split $d_i \in D$ the test for the power dissipation is performed by the loop in lines 11–20. Before the loop the variable P^* is assigned with the current best power dissipation.

For each split $d \in D$ the state assignment is performed and then the power dissipation is calculated (lines 12–14). If the power dissipation is better than P^*, the split is stored (lines 15–18). Then the tested split is removed from the set D (line 19).

If the power dissipation P^* is better than the current best P_{best} the split d^* is applied to the FSM (lines 21–24). If the state splitting didn't minimize the power the state a_i is restored to the FSM.

4.2   Transforming into Class ADE

The next step is to deal with the problem of transforming the input FSM into the FSM of class ADE, where the states' codes are split into three parts: a part associated with the input vector, a part associated with the output vector and a part stored in the internal registers and needed to preserve the orthogonality of the states' codes.

To find the orthogonal parts of the input as well as the output vectors one need to find the input variables that preserve their values during the transition to the particular state a_i.

Let $X(a_i, a_j)$ denotes the input vector that initiates transition from the state a_i to the state a_j. Let $V^b(X)$ denotes the value of the b-th variable of vector X. The condition function $OX_k(a_i)$ for k-th input variable of transition to the state a_i is presented below:

$$OX_k(a_i) = \begin{cases} 1, & \forall m \in \langle 1, M \rangle, m \neq i, V^k(X(a_m, a_i)) = 1 \\ 0, & \forall m \in \langle 1, M \rangle, m \neq i, V^k(X(a_m, a_i)) = 0 \\ -, & \text{otherwise} \end{cases} \quad (7)$$

Let $Y(a_i, a_j)$ denotes the output vector after the transition from the state a_i to the state a_j. Let $V^b(Y)$ denotes the value of the b-th variable of vector Y. The condition function $OY_k(a_i)$ for k-th output variable after the transition to the state a_i is presented below:

$$OY_k(a_i) = \begin{cases} 1, & \forall m \in \langle 1, M \rangle, m \neq i, V^k(Y(a_m, a_i)) = 1 \\ 0, & \forall m \in \langle 1, M \rangle, m \neq i, V^k(Y(a_m, a_i)) = 0 \\ -, & \text{otherwise} \end{cases} \quad (8)$$

Two states a_i and a_j are indiscernible when:

$$\forall k \in \langle 1, L \rangle, OX_k(a_i) = OX_k(a_j) \text{and} OY_k(a_i) = OY_k(a_j) \quad (9)$$

Set of the indiscernible states are called the indiscernibility class of the state. To find the sets of states indiscernible by the input and the output variables one can use the presented below algorithm.

Algorithm 2 for finding the sets of states indiscernible by the input and the output variables.

INPUT: Finite state machine FSM
OUTPUT: Set C of indiscernibility classes of states
1: $C \leftarrow \emptyset$
2: **while** $A \neq \emptyset$ **do**
3:   $a \leftarrow a_i \in A : P(a_i) = max$
4:   $C_a \leftarrow \emptyset$
5:   **for** $a_x in A$ **do**
6:     **if** $OX_k(a_x) = OX_k(a), \forall k \in \langle 1, L \rangle$ **then**
7:       **if** $OY_k(a_x) = OY_k(a), \forall k \in \langle 1, L \rangle$ **then**
8:         $C_a \leftarrow C_a \cup a_x$
9:       **end if**
10:     **end if**
11:   **end for**
12:   $A \leftarrow A \setminus C_a$
13:   $C \leftarrow C \cup C_a$
14: **end while**

Loop enclosing the lines from 2 to 14 is repeated while inside the set of states A there are states that were not included in any indiscernibility class. Line 3 selects the state connected with maximum static probability (see Eq. 5). Then in lines 5–11, the indiscernibility class is evaluated by testing all the states from the set A for the condition (9) (lines 6 and 7). In line 12 the states assigned to the indiscernibility class are removed from the set A.

Every state in the particular indiscernibility class C_a must have assigned a different code, but the states from the other class $C_b \neq C_a$ can be assigned the codes that were previously assigned to the any of the states from the class C_a. The assignment can be achieved with any power minimizing algorithm, i.e. sequential algorithm [23]. Thus the Algorithm 2 can be supplemented with the shown below lines to provide the state assignment and form the *Algorithm 2+* of the state assignment using the state splitting.

15: **while** $C \neq \emptyset$ **do**
16:     $c_i \leftarrow c \in C$
17:     $Encode(FSM, c_i)$
18:     $C \leftarrow C \setminus c_i$
19: **end while**

Loop in lines 15–19 enumerates all indiscernibility classes. All the states from each indiscernibility class are assigned the code in line 17, and the class c_i is removed from the set C in line 18.

4.3   Power Minimization Algorithm

Simple linking the Algorithm 1 with the Algorithm 2+, the algorithm of the power minimization using the special architectural model of an FSM and the multiple codes assignment is formed. Below one can find the final shape of the algorithm.

Algorithm 3 for power minimization using the special architectural model of an FSM and the multiple codes assignment.
INPUT: Finite state machine FSM
OUTPUT: Finite state machine FSM with state assignment
 1: $Algorithm_1(FSM)$
 2: $Algorithm_{2+}(FSM)$

In line 1 the Algorithm 1 is applied to the FSM, then in line 2 the Algorithm 2+ is applied.

5   Experimental Results

Experimental results presented in Table 1 were obtained using the standard benchmarks [1]. Calculations were performed according to the procedure described in Sect. 2, assuming the values: $C = 1\mathrm{pF}$, $f = 50\mathrm{MHz}$, $V_{DD} = 5\mathrm{V}$ and $P(x_i = 1) = 0.5$. Every value represents the power dissipated in [mW] on registers storing the state code. Algorithms used in the experiment were: NOVA (P_N), JEDI (P_J), column-based [15] (P_C), sequential [23] (P_S), iterative [22] (P_I), state splitting only Algorithm 1 (P_L), common model only Algorithm 2+ (P_M) and Algorithm 3 (P_T).

Table 1. Dynamic power dissipation for the benchmarks with the codes assigned using algorithms: NOVA (P_N), JEDI (P_J), column-based (P_C), sequential (P_S), iterative (P_I), state splitting only Algorithm 1 (P_L), common model only Algorithm 2+ (P_M) and Algorithm 3 (P_T).

Benchmark	P_N[mW]	P_J[mW]	P_C[mW]	P_S[mW]	P_I[mW]	P_L[mW]	P_M[mW]	P_T[mW]
bbara	279.70	198.13	187.53	175.90	175.90	172.37	189.07	184.63
bbtas	480.97	375.00	277.17	277.17	277.17	277.17	277.17	277.17
beecount	535.00	360.17	363.07	298.07	298.07	298.07	251.23	251.23
cse	311.20	217.80	186.17	149.90	149.87	148.90	149.00	148.90
dk16	1626.20	1388.67	1258.43	1030.30	968.03	970.67	970.23	971.03
dk27	997.03	1086.30	744.03	744.03	744.03	729.17	505.90	496.43
dk512	1268.60	1502.97	1065.83	796.13	718.00	741.27	638.97	638.97
donfile	1080.73	1171.87	885.43	742.20	690.10	696.60	468.77	468.77
ex1	1460.70	1025.83	525.67	461.83	444.30	391.17	448.03	406.43
keyb	638.00	405.57	404.17	347.83	347.83	347.73	346.40	346.40
pma	912.43	678.43	351.83	349.20	347.60	310.20	316.43	315.70
s27	722.17	568.10	561.10	561.10	554.10	550.60	289.73	260.37
s8	177.37	141.37	113.00	113.00	113.00	113.00	120.97	113.00
shiftreg	937.50	937.50	859.37	703.13	625.00	664.07	625.00	625.00
train11	357.80	258.17	289.87	211.73	211.73	211.73	172.10	164.70
Mean	785.69	687.72	538.18	464.10	444.32	441.51	384.60	377.92

Results in Table 1 show that the best state assignment was obtained for the Algorithm 3 (mean power of 377.92 mW), and the second was common model only Algorithm 2+ (mean power of 384.60 mW). The mean power for all other algorithms was at least about 55 mW bigger than the power for Algorithm 2+ and Algorithm 3. In most cases the Algorithm 3 gave the best results (12 out of 15 results), the Algorithm 1 gave the best results for 7 out of 12 cases, and the Algorithm 2+ for 6 out of 12 cases.

In Table 2 the comparison of the results for the benchmarks with the codes assigned using algorithms: NOVA, JEDI, column-based, sequential, iterative, state splitting only Algorithm 1, common model only Algorithm 2+ with the results for the Algorithm 3. Particular columns $\frac{P_X}{P_T}$ contain the ratios of the power dissipation for the algorithm "X" (where "X" can be one of: N – NOVA, J – JEDI, C – column based, S – sequential, I – iterative, L – state splitting only

Algorithm 1, M – common model only Algorithm 2+) to the power dissipation of the Algorithm 3 P_T.

Table 2. Comparison of the dynamic power dissipation for the algorithms: NOVA, JEDI, column-based, sequential, iterational, state splitting only Algorithm 1, common model only Algorithm 2+ to the Algorithm 3.

Benchmark	$\frac{P_N}{P_T}$	$\frac{P_J}{P_T}$	$\frac{P_C}{P_T}$	$\frac{P_S}{P_T}$	$\frac{P_I}{P_T}$	$\frac{P_L}{P_T}$	$\frac{P_M}{P_T}$
bbara	1.51	1.07	1.02	0.95	0.95	0.93	1.02
bbtas	1.74	1.35	1.00	1.00	1.00	1.00	1.00
beecount	2.13	1.43	1.45	1.19	1.19	1.19	1.00
cse	2.09	1.46	1.25	1.01	1.01	1.00	1.00
dk16	1.67	1.43	1.30	1.06	1.00	1.00	1.00
dk27	2.01	2.19	1.50	1.50	1.50	1.47	1.02
dk512	1.99	2.35	1.67	1.25	1.12	1.16	1.00
donfile	2.31	2.50	1.89	1.58	1.47	1.49	1.00
ex1	3.59	2.52	1.29	1.14	1.09	0.96	1.10
keyb	1.84	1.17	1.17	1.00	1.00	1.00	1.00
pma	2.89	2.15	1.11	1.11	1.10	0.98	1.00
s27	2.77	2.18	2.16	2.16	2.13	2.11	1.11
s8	1.57	1.25	1.00	1.00	1.00	1.00	1.07
shiftreg	1.50	1.50	1.37	1.13	1.00	1.06	1.00
train11	2.17	1.57	1.76	1.29	1.29	1.29	1.04
Mean	2.00	1.61	1.32	1.17	1.14	1.12	1.02

Results presented in Table 2 show that the Algorithm 2+ gave the results 1.02 times bigger than the Algorithm 3 and the Algorithm 1 gave the results 1.12 times bigger than the Algorithm 3. Algorithm 1 gave better results for the benchmarks *bbara* (0.93 times), *ex1* (0.96 times) and *pma* (0.98 times).

Results presented in the Table 1 include only the dynamic power and were obtained from the switching activity for the general model of the sequential circuit. For real applications, the dedicated software should be used. For that reason, the results were confirmed using the Altera Quartus Prime 17.1 Lite for the Cyclone V device and presented in Table 3. Column "Instances" present the number of the instances of FSM, next 3 columns have the same meaning, as in Table 1.

Results presented in the Table 3 confirm that for benchmark *pma* the best results gave the Algorithm 1, independent of the number of the instances of the FSM in the FPGA.

Table 3. Total power dissipation for the algorithms: state splitting only Algorithm 1, common model only Algorithm 2+ and the Algorithm 3 for benchmark *pma*.

Instances	P_L [mW]	P_M [mW]	P_T [mW]
1	355.41	357.44	357.02
10	370.47	376.27	371.92
100	468.11	493.08	478.45

6   Conclusions and Future Work

All the presented algorithms proved their usability in the power minimization of the FSM. Algorithm 1 that assigns multiple codes to the states is the worst of the three proposed algorithms in terms of the mean power regarding the set of benchmarks used in the experiment. But in 3 cases (*bbara*, *ex1* and *pma*) power dissipation was lower than the power for the Algorithm 3. This means that the Algorithm 2 worsened results obtained at the stage of state splitting, therefore in such cases, the intermediate results obtained with Algorithm 1 and Algorithm 2 should be remembered for future use.

Algorithm 1 needs a lot of the computational power because of the operation of the creating the splits for all states. This operation is very time consuming, especially when the FSM consists of the big amount of the states and there are a lot of transitions to every state. In future work, this operation should be optimized using some heuristics.

Also the next researches may be connected with implementing additional equivalent transformations, such as the state merging.

Acknowledgments. This work was supported by grant S/WI/1/2018 from Bialystok University of Technology and funded with resources for research by the Ministry of Science and Higher Education in Poland.

References

1. Yang, S.: Logic synthesis and optimization benchmarks user guide. Version 3.0., Technical Report. North Carolina. Microelectronics Center of North Carolina (1991). 46 p
2. Avedillo, M.J., Quintana, J.M., Huertas, J.L.: State merging and state splitting via state assignment: a new FSM synthesis algorithm. In: IEEE Proceedings - Computers and Digital Techniques, vol. 141, No. 4, 229–237 (1994)
3. Tsui, C.-Y., Monteiro, J., Devadas, S., Despain, A.M., Lin, B.: Power estimation methods for sequential logic circuits. IEEE Trans. VLSI Syst. **3**(3), 404–416 (1995)
4. Solovjev, V.: Synthesis of sequential circuits on programmable logic devices based on new models of finite state machines. In: Proceedings of the EUROMICRO Symposium on Digital Systems Design (DSD2001), September 4–6, Warsaw, Poland, pp. 170–173 (2001)

5. Iranli, A., Rezvani, P., Pedram, M.: Low power synthesis of state machines with mixed D and T flip flops. In: Proceedings of the Asia South Pacific Design Automation Conference (ASP-DAC), Kitakyushu, Japan, pp. 803–808. IEEE (2003)
6. Cao, C., Oelmann, B.: Mixed synchronous/asynchronous state memory for low power FSM design. In: Proceedings of the Euromicro Symposium on Digital System Design (DSD), Rennes, France, pp. 363–370. IEEE (2004)
7. Shiue, W.-T.: Novel state minimization and state assignment in finite state machine design for low-power portable device. Integration, the VLSI Journal **38**(3), 549–570 (2005)
8. Solov'ev, V.V.: Splitting the internal states in order to reduce the number of arguments in functions of finite automata. J. Comput. Syst. Sci. Int. **44**(5), 777–783 (2005)
9. Salauyou, V., Klimowicz, A., Grzes, T., Bulatowa, I., Dimitrova-Grekow, T.: Synthesis methods of finite state machines Implemented in Package ZUBR. In: Proceedings of the Sixth International Conference Computer-Aided Design of Discrete Devices (CAD DD7), Minsk, Belarus, pp. 53–56 (2007)
10. Kumar, M. T., Pradhan, S. N., Chattopadhyay, S.: Power-gated FSM Synthesis Integrating Partitioning and State Assignment. In: Proceedings of IEEE Region 10 Conference: Tencon vols. 1–4, pp. 2076–2081 (2008)
11. Stepaniuk, J.: Rough-Granular Computing in Knowledge Discovery and Data Mining. Springer, Heidelberg (2008). https://doi.org/10.1007/978-3-540-70801-8
12. Yuan, L., Qu, G., Villa, T., Sangiovanni-Vincentelli, A.: An FSM reengineering approach to sequential circuit synthesis by state splitting. IEEE Trans. CAD **27**(6), 1159–1164 (2008)
13. Choudhury, S., Sistla, K.T., Chattopadhyay, S.: Genetic algorithm-based FSM synthesis with area-power trade-offs. Integration - The VLSI J. **42**(3), 376–384 (2009)
14. Le Gal, B., Ribon, A., Bossuet, L., Dallet, D.: Reducing and smoothing power consumption of ROM-based controller implementations. In: 23rd Symposium on Integrated Circuits and Systems Design SBCCI 2010, pp. 8–13 (2010)
15. Grzes, T., Salauyou, V., Bulatova, I.: Algorithms of coding the internal states of finite-state machine focused on the reduced power consumption. Radioelectron. Commun. Syst. **53**(5), 265–273 (2010)
16. Klimovich, A.S., Solovev, V.V.: Transformation of a Mealy finite-state machine into a Moore finite-state machine by splitting internal states. J. Comput. Syst. Sci. Int. **49**(6), 70–79 (2010)
17. Pradhan, S.N., Kumar, M.T., Chattopadhyay, S.: Low power finite state machine synthesis using power-gating. Integr. VLSI J. **44**(3), 175–184 (2011)
18. Mrozek, I., Yarmolik, V.N.: Iterative Antirandom Testing. J. Electron. Test **28**(3), 301–315 (2012). Kluwer Academic Publishers
19. Mukati, M.A.: A heuristic approach of code assignment to obtain an optimal FSM Design. In: Advanced Information Technology in Education, Advances in Intelligent and Soft Computing, vol. 126, pp. 23–31 (2012)
20. Sait, S.M., Oughali, F.C., Arafeh, A.M.: FSM state-encoding for area and power minimization using simulated evolution algorithm. J. Appl. Res. Technol. **10**, 845–858 (2012)
21. Solovev, V.V.: Changes in the length of internal state codes with the aim at minimizing the power consumption of finite-state machines. J. Commun. Technol. Electr. **57**(6), 642–648 (2012)
22. Solovev, V.V., Grzes, T.N.: An iteration algorithm of coding internal states of finite-state machines for minimizing the power consumption. Russian Microelectr. **42**(3), 189–195 (2013)

23. Grzes, T.N., Solovev, V.V.: Sequential algorithm for low-power encoding internal states of finite state machines. J. Comput. Syst. Sci. Int. **53**(1), 92–99 (2014)
24. Grzes, T.N., Solovev, V.V.: Minimization of power consumption of finite state machines by splitting their internal states. J. Comput. Syst. Sci. Int. **54**(3), 367–374 (2015)
25. Pradhan, S.N., Choudhury, P.: Low power and high testable finite state machine synthesis. In: Proceedings of the International Conference on and Workshop on Computing and Communication (IEMCON), Vancouver, Canada. IEEE (2015)
26. El-Maleh, A.H.: Majority-based evolution state assignment algorithm for area and power optimisation of sequential circuits. IET Comput. Digit. Tech. **10**(1), 30–36 (2016)

SME: A New Software Transactional Memory Based Mutual Exclusion Algorithm for Distributed Systems

Sukhendu Kanrar[(✉)]

Narasinha Dutt College, Howrah, India
sukhen2003@gmail.com

Abstract. The utilization of concurrent computing has significantly increased in the last three decades for various commercial and scientific applications. However, concurrent systems often have an astronomically large number of possible executions. These executions may proceed in many different ways depending on scheduling of processes, sequence of inputs, etc. Such non-determinism often leads to gaps or malfunctions in the system design. Thus synchronization of resources became a great issue and programmers had to put huge effort solving this. Transactional memory is one of those measures to solve these inconsistencies. The goal of a transactional memory system is to transparently support the definition of regions of code that are considered in a transaction to maintain the ACID properties of transactions. This paper explores the possibility of designing a STM based mutual exclusion algorithm and compares its performance in terms of time and message complexity. A new STM-based mutual exclusion algorithm known as SME has been proposed and the results have been compared with those due to traditional FAPP algorithm. Besides, the proposed SME implementation is on the ring topology that provides a stable structure suitable for increasing the degree of multiprogramming.

Keywords: Software transactional memory (STM)
Mutual exclusion · Correctness · Fairness

1 Introduction

The motivation of designing transactional memory (TM) lies in the programming interface of parallel programs. A transaction is a form of program execution borrowed from database system. TM offers a mechanism that allows portions of program in isolation, concurrently executing tasks. Most TM system provides simple atomic statements that execute a block of code as a transaction. A transaction in this context is a piece of code that executes a series of reads and writes to shared memory. These reads and writes logically occur at a single instant in time; intermediate states are not visible to other (successful) transactions. TM allows programmer to define customized read,

© Springer Nature Switzerland AG 2018
K. Saeed and W. Homenda (Eds.): CISIM 2018, LNCS 11127, pp. 354–369, 2018.
https://doi.org/10.1007/978-3-319-99954-8_30

write and modify operations that apply to memory. TM allows writing coding like in this example:

$$def\_transfer\_data(source, destination, data):$$
$$transaction:$$
$$source = source - data$$
$$destination = destination + data$$

In the code above, the block defined by "transaction" has the atomicity, consistency and isolation guarantees and the underlying transactional memory implementation must assure those guarantees transparently. A transaction is a finite sequence of instruction, executed by a single processor, satisfying the serializability (i.e., transaction appear to execute serially) and atomicity properties. TM can be implemented entirely in software called Software Transactional Memory (STM). STM is a concurrency control mechanism analogous to database transactions for controlling access to shared memory in concurrent computing. It is an alternative to lock-based synchronization. STM has been perceived as a tool to handle distributed mutual exclusion problems with an ease of programming skill and keeping the ACID property intact (Fig. 1).

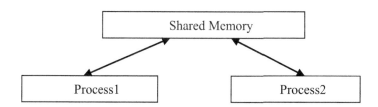

Fig. 1. Concurrency control with share memory equals to TM

2 Design State of the Art Review

The mutual exclusion criterion states that at a given instance of time, only a single process can be allowed access to a particular resource, in the respective Critical Section (CS) of code. Distributed mutual exclusion algorithms are either token-based or non token-based. A number of solutions have been proposed for prioritized mutual exclusion in a distributed system. Some of these approaches are suitable for real-time application. However, these may impose a higher message passing overhead. In Raymond's [2] token based mutual exclusion algorithm, requests are sent over a static spanning tree of the network, toward the token holder. In one of our earlier works, both fairness and priority have been addressed in proposing an algorithm MRA-P. However, MRA-P [3] suffered from some major shortcomings like lack of liveness, high message complexity, etc. Then I introduced a token based Fairness Algorithm for Priority Processes (FAPP) [1] that addresses both the issues (i.e., liveness, high message complexity) and keeps the control message traffic reasonably low. The proposed solution, in spite of considering priority of processes, ensures liveness in terms of token requests from low priority processes.

Several researchers have implemented TM language constructs. In one approach, languages provide block-structured atomic sections, so a programmer may reason as if each atomic section is executed as a single step, serialized with respect to all other atomic sections. I adopt their techniques for cloning methods in the JVM and dealing with native method calls, and I build on their technique for detecting conflicts at the memory word granularity. Shavit and Touitou [5] introduce the term STM and present a static STM, which requires advance knowledge of the memory locations involved in a transaction.

Another issue is strong and weak atomicity [6]. STM system generally implements weak atomicity, which means non-transaction code is not isolated from code in transaction.

Abadi, Birrell, Harris and Isard [7] develop semantics type systems for the constructs of the Automatic Mutual Exclusion (AME) programming model. With this semantics as a point of reference, they studied several implementation strategies and model STM systems that use in-place update, optimistic concurrency, lazy conflict detection, and roll-back. These strategies are correct only under non-trivial assumptions that I identify and analyze. The limitations of conventional synchronization techniques, based on locks and condition variables, are well known [9]. Coarse-grained locks, which protect relatively large amounts of data, simply do not scale well. Threads block one another even when they do not really interfere, and the lock itself becomes a source of contention.

Fine-grained locks are more scalable, but they are difficult to use effectively and correctly. Hagit Attiya [10] finds the answers of the question "What should be incorporated in a theory for transaction memory – and in a broader perspectives, concurrent data structures?"

Today, programmers use lock-based synchronization to control concurrent access to shared data. Lock based synchronization is difficult to compose, and can lead to problems such as deadlock. Transactional memory (TM) provides an alternate concurrency control mechanism that eliminates or alleviates these pitfalls, and significantly eases parallel programming. Although several researchers have implemented TM language constructs [4] and language designers have included TM constructs in new concurrent language specifications [12], no prior work has addressed how to support transactions in traditional OS programming approaches. Herlihy et al. [13] propose a new form of software transactional memory (STM) designed to support dynamic-sized data structures, and they describe a novel non-blocking implementation. The non-blocking property, I consider is obstruction-freedom.

Dynamic Software Transactional Memory (DSTM) is a low-level application programming interface (API) for synchronizing shared data without using locks. A transaction is a sequence of steps executed by a single thread. Transactions are atomic; i.e., each transaction either commits (it takes effect) or aborts (its effects are discarded). Transactions are serializable [14]; i.e., they appear to take effect in a one-at-a-time order. Transactional memory supports a computational model in which each thread announces the start of a transaction, executes a sequence of operations on shared objects, and then tries to commit the transaction. If the commit succeeds, the transaction's operations take effect; otherwise, they are discarded. Although transactional memory was originally proposed as hardware architecture [9], there have been several proposals for non-blocking software transactional memory (STM) and similar constructs [15, 16].

FAPP [1] is an improvement of Raymond's algorithm, which is a tree-based ME algorithm. FAPP is a priority based algorithm. Besides, it also maintains the FCFS order in allocating token amongst equal priority jobs. While the algorithm exchanges minimal information to select the next process that would enter critical sections, the overhead due to information that are maintained in the nodes is also very little. The FAPP algorithm has been described in Fig. 2 for the sake of completeness of the present text.

FAPP, however, suffers from several limitations as well. Firstly, Tree as a data structure has a strict hierarchy. Although FAPP is proposed for distributed environment, failure of a parent node may become critical. Secondly, the execution time and the message complexity both are O (log N), the height of the tree, where the N is total number of nodes in the system. Besides, in FAPP two or more token requests propagated through overlapping paths to the root node of the tree are handled one after another. It would be more efficient for a concurrency control algorithm if such requests are handled simultaneously.

Request Part:

Step 1: When a process N with priority P_N wants to enter the critical section (CS).According to priority, it adds tuple <N, P_N>into Path-list of N i.e., PL_N and send a request to other process with <N, P_N>.

Step 2: When process H which may or may not the token holder, receives a token request <N, P_N>. At first H updates the priorities by 1 for received earlier. Then insert <N, P_N> into its PL_H in descending order of priority otherwise insert at end ;
If process H $\neq P_{hold}$ then this process do additional task which is send a token request on behalf of <N, P_N>.

Execution Part:

Step 1: The new root process S = P_{hold} that receives token then removes the first tuple <N, P_N> from PL_S. if (S= = N) then enter CS otherwise, Process S send the token To <N, PN>.If (PLS[] $\neq$null) then S   send a dummy token_request<S, x> to <N, P_N>; Where x is the highest priority which received by S.

Fig. 2. FAPP algorithm

In this paper, I propose a new STM-based mutual exclusion algorithm that proposes to overcome these limitations of traditional tree based ME algorithm like FAPP. The proposed STM based algorithm has been implemented on Java platform. The rest of the paper has been organized as follows: a brief discussion on the implementation requirements for STM is in Sect. 3 of this paper; Sect. 4 presents the proposed algorithm in a modular approach; the performance evaluation and a comparative analysis of the proposed algorithm against traditional FAPP approach is recorded in Sect. 5; the paper ends with concluding remarks in Sect. 6.

3   Implementation of STM

Here I have implemented our STM by arranging a large amount of memory and giving it to the user's as per requirement. The main goal is to provide a concurrent shared memory, which will not have anomalies when multiple update requests are invoked on it simultaneously. I have used JAVA's synchronized (Object) method to make such a memory. The Structure of STM here is to have a 2D array of memory. Each row is to be considered as a block which will be synchronized to prevent race conditions. So, if a huge memory is considered still I can lock a minimal portion to make it faster as the other threads working on the same data structure but on other memory locations will not have to wait. The structure is as follows (Fig. 3).

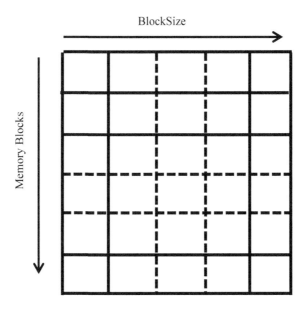

Fig. 3. STM memory structure

3.1   STM Memory Management

I have implemented first fit strategy to allocate memory. So, this is an O (n) procedure (here 'n' is the current number of full or partially used memory blocks) as I am scanning all the memory blocks that are partially filled from start to get a sufficiently long memory chunk. If a single block is not available, then I am assigning one or more new chunks. However if the request is greater than chunk size I am directly assigning new chunks which are O (1) operation.

STM_MALLOC (memory size)
/* This module used for allocating a chunk of memory containing max 100 blocks in each row. */

1	I have stored start block index, end block index, start index, end index, no. of blocks required for each STM variable and used array's 0 based indexing.
2	if memory_size>=block_size
3	block_required=(memory_size/block);
4	Synchronized memory_pool
5	for i=0 to block_required
6	Add new block to memory pool with 0 empty cells except the last block which may have N empty_cells, where N=block_size-(memory_size%block_size)
7	Synchronized memory_log
8	Make suitable entry in corresponding line in the log with variable name, start_index and end_index
9	end_block=memory_pool_size-1
10	start_block=end_block-block_required
11	End for loop
12	else
13	memory_found =false
14	for i=0 to memory_pool_size
15	if i-th block has enough free cells
16	Synchronized block$_i$
17	start_block=end_block=i;
18	start_index=block_size-block$_i$.empty_cells
19	end_index=start_index+memory_size-1
20	memory_found=true
21	Synchronized memory_log
22	concat with the entry of memory_log$_i$ the new variables name, start and end index
23	break
24	end if
25	end for loop
26	if ! memory_found
27	Synchronized memory_pool
28	assign a new memory block in the memory_pool with
29	start_block=end_block=memory_pool_size
30	start_index=0
31	end_index=memory_size-1
32	Synchronized memory_log
33	Make new log entry with variable name, start and end index
34	end if

3.2   Read and Write Operation

For each STM variable I have used array's 0 based indexing. Also I have stored start block index, end block index, start index, end index, no. of blocks required. So it is an $O(1)$ operation to find out which memory chunk's which memory cell will be updated. However, there may be some complexity rise due to the use of JAVA's synchronize (Object) method.

STM_READ (index)
/*This module reads from a list using an index pointing to the particular entry. */
1   block_number=0
2   if start_block_number==end_block_number
3   block_number=start_block_number
4   else
5   block_number=start_block_number+(index%block_size)
6   end if
7   Synchronized block$_{block\_number}$
8   return block$_{block\_number}$.memory$_{start\_index+(index\%block\_size)}$

STM_WRITE(index,new_val)
/*This module used for updating or writing in particular index of a list. */
1   block_number=0
2   if start_block_number==end_block_number
3   block_number=start_block_number
4   else
5   block_number=start_block_number+(index%block_size)
6   end if
7   Synchronized block$_{block\_number}$
8   block$_{block\_number}$.memory$_{start\_index+(index\%block\_size)}$=new_val

3.3   Checkpoint

I have used to maintain the log of the STM shared by all STM variables to recover from a damaged state if reached somehow. However, when checkpoint method is run the total memory pool is locked and I have to check each cell of each used chunk. So it is basically an $O(n^2)$ operation (basically O (chunks used $\times$ chunk length) operation).

STM_CHECKPOINT()

/*This module used for maintaining the log of the STM shared by all STM variable to recover from a damaged state */

1	Synchronized memory_pool
2	Synchronized memory_log
3	For each variable in memory_log's each line from the start and end index get the values of corresponding variable from memory_pool and suitably concatenate to update the memory log with current value.

4 Proposed STM-Based Mutual Exclusion (SME) Algorithm

The objective of the proposed algorithm is to improve upon the limitations of existing tree-based ME algorithms. The system would be more stable with a new type of interconnection other than a balanced tree. In distributed system (Hybrid P2P System), the control is divided to more than one central node. In order to evaluate whether STM is giving better output than conventional approach or not I have selected the FAPP Algorithm which is an extension of Raymond's Algorithm for Distribute Mutual Exclusion problem.

4.1 STM Implementation for SME

The proposed STM-based Mutual Exclusion algorithm (SME) uses a few independent modules. Let's discuss the objective of each module before the SME algorithm is described.

initialize_tree (..): All the nodes of the tree are initialized and its process queues are allocated memory using stm_malloc.

insert_in_process_queue (..): First, insert in the process queue of the node that is the parameter of the function using stm_write. Then the same node is inserted in its parent's process queue till it reaches the root of the tree.

Here basically, the process queues of the nodes are filled with the respective entries before the CS execution starts.

after_CS_execution(..): Here the P_{hold} starts execution. It removes the first tuple from its process queue.If the size of the queue is greater than zero, then a dummy token request function with parameters (E,x) is sent. Else if the dequeued node's queue_size is greater than zero, then the function start_CS_execution is called recursively. Else, the CS of all the requesting nodes is executed.

send_dummy_token_request(..): First, the new P_{hold} writes the dequeued node in its own queue using stm_write. Then the first tuple is removed from its queue and the identifier names of the node and the dequeued one's are checked. If they are same, CS is entered and start_CS_execution() is called again.

Else the send_dummy_token_request() function is called recursively.

Class ProcessNode has four member fields:

a. Identifier name
b. Priority
c. Parent Pointer.
d. Self list(containing the requests of itself and the child nodes)

   INITIALIZE_TREE()
       /* This module is for initializing the nodes and its process queues */
1 list.stm_malloc(.....)
  /*dynamic allocation of memory of the self list of each process queue */
INSERT_IN_PROCESS_QUEUE(requesting_node)
 /* This module is for updating the process queues of the participating nodes */

1	write in its own ID in process_queue and increment the front of the queue.
2	list.stm_write(queue_front,requesting_node)
3	while(requesting_node's parent not equal to NULL)
4	do
5	if(node's parent's queue_size > 0)
6	If(parent's list has nodes having priority > requesting_node's priority)
7	increment the priority of each node in parent's list.

                        /*this ensures starvation won't occur.*/

8	endif
9	for i=0 to node's parent's queue_size
10	if(node's parent's list stm_read(i).Identifier name equals node.Identifier name)
11	if(node's parent's list stm_read(i).priority < node.priority)
12	replace the list's node with the current node

         /*node.parent.list.stm_write(i,curr_node).*/

13	endif
14	endif
15	if(node's parent's list identifier names donot match withthe current node's identifier's name)

                  /*I take a flag variable to distinguish them.*/

16	write in the parent's process queue and increment the front of the parent's queue.
17	sort the process queue of node(in descending order of priorities)
18	node = node.Parent
19	endif
20	endif
21	done.

AFTER_CS_EXECUTION(ProcessNode node)
  /*This module is for CS execution begins here and its end is also validated here.*/
  1   remove the first tuple from the token holder's list of process_nodes
  2   if(node's queue_size > 0)
  3   replace node's priority with the priority of the current first node of the
       process queue
                      /* node's priority = stm_read(queue_rear).Priority. */
  4   send dummy_token_request(node,dequeued node)
  5   endif
  6   if(dequeued node's queue_size > 0)
  7   recursively call the same function i.e after_CS_execution(dequeued
node)
  8   finally the node completes CS execution and thus all requests are
       served ensuring liveness.
  9   endif

SEND_DUMMY_TOKEN_REQUEST(...., ...)
  /* This module used here the P_{hold} changes and it is concerned with the
  intermediate stage of the CS Execution.*/
  The newly designated root process R = P_{hold} that receives token <N,N$_P$> performs the
  following
  1   delete the first entry <N,N$_P$> from PL$_R$;

  2   if (R== N)
       /* after executing CS, process works with itsoriginal initial priority.*/
  3   enter CS;
  4   else
  5   send token<N,N$_P$>;
       /* N would be the new P_{hold} - the token ispassed to N from R.*/
  6   endif
  7   if (PL$_R$[] not equal to null)
  8   send dummy token_request <R, x>;
       /* N placcs a token request to R along withhighest priority x.*/
  9   endif.

5   Performance Analysis

I shell observe the performance of our algorithms using following performance
parameters: message complexity, Time complexity, Managing the ring structure, Load
Balancing and relative performance evaluation between FAPP and SME.

5.1   Message Complexity

Compared to traditional FAPP, here tree height is always 1. So, message complexity is of O (height of tree) = O (1). It is because only one message is sufficient to make the request to super node.

5.2   Time Complexity

Compared to traditional FAPP where time complexity is $2*(H-1) = O(\log n)$ [where H is the height of tree] our time complexity should be $O(1)$ [as $H = 1$]. However, I should consider the sorting time also which is $O(n\log n)$ normally and some concurrency management in the STM.

5.3   Managing the Ring Structure

It is possible that one child node may try to attach with some other child node. Then I simply provide to the new child node the old one's parent super node. This is also an $O(1)$ operation (Fig. 4).

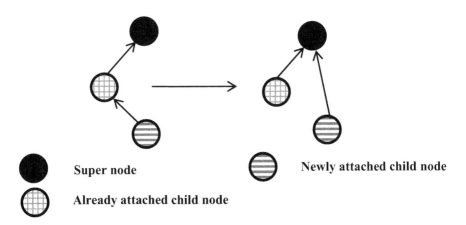

Fig. 4. Different types of node

5.4   Load Balancing

Considering there are $(n + 1)$ super nodes in ring and one of the super nodes has m excess child nodes, let rest n super-nodes each have (m/n) empty spaces (say m is divisible by n).

T(balance in n super-nodes) = T(insertion in next) + T(balance in next (n−1) super-nodes)

$$= O(m/n) + [T(\text{next}) + T(\text{balance in next}(n-2)\text{super} - \text{nodes})]$$
$$= 2 * O(m.n) + T(\text{next}) + T(\text{balance in next}(n-3)\text{super} - \text{nodes})$$
$$= \ldots\ldots\ldots\ldots\ldots\ldots\ldots\ldots\ldots\ldots$$
$$= n * O(m/n)$$
$$= O(m)$$

Hence, Load balancing is of O(number of excess child nodes).

5.5 Simulation Result

FAPP is a token based system where always a root node is present (the token holding node) due to its tree structure. One major limitation of the token based mutual exclusion algorithms for distributed environment like Raymond's well-known work on inverted-tree topology where root is present. So, ROOT crash implies System crash. Though proposed time complexity is O(log N) the complexity of sorting each list is not mentioned. Message complexity is also O(log N) due to its tree structure.

Token based protocol has no scope for parallel programming since the user shall have to wait to get all the requests for CS (critical section). I try to improve FAPP Algorithm using STM. To make the system more stable I need a new type of inter-connection other than a balanced tree.

I got the idea from Distributed System (Hybrid P2P System) where the control is divided into more than one central node. I use more stable structure, namely, Ring Structure. I can extend the ring if necessary.

In this section, I present the simulation results for our proposed algorithm and the tree based FAPP [1] solution. I have conducted multiple sets of simulations on different networks by choosing different link connection from a connected graph of different number nodes. The requesting nodes and the order of requests are also selected at random for different sizes of request queues. The average for each selection is plotted. The simulation is done using JAVA. The simulation parameters are listed in Table 1.

The results that have been plotted in different figures represent average of multiple executions. Thus the analysis based on these randomly selected executions may be considered unbiased and represents the generic behavior of the system for the proposed algorithm.

Table 1. Simulation parameters

Parameters	Value
Connection topology	Ring Structure
Minimum number of nodes in the graph	16
Maximum number of nodes in the graph	60000
Edge length	Static
Maximum Out-degree	2
Maximum degree	3
Minimum degree	1
Types of graphs	6
For each case, number of samples	6
System	In distributed system (Hybrid P2P System)
Two types of node	Server and Client
Priority of nodes in the graph	1, 2, ….. (user choice)
Implement the queues of each site	using java.util.ArrayList

From this comparison and graph I can state that STM is giving better output than the conventional implementation.

Again I have taken 6 types of graphs and for each case I have increased the number of nodes exponentially. For each case I have taken 6 samples.

Each sample consists of same number of nodes but the link connections are different, i.e. different graph with same number of nodes and same requesting nodes but different link connections and calculated execution times for each sample and made averages (Fig. 5).

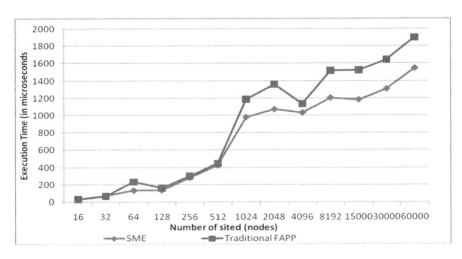

Fig. 5. Graph of execution time compared between SME and traditional FAPP

With an exponential increase in number of nodes I found that execution time changes in a manner between exponential and linear (for first 2 point and last 4 points almost linear, overall tends to an exponential nature) (Fig. 6).

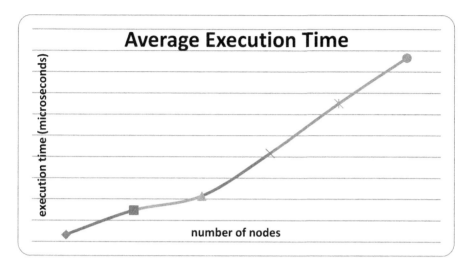

Fig. 6. Graph of execution time in SME

I can see that for networks with same number of node the outcomes are more or less same, i.e. if load is same execution time is more or less same (though not identical) which implies a linear nature on same workload and states that the system is stable and correct (Fig. 7).

Fig. 7. Graph of execution time, where no. of nodes gradually increases

6 Conclusion

I have implemented a new STM-based mutual exclusion algorithm known as SME and using that I have implemented this algorithm to traditional FAPP algorithm and found better outcome. Moreover using SME I have implemented the Ring based approach which removes the flaws of any token based algorithm like FAPP by providing more stable structure and implementing cloud like environment degree of multiprogramming may arise. Using SME I solve the problem of monitoring of processes for executing Mutual Exclusion.

References

1. Kanrar, S., Chaki, N.: FAPP: a new fairness algorithm for priority process mutual exclusion in distributed systems. Spec. Issue Recent. Adv. Netw. Parallel Comput. Int. J. Netw. **5**(1), 11–18 (2010)
2. Raymond, K.: A tree-based algorithm for distributed mutual exclusion. ACM Trans. Comput. Syst. **7**, 61–77 (1989)
3. Kanrar, S., Chaki, N.: Modified Raymond's algorithm for priority (MRA-P) based mutual exclusion in distributed systems. In: Madria, S.K., Claypool, K.T., Kannan, R., Uppuluri, P., Gore, M.M. (eds.) ICDCIT 2006. LNCS, vol. 4317, pp. 325–332. Springer, Heidelberg (2006). https://doi.org/10.1007/11951957_29
4. Harris, T., Fraser, K.: Language support for lightweight transactions. In: 18th Annual ACM SIGPLAN Conference on Object-Oriented Programming, Systems, Languages, and Applications. OOP-SLA 2003, pp. 388–402 (2003)
5. Shavit, N., Touitou, D.: Software transactional memory. In: 14th ACM Symposium on Principles of Distributed Computing. PODC 1995, pp. 204–213 (1995)
6. Naik, M., Aiken, A., Whaley, J.: Effective static race detection for Java. In: PLDI 2006: Proceeding of 2006 ACM SIGPLAN Conference on Programming Language Design and Implementation, pp. 308–319(2006)
7. Abadi, M., Birrell, A., Harris, T., Isard, M.: Semantics of transactional memory and automatic mutual exclusion. In: Proceedings of the 35th Annual ACM SIGPLAN-SIGACT Symposium on Principles of Programming Languages, vol. 20, pp. 1–49 (2008)
8. Harris, T., Plesko, M., Shinnar, A., Tarditi, D.: Optimizing memory transactions. In: ACM SIGPLAN Conference on Programming Language Design and Implementation. PLDI 2006, pp. 14–25 (2006)
9. Herlihy, M., Moss, J.E.B.: Transactional memory: architectural support for lock-free data structures. In: 20th Annual International Symposium on Computer Architecture, pp. 289–300 (1993)
10. Attiya, H.: Needed: foundations for transactional memory. Newsl. ACM SIGACT News Arch. **39**(1), 59–61 (2008)
11. Shpeisman, T., et al.: Enforcing isolation and ordering in STM. In: PLDI 2007: Proceedings of 2007 ACM SIGPLAN Conference on Programming Language Design and Implementation, pp. 78–88 (2007)
12. Charles, P., et al.: X10: an object-oriented approach to non-uniform cluster computing. In: OOPSLA 2005: Object-Oriented Programing, Systems, Languages, and Applications (2005)
13. Herlihy, M., Luchangcogton, V., Moir, M.N., Scherer III, W.: Software transactional memory for dynamic-sized data structure. In: 22nd Annual Symposium on Principles of Distributed Computing, PODC 2003, pp. 13–16. ACM, USA (2003)

14. Herlihy, M., Linearizability, J.W.: A correctness condition for concurrent objects. ACM Trans. Program. Lang. Syst. **12**(3), 463–492 (1990)
15. Afekn, Y., Dauber, D., Touitou, D.: Wait-free made fast. In: 27th Annual ACM Symposium on Theory of Computing, pp. 538–547 (1995)
16. Shavit, N., Touitou, D.: Software transactional memory. Distrib. Comput. Spec. Issue **10**, 99–116 (1997)
17. Banerjee, S., Mukherjee, P., Kanrar, S., Chaki, N.: A novel symmetric algorithm for process synchronization in distributed systems. In: Conference on Algorithms and application (ALAP 2018), pp. 69–82 (2018)

Area Targeted Minimization Method of Finite State Machines for FPGA Devices

Adam Klimowicz[(✉)]

Bialystok University of Technology, Bialystok, Poland
a.klimowicz@pb.edu.pl

Abstract. A new method for the minimization of finite state machines (FSMs) is proposed. In this method, such optimization criterion as the number of used logic elements is taken into account already at the stage of minimizing internal states. The method is based on sequential merging of two internal states. For this purpose, the set of all pairs of states that can be merged is found, and the pair that best satisfies the optimization criteria is chosen for merging. In addition, the proposed method allows one to minimize the number of transitions and input variables of the FSM. The binary, one-hot and JEDI state assignment methods are used. Experimental results show, that the used FPGA area is less on average by 18% comparing to traditional methods.

Keywords: Finite state machine (FSM) · State minimization · Logic synthesis
Area minimization · FPGA

1 Introduction

Finite state machines (FSMs) are widely used as behavioral models of control units implemented on devices of programmable logic such as field-programmable gate arrays (FPGA). Taking into account the specific characteristics of FPGA architectures in the early stages of design allows to increase the efficiency of synthesis methods, which means e.g. reducing the hardware complexity.

The conventional approach to the synthesis of FSMs includes the following stages, which are executed sequentially: minimization of the number of internal states, state assignment and synthesis of the combinational part of the FSM. Under the conventional approach, a developer has only two methods of optimizing the FSM: minimization of the number of internal states and state assignment. Often, even the exact minimization of the number of internal states does not make it possible to solve the optimization problems at the stage of logic synthesis.

In work [1], the problem of minimization and state assignment was considered for asynchronous FSMs. The method proposed in [2] is applicable only to FSMs with the number of states not exceeding 10. In [3], a program for concurrent state reduction and state encoding was presented, which made it possible to build incompletely specified state codes. In [4], a program called STAMINA that runs in exact and heuristic modes and uses explicit enumeration for the solution of state minimization problem is presented.

© Springer Nature Switzerland AG 2018
K. Saeed and W. Homenda (Eds.): CISIM 2018, LNCS 11127, pp. 370–379, 2018.
https://doi.org/10.1007/978-3-319-99954-8_31

In [5–11], the chip area (implementation cost) is minimized simultaneously with the minimization of the power consumption at the stage of state assignment. In [5], the problem is solved for two level circuits like programmable logic arrays (PLAs). In the majority of works [6–9] genetic algorithms are used. In [10], an internal state splitting procedure is used; in this case, no minimization of the number of internal states of the FSM is required. The parametric method of the minimization of finite state machines is proposed in [11]. In this method, such optimization criteria as the power consumption and possibility of merging other states are taken into account already at the early stage of minimization of internal FSM states.

The analysis of available studies showed that the number of internal states and area are not often simultaneously minimized. The methods that claim to simultaneously take into account several optimization criteria actually reduce to the conventional approach in which several different algorithms are proposed for each stage. In the present paper, we propose a heuristic method for the minimization of incompletely specified FSMs that makes it possible to optimize a used area already at the stage of minimization of the number of internal states. The proposed approach suits well for the implementation of FSMs on FPGA devices.

2 Idea of the Approach

A FSM behavior may be described by the *transition list*. The transition list is a table with four columns: a_m, a_s, $X(a_m, a_s)$, and $Y(a_m, a_s)$. Each row of the transition list corresponds to one FSM transition. The column a_m contains the present, the column a_s contains the next state, the column $X(a_m, a_s)$ contains the set of values of the input variables that initiates this transition (*a transition condition* or *an input vector*), and the column $Y(a_m, a_s)$ contains the set of values of the output variables that is generated by FSM at this transition (*an output vector*).

The proposed approach is based on the method for the minimization of the number of internal states of FSMs proposed in [12]. The idea of the method [12] is to sequentially merge two states. For this purpose, the set G of all pairs of internal states of the FSM satisfying the merging condition is found at each step. Then, for each pair in G, a trial merging is done. Next, the pair (a_i, a_j) that leaves the maximum possibilities for merging other pairs in G is chosen for real merging.

In distinction from [12], in the present paper we chose for merging at each step the pair (a_i, a_j) that best satisfies the optimization criteria in terms of area occupation, and leaves the maximum possibilities for merging other pairs in G. This procedure is repeated while at least one pair of states can be merged.

Let (a_s, a_t) be a pair of states in G, where C_{st} is the estimate of cost of FSM implementation, and M_{st} is the estimate of the possibility to merge other states. Then, with regard to the above considerations, the main FSM minimization algorithm can be described as on Fig. 1.

Algorithms of minimization of the number of transition an input variables are based on some observations. Suppose, for instance, that one transition from a state a_1 under condition x_1 leads to a state a_2 and the second transition from a_1 under condition $\bar{x}_1$ leads to another state a_3 and on each of these transitions not orthogonal output vectors are formed ($\bar{x}_1$ is an inversed form of the variable x_1). Suppose that the states a_2 and a_3 can be merged. After merging a_2 and a_3, a new state a_{23} is formed. Now two transitions lead from a_1 to a_{2_3}, one under condition x_1 and the second under condition $\bar{x}_1$. The latter means that the transition from a_1 to a_{23} is unconditional and two transitions can be replaced by one unconditional transition. Notice that in general transition conditions from a state a_1 can be much more complicated.

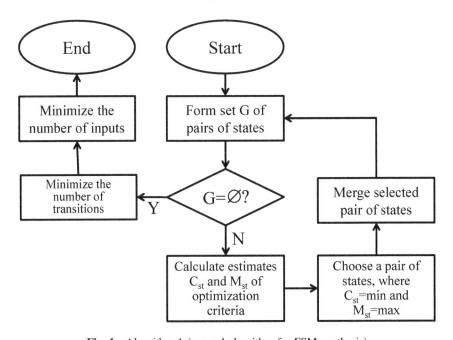

Fig. 1. Algorithm 1 (general algorithm for FSM synthesis)

At minimization of the number of FSM transitions one can arrive at a situation when certain input variables have no impact on the transition conditions. Suppose, for instance, that one transition from a state a_1 under condition x_1 leads to a state a_2 and another transition from a_1 under condition $\bar{x}_1$ leads to a state a_3 and the variable x_1 does not meet anywhere else in transition conditions of the FSM. Suppose that after the states a_2 and a_3 have been merged, the transition from the state a_1 to the state a_{23} becomes unconditional, i.e. it does not depend on values of input variables. The latter means that the variable x_1 has no impact on any FSM transition and therefore it is redundant.

3   Estimation of Optimization Criteria

To estimate the optimization criteria, all pairs of states in G are considered one after another. For each pair of states (a_s, a_t) in G, a trial merging is performed. Next the internal states are encoded using one of three state assignment methods (binary, one-hot and JEDI [13]) and the system of Boolean functions corresponding to the combinational part of the FSM is built. Next, for the pair (a_s, a_t), power consumption C_{st}, and the possibility of minimizing other states M_{st} are estimated. The optimization criteria for each pair of states (a_s, a_t) in G are estimated using the algorithm presented on Fig. 2.

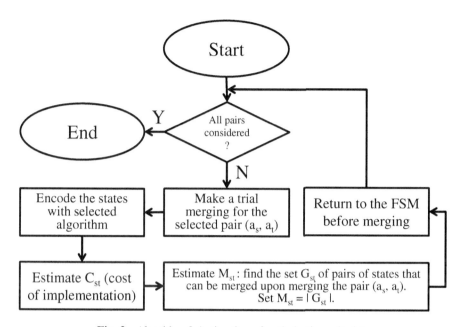

Fig. 2. Algorithm 2 (estimation of optimization criteria).

The estimate M_{st} is determined by the number of pairs of the FSM that can be merged after merging the pair (a_s, a_t). To provide the best possibilities for merging other states, M_{st} should be maximized. Using the method described in [12], the set G_{st} of pairs of states that can be merged upon merging the pair (a_s, a_t) must me find. After that, the parameter M_{st} can be calculated as the cardinality of the set G_{st} ($M_{st} = |G_{st}|$). Merging of the states a_i and a_j, minimization of the number of transitions and minimization of the number of input variables are performed as described in [14].

4 Estimation of Implementation Cost

When the cost of implementation of the FPGA based FSM is estimated, the implementation of the FSM memory is ignored and the cost is determined only by the cost of the combinational part of the FSM. The point is that the logic elements of the FPGA admit configurations with the combinational or register output. For that reason, in order to introduce a memory flip-flops in the FSM circuit, it suffices to configure the logic element output on which the activation function of the corresponding memory element is realized as a flip-flop output. No additional resources of FPGA are needed; therefore, the cost of the FSM memory implementation does not increase.

Note that, before calculating the implementation cost, the system of Boolean functions corresponding to the combinational part of the FSM can be minimized using the method that will be used for synthesis.

In the general case, the architecture of modern FPGAs can be represented as a set of logic elements based on functional LUT generators. A feature of LUT functional generators is that they can realize any Boolean function but with a small number of arguments (typically, 4–6 and more often 4). In the case when the number of arguments of functions to be realized exceeds the number of LUT inputs n, the Boolean function must be decomposed with respect to the number of arguments [15]. When the cost of implementation of a function w_i ($w_i \in W$) is calculated, only the restriction on the number of LUT inputs is taken in account. Among the great number of decomposition methods for Boolean functions with respect to the number of arguments, linear decomposition methods are most popular. They are used in the majority of industrial EDA systems. The Fig. 3 shows the general block diagram of the linear decomposition of a Boolean function y, where $FB_1, \ldots, FB_T$ are functional FPGA units, and $X_1, \ldots, X_T$ are subsets of the set of input variables X.

Fig. 3. Linear decomposition of a Boolean function

With regard to the above considerations, the algorithm for calculating the cost of implementation of an FSM for FPGA devices can be described as follows.

Algorithm 3 (for the estimation of the implementation cost of the FSM).

1. Calculate the implementation cost $C(w_i)$ for each function $w_i \in W$.
2. In the case of implementation of the FSM on the basis of FPGA, the cost $C(w_i)$ is calculated as

$$C(w_i) = 1 +](|Z(w_i)| - n)/(n - 1)[, \tag{1}$$

where $|A|$ is the cardinality of the set A, $Z(w_i)$ is the set of arguments of the function w_i and $]A[$ is the minimum integer greater than or equal to A.

3. Estimate the implementation cost of the FSM using the rule:

$$C_{st} = \sum_{w_i \in W} C(w_i) \tag{2}$$

4. Stop.

5 Experimental Results

The method of minimization of finite state machines was implemented in a program called ZUBR. To estimate the efficiency of the offered method we used MCNC FSM benchmarks [16] and well-known STAMINA minimization program [4] for comparison. The experiments were performed using IntelFPGA Quartus Prime version 17.1 EDA tool. All benchmarks in all three cases (without minimization, minimized with STAMINA and synthesized with proposed method) were implemented using identical design flow optimization parameters. Three parameters were taken from report files for further analysis: Total Logic Elements (C), Core Dynamic Power (P) and Maximum Clock Frequency - Fmax (F). For an implementation author has chosen the EP4CE115F29I8L device – a popular low cost FPGA from the Cyclone IV E family. For estimation of cost and further implementation three state assignment methods have been chosen: binary encoding, one-hot encoding and encoding obtained from JEDI tool using the default output dominant algorithm [13].

Table 1. The experimental results for binary encoding

Name	M_{OB}	C_{OB}	F_{OB}	P_{OB}	M_{1B}	C_{1B}	F_{1B}	P_{1B}	M_{2B}	C_{2B}	F_{2B}	P_{2B}	C_{OB}/C_{2B}	C_{1B}/C_{2B}
BBARA	10	22	296.12	0.20	7	23	318.57	0.20	7	22	296.30	0.20	1.00	1.05
BBSSE	16	70	185.56	0.22	13	142	139.66	0.24	13	57	210.39	0.22	1.23	2.49
DK15	4	15	631.71	0.20	4	15	654.02	0.20	4	15	497.76	0.20	1.00	1.00
LION9	9	15	383.00	0.20	4	3	899.28	0.20	4	3	911.58	0.20	5.00	1.00
S1488	48	491	62.02	1.16	48	491	98.38	0.87	48	468	66.54	1.04	1.05	1.05
S1494	48	468	63.90	0.95	48	468	100.11	0.81	48	426	64.69	0.95	1.10	1.10
S208	18	145	89.95	0.26	18	145	124.05	0.24	18	122	90.92	0.25	1.19	1.19
S420	18	151	88.61	0.26	18	151	128.14	0.25	18	133	98.54	0.24	1.14	1.14
S820	25	247	61.90	0.42	24	262	118.91	0.40	25	216	81.84	0.33	1.14	1.21
S832	25	297	78.24	0.38	24	255	113.11	0.31	25	222	72.65	0.37	1.34	1.15
SAND	32	328	69.74	0.55	32	328	100.83	0.47	32	266	75.00	0.36	1.23	1.23
SSE	16	70	185.56	0.22	13	142	139.66	0.24	13	57	210.39	0.22	1.23	2.49
TBK	32	774	59.56	0.85	16	474	106.83	0.38	32	346	78.98	0.42	2.24	1.37
TMA	20	118	156.52	0.24	18	118	180.31	0.23	18	105	164.99	0.23	1.12	1.12
TRAIN11	11	19	323.42	0.20	4	3	894.45	0.20	4	3	905.80	0.20	6.33	1.00
Mean	**22.13**	**215.33**	**182.39**	**0.42**	**19.40**	**201.33**	**274.42**	**0.35**	**20.60**	**164.07**	**255.09**	**0.36**	**1.48**	**1.24**

The experimental results for binary encoding are presented in Table 1, where M_{OB}, C_{OB}, ed be descrimples lower than frithm)speed) than for initial FSM, F_{OB} and P_{OB} are, respectively, the number of internal states, the number of used logic elements, maximum working frequency and dissipated dynamic power of the initial FSM (without minimization); M_{1B}, C_{1B}, F_{1B} and P_{1B} are, respectively, the number of internal states, number of logic elements, maximum frequency and dissipated power after minimization using STAMINA. Finally, parameters M_{2B}, C_{2B}, F_{2B} and P_{2B} are, respectively, the number of internal states, number of logic elements, maximum frequency and power after synthesis using proposed method. C_{OB}/C_{2B} and C_{1B}/C_{2B} are ratios of the corresponding implementation cost parameters. *Mean* row contains the average values.

The analysis of Table 1 shows that application of the proposed method allows to reduce the number of internal states of the initial FSM in 6 cases. Similarly, for binary encoding, the average area reduction of the FSM makes 1.48 times, and on occasion (example *train11*) 6.33 times. In comparison to STAMINA the number of states is higher in 3 cases but the average reduction of number of logic elements of the FSM implementation makes 1.24 times, and on occasion (example *SSE*) 2.49 times.

An application of the proposed method also allows to reduce the dissipated power in 7 of 15 cases in relation to FSMs without any minimization and in 4 of 15 cases in relation to FSMs minimized by STAMINA. In addition the maximum clock frequency in benchmarks realized with proposed method was higher than in base FSMs in 13 of 15 cases and higher than in STAMINA minimized benchmarks in 6 of 10 cases. Of course, there are examples where the power and the speed were worse in relation to initial machines or FSMs minimized with STAMINA. It is related to fact, that in minimization method with area criterion, sometimes the full minimization of states is not performed. There is always selected a result with smaller cost of implementation, which is not always the same as one with minimal number of states. Average speed and power parameters for presented method are slightly worse than ones obtained from STAMINA.

Table 2. The experimental results for one-hot encoding

Name	M_{0O}	C_{0O}	F_{0O}	P_{0O}	M_{1O}	C_{1O}	F_{1O}	P_{1O}	M_{2O}	C_{2O}	F_{2O}	P_{2O}	C_{0O}/C_{2O}	C_{1O}/C_{2O}
DK15	4	36	331.13	0.21	4	36	448.23	0.21	4	34	411.86	0.21	1.06	1.06
EX1	18	216	98.47	0.31	18	216	166.17	0.30	18	158	181.49	0.27	1.37	1.37
EX4	14	26	410.85	0.21	14	24	516.26	0.21	14	24	516.26	0.21	1.08	1.00
PLANET	48	130	290.19	0.29	48	132	423.01	0.29	48	125	454.34	0.26	1.04	1.06
S1	20	134	129.85	0.27	20	132	204.33	0.28	20	132	204.33	0.28	1.02	1.00
S1488	48	364	102.13	0.43	48	364	169.89	0.47	48	335	175.44	0.46	1.09	1.09
S1494	48	328	100.36	0.40	48	328	159.57	0.42	48	313	159.34	0.38	1.05	1.05
S208	18	150	102.28	0.27	18	150	178.16	0.27	18	115	185.70	0.25	1.30	1.30
S386	13	46	294.03	0.22	13	46	359.58	0.22	13	44	298.86	0.21	1.05	1.05
S420	18	141	109.03	0.28	18	141	169.78	0.27	18	127	193.50	0.25	1.11	1.11
S510	47	72	360.49	0.28	47	71	641.85	0.24	47	71	641.85	0.24	1.01	1.00
S820	25	227	95.68	0.33	24	238	157.75	0.35	25	209	160.08	0.43	1.09	1.14
S832	25	247	81.43	0.35	24	228	139.92	0.34	25	204	164.18	0.42	1.21	1.12
SAND	32	221	104.22	0.33	32	221	164.10	0.34	32	189	192.46	0.31	1.17	1.17
TRAIN11	11	19	519.21	0.21	4	7	579.71	0.20	4	7	577.03	0.20	2.71	1.00
Mean	25.93	157.13	208.62	0.29	25.33	155.60	298.55	0.29	25.47	139.13	301.11	0.29	1.18	1.10

The experimental results for one-hot encoding are presented in Table 2, where M_{0O}, C_{0O}, F_{0O} and P_{0O} are, respectively, the number of internal states, the number of used logic elements, maximum working frequency and dynamic power of the initial FSM (without minimization); M_{1O}, C_{1O}, F_{1O} and P_{1O} are, respectively, the number of states, number of logic elements, maximum frequency and dissipated power after minimization using STAMINA. Finally, parameters M_{2O}, C_{2O}, F_{2O} and P_{2O} are, respectively, the number of internal states, number of logic elements, maximum frequency and power after synthesis using proposed method. C_{0O}/C_{2O} and C_{1O}/C_{2O} are ratios of the implementation cost corresponding parameters. *Mean* row contains the average values.

For one-hot encoding (Table 2), the average area reduction of the FSM makes 1.18 times, and on occasion (example *train11*) 2.71 times. In comparison to STAMINA the number of states is higher in 2 cases but the average reduction of the cost of the FSM implementation makes 1.10 times, and on occasion (example *ex1*) 1.37 times.

An application of the proposed method also allows to reduce the dissipated power in 10 of 15 cases in relation to FSMs without any minimization and in 8 of 15 cases in relation to FSMs minimized by STAMINA. In addition the maximum clock frequency in benchmarks realized with proposed method was higher than in base FSMs in all of 15 cases and higher than in STAMINA minimized benchmarks in 8 of 10 cases. Average speed and power parameters for presented method are slightly better than ones obtained from STAMINA and even 2 times better (in case of speed) than for initial FSM.

Table 3. The experimental results for JEDI default encoding

Name	M_{0J}	C_{0J}	F_{0J}	P_{0J}	M_{1J}	C_{1J}	F_{1J}	P_{1J}	M_{2J}	C_{2J}	F_{2J}	P_{2J}	C_{0J}/C_{2J}	C_{1J}/C_{2J}
BBSSE	16	66	146.41	0.23	13	153	146.89	0.24	13	50	230.57	0.21	1.32	3.06
DK17	8	12	451.26	0.20	8	12	454.75	0.20	8	11	496.77	0.20	1.09	1.09
EX1	18	285	73.26	0.41	18	285	109.60	0.36	18	216	101.15	0.31	1.32	1.32
LION9	9	14	417.89	0.20	4	3	899.28	0.20	4	3	911.58	0.20	4.67	1.00
S1488	48	462	72.36	0.87	48	462	109.51	0.74	48	418	73.20	0.55	1.11	1.11
S1494	48	445	59.89	0.74	48	445	106.34	0.72	48	434	69.03	0.74	1.03	1.03
S208	18	172	89.18	0.28	18	172	140.77	0.37	18	107	100.52	0.23	1.61	1.61
S386	13	59	216.31	0.21	13	59	270.71	0.22	13	51	209.51	0.21	1.16	1.16
S420	18	135	85.16	0.29	18	135	142.78	0.24	18	131	84.40	0.28	1.03	1.03
S510	47	153	122.19	0.26	47	153	185.08	0.26	47	148	114.64	0.30	1.03	1.03
S820	25	285	77.59	0.43	24	279	120.03	0.37	25	227	77.00	0.31	1.26	1.23
S832	25	293	74.36	0.47	24	273	119.05	0.36	25	233	75.06	0.30	1.26	1.17
SAND	32	313	64.16	0.61	32	313	102.81	0.53	32	257	79.33	0.37	1.22	1.22
TMA	20	112	158.83	0.23	18	117	165.92	0.24	18	109	166.64	0.24	1.03	1.07
TRAIN11	11	18	356.13	0.20	4	3	893.66	0.20	4	3	905.80	0.20	6.00	1.00
Mean	**23.73**	**188.27**	**164.33**	**0.38**	**22.47**	**190.93**	**264.48**	**0.35**	**22.60**	**159.87**	**246.35**	**0.31**	**1.44**	**1.22**

The experimental results for JEDI output dominant encoding are presented in Table 3, where M_{0J}, C_{0J}, F_{0J} and P_{0J} are, respectively, the number of internal states, the number of used logic elements, maximum working frequency and dissipated dynamic power of the initial FSM (without minimization); M_{1J}, C_{1J}, F_{1J} and P_{1J} are, respectively, the number of internal states, number of logic elements, maximum frequency and dissipated power after minimization using STAMINA. Finally, parameters M_{2J}, C_{2J}, F_{2J} and P_{2J} are, respectively, the number of internal states, number of logic elements, maximum frequency and power after synthesis using proposed method. C_{0J}/C_{2J} and C_{1J}/C_{2J} are ratios of the corresponding implementation cost parameters. *Mean* row contains the average values.

The analysis of Table 3 shows that the average area reduction of the FSM makes 1.44 times, and on occasion (example *train11*) 6 times (when using JEDI encoding algorithm). In comparison to STAMINA the number of states is higher in 2 cases but the average reduction of number of logic elements of the FSM implementation makes 1.22 times, and on occasion (example *BBSSE*) 3.06 times.

An application of the proposed method also allows to reduce the dissipated power in 8 of 15 cases in relation to FSMs without any minimization and in 8 of 15 cases in relation to FSMs minimized by STAMINA. In addition the maximum clock frequency in benchmarks realized with proposed method was higher than in base FSMs in 11 of 15 cases and higher than in STAMINA minimized benchmarks in 5 of 10 cases. Average speed parameter for presented method is slightly worse than one obtained from STAMINA, but average power for presented method are better than ones from initial FSM and those obtained from STAMINA.

The cost of the implementation obtained using JEDI and binary encoding methods is smaller than that obtained using one-hot encoding. In lot of cases the cost obtained from proposed method was lower than obtained from STAMINA or initial FSM, although the number of the states was identical. It is related to the fact that the proposed method allows to minimize not only the number of FSM states, but also the number of FSM transitions and input variables what has an impact on the cost of synthesized circuits.

6   Conclusion

In this paper we presented an efficient method for FSM synthesis. Using the proposed method there are always obtained machines with less or the cost of FSM implementation as the initial machines or STAMINA minimized FSMs. The proposed method allows, at the first stage, to take into account the parameters of the target programmable system in order to optimize the cost of the machine. The presented method in many cases exceeds the STAMINA in terms of cost of implementation and in many cases, also in terms of power consumption and speed of operation.

Presented method is the part of future work on the complex minimization method, where not only area, but also speed and power consumption parameters will be taken in consideration. In the general case, the problem of choosing the pair of states for merging is a multicriteria discrete optimization problem, which can be solved by various algorithms. In the offered method of FSM minimization only two states merging is considered. The given algorithm can be modified to merge a group of states containing more than two states.

Acknowledgements. The research has been done in the framework of the grant S/WI/3/2018 and financed from the funds for science by MNiSW.

References

1. Hallbauer, G.: Procedures of state reduction and assignment in one step in synthesis of asynchronous sequential circuits. In: Proceedings of the International IFAC Symposium on Discrete Systems, Riga, 1974, pp. 272–282. Pergamons (1974)
2. Lee, E.B., Perkowski, M.: Concurrent minimization and state assignment of finite state machines, In: Proceedings of the IEEE International Conference on Systems, Man and Cybernetics, Minneapolis. IEEE Computer Society (1984)

3. Avedillo, M.J., Quintana, J.M., Huertas, J.L.: SMAS: a program for concurrent state reduction and state assignment of finite state machines. Proceedings of the IEEE International Symposium on Circuits and Systems (ISCAS), Singapore, 1991, pp. 1781–1784. IEEE (1991)
4. Rho, J.-K., Hachtel, G., Somenzi, F., Jacoby, R.: Exact and heuristic algorithms for the minimization of incompletely specified state machines. IEEE Trans. Comput. Aided Des. **13**, 167–177 (1994)
5. Wang, K.H., Wang, W.S., Hwang, T.T., et al.: State assignment for power and area minimization. In: Proceedings of the IEEE International Conference on Computer Design: VLSI in Computers and Processors, Cambridge, USA, pp. 250–254. IEEE Computer Society (1994)
6. Xia, Y., Almaini, A.E.A.: Genetic algorithm based state assignment for power and area optimization. IEE Proc. Comput. Digital Techn. **149**(4), 128–133 (2002)
7. Chaudhury, S., KrishnaTejaSistla, K.T., Chattopadhyay, S.: Genetic algorithmbased FSM synthesis with area-power trade-offs. Integr. VLSI J. **42**, 376–384 (2009)
8. Chattopadhyay, S., Yadav, P., Singh, R.K.: Multiplexer targeted finite state machine encoding for area and power minimization. In: Proceedings of the IEEE India Annual Conference on Kharagpur, India, 2004, pp. 12–16. IEEE Computer Society (2004)
9. Aiman, M., Sadiq, S.M., Nawaz, K.F.: Finite state machine state assignment for area and power minimization. In: Proceedings of the IEEE International Symposium on Circuits and Systems (ISCAS), Island of Kos, Greece, 2006, pp. 5303–5306. IEEE Computer Society (2004)
10. Yuan, L., Qu, G., Villa, T., Sangiovanni-Vincentelli, A.: An FSM reengineering approach to sequential circuit synthesis by state splitting. IEEE Trans. CAD **27**, 1159–1164 (2008)
11. Klimowicz, A., Solov'ev, V., Grzes, T.: Minimization method of finite state machines for low power design. In: Proceedings of Euromicro Conference on Digital System Design, Funchal, 2015, pp. 259–262 (2015)
12. Klimovich, A., Solov'ev, V.V.: Minimization of mealy finite-state machines by internal states gluing. J. Comput. Syst. Sci. Int. **51**(2), 244–255 (2012)
13. Lin, B., Newton, R.A.: Synthesis of multiple level logic from symbolic high-level description languages. In: Proceedings of the International Conference on VLSI, pp. 187–196 (1989)
14. Klimowicz, A., Solov'ev, V.V.: Minimization of incompletely specified Mealy finite-state machines by merging two internal states. J. Comput. Syst. Sci. Int. **52**(3), 400–409 (2013)
15. Zakrevskij, A.D.: Logic synthesis of cascade circuits. Nauka, Moscow (1981). [in Russian]
16. Yang, S.: Logic synthesis and optimization benchmarks user guide. Version 3.0. Technical Report. North Carolina. Microelectronics Center of North Carolina (1991)

Additivity and Superadditivity in N-Person Cooperative Games with Attanassov Intuitionistic Fuzzy Expectations

Elena Mielcová$^{(\boxtimes)}$ and Radomír Perzina

Silesian University in Opava, School of Business Administration in Karvina,
Univerzitní Nám. 1934/3, 733 40 Karviná, Czech Republic
{mielcova,perzina}@opf.slu.cz

Abstract. In agent-based models, agents are expected to coordinate mutual actions – to cooperate. The cooperation among agents is usually described by tools of game theory. In general, the cooperation of autonomous agents is based on information of perspective gain from cooperation. If the gain from cooperation is at least as high as the gain which agents can receive without cooperation, then this situation can be described by tools of superadditive cooperative games. The information received by agents in the case of real-world systems is not deterministic, and the use of more sophisticated tools is required. Hence, the main aim of this paper is to discuss additivity and superadditivity issues in the case of cooperative games with expectations given as Atanassov intuitionistic numbers.

Keywords: Atanassov intuitionistic fuzzy sets · Additivity
Superadditivity · Cooperative games

1 Introduction

Nowadays, the agent based models use the bases of the cooperative game theory to model hierarchical complex systems [1]. These systems can be modeled as multiagent systems using agent-based modeling. However, a key issue in such models is to understand the dynamics of agent interaction. Game theory offers techniques and tools for modeling communication problems among agents. For example, in a multiagent problem, the cooperative outcome of decision making cooperating agents with different preference functions is described by the theory of cooperative games. In the first step agents (in game theory described as players of a model game) are cooperating in order to increase a mutual gain. Rational agents cooperate under the condition that the cooperation brings them higher gain that agents can get without cooperation – which means under condition of superadditivity.

This work was supported by a GACR 18-01246S.

K. Saeed and W. Homenda (Eds.): CISIM 2018, LNCS 11127, pp. 380–391, 2018.
https://doi.org/10.1007/978-3-319-99954-8_32

In order to model real-world situations, the use of some level of uncertainty is necessary. One of the possibilities how to incorporate uncertainty into the system is the introduction of fuzzy sets theory into a used system model. Since 1960 s, when Zadeh published his now famous article "Fuzzy Sets" [2], the fuzzy sets theory became one of the basic tools for description of hesitation in mathematical models; in fuzzy sets theory every fuzzy set is composed of elements characterized by a membership degree to the set. However, the better alternative emerged with Atanassov's intuitionistic fuzzy sets [3]. Atanassov extended Zadeh's idea by incorporating the indecisiveness part into the original fuzzy set theory. In Atanassov's intuitionistic fuzzy sets, both the membership degree and nonmembership degree are assigned to each of their elements. As in fuzzy sets theory, the Atanassov's intuitionistic fuzzy sets have been studied and applied in various areas of mathematics and computer science. Considering the discussion about terminological difficulties concerning intuitionistic fuzzy sets, see [4], throughout this paper term "I-fuzzy set", is used instead of "Atanassov's intutitionistic fuzzy set".

Similarly as in the fuzzy set theory, the theory of I-fuzzy sets covers also definition and operations over I-fuzzy numbers (defined and discussed for example in [5]). One of the basic operations, needed in the decision-making process of agents, is an ordering relation. In order to compare two I-fuzzy quantities or numbers, there exist several definitions of relations. Usually these relations corresponds to specific needs in particular applications. Hence, the main aim of this paper is to discuss issues of additivity and superadditivity in I-fuzzy cooperative games – in this case games with characteristic function given as I-fuzzy numbers. The additivity and superadditivity issues will be discussed with respect to several possible types orderings of I-fuzzy numbers with respect to their basic properties.

2   I-Fuzzy Sets

As mentioned in the introduction, I-fuzzy sets were first defined by Atanassov (1986) [3], this definition comes from his book "*Intuitonistic Fuzzy Sets: Theory and Applications*" (1999) [7]:

Definition 1 *(Atanassov). Let X be a nonempty set. Then the I-fuzzy subset $\tilde{A}$ of X is defined as a set of triples $\tilde{A} = \{\langle x, \mu_{\tilde{A}}(x), \nu_{\tilde{A}}(x) \rangle; x \in X\}$, where functions $\mu_{\tilde{A}} : X \to L$ and $\nu_{\tilde{A}} : X \to L$ for the unit interval $L = [0,1]$ define the degree of membership and the degree of nonmembership of the element $x \in X$ to $\tilde{A} \subset X$, respectively. For an I-fuzzy set, the condition $0 \leq \mu_{\tilde{A}}(x) + \nu_{\tilde{A}}(x) \leq 1$ holds for all $x \in X$.*

Usually, an I-fuzzy subset of $\tilde{A}$ on X is called simply as an 'I-fuzzy set'. The class of all I-fuzzy subsets of X is denoted by $IF(X)$.

From the definition we can see that each element $x \in X$ is to some extent a member of the set $\tilde{A}$, and to some extent is not a member of the set $\tilde{A}$. The degree of membership and nonmembership of an element to the set is described by its membership function $\mu_{\tilde{A}}(x)$, and nonmembership function $\nu_{\tilde{A}}(x)$, respectively.

Moreover, there is a missing part of an information about a membership of $x \in X$ in the set $\tilde{A}$. This missing part is in fact 'indecisiveness' or 'uncertainty' part, and it is evaluated by a value $\pi_{\tilde{A}}(x)$ called a 'hesitancy degree', or an 'I-fuzzy index' of an element x in $\tilde{A}$ [5]:

$$\pi_{\tilde{A}}(x) = 1 - \mu_{\tilde{A}}(x) - \nu_{\tilde{A}}(x). \tag{1}$$

Obviously, $\pi_{\tilde{A}}(x) \leq 1$ for any $x \in X$; moreover for any fuzzy set $\pi_{\tilde{A}}(x) = 0$ because in the case of fuzzy sets $\mu_{\tilde{A}}(x) + \nu_{\tilde{A}}(x) = 1$. Hence, the decisiveness space of I-fuzzy sets is not 'closed' while the decisiveness space of fuzzy sets is 'closed'. This can be considered the main difference between the definition of Atanassov's I-fuzzy sets and the classical fuzzy sets.

Atanassov also defined two operators which allow to transform every I-fuzzy set into a fuzzy set. These two operators can be viewed as operators of 'necessity' and 'possibility' [3]:

- Necessity operator: $\Box \tilde{A} = \{\langle x, \mu_{\tilde{A}}(x) \rangle; x \in X\}$.
- Possibility operator: $\Diamond \tilde{A} = \{\langle x, 1 - \nu_{\tilde{A}}(x) \rangle; x \in X\}$.

There are even more possibilities how to transform an I-fuzzy set into a fuzzy set. For example there is a possibility to use normalized score degree or accuracy degree as a fuzzy membership function of a transformed I-fuzzy set. According to Xu and Xia (2011) [8] the pair $(\mu_{\tilde{A}}(x), \nu_{\tilde{A}}(x))$ for $x \in X$, $\tilde{A} \in IF(X)$ is called an I-fuzzy value $\tilde{\alpha}(x)$, simply denoted as $\tilde{\alpha} = (\mu_{\tilde{\alpha}}, \nu_{\tilde{\alpha}})$ where $\mu_{\tilde{\alpha}} \in [0,1], \nu_{\tilde{\alpha}} \in [0,1]$. Value $s_{\tilde{\alpha}}$ defined as

$$s_{\tilde{\alpha}} = \mu_{\tilde{\alpha}} - \nu_{\tilde{\alpha}} \tag{2}$$

is called a score degree; similarly value $h_{\tilde{\alpha}}$ defined as

$$h_{\tilde{\alpha}} = \mu_{\tilde{\alpha}} + \nu_{\tilde{\alpha}} \tag{3}$$

is called an accuracy degree.

Elementary arithmetic operations over I-fuzzy sets are derived, similarly as in the classical fuzzy sets theory, by using so-called extension principle. In general, the extension principle is a method udes to extend the typical operations of classical set theory to I-fuzzy set theory; it gives a directions how to calculate membership and nonmembership degree of elements or functions of I-fuzzy sets which are results of operations. The extension principle for fuzzy sets was defined by Zadeh [2], the extension principle was reformulated for I-fuzzy setting by Çoker [6] in his article discussing the topology of I-fuzzy sets:

Definition 2. *Let X and Y be sets, $f : X \to Y$ be a mapping. The mapping $\tilde{f} : IF(X) \to IF(Y)$ defined for all $\tilde{A} \in IF(X)$ with $\mu_{\tilde{A}} : X \to [0,1]$, $\nu_{\tilde{A}} : X \to [0,1]$ and $y \in Y$ by*

$$\mu_{\tilde{f}(\tilde{A})}(y) = \begin{cases} \sup\{\mu_{\tilde{A}}(x) | x \in X, f(x) = y\} & \text{if } f^{-1}(y) \neq \emptyset, \\ 0 & \text{otherwise,} \end{cases} \tag{4}$$

$$\nu_{\tilde{f}(\tilde{A})}(y) = \begin{cases} \inf\{\nu_{\tilde{A}}(x) | x \in X, f(x) = y\} & \text{if } f^{-1}(y) \neq \emptyset, \\ 1 & \text{if otherwise,} \end{cases} \tag{5}$$

is called an I-fuzzy extension of f.

The inverse mapping $\tilde{f}^{-1}$ is defined such that for any $\tilde{B} \in IF(Y)$, the membership and nonmembership function is $\mu_{\tilde{f}^{-1}(\tilde{B})}(x) = \mu_{\tilde{B}}(f(x))$, and $\nu_{\tilde{f}^{-1}(\tilde{B})}(x) = \nu_{\tilde{B}}(f(x))$ for every $x \in X$. The extension principle allows $f : X \to Y$ to be extended to $\tilde{f} : IF(X) \to IF(Y)$.

The main aim of this paper is to discuss the additivity and superadditivity issues of cooperative games with pay-off functions determined as I-fuzzy numbers. In general, an I-fuzzy number is the generalization of a real number in the sense that it does not refer to one single value but to a connected set of possible values with evaluation of their membership and nonmembership degree. This definition of I-fuzzy numbers is based on paper of Mahapatra and Roy [9]:

Definition 3. *An I-fuzzy subset of the real line $\tilde{A} = \{\langle x, \mu_{\tilde{A}}(x), \nu_{\tilde{A}}(x) \rangle; x \in R\}$ is called an I-fuzzy number if:*

(a) *$\tilde{A}$ is normal (there exist at least two elements $x_0, x_1 \in R$, not necessarily different, such that $\mu_{\tilde{A}}(x_0) = 1$ and $\nu_{\tilde{A}}(x_1) = 0$).*

(b) *The membership function of $\tilde{A}$ denoted by $\mu_{\tilde{A}}$ satisfies: $\mu_{\tilde{A}}(\lambda x_1 + (1 - \lambda)x_2) \geq \min(\mu_{\tilde{A}}(x_1), \mu_{\tilde{A}}(x_2)) \quad \forall x_1, x_2 \in R, \quad \lambda \in [0, 1]$, i.e. the membership function is quasiconcave.*

(c) *The nonmembership function of $\tilde{A}$ denoted by $\nu_{\tilde{A}}$ satisfies: $\nu_{\tilde{A}}(\lambda x_1 + (1 - \lambda)x_2) \leq \max(\nu_{\tilde{A}}(x_1), \nu_{\tilde{A}}(x_2)) \quad \forall x_1, x_2 \in R, \quad \lambda \in [0, 1]$, i.e. the membership function is quasiconvex.*

(d) *The membership function $\mu_{\tilde{A}}$ is upper semi-continuous and the nonmembership function $\nu_{\tilde{A}}$ is lower semi-continuous.*

(e) *$\{x \in X; \nu_{\tilde{A}}(x) < 1\}$ is bounded.*

For illustration, all numerical examples in this paper are given using triangular I-fuzzy numbers. In general, triangular I-fuzzy number is fully described by a six-tuple $\tilde{A}_{TIFN} = (a_1, a_2, a_3, a_1', a_2, a_3')$ of real numbers $a_1, a_2, a_3, a_1', a_2, a_3'$ where $a_1 \leq a_2 \leq a_3$ and $a_1' \leq a_2 \leq a_3'$ such that $\tilde{A}_{TIFN}$ is a subset of I-fuzzy sets in R with membership function and non-membership functions [9]:

$$\mu_{\tilde{A}_{TIFN}}(x) = \begin{cases} \frac{x - a_1}{a_2 - a_1} & \text{for } a_1 \leq x \leq a_2, \\ \frac{a_3 - x}{a_3 - a_2} & \text{for } a_2 \leq x \leq a_3, \\ 0 & \text{otherwise,} \end{cases} \tag{6}$$

$$\nu_{\tilde{A}_{TIFN}}(x) = \begin{cases} \frac{a_2 - x}{a_2 - a_1'} & \text{for } a_1' \leq x \leq a_2, \\ \frac{x - a_2}{a_3' - a_2} & \text{for } a_2 \leq x \leq a_3', \\ 1 & \text{otherwise,} \end{cases} \tag{7}$$

where $a_1 \leq a_2 \leq a_3$ and $a_1' \leq a_2 \leq a_3'$.

For two I-fuzzy numbers $\tilde{A}_{TIFN} = (a_1, a_2, a_3, a_1', a_2, a_3')$, and $\tilde{B}_{TIFN} = (b_1, b_2, b_3, b_1', b_2, b_3')$, the addition operation expressed in a form of six-tuple [9]: $\tilde{C}_{TIFN} = \tilde{A}_{TIFN} \tilde{+} \tilde{B}_{TIFN} = (a_1 + b_1, a_2 + b_2, a_3 + b_3, a_1' + b_1', a_2 + b_2, a_3' + b_3')$.

The membership and non-membership functions of $\tilde{C}_{TIFN} = \tilde{A}_{TIFN} \tilde{+} \tilde{B}_{TIFN}$ are:

$$\mu_{\tilde{C}_{TIFN}}(z) = \begin{cases} \frac{z-(a_1+b_1)}{(a_2+b_2)-(a_1+b_1)} & \text{for } a_1 + b_1 \leq z \leq a_2 + b_2 \\ \frac{(a_3+b_3)-z}{(a_3+b_3)-(a_2+b_2)} & \text{for } a_2 + b_2 \leq z \leq a_3 + b_3 \\ 0 & \text{otherwise} \end{cases} \quad (8)$$

$$\nu_{\tilde{C}_{TIFN}}(z) = \begin{cases} \frac{(a_2+b_2)-z}{(a_2+b_2)-(a_1'+b_1')} & \text{for } a_1' + b_1' \leq z \leq a_2 + b_2 \\ \frac{z-(a_2+b_2)}{(a_3'+b_3')-(a_2+b_2)} & \text{for } a_2 + b_2 \leq z \leq a_3' + b_3' \\ 1 & \text{otherwise} \end{cases} \quad (9)$$

In the cooperative game theory, the idea of game solution is based on the possibility to find a rank of evaluated alternatives. However, in the case of I-fuzzy numbers, it is not always easy to determine order of two values. In this paper, three possible rankings of I-fuzzy numbers with its consequences on additivity and superadditivity of I-fuzzy cooperative game are discussed. The first is the ranking based on deterministic representation, the second is a ranking based on I-fuzzy representation and the third is a ranking using fuzzy representation.

2.1   Ordering Using Deterministic Representation

Ordering using deterministic representation expect a setting of a crisp value representing I-fuzzy number, and consequently comparing these crisp values using crisp relations. Two of possible examples of such values could be modal values (the same as in the case of fuzzy numbers), or extreme α, β-cut values. In the case of I-fuzzy sets we can define:

- Ordering using modal values:

$$\tilde{A} \preccurlyeq \tilde{B} \text{ iff } \sup\{x; \mu_{\tilde{A}}(x) = 1\} \leq \sup\{x; \mu_{\tilde{B}}(x) = 1\} \quad (10)$$
$$\tilde{A} \approx \tilde{B} \text{ iff } \sup\{x; \mu_{\tilde{A}}(x) = 1\} = \sup\{x; \mu_{\tilde{B}}(x) = 1\} \quad (11)$$

- Ordering using α, β-modal values for given $\alpha \in (0,1)$, and $\beta \in (0,1)$:
  Let

$$a = \sup\{x; \mu_{\tilde{A}}(x) \geq \alpha, \nu_{\tilde{A}}(x) \leq \beta\},$$
$$b = \sup\{x; \mu_{\tilde{B}}(x) \geq \alpha, \nu_{\tilde{B}}(x) \leq \beta\}.$$

Then

$$\tilde{A} \preccurlyeq \tilde{B} \text{ iff } a \leq b, \quad (12)$$
$$\tilde{A} \approx \tilde{B} \text{ iff } a = b. \quad (13)$$

2.2 Ordering Using I-Fuzzy Representation

An I-fuzzy ordering relation can be derived from the extension principle (4):

Definition 4. *Let $IFN(R)$ be the set of all I-fuzzy numbers. For $\tilde{A}, \tilde{B} \in IFN(R)$ we define fuzzy relations $\tilde{A} \preccurlyeq \tilde{B}$ and $\tilde{A} \approx \tilde{B}$ with membership functions $\mu_{\preccurlyeq} : IFN(R) \times IFN(R) \to [0,1]$, $\mu_{\approx} : IFN(R) \times IFN(R) \to [0,1]$ and nonmembership functions $\nu_{\preccurlyeq} : IFN(R) \times IFN(R) \to [0,1]$, $\nu_{\approx} : IFN(R) \times IFN(R) \to [0,1]$ such that:*

$$\mu_{\preccurlyeq}(\tilde{A}, \tilde{B}) = \sup_{x \le y}(\min(\mu_{\tilde{A}}(x), \mu_{\tilde{B}}(y))); \tag{14}$$

$$\nu_{\preccurlyeq}(\tilde{A}, \tilde{B}) = \inf_{x \le y}(\max(\nu_{\tilde{A}}(x), \nu_{\tilde{B}}(y))); \tag{15}$$

$$\mu_{\approx}(\tilde{A}, \tilde{B}) = \sup_{x \in R}(\min(\mu_{\tilde{A}}(x), \mu_{\tilde{B}}(x))); \tag{16}$$

$$\nu_{\approx}(\tilde{A}, \tilde{B}) = \inf_{x \in R}(\max(\nu_{\tilde{A}}(x), \nu_{\tilde{A}}(x))). \tag{17}$$

2.3 Ordering Using Fuzzy Representation

A fuzzy ordering relation can be derived from the extension principle (4) applied on fuzzy number derived from I-fuzzy number. In this case, fuzzy ordering relation should give the membership degree of given ordering relation, analogically to fuzzy case [10]. In this case, the fuzzy number used to compare two I-fuzzy numbers is based on score degree of I-fuzzy numbers. The expected ordering relation is based on the idea of fuzzy ordering relation, and it evaluates the possibility of relation by a real number $r_{\preccurlyeq}(\tilde{A}, \tilde{B})$ and $r_{\approx}(\tilde{A}, \tilde{B})$. In order to maintain the compatibility with fuzzy relations and with idea of comparison of intuitionistic fuzzy values with respect to their score degree described in [11], the possibility of relation is described as follows: For any pair of I-fuzzy numbers $\tilde{A}, \tilde{B}$ the possibility of the relation $(\tilde{A} \preccurlyeq \tilde{B})$ is defined as a real number $r_{\preccurlyeq}(\tilde{A}, \tilde{B}) \in [0,1]$ that:

$$r_{\preccurlyeq}(\tilde{A}, \tilde{B}) = \frac{(\sup_{x \le y}(\min(s_{\tilde{A}}(x), s_{\tilde{B}}(y)))) + 1}{2}. \tag{18}$$

Analogically, the possibility of the relation $(\tilde{A} \approx \tilde{B})$ is defined as a real number $r_{\approx}(\tilde{A}, \tilde{B}) \in [0,1]$ that:

$$r_{\approx}(\tilde{A}, \tilde{B}) = \frac{(\sup_{x,y \in R}(\min(s_{\tilde{A}}(x), s_{\tilde{B}}(y)))) + 1}{2}. \tag{19}$$

3 Cooperative Games

In agent-based models, agents are expected to coordinate mutual actions – to cooperate. Cooperation of agents is usually described by cooperative games. Let $N = \{1, 2 \ldots n\}$ be a set of n players (= agents) from a universe of players U, let 2^N be the collection of all subsets of N. Any nonempty subset of N is called a coalition. Formally, a cooperative game in a form of characteristic function is defined as:

Definition 5. *A cooperative game is a pair* (N, v) *where* $N = \{1, 2 \ldots n\}$ *is a set of* n *players* $v : 2^N \to R$ *is a mapping defined on subsets of* N *with the property* $v(\emptyset) = 0$.

The function v *is called a characteristic function of a game.*

The characteristic function v connects each subcoalition of players $K \subseteq N$ with a real number $v(K) \in R$ representing total gain (also called a pay-off or profit) of coalition K; in cooperative games we assume $v(\emptyset) = 0$. A cooperative game can be shortly denoted as (N, v), or simply determined only by a characteristic function v.

Example 1. Example of a cooperative game: Let (N, v) be a cooperative game with $N = \{1, 2, 3\}$. This game is set by a characteristic function such that $v(\emptyset) = 0$, $v(\{1\}) = 5$, $v(\{2\}) = v(\{3\}) = v(\{1, 2\}) = v(\{1, 3\}) = v(\{2, 3\}) = 6$, $v(\{1, 2, 3\}) = 15$.

Characteristic functions are usually assumed to be superadditive [12]; this means that for any pair of disjoint coalitions $K, L \subset N$, $K \cap L = \emptyset$, the value of a union of disjoint coalitions is not smaller than the sum of the coalitions' separate values: $v(K \cup L) \geq v(K) + v(L)$.

Analogically, the characteristic function is subadditive if for any pair of disjoint coalitions $K, L \subset N$, $K \cap L = \emptyset$ the characteristic function satisfies condition $v(K \cup L) \leq v(K) + v(L)$, while it is additive if $v(K \cup L) = v(K) + v(L)$.

A game (N, v) is additive if and only if it is superadditive and subadditive. Might happen that the game is nor superadditive, nor subadditive.

Example 2. Let (N, v) be a cooperative game with $N = \{1, 2, 3\}$ and a characteristic function v such that $v(\emptyset) = 0$, $v(\{1\}) = 2$, $v(\{2\}) = v(\{3\}) = v(\{1, 2\}) = v(\{1, 3\}) = v(\{2, 3\}) = 4$, $v(\{1, 2, 3\}) = 12$. This game is nor superadditive, nor subadditive:

$$\underbrace{v(\{2\}) + v(\{3\})}_{4+4=8} > \underbrace{v(\{2, 3\})}_{4} \qquad \text{and} \qquad \underbrace{v(\{1\}) + v(\{2, 3\})}_{2+4=6} < \underbrace{v(\{1, 2, 3\})}_{12}.$$

We say that a cooperative game (N, v) is convex if for every pair of coalitions $K, L \subset N$:

$$v(K \cup L) + v(K \cap L) \geq v(K) + v(L). \tag{20}$$

Directly from he definition of convexity it is clear that convexity implies superadditivity, inverse implication is not valid, as shown in the next example:

Example 3. Let (N, v) be a cooperative game with $N = \{1, 2, 3\}$ and a characteristic function v such that $v(\emptyset) = 0$, $v(\{1\}) = 2$, $v(\{2\}) = v(\{3\}) = 4$, $v(\{1, 2\}) = v(\{1, 3\}) = v(\{2, 3\}) = 8$, $v(\{1, 2, 3\}) = 12$. This game is superadditive, however it is not convex:

Let $K = \{1, 2\}$, and $L = \{1, 3\}$. Then $v(K) = v(L) = 8$, $v(K \cup L) = v(\{1, 2, 3\}) = 12$ and $v(K \cap L) = v(\{1\}) = 2$.

$$\underbrace{v(K \cup L) + v(K \cap L)}_{12+2=14} \not\geq \underbrace{v(K) + v(L)}_{8+8=16}.$$

4 I-Fuzzy Cooperative Games

The main aim of this paper is to discuss the superadditivity issues of cooperative games with vague payoffs, in this case described as I-fuzzy numbers:

Definition 6. *Let* (N, v) *be a cooperative game and let* $\tilde{w}(K) = \langle x, \mu_{\tilde{w}(K)}(x), \nu_{\tilde{w}(K)}(x) \rangle$ *be an I-fuzzy number for any* $K \subset N$ *with the membership function* $\mu_{\tilde{w}(K)} : R \to [0,1]$, *non-membership function* $\nu_{\tilde{w}(K)} : R \to [0,1]$ *fulfilling condition* $0 \leq \mu_{\tilde{w}(K)}(x) + \nu_{\tilde{w}(K)}(x) \leq 1$; *such that*

- $\mu_{\tilde{w}(K)}(v(K)) = 1$;
- $\mu_{\tilde{w}(K)}(x)$ *is non-decreasing for* $x < v(K)$ *and non-increasing for* $x > v(K)$;
- $\nu_{\tilde{w}(K)}(x)$ *is non-increasing for* $x < v(K)$ *and non-decreasing for* $x > v(K)$;
- $\mu_{\tilde{w}(\emptyset)}(x) = 1$ *iff* $x = 0$, *and* $\nu_{\tilde{w}(\emptyset)}(x) = 1$ *for all* $x \neq 0$.

Then $\tilde{w}$ *is the I-fuzzy characteristic function, and the pair* $(N, \tilde{w})$ *is called an I-fuzzy extension of the cooperative game* (N, v).

Example 4. Let's consider two-player coalition game (N, v) such that $N = \{1, 2\}$, $v(\{1\}) = 2$, $v(\{2\}) = 3$, $v(\{1, 2\}) = v(N) = 6$. I-fuzzy extension $(N, \tilde{w})$ of the game (N, v) can be for example of the form:

$$\mu_{\tilde{w}(\{1\})}(x) = \begin{cases} x - 1 & \text{for } 1 \leq x \leq 2 \\ 3 - x & \text{for } 2 \leq x \leq 3 \\ 0 & \text{otherwise} \end{cases} , \ \nu_{\tilde{w}(\{1\})}(x) = \begin{cases} 2 - x & \text{for } 1 \leq x \leq 2 \\ x - 2 & \text{for } 2 \leq x \leq 3 \\ 1 & \text{otherwise} \end{cases}$$

$$\mu_{\tilde{w}(\{2\})}(x) = \begin{cases} \frac{x-1}{2} & \text{for } 1 \leq x \leq 3 \\ \frac{5-x}{2} & \text{for } 3 \leq x \leq 5 \\ 0 & \text{otherwise} \end{cases} , \ \nu_{\tilde{w}(\{2\})}(x) = \begin{cases} 3 - x & \text{for } 2 \leq x \leq 3 \\ \frac{x-3}{2} & \text{for } 3 \leq x \leq 5 \\ 1 & \text{otherwise} \end{cases}$$

$$\mu_{\tilde{w}(N)}(x) = \begin{cases} x - 5 & \text{for } 5 \leq x \leq 6 \\ 7 - x & \text{for } 6 \leq x \leq 7 \\ 0 & \text{otherwise} \end{cases} , \ \nu_{\tilde{w}(N)}(x) = \begin{cases} 6 - x & \text{for } 5 \leq x \leq 6 \\ x - 6 & \text{for } 6 \leq x \leq 7 \\ 1 & \text{otherwise} \end{cases}$$

5 Superadditivity in I-Fuzzy Cooperative Games

Let a pair $(N, \tilde{w})$ be an I-fuzzy extension of the cooperative game (N, v). Then $(N, \tilde{w})$ is superadditive, if for any two disjoint coalitions K and L, $K, L \subset N$, $K \cap L = \emptyset$ the next inequality holds:

$$\tilde{w}(K \cup L) \succcurlyeq \tilde{w}(K) \tilde{+} \tilde{w}(L) \tag{21}$$

Example 5. Let's consider the same two-player I-fuzzy cooperative game as defined in previous example. In order to decide whether the game is superadditive, we have to compare $\tilde{w}(N)$ of an I-fuzzy extension $(N, \tilde{w})$ with membership and nonmembership functions:

$$\mu_{\tilde{w}(N)}(x) = \begin{cases} x - 5 & \text{for } 5 \leq x \leq 6 \\ 7 - x & \text{for } 6 \leq x \leq 7 \\ 0 & \text{otherwise} \end{cases} , \ \nu_{\tilde{w}(N)}(x) = \begin{cases} 6 - x & \text{for } 5 \leq x \leq 6 \\ x - 6 & \text{for } 6 \leq x \leq 7 \\ 1 & \text{otherwise} \end{cases}$$

with the result of $\tilde{w}(\{1\})\tilde{+}\tilde{w}(\{2\})$ of the same I fuzzy cooperative game given by these membership and nonmembership functions:

$$\mu_{\tilde{w}(\{1\})\tilde{+}\tilde{w}(\{2\})}(x) = \begin{cases} \frac{x-2}{3} & \text{for } 2 \leq x \leq 5 \\ \frac{8-x}{3} & \text{for } 5 \leq x \leq 8 \\ 0 & \text{otherwise} \end{cases}$$

$$\nu_{\tilde{w}(\{1\})\tilde{+}\tilde{w}(\{2\})}(x) = \begin{cases} \frac{5-x}{2} & \text{for } 3 \leq x \leq 5 \\ \frac{x-5}{3} & \text{for } 5 \leq x \leq 8 \\ 1 & \text{otherwise} \end{cases}$$

In general, the result of the comparison as mentioned in the example is highly dependent on a choice of of comparison relation $\succcurlyeq$. The next three parts of this section demonstrate how the three possible ordering relations influence the concept of additivity in cooperative games.

5.1 Superadditivity with Deterministic Ordering Relation

The case when the deterministic ordering relation is used to evaluate superadditivity of the game is the easiest possibility; a real value is assigned to each of compared numbers, and then the real values are compared. The only problem is, that different ordering realtions give different results in cooperative game superadditivity decision, as demonstrated at in the next three examples.

Example 6. Let $(N, \tilde{w})$ be the I-fuzzy cooperative game from Example 4. In order to determine that this game is superadditive, we have verify validity of relation $\tilde{w}(N) \succcurlyeq \tilde{w}(\{1\})\tilde{+}\tilde{w}(\{2\})$. Left- and right-hand sides of the equation are expressed in Example 5. When taking into account the ordering using modal values (10), we can easily see that the left hand side (LHS) of the equation is $LHS = 6$, while the right hand side (RHS) of the equation is $RHS = 5$. Thus $LHS \geq RHS$, this imply that $\tilde{w}(N) \succcurlyeq \tilde{w}(\{1\})\tilde{+}\tilde{w}(\{2\})$, the game is superadditive.

Example 7. Let $(N, \tilde{w})$ be the I-fuzzy cooperative game from Example 4. When taking into account the ordering using $\alpha, \beta-$modal values (12) with $\alpha = 0.5$ and $\beta = 0.5$, we can easily see that the left hand side of the equation is $LHS = a = \frac{13}{2}$, while the right hand side of the equation is $RHS = b = \frac{13}{2}$. Thus $LHS = RHS$, this imply that $\tilde{w}(N) \approx \tilde{w}(\{1\})\tilde{+}\tilde{w}(\{2\})$, the game is additive.

Example 8. Similarly as in two previous examples, let $(N, \tilde{w})$ be the I-fuzzy cooperative game from Example 4. When taking into account the ordering using $\alpha, \beta-$modal values (12) with $\alpha = \frac{1}{3}$ and $\beta = \frac{2}{3}$, we can easily see that the left hand side of the equation is $LHS = a = \frac{20}{3}$, while the right hand side of the equation is $RHS = b = 7$. Thus $RHS \geq LHS$, this imply that $\tilde{w}(\{1\})\tilde{+}\tilde{w}(\{2\}) \succcurlyeq \tilde{w}(N)$, the game is subadditive.

From the above examples we can see, that in cooperative game theory it is crucial to determine the ordering relation equivalent to ordering of all players, otherwise the game is not suitable model of real-world behavior. The ambiguity of ordering relation in the case of the cooperative game superadditivity is partially covered when determining superadditivity using I-fuzzy or fuzzy ordering relation.

5.2   Superadditivity with I-Fuzzy Ordering Relation

The problem is the same as above: to determine if $\tilde{w}(K \cup L) \succcurlyeq \tilde{w}(K)\tilde{+}\tilde{w}(L)$ is valid. From (14) and (15) we receive:

$$\mu_\succcurlyeq(\tilde{w}(K \cup L), \tilde{w}(K)\tilde{+}\tilde{w}(L)) = \sup_{x \geq y}[\min(\mu_{\tilde{w}(K \cup L)}(x), \mu_{\tilde{w}(K)\tilde{+}\tilde{w}(L)}(y))]; \quad (22)$$

$$\nu_\succcurlyeq(\tilde{w}(K \cup L), \tilde{w}(K)\tilde{+}\tilde{w}(L)) = \inf_{x \geq y}[\max(\nu_{\tilde{w}(K \cup L)}(x), \nu_{\tilde{w}(K)\tilde{+}\tilde{w}(L)}(y))]. \quad (23)$$

The membership function of a possibility that the I-fuzzy coalition game (N, w) is I-fuzzy superadditive:

$$\mu_{super}(N, \tilde{w}) = \min(\mu_\succcurlyeq(\tilde{w}(K \cup L), \tilde{w}(K)\tilde{+}\tilde{w}(L)); K, L \subset N, \ K \cap L = \emptyset); \quad (24)$$

the nonmembership function of an impossibility that the I-fuzzy coalition game (N, w) is I-fuzzy superadditive:

$$\nu_{super}(N, w) = \max(\nu_\succcurlyeq(w(K \cup L), w(K)\tilde{+}w(L)); K, K \subset N, \ K \cap L = \emptyset). \quad (25)$$

Example 9. Let $(N, \tilde{w})$ be the I-fuzzy cooperative game from Example 4. In order to determine that this game is superadditive, we have verify that

$$\tilde{w}(N) \succcurlyeq \tilde{w}(\{1\})\tilde{+}\tilde{w}(\{2\}). \quad (26)$$

We can easily calculate that $\mu_\succcurlyeq(\tilde{w}(K \cup L), \tilde{w}(K)\tilde{+}\tilde{w}(L)) = 1$, and $\nu_\succcurlyeq(\tilde{w}(K \cup L), \tilde{w}(K)\tilde{+}\tilde{w}(L)) = 0$, so we can expect that the game is superadditive. However, values $\mu_\succcurlyeq(\tilde{w}(K)\tilde{+}\tilde{w}(L), \tilde{w}(K \cup L)) = \frac{3}{4}$, and $\nu_\succcurlyeq(\tilde{w}(K)\tilde{+}\tilde{w}(L), \tilde{w}(K \cup L)) = \frac{1}{4}$, thus this I-fuzzy game is to some extent not superadditive.

The next two remarks are valid for the I-fuzzy extension of the cooperative games, both of them demonstrate connection of the crisp cooperative game and its I-fuzzy extension. Proof of both remarks can be found in [13].

Remark 1. Let $(N, \tilde{w})$ be an I-fuzzy extension of the cooperative game (N, v). Then for two disjoint coalitions K, L such that $K, L \subset N, K \cap L = \emptyset$ inequality $v(K \cup L) \geq v(K) + v(L)$ implies $\mu_\succcurlyeq(\tilde{w}(K \cup L), \tilde{w}(K)\tilde{+}\tilde{w}(L)) = 1$ and $\nu_\succcurlyeq(\tilde{w}(K \cup L), \tilde{w}(K)\tilde{+}\tilde{w}(L)) = 0$.

Remark 2. Let $(N, \tilde{w})$ be an I-fuzzy extension of the cooperative game (N, v), and let $(N, \tilde{w})$ be I-fuzzy superadditive. Then values $\mu_{super}(N, \tilde{w}) = 1$ and $\nu_{super}(N, \tilde{w}) = 0$.

5.3   Superadditivity with Fuzzy Ordering Relation

The problem of superadditivity with fuzzy ordering relation is similar to the problem with I-fuzzy ordering relation. The main task is to determine if the relation $\tilde{w}(K \cup L) \succcurlyeq \tilde{w}(K)\tilde{+}\tilde{w}(L)$ is valid. From (18) we receive:

$$r_\succcurlyeq(\tilde{w}(K \cup L), \tilde{w}(K)\tilde{+}\tilde{w}(L)) = \frac{\sup_{x \geq y}[\min(s_{\tilde{w}(K \cup L)}(x), s_{\tilde{w}(K)\tilde{+}\tilde{w}(L)}(y))] + 1}{2}. \quad (27)$$

Then the possibility that the I-fuzzy coalition game (N, w) is fuzzy superadditive is:

$$r_{super}(N, \tilde{w}) = \min(r_{\succcurlyeq}(\tilde{w}(K \cup L), \tilde{w}(K) \tilde{+} \tilde{w}(L)); K, L \subset N, \ K \cap L = \emptyset). \, (28)$$

Example 10. Let $(N, \tilde{w})$ be the I-fuzzy cooperative game from Example 4. In order to determine that this game is superadditive, we have verify that

$$\tilde{w}(N) \succcurlyeq \tilde{w}(\{1\}) \tilde{+} \tilde{w}(\{2\}). \tag{29}$$

In order to determine values of r_{super} we need to calculate values of score degree or I-fuzzy numbers $\tilde{w}(N)$, and $\tilde{w}(\{1\}) \tilde{+} \tilde{w}(\{2\})$:

$$s_{\tilde{w}(N)}(x) = \begin{cases} 2x - 11 & \text{for } 5 \leq x \leq 6 \\ 13 - 2x & \text{for } 6 \leq x \leq 7 \\ -1 & \text{otherwise} \end{cases}$$

$$s_{\tilde{w}(\{1\}) \tilde{+} \tilde{w}(\{2\})}(x) = \begin{cases} \frac{x-5}{3} & \text{for } 2 \leq x \leq 3 \\ \frac{5x-19}{6} & \text{for } 3 \leq x \leq 5 \\ \frac{13-2x}{3} & \text{for } 5 \leq x \leq 8 \\ -1 & \text{otherwise} \end{cases}$$

We can easily calculate that $r_{\succcurlyeq}(\tilde{w}(K \cup L), \tilde{w}(K) \tilde{+} \tilde{w}(L)) = 1$, so we can expect that the game is superadditive. However, similarly as in the I-fuzzy case, value $r_{\succcurlyeq}(\tilde{w}(K) \tilde{+} \tilde{w}(L), \tilde{w}(K \cup L)) = \frac{3}{4}$, thus this I-fuzzy game is to some extent not superadditive.

6   Conclusions

In this article we discussed the superadditivity issues of the I-fuzzy extension to class of transferable utility function coalitional games when expected gains are I-fuzzy numbers. Intuition behind cooperative games is bound with superadditivity issues; players may decide not to create coalitions if the game is not superadditive. However, the intuition behind the superadditive games is not straightforward when uncertainty issues are present. As was discussed in the above paper, the evaluation of superadditivity of a game with I-fuzzy characteristic function is highly dependent on the chosen ordering relation. Even with the easiest type of the order – the deterministic ordering – the situation can be difficult – one game can be superadditive, additive, or subadditive for different types of ordering relations. The situation is complicated by a fact that players may have different preference relations. Both I-fuzzy ordering relation, as well fuzzy ordering relation can catch the uncertainty behind the issue of superadditivity of I-fuzzy cooperative games as they work with the full information of membership and nonmembership of characteristic function of the game. However, the use of I-fuzzy ordering relation as well as fuzzy ordering relation is limited due to the computational difficulties as well as problems with transitivity of relations.

References

1. Shoham, Y., Leyton-Brown, K.: Multiagent Systems: Algorithmic, Game-Theoretic, and Logical Foundations. Cambridge University Press, Cambridge (2009)
2. Zadeh, L.A.: Fuzzy sets. Inf. Control. **8**(3), 338–353 (1965). https://doi.org/10.1016/S0019-9958(65)90241-X
3. Atanassov, K.T.: Intuitionistic fuzzy sets. Fuzzy Sets Syst. **20**(1), 87–96 (1986)
4. Dubois, D., Gottwals, S., Hajek, P., Kacprzyk, J., Prade, H.: Terminological difficulties in fuzzy set theory - the case of 'intuitionistic fuzzy sets. Fuzzy Sets Syst. **156**(3), 485–491 (2005). https://doi.org/10.1016/j.fss.2005.06.001
5. Li, D.-F.: Decision and Game Theory in Management with Intuitionistic Fuzzy Sets. SFSC, vol. 308. Springer, Heidelberg (2014). https://doi.org/10.1007/978-3-642-40712-3
6. Çoker, D.: An introduction to intuitionistic fuzzy topological spaces. Fuzzy Sets Syst. **88**(1), 81–89 (1997). https://doi.org/10.1016/S0165-0114(96)00076-0
7. Atanassov, K. T.: Intuitionistic Fuzzy Sets: Theory and Applications. Studies in Fuzziness and Soft Computing. Physica-Verlag, New York (1999). https://doi.org/10.1007/978-3-7908-1876-83
8. Xu, Z.S., Xia, M.: Induced generalized intuitionistic fuzzy operators. Knowl. Based Syst. **24**(2), 197–209 (2011). https://doi.org/10.1016/j.knosys.2010.04.010
9. Mahapatra, G.S., Roy, T.K.: Intuitionistic fuzzy number and its arithmetic operation with application on system failure. J. Uncertain Syst. **7**(2), 92–107 (2013)
10. Mareš, M.: Weak arithmetics of fuzzy numbers. Fuzzy Sets Syst. **91**, 143–153 (1997). https://doi.org/10.1016/S0165-0114(97)00136-X
11. Xu, Z.S., Yager, R.R.: Some geometric aggregation operators based on intuitionistic fuzzy sets. Int. J. Gen. Syst. **35**, 417–433 (2006). https://doi.org/10.1080/03081070600574353
12. Owen, G.: Game theory, 3rd edn. Academic Press, San Diego (1995)
13. Mielcová, E.: Core of n-Person transferable utility games with intuitionistic fuzzy expectations. In: Jezic, G., Howlett, R.J., Jain, L.C. (eds.) Agent and Multi-Agent Systems: Technologies and Applications. SIST, vol. 38, pp. 167–178. Springer, Cham (2015). https://doi.org/10.1007/978-3-319-19728-9_14

Congestion Control for IoT Using Channel Trust Based Approach

Moumita Poddar[1($\boxtimes$)], Rituparna Chaki[2], and Debdutta Pal[1]

[1] Calcutta Institute of Engineering and Management, Kolkata, India
pdmoumita@gmail.com
[2] University of Calcutta, Kolkata, India

Abstract. Nowadays in the area of Internet of Things (IoT), congestion control has become an essential research area because of people and devices are progressively get connected over the network. The idea behind congestion control mechanisms originated from the point of network bandwidth, node processing ability, server capacities, channel capacity, flow of the link, number and size of distinct flow and channel reliability. Here we have used the concept of different RED, AMID and COAP based congestion control mechanisms. We have measure two level of congestion control that is node level and channel trustability. In this paper we have presented literature review of some of existing congestion control mechanisms. A congestion control model has also been proposed, which uses the measure of node level congestion and channel-trust for decision making.

Keywords: Internet of Things (IoT) · Congestion control · RED
AMID · COAP

1 Introduction

Internet of Things is spreading widely so efficient communication between the nodes is getting more important. In IoT, [1] especially in sensor networks and wireless access networks, there are limited network bandwidths and energy [2, 3] and processing platform also have finite capacities, thus congestion control plays an important role in IoT for providing satisfactory services. The idea behind congestion control originated from the perspective of network bandwidth, node processing ability and server capacities. As more and more people and devices get connected over the net, the need for congestion control increases. In IoT, the monitoring device observes such network features like flow and capacity of a link in network, number and size of distinct flows.

2 Review

In the literature various congestion control methodologies are studied for the solution of congestion problem. One of the major techniques depends window based Additive increase multiplicative decrease (AMID) [5]. In AMID there are three phases - slow start, congestion avoidance, congestion detection. Here congestion window is increased

© Springer Nature Switzerland AG 2018
K. Saeed and W. Homenda (Eds.): CISIM 2018, LNCS 11127, pp. 392–404, 2018.
https://doi.org/10.1007/978-3-319-99954-8_33

by a after per round trip time when there is no congestion but if congestion is detected congestion window is reduced by increase decrease rule constant accordingly. The other well-known congestion technique is Random early detection (RED) [6, 7]. It employs AQM (Active queue management) mechanism which is a router congestion control. First the average queue length is calculated and based on this length probability of packet loss is notified. In the buffer zone, if the queue length is greater than a certain threshold, there is a sign of congestion happening.

In [10, 13, 15], all the congestion control mechanisms are based on AMID. In [13] authors have proposed modified TCP congestion control mechanism based on bandwidth estimation [14] and double AIMD (Additive-Increase Multiplicative-Decrease) [12], named Switch-TCP. Here double AIMD is used to control the window size effectively and alleviate the network congestion. This mechanism uses ABSE (Adaptive Bandwidth Share Estimation) filter to estimate available bandwidth after comparing with present bandwidth and previous bandwidth. Finally according to the state of the network, congestion window can be increased or decreased. In [15] author has developed a novel delay-based additive increase, multiplicative decrease (AIMD) congestion control algorithm [16] which can be used to solve the coexistence problem by carefully choosing the probabilistic back off function while avoiding many of the side effects of the PERT [17] strategy. Permissible features of this algorithm are: (1) low standing queues and delay in homogeneous environments (with delay-based flows only); (2) fair coexistence of delay and loss based flows in heterogeneous environment; (3) delay-based flows behave as loss-based flows when loss-based flows are present in the network; otherwise they revert to delaybased operation. Switching between loss and delay based flow is possible thus the loss rate is low when loss and delay based flows coexist together. The network in which author has deployed (and in which no loss-based flows are present) their mechanism, have similar characteristics to networks where RED AQM [18, 19] schemes are deployed. In [10], authors have used a distributed congestion control algorithm that allocates transmission rates to M2M (machine to machine) flows in proportion to their demands. Here the key idea to achieve utility max-min rate allocation [11] is to replace additive increase procedure in AMID with one which additively increases the sending rate of a flow with an amount of proportional to the target sending rate and returns selectively instead of multiplicative decrease in AMID. Hence this algorithm maintains stable throughputs of M2M flows and named PAISMD algorithm.

In the papers [20, 23–25] all the mechanisms are based on RED. In [20], authors has proposed improved Random Early Drop (IRED) algorithm where hierarchical system framework and queuing theory are used. This algorithm employs the instantaneous queue length to calculate drop rate of the systems. The performance metrics of this algorithm are average queue length, average delay and total loss probability. Active Queue Management (AQM) [19] mechanism is also used to avoid congestion. Standard RED does not accommodate Quality of Service (QoS). In contrast to standard RED [21, 22] in IRED drop rate is calculated by instantaneous queue size and the probability of packet dropping is reduced. IRED is not capable to consider packets coming from multiple sources which are considered as a drawback. In [22–24], authors have used hop-to-hop controlled hierarchical multicast congestion control mechanism which can achieve multicast communication of heterogeneous network effectively. It combines the techniques of RED and HTH [Hop to Hop] and named HTHRED. This Hop-to-hop congestion control manner is implemented on all routers along the path. In this mechanism, each router determines its congestion status based on current network state. When a route suffers from congestion, it is discarded with certain probability and report is sent to upstream router. After a router receives congestion status update other routers, it takes appropriate measures to increase or decrease transmission rate to some downstream router. At the same time, packet discards number of each link which was considered to ensure the fairness.

In [26], authors has presented an optimization technique for M2M [27] communication for IoT which increases the quality of the mobile communication networks. Here the framework of communication for IoT data test-bed is totally based on LTE (Long Term Evolution) communication systems. LTE is a one type of standard for wireless communication of high-speed data for mobile phones and data terminals. It increases the channel capacity and speed. LTE network supports (1) high data rates, (2) low latency, (3) all IP network packet-optimized, (4) provides service continuity across heterogeneous access networks. In this paper authors have achieved the test-bed framework by constructing Evolve Packet Core (EPC) and have used Net Field Programmable Gate Array (NetFPGA) [28] and Open Flow platforms. The NetFPGA is a low-cost open platform and is designed only for a router implementation. The advantages of NetFPGA, includes line-rate, flexible, open platform, and enable fast networking hardware prototyping (e.g. modified Ethernet switches and IP routers) for research, and classroom experimentation. In this Open Flow network author has implemented the concept of network virtualization for controlling the packets routing, load balance by sharing the load to other unused wire. Test-bed model which is used in this system, offers more sensitive control for M2M communication over LTE network.

[28, 30] all are based on Constraint Application Protocol (CoAP) which is becoming popular and important in IoT messaging protocol. It is the communication protocol developed for constrained network of low-power and lossy environment. CoAP specifies conservative value for the number of open requests, retransmission time, and transmission rate. It is based on a client–server model and handled asynchronously over a datagram transports such User Datagram Protocol (UDP). Since CoAP operates on top of UDP, CoAPis expected to support additional congestion control and reliability mechanisms. Originally, CoAP is designed to allow implementations that do not maintain any end-to-end connection information. Thus, the default congestion control mechanisms are not capable of adapting to network conditions.

In [28], authors aim to meet the various limitations of CoAP. It uses round trip an estimation technique which includes variable backoff factor and aging mechanism to provide dynamic and controlled retransmission timeout adaption suitable IoT communication. CoCoAintroduces novel Round Trip Time (RTT) estimation techniques, together with a Variable Backoff Factor (VBF) and aging mechanisms in order to provide dynamic and controlled Retransmission Timeout (RTO) adaptation suitable for the peculiarities of IoT communications.

In [30], authors focus to meet one of the primary limitations of CoCoA in presence of wireless losses. Basically it helps to distinguish wireless losses and Congestion losses and gives higher throughput as compared to the default CoCoA scheme.

3 Proposed Work

3.1 Assumptions

In the proposed work following assumptions are taken to perform trust based congestion control

- Each node is capable of sensing different types of data and sends those data to Monitoring Node (MN).
- MN dynamically assigns higher priority to HOP Data (HOPDATA) than NODE data (NODEDATA).
- The congestion control functionality at the transport layer has been transferred to the network layer.

3.2 Description

Data dictionary
$i=1\ldots n$ time index
R_{gr}^i= Data rate generation
obj_{inter_rank}= Inter queue value
obj_{intra_rank}= Intra queue rank
R_{sch}^i= Scheduling data rate in i^{th} instance of time
R_{fwd}^i= Forwarding data rate in i^{th} instance of time
$t_{pkt\_trans\_time}$=Packet transmission time
Ch_{trust}^i= Channel trust
$Ch_{pkt\_flow\_rate}$ = channel packet flow rate
$Ch_{ack\_flow\_rate}$ = acknowledge packet flow rate
RTT = Round Trip Time
RTO = Retransmission time out
Ch_{Trust} = Channel trust

The proposed logic aims to detect whether channel is reliable for transmission of the packet from source to destination using the metrics: node level congestion and channel trust. A priority scheme is chosen to ascertain quicker response time in case of urgency. Each node has a number of equal sized priority queues for two types of sensed data. In the proposed model network layer interact with the MAC layer to perform congestion control function. Here, the application layer generates node data (if it is a source node) and the hop data (if it is not a source node) from the other nodes and the combined data traverse through the network layer. Queue scheduler has been provisioned to schedule the diverse traffic with different priority from the priority queues.

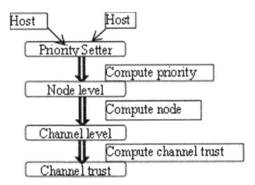

Fig. 1. Block diagram of proposed model

Figure 1 shows the block diagram of proposed model. Proposed work has been divided into three sub phases, Priority setter, node_level_congestion measure and compute_channel_trust.

PHASE 1: Priority Setter

In this phase a node with maximum number of link with the neighboring nodes in the network is designated as monitoring node and it assigns the priorities for heterogeneous traffic data. This heterogeneous traffic data are two types. One is HOP data and another one is NODE data. These NODE and HOP data contain packets which are collected from different sources and have already traversed some hop(s) hence loss of any HOP data would cause more wastage of network resources than Node data because NODE data are collected from single source and there is less possibility of traversing multi-hop. Basically every packet is associated with Inter_queue_valuewhich is a structure. Hence according to the values of the members of this structure, Hop data are given more priority than Node data. The Inter_queue_valuehas the attribute set as {Type, Packet_index, Status, Source_addr, Des_Addr, Hop_count}. Each data queue has its dynamic priority (high to low) for inserted data. These priority is represented by Intra_queue_rank (obj_{intra_rank}) which is associated to packets for each source. Round robin scheduling is used for scheduling transmission of the packets from as per their Intra_queue_rank in the queue.

The classifier assigns the priority between the Node_data and Hop_data by examining Inter_queue_value (obj_{inter_rank}). The following Fig. 2 is the priority setter model.

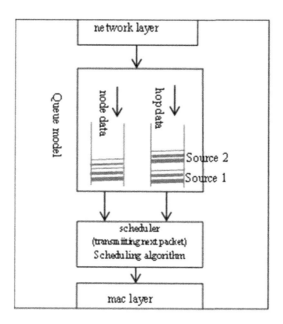

Fig. 2. Priority setter model

PHASE 2: Measure_Node_Level_Congestion

In this phase Scheduling_rate and Forwarding_rateare used to determine node level congestion. The Scheduling_rate (R^i_{sch}) is defined as how many packets the scheduler schedules per unit time from the queues. The scheduler forwards the packets to the MAC layer from which the packets are delivered to the next node $(i + 1)$ along the path towards the Monitoring node (MN).

$$R^i_{sc}h = (queue_{len})/T \qquad (1)$$

Where $queue_{len}$ is the number of packets in the queue at i^{th} instance of time and T is time period required to forward total number of packets.

Forwarding_ rate (R^i_{fwd}) is the rate at which packets are forwarded from MAC layer at i^{th} instance of time to the next node.

$$R^i_{fwd} = 1/t_{pkt\_trans\_time} \qquad (2)$$

Then we compute the Node_level_congestion (C^i_t) for i^{th} node at t^{th} instance of time as the ratio of Forwarding_rate (R^i_{fwd}) to Scheduling_rate (R^i_{sch}) of a node.

$$C^i_t = R^i_{fwd}/R^i_{sch} \qquad (3)$$

When $(R_{fwd}/R_{sch} = 1)$, we have scheduling rate = forwarding rate hence this status is considered as low congestion.

If $(R_{fwd}/R_{sch} > 1)$ then Scheduling_rate < Forwading_rate hence this status is consider as low congestion.

When$(R_{fwd}/R_{sch} < 1)$ then Scheduling_rate > Forwarding_ratehence this status is considered as High congestion.

We then calculate the Packet_transmission_time ($t_{pkt\_trans\_time}$) which is the time required to successfully send packet from the current node to the next hop node. It is calculated using Exponential Weighted Moving Average formula (EWMA). It is a moving filter that applied to older values in a time series and analyses whether the value of the parameter(s) being observed in a given time interval, exceeds a particular threshold value.$t_{pkt\_trans\_time}$is updated by

$$t^i_{pkt\_trans\_time} = \left(1 - \beta_{pkt_{conts}}\right) \times t_{pkt\_trans\_time} + \beta_{pkt\_conts} \times prompt\left(t_{pkt\_trans\_time}\right) \tag{4}$$

Here β_{pkt_conts} is a constant where $0 < \beta_{pkt\_conts} < 1$

PHASE 3: Compute_channel_trust

Channel_ trust (Ch^i_{trust}) is used to decide whether the selected channel is dependable for secure transmission of packets to the next node or not. Round Trip Time (RTT) and Retransmission Timeout (RTO) are used to measure the Channel Trust.

The channel packet flow rate ($Ch_{pkt\_flow\_rate}$) and channel acknowledge packet flow rate ($Ch_{ack\_flow\_rate}$) are used to determine RTO.

$$Ch_{pkt\_flow\_rate} = n/t1$$

$$Ch_{ack\_flow\_rate} = m/t2 \quad m \leq n$$

where n: No of pkt transmitted, m: total ACKs between receiver and sender, t2: Total time to transmit the ACKs.

The difference between channel packet flow rate ($Ch_{pkt\_flow\_rate}$) and channel acknowledge packet flow rate ($Ch_{ack\_flow\_rate}$) is depending on RTO.

$$(n/t1 - m/t2)\alpha RTO \quad n \geq m$$

$$So, \quad K = \frac{(n/t1 - m/t2)}{RTO}$$

$$Where \quad RTO = RTT + \max(L, beta \times RTT)$$

$$and \quad RTT = (2n/t1)$$

$$and \quad beta = \int_1^n Ch_{pkt\_flow\_rate} dt \Big/ \int_1^m Ch_{ack\_flow\_rate} dt$$

L is the lower bound of the time out and beta is the delay variance factor.

We use the term buffer_rate to represent the ratio of the number of packet flow at sender end (y) and the number of packet flow at receiver end (x).

$$\text{Thus buffer\_rate} = y/x$$

After obtaining RTO, it is denoted as ACK which is the time required to get the confirmation whether the packet is transmitted from sender to receiver successfully or not. The algorithm for our proposed work is as follows

/ Algorithm for determining node level congestion /

```
Begin
Compute data generation rate for a node
```
$$R_{gr}^i = \frac{\sum_{i=1}^n D_i}{s}$$
```
Computepacket transmission time
```
$$t_{pkt\_trans\_time}^i = (1 - \beta_{pkt_{conts}}) \times t_{pkt\_trans\_time} + \beta_{pkt\_conts} \times prompt(t_{pkt\_trans\_time})$$
```
Compute Forwading rate ( R_fwd^i )
```
$$R_{fwd}^i = \frac{1}{t_{pkt\_trans\_time}}$$
```
Compute Scheduling rate (R_sch^i ) for i^th node
```
$$R_{sch}^i = \frac{queue_{len}}{T}$$
```
Compute Node level congestion (C_t^i ) for i^th nodeat t^th instance
of time as
```
the ratio of the Forwading rate to Scheduling
```
rate
```
$$C_t^i = \frac{R_{fwd}^i}{R_{sch}^i}$$
```
if  (C_t^i  = 1 ) then node level congestion is low
            if ( C_t^i>1 ) then node level congestion is low
            if ( C_t^i<1 ) then node level congestion is high
End
```

/ Algorithm for determining channel trust /

```
Begin
Compute Channel packet flow  (Ch_pkt_flow_rate )
Ch_pkt_flow_rate = n/t1
ompute Channel acknowledge packet flow ( Ch_ack_flow_rate)
Ch_ack_flow_rate = m/t2          m≤n
ompute Beta which is a delay variance
beta = ∫₁ⁿ Ch_pkt_flow_rate dt / ∫₁ᵐ Ch_ack_flow_rate dt

Compute Round trip time ( RTT )
RTT = ( 2n/t1 )
Compute Retransmission time out ( RTO )
RTO = RTT + max ( L , beta × RTT )
Compute the constant K in the following way
  (n/t1 - m/t2 ) α RTO
  where n ≥ m , So (n/t1 - m/t2 ) = K . RTO
thus, K = (n/t1 - m/t2 ) / RTO
if (buffer_rate>Th) and (Ack≤RTT )
Then Channel_Trust (Ch_Trust) is increased
else if ( Ack> RTT )
                    If ( buffer_rate< Th )
                    Then Channel_Trust ( Ch_Trust ) is decreased
                    else Channel_Trust ( Ch_Trust ) is increased
End
```

3.3   Performance Analysis

Metrics: The metrics used to evaluate the performance are given below.

Originating_rate (R_{gr}^i): The rate of data generation by a specific node is calculated as the originating_rate (R_{gr}^i) where R_{gr}^i of node i is:

$$R_{gr}^i = \sum_{i=1}^{n} D_i/s$$

Here, D_i represents data originating at i^{th} instance, for all i, $R_{gr}^i > 0$.

Scheduling_rate (R_{sch}^i). is defined as how many packets the scheduler schedules per unit time from the queues.

$$R_{sch}^i = queue_{len}/T$$

Forwarding_ rate (R^i_{fwd}): It is the rate at which packets are forwarded from MAC layer at i^{th} instance of time to the next node.

$$R^i_{fwd} = 1/t_{pkt\_trans\_time}$$

We have computed node level congestion using originating_rate, forwarding rate, scheduling rate, packet transmission rate according to our proposed algorithm (Fig. 3).

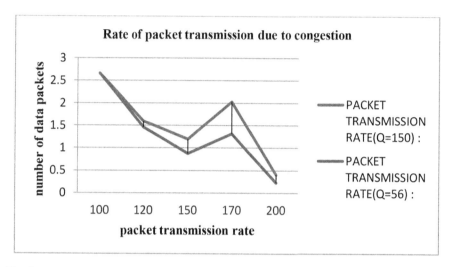

Fig. 3. Rate of packet transmission due to congestion Y-axis: number of data packets and X-axispacket transmission rate

Packet transmission rate is one of the important factor which can be effected due to the congestion. In a network if nodes are congested due to high data traffic then forwarding rate of packet transmission will also be reduced. The queue length is key factor that determine the performance of the network during packet transfer. If the queue length is high then it can buffer more data packets and transmission rate becomes high. Queue with small buffering capacity, drop packets that reduce packet transfer rate in the network.

Figure 4 shows as queue length with respect to data originating rate is decreased, packet transmission rate gets effected.

It shows how forwarding rate is changed due to different queue length. When a particular node is congested then packet forwarding rate from it to the next node is observed to decreased. Thus we can easily determine whether a node is congested or not.

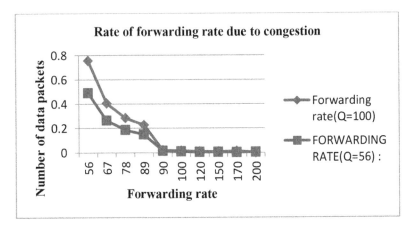

Fig. 4. Rate of forwarding rate due to congestion. Y- axis: number of data packets and X-axis forwarding rate

4   Conclusion and Future Work

This paper deals with on the problem of congestion control in IoT environment, which is observed to be increasing at an alarming rate. It is required to develop an effective congestion control protocol that will reduce the chance of delayed communication and loss of packets in IoT environment. The performance of congestion control protocols depends on a number of parameters. We have done ameticulous survey and comparison of different classes of congestion control protocols leading to a new approach towards efficient congestion control mechanism. We have identified certain parameters for efficient congestion control. Measuring Node level congestion and Channel_trustarethe key parameter which are used to measure the channel reliability or trust. The performance evaluation shows that our approach efficiently controls congestion in IoT and maintains an optimal data rate during packet transmission.

References

1. Atzori, L., Iera, A., Morabito, G.: The internet of things: a survey. Comput. Netw. **54**(15), 2787–2805 (2010)
2. Chen, J., He, S., Sun, Y., Thulasiraman, P.: Optimal flow control for utility-lifetime tradeoff in wireless sensor networks. Comput. Netw. **53**, 3031–3041 (2009)
3. Chen, J., Xu, W., He, S., Sun, Y., Thulasiraman, P., Shen, X.: Utility-based asynchronous flow control algorithm for wireless sensor networks. IEEE J. Sel. Areas Commun. **28**, 1116–1126 (2010)
4. Palattella, M.R., Accettura, N., Dohler, M., Grieco, L.A., Boggia, G.: Traffic aware scheduling algorithm for reliable low power multi hop IEEE 802.15.4e networks. In: 23rd IEEE International Symposium on Personal, Indoor and Mobile Radio Communications, PIMRC, September 2012

5. Jain, R., Ramakrishnan, K.K., Chiu, D.-M.: Congestion avoidance in computer networks with a connectionless network layer. Digital Equipment Corporation, Technical report DEC-TR-506 (1987)
6. Bonald, T., May, M., Bolot, J.C.: Analytic evaluation of RED performance. Proc. INFOCOM 1(3), 1415–1424 (2000)
7. Bauso, D., Giarre, L., Neglia, G.: Active queue management stability in multiple bottleneck networks control. Commun. Sig. Process., 369–372 (2004)
8. Winter, T., et al.: IPv6 routing protocol for low-power and lossy networks. In: RFC 6550, IETF RFC 6550 (2012)
9. Accettura, N., Palattella, M.R., Boggia, G., Grieco, L.A., Dohler, M.: Decentralized traffic aware scheduling for multi-hop low power lossy networks in the internet of things. IEEE (2013)
10. Lam, R.K., Chen, K.-C.: Congestion control for M2M traffic with heterogeneous throughput demands. In: IEEE WCNC, pp. 1452–1457 (2013)
11. Miller, K., Harks, T.: Utility max-min fair congestion control with time-varying delays. In: Proceedings of IEEE INFOCOM, pp. 331 –335 (2008)
12. Chiu, D.-M., Jain, R.: Analysis of the increase and decrease algorithms for congestion avoidance in computer networks. Comput. Netw. ISDN Syst. 17(1), 1–14 (1989)
13. Changbiao, X., Wei, S.: New TCP mechanism over heterogeneous networks. In: International Conference on Embedded Software and Systems, pp. 303–307 (2008)
14. Capone, A., Fratta, L.: Martignon: F.: Bandwidth estimation schemes for TCP over wireless networks. IEEE Trans. Mob. Comput. 3(2), 129–143 (2004)
15. Budzisz, L., Stanojevic, R., Schlote, A., Baker, F., Shorten, R.: On the fair coexistence of loss- and delay-based TCP. IEEE/ACM Trans. Network. 19(6) (2011)
16. Leith, D., Heffner, J., Shorten, R., McCullagh, G.: Delay-based AIMD congestion control. In: Proceedings 5th PFLDnet, pp. 1–6 (2007)
17. Bhandarkar, S., Reddy, A., Zhang, Y., Loguinov, D.: Emulating AQM from end hosts. Comput. Commun. Rev. 37(4), 349–360 (2007)
18. Que, D., Chen, Z., Chen, B.: An improvement algorithm based on RED and its performance analysis. In: ICSP Proceedings (2008)
19. Firoiu, V., Borden, M.: A study of active queue management for congestion control. In: IEEE INFOCOM (2000)
20. Huang, J., et al.: Modeling and analysis on congestion control in modeling and analysis on congestion control in IoT. In: IEEE ICC - Ad-hoc and Sensor Networking Symposium, pp. 434–439 (2014)
21. Floyd, S., Jacobson, V.: Random early detection gateways for congestion avoidance. IEEE/ACM Trans. Network. 1(4), 397–413 (1993)
22. Zhang1, J.-C., Zhao, R.-X., Chen1, J.-J.: A hop to hop controlled hierarchical multicast congestion control mechanism. In: Hu, W. (ed.) Electronics and Signal Processing, LNEE 97, pp. 363–369. Springer, Heidelberg (2011). https://doi.org/10.1007/978-3-642-21697-8_46
23. Liu, J.-C., Li, B., Zhang, Y.-Q.: A hybrid adaptation protocol for tcp-friendly layered multicast and its optimal rate allocation. In: Proceedings of IEEE INFOCOM, pp. 1520–1528 (2001)
24. Byers, J.W., Horn, G., Luby, M.: FLID-DL, "congestion control for layered multicast". IEEE J. Sel. Areas Commun. 20, 1558–1570 (2002)
25. Liu, K.-J., Cheng, Z.-Q., Zhao, Y.-P.: Multicast congestion control based on hop to hop. Comput. Eng. 33, 99–101 (2007)
26. Hsieh, H.-C., Larosa, Y.T., Chen, J.-L.: Congestion control optimization of M2M in LTE network. Adv. Commun. Technol. (ICACT), 823–827 (2013)

27. Olivier, H., David, B., Omar, E.: The Internet of Things: Key Applications and Protocols, pp. 223–246. Wiley (2012)
28. Naous, J., Gibb, G., Bolouki, S., McKeown, N.: NetFPGA: reusable router architecture for experimental research. In: Proceedings of the ACM Workshop on Programmable Routers for Extensible Services of Tomorrow (PRESTO 2008), pp. 1–7 (2008)
29. Betzler, A., Gomez, C., Demirkol, I., Paradells, J.: CoAP congestion control for the internet of things. IEEE Commun., 154–160 (2016)
30. Bhalerao, R., Subramanian, S.S., Pasquale, J.: An analysis and improvement of congestion control in the CoAP internet-of-things protocol. In: Consumer Communications & Networking Conference (CCNC), pp. 889–894. IEEE (2016)
31. Poddar, M., Chaki, R., Pal, D.: A channel trust based approach for congestion control in IoT. In: AICT, pp. 319–324. IEEE (2015)

Synthesis of High-Speed ASM Controllers with Moore Outputs by Introducing Additional States

Valery Salauyou and Irena Bulatowa$^{(\boxtimes)}$

Bialystok University of Technology, Bialystok, Poland
{v.salauyou,i.bulatowa}@pb.edu.pl

Abstract. In the paper, we propose a new method for FPGA-based design of high-speed Algorithmic State Machine (ASM) controllers. The method is based on the introduction of additional states of the state machine in order to implement all transition functions in the single-level structures. In this method, such an optimization criterion as a critical path delay is applied already at the stage of converting the ASM chart to the state machine HDL description. The proposed method consists of two steps: determining the place of additional labels on the ASM chart and introducing additional states of FSM. Experimental results show that our approach achieves an average performance gain of 20.43% to 27.41% (for various FPGA devices) compared with the traditional synthesis method. The maximum performance increase achieved is 59.17%. At the same time, the method slightly increases the cost of implementation by an average of 5.13% to 5.19%, but in some cases even reduces the cost.

Keywords: Algorithmic State Machine (ASM) · ASM chart
Finite State Machine (FSM) · Performance optimization

1 Introduction

An Algorithmic State Machine (ASM) controller is a control unit whose hardware algorithm is specified by an ASM chart. An ASM controller can be implemented as a finite state machine (FSM). The ASM chart is a high-level graphical notation to represent the flow of operations performed by the digital system. It is a powerful method for specifying the behavior of finite state machines, especially well-suited for more complex systems designs.

Nowadays, Field Programmable Gate Arrays (FPGAs) are widely used for digital systems design. The flexibility and performance of the FPGA devices make them an ideal platform for developing high-speed systems that require real-time operation. The main optimization criteria used in FPGA designs are performance, area, and power consumption. Since FPGAs have huge resources of logic elements, the utilized area is not often a critical parameter. However, the performance of digital systems is a significant requirement for many applications such as telecommunications, cryptography, digital signal processing, specialized equipment, and others.

K. Saeed and W. Homenda (Eds.): CISIM 2018, LNCS 11127, pp. 405–416, 2018.
https://doi.org/10.1007/978-3-319-99954-8_34

The speed of the FSM design can be evaluated based on the maximum clock frequency, which is determined by the worst-case delay through its combinational block. FSM performance optimization is usually considered in the context of state assignment and combinational logic optimization. The maximum possible clock rate of a sequential logic circuit is decided by the largest of the path delays, so in the case of FPGA design it depends on the number of LUTs and interconnects delays on the critical path.

ASM-based synthesis methods have been widely developed by several authors. In [1], an algorithmic state machine model has been introduced. In this work, it was proposed to represent a digital system as a composition of data path and control automaton, where the data path performs the data processing according to the order of microoperations generated by the control automaton on the base of the microprogram to be executed. The ASM charts for specifying digital designs were first documented in [2]. Since then, the ASM design methods have been widely applied and developed in many studies.

In [3], the techniques for converting ASM charts into PLA-, PAL-, and multiplexer-based implementations are described. Various ASM-based synthesis methods were developed in [4]. Paper [5] proposes the algorithmic register transfer language for formal text representation of the ASM charts. In [6], the technique for minimizing the number of ASM vertices, which results in state and logic circuit minimization, is presented. Paper [7] proposes a method for the synthesis of self-checking FPGA-based ASM controllers. In [8], a new notation called "ASM++ diagrams", which improves the ASM charts for more complex designs and allows for the automatic conversion into HDL code, is considered. A synthesis method targeted at area optimization for ASM controllers implemented in FPGAs is presented in [9]. In [10], synthesis methods for ASM controllers based on ASM charts with linear chains of states are proposed.

In a series of papers [11–17], different techniques for FSM performance optimization were developed. These techniques improve FSM performance by minimizing the longest path delay, which results in maximum speed. In contrast to all the above approaches, we propose to apply our technique at an earlier stage of ASM conversion to the FSM description. As a result, we get such an FSM specification in HDL language that already provides an increase in the designed system speed.

In this paper, we propose a novel synthesis method for high-speed ASM controllers implemented in FPGAs. As a model for the ASM controller, the Moore finite state machine is used. The proposed approach is based on introducing additional states to implement all the transition functions in the single-level structure with a minimal path delay. The method is targeted at FPGA implementation and considers specific features of FPGA logics.

2   Idea of the Proposed Approach

An ASM chart is a graphical notation to specify the operation of a control unit. An ASM chart is a directed connected graph containing one initial vertex, one final vertex, and a finite number of operator and decision vertices. The operator vertex, represented as a rectangle, corresponds to one FSM state and lists the output signals (microoperations) that are asserted in that state. The subset Yt of the set of microoperations $Y = \{y_1,...,y_N\}$ is indicated inside each operator vertex. The decision vertex, represented as a diamond, contains the input condition on which the branching from a given state depends. Only one logical condition from the set $X = \{x_1,...,x_L\}$ is placed within each decision vertex. The choice of the branch 0 or 1 is made depending on the value of the input signal (logical condition). An example of an ASM chart with $Y = \{y_1,...,y_8\}$ and $X = \{x_1,...,x_8\}$ is shown in Fig. 1.

To design the Moore machine from the ASM chart, we have to mark the ASM chart with the state labels $a_1,..., a_M$. This is done in the following way: the initial and final vertices are marked with the same label a_1, and the remaining state labels $a_2,...,a_M$ are assigned to the ASM operator vertices. The state labels $a_1,...,a_M$ correspond to the FSM internal states. Such labels are called *main state labels* and the corresponding FSM states are called *main internal states*. The example ASM chart in Fig. 1 is marked with the main state labels $a_1,...,a_9$. In addition, *additional state labels*, which are placed at the inputs of decision boxes, can be introduced (the labels a_{10} and a_{11} in Fig. 1). We refer to the corresponding FSM states as *additional internal states*.

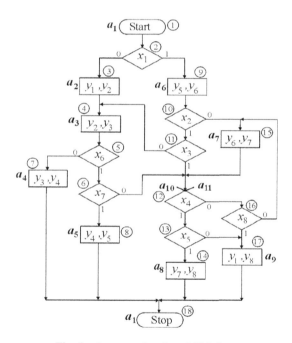

Fig. 1. An example of an ASM chart

To design FSM from the marked ASM chart, we must describe all transition paths between the internal states. We can describe the FSM behavior by the *transition table*, which contains four columns: a_m is the present state, a_s is the next state, $X(a_m, a_s)$ is the transition condition, and $Y(a_m)$ is the set of output variables asserted at state a_m. Each row of the table corresponds to one FSM transition. The logical condition $X(a_m, a_s)$ is specified as a conjunction of input variables that initiate this transition. The Moore FSM outputs $Y(a_m)$ are only present state dependent. The transition table for the ASM chart shown in Fig. 1 is presented in Table 1.

The most commonly used FPGAs implement the logic functions using look-up tables (LUT). The n-input LUT (n-LUT) is a small static RAM with 1-bit output that is used to implement the truth table of an arbitrary n-input function. The n-input LUT can implement any logical function of up to n variables. In practice, LUTs have a number of inputs limited to 4–6. A function of more than n variables can be implemented as a multi-level network of LUT components, which causes an increase in output signal delay. In the case of FSM design, the maximum clock frequency of synchronous circuit is determined by the maximum propagation delay through the combinational block. Therefore, a reliable method to increase FSM performance is to reduce the worst-case delay for FSM transition functions.

Table 1. Moore FSM transition table for ASM from Fig. 1.

No	a_m	$X(a_m, a_s)$	a_s	$Y(a_m)$
1	a_1	x_1	a_6	–
2	a_1	$\bar{x}_1$	a_2	–
3	a_2	1	a_3	y_1, y_2
4	a_3	$x_6 x_7$	a_5	y_2, y_3
5	a_3	$x_6\, \bar{x}_7\, x_4 x_5$	a_8	y_2, y_3
6	a_3	$x_6\, \bar{x}_7\, x_4\, \bar{x}_5$	a_9	y_2, y_3
7	a_3	$x_6\, \bar{x}_7 \bar{x}_4\, x_8$	a_9	y_2, y_3
8	a_3	$x_6\, \bar{x}_7 \bar{x}_4 \bar{x}_8$	a_7	y_2, y_3
9	a_3	$\bar{x}_6$	a_4	y_2, y_3
10	a_4	1	a_1	y_3, y_4
11	a_5	1	a_1	y_4, y_5
12	a_6	$x_2 x_3 x_4 x_5$	a_8	y_5, y_6
13	a_6	$x_2 x_3 x_4\, \bar{x}_5$	a_9	y_5, y_6
14	a_6	$x_2 x_3\, \bar{x}_4\, x_8$	a_9	y_5, y_6
15	a_6	$x_2 x_3\, \bar{x}_4 \bar{x}_8$	a_7	y_5, y_6
16	a_6	$x_2\, \bar{x}_3$	a_3	y_5, y_6
17	a_6	$\bar{x}_2$	a_7	y_5, y_6
18	a_7	$x_4 x_5$	a_8	y_6, y_7
19	a_7	$x_4\, \bar{x}_5$	a_9	y_6, y_7
20	a_7	$\bar{x}_4\, x_8$	a_9	y_6, y_7
21	a_7	$\bar{x}_4 \bar{x}_8$	a_7	y_6, y_7
22	a_8	1	a_1	y_7, y_8
23	a_9	1	a_1	y_1, y_8

We propose a method for high-speed FSM design that ensures single-LUT-level implementation of all transition functions, which results in FSM performance improvement. One-hot encoding is the most suited state assignment approach to high-speed FSM design, because it attempts to improve performance by simplifying decode logics. In one-hot encoding, each state is associated with one code bit and therefore one flip-flop to each state. Only one flip-flop is set at a time, which indicates the current FSM state. When one hot is used, only one state variable is asserted on each transition and therefore only one LUT input is utilized to check for each state. This is important for our approach, because we try to simplify transition functions by limiting the number of input variables to enable a single-LUT-level logic function implementation. The n-LUT based implementation of some transition function from state a_i needs only one LUT input to the current state decoding, and the remaining n-1 inputs of LUT can be used to check the transition condition.

Let $A = \{a_1,\ldots,a_M\}$ be the set of main internal states of FSM; $X(a_m, a_s)$ be the set of input variables that affect the transition from a_m to a_s, which we refer as transition condition. If $|X(a_m, a_s)| > n$-1, then it is impossible to implement the transition from a_m to a_s in a single LUT block. Such a transition function can be implemented by a network consisting of more LUTs, but it leads to an increase in signal propagation delay.

In our approach, we propose to introduce additional internal states of FSM to simplify the transition functions and enable their implementation in fast single-LUT-level structures. Additional states should be introduced to satisfy the following condition for all FSM transitions:

$$|X(a_i, a_j)| \leq n - 1, \forall a_i, a_j \in A. \tag{1}$$

If condition (1) is satisfied, each transition function can be implemented in a single LUT and the whole combinational block of the FSM can be realized in a single-logic-level structure. This helps in reducing the worst-case propagation delay and thereby increasing the maximum clock frequency.

Additional states are introduced at those state transitions for which the condition (1) is not met. The output signals $Y(a_i)$ generated at an additional state are the same as those generated at the initial state a_i of this transition. If several transitions from different states pass through the ASM vertex marked by an additional state label, then the appropriate number of additional states is introduced. The output signals $Y(a_i)$ at the additional states repeat those generated at the initial states of each transition. The introduction of additional states does not change FSM behavior, because the additional states keep the same output signals that are generated at the states a_i. However, such transitions need more clock cycles to pass though all additional states. But all other changes in the FSM states occur in a single clock cycle. The proposed approach allows reducing the critical path delay and the minimum clock period, resulting in a maximum speed.

3 Synthesis Method for High-Speed ASM Controllers

The proposed method for high-speed ASM controllers synthesis consists of two stages. In the first stage, the places for entering the additional labels on the ASM chart are determined, and in the second stage, the additional FSM states are introduced. The ASM-based high-speed FSM synthesis algorithm can be described as follows.

Algorithm 1 *(general algorithm for high-speed ASM controllers synthesis)*

Step 1. *Mark the ASM chart by state labels for Moore FSM synthesis. Obtain the transition table from marked ASM chart.*
Step 2. *If the condition (1) is met for all FSM transitions, then go to step 5.*
Step 3. *Using Algorithm 2, determine the place of the additional state label (or labels) on the ASM chart.*
Step 4. *Using Algorithm 3, introduce the additional states of the FSM. Create a new transition table that includes the additional states. Go to step 2.*
Step 5. *Stop.*

To determine the place of the additional label on the ASM chart, we propose to build the chains of the decision vertices for all transition paths that do not meet the condition (1), and to identify the potential places for additional labels on these chains. Next, the most often pointed vertex can be chosen as a place for an additional label. The algorithm for determining the place of the addition label on the ASM chart is as follows.

Algorithm 2 *(to determine the place of an additional state label)*

Step 1. *Build the chains of decision vertices for all ASM transition paths that do not meet the condition (1).*
Step 2. *Place the SL labels through every n-1 vertex starting from the beginning of the transition chain.*
Step 3. *Place FL labels through every n-1 vertex starting from the end of the transition chain.*
Step 4. *For each chain, all vertices labeled with SL and FL and those that are between the corresponding SL and FL labels, are counted among the potential vertices for the additional state label introduction.*
Step 5. *To select one of the potential vertices as a place for an additional label, create matrix W. The rows of matrix W correspond to the chains of decision vertices defined in step 2. The columns of matrix W correspond to the vertices pointed out in step 4 as potential vertices to introduce additional labels. The entry w_{ij} of matrix W is equal to 1 if the vertex in column j is counted among the potential vertices of the chain occurring in row i.*
Step 6. *To determine the place of the additional label on the ASM, select the matrix column with the maximum number of 1 s. If there is more than one such column, choose the vertex with more edges leading to it in the ASM chart.*
Step 7. *Stop.*

Let v_i be the ASM decision vertex chosen according to Algorithm 2. The additional state label is placed at the input of vertex v_i. Since transitions from several different states in which the different outputs are generated may lead to vertex v_i, then more than one additional labels may be placed at the input of v_i. The output signals formed in the corresponding additional states are the same as those generated in the initial state of each transition. Let us denote by $p(a_m)$ a transition beginning at the state a_m, $a_m \in$ A. Let $P(v_j)$ be the set of transitions for which vertex v_j has been pointed as a potential place to introduce the additional label. The transitions of the set $P(v_j)$ are marked by 1 in column v_j of matrix W. The algorithm of introducing additional states is presented as follows.

Algorithm 3 *(introducing additional states)*

Step 1. Determine the set $A^* = \{a_{j1}, ..., a_{jK}\}$ of the initial internal states for transitions of the set $P(v_j)$.

Step 2. Mark the input of vertex v_j using additional labels $a_{M+1}, ..., a_{M+K}$.

Step 3. Include the additional states $a_{M+1}, ..., a_{M+K}$ in the FSM transition table.

Step 4. Describe the transitions from the additional states $a_{M+1}, ..., a_{M+K}$ in the FSM transition table.

Step 5. Define the sets $Y(a_{M+k})$ of the output signals in the additional states $a_{M+1}, ..., a_{M+K}$ as $Y(a_{M+k}) = Y(a_{jk})$, $k = \overline{1, K}$.

Step 6. Modify the transitions of the set $P(v_j)$ so that each transition $p(a_{jk}) \in P(v_j)$ is ended in the additional state a_{M+k} in which the outputs $Y(a_{jk}) = Y(a_{M+k})$, $k = \overline{1, K}$ are generated.

Step 7. Stop.

To illustrate the synthesis procedure, consider again the example of the ASM chart shown in Fig. 1. The ASM chart contains 18 vertices. The vertex numbers are circled in Fig. 1. To synthesize the Moore FSM, the ASM chart has been marked with the main state labels $a_1, ..., a_9$, and the transition table (shown in Table 1) has been obtained from the marked ASM chart. Let $n = 4$, then there are eight FSM transitions numbered as 5, 6, 7, 8, 12, 13, 14, and 15 for which the condition (1) is not satisfied.

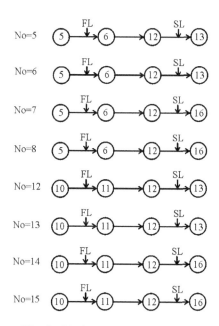

Fig. 2. Marked chains of transitions

According to Algorithm 2, the chains of decision vertices are built for these transition paths. For our example, all the chains are of the same length. The transition chains marked with SL and FL labels are depicted in Fig. 2. Matrix W is created according to step 5 of Algorithm 2 as is shown in Table 2, where column a_m additionally contains the initial state for each transition. The largest number of 1 s in column "12" in Table 2 indicates vertex v_{12} to be selected for marking with an additional label.

Table 2. Matrix W

a_m	No	Vertex number				
		6	12	13	11	16
a_3	5	1	1	1		
a_3	6	1	1	1		
a_3	7	1	1			1
a_3	8	1	1			1
a_6	12		1	1	1	
a_6	13		1	1	1	
a_6	14		1		1	1
a_6	15		1		1	1
$\sum$		4	8	4	4	4

Table 3. FSM transition table after introducing the additional states

No	a_m	$X(a_m, a_s)$	a_s	$Y(a_m)$
1	a_1	x_1	a_6	–
2	a_1	$\bar{x}_1$	a_2	–
3	a_2	1	a_3	y_1, y_2
4	a_3	$x_6 x_7$	a_5	y_2, y_3
5	a_3	$x_6 \bar{x}_7$	a_{10}	y_2, y_3
6	a_3	$\bar{x}_6$	a_4	y_2, y_3
7	a_4	1	a_1	y_3, y_4
8	a_5	1	a_1	y_4, y_5
9	a_6	$x_2 x_3$	a_8	y_5, y_6
10	a_6	$x_2 x_3$	a_9	y_5, y_6
11	a_6	$\bar{x}_2$	a_7	y_5, y_6
12	a_7	$x_4 x_5$	a_8	y_6, y_7
13	a_7	$x_4 \bar{x}_5$	a_9	y_6, y_7
14	a_7	$\bar{x}_4 x_8$	a_9	y_6, y_7
15	a_7	$\bar{x}_4 \bar{x}_8$	a_7	y_6, y_7
16	a_8	1	a_1	y_7, y_8
17	a_9	1	a_1	y_1, y_8
18	a_{10}	$x_4 x_5$	a_8	y_2, y_3
19	a_{10}	$x_4 \bar{x}_5$	a_9	y_2, y_3
20	a_{10}	$\bar{x}_4 x_8$	a_9	y_2, y_3
21	a_{10}	$\bar{x}_4 \bar{x}_8$	a_7	y_2, y_3
22	a_{11}	$x_4 x_5$	a_8	y_5, y_6
23	a_{11}	$x_4 \bar{x}_5$	a_9	y_5, y_6
24	a_{11}	$\bar{x}_4 x_8$	a_9	y_5, y_6
25	a_{11}	$\bar{x}_4 \bar{x}_8$	a_7	y_5, y_6

Once a vertex for labeling is found, the additional states can be introduced according to Algorithm 3. The set $A*$ of initial states for the transition paths of the set P (v_{12}) is defined as $A* = \{a_3, a_6\}$. Because $K = |A*| = 2$, two additional labels a_{10} and a_{11} should be placed at the entrance of vertex v_{12}, and therefore two additional FSM states a_{10} and a_{11} will be introduced. These additional states differ only in the output signals generated: at state a_{10} the output set $Y(a_{10}) = Y(a_3) = \{y_2, y_3\}$ corresponding to state a_3 is generated; but at state a_{11} the same output set $Y(a_{11}) = Y(a_6) = \{y_5, y_6\}$ as at state a_6 will be asserted. The modified transition table is shown in Table 3.

The long transitions from states a_3 and a_6 have been modified so they lead to the additional states a_{10} and a_{11}, respectively, and the new transitions from states a_{10} and a_{11} have been inserted into the state table. Note that the transitions from state a_7 are not modified because they meet the condition (1).

4 Experimental Results

To estimate the efficiency of the proposed method, we applied it to the ASM chart examples from the benchmark dataset of the ZUBR design system [18]. The size parameters of the test examples are shown in Table 4, where L, N, M, and P are the number of inputs, outputs, states, and transitions of the original FSM, respectively; $M*$ and $P*$ are the number of states and transitions of the FSM synthesized using the proposed method. FPGA implementation was performed using the Intel Quartus Prime Lite Edition v.16.1 tool with both the default option *Balanced* and the speed optimizing option *Performance*.

Table 4. Parameters of the ASM examples

Example	L	N	M	P	M*	P*
prim2r	9	6	12	29	17	33
std2r	10	10	13	44	18	43
dst	14	14	21	57	29	64
gsa4d	16	15	22	67	31	76
gsa5d	16	12	20	61	29	69
sstr6	16	14	21	60	28	68
dst7	12	11	14	41	19	39
mnst	18	16	26	74	36	84
sstr2r	12	12	21	52	27	59
gsa10	12	13	22	74	28	60

The results of comparing the performance of the implemented FSMs are shown in Tables 5 and 6, where F and $F*$ are the rounded maximum clock frequencies (in MHz) for the conventional method (without the additional states) and the proposed synthesis method, respectively; and "%" is the percentage increase in the maximum clock frequency when using our synthesis method.

Table 5. Performance comparison results for implementation with the *Balanced* option

Example	MAX II			MAX V			MAX 10			Cyclone IV E			Cyclone IV GX		
	F	F*	%	F	F*	%	F	F*	%	F	F*	%	F	F*	%
prim2r	330	405	22.89	178	222	24.26	454	565	24.58	634	710	12.00	631	720	14.12
std2r	272	348	28.20	135	186	37.60	333	477	43.08	521	597	14.50	452	659	45.68
dst	311	335	7.43	158	201	27.11	418	471	12.73	543	628	15.51	522	637	21.83
gsa4d	273	324	18.28	161	179	10.89	388	434	11.89	468	536	14.64	501	539	7.65
gsa5d	234	356	52.33	132	174	31.91	323	430	32.87	473	539	14.08	465	550	18.26
sstr6	269	339	25.90	142	198	39.45	385	470	22.11	524	597	13.98	511	568	11.01
dst7	285	360	26.22	157	180	14.82	340	466	37.12	500	682	36.47	523	590	12.46
mnst	299	354	18.67	157	173	10.60	359	439	22.50	521	620	18.98	532	630	18.,32
sstr2r	297	335	13.04	158	174	10.12	469	585	24.87	578	685	18.51	569	708	24.27
gsa10	321	383	19.21	173	217	25.50	390	510	30.58	443	705	59.17	535	711	32.83
mean			23.22			23.23			26.23			21.78			20.64
max			52.33			39.45			43.08			59.17			45.68

Table 6. Performance comparison results for implementation with the *Performance* option

Example	MAX II			MAX V			MAX 10			Cyclone IV E			Cyclone IV GX		
	F	F*	%	F	F*	%	F	F*	%	F	F*	%	F	F*	%
prim2r	341	418	22.51	201	224	11.68	514	5847	13.54	647	717	10.75	647	718	10.98
std2r	257	375	45.82	149	202	35.58	337	522	54.70	526	658	25.13	495	657	32.57
dst	315	347	10.21	163	196	20.48	423	517	22.06	508	583	14.88	505	646	27.91
gsa4d	298	360	20.60	158	172	9.04	364	483	32.53	494	578	16.93	491	631	28.52
gsa5d	244	348	42.58	143	181	26.42	327	436	33.52	452	596	31.80	417	553	32.69
sstr6	260	359	37.82	139	192	38.26	400	478	19.56	483	600	23.76	507	614	20.92
dst7	313	360	14.75	180	189	4.98	419	466	11.37	530	661	24.89	533	585	9.78
mnst	308	349	13.55	157	197	25.44	368	454	23.43	496	599	20.59	499	582	16.66
sstr2r	318	347	9.06	159	173	8.46	463	577	24.77	581	716	23.19	586	720	22.82
gsa10	337	403	19.65	174	216	24.00	384	532	38.62	528	711	34.71	533	677	26.78
mean			23.66			20.43			27.41			22.66			22.96
max			45.82			38.26			54.70			34.71			32.69

The results in Table 5 show that applying the proposed method can improve performance, on average, by 20.64% to 26.23% (for different FPGA series) when implementing with the *Balanced* option. The maximum performance increase achieved is 59.17% for test example *gsa10* targeted at Cyclone IV E FPGA devices. Similarly, with the *Performance* option (as shown in Table 6), the maximum clock frequency increases significantly, by an average of 20.43% to 27.41%, and in the best case a performance gain of 54.7% was achieved (for test example *std2r* implemented in the MAX 10 device).

Table 7 shows the results of area utilizing, where C and C^* are the number of LUTs used in the design using the conventional synthesis method and the proposed synthesis method, respectively; "%" is the percentage increase in hardware when using the

Table 7. Area comparison results

Example	MAX II			MAX V			MAX 10			Cyclone IV E			Cyclone IV GX		
	C	C*	%	C	C*	%	C	C*	%	C	C*	%	C	C*	%
prim2r	34	41	20.59	34	41	20.59	38	38	0.00	37	37	0.00	38	37	−2.63
std2r	34	39	14.71	34	39	14.71	38	40	5.26	37	39	5.41	37	39	5.41
dst	87	92	5.75	87	92	5.75	76	89	17.11	75	88	17.33	75	88	17.33
gsa4d	90	96	6.67	90	96	6.67	74	89	20.27	73	88	20.55	73	88	20.55
gsa5d	93	94	1.08	93	94	1.08	89	87	−2.25	88	86	−2.27	88	86	−2.27
sstr6	95	82	−13.68	95	82	−13.68	90	69	−23.33	88	68	−22.73	88	68	−22.73
dst7	46	59	28.26	46	59	28.26	48	55	14.58	46	54	17.39	46	54	17.39
mnst	120	107	−10.83	120	107	−10.83	109	100	−8.26	108	99	−8.33	108	99	−8.33
sstr2r	74	77	4.05	74	77	4.05	52	59	13.46	51	58	13.73	51	58	13.73
gsa10	84	85	1.19	84	85	1.19	69	79	14.49	68	78	14.71	68	78	14.71
mean			5.78			5.78			5.13			5.58			5.31

proposed synthesis method. The results indicate that mainly we have a small increase in area by an average of 5.13% to 5.78% (for different FPGAs), but in some cases even a cost reduction is obtained.

5   Conclusions

In this paper a new method for the design of high-speed ASM controllers was presented. The method is based on the introduction of additional FSM states, which allows to simplify the transition functions logics to implement all the functions in the faster one-LUT-level structures. The experimental results show that the proposed synthesis method provides high improvement of speed with a rather small hardware overhead. Because the method is applied at the early stage of converting the ASM to the state machine HDL description, it can be used with other known optimization methods to improve the performance result.

Acknowledgments. This work was supported by grant S/WI/3/2018 (from the Bialystok University of Technology, Bialystok, Poland) founded by the Polish Ministry of Science and Higher Education.

References

1. Glushkov, V.: Automaton theory and formal microprogram transformation. Cybernetics **1**, 1–8 (1968)
2. Clare, C.: Designing Logic Systems Using the State Machines. McGraw-Hill, New York (1973)
3. Green, D.H., Chughtai, M.A.: Use of multiplexers in the direct synthesis of ASM-based designs. IEEE Proc. E, Comput. Digit. Tech. **133**(4), 194–200 (1986)
4. Baranov, S.: Logic Synthesis for Control Automata. Kluwer Academic Publisher, Boston (1994)

5. Lu, J.Y., Kim, J.D., Chin, S.K.: Hardware composition with hardware flowcharts and process algebras. In: 2nd IEEE International Conference on Engineering of Complex Computer Systems Proceedings, pp. 352–364. IEEE, Montreal, Canada (1996)

6. Baranov, S.: Minimization of algorithmic state machines. In: 24th Euromicro Conference Proceedings, pp. 176–179. IEEE, Vasteras, Sweden (1998)

7. Levin, I., Sinelnikov, V., Karpovsky, M.: Synthesis of ASM-based self-checking controllers. In: Euromicro Symposium on Digital Systems Design Proceedings, pp. 87–93. IEEE, Warsaw, Poland (2001)

8. De Pablo, S., Cáceres, S., Cebrián, J.A., Berrocal, M.: A proposal for ASM ++ diagrams. In: Design and Diagnostics of Electronic Circuits and Systems Proceedings, pp. 1–4. IEEE, Krakow, Poland (2007)

9. Barkalov, A., Titarenko, L., Bieganowski, J.: Reduction in the number of LUT elements for control units with code sharing. Int. J. Appl. Math. Comput. Sci. **20**(4), 751–761 (2010)

10. Barkalov, A., Titarenko, L., Bieganowski, J.: Logic Synthesis for Finite State Machines Based on Linear Chains of States. SSDC, vol. 113. Springer, Cham (2018). https://doi.org/10.1007/978-3-319-59837-6

11. Hertwig, A., Wunderlich, H.: Fast controllers for data dominated applications. In: European Design and Test Conference (ED & TC 1997) Proceedings, pp. 84–89. IEEE, Paris, France (1997)

12. Czerwinski, R., Kania, D.: State assignment and optimization of ultra-high-speed FSMs utilizing tristate buffers. ACM Trans. Des. Autom. Electron. Syst. (TODAES) **22**(1) (2016). Article 3

13. Kim, E., Lee, D., Saito, H., Nakamura, H., Lee, J., Nanya, T.: Performance optimization of synchronous control units for datapaths with variable delay arithmetic units. In: ASP-DAC Asia and South Pacific Design Automation Conference Proceedings, pp. 816–819. IEEE, Kitakyushu (2003)

14. Weng, S., Kuo, Y., Chang, S.: Timing optimization in sequential circuit by exploiting clock-gating logic. ACM Trans. Des. Autom. Electron. Syst. (TODAES) **17**(2) (2012). Article 16

15. Bommu, S., O'Neill, N., Ciesielski, M.: Retiming-based factorization for sequential logic optimization. ACM Trans. Des. Autom. Electron. Syst. (TODAES) **5**(3), 373–398 (2000)

16. Huang, S.: On speeding up extended finite state machines using catalyst circuitry. In: ASP-DAC 2001 Asia and South Pacific Design Automation Conference (DAC 2006) Proceedings, pp. 583–588. IEEE, Yokohama (2001)

17. Gupta, G.R., Gupta, M., Panda, P.R.: Rapid estimation of control delay from high-level specifications. In: 43rd Design Automation Conference Proceedings, pp. 455–458. ACM, San Francisco, USA (2010)

18. Salauyou, V., Klimowicz, A., Grzes, T., Bulatowa, I., Dimitrowa-Grekow, T.: Synthesis methods of finite state machines implemented in package ZUBR. In: 6th International Conference Computer-Aided Design of Discrete Devices (CAD DD2007) Proceedings, pp. 53–56. National Academy of Sciences of Belarus, Minsk (2007)

Impact of Address Generation on Multimedia Embedded VLIW Processors

Guillermo Talavera[1]([⊠]) (iD), Antoni Portero[2]([⊠]) (iD), and Francky Catthoor[3]([⊠]) (iD)

[1] Institut de Bioenginyeria de Catalunya, Baldiri Reixac, 10-12,
08028 Barcelona, Spain
gtalavera@ibecbarcelona.eu
[2] IT4Innovations National Supercomputing, Center VSB-Technical University
of Ostrava, 17. listopadu 15/2172, 708 33 Ostrava - Poruba, Czech Republic
antonio.portero@vsb.cz
[3] imec, Kapeldreef 75, 3001 Leuven, Belgium
catthoor@imec.be
http://www.ibecbarcelona.eu, http://www.it4i.cz, http://www.imec-int.com

Abstract. Embedded multimedia devices need to be more and more energy efficient while dealing with applications of increasing complexity. These applications are characterised by having complex array index manipulation, a large number of data accesses and require high performant specific computation at low energy consumption due to battery life.

In many cases, the principal component of such systems is a programmable processor, and often, a Very Large Instruction Word (VLIW) processor (alone or integrated with other processor cores). A VLIW processor seems a good solution providing enough performance at low power with sufficient programmability but optimising the access to the data is a crucial issue for the success of those devices. Some modern embedded architectures include a dedicated unit that works in parallel with the central computing elements ensuring efficient feed and storage of the data from/to the data path: the Address Generation Unit.

In this paper, we present an experimental work that shows, on real and complete applications and benchmarks, the impact of address generation in VLIW-like processor architectures. We see how address generation in multimedia embedded systems has a very significant contribution to the energy budget and a careful analysis an optimisation is needed to extend battery life as much as possible while keeping enough performance to satisfy the quality of service requirements. We also present the framework used to create and evaluate the impact of address generation on the overall system.

Keywords: Address generation · VLIW processors
Energy optimisation

© Springer Nature Switzerland AG 2018
K. Saeed and W. Homenda (Eds.): CISIM 2018, LNCS 11127, pp. 417–433, 2018.
https://doi.org/10.1007/978-3-319-99954-8_35

1   Introduction

The Application Specific Instruction set Processors (ASIPs) solution can provide better compromise regarding Giga-Operations per second per Watt (GOPs/W) than other hardware architectures like Field Programmable Gate Array (FPGA) and still be more flexibility than a dedicated Application Specific Integrated Circuit (ASIC). Or even x86-64 architectures with data-flow extensions [1,2]. The ASIPs have broad use in cryptography [3], computer vision [4], or neural networks [5]. Such embedded applications, as speech [6] and image recognition, high bandwidth wireless communications [7] or multimedia applications [8], are often characterised by having a complicated array index manipulation scheme, and a large number of data accesses [9]. These datasets are typically stored in main memory, which means that the processor needs to generate the address of the memory location to retrieve and store them.

Address calculations often involve linear and polynomial arithmetic expressions which have to be calculated during program execution under strict timing constraints. Memory address computation can significantly degrade the performance and increase power consumption: memory causes 50%–75% of the power consumption on embedded multimedia systems accesses [10,11]. Hence, it is essential to carry out these accesses and related addresses computations in a productive way.

Different optimisations can boost performance and reduce energy consumption. Data Transfer and Storage Exploration (DTSE) optimizations [12–16] are crucial to efficiently map data-intensive applications onto programmable platforms. Those transformations modify the initial code to minimise the load of shared memory buses, which is the main source of power consumption [10]. The data memory access related impact on energy and cycle count is usually dominant in such data-intensive applications. Hence, it is motivated that applying these transformations to the source code is initially performed without worrying yet about the impact on other components in the platform. Hence, after this optimisation stage, a direct implementation of the resulting code would lead to a high expense on addressing and local control. That is not desirable, so, in the overall methodology [12,13], a post-processing address optimisation stage is proposed where this overhead is largely removed again.

Falk et al. [19,20] give a detailed explanation on how to reduce control flow at source code level. With these techniques, the control flow overhead introduced by the previous optimisations is significantly reduced (even concerning the original code). Also related to the address generation itself, several techniques have been proposed to alleviate the cost, as shown in our review in [21]. Combining all these post-processing steps should give us already a significant reduction of the overhead. However, at the level of the address generation itself, we can go further in the improvement to provide even more optimal results. The principal contribution of this paper is to present an experimental work that shows in real and complete applications the impact (on energy consumption and performance) of the address generation on the overall system. We show how address generation plays an essential role in the multimedia embedded domain and address calculations must be done with extreme care to improve the energy efficiency and performance of the system. For our work, we used a set of real applications and benchmarks commonly used in the embedded multimedia domain and a complex architectural exploration framework.

In Sects. 2 and 3 we introduce the complete framework that allows to create and evaluate the impact of address generation on VLIW-like processor architectures. In Sect. 4 we briefly describe the set of real-life applications and benchmarks used to validate our work. Section 5 shows the experimental results of this work and finally, in Sect. 6, we conclude.

2   AGU Mapping and Exploration Framework

For the Address Generation Unit (AGU) template design, we used novel the AGU mapping and exploration framework proposed by Taniguchi et al. [23]. In this section, we summarise the AGU mapping and exploration framework based on reconfigurable AGU model. First of all, the reconfigurable AGU model is introduced, and AGU mapping framework which is performance evaluation framework is described. Then, the architecture exploration framework for reconfigurable AGU model is introduced.

2.1   Reconfigurable AGU Model

The reconfigurable AGU model is a novel AGU model for AGU architecture exploration. Reconfigurable AGU model is based on reconfigurable architecture concept and has n_{PE} PEs and their corresponding pipeline registers. Each Processing Element (PE) has a heterogeneous function with its specific latency and is fully connected to any other PE output (except its output). Because of this full connection, placement and routing do not have to be considered. For AGU architecture exploration, design parameters of the reconfigurable AGU model are (1) n_{PE} and (2) assignment of functions for each PE.

Figure 1 shows one example of the proposed reconfigurable AGU model which has four PEs. PE0 and PE1 have a latency of 1 cycle and implement *add* and *sub* instructions indicated by '+' and '−'; and PE2 has 4-cycle-latency *multiply* instruction indicated by '*'; and finally, PE3 has 30-cycles-latency *modulo* instruction indicated by '%'. Because of the full connection, the order in which the PEs are organized is not important. For example, the array would have the same functionality if PE0 was swapped with PE3. Thus, we can consider the AGU model in which any PE can be swapped with any other, as shown for example in Fig. 1.

2.2   AGU Mapping Framework

Figure 2 shows an overview of the AGU mapping framework. For a given Data Flow Graph (DFG) of address calculation and reconfigurable AGU specification, the AGU mapping framework does the scheduling and the mapping of the DFG onto a specific architecture using the Simulated Annealing algorithm to minimise cycle count. By AGU mapping framework, the DFG of address calculation is partitioned into sub-DFGs (AC0, AC1, AC2, and AC3 shown in Fig. 2) and each node is assigned to one PE in the configuration. For more information on the algorithm used for scheduling and allocation, the reader can refer to [24].

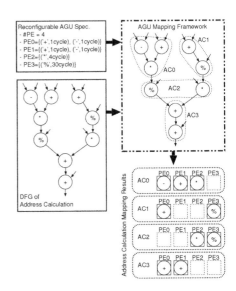

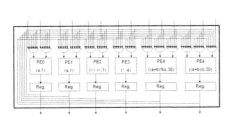

Fig. 1. Example of a reconfigurable AGU Model

Fig. 2. Overview of AGU mapping Framework

2.3   AGU Exploration Framework

In this section, we explain the proposed AGU exploration technique. The AGU exploration framework iterates over the AGU mapping (as explained in the previous section) using the AGU mapping framework over different architecture candidates in the solution space. To prune the search space of AGU architecture candidates, we assume that each PE is capable of implementing a set of small DFGs. The PE implementation pattern set includes all possible combinations of PE implementation patterns. Note that the exploration of the pattern itself is outside the scope of this paper. Various works, like [25,26] and others, tackle this problem. The AGU exploration framework iterates over all possible combinations of the PE implementation patterns corresponding to one architecture configuration. The AGU mapping framework is in turn called to perform scheduling and allocation on this architecture to evaluate its costs. Table 1 shows an example of a PE implementation pattern set. PE implementation patterns (+) and (−) indicate a PE which executes *add* instructions and *sub* instructions,

Table 1. Example of PE implementation pattern

Pattern	Specification
$(+)$	add
$(-)$	sub
$(+,-)$	add, sub

Table 2. Architecture candidates: all combination of PE implementation patterns shown in Table 1 in case of $max_{PE} = 3$

No.	#PE	Architecture candidate	#add	#sub
0	1	$(+)$	1	0
1	1	$(-)$	0	1
2	1	$(+,-)$	1	1
3	2	$(+),(+)$	2	0
4	2	$(+),(-)$	1	1
5	2	$(+),(+,-)$	2	1
6	2	$(-),(-)$	0	2
7	2	$(-),(+,-)$	1	2
8	2	$(+,-),(+,-)$	2	2
9	3	$(+),(+),(+)$	3	0
10	3	$(+),(+),(-)$	2	1
11	3	$(+),(+),(+,-)$	3	1
12	3	$(+),(-),(-)$	1	2
13	3	$(+),(-),(+,-)$	2	2
14	3	$(+),(+,-),(+,-)$	3	2
15	3	$(-),(-),(-)$	0	3
16	3	$(-),(-),(+,-)$	1	3
17	3	$(-),(+,-),(+,-)$	2	3
18	3	$(+,-),(+,-),(+,-)$	3	3

respectively. PE implementation pattern $(+,-)$ designates a PE which executes *add* or *sub* instructions.

Let n_{ptn} and m be the number of PE implementation patterns and assumed PEs, respectively. The number of architecture candidates in the solution space equals $(n_{ptn})^m$ because each PE has n_{ptn} implementation patterns. However, because of full connection of reconfigurable AGU model, the AGU can implement the same functionality as the AGU whose PEs are swapped. Therefore, the number of architecture candidates with m PEs can shrink to $_{n_{ptn}}H_m$, which means repeated m-combinations from n_{ptn} elements. Finally, the number of architecture candidates N_{cand} is described as follows:

$$N_{cand} = \sum_{m=1}^{max_{PE}} {}_{n_{ptn}}H_m = \sum_{m=1}^{max_{PE}} \frac{(n_{ptn} + m - 1)!}{m!(n_{ptn} - 1)!}, \tag{1}$$

where max_{PE} is the maximum number of PEs. Usually, the number of functional units in embedded processors is limited, and the maximum number of PEs

max_{PE} may realistically not increase so much. The number of PE implementation patterns (n_{ptn}) is expected to increase when we consider special instructions for more effective address calculation. Then, N_{cand} may explode because N_{cand} increases in factorial order of n_{ptn}.

Let min_i, and max_i be the minimum and the maximum number of instructions of type i that can be instantiated, respectively. Let n_i^{arch} be the number of instructions of type i in an architecture candidate $arch$. AGU exploration framework tries to perform a mapping only for architecture candidates which satisfy following equation.

$$\forall i (n_i^{arch} \geq min_i) \wedge (n_i^{arch} \leq max_i) = 1 \qquad (2)$$

When n_i^{DFG} means the number of instructions of type i contained in given DFG, we decide min_i and max_i as follows.

$$min_i = \begin{cases} 0 \text{ if } n_i^{DFG} = 0 \\ 1 \text{ otherwise} \end{cases} \qquad (3) \qquad\qquad max_i = \begin{cases} 1 \text{ if } n_i^{DFG} = 0 \\ n_i^{DFG} \text{ otherwise} \end{cases} \qquad (4)$$

As a practical example, Table 2 shows all architecture candidates for a given PE implementation pattern (shown in Table 1) for the case of $max_{PE} = 3$. Notice that each architecture candidate has different functionality, that is, it contains a different number of add and sub. When we assume an input DFG which consists in only add, architecture candidates No. 1, 6, and 15 cannot execute given DFG because they do not contain any add. In the same way, by focusing on the number of instructions like add, sub, etc. in each candidate, architectures can be explored effectively.

Based on the Eq. 2, the AGU exploration framework can efficiently eliminate architecture candidates that do not fall into the relevant design space, as specified by the above constraints. The elimination of candidates reduces the worst-case exploration effort significantly. For a more detailed algorithm to enumerate architecture candidate for architecture exploration, the reader can refer to [23].

3   COFFEE Framework

Architectures form the bridge between the application and the technology. Therefore, to optimise an ASIP processor architecture, the designer must take into account the application requirements. An active ASIP architecture exploration has to cover a wide range of architectures to find the one which is optimal for the application and system cost trade-offs (e.g. reduce the energy consumption while providing the required real-time constraints and quality). From the implementation side, it is essential to take the physical design method (e.g. custom design vs standard cell design) and high-level technology inputs (e.g. poor interconnect scaling in deep sub-micron technologies, leakage) into account early in the design flow to ensure a more optimal outcome. If the implementation allows the designer to give guidelines on the floorplan, it is essential to take this into account. Architecture exploration, therefore, forms the cornerstone of any processor design. Note that variability and reliability are also crucial issues in deep sub-micron technologies, but the mitigation of these effects can be handled in a complementary way [27,28] that is compatible with our approach. Therefore this part is not tackled in this work.

3.1   Feenecs Template

Figure 3 combines the optimizations for different components that have been presented in the previous Sections. The presented processor design is still a template and architecture exploration within this template is required to find the optimal architecture for one application or a set of applications. Based on the performance requirements and initial feedback from synthesis for a certain technology node, the pipeline depth of this in-order processor has to be fixed.

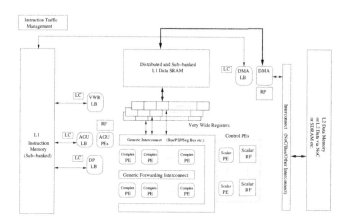

Fig. 3. Complete high level efficient architecture: FEENECS architecture template

The most notable components of Fig. 3 are the data memory hierarchy, that consists of an L2 background data memory that is accessed through a generic global communication architecture (Network on Chip, Bus or other). Data is transferred from this L2 memory into the L1 data memory, a scratchpad memory, by the direct memory access controller. From there on, complete lines of the scratch-pad memories are moved to very wide register files for data parallel computations and single values can be copied to a scalar register file. The AGU units are also placed close to the background or foreground memory units between which organise the transfers. Preferably they are evenly split over reading and write ports so that they can be fully local to the port they are providing addresses to. The data-path functional units also come in two types: (1) a set of complex functional units that balance data-level parallelism and instruction-level parallelism (a set of "Single-Input-Multiple-Data" functional units). Also, use extensive forwarding to reduce register file accesses, and (2) a set of functional control units that are of a scalar type and access the scalar register file. On the instruction side, the L1 Instruction memory can be accessed directly by the control code, but for the kernels, a set of physically distributed loop buffers are used (placed next to the components they control). These loop buffers also have distributed control and can synchronise at specific points using local controllers to improve the efficiency of the instruction memory As they do not follow a single program counter, the number of NOP (no operation) entries is massively reduced in applications that exhibit very different activation frequencies for the different components. The communications between different processors of this type (interprocessor communication) are compatible with other related work like [29], while the intra-processor connections can be optimised using techniques [30] like segmented buses.

In this architecture template, the implementation and layout guidelines that have been discussed in the previous sections have been used to group the different architectural components based on their communication requirements to reduce the interconnect cost. Hierarchically structured hardware design using *Data-path Generation* [31] and *Energy-aware floor-planning* [32] can be used to propagate these constraints down to the physical implementation.

The set of architecture modifications that is presented above has led to the filing of a patent, as described in [33]. To make use of any efficient architecture, a scalable and retargetable compiler that can compile to it is required. The next section explains a high-level compiler flow to perform a phase decoupled compilation for such a processor template.

3.2   Energy Estimation Model

The COFFEE framework enables early estimates with enough accuracy since, at this abstraction level, the full hardware description is not yet needed and therefore exploration can be faster. After architectural exploration and optimisations, when the hardware is fixed, a complete and more accurate gate level simulation and estimation are then possible. In the COFFEE framework, different instances of the components of the processor (register file, arithmetic logic unit, pipeline registers) were designed at register transfer level with an optimised VHDL description. For each instance, logic synthesis is done with the UMC90nm general purpose standard cell library from Faraday [34] also used for the ASIC power model [22]. The result of the whole process is a library of parametrised energy models. The energy per activation and leakage power for the different components are estimated from the activity information from gate level simulation and the parasitic information. Since memories are highly optimised custom hardware blocks, the standard cell hardware design flow cannot be used. Instead, different memories were modelled using a commercial memory compiler from Artisan [35]. Finally, the precomputed library contains the energy annotations (dynamic and leakage) for various components of the processor using standard cell flow, and for memories, using the commercial memory compiler. A detailed description of the complete energy model is fully described in Raghavan et al. [36].

4   Benchmarks and Applications

A benchmark is a standard program or set of programs which can run on a computer to assess the relative performance. It must be representative of the application domain to stress the critical processor and compiler features necessary to run efficiently. In this work, we used several benchmarks and some complete applications to test the effectiveness of the proposed AGU.

4.1   Benchmarks:

The MediaBench [38] benchmark suite includes typical applications from the multimedia domain that are expected to be part of representative future multimedia applications. This includes video, image and audio coding and decoding, encryption algorithms, and 3D rendering.

JPEG: JPEG is a standardised compression method for full-colour and grey-scale images. JPEG is lossy, meaning that the output image is not precisely identical to the input image. Two applications are extracted from the JPEG source code; *cjpeg* does image compression and *djpeg* does decompression.

ME: The ME (Motion Estimation) is a fundamental part of video compression used by MPEG 1, 2 and four as well as many other video codecs. The ME is the process of determining motion vectors that describe the transformation from one 2D image to another; usually from adjacent frames in a video sequence. The motion vectors are related to the complete picture (global motion estimation) or specific parts, such as rectangular blocks, arbitrarily shaped patches or even per pixel. The motion vectors may be composed of a translational model or multiple other models that approximate the motion of a video camera, such as translation, rotation and in all three dimensions.

MPEG2: MPEG-2 is the current dominant standard for high-quality digital video transmission. The vital computing kernel is a discrete cosine transform for coding and the inverse transform for decoding. The two applications used are mpeg2enc and mpeg2dec for encoding and decoding respectively.

GSM: European GSM 06.10 provisional standard for full-rate speech transcoding, prI-ETS 300 036, which uses residual pulse excitation/long-term prediction coding at 13 kbit/s. GSM 06.10 compresses frames of 160 13-bit samples (8 kHz sampling rate, i.e. a frame rate of 50 Hz) into 260 bits.

ADCPM: Adaptive differential pulse code modulation is one of the simplest and oldest forms of audio coding. Adcpm decode is the decoder and adpcm encode is the encoder.

4.2 Real-Life Applications

In addition to the benchmarks, we also want to evaluate the proposed techniques with a consistent set of real-life applications.

Cavity_detector: The cavity detection benchmark [39] is part of a medical imaging application to detect cavities on tomography scans. The role of the application that is used as a benchmark is a chain of custom imaging filters.

QSDPCM: Quad-tree Structured Difference Pulse Code Modulation algorithm is an inter-frame compression technique for video images. It involves a hierarchical motion estimation step, and a quad-tree based encoding of the motion compensated a frame-to-frame difference signal.

MPEG4: The MPEG4 is a complete application that drove our work on [22].

5 Experimental Results and Final Template

Data-flow dominated applications are based on intensive computations in the innermost loops of the codes, and Amdahl's law [40] argues in favour of speeding up these parts of the algorithms. Moreover, accessing memories to bring data to the data path is costly regarding energy. As we saw in [22], many optimisations are possible, both architecture-dependent and independent. Those optimisations are crucial to improve speed and the energy efficiency but introduce a high expense on addressing and local control, for example by adding complex modulo operations. To obtain a sound general address generation unit capable of dealing with many multimedia applications efficiently, we have used the applications and benchmarks mentioned in the previous section in the AGU mapping framework with different architectures. The three real-life applications (cavity detector, QSDPCM and MPEG4) and the ME benchmark have been optimised with some DTSE [12–16] and some control flow techniques explained in [17–20] before the AGU exploration.

In this work, we have considered the three innermost loops being k, j and i the iterators of the loops from the outer to the inner iterator as we can see in Fig. 4.

```
for (k=init_val_k; k<lim_val_k; k++){
  for (j=init_val_j; j<lim_val_j; j++){
    for (i=init_val_i; i<lim_val_i; i++){
      code_to_be_executed;
    }
  }
}
```

Fig. 4. Aspect of the inner most loops of the different benchmarks

Table 3 shows the needed operations used in the inner loops of the different benchmarks or applications and these operations are the ones required to be mapped to the PEs of the AGU. We can then construct the template AGU which

Table 3. Operations needed for the different benchmarks and applications

Benchmark/ application	Source code optimizations	Operations needed
JPEG	NO	$i + 1$
		$i - 1$
MPEG2	NO	$i + 1$
		$i - 1$
		$i{*}j$
		$i >> j$
GSM	NO	$i + 1$
		$i - 1$
		$i{*}j$
		$i >> j$
ADCPM	NO	$i + 1$
		$i - 1$
		$i >> j$
ME	Yes	$i + 1$
		$i{*}j$
		$(i + j)\%N_0$
		$(i + j)/N_0 * N_1 + N_2$
Cavity Detector	Yes	$i - j - k$
		$i{*}j$
		$i + j + k$
		$i + j$
		$i - j$
		$i+j{*}N_0+N_1$
QSDPCM	Yes	$i + j$
		$i{*}j$
		$i+j+k-N_0$
		$i{*}N_0 + j$
		$(i+j){*}N_0+k$
MPEG4	Yes*	$i + N_0$
		$i{*}j$
		$i >> j$

Table 4. Operations on the PE

PE	Implements	Latency
PE0	$\pm$	1
PE1	$\pm$	1
PE2	$<< >>$	1
PE3	$*$	4
PE4	$(a + b)\%c$	30
PE5	$(a + b)/c$	30

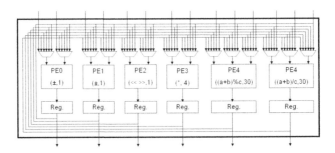

Fig. 5. Reconfigurable AGU template

is capable of dealing with these operations speeding up the process of address generation. Table 4 shows the proposed PEs for the AGU template targeting the applications and benchmarks used, and Fig. 5 shows the template in a similar fashion to Fig. 1.

Once the topology of the PEs of the AGU has been determined, we can then integrate this AGU in the machine description used in the COFFEE framework (Sect. 3) to simulate the behaviour of the processor. For those experiments, we used two different processors. The first processor (a.k.a base processor) was built similarly to the Texas Instruments TMS c67 family [37]. This digital signal processor has two clusters with four functional units each, as we can see in Fig. 6. Each cluster has one functional unit with a multiplier, and the remaining functional units have a general arithmetic and logic unit and a shifter; besides hardware support for cluster copy and branch operations. The second version of the processor (processor with AGUs) substitutes, in each cluster, two simple, functional units for the reconfigurable AGU (see Fig. 7).

Not all the hardware resources are used in all cases. For example, QSDPCM and ME need the complete set of PEs on Table. 4 but MPEG2, MPEG4 and cavity detector do not need the PE4 and PE5 [$(a + b)\%c$ and $(a + b)/c$] since they are are not used in these algorithms. For our experiments, we used the complete template (Fig. 5) for the QSDPCM and ME applications and a reduced version of the template without the PE4 and PE5 for the rest of the applications. If we know in advance that just a small set of applications is executed, tuning the template for the specific applications gives us better results, regarding the area. Because of the reduction of unnecessary hardware and concerning energy, because with fewer hardware resources accessing the foreground memories, fewer ports are needed. Hence, the energy per access of the memory is smaller.

Figures 8 and 9 show the different implementations of the benchmarks and applications (except for the MPEG4 application. The "original" and "optimized" results were run with the base processor (Fig. 6) and the AGU with the "processor with the reconfigurable AGU" (Fig. 7). As we can see, the usage of a specific AGU improves both cycles and energy consumption. In the case of the optimised codes (Fig. 8), we can see gains in the execution cycles of 30% compared to the optimised versions and between 50 and 60% compared to the original versions.

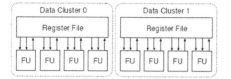
Fig. 6. Base processor

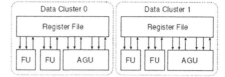
Fig. 7. Processor with the reconfigurable AGU

Regarding the energy, the improvements over the optimised code are around 20% and compared to the original implementations around 50%. These results show the effectiveness of adding specialised AGUs explicitly dedicated to the costly operations needed, effects of the DTSE optimisations. In Fig. 9, we notice that even in the case of a benchmark without that complex addressing operations (no DTSE optimisations accomplished), which could be easily managed without an AGU, we can notice a considerable improvement: between 10% and 30% in execution cycles and between 15% and 33% regarding energy. Adding the AGUs offers more explicit parallelism to the compiler which can then execute more instructions at the same time, and hence, finish earlier the needed calculations. The hardware overhead introduced by the AGUs is shown in Fig. 10. The first configuration corresponds to the base processor (Fig. 6) which is used as a reference. For the comparisons, we just considered the functional units and processing elements (not foreground memory). For the experiments we used the processor presented in Fig. 7 but with different configurations of the AGUs. For the QSD-PCM and ME we used the complete template and the overhead introduced is considerable: around 200%. This is basically because with this configuration we removed four basic functional units (with a general ALU and a shifter) and we replace them with two AGUs with a modulo and a divider processing element each, and the hardware needed to implement these operations is large. This substantial overhead could have been partially reduced using the next configuration ("processor with 2 AGUs with shared modulo and divider operations"), since

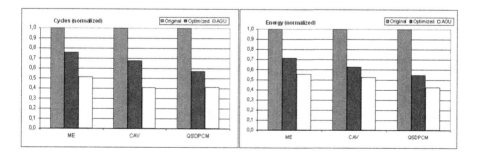

Fig. 8. (a) Cycles and (b) Energy comparison of the different benchmarks/applications after optimizations and AGU inclusion.

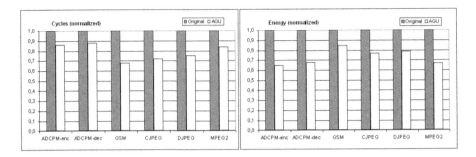

Fig. 9. (a) Cycles and (b) Energy comparison of the different benchmarks/applications after AGU inclusion.

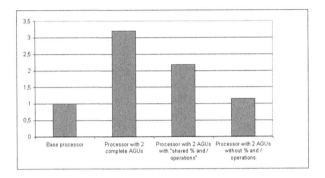

Fig. 10. Hardware overhead introduced by the different configurations of the processor

modulo operations are based on divider operations and, hence, the related hardware is similar. In this case, the hardware overhead would have been smaller, but the execution time and the energy needed would have been higher. As seen in [21], area for AGUs is not anymore a crucial metric and is not a critical metric in future designs. Nevertheless, it has to be taken into account. Even with the configuration of the two complete AGUs, the processor core accounts for less than 10% of the total processor taking into account data and instruction memories, register files, pipeline registers and functional units.

The rest of the applications and benchmarks used the "processor with 2 AGUs without modulo or divider operations". In this case, the hardware overhead accounts for 15% of the processor core.

6   Conclusions

In this paper, we have shown the importance of the impact of the address generation calculations on multimedia applications and how crucial is to explore and evaluate this impact on the overall design efficiently. For that exploration, we have introduced an AGU exploration framework which is capable of exploring many architecture candidates which satisfy constraints and then insert those results on a complete ASIP architecture exploration framework. With this entire framework, we have identified the primary computing elements required to perform an adequate address generation, and we have used the architecture and compiler simulator framework, to validate our results with several benchmarks an real applications. In all the cases we have seen that exploring and optimising the address generation brings considerable improvements in energy and cycle count on already optimised codes and even on non-optimized ones.

Acknowledgment. This work is supported by the Ministry of Education, Youth and Sports of the National Programme for Sustainability II (NPU II) under the project "IT4Innovations excellence in science – LQ1602" and by the EC under the grant HARPA FP7-612069.

References

1. Ho, N., et al.: Simulating a multi-core x86-64 architecture with hardware ISA extension supporting a data-flow execution model. In: AIMS 2014, pp. 264–269 (2014). https://doi.org/10.1109/AIMS.2014.41
2. Ho, N., et al.: Enhancing an x86_64 multi-core architecture with data-flow execution support. In: CF 2015. ACM, New York (2015). Article 41, 2 pp. https://doi.org/10.1145/2742854.2742896
3. Huo, Y., Liu, D.: High-throughput area-efficient processor for 3GPP LTE cryptographic core algorithms. In: 28th IEEE International Conference on Application-Specific Systems, Architectures and Processors, ASAP, p. 210 (2017)
4. Zhang, B., Zhao, C., Mei, K., Zhao, J., Zheng, N.: Hierarchical and parallel pipelined heterogeneous SoC for embedded vision processing. IEEE Trans. Circuits Syst. Video Technol. **28**, 1434–1444 (2018). https://doi.org/10.1109/TCSVT.2017.2665489
5. Iandola, F., Keutzer, K.: Keynote: small neural nets are beautiful: enabling embedded systems with small deep-neural-network architectures. In: 2017 International Conference on Hardware/Software Codesign and System Synthesis (CODES+ISSS), Seoul, pp. 1–10 (2017). https://doi.org/10.1145/3125502.3125606
6. Bouraoui, H., Jerad, Ch., Chattopadhyay, A., Hadj-Alouane, N.B.: Hardware architectures for embedded speaker recognition applications: a survey. ACM Trans. Embed. Comput. Syst. **16**(3) (2017). Article 78, 28 pp. https://doi.org/10.1145/2975161
7. Yoshida, N., Lanante, L., Nagao, Y., Kuron,ki, M., Ochi, H.: A hybrid HW/SW 802.11ac/ax system design platform with ASIP implementation. In: 2017 International Symposium on Intelligent Signal Processing and Communication Systems (ISPACS), Xiamen, pp. 827–831 (2017). https://doi.org/10.1109/ISPACS.2017.8266590
8. Khan, S., Rashid, M., Javaid, F.: A high performance processor architecture for multimedia applications. Comput. Electr. Eng. **66**, 14–29 (2017). https://doi.org/10.1016/j.compeleceng
9. Kuhn, P.: Algorithms, Complexity Analysis and VLSI Architectures for MPEG-4 Estimation. Kluwer, Norwell (2004)

10. Wuytack, S., Catthoor, F., Nachtergaele, L., De Man, H.: Power exploration for data-dominated video applications. In: ISLPED 1996: Proceedings of the 1996 International Symposium on Low Power Electronics and Design, pp. 359–364. IEEE Press, Piscataway (1996)

11. Moolenaar, D., Nachtergaele, L., Catthoor, F., De Man, H.: System-level power exploration for MPEG-2 decoder on embedded cores: a systematic approach. J. VLSI Sig. Process. Syst., 395–404 (1997)

12. Catthoor, F.: Data Access and Storage Management for Embedded Programmable Processors. Kluwer, New York (2002). https://doi.org/10.1007/978-1-4757-4903-8

13. Catthoor, F., Balasa, F., Greef, E.D., Nachtergaele, L.: Custom Memory Management Methodology: Exploration of Memory Organization for Embedded Multimedia System Design. Kluwer Academic Publisher, US (1998). https://doi.org/10.1007/978-1-4757-2849-1

14. Catthoor, F., Dutt, N.: Hot topic session: how to solve the current memory access and data transfer bottlenecks: at the processor architecture or at the compiler level? In: DATE (2000)

15. Catthoor, F.: Energy-delay efficient data storage and transfer architectures and methodologies: current solutions and remaining problems. J. VLSI Sig. Process. **21**, 219–231 (1999)

16. Gonzalez, R., Horowitz, M.: Energy dissipation in general purpose microprocessors. IEEE J. Solid-State Circuits **31**, 1277–1284 (1996)

17. Falk, H., Marwedel, P.: Control flow driven splitting of loop nests at the source code level. In: DATE 2003: Proceedings of the Conference on Design, Automation and Test in Europe, pp. 410–415. IEEE Computer Society, Washington (2003)

18. Falk, H., Verma, M.: Combined data partitioning and loop nest splitting for energy consumption minimization. In: Schepers, H. (ed.) SCOPES 2004. LNCS, vol. 3199, pp. 137–151. Springer, Heidelberg (2004). https://doi.org/10.1007/978-3-540-30113-4_11

19. Falk, H., Marwedel, P.: Source Code Optimization Techniques for Data Flow Dominated Embedded Software. Springer, New York (2004). https://doi.org/10.1007/978-1-4020-2829-8

20. Falk, H.: Control flow driven code hoisting at the source code level. In: ODES 2005: Proceedings of The 3rd Workshop on Optimizations for DSP and Embedded Systems, March 2005

21. Talavera, G., Jayapala, M., Carrabina, J., Catthoor, F.: Address generation optimization for embedded high-performance processors: a survey. J. Sig. Process. Syst. Sig. Image Video Technol. **53**, 271–284 (2008)

22. Portero, A., Talavera, G., Moreno, M., Carrabina, J., Catthoor, F.: Methodology for energy-flexibility space exploration and mapping of multimedia applications to multiple platform styles. IEEE Trans. Circuits Syst. Video Technol. **21**(8), 1027–1039 (2011)

23. Taniguchi, I., Raghavan, P., Jayapala, M., Catthoor, F., Takeuchi, Y., Imai, M.: Reconfigurable AGU: an address generation unit based on address calculation pattern for low energy and high performance embedded processors. IEICE Trans. Fundam. Electron. Commun. Comput. Sci. **E92.A**(4), 1161–1173 (2009)

24. Taniguchi, I., Sakanushi, K., Ueda, K., Takeuchi, Y., Imai, M.: Dynamic reconfigurable architecture exploration based on parameterized reconfigurable processor model. In: De Micheli, G., Mir, S., Reis, R. (eds.) VLSI-SoC 2006. IIFIP, vol. 249, pp. 357–376. Springer, Boston, MA (2008). https://doi.org/10.1007/978-0-387-74909-9_20

25. Biswas, P., Choudhary, V., Atasu, K., Pozzi, L., Ienne, P., Dutt, N.: Introduction of local memory elements in instruction set extensions. In: DAC 2004: Proceedings of the 41st Annual Conference on Design Automation, NY, USA, pp. 729–734 (2004)
26. Yu, P., Mitra, T.: Scalable instructions identification for instruction-set extensible processors. In: Proceedings of CASES, September 2004
27. Wang, H., Miranda, M., Catthoor, F., Dehaene, W.: Synthesis of runtime switchable Pareto buffers offering full range fine grained energy/delay trade-offs. J. Sig. Process. Syst. **52**, 193–210 (2007)
28. Wang, H., Miranda, M., Dehaene, W., Catthoor, F.: Design and synthesis of Pareto buffers offering large range run-time energy-delay trade-off via combined buffer size and supply voltage tuning. IEEE Trans. VLSI Syst. **17**, 117–127 (2009)
29. Leroy, A., Milojevic, D., Verkest, D., Robert, F., Catthoor, F.: Concepts and implementation of spatial division multiplexing forguaranteed throughput in networkson-chip. IEE Trans. Comput. **57**(9), 1182–1195 (2008)
30. Papanikolaou, A.: Application-driven software configuration of communication networks and memory organizations. Ph.D. thesis, CS Dept., U. Gent, Belgium, December 2006
31. RWTH Aachen - University of Technology. DPG User Manual Version 2.8, October 2005. http://www.eecs.rwth-aachen.de/dpg/info.html
32. Guo, J.: Analysis and optimization of intra-tile communication network. Ph.D. thesis, ESAT/EE Dept., K.U.Leuven, August 2008
33. Raghavan, P., Catthoor, F.: Ultra low power asip (application-domain specific instruction-set processor) micro-computer. EU Patent Filed EP 1 701 250 A1, September 2006
34. Faraday Technology Corporation: Faraday UMC 90 nm RVT Standard Cell Library (2007)
35. ARM: Artisan Memory Generator. http://www.arm.com/products/physicalip/memory.html
36. Raghavan, P., Lambrechts, A., Absar, J., Jayapala, M., Catthoor, F., Verkest, D.: COFFEE: COmpiler framework for energy-aware exploration. In: Stenström, P., Dubois, M., Katevenis, M., Gupta, R., Ungerer, T. (eds.) HiPEAC 2008. LNCS, vol. 4917, pp. 193–208. Springer, Heidelberg (2008). https://doi.org/10.1007/978-3-540-77560-7_14
37. IDSPS Fixed/Floating Point Digital Signal Processor (TI TMS320c67). http://www.ti.com/product/TMS320C6748. Accessed February 2018
38. Lee, C., Potkonjak, M., Mangione-Smith, W.H.: Mediabench: a tool for evaluating and synthesizing multimedia and communications systems. In: MICRO 30: Proceedings of the 30th Annual ACM/IEEE International Symposium on Microarchitecture, pp. 330–335. IEEE Computer Society (1997)
39. Bister, M., Taeymans, Y., Cornelis, J.: Automated segmentation of cardiac MR images. In: 1989 Proceedings of the Computers in Cardiology, pp. 215–218, September 1989
40. Amdahl, G.M.: Validity of the single processor approach to achieving large scale computing capabilities. In: AFIPS 1967 (Spring): Proceedings of the Spring Joint Computer Conference, 18–20 April 1967, NY, USA, pp. 483–485 (1967)

A Process Mining-Based Solution for Business Process Model Extension with Cost Perspective Context-Based Cost Data Analysis and Case Study

Dhafer Thabet[(✉)], Sonia Ayachi Ghannouchi,
and Henda Hajjami Ben Ghezala

RIADI Laboratory, National School of Computer Sciences, Mannouba
University, Mannouba, Tunisia
dhafer.thabet@isetso.rnu.tn,
sonia.ayachi@isgs.rnu.tn,
henda.benghezala@ensi.rnu.tn

Abstract. Several organizations look for improving their business processes in order to enhance their efficiency and competitiveness. The lack of integration between the business process model and its incurred financial cost information hampers for better decision making support allowing business process incurred cost reduction. In previous work, we proposed a solution for business process model extension with cost perspective based on process mining, independently of the business process model notation. The proposed solution provides cost data description and analysis at the process and the activity levels. Cost data analysis allows to extract knowledge about factors influencing on cost at each of the process and the activity levels. The proposed solution also involves cost data analysis through the use of classification algorithms which can be selected by the user. However, the lack of support during this selection may affect the accuracy of the obtained results. Furthermore, the performance of the same classification algorithm may vary from a case to another depending on its context: (1) data features and (2) the considered performance criteria. Thus, in this paper, we propose to adopt a context-based cost data analysis allowing to select and apply the classification algorithm the most suited to the case in hand. This supports improving the accuracy of the obtained results. In order to validate the proposed solution, a case study is conducted on the business process of a maternity department in a Tunisian clinic. The results of this case study confirm the expected goals.

Keywords: Business Process improvement · Process mining
Business Process model cost extension · Context-based cost data analysis
Classification algorithm selection

© Springer Nature Switzerland AG 2018
K. Saeed and W. Homenda (Eds.): CISIM 2018, LNCS 11127, pp. 434–446, 2018.
https://doi.org/10.1007/978-3-319-99954-8_36

1 Introduction and Research Questions

Nowadays, organizations are encountering an increasing competition. This requires not only an efficient business process management (BPM) in order to satisfy customers' requirements, but also an important need for reducing the financial cost incurred by business process (BP) execution in order to maintain organization competitiveness. Therefore, the ability of closely monitoring BP financial costs and making the required BP improvements is highly desirable [11]. On one hand, the extracted knowledge should arise from analysis of operational level data. In this context, process mining includes techniques allowing to explore and analyze event logs generated during BP execution. These event logs can be used to extend BP model with additional information useful for decision making support [15]. On the other hand, management accounting techniques allow capturing business operations costs used to produce reports for decision making support.

Nevertheless, the lack of integration between the BP model and the financial incurred cost information represents a constraint on providing better support to reduce these costs. Moreover, it is important that this integration takes into account the diversity of BP model types. Therefore, in [13, 14], we proposed a solution for the extension of BP models with cost perspective independently of their notations. The proposed solution provides cost data description and analysis at the process and the activity levels. The proposed solution provides cost data analysis based on classification algorithm selected by the user.

However, if the classification algorithm is simply selected by the user, it may negatively affect accuracy of the obtained results. Furthermore, a classification algorithm performance may vary from a case to another depending on the context (of the case in hand) which consists mainly of data features and the considered criteria of performance. Thus, in this paper, a context-based cost data analysis based on classification algorithms proposed. Moreover, a case study is conducted on the BP of a maternity department in a Tunisian clinic in order to validate the proposed solution.

The remainder of this paper is organized as follows: Sect. 2 gives an overview of the related work. Section 3 recalls the proposed general solution and describes the proposed context-based cost data analysis approach. Section 4 presents the conducted case study and a discussion of the obtained results. In Sect. 5, a summary of the contributions and future work are presented.

2 Related Work

In [9], Nauta proposed a solution as a bridge between management accounting and process mining. The general architecture of this solution consists of three main steps: (1) cost model creation; (2) event log cost annotation; and (3) cost reports creation. The cost model includes all information required to annotate event logs with cost information. The cost model and the event log are the inputs for annotating this event log with cost information. In [7, 19, 20], Low proposed a solution based on the work of Nauta. It consists of three main phases: (1) cost model creation; (2) event log cost annotation; and (3) cost analysis. The solution of Low provides cost prediction which allows to extract patterns from cost annotated event logs in order to predict the cost to be incurred by the ongoing process instance. Low's approach is also based on the solution proposed in [16] which allows to generate a transition system from event logs and to store time statistics about each state of the transition system. The solution of Conforti et al. presented in [2] is a part of a wider approach for process risks management. This approach aims at enriching the four phases of the BPM lifecycle with elements of risk management. The solution focuses on the diagnosis phase as it supports participants at the process execution level by providing risk predictions in terms of probability and gravity whenever the participant takes a decision that may lead, among others, to exceed the expected cost. Predictions are provided in the form of recommendations in order to reduce these risks. Through the study of the presented solutions, we drew that all of them are based on a single algorithm for cost analysis and do not take into account the context in hand.

3   Proposed Solution

The overall proposed solution is a general approach for BP model extension with cost perspective based on process mining, which provides context-based cost data analysis. In the following, we give a general overview of the proposed solution and we focus on the provided context-based cost data analysis.

3.1   General Overview of the Proposed Solution

The proposed approach is an extension of a BP model with cost perspective [13, 14]. The first step is to extract cost data from the annotated event log obtained through the application of Nauta's approach [9]. The second step is to associate the extracted cost data to the corresponding BP model in order to construct a cost extended BP model as an instance of a general cost-extended meta-model (High-level Process Structure - HLPS) [13, 14]. The next step allows to visualize the obtained BP model with the corresponding notation. Then, the proposed approach provides cost data handling at two levels: (1) process-level: cost data handling at this level consists in the description and the analysis of cost data related to the whole BP. Cost description allows to get views about costs incurred by the execution of the BP instances. Cost analysis allows to get deeper views on BP incurred costs by extracting and presenting knowledge about cost-influencing factors; and (2) activity-level: cost data handling at the activity level corresponds to cost description and analysis of cost data related to each activity of the BP. Cost description allows to have views about costs incurred by the execution of a user-selected activity. Cost data analysis allows to have deeper views on the activity incurred costs.

3.2   Context-Based Cost Data Analysis

Cost data analysis presented in this section is based on the application of the appropriate classification algorithm to extract knowledge about cost-influencing factors, by taking into account the context of the case in hand.

Machine Learning and Classification Algorithms. Machine learning algorithms are widely used to extract knowledge from massive data [12, 18]. Thus, we capitalize on these algorithms in order to extract tacit knowledge about factors influencing on BP incurred costs. Particularly, we focus on classification algorithms which "learn" to distinguish between classes of a training set based on some attributes. On one hand, for each process (respectively activity) instance, cost data and other associated attributes (resource, time, etc.) are available. On the other hand, we aim at knowing how these attributes may influence on the process (respectively activity) incurred costs. Otherwise, the question may be translated: how can these attributes be the cause of incurring high (or low) costs? We consider that costs are high when they exceed the expected cost. Thus, it is possible to answer to this question by using a classification algorithm with the following inputs: process (respectively activity) instances for the training set, process (respectively activity) related data for attributes, and "high cost, expected cost, and low cost" for classes.

Proposed Approach for Cost Data Analysis Based on Classification Algorithms. In order to provide cost data analysis based on a classification algorithm, it is obvious to start by looking for the algorithm with the best performance. However, in [1] and many other studies as [3, 5, 6, 8, 10, 17], authors showed that there is no best classification algorithm for all data sets. In fact, performance of a classification algorithm, mainly, depends on data features (number of instances, number of attributes, number of classes, etc.) and the considered criteria of performance (accuracy, precision, recall, etc.) As shown in Fig. 1, the proposed approach allows to analyze cost data by selecting and then applying the appropriate classification algorithm by taking into account input data features and user's preference in terms of algorithm performance. A classification algorithm is selected based on a set of criteria and from a classification algorithms database which stores different features about experiences carried out on classification algorithms. For each experience, two types of features are retained: features related to input data (classes number, attributes number, instances number, and application domain) and features related to algorithm performance (accuracy, precision, and recall). These features are defined based on comparison works in the literature. They represent an illustrative common set of features to be adopted as criteria for classification algorithm selection. The number of classes, the number of attributes, and the number of instances are derived from the input data while the application domain and priority criterion of performance are specified by the user. The application domain corresponds to the domain in which the BP belongs (health, agriculture, etc.). The priority criterion of performance is specified based on user's preferences: accuracy (required percentage of correctly classified instances among the total number of instances), precision (required percentage of correctly classified instances for a given class among the total number of classified instances of this class), and recall (required percentage of correctly classified instances among the total number of this class). Once the classification algorithm is selected, it is applied on the input data which allows to extract knowledge about the influence of the considered attributes on cost data. Results about performance of the applied algorithm can be used to enrich the classification algorithms database with a new experience.

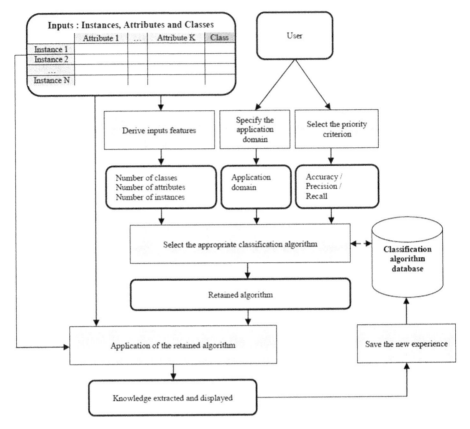

Fig. 1. Proposed approach for context-aware cost data analysis

Selection of the Appropriate Classification Algorithm. All the studied works on the comparison between different classification algorithms showed that their performances depend closely on features of the input data. Thus, as shown in Fig. 2, the proposed selection of the appropriate classification algorithm is based, firstly, on the input data features and, secondly, on user-selected priority criterion of performance. The classification algorithms database stores a set of experiences each of which is characterized by a set of features. The first step consists in representing the features of the case in hand as a vector while features of previous experiences are represented as a matrix. The selection of the appropriate classification algorithm consists in looking for the experience(s) having the closest features to those of the case in hand, among the experiences available in the classification algorithms database. Then, this could be calculated by the minimal distance between the case in hand and the available experiences. In order to calculate this distance, several functions could be adopted, such as the Euclidean or the Manhattan or Minkowski distance. In [4], the author showed that the Euclidean distance is the most used for such calculation. Thus, we retained to use the Euclidean distance to calculate distances between features of the case in hand and those of the available experiences. As shown in Fig. 2, the step for calculating Euclidean distances

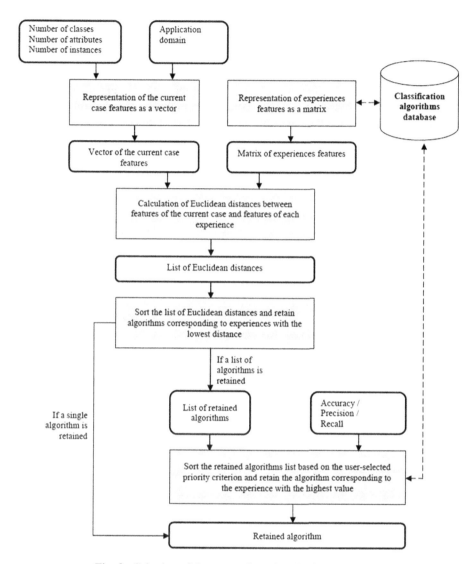

Fig. 2. Selection of the appropriate classification algorithm

provides a list of distances each of which represents the Euclidean distance between the case in hand and a particular experience.

As we are looking for the closest experience to the case in hand, the next step consists in sorting the obtained list and retaining the algorithm(s) corresponding to the smallest distance. If a single algorithm is obtained, then it is retained. However, if a list of algorithms is obtained, then the next step consists in sorting this list based on the user-selected priority criterion. Thus, the algorithm having the highest value, for the selected criterion, will be retained.

4   Case Study and Discussion

The proposed solution was implemented as standalone tool [13, 14] which takes two inputs: (1) the file representing the BP model and (2) the file representing the corresponding cost annotated event log. The main role of this tool is to extend a BP model with cost perspective based on cost data extracted from the annotated event log. Thus, the output is an extended BP model with cost perspective at process and activity levels. In this section, we present the carried out case study using the developed tool followed by a discussion about advantages and limits of the proposed solution.

4.1   Case Study

In the following, we present the case study we carried out in a Tunisian clinic by applying the proposed solution on its business process of deliveries.

Presentation of the Clinic and the Business Process of Deliveries. The considered clinic is a multidisciplinary Tunisian health facility in which we conducted a case study on its BP of deliveries. To do so, we were provided with an "anonymized" report about the acts of deliveries, in the form of a Microsoft Excel file, a sample of which is illustrated by Table 1. This report includes information about the resources involved in the delivery BP and its associated data attributes.

Table 1. Sample of the report on acts of deliveries

Admission number	Activity	Resource	Activity start	Activity end	Operating theater	Room	Participant
12000003	Admission	AdAg	01/01/2012	01/01/2012			
12000003	Simple delivery	SimTm2	01/01/2012 11:00:00	01/01/2012 12:00:00	02	Ml	P15
12000003	Billing	BillAg	03/01/2012	03/01/2012			

Business Process Model of Deliveries. Figure 3 illustrates the deliveries BP model with Petri Net notation. We defined this model according to the data contained in the report of deliveries. This BP begins with the admission of the patient.

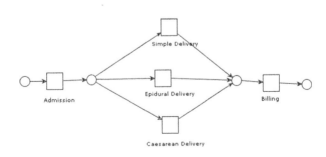

Fig. 3. BP model of deliveries (Petri Net notation)

Then, depending on several factors, often related to the patient's condition, the doctor in charge decides the type of delivery to be performed. Thus, the doctor will decide whether the patient will undergo a simple, epidural or caesarean delivery. After the delivery, the patient can pay her bill and leave the clinic.

Cost Annotated Event Log. The first step consists in transforming the report on acts of deliveries to an event log in the standard format (XES). Figure 4 illustrates a sample of the obtained event log which consists of traces each of which includes events. Each event is characterized by a set of attributes described by their types, names, and values. Figure 4 presents the end event of an instance of the "Epidural Delivery" activity.

```
<log>
    ...
    <trace>
        ...
        <event>
            <string key="Theater" value="2"/>
            <string key="org:resource" value="EpiTm4"/>
            <string key="Participant" value="P23"/>
            <string key="concept:name" value="Epidural Delivery"/>
            <string key="Room" value="M1"/>
            <string key="lifecycle:transition" value="complete"/>
            <date key="time:timestamp" value="2012-03-08T02:00:00.000+01:00"/>
        </event>
        ...
    </trace>
    ...
</log>
```

Fig. 4. Sample of the initial event log

Next, we were provided with the cost drivers corresponding to the BP of deliveries. Each cost driver is characterized by the cost type, activity, value, unit and eventually the corresponding resource and/or data variable (with its value). We used these cost drivers to define the corresponding cost model. In order to perform event log cost annotation, two inputs are required: the initial event log and the cost model corresponding to the considered BP. Thus, the application of the solution of Nauta on these inputs provided a cost annotated event log, a sample of which is illustrated in Fig. 5.

Application of the Proposed Solution: Results and Interpretation. The proposed solution takes as inputs: a file representing the BP model with the format corresponding to its notation, and the corresponding cost annotated event log file in XES format. For the BP of deliveries, we defined three files representing the BP model corresponding,

```
<log>
    ...
    <trace>
        ...
        <event>
            <string key="concept:name" value="Epidural Delivery"/>
            <float key="cost:type:Equipment Charges" value="0.306">
                <float key="0df67gdb7-67jf-4695-8d66-3d4amvd387d9" value="0.306"/>
            </float>
            ...
            <float key="cost:type:Building Charges" value="11.485">
                <float key="0df67gdb7-67jf-1234-mvog66-3d4amvd387d9" value="11.485"/>
            </float>
            <float key="cost:type:Staff Charges" value="138.213">
                <float key="f4957365-1c47-442b-9950-1bgd53g0a28d69" value="14.931"/>
                <float key="f22465d9-8a6a-4613-ab8e-01613050ef5" value="123.282"/>
            </float>
            <string key="cost:currency" value="TND"/>
            <string key="lifecycle:transition" value="complete"/>
        </event>
        ...
    </trace>
    ...
</log>
```

Fig. 5. Sample of the cost annotated event log corresponding to the BP of deliveries

respectively, to Petri Net, EPC and BPMN notations. The file representing the cost annotated event log is obtained by the application of Nauta's solution on the initial event log. Thus, the proposed solution can be applied to the case of this BP. The results are presented in the following sub-sections.

Business Process Model Cost Extension. The first step is to import the BP model file and the corresponding cost annotated event log file. The background frame of Fig. 6 displays the BP model with an arbitrarily chosen notation (BPMN) among the three tested notations (Petri Net, EPC and BPMN). Thus, the corresponding cost data description and analysis steps could be applied. The results of the application of these steps are presented in the following sub-sections.

Cost Description. In order to have a general view about the BP incurred cost, we start by getting a view on costs incurred by the activities of the BP. Thus, we choose a cost description, at the process level, by cost representation based on activities. Figure 6 illustrates the percentage of the average total cost incurred by each activity in the BP, distinguishing the one that incurred the highest average total cost.

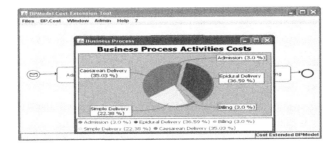

Fig. 6. Graphical representation of deliveries BP cost based on activities (process level)

Figure 6 shows that the "Epidural Delivery" activity incurred the highest total cost with a percentage of 36.59%. Thus, we opt for a more detailed view on the cost incurred by this activity. A representation of the average cost incurred by the "Epidural Delivery" activity based on cost types shows that the cost type "Staff Charges" represents the major part (318.64 TND) of the average total cost incurred by the activity "Epidural Delivery" (330.43 TND). Thus, we choose to focus on details about this cost type. The "Staff Charges" cost type corresponds to staff salaries and in the case of the "Epidural Delivery" activity, this cost type is related to salaries of teams' members executing this activity. This leads to analyze the "Staff Charges" cost type corresponding to "Epidural Delivery" activity in a deeper way by using the cost analysis offered by the proposed solution. In order to find out factors influencing on this activity incurred cost, we opt for cost analysis based on classification algorithms.

Cost Analysis. Figure 7 illustrates the window for customizing cost data analysis parameters for the "Epidural Delivery" activity using the classification algorithms. Since we are interested in analyzing "Staff Charges" cost type, it is selected in this

Fig. 7. Customizing parameters of classification algorithms-based cost analysis

window. In addition, we have an expected cost value of 317 TND, calculated on the basis of the average duration of the "Epidural Delivery" activity.

Moreover, we choose "accuracy" as a priority criterion for the selection of classification algorithms and we add a new domain of application ("Medical") since no domain, among those proposed in this window, corresponds to the domain of application of the this case. Validation of these options triggers the automatic selection of the algorithm appropriate to the case in hand according to the specified options. Thus, the retained classification algorithm is applied to the input data and the obtained results are illustrated in Fig. 8 which, mainly, shows the inferred knowledge. The retained classification algorithm is the J48 algorithm. The inferred knowledge is represented as a decision tree which can be summarized as the following of decision rules:

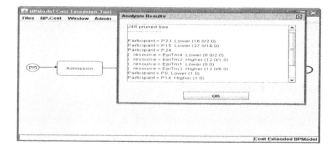

Fig. 8. Results of the analysis of "Epidural Delivery" activity cost based on classification algorithms

First, the inferred knowledge indicates that P23, P15 and P8 participated in instances of the "Epidural Delivery" activity that incurred costs lower than the expected cost value. This demonstrates the efficiency (in terms of cost) of these participants in executing this activity. Second, the participation of P14 in instances of the "Epidural Delivery" activity incurred costs higher than the expected cost value. This indicates a lack of efficiency in P14 participations in the execution of the "Epidural Delivery" activity. Third, the participation of P24 in the execution of this activity leads to a cost lower than the expected value if it is part of one of the teams EpiTm4 or EpiTm1.

However, P24's participation incurred a cost higher than the expected value if it is part of one of the teams EpiTm2 or EpiTm3. This knowledge and its interpretations could be very useful for decision makers at the considered clinic as it would support them in making decisions to reduce the costs incurred by "Epidural Delivery" activity execution. For example, on the one hand, the third inferred rule could be adopted to permanently assign the participant P24 to one of the teams EqPer1 or EqPer4 in order to ensure its efficiency in terms of cost. On the other hand, it is also possible to study the possibility of assigning the participant P14 to the teams executing the simple or caesarean delivery activities.

4.2 Discussion

The experimentation of the proposed solution with a BP from real world showed several advantages in comparison with related work. Indeed, regardless of the cost perspective integration into the BP model, the proposed solution provides context-based cost data analysis which is not provided by all the studied solutions. The proposed cost data analysis allows to select the appropriate classification algorithm according to the case in hand by capitalizing on past experiences. This allows to improve accuracy of the obtained results which would positively affect on decision making. Moreover, the conducted real case study allowed to validate the general solution.

Yet, the proposed solution has some limits. Indeed, the selection of the appropriate classification algorithm to the case in hand is based on static comparisons with past experiences, which makes results closely dependent on these experiences. Moreover, the proposed solution only focuses on the influence of organizational and data perspectives on cost perspective. Furthermore, more complex real world business processes should be considered for additional case studies in order to consolidate the proposed general solution validation.

5   Conclusion and Future Work

In this paper, we proposed an improvement of a general solution for BP model extension with cost perspective based on process mining including cost data analysis. On one hand, we enriched the proposed approach with a context-based cost data analysis based on the selection of the appropriate classification algorithm to be applied. Indeed, the proposed selection takes into account data features and performance criteria. On the other hand, for validation purpose, we applied the whole general approach on the BP of deliveries corresponding to a real world Tunisian clinic. Based on this case study, a discussion about the advantages as well as the limits of the proposed solution was presented. In future work, cost data analysis would be improved by adopting a meta-learning [1] approach to enhance accuracy of the classification algorithm selection. Moreover, the influence of the control-flow perspective on the cost perspective would be studied and included in cost data analysis. Furthermore, more complex case studies would be conducted along with an evaluation of the proposed approach.

References

1. Bhatt, N., Thakkar, A., Ganatra, A.: A survey & current research challenges in meta learning approaches based on dataset characteristics (2012). metalearning.wordpress.com. http://www.ijsce.org/attachments/File/v2i1/A0426022112.pdf. Accessed 2015
2. Conforti, R., de Leoni, M., La Rosa, M., van der Aalst, W.: Supporting Risk-Informed Decisions during Business Process Execution. CAiSE, Valencia (2013)
3. Doran, M., Stan Raicu, D., Furst, J., Settimi, R., Schipma, M., Chandler, D.: an empirical comparison of machine learning algorithms for the classification of Anthracis DNA using microarray data (2006). http://www.depaul.edu/: http://facweb.cs.depaul.edu/research/vc/publications/MLComparison_paper.pdf. Accessed 2015
4. Kalakech, M.: Sélection semi-supervisée d'attributs: application à la classification de textures couleur, Lille (2011)
5. Khorshid, M., Abou-El-Enien, T., Soliman, G.: A comparison among support vector machine and other machine learning classification algorithms (2015). http://www.ipasj.org/. http://ipasj.org/IIJCS/Volume3Issue5/IIJCS-2015-05-11-23.pdf. Accessed 2015
6. Kotsiantis, S.: Supervised machine learning: a review of classification techniques (2007). https://datajobs.com.   https://datajobs.com/data-science-repo/Supervised-Learning-[SB-Kotsiantis].pdf. Accessed 2015
7. Low, W.Z.: Cost-aware workflow systems: support for cost mining and cost reporting, Queensland (2011)
8. Narwal, S., Mintwal, K.: www.ijarcsse.com. http://www.ijarcsse.com/docs/papers/Volume_3/12_December2013/V3I12-0140.pdf. Accessed 2015
9. Nauta, W.E.: Towards cost-awareness in process mining, Eindhoven (2011)
10. Nitze, I., Schulthess, U., Asche, H.: Comparaison of machine learning algorithms random forests, artificial neural network and support vector machine to maximum likelihood for supervised crop type classification. In: GEOBIA, Rio de Janeiro (2012)
11. QUT BPM Discipline: Cost-aware business process management (2013). http://yawlfoundation.org/cost/costreporting.html. Accessed 2014
12. Rozinat, A.: Process Mining: Conformance and Extension. University Press Facilities, Eindhoven (2010)
13. Thabet, D., Ghannouchi, S.A., Ben Ghezala, H.H.: General solution for business process model extension with cost perspective based on process mining. In: International Conference on Software Engineering Advances (ICSEA 2016), Rome (2016)
14. Thabet, D., Ghannouchi, S.A., Ben Ghezala, H.H.: Towards a general solution for business process model extension with cost perspective based on process mining. In: International Business Information Management (IBIMA 2016), Seville (2016)
15. van der Aalst, W.M.: Process Mining: Discovery, Conformance and Enhancement. Springer, Heidelberg (2011). https://doi.org/10.1007/978-3-642-19345-3
16. van der Aalst, W., Schonenberg, M., Song, M.: Time prediction based on process mining. Inf. Syst. 36(2), 450–475 (2011)
17. Williams, N., Zander, S., Armitage, G.: A preliminary performance comparison of five machine learning algorithms for practical IP traffic flow classification (2006). http://sigcomm.org/. http://ccr.sigcomm.org/online/files/p7-williams.pdf. Accessed 2015

18. Witten, I., Frank, E.: Data Mining: Practical Machine Learning Tools and Techniques. Morgan Kaufmann, San Francisco (2005)
19. Wynn, M.T., Low, W.Z., ter Hofstede, A.H., Nauta, W.: A framework for cost-aware process management: cost reporting and cost prediction. J. Univers. Comput. Sci. **20**(3), 406–430 (2014)
20. Wynn, M.T., Low, W.Z., Nauta, W.: A framework for cost-aware process management: generation of accurate and timely management accounting cost reports (2013)

Various Aspects of Computer Security

Model of Secure Data Storage
in the Cloud for Mobile Devices

Mateusz Kłos[1] and Imed El Fray[1,2(✉)]

[1] Faculty of Computer Science,
West Pomeranian University of Technology, Szczecin, Poland
{mklos,ielfray}@wi.zut.edu.pl
[2] Faculty of Applied Informatics and Mathematics,
Warsaw University of Life Sciences - SGGW, Warsaw, Poland
imed_el_fray@sggw.pl

Abstract. Storing data in the cloud environment becomes more and more popular for users and also for entrepreneurs. It offers high scalability, efficiency and good price. However, it's not always secure, even if providers ensures about high security of their service. "Arms race" never stops, attackers have sophisticated tools and often specialized knowledge. Combination of these two may result in danger for data stored in clouds. Furthermore, by uploading data on cloud, we're giving away control about them. Rapid technological progress and popularity of mobile devices results with users increasing awareness about threats. On the other hand, there's not as many solutions for mobile devices as for desktop devices. Also their quality is not always very high. Proposed model reduces the role of "third-parties", offering much more control for user, the owner of stored data.

Keywords: Data storage · Cloud computing · Mobile device
Mobile device security · Raspberry pi

1   Introduction

The concept of cloud computing exists for over a decade. Furthermore, most of users use clouds every day [1]. Every online service offering sending and receiving e-mails, watching videos, playing music, storing files etc. probably utilizes cloud computing. This phenomenon is constantly improving and it's used by start-ups as well as huge corporations and governments [2, 3]. Clouds have a lot of advantages like low price, speed, scalability, performance, efficiency and reliability.

Number of cloud types is dependent on strictness of definition. The oldest, widest and simplest form of cloud computing, defined as relocation of information systems out of one's business or server room, is colocation. In this case, the provider offers the location, energy and the network. Client has to equip this location with software and hardware.

© Springer Nature Switzerland AG 2018
K. Saeed and W. Homenda (Eds.): CISIM 2018, LNCS 11127, pp. 449–460, 2018.
https://doi.org/10.1007/978-3-319-99954-8_37

The most common practice is to distinguish the following types of clouds [4]:

- IaaS (Infrastructure as a Service) – extension for colocation. In this case, the provider offers not only the location but also hardware and security. Nowadays there's increasing use of virtualization for IaaS: client has to deliver just a virtual machine to a provider. It makes moving to new servers much simpler.
- PaaS (Platform as a Service) – it has the same benefits as IaaS and, additionally, the provider gives to a client the whole application platform with an operating system. The provider takes care about it, keeps it up to date and secure. The client pays only for used resources.
- SaaS (Software as a Service) – SaaS is the extension of IaaS and PaaS. It's more similar to what is understood as the cloud in a common language. The provider not only offers the location and hardware but also software. The client utilizes only functionality of given application. The cost is generally counted per 1 month for each user.
- MaaS (Monitoring as a Service) – security monitoring for clients (e.g. securing big enterprises and governments from cyber threats) who utilizes the internet for their business. The main purpose of MaaS is the monitoring of SaaS, PaaS and IaaS.

The proposed model of secure data storage is SaaS as it offers software (mobile application) with hardware and servers.

2   The Analysis of Existing Solutions

There are solutions offering secure data storing in cloud but most of them is not designed for mobile devices. Also they're not free of threats. Existing applications and services like: Tresorit [5], Livedrive [6], SpiderOak [7], BackBlaze [8] are definitely better alternative for non-secure clouds. These services have a lot in common. They utilizes advantages of symmetric and asymmetric cryptography, client-side encryption and decryption and cryptographic hash algorithms. Most of them are seeking for compromise between security and performance. User's data is usually client-side encrypted and then it's sent to a server using one of secure protocols (SFTP, FTPS, TLS/SSL) [9].

The disadvantage of this solution is giving away the data (often containing sensitive information) to a third-party provider. Even if the encryption algorithm won't be cracked, what is theoretically possible [10], the responsibility for access depends only on a third-party.

Examples of existing solutions include:

- securing with authentication mechanism: using login and the password to access files. Often used for non-secure services. Insecure in case of a cyber attack, where the intruder may gain access to credentials easily [11] and also because of the risk from the service provider who has unlimited access to user's data,
- client-side encryption: by utilization of the strong cryptography, even the service provider has no access to data because he receives it already encrypted. However, chosen cryptographic methods are often barely sufficient. Trying to offer the best performance sometimes we forget about fast increase of computing power [12, 13]. Data sent by client should be safe for longer time period than just few years,

- sending whole data to a single server: the most common practice when the data is encrypted. If the encryption algorithm is cracked, the data is no longer safe and can be accessed by both the service provider and the attacker who gained access to a server [10],
- biometrics: sometimes used as an alternative to authentication mechanism and/or encryption algorithms. This practice is criticized by some authorities who are aware that the idea behind passwords is their secrecy. Also the security of access cards is based on the fact that only authorised user has an access to them. Biometric data is entirely public what may be considered as a vulnerability of this concept [14].

Effectiveness of these methods is highly dependent on the implementation. The model of secure data storage proposed in this paper utilizes all of them, maximizing their efficiency.

Table 1 shows the comparison of some of mobile cloud solutions (chosen by their popularity or declared high security level) with proposed solution, called SecureCloud.

Table 1. Comparison of existing solutions

	Dropbox	Google Drive	Livedrive	Tresorit	SpiderOak	BackBlaze	SecureCloud
Client-side encryption	AES128	AES128	No	AES256	AES256	AES128	AES256
Storing data encrypted	AES256	AES128	AES256	AES256	AES256	AES128	AES256
Transfer encryption	SSL/TLS	SSL/TLS	SSL/TLS	SSL/TLS	SSL/TLS	SSL/TLS	SFTP
Two-factor authentication	Yes	Yes	No	Yes	Yes	Yes	Yes
Biometrics as login	No	No	No	No	No	No	Yes (optional)
Split data mechanism	No	No	Yes (optional)	No	No	No	Yes
Securing volatile memory	No	No	No	No	No	No	Yes
Private Key Encryption	No	No	No	Yes	Yes	No (vulnerable)	Yes
Provider's "zero knowledge"	No	No	No	Yes	No (mobile app)	No (vulnerable)	Yes
Open source	No	No	No	No	No	No	Yes

Compared features are related to overall security and privacy of each solution. Client-side encryption means that data are encrypted locally, by client application. It's far more secure than server-side encryption and it's used by most of existing clouds just like storing user's data (sent files) encrypted. Transfer encryption gives end-to-end security by using protocols such as SSL/TLS or SFTP. Two-factor authentication becomes a standard advised by most of cloud providers. "Biometrics as login" is a feature adding additional layer of security by using biometrics not instead of user's password but instead of a login, to identify user. From compared solutions, only SecureCloud utilizes biometrics this way (as an optional feature). "Split data mechanism" is used for sending user's data, that was client-side splitted, to at least two servers. It's additional security layer used by SecureCloud, not present in most of existing solutions. Also securing credentials and keys in client device's volatile memory is not used by most of mobile clouds or it's not documented. SecureCloud protects sensitive data in volatile memory (client-side) by using one-time session keys and encrypting it. All mechanisms used by SecureCloud are described in detail in another chapter. Private Key Encryption is very important feature, making storing data in cloud much more secure. It gives all the responsibility for access to the cloud in hands of the user. Downside is that, if the password is lost, access to user's data is lost. Provider can't restore user's password but this inconvenience is the price of maximizing security. It's also the part of provider's "zero knowledge" policy. It means, even if provider would like to access user's data (e.g. authorities order), he has no ability to do that. This feature is related not only with security of solution but, above all, with privacy. Some of providers declare this policy but it's not guaranteed by their security architecture. SecureCloud guarantees providers (server administrator) "zero knowledge" by its architecture and open source (from compared solutions only SecureCloud offers open source).

Motivation behind proposed solution is to create the free, open source cloud for mobile devices, giving maximum security and privacy. The solution that can be utilized not only by "security geeks" but also adapted by corporations, governments or any private user seeking for a highly secure way of accessing sensitive data from his device (e.g. lawyer accessing clients data).

3   Model of Secure Data Storage in the Cloud for Mobile Devices

Proposed solution offers comfort and intuitiveness of cloud with high security level contains the application developed for Android devices and the servers used for storing any file chosen by the user. The communication with server is depend on SFTP so security of the communication between client and server is guaranteed by SSH protocol. Application has two modules. The first one is responsible for authentication, browsing the list of files on the device and on the server. The second module is the Encrypter. It's responsible for cryptographic operations in the background.

Figure 1 shows the flow of a data in the application. It's widely described further, in points "a" and "b", focused on sending and receiving files to and from a server.

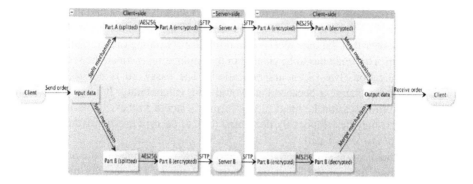

Fig. 1. Data flow in the application

Figure 2 shows the two-factor authentication when user is logging to the application using login and password. Alternatively login may be replaced with user's fingerprint if the device has a fingerprint reader. It's used for additional security but the password is still obligatory. After 5 unsuccessful authentication tries, there's 15 min of lockdown when another tries are not possible. It's the way to prevent brute force and dictionary attacks. What's more, in this case the user receives an e-mail or sms with the link to permanently block his account.

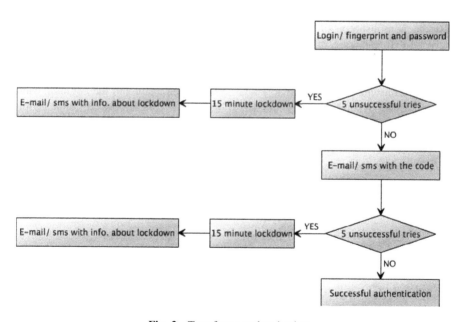

Fig. 2. Two-factor authentication

Hash received from user's password is compared with the hash stored in the device. We're using the BCrypt algorithm. If hashes are equal, the first phase of authentication is successful. After that the user receives an e-mail/sms with the one-off code which is valid for 5 min. This code has to be entered in the application to finish the second phase of the authentication (two-factor authentication). The password is not stored in the device memory in plaintext because that would be a vulnerability. It's encrypted with generated one-time session key and in this form it's stored in the volatile memory. If it's necessary it may be temporarily decrypted (e.g. to decrypt user's private key or to compute the password's hash).

When authentication is finished, user's private key is decrypted in the background. This key is used for authentication with the SFTP server. For security purpose, it's stored on the device in the encrypted form (Serpent algorithm with 256-bit key). After user is authenticated, his password is used to decrypt his private key. Both the password and the private key are encrypted with the same one-time session key to store it in device's volatile memory in the more secure way.

Android utilizes the ASLR technology (Address Space Layout Randomization) which means that the memory location used for storing user's private key and password is variable. That makes some of client-side attacks more difficult (Fig. 3).

To eliminate third-parties from proposed project, two Raspberry Pi 2B devices with an access to the Internet and equipped with memory cards (alternatively external HDDs) were used. With the usage of private servers, the user is responsible for their security and regular back-ups. Also it's up to user to place the public key on the server. The public key is stored in plain-text, server-side, by default. Optionally, user (who is also the administrator of servers) can use additional, secure feature: public key encryption. In this case, the public key will be decrypted when the administrator is authenticated. Administrator authenticates himself using login and password after booting up the server. He may also set the timeout and then, after specific time, authentication will expire, public key will be encrypted again and the communication between client (Android device) and server will be no longer possible, until another authentication by the administrator. It gives more security by protecting access to user's public key.

Kernel-level Protection : ASLR

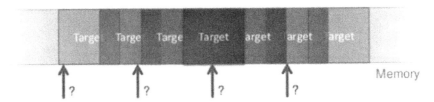

- Randomize Memory Layout to prevent exploits
  - Many of recent exploits utilize *specific* address

Fig. 3. ASLR; reference: [15]

Below there's schema and fragment of implementation (Fig. 4) of proposed solution:

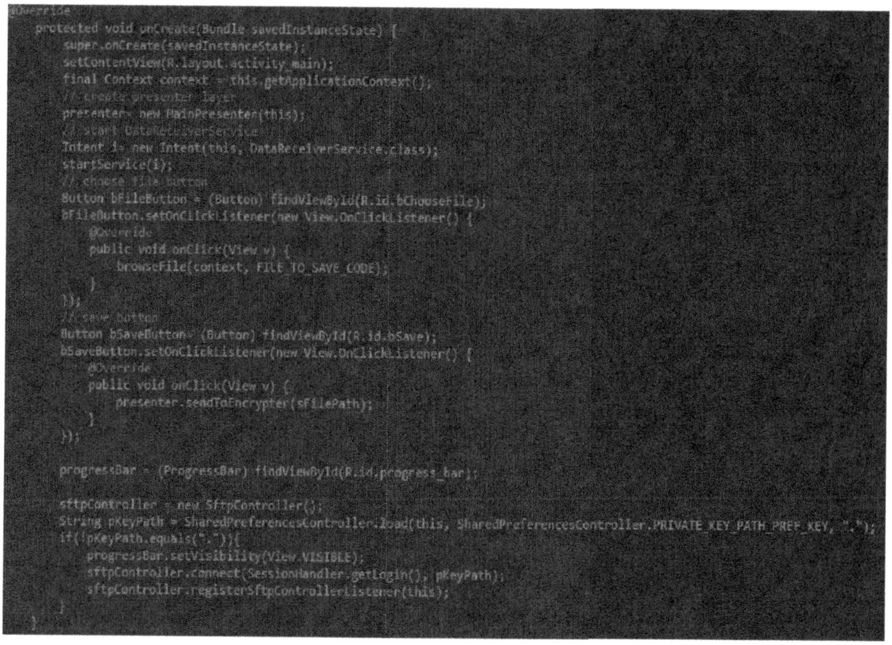

```
@Override
protected void onCreate(Bundle savedInstanceState) {
    super.onCreate(savedInstanceState);
    setContentView(R.layout.activity_main);
    final Context context = this.getApplicationContext();
    // create presenter layer
    presenter= new MainPresenter(this);
    // start DataReceiverService
    Intent i= new Intent(this, DataReceiverService.class);
    startService(i);
    // choose file button
    Button bFileButton = (Button) findViewById(R.id.bChooseFile);
    bFileButton.setOnClickListener(new View.OnClickListener() {
        @Override
        public void onClick(View v) {
            browseFile(context, FILE_TO_SAVE_CODE);
        }
    });
    // save button
    Button bSaveButton= (Button) findViewById(R.id.bSave);
    bSaveButton.setOnClickListener(new View.OnClickListener() {
        @Override
        public void onClick(View v) {
            presenter.sendToEncrypter(sFilePath);
        }
    });

    progressBar = (ProgressBar) findViewById(R.id.progress_bar);

    sftpController = new SftpController();
    String pKeyPath = SharedPreferencesController.load(this, SharedPreferencesController.PRIVATE_KEY_PATH_PREF_KEY, ".");
    if(!pKeyPath.equals(".")){
        progressBar.setVisibility(View.VISIBLE);
        sftpController.connect(SessionHandler.getLogin(), pKeyPath);
        sftpController.registerSftpControllerListener(this);
    }
}
```

Fig. 4. Code fragment of the application's main class

Possible attacks on the client would require cracking BCrypt hash to obtain user's password or cracking Serpent encryption to obtain user's private key. BCrypt was designed to remain secure despite hardware improvements and to be resistant to brute-force attacks [15].

Attacker using Hashcat software on the system with 8x Nvidia GTX 1080 GPUs would be able to crack 8624.7 MH/s (millions of hashes per second).

In case of BCrypt, using the same system, attacker would be able to crack only 105.7 kH/s (thousands of hashes per second) [16].

3.1 Sending Files to the Server

User clicks the FILE button and chooses any file he wants from device's memory to send it to the cloud. It may be the music, pdf, pictures etc. After choosing the file, he saves it with the SAVE button. In this moment, the Encrypter module is activated. It receives user's password, private key to make SFTP connection and the file's path. The file is now splitted to two parts. Both parts are encrypted using PBE AES-256 CBC algorithm, using user's password which he entered during authentication process (it's entered only once- during authentication). After that, the connection with the first server is made. The first part of the file is sent to the first server securely (SSH connection) and then the second part is sent to the second server. This file is still accessible on client-side because physical security of an Android device with its files stored in plaintext is not purpose of this project.

By splitting the file, encrypting it and sending via secure channel, the high security level is given. Sniffing traffic between client and server, physical access to one of servers or even cracking the encryption algorithms doesn't give access to user files. Similar solutions exist for desktop devices [17].

Figure 5 shows the main menu of discussed application. From this level, user can make an order to receive or send files to the cloud.

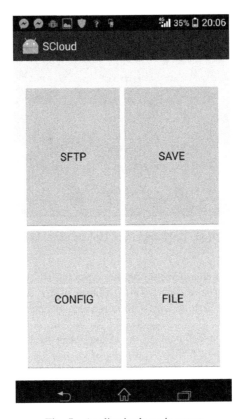

Fig. 5. Application's main menu

Figure 6 is the fragment of this paper (pdf file) in plaintext. Figure 7 is the same file encrypted with AES256-CBC after it was splitted. It's the moment when both parts of the file can be send to servers and stored there securely.

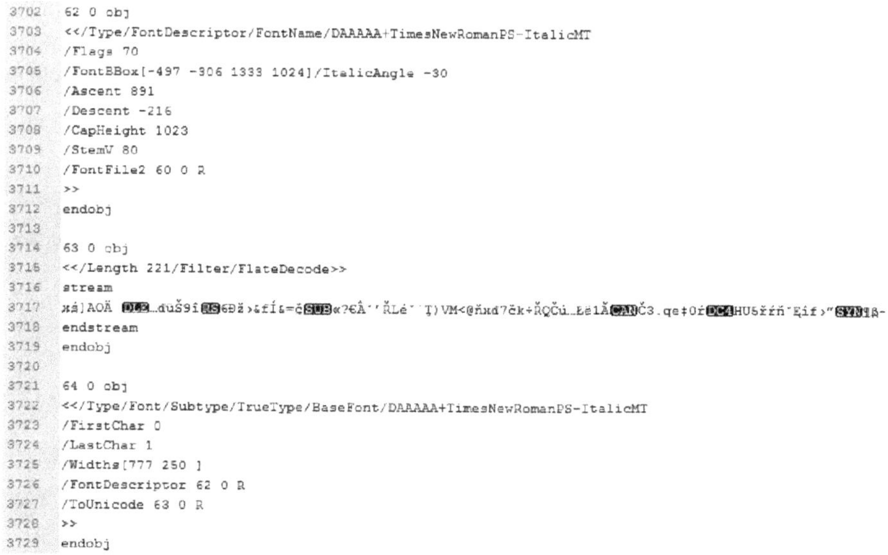

```
3702   62 0 obj
3703   <</Type/FontDescriptor/FontName/DAAAAA+TimesNewRomanPS-ItalicMT
3704   /Flags 70
3705   /FontBBox[-497 -306 1333 1024]/ItalicAngle -30
3706   /Ascent 891
3707   /Descent -216
3708   /CapHeight 1023
3709   /StemV 80
3710   /FontFile2 60 0 R
3711   >>
3712   endobj
3713
3714   63 0 obj
3715   <</Length 221/Filter/FlateDecode>>
3716   stream
3717   ¤á]AOÄ  ████…ƒuŠ9î██6Ðž›¢ƒÍ¢=¢███«?Ê´´ʼRLé´ T)VM<@ñ¤d7 Čk+ÑQČú Ŀ¢1Ä████Č3.qe‡0f███HU¢žñ´Ẹíf)"███¶§-
3718   endstream
3719   endobj
3720
3721   64 0 obj
3722   <</Type/Font/Subtype/TrueType/BaseFont/DAAAAA+TimesNewRomanPS-ItalicMT
3723   /FirstChar 0
3724   /LastChar 1
3725   /Widths[777 250 ]
3726   /FontDescriptor 62 0 R
3727   /ToUnicode 63 0 R
3728   >>
3729   endobj
```

Fig. 6. Fragment of this paper in plaintext (pdf)

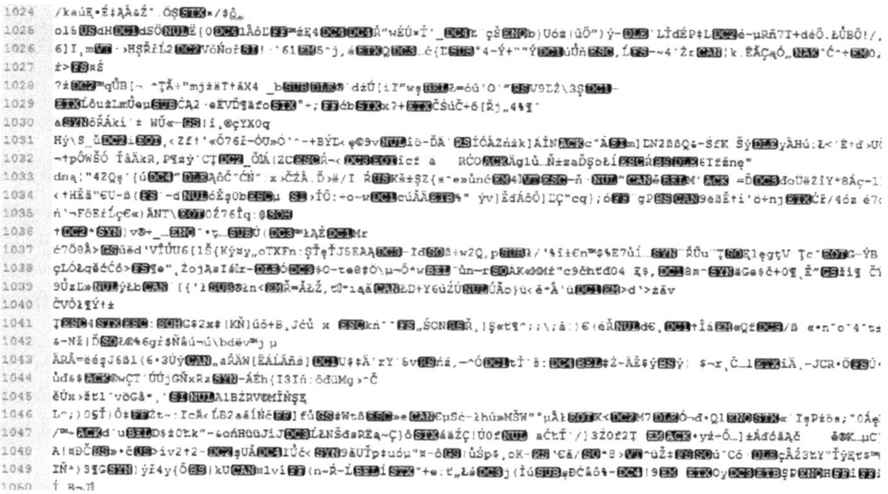

Fig. 7. Fragment of the same file after splitting and encryption

3.2 Receiving Files from the Server

It's the process similar to sending. User authenticates with the application (if he's not already authenticated). He clicks the SFTP button and the connection to one of servers is made. User browses the list of files stored on the server. Both parts of chosen file are sent from the servers to user's device. They're decrypted with the Encrypter module and then they're merged. From now on, user has access to them.

This process is intuitive and implemented security mechanism are transparent to the user. Security of files between server and client is based not only on SSH protocol but also the fact that they're decrypted and merged only after they're received by the client (Figs. 8 and 9).

```java
public void connect(final String userName, final String privateKeyPath){
    Thread thread = new Thread(new Runnable() {
        @Override
        public void run() {
            try {
                JSch jsch = new JSch();
                jsch.addIdentity(privateKeyPath);
                session = jsch.getSession(userName, HOST_NAME, PORT_NUMBER);
                session.setConfig("StrictHostKeyChecking", "no");
                session.connect();
                channelSftp = (ChannelSftp) session.openChannel(PROTOCOL_NAME);
                channelSftp.connect();
                notifyAboutEstablishedConnection();
                Log.d(TAG, PROTOCOL_NAME + " connection established!");
            } catch (JSchException e) {
                notifyAboutFailedConnection();
                e.printStackTrace();
            }
        }
    });
    thread.start();
}
```

Fig. 8. Code fragment responsible for making a secure connection with the server

Due to the nature of the application, the files security is only ensured on the way to and from the server and on the server itself, thanks to their encrypted storage as the encrypted private key of the user on the Android device. Files in the plaintext form are still at the device. The application is not responsible for the files stored at the device, only creates their copies, encrypts them and securely transfers them to the server, from which they can also be downloaded as a copy.

If the user loses the server in the form of a Raspberry Pi device, it also loses an access to the files stored in it. The loss of Android device may also result in lack of access because it stores the user's private key. In order to protect the user against the loss of the key, one can copy it and store it in another place.

To increase the security, it's possible to use a different SSH port than the default one (port 22), which may prevent many automated bot attacks.

Fig. 9. Encrypted communication between client and server (Tcpdump)

4 Summary

Proposed model of secure data storage in the cloud for mobile devices meets its requirements. It offers high security level both for daily use and for clients who consider the security as their priority. This model combines advantages of existing desktop device solutions and moves it to the mobile device level with improvements and independence from third-parties using own servers. User is no longer obligated to trust third-parties, even if it's "just" the matter of access to his data.

Possible improvements include:

- stronger cryptography
- more advanced biometric readers
- using front camera of the device for face recognition (as another authentication component with fingerprint and password)
- cryptographic cards and tokens
- mobile devices and servers designed for security purpose, maximizing the security.

References

1. https://www.newgenapps.com/blog/top-10-cloud-computing-examples-and-uses
2. Chang, V., Ramachandran, M.: Towards achieving data security with the cloud computing adoption framework. IEEE Trans. Serv. Comput. 9(1), 138–151 (2016)
3. Popovicand, K., Hocenski, Z.: Cloud computing security issues and challenges. In: MIPRO, 2010 Proceedings of the 33rd International Convention, pp. 24–28, May 2010
4. Mell, P., Grance, T.: The NIST definition of cloud computing. U.S. Department of Commerce, National Institute of Standards and Technology (2011)
5. https://tresorit.com/
6. https://www2.livedrive.com/
7. https://spideroak.com/
8. https://www.backblaze.com/
9. Wheeler, A., Winburn, M.: Cloud Storage Security: A Practical Guide, 1st edn. Elsevier, Amsterdam (2015)
10. Swenson, Ch.: Modern Cryptanalysis: Techniques for Advanced Code Breaking. Wiley, Indianapolis (2008)
11. Mitnick, K.: The Art of Deception: Controlling the Human Element of Security. Wiley, Indianapolis (2003)
12. Moore, G.E.: Cramming more components onto integrated circuits. Electronics 38 (1965)
13. https://www.economist.com/news/leaders/21694528-era-predictable-improvement-computer-hardware-ending-what-comes-next-future
14. https://www.wired.com/2016/03/biometrics-coming-along-serious-security-concerns/. Accessed 03 Apr 2018
15. https://www.usenix.org/system/files/conference/woot14/woot14-malvoni.pdf
16. https://gist.github.com/epixoip/a83d38f412b4737e99bbef804a270c40
17. Rajasekhar Reddy, M., Akilandeswari, R., Priyadarshini, S., Karthikeyan, B., Ponmani, E.: A modified cryptographic approach for securing distributed data storage in cloud computing. In: International Conference on Networks and Advances in Computational Technologies (NetACT) (2017)
18. https://www.dropbox.com/
19. https://www.google.com/drive/

MySQL Extension Automatic Porting to PDO for PHP Migration and Security Improvement

Fabio Mondin and Agostino Cortesi[✉]

DAIS - Università Ca' Foscari, Venice, Italy
fabiomondin08@gmail.com, cortesi@unive.it

Abstract. In software management, the upgrade of programming languages may introduce critical issues. This is the case of PHP, the fifth version of which is going towards the end of the support. The new release improves on different aspects, but removes the old deprecated MySQL extensions, and supports only the newer library of functions for the connection to the databases. The software systems already in place need to be renewed to be compliant with respect to the new language version. The conversion of the source code, to be safe against injection attacks, should involve also the transformation of the query code. The purpose of this work is the design of specific tool that automatically applies the required transformation yielding to a precise and efficient conversion procedure. The tool has been applied to different projects to provide evidence of its effectiveness.

Keywords: Static analysis · Code conversion · PHP · Deprecated MySQL

1 Introduction

1.1 Aim of the Work

Every framework, library or language for application development is constantly updated in order to take full advantage of new features but also to fix some vulnerabilities. A software system, in order to satisfy the basic protection rules and keep safe, has to be always updated to the latest version of the components from which it depends. However sometimes the old version of a component is not directly adaptable to the new one, and it requires the modification of the instructions of the source code or even of its structure.

This paper focuses on the PHP language. The old stable PHP release is the 5.6 that is going towards the end of the support, while the current supported version is version 7. The new version introduces many new features and improvements, but on the other side it brings some incompatibilities with the old source code. In particular, it removes many functionalities that were just deprecated in the previous version. Among these, one of most significant change is the removal of the MySQL extensions. This set of functions allows to access the functionality provided by MySQL that are fundamental for the interaction with the database [15–18].

© Springer Nature Switzerland AG 2018
K. Saeed and W. Homenda (Eds.): CISIM 2018, LNCS 11127, pp. 461–473, 2018.
https://doi.org/10.1007/978-3-319-99954-8_38

It is important to notice that many software systems written in PHP, while interacting with the MySQL database component, make use heavily of this set of instructions.

This work focuses on the transformation of the MySQL extension to the more recent PHP Data Objects (PDO), avoiding to treat all the other changes related with the new PHP version. PDO are chosen against MySQLi because they are an abstraction layer for accessing different databases providing a lightweight and consistent common interface. We address only this specific aspect because it is the more relevant from a security perspective. In fact, differently from the old MySQL functions, the PDO class supports the prepared statement, that is the method considered more secure against the possibility of injection attacks. This technique to be effective requires that the code of the query executed for the access to the database is corrected accordingly [1, 4, 6, 10]. Consequently, the project to achieve reliable results has to take into account this aspect too.

The system developed for the transformation has to take as input many files simultaneously and apply the conversion to each of them. It has to be sufficiently general to solve all the conversion problems, and at the same time to modify only the proper functions, without the alteration of the ones that don't need to be modified. It has to be capable to treat all the possible directives that have to be altered, according to the distinct models and styles of source code taken as input.

1.2 Methodology

First of all, to convert the input source code it is essential to follow a source to source type of transformation technique. This kind of translation takes as input a source code written in a given programming language that is analysed and then modified to obtain a new source code written in a language with the same level of abstraction, in this case exactly with the same PHP language. In particular, the changes made should not alter the external behavior of the software: the results obtained from the execution of the old and the new scripts should be exactly the same [7].

To perform a precise conversion, a preliminary analysis phase is needed that scans the entire code to look for the parts that have to be treated. All the old MySQL functions, which must be replaced, have as parameter the variable for the connection to the database. All of them, in order to interact with the database, have to know its specification and then must get it as parameter. As a result, the first analysis search for this variable initialization to obtain the source of this information. Then, in order to find all the MySQL functions to be converted, a data flow analysis is performed [4]. This can be compared to the taint analysis methods [2] to mark all the variable that derive from a source one. This way, the search gets exactly the only interesting instructions that have to be modified, by removing any possibilities of mistakes. In the case this approach does not discover any variable, a normal scan of the entire source code is executed to search among all the instructions the only ones that have to be changed.

We design proper rules for each single transformation. So, it is possible to handle program written in different styles and to obtain the more advantageous substitution to integrate with the other settings.

1.3 Results

The resulting tool comprises a set of algorithms that analyze, find and transform all the instructions belonging to the old MySQL library to the currently supported PDO. Moreover, the MySQL query code is translated to be suitable to be executed with the prepared statement of the PDO methods. So, the code once processed will treat all the user inputs as parameters avoiding every injection hazards.

The transformation structure is based on an algorithm that reads a set of rules taken as input, process and then executes them. These rules contain the pattern of the old function to be searched inside the code and the corresponding replacement instruction. Each rule is related to a single type of conversion, that is an individual pattern to be found. The conversion algorithm looks for the pattern of the rules in correspondence of the lines of code found by the previous phase of data flow analysis.

After the first conversion phase dedicated to the MySQL functions, a second automatic conversion is performed, specific this time for the MySQL code. This starts from a particular MySQL instruction, the "mysql_query", it gets the variable containing the query string, and then it searches all the line of code that deal with this string, with a backwards data flow analysis technique. Each input is replaced by a place-holder within the query code, while its value is saved in a ad-hoc array for the parameters. Finally, the array is passed to the new proper function for the binding of all the values.

The tool interface allows users to select one or more files in input and possibly to modify the list of selected files. It presents a basic list of rules for the most common case of functions to be changed that can be further improved, by adding new rules, or by modifying them.

1.4 Structure of the Paper

The paper is structured as follows. Section 2 discusses related work. Section 3 introduces the conversion of deprecated MySQL statements. In Sects. 4 and 5 the conversion rules and the transformation methods are presented, respectively. The experimental results on the application of the conversion procedure are discussed in Sect. 6. Section 7 concludes.

2 Related Work

Many automatic source code transformers have been developed, focusing on performance improvement, on the automatic migration of deprecated or no more supported code to the corresponding newer version. From trivial scripts to improve small aspects of a particular source code to complete converter tool from a particular language to a completely different one, or even to expert systems that are able to generically manipulate different computer languages.

Among the other, we may refer to PIPS [20, 21], an open and extensible source-to-source compilation framework that automatically analyze and transform programs written in C and Fortran programming languages; the C2CUDATranslator [13], a source-to-source compiler with the purpose of transforming an application in C language to an equivalent one in CUDA C, a toolkit that is integrated in the C language and that is needed to use the NVIDIA GPU; the error fixing tool proposed by Khmelevsky et al. [5], a source-to-source transformation tool developed for C and C++ for the mistake detection and the subsequent fixing; Spoon [8], a meta-analysis tool to analyze, rewrite and transform any program written in Java; Rose [21], an open source software for developing tool with the task of automatically analyse, debug and optimize the source code in C, C++, Fortran, Java, Python and PHP; Grumpy [14], a source code transcompiler for translating code from Python to Go.

Focussing on the PHP language, the main reference is the MySQLConverterTool [12]. The intent of this small tool is to convert the old deprecated MySQL extension to the corresponding MySQLi functions, that is the current supported extensions. It is written in PHP, so it is usable as a web server. It can transform any PHP file although it has some limitation such as the problem of finding an equivalent to mysql_result that does not exist in MySQLi. This tool has limited applications because it supports only MySQLi extension and it does not have any functionality for the transformation to the PDO class neither it has any method for the translation of the MySQL code called in order to be really protected against injection.

A similar application with the same aim is YAK Pro – mysql to mysqli converter [22]. This is another free and open source tool to transform the PHP scripts from the abandoned MySQL functions to the similar procedural version of the current MySQLi extension. It is written in PHP too, and it is based upon the PHP-Parser to parse the PHP files given in input for the initial static analysis. However, like MySQLConverterTool, this tool has many limitations on the supported.

Finally, the PHP 5.4 Short Array Syntax Converter [18] is designed only for a specific and limited type of code manipulation. It builds a PHP command line script that is able to convert or revert the input PHP scripts from the old array syntax to the current short array syntax. It transforms the array objects instantiated with the syntax "array()" to the new short syntax presented from the PHP version 5.4 that let an array to be instantiated simply with the characters "[]". Hence this translation can help to simplify and make more clear the source code of the PHP scripts.

The projects above that try to achieve the transformation in question, or an analogous one like MySQL Converter Tool and YAK Pro, are able to convert in a basic way the MySQL functions, but they do not even take into account the adjustment of the MySQL code. So, even if the new code will be executed throw the secure PDO technique, or the MySQLi for the mentioned application, the input will not be prevented from the injection, because they do not entrust on the prepared statement.

3 Deprecated MySQL Conversion

The conversion method is defined in different components. The first one that treat only the replacement of the MySQL functions and a second one that is suited exclusively for the MySQL code that executes an operation inside the database. It is chosen to keep them separate because they imply two completely different procedures of dealing with the code, even if one relies on the other. The two are strictly related and cannot be accomplished separately. So the first, that treats the MySQL functions, once concluded, directly calls the second, so that it is not possible the completion of only one of the two. The two approaches are dissimilar because they have to achieve a different purpose. The first has to be more universal possible to fit to the different situations, because the different inputs can employ the MySQL functions in different way. While the MySQL code is more standard and has a precise predefined form that implies a rigorous structure. In addition, its processing has only to identify the user input and mechanically substitute them. Consequently, the two procedures have been designed in different ways. The first that takes in input the subject of its job in the form of rules for each element to be altered, while the second that is simply codified to search and replace a defined class of instructions. In any case they are implemented in different components to make the system more structured and ordered.

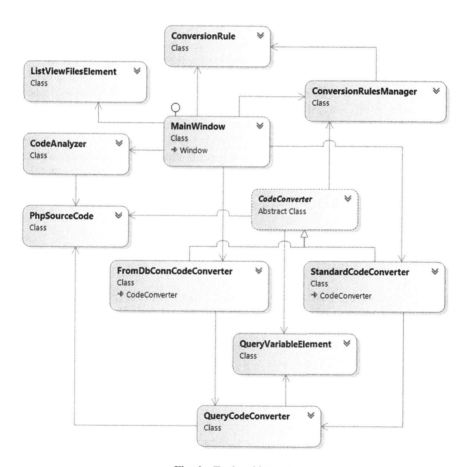

Fig. 1. Tool architecture

The diagram depicted in Fig. 1 represents the different components of the conversion tool. The structure is based on the *Model-View-ViewModel* pattern to provide a clear separation between the user interface with its controls and the remaining logic of the software. The class *MainWindow* contains all the methods that handle the events occurred inside the user interface and then shows the results of the computation on it. The view component, that is the graphic interface, is symbolized throw the small white spot linked to the *MainWindow* class. The *CodeAnalyzer* is the first object instantiated to execute the basic analysis of the code for obtaining the instruction for the connection to the database. As other components, it employs the methods of the *PhpSourceCode* object to realize its functionalities. This is an entity to implement all the common utilities to deal with the PHP source code that are used as basic action by the other operations. The conversion phase is stated by distinct classes. The basic services are gathered in the *CodeConverter* abstract class, while the complete task is achieved by one of two concrete class that realizes it in the two different ways. *FromBdConnCodeConverter* is the normal and more accurate option, that performs the process starting from the value obtained by the analysis phase. The *StandardCodeConverter* is executed only if the database connection field is empty. Both cases receive the rules declared by the user and elaborated through the *ConversionRuleManager* object. The latter has the role of computing the pattern and the regular expression used to identify the code to be replaced for each rule. In this way, the effort is done only once at first improving also the efficiency. After the substitution of the MySQL functions, the converter performs the replacement of the inputs within the MySQL code through the execution of a specific module. The *QueryCodeConverter* class implements this process separately from the rest of the procedure because it is achieved in a distinct manner. Finally, the class *QueryVariableElement*, *ConversionRule* and *ListViewElement* are the objects for the relative concrete items, without any specific method, used for representing the corresponding basic elements.

4   Conversion Rules

The analysis of various PHP source code that resolve different problems allowed to gather the main relevant instructions that have to be replaced. They have been partitioned and organized to obtain clear distinct transformation rules.

> Rule 1: database connection
>   Source function: mysql_connect
>   PDO equivalent: new PDO (PDO object constructor)
>   Wrapper function: new DatabasePDOConnection

The function that opens a connection to a MySQL server database, with the corresponding parameters passed, is replaced by the creation of an instance of the object PDO. The corresponding custom directive created is an object that handles the creation of the connection to the database and the error reporting.

Rule 2: query execution
  Source function: mysql_query
  PDO equivalent: prepare, bindParam, execute
  Wrapper function: execQuery

The function that send a MySQL query to the connected database through the link identifier is replaced by the three PDO methods that prepare the query to be executed, add the parameters to the query, according to the prepared statement technique, and finally execute the request set. The wrapper function executes all the three methods, automatically binding the input of the query passed as parameter, including a proper error handling.

Rule 3: results fetch as associative array
  Source function: mysql_fetch_assoc
  PDO equivalent: fetch(PDO::FETCH_ASSOC)
  Wrapper function: fetchAssocQuery

The instruction that fetches the next row of results in the form of an associative array is replaced by the method that fetches the next row from a result set in the same way. The custom function is a wrapper that executes one of the two instructions based on the type of the query result parameter passed.

Rule 4: results fetch as associative and numeric array
  Source function: mysql_fetch_array
  PDO equivalent: fetch(PDO::FETCH_BOTH)
  Wrapper function: fetchArrayQuery

The deprecated function that returns the next row of results as both an associative and a numeric array is substituted by the equivalent PDO method or wrapper function that returns the same results in the same manner.

Rule 5: results fetch as enumerated array
  Source function: mysql_fetch_row
  PDO equivalent: fetch(PDO::FETCH_NUM)
  Wrapper function: fetchRowQuery

As the previous rule, the old MySQL instruction is replaced by the corresponding method or wrapper all, which returns the results of a query as an array indexed only by numbers.

Rule 6: number of row changed
   Source function: mysql_affected_rows
   PDO equivalent: rowCount
   Wrapper function: affectedRowsQuery

The function that counts the number of rows affected by a previous MySQL operation is replaced by the method that obtains the same result for the last statement executed by the object from which it is called, or by the custom function with the same instructions.

Rule 7: id of the last row generated
   Source function: mysql_insert_id
   PDO equivalent: lastInsertId
   Wrapper function: lastInsertIdQuery

The source function retrieves the identifier automatically generated, in a field with the properties of auto-increment, by the previous query of insert type. The equivalent PDO returns either the ID of the last row inserted or the last value from a sequence object according to the driver on which it is based. So, they can be considered interchangeable for the same underlying database. The wrapper function executes one of the two solutions depending on the type of database link which is passed.

Rule 8: special characters escape
   Source function: mysql_real_escape_string
   PDO equivalent: quote
   Wrapper function: -

This source function makes the escape of the special characters in a query string. The quote method quotes around the input string but also it escapes special characters. No wrapper function is developed to replace the original instruction because with the prepared statements the escapes of special characters is unnecessary or even useless. So, this function is simply removed without any substitution.

Rule 9: error reporting
   Source function: mysql_error / mysql_errno
   PDO equivalent: errorInfo
   Wrapper function: -

The functions that return the text or the numerical value of the error message from the preceding operation can be replaced by the PDO method that performs the similar task. It is completely removed by the custom function because the error reporting is already accomplished by the other wrapper functions.

5   Transformation Methods

The transformation of the MySQL query code is quite standard and it does not need to be taken as input. Its adjustment is in fact independent on the different applications because its syntax is not altered and only the input components are substituted. So, in this case it is not necessary to formulate the conversion as a set of rules: it is enough to state which method has to be applied. These procedures are then directly implemented throw the tool code, without the need to create a parametrized structure with the rules as input.

> Method 1: base case, standard input
> *Pseudocode pattern:*
> $queryString .= "AND fieldName operator ' " . $input . " ' ";
> *Replacement:*
> $queryString .= "AND fieldName operator :" . ++$placeholder. " ";
> $bindParamsArray[":$placeholder"] = $input;

The basic case of input by the user is the direct concatenation of the variable containing the input to the query code. Originally this input is escaped throw the function "mysql_real_escape_string" or even it is simply copied. The transformation inserts the value of a placeholder in place of the old input inside the query and it saves the real input value in the specific array at the position indexed by the placeholder. The function that executes the query binds this value to its position before the actual execution.

> Method 2: fixed operator
> *Pseudocode pattern:*
> $queryString .= "AND fieldName >= ' " . $input . " ' ";
> *Replacement:*
> $queryString .= "AND fieldName >= :" . ++$placeholder. " ";
> $bindParamsArray[":$placeholder"] = $input;

If the query contains a settled operator, such as a mathematical operator, the transformation is applied exactly as in the previous method. The input is replaced by a placeholder and saved in the common array.

> Method 3: query without input
> *Pseudocode pattern:*
> $queryString .= "AND fieldName IS NULL / NOT NULL";
> *Replacement:*
> $queryString .= "AND fieldName IS NULL / NOT NULL";

For some MySQL operator it is not expected any parameter as input. For these cases it is not necessary any input substitution, so the transformation does not alter the original code that remains unchanged.

Method 4: IN keyword

   Pseudocode pattern:

$queryString .= "AND fieldName IN (". $input .") ";

   Replacement:

$InValues = explode(",", $input);

      $INElem = '';

      for($i=0; $i<count($InValues); $i++){

         $INElem.=":".++$placeholder.",";

         $bindParamsArray [":$placeholder"] = $InValues[$i];

      }

      $queryString .= "AND fieldName IN (". substr($INElem, 0, -1) .")";

The input relative to the MySQL keyword IN is completely rewritten always to substitute the inputs with placeholders. In this case the different input values are separated by a comma, so firstly they are divided in single input values. Then each one is replaced by the placeholder while its value is saved on the parameters array. Finally, the original string is corrected with the string of the placeholders.

Method 5: BETWEEN keyword

   Pseudocode pattern:

$queryString .= "AND fieldName BETWEEN '". $inputFrom ."' AND '". $inputTo ."' ";

   Replacement:

      $queryString .= "AND fieldName BETWEEN :".++$placeholder." AND :".++$placeholder." ";

      $bindParamsArray[":$placeholder-1"] = $inputFrom;

      $bindParamsArray[":$placeholder"] = $inputTo;

The BETWEEN keyword expects two different inputs, the first for the start and the second for the end of the range that it selected. They are consequently substituted by two placeholders that are used as index for the array of inputs to bind. In particular, the first placeholder value is corrected to index the first of the two inputs.

The placeholder of the various methods is simply an integer variable that is incremented for each input. In this way every input has a different placeholder value, that is also the index of the array where the actual values of the inputs are saved.

6   Experimental Evaluation

We applied the conversion tool (whose interface is depicted in Fig. 2) on a complex management system. This is made of many PHP scripts that manage the entire production process of a medium-size company. It allows to generate different kind of documents like invoices and reports. Its structure is based on different modules, that represent the activities executed by the corresponding production phases. Each one is mainly structured in three different files. The first one contains the graphical interface, the second one contains all the operations on data, and the last implements the basic functionalities.

The GUI files are about 150 different scripts. The number of the operation files is the same, as each of them is related to the corresponding interface module. The class files are about 200. The management system is made of more than 500 files, considering only the ones containing the PHP code. The code of every unit is produced through a framework that automatically creates the basic structure of the reports and the elementary operations, facilitating the development process. All the fundamental programs generated are widely customized, to adapt the product to the existing needs. All the transformation rules introduced in Sect. 4 have been proven effective while applied to this system, yielding to an almost complete transformation of all the functions.

The analysis phase of all the 500 files needed about half a second, while the conversion of the entire code, performed through the database link based conversion process, takes about 20 s.

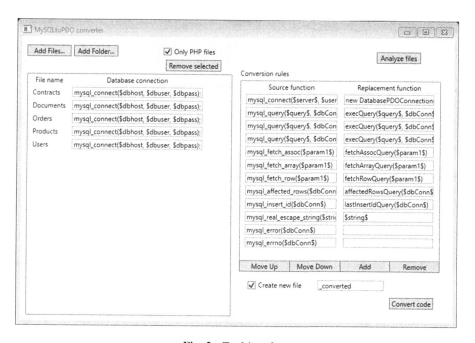

Fig. 2. Tool interface

When considering the impact of the code transformation on the execution, it results that there is no significant difference between the old version and the new one both for the execution time and for the memory space usage.

7 Conclusions

The system presented in this paper covers most of the relevant issues in the migration to PHP 7. Unfortunately, there are a few scenarios where the conversion procedure is not able to provide a complete and accurate transformation. This is the case when there are two or more inputs inside the same portion of query code. If the instruction that produces a part of the query string concatenates the MySQL code to more than one variable, the transformation algorithm is able to substitute only the first one of them. Another problem that remains to be solved is related to the conversion rule defined for the mysql_affected_rows function: the original MySQL instruction takes as parameter the database link while the corresponding replacement method of the PDO class takes as parameter the variable that stores the result of the query execution. These open issues are currently under investigation to fully automatize the conversion process, providing an interesting workbench for applying static analysis techniques for security enforcement [3, 9, 11].

References

1. Artzi, S., et al.: Finding bugs in web applications using dynamic test generation and explicit-state model checking. IEEE Trans. Softw. Eng. **36**(4), 474–494 (2010)
2. Clause, J.A., Li, W., Orso, A.: Dytan: a generic dynamic taint analysis framework. In: ISSTA 2007, pp. 196–206 (2007)
3. Costantini, G., Ferrara, P., Cortesi, A.: Static analysis of string values. In: Qin, S., Qiu, Z. (eds.) ICFEM 2011. LNCS, vol. 6991, pp. 505–521. Springer, Heidelberg (2011). https://doi.org/10.1007/978-3-642-24559-6_34
4. Hauzar, D., Kofron, J.: Framework for static analysis of PHP applications. In: ECOOP 2015, pp. 689–711 (2015)
5. Khmelevsky, Y., Rinard, M., Sidiroglou-Douskos, S.: A source-to-source transformation tool for error fixing (2013)
6. Kiezun, A., Guo, P.J., Jayaraman, K., Ernst, M.D.: Automatic creation of SQL injection and cross-site scripting attacks. In: ICSE 2009, pp. 199–209 (2009)
7. Loveman, D.B.: Program improvement by source-to-source transformation. J. ACM **24**(1), 121–145 (1977)
8. Pawlak, R., Monperrus, M., Petitprez, N., Noguera, C., Seinturier, L.: SPOON: a library for implementing analyses and transformations of Java source code. Softw. Pract. Experience **46**, 1155–1179 (2015)
9. Pollet, I., Le Charlier, B., Cortesi, A.: Distinctness and sharing domains for static analysis of Java programs. In: Knudsen, J.L. (ed.) ECOOP 2001. LNCS, vol. 2072, pp. 77–98. Springer, Heidelberg (2001). https://doi.org/10.1007/3-540-45337-7_5
10. Wassermann, G., Su, Z.: Sound and precise analysis of web applications for injection vulnerabilities. PLDI **46**, 32–41 (2007)
11. Zanioli, M., Ferrara, P., Cortesi, A.: SAILS: static analysis of information leakage with sample. In: ACM SAC 2012, pp. 1308–1313 (2012)
12. A MySQL Converter Tool. https://github.com/philip/MySQLConverterTool
13. C2CUDATranslator. https://github.com/prem30488/C2CUDATranslator
14. Grumpy: Go running Python. https://github.com/google/grumpy
15. Migrating from PHP 5.6.x to PHP 7.0.x. http://php.net/manual/en/migration70.php

16. PHP Backward incompatible changes. http://php.net/manual/en/migration70.incom-patible.
    php
17. PHP Supported Versions. http://php.net/supported-versions.php
18. PHP 5.4 Short Array Syntax Converter. https://github.com/thomasbachem/php-short-array-
    syntax-converter
19. PIPS: Automatic Parallelizer and Code Transformation Framework. https://pips4u.org
20. The PIPS Workbench Project. http://www.cri.ensmp.fr/PIPS/home.html
21. ROSE compiler infrastructure. http://rosecompiler.org
22. YAK Pro - mysql to mysqli converter. http://mysql-to-mysqli.yakpro.com/

Network Electronic Devices Authentication by Internal Electrical Noise

Elena Nyemkova[1] ⬥, Zynovii Shandra[1] ⬥,
Aleksandra Kłos-Witkowska[2] ⬥, and Łukasz Więcław[2(✉)] ⬥

[1] Lviv Polytechnic National University, 12 Bandera St., Lviv 79013, Ukraine
cyberlbil2@gmail.com, zshandra@gmail.com
[2] University of Bielsko-Biala, 2 Willowa St., 43-309 Bielsko-Biala, Poland
{awitkowska, lwieclaw}@ath.bielsko.pl

Abstract. The article is devoted to dynamic authentication method of electronic network devices with built-in analog-to-digital converters (ADCs) based on authentication templates. The following results were obtained: the authentication of each electronic device can be carried out uniquely by its internal electrical noise (like biometric authentication of a person). Uniqueness of authentication is provided by the invariants of the noise signal such as the shape of the graph of the autocorrelation function of noise and the set of resonance frequencies of the device. The electronic device authentication template is obtained from the sequence of values of the autocorrelation function of the noise. It consists from the bit template and the amplitude template. The technique of obtaining an authentication template is presented. The required duration of the noise signal is 0.5 s for reliable authentication at a sampling frequency of 44.1 kHz. The results of authentication of several computers are presented.

Keywords: Device authentication · Internal electrical noise
Stochastic autooscillations · Phase portrait · Bit template · Hamming distance

1 Introduction

Commercialization of technologies Internet of Things, SCADA and others led to a sharp decline in the information security of computer network systems. A low level of security makes possible of cyber-attacks, where the targets can be either directly specific cyber-physical systems, or remote servers that are not related to particular systems, but related to specific cyber-physical systems through telecommunications. The inclusion in the interconnecting protocols of logical names of devices does not solve the problem of information security; logical names can be substituted by various attack technologies.

Modern computer networks are exposed to large number of different attacks every day. A significant part of the attacks is due to an access violation when the attacker becomes a legitimate user. This is made possible by weak authentication attributes of legal user. For electronic devices need to develop techniques (similar to biometrics techniques for people) that would make it possible to uniquely identify electronic device in a network.

© Springer Nature Switzerland AG 2018
K. Saeed and W. Homenda (Eds.): CISIM 2018, LNCS 11127, pp. 474–485, 2018.
https://doi.org/10.1007/978-3-319-99954-8_39

The challenge is to develop methods of recognition, which would provide unambiguous information on the specific unique device. Many researchers have come to the conclusion that such information may be inherent noise signals [1–3] and ambient noise signal [4].

Any electronic device consists of a set of elements that are different in the parameters within limit variations. Nobody can make exactly the same elements at the micro-level, so that these differences are manifested in deviations of parameters at the macro level of devices: linear gain tract characteristics, resonant frequencies, noise ratio and others [5]. For example, impulse noise is used to identify the chip by implementing physical unclonable function [2].

Authentication accuracy is determined by quality measure which depends on the technical equipment, measurement methodology and the selected identifier. Therefore, comprehensive approach is needed to meet the challenges of authentication of electronic devices.

Uncontrolled changes in signals occur during the operation of electronic devices due to fluctuations in internal electromagnetic fields. Fluctuations can spread along cables or wires or by radiation in the form of electromagnetic waves. As a result, interference appears, it is undesirable for the normal operation of the device. There are many causes of interference. A sudden change in current or voltage is the main reason. A complex interference pattern of electromagnetic fields arises inside the electronic device connected to the power source; it is caused by the mutual influence of the components of the device. As a result, parasitic signals appear in the output circuit of the electronic device. When designing devices, developers try to minimize these parasitic signals, but reducing their level to zero is impossible.

Parameters of parasitic signals (for example: phase, amplitude, frequency, dynamic spectrum) are determined by these internal electromagnetic fields, which in turn depend on the elements base and design features of the device. Complete similarity of devices cannot be provided because of the natural scatter of parameters at the micro level even with the same selection of elements and their internal arrangement. The interaction of electromagnetic fields in the middle of the device depends on the values of the resonant frequencies of the device, which are the consequence of processes in circuits with distributed parameters. At the output of the device, signals will be present, which have fallen into the region of resonant frequencies. The signals at the output will be different for different devices of the same type, in other words, the parasitic signals at the output are individual similarly to the biometric indicators of different people. Therefore, it can try to use them to identify electronic devices. Parasitic signals due to their minimization are very small, as a rule, there are speaking about the noise at the output of the device.

It is necessary to determine the characteristics for identification. Noise signals are characterized by a level and a spectrum. In measuring practice, the concept of the noise coefficient is used - measuring the ratio of the output signal to the signal at the input. This is an integral parameter and it is not suitable for the identification indicator. It is necessary to find processes that could unambiguously characterize the features of this device. The appearance of parasitic signals at the output is associated with the internal structure of the device, and it becomes possible to determine the identification feature (identifier) with an appropriate choice of the parasitic signal parameter.

The task of recognizing digital microphones was partially solved by using frequency analysis with the construction of spectrograms (creating a spectral image of the device) [6].

The possibility of identifying electronic devices based on their low frequency electromagnetic emissions (0–500 kHz) was demonstrated in [5]. Researchers proposed the technique by which both type of electronic devices and individual devices within a type can be distinguished.

The software "Fractal" is designed for detection of phonograms compilation [7]. The recording of a phonogram is characterized by the influence of the noise of the recording device, therefore, in the case of rewriting on other equipment, the own noises of phonograms have other characteristics. This makes it possible to detect the compilation of an audio file.

The possibility of using the Hearst coefficient of the noise signal was investigated for identification purposes [8]. The method for identifying computers on the network is proposed using the phase portraits of Fourier components of the noise of integrated audio cards [9]. Identification of the audio device is carried out by constructing phase portraits of different Fourier components and calculating their parameters, namely the displacement of the centers of the strange Fourier component attractors relative to the origin.

The main idea of the research is based on the assumption that individual differences of electronic devices, such as design features and different parameters of components, is displayed on correlation and spectral characteristics of noise. The goal is to develop the dynamic authentication method of these devices based on authentication templates. This method realizes the obtaining of individual invariant characteristics of noise signals for each electronic device, as well as an authentication algorithm. The noise signal for authentication is different each time, which provides protection from the substitution attack. The tasks are obtaining the invariant characteristics of the noise signal; constructing an authentication template; experimental determination of the noise signal duration for reliable authentication, development of an authentication algorithm.

2   Techniques Identification of Complex Systems

The problems of identifying complex systems attract the stable interest of researchers. The two main tasks are solved in the study of complex systems. The first task is the identification of the system. Identification of the system means finding certain invariant characteristics. The second task is the prediction of the behavior of the system.

Usually, complex systems are non-linear systems with dissipation (such as electronic devices), in which the development of chaotic processes is happened [10–15]. Today it has become known a growing number of relatively simple examples of spontaneous appearance of temporary structures in disordered systems [13]. An autooscillations are occurred in electronic devices. Nonlinear oscillator model is used in the research of noise in radio frequency integrated circuits [14].

Active and passive methods for the identification of complex systems are currently used. The passive method is based on the analysis of the system's own signals [16]. This is actually in those cases when the process under study is almost impossible to describe mathematically. Suppose the observed variable, a series of N numbers, is present. These are the values of some measured dynamic variable $x(t)$ with a constant step τ in time, $t_i = t_0 + (i - 1)\tau$: $x_i = x(t_i)$, $i = 1,..., N$. The main requirement for identification is the following. The invariant characteristics of the initial system and those obtained from the time series must coincide. These characteristics can be determined from the experiment without knowing all the dynamic variables of the system.

Identification should be based not only on the logical name of the system, but on the essence of the processes occurring in the system itself. Since each system is unique at the microscopic level, the dynamic variable $x(t)$ will have a unique trajectory. If it is possible to find invariant characteristics for each complex system based on the sequence $x(t)$, then this is a solution to the problem of identifying the system without constructing mathematical models.

There are deep analogies in the organization and functioning of complex systems, despite the fact that they can differ significantly in specific manifestations and details. It should be noted that most complex systems are characterized by flicker noise. Dynamic variable shows the properties of flicker noise. This property is inherent in natural systems [17].

Infrequently, the identification of specific complex system provide by means of the autocorrelation function [18]. Most real systems are dissipative with chaotic dynamics. As shown in [19], reconstruction of attractors is possible. Usually, researchers use the calculated spectrum of a dynamic variable to identify complex systems [5, 7, 20]. At the same time, the danger of aliasing is with uniform sampling. For signals in telecommunication systems, the process of digitizing an analog signal is preceded by filtration, and the aliasing effect disappears. For some practical cases, the dynamic variable is represented only as a discrete series, filtration is impossible in principle. The use of non-uniform sampling is also impossible. Therefore, additional confirmation must be made about the limited spectrum.

An external signal is applied to the system and its response is examined at an active approach. The study of the response can be carried out on the basis of a mathematical model of a complex system or with the help of neural networks, as shown in [21]. The method was improved significantly [22]. But this method requires a large amount of calculations, a lot of time and many examples for training.

The identification of complex systems is necessary to obtain access rights to confidential information or a control system for the tasks of the Internet of Things. The main requirements for such identification are as follows. First, among the many such systems, it is necessary to identify the one that has access rights. Secondly, identification should be carried out in real time, i.e. for a very short time. Thirdly, the identification procedure should not require many calculations. The second and third conditions limit the volume of mathematical operations with the time series of the dynamic variable $x(t)$. Now identification of devices in telecommunications networks is carried out using logical names or cryptographic protocols. Evaluation of parameters of mathematical models of technical devices takes a long time and involves the participation of a man.

A stochastic process is called stationary, if the autocovariance $cvar(x, x_l)$ and the autocorrelation function $corr(x, x_l)$ of the time series x_i are depends only from the lag value l. Thus, each stationary process can be characterized by its autocorrelation function. The autocorrelation function can be taken as a template - an identifier for a complex system. All assumptions made about the behavior of systems should be tested experimentally for each type of complex systems that require identification.

3   Research Methodology

Due to the low level of the noise signal, it was necessary to develop a technique for processing the output signal of an electronic device, which would enable to detect differences between different devices, i.e. determine the authenticator.

Measurements of the noise signal at the output of the electronic device were carried out using software Oscillometr (Shmelev) [23], which allows measuring signals at a level of 200 µV. The noise signal to the input of the ADC is recorded in a file with the extension wav. This software oscilloscope allows changing the sampling frequency from 2 kHz to 400 kHz. In this case, it is possible to observe visually on the monitor screen the spectrum of the signal and its variation in time. The microphone and line inputs were disconnected programmatically.

The measurements were carried out on computers with a sampling frequency of 44.1 kHz. A total of 20 stationary computers were examined from computer classes of National University Lviv Polytechnic. On each computer, several measurements were taken at different time intervals from a few seconds to several tens of days. The duration of each file was up to 10 s. The number of samples in the file for each channel (right and left channels) was up to 440 thousand samples. The steady-state processes occurred in each record for the first 1500 counts. In further calculations, the stable mode exit section was excluded, the 100000-sample recording sections were analyzed, these sections were taken from different parts of the recording file and for them, and the autocorrelation functions were calculated for the analysis.

Plot of noise signal are showed in Fig. 1. One division along the y axis corresponds to 100 µV.

Preliminary statistical processing of the noise signal was done. Mathematical expectation $(mean(x))$, variance $(Var(x))$ and mean square deviation $(Stdev(x))$ were estimated [24, 25]:

$$mean(x) = \frac{1}{n} \sum_{i=0}^{n-1} x_i \qquad (1)$$

$$Var(x) = \frac{1}{n-1} \sum_{i=0}^{n-1} (x_i - mean(x))^2 \qquad (2)$$

$$Stdev(x) = Var^{0.5}(x) \qquad (3)$$

For 20 000 samples: $mean(x) = 0.018$, $Var(x) = 7.203$, $Stdev(x) = 2.684$.
For 100 000 samples: $mean(x) = 0.006$, $Var(x) = 6.039$, $Stdev(x) = 2.457$.

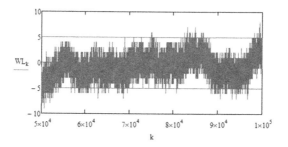

Fig. 1. Oscillogram of the noise signal of a stationary computer (left channel, ADC). The discrete samples are plotted along the abscissa axis. Voltage is plotted along the ordinate axis.

The histogram is obtained for 100 000 samples and 20 000 samples. The form of histogram is similar to the Gaussian distribution. For comparison, a histogram for a Gaussian distribution with an average value (*mean(x)*) and variance (*Var(x)*) for the noise signal is plotted, Fig. 2.

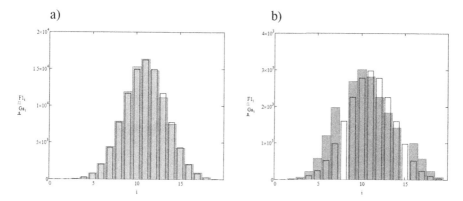

Fig. 2. The histogram of noise signal distribution F1 (solid gray bars) and Gaussian Ga with parameters calculated from the noise signal (contour bars): (a) 100000 samples, (b) 20000 samples.

Asymmetry (*skew(x)*) and kurtosis (*kurt(x)*) were calculated to accurately compare the resulting distribution with the Gaussian distribution (*Ga_i*). The formulas were used:

$$skew(x) = \frac{n}{(n-1)(n-2)Stdev(x)^3} \sum_{i=0}^{n-1} (x_i - mean(x))^3 \tag{4}$$

$$kurt(x) = \frac{n(n+1)}{(n-1)(n-2)(n-3)Stdev(x)^4} \sum_{i=0}^{n-1} (x_i - mean(x))^4 - \frac{3(n-1)^2}{(n-2)(n-3)} \tag{5}$$

$$Ga_i = \frac{A}{\sqrt{2\pi Var(x)}}\exp(\frac{-(i-11)^2}{2Var(x)})$$ (6)

where A = 100 000, A = 20 000.

For 20 000 samples: $skew(x) = 0.192$, $kurt(x) = -0.272$.
For 100 000 samples: $skew(x) = 0.06$, $kurt(x) = -0.016$.

In our case, the autocorrelation function cannot be calculated from the joint probabilities distribution densities, since they are not known. Averaging over the ensemble is also impossible, since we are dealing with only one implementation.

The only possible operation is the calculation of the temporal autocorrelation function on a limited interval under the assumption that the random process is ergodic.

$$corr_k(x,x) = \frac{1}{var(x)(N+1)}\sum_{i=1}^{N}(x_{k+i}-mean(x))(x_i-mean(x))$$ (7)

The results of the experiment show that the form of the autocorrelation function for each particular computer does not change, whereas for different computers the form differs significantly (Fig. 3). Averaging was performed for 20 000 samples.

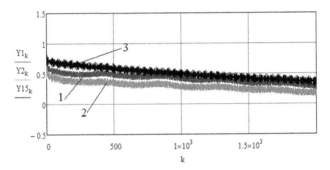

Fig. 3. Functions of autocorrelation of noise of two different computers: plots 1 and 2 are from files of first computer and plot 3 is from file of second computer.

The form of small-scale changes of autocorrelation function does not change for one computer. It remains constant for different offsets from the beginning of the file, as well as for files recorded with one computer at different times. It is practically constant for noise signal files recorded at different instants of time. The form of small-scale changes of autocorrelation function depends on the particular computer (Fig. 4).

The form of small-scale changes of autocorrelation function does not change as the number of samples exceeds 20 000. Thus, the form of the autocorrelation function can be used for identification.

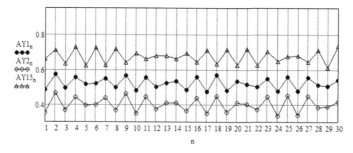

Fig. 4. Autocorrelation functions of the noise signal of two computers: top plot is corresponded to first computer; middle and lower plots are corresponded to second computer.

4 Definition of the Authentication Signs

The task of authentication of electronic devices by internal electrical noise is based on the uniqueness of the component parameters as a base at the microscopic level, and their constructive location. The task is solved by the method of calculating the auto-correlation function of the noise signal, which is characteristic for each electronic device and characterizes its own resonant frequencies. Based on the autocorrelation function, the bit and amplitude templates of the device are calculated. Although the autocorrelation function is practically individual for each device, different autocorre-lation functions are used for authentication. It is necessary to compare. As such a value the template is proposed, it consists of a bit sequence (bit template) and a sequence that characterizes the amplitude of the samples (amplitude template).

The bit template is a sequence of zeros and ones that is formed by the following rule: if the next value of the autocorrelation function a_{n+1} is not less than the previous an a_n ($a_{n+1} \geq a_n$), then one is written to the bit sequence, if less, ($a_{n+1} < a_n$), then zero is written. For a computer with the number I there can be written:

$$B_n^I = \begin{cases} 1, a_{n+1} \geq a_n \\ 0, a_{n+1} < a_n \end{cases} \qquad (8)$$

The length of this bit sequence is one less than the number of samples of the autocorrelation function and is $N - 1$. Each autocorrelation function I is matched to the bit templates. To compare two bit sequences, which obtained from different autocor-relation functions, the Hamming distance is calculated. The Heming distance is nor-malized to the length of the sequence of autocorrelation values:

$$H(B^I, B^J) = \frac{1}{N-1} \sum_{n=1}^{N-1} |B_n^I - B_n^J| \qquad (9)$$

Here (and further) the upper indices I and J denote the autocorrelation functions obtained from the I and J record files. It is important the necessary length of the

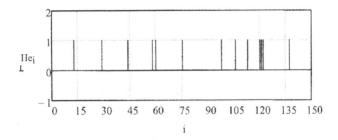

Fig. 5. Set of the not equal bits of bit sequence for files from two computers.

autocorrelation function for needed accuracy. Not equal bits in bit sequence are not equidistant. The set of the not equal bits for files from two computers are shown in the Fig. 5.

The set of the not equal bits for files from one computer are shown in the Fig. 6.

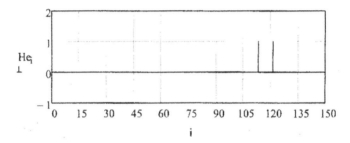

Fig. 6. Set of the not equal bits of bit sequence for files from one computer.

The comparisons of normalized Hamming distanced for bit sequence of two computers and the one of one computer shown, that the length 1000 bit is enough for computer authentication. The results are in the Table 1.

Amplitude template A^I of the device is a sequence of modules of differences of neighboring values of the autocorrelation function:

$$A_n^I = |a_{n+1} - a_n| \tag{10}$$

The normalized sum of the modules of difference between A^I and A^J is calculated to compare two amplitude templates obtained from various autocorrelation functions:

$$M(A^I, A^J) = \frac{1}{N-1} \sum_{n=1}^{N-1} |A_n^I - A_n^J| \tag{11}$$

Table 1. Normalized distances

Length of bit sequence or amplitude sequence	Normalized Hamming distance for files from two computers	Normalized Hamming distance for files from one computer	Normalized amplitude distance for files from two computers	Normalized amplitude distance for files from one computer
10	0.000	0.000	0.0170	0.0017
50	0.060	0.000	0.0160	0.0017
100	0.070	0.000	0.0160	0.0015
150	0.087	0.013	0.0160	0.0015
200	0.095	0.010	0.0160	0.0014
300	0.100	0.010	0.0160	0.0015
400	0.103	0.010	0.0160	0.0015
500	0.098	0.008	0.0160	0.0014
600	0.095	0.007	0.0160	0.0014
700	0.099	0.009	0.0160	0.0014
800	0.101	0.009	0.0160	0.0014
900	0.102	0.009	0.0160	0.0014
1000	0.100	0.009	0.0160	0.0014

Table 1 shows the values of the normalized distance between the amplitude sequences, taken for file from one computer for different offsets from the beginning of the file, and for files from two computers.

A difference of one order of magnitude for the amplitude template is observed for two computers, like a bit template.

The normalized Hamming distances for files from two computers and from one computer are differing by approximately in 10 times. This makes it possible to reliably distinguish these computers on the network.

5 Authentication Algorithm

Authentication algorithm is carried out as follows. The time samples sequence of the internal noise signal of the PC^I is recorded from ADC. This sequence is fed to the input of the autocorrelation calculation program. The computed bit template B^I and amplitude template A^I are recorded in the template folder of the PC^I. This procedure is carried out for all N personal computers of the corporate network. Templates are stored on the server in the authentication database.

When authentication should be done for PC^J computer, the B and A are calculated:

$$B = \begin{cases} 1, H(B^J, B^I) \cong H(B^J, B^J), I = \overline{1,N} \\ 0, H(B^J, B^I) >> H(B^J, B^I), I = \overline{1,N} \end{cases} \tag{12}$$

$$A = \begin{cases} 1, M(A^J, A^I) \cong M(A^J, A^J), I = \overline{1,N} \\ 0, M(A^J, A^I) > > M(A^J, A^J), I = \overline{1,N} \end{cases} \tag{13}$$

Authentication result AUT is written as a logical product:

$$AUT = B \wedge A \tag{14}$$

Thus, the conditions $B = 1$, $A = 1$ must be fulfilled to confirm authentication $AUT = 1$ on two templates simultaneously.

Experiments and calculations for 20 PC showed that there is an error of the authentication of computers PC^5 and PC^6. A detailed examination showed that the bit and amplitude patterns of these computers are the same within the change for different recording files. All the other 18 computers were authenticated correctly.

6   Conclusion

The authentication method for electronic devices is proposed, which is based on invariants of internal electrical noise signals. The method does not require large computational powers and can be used for real-time authentication. Such authentication is suitable for the Internet of Things, network identification of computers and smartphones.

The following results were obtained: the authentication of each electronic device can be carried out uniquely by its internal electrical noise (like biometric authentication of a person). Uniqueness of authentication is provided by the invariants of the noise signal such as the shape of the graph of the autocorrelation function of noise and the set of resonance frequencies of the device. The electronic device authentication template is obtained from the sequence of values of the autocorrelation function of the noise. It consists from the bit template and the amplitude template. A set of resonance frequencies is obtained from data for the phase portrait of the noise signal. The required duration of the noise signal is 0.5 s for reliable authentication at a sampling frequency of 44.1 kHz. The authentication algorithm is presented.

References

1. Hasse, J., Gloe, T., Beck, M.: Forensic Identification of GSM Mobile Phones. http://www.dence.de/publications/Hasse13_GSMMobilePhoneIdentification.pdf. Accessed 19 Mar 2018
2. Toshiba Develops New Chip Authentication Technology Using Transistor Noise. http://www.toshiba.co.jp/rdc/rd/detail_e/e1506_03.html. Accessed 19 Mar 2018
3. Laput, G., Yang, C., Xiao, R., Sample, A., Harrison, C.: Em-sense: touch recognition of uninstrumented, electrical and electromechanical objects. In: 28th Annual ACM Symposium on User Interface Software Technology, pp. 157–166. UIST, New York (2015)
4. Karapanos, N., Marforio, C., Soriente, C., Capkun, S.: Sound-proof: usable two-factor authentication based on ambient sound. In: 24th USENIX Security Symposium, pp. 483–498. USENIX, Washington (2015)

5. Yang, C., Sample, A.P.: EM-ID: tag-less identification of electrical devices via electromagnetic emissions (2016). http://ieeexplore.ieee.org/document/7488014/
6. Chumachenko, A., Rublev, D., Makarevich, O., Fedorov, V.: Identification of digital microphones by the imperfections of the recording path. Issue SFU Tech. Sci. Thematic Issue Inf. Secur. Taganrog **8**, 84–92 (2007)
7. Rybalsky, O., Zhuravel, V., Solovyev, V.: Signalogramm structure and universality of the fractal approach to the development of the phonoscope assessment toolkit. Inf. Math. Methods Simul. **3**(3), 225–232 (2013)
8. Nyemkova, E., Chaplyha, V., Shandra, Z.: Technique of measuring of identification parameters of audio recording device. In: The 18th International Conference on Information Technology for Practice, Ostrava, pp. 209–218 (2015)
9. Nyemkova, E., Chaplyha, V., Shandra, Z., Kochan, R., Gancarczyk, T., Shaikhanova, A.: Computational device authentication via fluctuations of analog-to-digital converter. In: 9th IEEE International Conference on Intelligent Data Acquisition and Advanced Computing Systems: Technology and Applications (2017)
10. Nicolis, G., Prigogine, I.: Self-Organization in Nonequilibrium Systems. Wiley-Interscience, New York (1977)
11. Ebeling, W.: Stochastische Theorie der Nichtlinearen Irreversiblen Prozesse. W. Pieck U.P, Rostock (1977)
12. Mehrotra, A.: Simulation and modelling techniques for noise in radio frequency integrated circuits. University of California at Berkeley (1999)
13. Schuster, H.G., Just, W.: Deterministic Chaos. WILEY-VCH Verlag GmbH & Co. KGaA, Weinheim (2005)
14. Rabinovich, M.I., Afraimovich, V.S.: Stochastic auto oscillations and turbulence. Phys. Usp. **125**, 123–168 (1978)
15. Lichtenberg, A., Lieberman, M.: Regular and Chaotic Dynamics. Springer, New York (1992). https://doi.org/10.1007/978-1-4757-2184-3
16. Loskutov, A.: Lectures time series analysis. http://chaos.phys.msu.ru/loskutov/PDF/Lectures_time_series_analysis.pdf. Accessed 19 Mar 2018
17. Kuzovlev, Y.: Why nature needs 1/f noise. Phys. Usp. **58**(7), 719–729 (2015)
18. Dyvak M., Padletska N., Pukas, A., Kozak O.: Identification the recurrent laryngeal nerve by the autocorrelation function of signal as reaction on the stimulation of tissues in surgical wound. In: Proceedings of the XIIth International Conference CADSM 2013, Lviv, Ukraine, pp. 89–92 (2013)
19. Nikulchev, E.B.: Identification of Dynamic Systems Based on Symmetry of Reconstructed Attractors. Moscow State University of Printing Publishing, Moscow (2010)
20. Petrovich, V.N.: Identification of parameters of mathematical models of dynamic control system. Artif. Intell. **4**, 343–349 (2011)
21. Patra, J.C.: Identification of nonlinear dynamic systems using functional link artificial neural networks. IEEE Trans. Syst. Man Cybern. Part B (Cybern.) **29**(2), 254–262 (1999)
22. Patra, J.C., Kot, A.C.: Nonlinear dynamic system identification using Chebyshev functional link artificial neural networks. IEEE Trans. Syst. Man Cybern. Part B (Cybern.) **32**(4), 505–511 (2002)
23. OscilloMeter 7.30 - Multichannel Real-Time Spectrum Analyzer. http://soft-arhiv.com/load/47-1-0-95
24. Max, J.: Methods and Techniques for Signal Processing and Applications to Physical Measurements - Principles and Apparatus for Real-Time Processing. Masson, Paris (1980)
25. Bendat, J.S., Piersol, A.G.: Random Data: Analysis and Measurement Procedures. Wiley, New York (2010)

Proposal for a Privacy Impact Assessment Manual Conforming to ISO/IEC 29134:2017

Sanggyu Shin[✉], Yoichi Seto, Kumi Hasegawa, and Ryotaro Nakata

Advanced Institute of Industrial Technology, 1-10-40 Higashiooi, Shinagawa-ku,
Tokyo 140-0011, Japan
{shin,seto.yoichi}@aiit.ac.jp

Abstract. In this paper, we compared the requirements of previously developed manual and ISO/IEC 29134:2017 and analyzed the changes. As a result, there were no major differences in requirements. It is useful to conduct a privacy impact assessment (PIA) before actually operating the system to appropriately construct and operate a system that handles personal information. A manual (procedure manual) is necessary to implement PIA efficiently. In June 2017, ISO issued the ISO/IEC 29134:2017 as an international standard on PIA. Cause the past PIA manual developed based on ISO 22307:2008, development of a PIA manual conforming to ISO/IEC 29134:2017 was required. By our analysis, as a newly stated matter, ISO/IEC 29134:2017 explicitly indicated Due Diligence, stakeholder engagement, and risk countermeasures. Based on the analysis results, we propose a new PIA manual reflecting the requirements of ISO/IEC 29134:2017.

Keywords: Privacy information · Privacy impact assessment
Risk countermeasures · ISO 22307:2008 · ISO/IEC 29134:2017

1 Introduction

With the progress of computerization of personal information in the 90s, problems related to the leakage of personal information and infringement of privacy in the information system emerged. Performing the privacy impact assessment (from now on referred to as PIA) as a countermeasure of this problem was reviewed all over the world. Since the mid-1990s, the PIA was introduced in Canada, New Zealand, Australia, the United States, and South Korea. The British Commonwealth is implementing PIA as a social system, while the United States and South Korea regulate and enforce it by law [1, 2]. The EU stipulates the implementation of Data Protection Impact Assessment in the General Data Protection Regulation (from now on referred to as GDPR) scheduled to be in effect in 2018 [3–5].

© Springer Nature Switzerland AG 2018
K. Saeed and W. Homenda (Eds.): CISIM 2018, LNCS 11127, pp. 486–498, 2018.
https://doi.org/10.1007/978-3-319-99954-8_40

In Japan, the operation of a specific personal information protection evaluation in the *My Number* system has been adopted as a similar system, and administrative organizations are obliged to implement [6].

PIA is useful to properly construct and operate a system that handles personal information and to efficiently further implement PIA, a manual conforming to the international standard is necessary. The first international standard ISO 22307:2008 on PIA was issued in 2008 and in June 2017 the new standard ISO/IEC 29134:2017 was released. Since the PIA manual developed in the past is based on ISO 22307:2008, it was necessary to make a PIA manual conforming to ISO/IEC 29134:201 [7–10].

In this paper, we compare the past manual (based on ISO 22307:2008) with ISO/IEC 29134:2017 and introduce the proposed a new PIA manual reflecting ISO/IEC 29134:2017.

2   Brief of Privacy Impact Assessment

A privacy impact assessment (PIA) is a risk management method that evaluates the influence on privacy "in advance," in order to reduce or avoid privacy (personal information protection) problems when introducing or repairing a system involving the collection of personal information.

The purpose of PIA is to reduce costs reduction and increase trust among stakeholders. Based on the results of the implementation, the PIA urges the constructed system to change the specification as necessary. By making changes before operating the system, it is possible to reduce the operation stop due to the occurrence of privacy problems after an operation, business risks and system renewal costs incur thereby [7, 8, 11].

Also, with the implementing organization publishing the PIA report, it is possible to provide a base to discuss privacy and handling of personal information with the executing organization, stakeholders and other actors. The PIA will also indicate to stakeholders the fact that organizations are paying attention to the protection of individual rights. In other words, PIA is also a mean for communicating risks.

Requirements of PIA are stipulated in the international standards mentioned in Sect. 3 and in the EU with Data Protection Impact Assessment under General Data Protection Rules [5–7].

3   International Standards Related to Privacy Impact Assessment

3.1   ISO 22307:2008

ISO 22307:2008 (Privacy Impact Assessment) is the first international standard stipulating the privacy impact assessment issued in April 2008 by the International Standards Committee ISO/TC 68/SC 7 (Financial Services). It is also applicable to other industries than the financial one.

The following six common elements (six requirements) are required by any PIA process: (1) PIA plan, (2) assessment, (3) PIA report, (4) competent expertise, (5) degree of independence and public aspects and (6) use in the PFS (proposed financial system) decision-making.

Among them, the former three correspond to the PIA implementation procedure; the latter three correspond to the implementation system.

3.2   ISO/IEC 29134:2017

ISO/IEC 29134:2017 (Guidelines for privacy impact assessment) was issued in July 2017 from ISO/IEC JTC 1/SC 27. ISO/IEC 29134:2017 describing the stakeholder identification and consultation and the importance of risk response. Such a protocol stipulates the positioning and implementation procedure of PIA assuming its use in private organizations [8].

However, the description is a recommended expression and not a mandatory one, and the basic requirement follows the six requirements specified in ISO 22307:2008. Table 1 shows the comparison with ISO/IEC 29134:2017 with reference to the requirements of ISO 22307.

The purpose of PIA implementation is divided into three.

(1) Security measures on personal information: The PIA adopts the concept of "Privacy by Design," which considers privacy measures beforehand at the planning stage in the information system life cycle. In general, it is said that the cost of security measures for information systems would be higher if implemented after the process. Implementing PIA at the planning stage of the system can be a useful method of protecting personal information even for organizations that have budget constraints on security measures [11,12].

(2) Establishing trust between stakeholders: PIA evaluates the information system to be newly introduced, using the multi-stakeholder process method where each stakeholder discusses in a roundtable fashion from an unbiased viewpoint and reports the results as a PIA report, such as Web. By doing so, it becomes a means of building trust relationships with among stakeholders [13,14].

(3) Equivalent attention in the protection of personal information: PIA implementation can be used as Due Diligence. Due Diligence is the act of deciding the responsible branch point. The process of PIA that identifies and cope with potential privacy risks that may occur in the course of business is equivalent to Due Diligence [13].

3.3   ISO/IEC 29100:2011

The ISO/IEC 29100:2011 privacy framework is an international standard which prescribes the privacy framework (published in Japanese Industrial Standard JIS X 9250: 2017 in June 2017).

ISO/IEC 29100:2011 describes privacy considerations (11 principles). In the 11 principles of ISO/IEC 29100:2011, "Consent and choice," "Data minimization"

Table 1. Comparison between ISO 22307 and ISO/IEC 29134:2017.

	ISO 22307	ISO/IEC 29134:2017
Purpose	Identify methods to provide privacy impact assessment requirements to optimally protect privacy in the financial sector.	Provide of a procedure of privacy impact assessment, and composition and contents of PIA report.
Request	(1) PIA plan (2) Assessment (3) PIA report (4) competent expertise (5) degree of independence and public aspects (6) use in the PFS decision-making * (1)–(3) procedure, (4)–(6) system	(1) Preparation for PIA analysis (2) Procedure for PIA: 5 items ① Introduction ② Preliminary analysis ③ Preparation of PIA ④ Implementation of PIA ⑤ Follow up of PIA (3) PIA Report: 8 items ① Introduction ② Report structure ③ Scope of PIA ④ Privacy requirements ⑤ Risk assessment ⑥ Risk response plan ⑦ Conclusion and decision ⑧ PIA public summary
Quotation standard	· OECD Guidelines on the Protection of Privacy and Transborder Flows of Personal Data (1980, These Guidelines were updated in 2013)	· ISO/IEC 29100:2011 (Information technology - Security techniques - Privacy framework) · ISO/IEC 27000:2016 (Information technology - Security techniques - Information security management systems - Overview and vocabulary) · ISO/IEC 29151, 27001
Third Party Confirmation	No regulation	A third-party organization's review will give the PIA report reliability and improve transparency. Also, if the PIA is implemented by a third-party organization, a review does not necessarily need to be carried out by a third-party organization.
Other	· "shall" expression · Privacy compliance audit and privacy impact assessment are clearly separated	· "should" expression · ISO 31000 is not quoted · Risk assessment is mixed with ISMS · Quoted ISO/IEC 27001, 29151

and "Privacy compliance" were added as new items. Also, the contents of the items corresponding to the 8 principles of the OECD were also described clearly. Furthermore, ISO/IEC 29134:2017 quotes ISO/IEC 29100:2011 [8,15,16].

4   ISO/IEC 29134:2017 Requirement Analysis for PIA Manual Development

4.1   Assessment Method

The analysis was carried out by referring to the description section of the corresponding ISO/IEC 29134:2017 (from now on referred to as 29134) according to the section of the PIA manual conforming to ISO 22307:2008 (from now on referred to as 22307) previously developed. According to the result of the analysis, modification of the PIA manual, additional rewriting was carried out. Table 2 shows the table of contents of the previously developed manual for surveillance camera and the main review points for each chapter [8–10,17].

4.2   Analysis

Table 2 shows the table of contents of the PIA developed the manual and the corresponding part of the reference 29134, and the list of review points for manual revision. Details of the results of the examination are described below.

Definition of a PIA. 29134 has the description of the definition of PIA, we ascertained that the current manual (already proposed our Garde line) description was not inconsistent with the description of 29134.

Benefits of Carrying Out a PIA. In the description about benefits of carrying out a PIA in 29134, also regarding reducing the privacy risk by preliminary evaluation at the early stage of development, there is no difference from the description of PIA implementation purpose described in the current manual. The point of view on Due Diligence is the concept added in 29134, which is a concept complementing the purpose of PIA, so we added it to our new manual.

Procedure for Performing the PIA. 29134 clearly distinguishes between "business flow" and "data flow." In other words, should it separates "work" and "data." Although ISO 22307 (from now on referred to as 22307) also features the description "business process and data flow," the existing manual does not distinguish the description clearly. For this reason, we re-inspected the entire manual and revised it clearly to distinguish between "business" and "data flow."

Table 2. Main review points of the PIA manual revision

Table of PIA manual		Main chapter of the referenced ISO/IEC 29134:2017	Main review points
1. Introduction		Introduction	(1) Definition of a PIA
2. Privacy impact assessment		5.1 Benefits of carrying out a PIA	(2) Benefits of carrying out a PIA
3. Overview of implementation of privacy impact assessment in surveillance camera system		Whole of document	(3) PIA implementation procedure
4. Determine whether implement		6.2 Determine whether a PIA is necessary (threshold analysis)	(4) Determine whether implement
5. Perform the PIA	5.1 Creating a project plan 5.2 Preparation of evaluation	6.3 Preparation of the PIA 6.4.3 Determine the relevant privacy safeguarding requirements	(5) Prepare for evaluation (6) Preparation of evaluation sheet
	5.3 Risk analysis	6.4.1 Identify information flows of PII 6.4.2 Analyse the implications of the use case 6.4.4 Assess privacy risk	(7) System risk analysis (8) Risk analysis of business flow (9) Risk response
	5.4 Impact assessment	6.4.5 Prepare for treating privacy risks 7.5 Risk assessment	(10) Impact assessment
	5.5 Preparation of PIA report 5.6 Submission of PIA report	7.2 Report structure 7.4 Privacy requirements 7.8 PIA public summary	(11) Preparation of PIA report (12) Submission of PIA report

Determine Whether Perform or Not the PIA. The 29134 stipulates that preliminary analysis should be conducted before performing the PIA. Based on the result of this preliminary analysis, we can determine whether a PIA is necessary. If necessary, prepare a PIA implementation plan. Also, in 29134, there is a description "the organization decides and documents the appropriate scope of the PIA, the size of the PIA, and the PIA implementation process" when a PIA is required.

Even in the current manual, it is made clear that the organization requesting implementation determines the necessity of PIA evaluation and that it is not coercible to recommendations about PIA implementation in preliminary PIA report. The position of the preliminary PIA is not inconsistent with the current manual, and revision is unnecessary. Items that need to be documented when determining PIA implementation will be noted.

Prepare for Evaluation. The 29134 specifies the following as preparation process of PIA.

- Improvement of implementation system
- Identify scope
- Evaluation criteria
- Developing a schedule
- Stakeholder engagement.

Among them, the concept of stakeholder engagement was prescribed for the first time in 29134 as the implementation guideline of PIA. Stakeholder engagement is a series of procedures that identify individuals who may be affected by processing PIA or processing PII and minimizes the effect through consultation. The process of stakeholder engagement is important because the PIA incorporates a multi-stakeholder process under the agreement between various stakeholders. For this reason, as a statement on stakeholder engagement, we added about the "identify stakeholders," "establish consultation plan," and "consult with stakeholders."

Preparation of Evaluation Sheet. Regarding the implementation guidance in the evaluation sheet creation, the 29134 has a statement "to use related information available from the previous project." In Chapter 6.2 "Determine whether a PIA is necessary" in the 29134, the case of existing system remodeling is specified as a condition that it is desirable to implement PIA. In the case of existing system repair, there are cases where the situation differs from the case of newly developed systems, such as available information, a necessity of detailed evaluation and so forth. For this reason, it was revised that, in preparation to the evaluation sheet, it is selectable whether to make it by detailed PIA or simple PIA depending on the situation.

Also, in the 29134, in the creation of evaluation items, it is supposed to be based on the description of the 29100 as a privacy protection requirement. The manual of the previous version also refers to the 29100, but the 29134 explicitly refers to the safety measure requirement described in the 29100.

System Risk Analysis. The description about procedure of the system risk analysis in the 29134 also applies to the procedure of the system risk analysis. There was no inconsistency with the current manual.

Risk Analysis of Business Flow. There is no clear description regarding the method of risk analysis of business flow in the 29134. Therefore, we will not change the description of risk analysis method about business flow. We decided to continue to adopt the "baseline approach" and "informal approach" which are risk analysis methods described as examples in the previous PIA manual.

Risk Response. In the risk analysis method referred to as an example in the description of "guidance for conducting" of the 29134, a privacy risk map adopted in ISMS is cited. In the privacy risk map, control measures are selected from four options: relocation, avoidance, possession, and reduction. Basically, concerning personal information protection, the PII administrator is in a position to keep personal information from businesses or individuals, and the PII administrator should not judge the method (type) of risk control measures. Therefore, unlike the ISMS risk analysis method, risk analysis in PIA does not consider risk analysis using risk maps and risk control measures in developed manuals.

Control measures are needed to "reduce" or "avoid" risks, which is close to PMS (Personal Information Protection Management System) based on JIS Q 15001 shown in Table 3.

However, as PMS does not specify precise procedures for evaluating the degree of influence, it is desirable to adopt the implementation procedure prescribed by ISMS for impact assessment.

For the above reasons, we did not add the risk analysis example using the privacy risk map as an example in the description of the guidelines.

Table 3. Comparison between ISMS and PMS

	ISO 27005:2011 (ISMS)	JIS Q 15001:2006 (PMS)
Managed target	My assets (business process activities, information)	**Personal informa- tion of others**
Acceptable risk	Risk below level are accepted	**Prevent the remaining risk from becoming obvious**
Analysis method	Static analysis	**Analysis by lifecycle**
Threat analysis	Carry out	**Do not implement**
Impact evaluation	**Clear procedure**	Unclear procedure

[Bold]: Items do reference at PIA.

Impact Assessment. PIA is a process for evaluating whether requirements are in conformity or nonconformity with other conditions and for proposing improvement measures. On the other hand, in 29134, the concept of ISMS is reflected in the process of implementing risk response. Therefore, the impact assessment method does not require further revisions.

Also, as already discussed in the questionnaire analysis of "(9) Risk response," impact assessment is implemented with the objective of "reducing" or "avoiding" risks. For this reason, we will continue to adopt the two-way gap analysis shown in Fig. 1 as shown in the current PIA manual as an impact assessment method. In the two-way gap analysis reform two evaluations, "evaluation of risk management plan" which evaluates that realize the risk and whether response plan is being implemented or not, and "evaluation of completeness about requirement items" which assesses whether the identified risk covers every requirement.

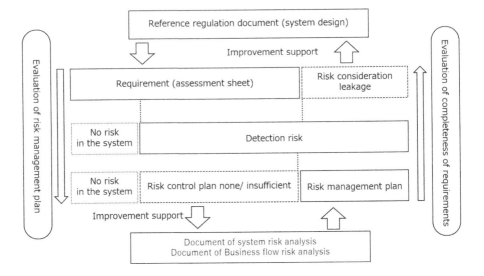

Fig. 1. Evaluation of impact by two-way gap analysis.

Preparation of PIA Report. In 29134, as a list to be described on the cover page of the PIA report, it is described. Since the description on the front page is not defined in the current PIA manual, it was added.

Submission of PIA Report. In 29134, about publishing the PIA report, it is description about the creation of the public summary assuming the disclosure on the website etc., in the current PIA manual, since there is no concrete description about this, and it was added.

4.3   Consideration

The 29134, the following 6 requirements of ISO 22307 have been followed.

- Elements concerning PIA implementation procedure
  (1) PIA plan
  (2) assessment
  (3) PIA report
- Elements concerning PIA implementation system
  (4) competent expertise
  (5) degree of independence and public aspects
  (6) use in the PFS decision-making.

Also, the following items which have been considered from a previous standard point of view, have been explicitly stated in 29134.

- Due diligence
- Stakeholder engagement
- Risk countermeasures
- Public summary

These are elements that clarify the positioning of the PIAs and should be indicated in the manual. Also, the 29134 provides a concrete description of the implementation procedures of PIAs not shown in ISO 22307, and the items in the order of implementation are reflected in the revision.

On the other hand, in the case of risk response, the policy of the current PIA manual was decided to be continued. The 29134 specifies ISO/IEC 27000 and ISO/IEC 29100 as quoted standards. The risk management adopted the ISMS approach (ISO/IEC 27005). The risk response is, as described in Sect. 4.2 (9) Risk response, (10) Impact assessment, and (11) Preparation of PIA report, which basically, countermeasures are needed to "reduce" or "avoid" the risk of personal information handled by an information system covered by the PIA. We will continue to adopt this policy [7–10].

5   The Process of the Implementation of PIA

Figure 2 shows the PIA implementation procedure according to ISO/IEC 29134. In each process of PIA, input, purpose, action, expected output (report) are shown explicitly in ISO/IEC 29134. Documents created in each process of PIA (expected results) were considered outputs, and the served as inputs to the next process. We also reflect on this configuration in the description of PIA manual.

	Preparation for implementation of PIA		Implementation of PIA evaluation		Report of PIA
	Preliminary assessment	Assessment preparation	Risk analysis	Impact assessment	Report / Review
Input	• System design document • Office work (Business) overview • Operation management provision etc.	• Documents related to an evaluation subject • Documents of a reference standard • Evaluation policy (simple, detail)	• Document of related to a target system • Document about reference rule • System analysis document • Business flow analysis document • Materials related to safety management measures	• System risk analysis document • Business flow risk analysis document • Materials related to safety management measures • Evaluation sheet	• Impact assessment report and related materials
Process	• Collection of evaluation related materials • Confirm evaluation scope • Extraction of personal information to be protected	• Analysis of target system • Analysis of business flow • Preparation of evaluation sheet	• Selection of system risk analysis method • System risk analysis	• Perform the impact assessment	• Prepare the PIA report
	• Analysis of target system/personal information flow	• Preparation implementation framework • Specify of assessment scope • Specify of reference rules documents, organizational regulations, etc. • Set the stakeholders and development of consultation plan	• Prepare for personal information management ledger • Selection of business flow risk analysis method • Business flow risk analysis	• Establish risk response plan	• Prepare the PIA public summary report
	• Impact assessment • Judgment of simplified or detailed PIA • Preparation of preliminary PIA report	• Decide the implementation schedule • Preparation of PIA implementation design document	• Hearing to stakeholders	• Hearing to stakeholders	• Review by stakeholders • Submission/disclosure of PIA report
Output	• Preliminary PIA report	• System analysis document • Business flow analysis document • Assessment sheet • PIA implementation design document	• System risk analysis document • Business flow risk analysis document	• Impact assessment report	• PIA report • PIA public summary report

Fig. 2. PIA implementation procedure according to ISO/IEC 29134.

5.1   Preparation for Implementation of PIA

Preliminary Assessment. Prior to the main assessment, preliminary evaluation (preliminary PIA) would be carried out. In the preparatory PIA, the implementation schedule, a system (personnel) securing, a decision of the embodiment
are summarized in the report. However, it is also possible to skip the implementation of preliminary PIA at the discretion of the responsible official of the
requesting organization, formulate the PIA implementation plan, and implement
the PIA (this evaluation) project. The decision on implementation (simple and
detailed) of PIA (this evaluation) based on the results of preliminary PIA was
taken by a judgment of organization supervisor.

Assessment Preparation. After the preliminary PIA is implemented, a plan
for evaluating PIA would be formulated in order to promote the PIA project,
improve PIA implementation structure, identify the scope of PIA, the laws and
standards to be referred, guidelines and internal regulations of the organization.
Based on the reference standard, evaluation criteria for evaluating the influence
of the privacy risk of the target system are summarized as evaluation sheets.
Also, based on the design document of the evaluation target system, the system
configuration - which is the basis of the evaluation - carries out the business
analysis and creates the system analysis book and the business flow analysis
report.

5.2   Implementation of PIA Evaluation

Risk Analysis. In order to evaluate the privacy risk of the target system,
the evaluation team analyzes the privacy risk after understanding the target
system (system analysis, business/data flow analysis, evaluation sheet creation).
If necessary, conduct hearings with concerned parties.

Impact Assessment. Evaluate impact based on evaluation sheet, system risk
analysis document, business flow risk analysis document.

5.3   Report/Review of PIA

Creating a PIA Report. The evaluation team prepares a PIA report based
on the results of the impact assessment of the privacy risk. We also prepare a
public report (public review).

Stakeholder Review. Publish the PIA report and receive reviews from stakeholders.

6   Conclusion

The ISO issued a new standard ISO/IEC 29134:2017 on PIA. For this reason, the current PIA manual developed under ISO 22307:2008 was revised to comply with this new standard through the comparative analysis of the already published our current PIA manual and ISO/IEC 29134:2017 was conducted. As a result, it has been confirmed that there is no significant difference between the PIA manuals already developed and ISO/IEC 29134:2017 regarding the basic requirements of PIAs. In ISO/IEC 29134:2017, it was confirmed that the description of "due diligence," "stakeholder engagement," and the "risk countermeasures" was described as the significance of PIA implementation.

On the other hand, the feature of the risk assessment method is ISO/IEC 29134 adopted ISO/IEC 27001 methods. In the PIA Manual, the risk assessment procedure is based on the procedures specified in ISO/IEC 29134. The risk assessment method will continue to adopt a bi-directional gap analysis method based on the idea of JIS Q 15001 (PMS) aimed at reducing and avoiding the risk of personal information in the already-developed PIA manager.

Acknowledgments. This research was carried out under the cooperation of team members as Project Based Learning of the Graduate School of Industrial Technology. I express my gratitude here.

References

1. Yoichi, S.: Privacy Impact Assessment (PIA) and Personal Information Protection. Chouokeizai-sha Inc., Tokyo (2010)
2. Yousuke, K.: The overseas trend of privacy impact assessment (PIA) and its application to Japan. In: Japan Data Communications, vol. 214, pp. 10–12. Japan Data Communications Association, Tokyo (2017)
3. Yoichi, S.: A Privacy Risk Countermeasure Technical Text: From the Concept of a Policy to the Risk Countermeasure Technology. Amazon Services International Inc., Tokyo (2017)
4. JETRO Brussel Office: Practical Handbook on the EU General Data Protection Rule (GDPR) (Introduction). JETRO, Brussel (2016)
5. JIPDEC: Regulation of the European Parliament and of the Council of on the protection of natural persons with regard to the processing of personal data and on the free movement of such data and repealing Directive 95/46/EC (General Data Protection Regulation) (Japanese translation) (2016)
6. Personal Information Protection Committee: Summary of Specific Personal Information Protection Assessment (2014). https://www.ppc.go.jp/files/pdf/gaiyou2.pdf. Accessed 15 June 2018
7. ISO 22307:2008 Financial services - Privacy impact assessment. https://www.iso.org/standard/40897.html
8. ISO/IEC 29134:2017(en) Information technology - Security techniques - Guidelines for privacy impact assessment. https://www.iso.org/obp/ui/#iso:std:iso-iec:29134:ed-1:v1:en
9. Satoru, N.: Development of guidelines for personal information impact assessment. J. Jpn. Soc. Secur. Manag. **29**(1), 3–16 (2015)

10. Advanced Institute of Industrial technology: Privacy impact assessment manual for surveillance camera system. AIIT (2016)
11. Yoichi, S.: Practical Privacy Risk Assessment Technique: Privacy by Design and Privacy Impact Assessment. Kindaikagakusha, Tokyo (2014)
12. Sadamu, T., Yoichi, S.: Privacy by Design. Automatic recognition, October issue, pp. 57–63. Japan Industrial Publishing Co. (2011)
13. Hasegawa, K., Yoichi, S.: Analysis of Adoption of Privacy Impact Assessment in Each Country. CSS2017, Yamagata (2017)
14. Yukari, U., Kensuke, S., Keisuke, S., Tian, J., Michitomo, N., Yoichi, S.: A Study of Privacy Impact Assessment in the Multi-Stakeholder Process. CSS2016, Akita (2016)
15. ISO/IEC 29100:2011 Information technology - Security techniques - Privacy framework. https://www.iso.org/obp/ui/#iso:std:45123:en
16. Ryotaro, N., Sanggyu, S., Yoichi, S.: Application of ISO/IEC 29100:2011 to the evaluation criteria of Privacy Impact Assessment. ISEC2017 (2017)
17. Yoichi, S.: Privacy Impact Assessment Guideline Practice Text. Inpress R&D, Tokyo (2016)

PHANTOM Protocol as the New Crypto-Democracy

Gautam Srivastava[1]([⊠]), Ashutosh Dhar Dwivedi[1,2], and Rajani Singh[2,3]

[1] Department of Mathematics and Computer Science, Brandon University, Brandon, MB, Canada
srivastavag@brandonu.ca
[2] Institute of Computer Science, Polish Academy of Sciences, Warsaw, Poland
[3] Faculty of Mathematics, Informatics, and Mechanics, University of Warsaw, Warsaw, Poland

Abstract. One of the biggest problems plaguing society today is that of fraudulent elections. The world's largest democracies still suffer from flawed electoral systems. In current voting systems, we see problems with vote rigging, hacking of the **EVM** (Electronic voting machine), election manipulation, and polling booth capturing. Looking closely at the current Cambridge Analytica scandal brings the validity of current voting systems into question. In this paper, we propose a novel voting model which can resolve these issues. Using a recently introduced blockchain protocol called PHANTOM, we try to alleviate known problems in voting systems. Furthermore, the advantage of using our model is, it is compatible with all voting schemes. So, one can implement our model using any voting scheme depending on the requirement of different type of elections.

1 Introduction

In the current architecture of the Internet, there is a strong asymmetry in terms of power between the entities that gather and process personal data (e.g., major Internet companies, telecom operators, cloud providers) and the individuals from which this personal data is issued. In particular, individuals have no choice but to blindly trust that these entities will respect their privacy and protect their personal data. In this paper, we address voting system issues by proposing an crypto-democracy model based on existing scientific achievements from the field of cryptography.

Some countries have already taken an initiative to improve their voting system by using blockchain technology [10] — a decentralized peer to peer network accompanied by a public ledger. The inability to change or delete information from blocks makes the blockchain the best technology for voting systems (Fig. 1). However, security and scalability of the voting system using blockchain methodology still needs to be answered. In a blockchain protocol, when a miner (responsible node for maintaining the blocks) extends the chain with a new block, it

© Springer Nature Switzerland AG 2018
K. Saeed and W. Homenda (Eds.): CISIM 2018, LNCS 11127, pp. 499–509, 2018.
https://doi.org/10.1007/978-3-319-99954-8_41

propagates in time to all honest nodes before the next one is created. The propagation of these long, data and electricity intensive blockchains brings on the
problems of the protocol that we have seen with many cryptocurrencies. Namely,
large electricity usage, large blockchains, and very slow computational speeds.
In the more than likely case when block creation rates are sped up or block
size increased, we will most definitely see these problems grow in an exponential
nature. Therefore to apply classic blockchain techniques to voting applications
for larger democratic countries having massive populations is not by any means
efficient or viable.

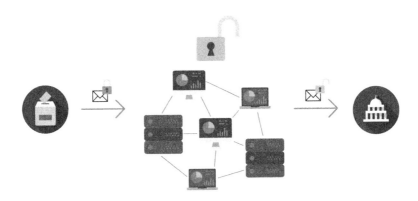

Fig. 1. The future of voting systems using blockchain technology

Recently, we have seen a major scandal hit the worldwide press involving
Cambridge Analytica [1]. The data analytics firm used personal information
harvested from more than 50 million Facebook profiles without permission to
build a system that could target US voters with personalised political advertise-
ments based on their psychological profile. This scandal has brought a major
international democratic voting system into question. The British data analysis
firm at the centre of Facebook's privacy scandal has declared bankruptcy and
has since shut down, confirming the public perception of such events.

1.1   Related Work

The migration of democratic voting systems to digital based platforms has
begun. Many digital voting systems are currently in use around the world. In
2005, Estonia started the first online voting system for municipal elections. In
2007, the Estonian parliamentary election also used internet voting. In 2015, they
used an i-voting system (Vabariigi Valimiskomisjon) for parliamentary election
system and 30.5% votes were made through i-voting.

In 2008, Satoshi Nakamoto invented the basis for what we now know as
blockchain technology [10]. The core concepts for this system were used in many
cryptocurrencies and other applications, with the reach of its applicable side still

not fully known. Built on the blockchain technology of Nakamoto was a protocol called **PHANTOM**, which we build on here [14]. **PHANTOM** has been proven to be secure under any throughput that the network itself can support, which makes it prime for use in a voting system where voters can number in the millions for large democracies.

In 2014, Lalley and Weyl proposed that blockchain lowers disorder and dictatorship costs of the voting and electoral process [8]. In addition to efficiency gains, this technological progress has implications for decentralized institutions of voting. One application that they proposed is Quadratic Voting (QV), which was further studied in [12]. Voters making a binary decision purchase votes from a centralized clearing house, paying the square of the number of votes purchased. They show that this process is both efficient and applicable to modern voting. Last year, it was suggested that

> Quadratic voting is the most important idea for law and public policy that has emerged from economics in (at least) the last ten years [4]

In 2015, the state of Virginia in the U.S.A. also implemented a blockchain-based solution to vote using *Follow My Vote* [2]. In this blockchain implementation, the voter has to install voting booth on a computer or smartphone. But there were too many flaws in this implementation and therefore the Follow My Vote project is still active but has lost funding.

In 2016, Kaspersky Labs and Economist newspaper [3] organized a competition where teams from the U.S.A. and UK had to implement voting systems using blockchain. The *Votebook* team from New York University in the U.S.A. came in first place who offered most effective case study on how a blockchain voting system might look like.

Voting systems are not alone showing the power on blockchains. IBM and Samsung have announced a collaboration to build decentralized Internet of Things (IoT) solutions by leveraging the Blockchain technology [6]. As the number of connected devices grows from billions to hundreds of billions, and as governments and corporations race to take control of devices and data, the authors feel the need to save IoT through the use of blockchains.

In this paper, we will further some of the initial ideas revolving around blockchain voting to a decentralized system that is efficient, secure, and most importantly realizable for large democracies. In depth surveys into the current uses of blockchain technology is given in [5,16].

Looking specifically more closely at blockchain based voting schemes, there have been a few works. In [15], the author explains that the blockchain is essentially a public ledger with potential as a worldwide, decentralized record for the registration, inventory, and transfer of all assets not just finances, but property and intangible assets such as votes, software, health data, and ideas. Lastly in [11], the author talks about how building upon the immutability, transparency and consensus inherent in blockchain technology, can help voting systems capitalize on every vote being recorded under a secure, cryptographic hash.

1.2 Security Problems in the Current Election System

Security of digital voting is always a problem in voting systems. During these digital voting elections, researchers identified many potential security risks with the system. Such risks could be malware in the client machine that can change votes for different candidate or another possibility is an attacker can directly infect servers. However a model using blockchain technology could prevent these issues. That being said, for larger democratic countries having massive populations and large geographical areas, using solely blockchain technology is not enough because of its slow computational speed. Some countries are also dealing with other problems in voting system like illiteracy, threatening voters, and booth capturing. Therefore current blockchain voting models are not enough to fight against these flawed election systems.

2 Our Model

We break down our model into the following two contributions:

1. In this paper, we introduce a more advanced blockchain voting management system. Instead of using the classic blockchain protocol, we use the **PHANTOM** protocol — a protocol for transaction confirmation that is secure under any throughput that the network can support. PHANTOM, unlike some of its predecessors, enjoys very large transaction throughput, which is a major downfall of bitcoin-like cryptocurrencies. PHANTOM utilizes a Directed Acyclic Graph of blocks, aka blockDAG, a generalization of blockchains which better suits a setup of fast or large blocks. PHANTOM uses a greedy algorithm on the blockDAG to distinguish between blocks mined properly by honest nodes and those mined by non-cooperating nodes that deviated from the DAG mining protocol.
2. The advantage of using our model is its compatibility with all voting schemes. So, one can implement our model using any voting scheme depending on the requirement of different type of elections.

2.1 Proposed Model

In this section we propose a model that does not entirely replace the present digital voting model but rather integrates new technology and other modifications in current system.

2.2 System Requirements

1. Security: Every vote should be counted, must be secure and accurate and can not be changed. For this purpose, we are using the PHANTOM protocol which is more secure than blockchain while still being as fast. Our model is compatible with all voting schemes. So, one can implement our model using any voting scheme depending on the requirement of different types of elections.

2. Authentication: Votes can only be made by authentic voters. In our system we do not need a specific registration process. Many countries provide a unique national identity card by using biometric and demographic data of people. As governments already have the biometric information of their constituents, we use fingerprint authentication to ensure an honest voter identity.

2.3 The PHANTOM

PHANTOM protocol has very large transaction throughput compared to blockchain. Miners in PHANTOM do not extend a single chain of blocks but structure blocks in the form of a Directed Acyclic Graph, a blockDAG, and refers to all blocks in the graph (that were not previously referenced, i.e. leaf-blocks). An example is shown in the Fig. 2.

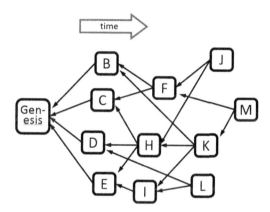

Fig. 2. 3-cluster of block DAG

In the example shown above, the DAG terminology is applied to block H as an example as follows:

- $past(H) = \{Genesis, C, D, E\}$ — blocks which reference H directly or indirectly and created before H.
- $future(H) = \{J, K, M\}$ — blocks which reference H directly or indirectly and created after H.
- $anticone(H) = \{B, F, I, L\}$ — order between these blocks and H is ambiguous. Deciding this order is the main challenge of protocol.
- $tips(G) = \{J, L, M\}$ — leaf blocks, with degree 0 and referenced in the header of the next block.

Security in PHANTOM

PHANTOM protocol ensures the security of votes by using these three operations:

1. By using block DAG structure, the protocol recognizes the cluster of well connected blocks. The blocks that were not mined honestly will not belong to this cluster and vice-versa.
2. It extends the partial ordered DAG graph to a full topological order in a way that penalizes blocks which are outside it and favours blocks which are inside it.
3. The order over the blocks induces an order over transactions; transactions in the same block are ordered accordingly to the order of their preference in it (Fig. 3).

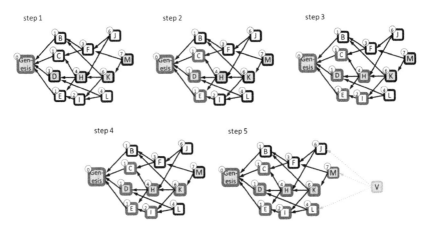

Fig. 3. An example of BlockDAG and its procedure to construct blue set consist of honest nodes

The small circle near each block X denotes the number of blue blocks (honest nodes) in the $past(X)$ called score. The algorithm selects the chain greedily, starting from the highest scoring tip M, then selecting its predecessor K (the highest scoring tip in past of M), then H, D (breaking the C, D, E tie arbitrarily), and finally $Genesis$. For methodological reasons, the chain is added to a hypothetical 'virtual' block V a block whose past equals the entire current DAG. Blocks in the chain $(genesis, D, H, K, M, V)$ are marked with a light-blue shade. Using this chain, DAGs are constructed consisting of a set of blue blocks, $BLUE_k(G)$ where k is the parameter which means that atmost $k+1$ blocks are assumed to be created within each unit of delay, so that typical anticone sizes should not exceed k.

The set of blue blocks is constructed recursively, starting with an empty one, as follows: In step 1 visit D and add genesis to the blue set (it is the only block in past (D)). Next, in step 2, visit H and add to $BLUE_k(G)$ blocks that are blue in $past(H)$, namely, C, D, E. In step 3 visit K and add H, I; note that block B is in $past(K)$ but was not added to the blue set, since it has 4 blue blocks in its anticone. In step 4 visit M and add K to the blue set; again, note that $F \in past(M)$ could not be added to the blue set due its large blue anticone. Finally, in step 5, visit the block $virtual(G) = V$, and add M and L to $BLUE_k(G)$, leaving J away due its large blue anticone.

Voting Architecture and Encryption of Votes
We use a multi-tiered, decentralized distributed ledger by dividing the protocol network into three tiers (Fig. 4):

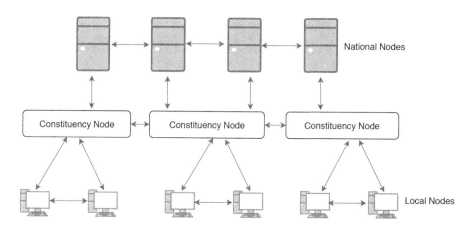

Fig. 4. Three tier node structure

1. National: The national tier (level 1) is the set of nodes which are not tied to any location. At this node, we apply the **PHANTOM** protocol. These nodes are only responsible to mine transactions and add blocks in the form of blockDAG instead of a long chain of blocks, as shown in Fig. 5. All national nodes are connected with each other and can communicate.
2. Constituency: The constituency also known as electoral area is a territorial subdivision for electing members. The constituency tier (level 2) contains all the nodes that are deemed to be at the constituency level. These nodes would be directly connected to each other and to a subset of polling stations under that constituency. A state or province of a given country would make for a good example of this tier.
3. Local: The local tier (leaf nodes) is a set of all polling stations across the country. A local node is setup to only communicate with the other local nodes under the associated constituency node and the constituency node itself. $B1, B2...B9$ represents the vote transactions by individual voters which is transferred to upper level nodes after encryption.

We are using an encryption method which is based on public and private keys. Each constituency level node generates the key pairs and different public key. The public keys are distributed to all lower level connected polling station nodes in the Local tier under the given constituency node. These nodes use public keys to encrypt votes made by polling stations. As each constituency has a different public key, a chunk of data under a given constituency is encrypted differently than the another chunk of data in another constituency. In such cases, if a hacker manages to recover a private key of a particular constituency then they will only be able to decrypt data under the current constituency. They will not be able to recover all data in other constituencies. Once the voting deadline passes, constituency nodes publish the private key to decrypt the data and count all the votes.

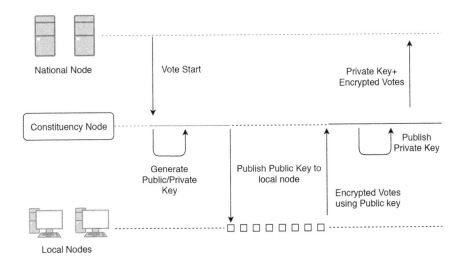

Fig. 5. Key pair encryption

We do not encourage voting through mobile apps in our model because the client side machines could potentially be infected with malware or other viruses. Since our voting system model also focusses on rural areas where literacy rates may be low and voters may not be familiar with the modern technologies, allowing the use of modern technology may become detrimental. Therefore, in our model, we emphasize that the voting should be performed by using polling booths which will prevent such attacks.

During the voting process, the voter is required to posses their national identification card which includes a unique identity number, biometric information and other related data. For example India provides a 12-digit unique identity number issued to all Indian citizens based on their biometric and demographic data, called UIDAI (Unique Identification Authority of India). As government has all the biometric and demographic information of the voters, we use fingerprint authentication to ensure an honest voter identity. Once the system can properly identify that the user's fingerprint is a match, they will be allowed to vote.

Some countries are also facing the problem of threatening voters to vote for a particular candidate or the known issue of booth capturing. Such problems can not be completely avoided but among the various voting schemes we plan to study types of vote counting schemes which can hopefully avoid a complete loss for honest candidates.

3   Voting Schemes Used by PHANTOM

The study of the effects of different voting schemes is called social choice theory. In other words, social choice theory or social choice is a theoretical framework for analysis of combining individual opinions, preferences, interests, or welfares to reach a collective decision or social welfare in some sense.

In social choice theory, according to Arrow's impossibility theorem (1951) or Arrow's paradox [9], when voters have more than two distinct alternatives (options), no ranked voting electoral system can convert the ranked preferences of individual voter into a nation-wide (complete and transitive) ranking. In short, there is no perfect voting scheme that always satisfies three *fairness* criteria.

- If every voter prefers candidate A over candidate B, then the people of the country prefer A over B.
- If every voter's preference between A and B remains unchanged, then the people of the nation's preference will also remain unchanged between A and B (even if the preferences of the voters between other pairs like A and C, B and C, or C and D change).
- There is neither *dictator* nor *prophet* meaning that no single voter possesses the power or the knowledge to always determine the people preference in that country.

Arrow's impossibility theorem is often most cited in discussions of voting theory that which voting scheme is best is further interpreted by the Gibbard-Satterthwaite theorem [13]. To that end, democratic countries have experimented with a number of different voting schemes. The advantage of using our model is, it is compatible with all voting schemes. So, one can implement our model using any voting scheme depending on the requirement of different type of elections.

Vote counting strategy plays an important role in any election process. Game theorists have suggested various types of voting schemes, each of them having pros and cons. Vote counting schemes that are being widely used are:

1. *Plurality voting* — where each voter is allowed to vote for only one candidate and who gets the most votes is elected.
2. *Ranked voting* — Instead of selecting only one candidate, voters rank all the candidates according to their preferences from most favorite to least. Each country has different political and local environment.

Moreover, the process to actually choose a good vote counting scheme based on country of election is another challenge altogether.

4   Future Work

Furthering this work is a natural decision, as we see this work as only a preliminary splash in the world of blockchain-based voting protocols. As a first step, it will be important to give some experimental evidence and credence to the security level of the PHANTOM protocol as to be used in this fashion. In [14], the authors describe the protocol at length giving detailed algorithms, but fail to show how applications of the protocol may cause security to be compromised for specific applications. We have see the original protocol [10] fail under recent scrutiny [7] therefore need to make sure PHANTOM is secure. Furthermore, it would be essential to address the security of the voters themselves during the voting process. Lastly, we have left the vote counting process open here. Originally championed by the Marquis the Condorcet and many others, majority rule has often been rejected as indeterminate, incoherent, or implausible. Majority rule's arch competitor is the Borda count, proposed by the Count de Borda, and there has long been a dispute between the two approaches. We wish to examine which counting process matches well with our process. Lastly, it would be pertinent to find a real world voting application to champion. Even something like a small University voting process would be a nice example to see the procedure at work.

5   Conclusion

Our model provides a perfect voting system for those places where the voting system is suffering from problems plaguing today's democracies like EVM hacking, and election manipulation. This model is also ideal for rural areas where literacy rates can be low. Our system does not use tablets or mobile devices, making it free from virus or malware attacks. When energy consumption and slow computational speed are major problems, our model provides a fast, secure and high throughput voting system compared to traditional blockchain voting schemes. As a complete package we have proposed a system that is easy to implement. It will be of interest to see how blockchain technology fits into its many proposed applications in the years to come, and how it can be used to further the needs of the many people who rely on technological advancement to help further our needs as a society. The advantage of using our model is, it is compatible with all voting schemes. So, one can implement our model using any voting scheme depending on the requirement of different types of elections.

References

1. Cambridge Analytica: The Story so Far. https://www.theguardian.com/news/2018/mar/26/the-cambridge-analytica-files-the-story-so-far
2. Blockchain Voting: The End To End Process. Follow My Vote https://followmyvote.com/blockchain-voting-the-end-to-end-process

3. Cyber Security Case Study Competition- Kaspersky. http://www.economist.com/sites/default/files/drexel.pdf
4. Allen, D.W., Berg, C., Lane, A.M., Potts, J.: The economics of crypto-democracy. Linked Democracy: AI for democratic innovation. In: 26th International Joint Conference on Artificial Intelligence, 19 August 2017 (2017)
5. Atzori, M.: Blockchain-based architectures for the internet of things: a survey (2016)
6. Brody, P., Pureswaran, V.: Device democracy: saving the future of the internet of things. IBM, September 2014
7. Conti, M., Kumar, S., Lal, C., Ruj, S.: A survey on security and privacy issues of bitcoin. IEEE Commun. Surv. Tutorials (2018)
8. Lalley, S.P., Weyl, E.G.: Quadratic voting. arXiv preprint arXiv:1409.0264 (2014)
9. MacKay, A.F.: Arrow's theorem: the paradox of social choice, a case study in the philosophy of economics. Technical report (1980)
10. Nakamoto, S.: Bitcoin: A peer-to-peer electronic cash system (2008)
11. Pilkington, M.: 11 Blockchain technology: principles and applications. In: Research Handbook on Digital Transformations, p. 225 (2016)
12. Posner, E.A., Weyl, E.G.: Voting squared: quadratic voting in democratic politics. Vand. L. Rev. **68**, 441 (2015)
13. Reny, P.J.: Arrows theorem and the gibbard-satterthwaite theorem: a unified approach. Econ. Lett. **70**(1), 99–105 (2001)
14. Sompolinsky, Y., Zohar, A.: PHANTOM: a scalable blockdag protocol. IACR Cryptol. ePrint Archive **2018**, 104 (2018)
15. Swan, M.: Blockchain: Blueprint for a New Economy. O'Reilly Media, Inc. (2015)
16. Zheng, Z., Xie, S., Dai, H.N., Wang, H.: Blockchain challenges and opportunities: a survey. Work Paper-2016 (2016)

Ensuring Database Security with the Universal Basis of Relations

Vitalii I. Yesin[1] , Maryna V. Yesina[1] , Serhii G. Rassomakhin[1] ,
and Mikolaj Karpinski[2(✉)]

[1] V. N. Karazin Kharkiv National University,
4 Svobody Square, Kharkiv 61022, Ukraine
{v.i.yesin, m.v.yesina, rassomakhin}@karazin.ua
[2] University of Bielsko-Biala, 2 Willowa Street, 43-309 Bielsko-Biala, Poland
mpkarpinski@gmail.com

Abstract. The subject matter of the article is methods and means of the databases (DBs) security ensuring, built on the basis of the database scheme that is invariant to subject domains (SDs). The goal is to develop a substantiated approach that implements the complex use of various mechanisms ensuring the databases security built on the database schema with the universal basis of relations. The task: based on the analysis of existing database protection mechanisms supported by various database management systems (DBMSs), and features of the destination, construction of the database schema with the universal basis of relations, to develop and present in a systematized form the means and methods ensuring the databases security built on this DB schema. The following results were obtained: solving the problem of protecting databases as the most important corporate resource, in the process of creating database schema invariant to subject domains, special means were developed (in the form of implemented schema objects such as triggers, procedures, packages, tables, functions) and rules of their use, ensuring: access control to schema objects; data protection and hiding of objects; data integrity support; recovery of incorrectly modified or lost data; monitoring of the state, changes introduced into the database; logging user actions.

Keywords: Database with the universal basis of relations · Database security
Data protection · Access control · Security policy

1 Introduction

The database (DB), as the most important corporate information resource, should be properly protected. And in the case of using a database, built on the basis of a scheme with the universal basis of relations, that allows to store simultaneously in the fixed structure of the relations of its scheme the data of various subject domains (SDs) necessary for the company, organization or institution according to its multidisciplinary activities, as a corporate repository, the problem of ensuring the database security, as the protection of its data from undesirable disclosure-use (violation of confidentiality), falsification (integrity violation), loss or decrease in availability measure, becomes even

© Springer Nature Switzerland AG 2018
K. Saeed and W. Homenda (Eds.): CISIM 2018, LNCS 11127, pp. 510–522, 2018.
https://doi.org/10.1007/978-3-319-99954-8_42

more actual. Herewith, it must be noted that the finished universal technique of integrated solution of the task ensuring of databases security today does not exist. This is explained by the variety of activities of enterprises, the structure of information systems, networks, database management systems (DBMS), data flows and ways to organize access to them. Therefore, in each specific situation, including when using a database with a universal basis of relations, this most important task requires an original approach, usually based on existing developments and solutions in this area.

2 Means and Methods for Protecting Databases Built on the Basis of the Scheme with the Universal Basis of Relations

The essence of the problem of ensuring the information security of databases is to develop methods and means that ensure the confidentiality, integrity, availability of their data under conditions of impact on them of any intentional or unintentional threats. Any threat should be considered as a potential possibility of security system violation that, if successful, can have some negative impact.

Existing approaches to solving this problem involves examining the database survey to identify possible threats that can lead to destruction, theft, data fraud, loss of confidentiality and data integrity, loss of availability and finding effective ways, means of confronting them. Herewith, first of all, the possibilities of means and methods of database protection that are supported by the database management system are analyzed.

The means and methods of databases protecting in various DBMS, on the platform of which the database scheme with the universal basis of relations [1–3] can be implemented, differ from each other. However, in varying degrees, often enough among them there are such as [4]: authorization, access control; views; backup and recovery; integrity support; encryption; the use of fault-tolerant hardware.

Below, without affecting the general security issues of computer systems, using the theory and the research results described in [4–12], we propose an approach implemented the complex use of various mechanisms ensuring databases security built on the basis of the database scheme that is invariant to subject domains (SDs) [1], taking into account the peculiarities of its structure.

It is known that to the violation of confidentiality leads both an intentional action aimed at the implementation of unauthorized access to the data and a random error of software or unskilled user action, which led to the disclosure of confidential information. Therefore, in the first place, the user authorization mechanism was analyzed to identify certain vulnerabilities in it and their subsequent elimination.

It is no secret that once a user get access right to database system, he can automatically be granted various privileges associated with his identifier. In particular, these privileges can include permission to access certain base (tables), virtual (views) relations of DB schema, its procedures, functions and other objects, as well as various actions with them. Such a method is sufficiently developed and flexible. It allows the database administrator to configure the access rights of users in accordance with their job responsibilities (the principle of access reasonableness). However, with it help, access is restricted only to named objects of the database schema, and, as a rule, only to a complete set of data that is provided to the respective users. While there is a need to control access at a lower level (although some DBMSs provide certain privileges for attributes of basic and virtual relations [5]). Using discretionary access control, it is impossible, for example, in full to restrict a subject access (a registered user) to only a part of DB relation tuples. And, taking into account the peculiarities of the database scheme with the universal basis of relations, which is invariant to subject domains and which allows to store data from different SDs in the fixed structure of the relations simultaneously, this is unacceptable. Thereby, analyzing the different approaches [4–8, 13] of the solution of this problem, it was concluded that it is advisable to use in this case of the mechanism of fine-grained access control, also known as row level security (RLS) [14].

That it was possible to take advantage of this mechanism benefits, as well as to simplify the procedure for registering the actions of database users (conducting an audit), ensuring auditability (one of the most important requirements of computer security), certain adjustments were made to the DB invariant scheme presented in [1] (in her base relations R^{sh}).

First, in each base relation of such database scheme $R_i^{sh} \in R^{sh}$ the following attributes were added: user identifier ($u_i \in at(R_i^{sh})$); the tuple recording time ($t_i^{ins} \in at(R_i^{sh})$); tuple component update time ($t_i^{upd} \in at(R_i^{sh})$). Secondly, since the specific user (its identifier) $u^j \in U_1$ is associated with the value of the attribute $u_i(U_1$ – the set of user identifiers) for which access privileges to the tuples of the base relations should be defined $R^{sh} - p_j \in U_3$ (where U_3 is the set of privileges granted to users for performing operations such as deletion, insert, update, select, as well as their combinations), the relation was defined whose extensions include data on the corresponding database user names, their identifiers and corresponding their access privileges. In a formalized form, such relation, referred to as the relation of users, can be represented as a subset of the Cartesian product $U_1 \times U_2 \times U_3$:

$$U = \{(u_1, u_2, u_3) | u_1 \in U_1 \wedge u_2 \in U_2 \wedge u_3 \in U_3\}, \tag{1}$$

where U_2 is the set of user names; $u_1 = u^j$; $u_3 = p_j$;

$$p_j = p_j^{gl} \cup p_j^{del} \cup p_j^{upd} \cup p_j^{sel} \cup p_j^{ins}, \tag{2}$$

$$p_j^{gl} = \begin{cases} p^{gl} \in P_{user}, & \text{if } u^j \text{ has the privilege to access data } \forall u^k, k = 1 \ldots |U_1|; \\ p^{none} = 0 \, (p^{none} \in P_{user}), & \text{else;} \end{cases}$$

$$p_j^{del} = \begin{cases} p^{del} \in P_{user}, & \text{if } u^j \text{ has the privilege to delete his data;} \\ p^{none} = 0 \, (p^{none} \in P_{user}), & \text{else;} \end{cases}$$

$$p_j^{upd} = \begin{cases} p^{upd} \in P_{user}, & \text{if } u^j \text{ has the privilege to update his data;} \\ p^{none} = 0 \, (p^{none} \in P_{user}), & \text{else,} \end{cases}$$

similarly for the privilege p_j^{sel} that allows to j user (u^j) to select the data available to him from the base relations R^{sh}, and data insert privilege – p_j^{ins}; $P_{user} = \{p^{none}, p^{del}, p^{upd}, p^{sel}, p^{ins}, p^{gl}\}$ is user privilege domain.

The result of mapping the relation U to the base relation $R_U^{sh} \in R^{sh}$ of the database scheme that is invariant to SDs is represented in the form of the main lines of data definition language code of the ISO SQL standard used in the CREATE (ALTER) TABLE operators:

```
USER_ID    NUMERIC(12)  PRIMARY KEY,  -- user id code(PK)
USER_NAME  VARCHAR(30)  not null,     -- user name
USER_ISUD  NUMERIC(2)   not null      -- user privileges.
```

Thirdly, to implement the possibility that the grantor (by one authorized user u^j) transferred the privileges belonging to him to other authorized users (grantees), the new mechanism was developed, since the traditional way (using GRANT command of the SQL standard) was not fully suitable for the database scheme with the universal basis of relations, taking into account its destination and structure of relations R^{sh}. Such mechanism implemented within RLS technology required the development of a new relation for the database scheme that is invariant to SD, namely so-called of the access privilege distribution relation to the data of other users. In a formalized form, it can be represented as a subset of the Cartesian product $U_1 \times U_1 \times U_3$:

$$G = \{(g_1, g_2, g_3) | g_1 \in U_1 \wedge g_2 \in U_1 \wedge g_3 \in U_3\}. \tag{3}$$

The relation (3) extension is a set of tuples, each of which is associated with a specific data owner (g_1), which transmits its access privileges (g_3) to another authorized user (g_2).

The result of mapping this relation to the base schema relation ($R_G^{sh} \in R^{sh}$) is shown below in the form of the following main lines of SQL code used in CREATE (ALTER) TABLE operators:

```
GRANT_ID   NUMERIC(12)  PRIMARY KEY,  -- primary key (PK)
GRANTOR    NUMERIC(12)  not null,     -- user-owner of data
GRANTEE    NUMERIC(12)  not null,
USER_ISUD  NUMERIC(2)   not null      -- user privileges.
```

Further in accordance with the RLS technology were determined:

- a set of declarative commands (RLS policies) that determine how and when have to apply users access restrictions to the tuples of the schema base relations R^{sh};
- a set of stored functions Ψ (combined in a package) that are called when the conditions specified in the security policy (RLS policy) are performed;
- predicates formed by functions Ψ that the DBMS automatically appends to the end of the WHERE clause of user-executable SQL statements (the consumption of system resources depends on the correct predicate formation).

In the aggregate, all this can be represented as the implementation of rules for protecting relations R^{sh} and formalized in the form of the following expression:

$$Sr = \{R_i^{sh}, oper_i^j, policy_i^k, \Psi_i^l, attr_i^{\mu kl}, pat_{contr}^{R_i^{sh}}\}, \tag{4}$$

where $oper_i^j$ is the j-th combination (from the values: select, update, delete, insert) of the allowed access operations to the relation $R_i^{sh} \in R^{sh}$; $policy_i^k$ is name of the k-th RLS policy, which is applied for the base relation R_i^{sh}; $\Psi_i^l \in \Psi$ is the name of the l-th function (specifying the package name) that generates the predicate for the base relation R_i^{sh}; $attr_i^{\mu kl}$ is the value of the μ-th parameter for the k-th RLS policy and the l-th function; $pat_{contr}^{R_i^{sh}}$ is pattern of the commands for managing access to R_i^{sh} (for implementation of the security policy).

Herewith, it should be noted that, for example, when implementing the database scheme with the universal basis of relations on the Oracle DBMS platform, in order to enhance the capabilities of RLS technology, guided by the recommendations [7, 8], it is also expediently to use the mechanism of so-called application contexts (named set of pairs "parameter-value"). The idea underlying the use of contexts is simple enough, but, at the same time, it allows to provide serious protection. The list of variables in memory (context), whose values are bound to sessions, is determined. Herewith, the session can get the current values of these variables, calling a special function, and variables in the context can be set only by calling a procedure associated with this context.

An example of the pattern of access control commands (of security policy implementation for Oracle DBMS) is given below.

```
create or replace package rls_utils is
...
function get_predicate(dml_stmt_p number, object_name_p
varchar2) return varchar2;
function get_access_rule_predicate(schema_p in varchar2,
object_p in varchar2) return varchar2;
...
end;
/
create or replace package body rls_utils is
...
   function get_access_rule_predicate
(schema_p varchar2, object_p varchar2) return varchar2
   as
   begin
     return (get_predicate(DML_access_rule, object_p));
   end;
...
end;
/
{
begin
dbms_rls.add_policy(object_schema   => '{user_name}',
         object_name      => '{table_name}',
         policy_name      => '{RLS_user_name_access_rule}',
         function_schema  => '{user_name}',
         policy_function  =>
'{RLS_UTILS.GET_access_rule_PREDICATE}',
         statement_types  => '[SELECT] [,INSERT] [,DELETE]
[,UPDATE]',
         update_check     => {TRUE|FALSE},
         enable           => {TRUE|FALSE},
         static_policy    => {TRUE|FALSE}
            );
end;
/
}
```

The following symbols are used in the above pattern:

- variables (in bold italic font): *user_name* is user name; *table_name* is base relation name $R_i^{sh} \in R^{sh}$ to be protected by policy; *access_rule* is combinations of access operations (select, update, delete, insert – $oper_i^j$, expression (4)) to the relation specified in *table_name*;

- parameters of the *add_policy* procedure of the standard Oracle package dbms_rls: *policy_name* is the name of the RLS policy that is applied to the base relation $R_i^{sh} \in R^{sh}$; *policy_function* is the name of the function owner that returns the condition; *policy_function* is the name of the function (with the name of the package) which generates a predicate for the base relation $R_i^{sh} \in R^{sh}$; *statement_types* is statement types to which the policy applies; *update_check* is optional argument for INSERT or UPDATE statement types (the default is false). Setting update_check to true causes the server to also check the policy against the value after INSERT or UPDATE; *enable* is a parameter indicating the activation of the policy immediately after its addition (the default is true); *static_policy* is a parameter (the default is true). If it is set to true, the server assumes that the policy function for the static policy produces the same predicate string for anyone accessing the object, except for SYS or the privileged user who has the EXEMPT ACCESS POLICY privilege.
- the braces are {}, the square brackets are [], the symbol | correspond to the notation taken from the extended Backus-Naur notation;
- all other alphanumeric characters are either language keywords, either by standard package names or by accepted string literals.

As a rule, today in relational DBMS separate records, from the point of view of the access organization to them of various users, are not specially protected, although there are examples known from practice when it is required [13, 15]. Therefore, in order to provide such functionality, based on the capabilities of the above fine-grained access control mechanism, taking into account the predetermined relation R^{sh} structure, a special additional relation of the DB scheme with the universal basis of relations was developed, the data of which is used by the function forming the predicate. This relation, referred to as the relation of access restrictions to a specific data item, can be presented in a formalized form as a subset of the Cartesian product $U_1 \times U_2 \times R_{name}^{sh} \times R_{ID}^{sh}$:

$$A = \{(a_1, a_2, a_3, a_4) | a_1 \in U_1 \wedge a_2 \in U_2 \wedge a_3 \in R_{name}^{sh} \wedge a_4 \in R_{ID}^{sh}\}, \qquad (5)$$

where R_{name}^{sh} is the set of schema relations R^{sh} names; $R_{ID}^{sh} = \cup_i R_i^{sh}[K_{PK_i}]$ is a set of identifiers that are primary keys (K_{PK_i}) in the corresponding relations R^{sh}, access to which is limited to a user with an identifier $a_1 \in U_1$ and a name $a_2 \in U_2$.

The result of mapping this relation to the base relation ($R_A^{sh} \in R^{sh}$) of the database scheme that is invariant to SD is represented as the following main lines of SQL code:

```
USER_ID     INTEGER not null,    -- user ID
USER_NAME   VARCHAR(255) not null, -- user name
CLASS_ID    INTEGER not null,-- object ID in TABLE_NAME

TABLE_NAME VARCHAR(255) not null-- table name( R_name^sh )
primary key (CLASS_ID, TABLE_NAME)-- PK.
```

The packet body fragment forming the context attributes and the predicate string is shown in [10].

Herewith, in general, it is necessary to understand that the implementation of the access mechanism of different users to specific individual data elements leads to an increase in the total time required to process the corresponding requests to the database.

In order to organize access to data and system resources in the development of the database schema with the universal basis of relations, its following objects were also identified: roles designed to simplify the management of system and object privileges; synonyms required to specify an alternate object name of the database; profiles as a named set of resource limits and password parameters that restrict database usage for a user.

To protect important information stored in the database, access to it from one side should be limited, and on the other side it is advisable to encrypt it. Data encryption is a key component in implementing the principle of multilevel protection. The desire to reduce the risk of data confidentiality loss, including due to insider threats of privileged users, has become a motivated start for: developing mechanisms that provide the possibility of effective use for the protection of cryptographic primitives supported by the DBMS (if there are any and they satisfy the consumer of the information product); developing their own cryptographic protection means (if they are not available or they do not fully meet the requirements of the consumer of the information product); or for their complex use.

For this purpose, a package of subprograms, a technique for its application was developed. Also recommendations on the use of existing technologies of information encryption and hiding have been determined.

The developed package of subroutines and the technique of its application provide for the integrated use of both the supported cryptographic primitives by the DBMS (for example, for Oracle DBMS it is cryptographic algorithms AES, 3DES168, RC4; cryptographic hash algorithms: MD5, SHA-1, SHA-2; keyed hash (MAC) algorithms: HMAC_MD5, HMAC_SH1, HMAC_SH512 and others) and the symmetric block cipher "Kalyna" from the national Ukrainian encryption standard DSTU 7624:2014.

Large amounts of data and discretionary access to information stored in a database based on a database schema with the universal basis of relations to a certain extent complicate the implementation of an effective mechanism when the content is pre-decrypted and then, after use, is encrypted back. Therefore, in order to preserve the habitual tools and operating procedure in the proposed approach, it is recommended to use the so-called "transparent encryption" method, in which the information is automatically decrypted when reading from the medium (if the correct key was entered) and automatically encrypted during recording. So transparent data encryption (TDE) allows you to selectively encrypt vulnerable data that is stored in database files, as well as all stream file components, such as redo logs, archive logs, backup tapes. The TDE technique is inherent in various DBMSs (IBM patent 7426745 [16]). The main purpose of TDE is to protect vulnerable data in the appropriate operating system files.

In addition, without resorting to the encryption procedure, for several reasons: observance of intellectual property rights; commercial value; the code provides the solution of problems of protection and distribution of data access rights; the inadmissibility of code modification by other users (especially after installing the software to the consumer of the information product, that the latter had no reason to declare after his own modification (in fact, hacking) about the inoperability and unreliability of software), code of the main procedures, functions, packages, triggers of the database schema with the universal basis of relations is advisable to hide. For this purpose, it is suggested to use the corresponding DBMS tools. For example, in Oracle DBMS, such the most suitable means is the special utility WRAP. This utility allows to hide PL/SQL code of main objects of the database schema quite simply and effectively, transforming this code into an unreadable form, which in its turn is uniquely understood by the server. The server can compile and execute it. Herewith the code is changed, and not encrypted with complex algorithms. Such a substitution does not greatly affect the performance, unlike the encryption/decryption procedure. However, using this mechanism, it should be kept in mind that if you need to change the source code, you will have to change the original again, hide it with the utility and load the hidden version into the database.

In addition to this mechanism, special pipelined-functions were developed to hide the composition and structure of the base and virtual relations of the database schema with the universal basis of relations. These functions with the parameter in the form of a meta-description line of the data model language (LDM) [17, 18] can be used in SQL statements (in FROM clause) instead of base and virtual relations of the database schema with the universal basis of relations.

An example of using pipelined-function:

```
SELECT '<ClassO>='||COLUMN_VALUE as name
FROM TABLE(get_spis_metadata('{<ClassO>=*.**;}'))
ORDER BY name;
```

where *get_spis_metadata* is a pipelined function with a parameter in the form of a meta-description line of the LDM that is used in the SELECT statement as a virtual table to obtain a list of certain requested data of the considered SD.

It is known that the loss of database data integrity can have the most serious consequences for the future work of the organization. Therefore, in the database scheme with a universal basis of relations, appropriate means of maintaining the data integrity were realized, which were considered in detail in [1], which contribute to the overall security of the database, preventing the possibility of data transition to an inconsistent state, thereby excluding the threat of receiving erroneous or incorrect results.

Using databases based on a database scheme with the universal basis of relations, it is recommended as one of the mechanisms that contribute to increasing the DB availability, to perform periodically backup their contents and organize the storage of created copies in places provided with the necessary protection. Today, almost any modern DBMS provides backup tools that allow you to restore a database. At the same time, in addition to the capabilities of standard backup and recovery tools, it became expedient to define one more relation of the database scheme with the universal basis of relations. Namely, a relation, referred to as a log of changed data. In a formalized form, this relation can be represented as a subset of the Cartesian product $OS_{user} \times IP \times U_2 \times DB_{name} \times L_{DM} \times T_{DB} \times T_{DDB} \times Op \times P_{name}$:

$$L = \{(l_1, l_2, l_3, l_4, l_5, l_6, l_7, l_8, l_9) | l_1 \in OS_{user} \wedge l_2 \in IP \wedge l_3 \in U_2 \wedge l_4 \in DB_{name}$$
$$\wedge l_5 \in L_{DM} \wedge l_6 \in T_{DB} \wedge l_7 \in T_{DDB} \wedge l_8 \in Op \wedge l_9 \in P_{name}\}, \quad (6)$$

where OS_{user} is the set of device names (host-machines of clients) from which the session was activated; IP is the set of IP addresses of the devices from which the session was activated; DB_{name} is set of database names; L_{DM} is the set of meta description lines of LDM, leading to a change in the data stored in the database; T_{DB} is the set of times when changes were made to the current database; T_{DDB} is the set of times of data output to other databases (when replication, distribution of data in a distributed system); Op is the set of statement that lead to the modification of data stored in the database ($Op = \{insert, delete, update\}$); P_{name} is the set of procedure names of the LDM interpreter [18] ($P_{name} = \{Proc_{metadata}, Proc_{data}\}$).

The result of mapping this relation to the base relation of the database schema with the universal basis of relations ($R_L^{sh} \in R^{sh}$) is presented below in the form of the main lines of SQL code:

```
HOST                VARCHAR2(255) not null, -- host name
IP_ADDRESS          VARCHAR(255) not null,  -- IP address
SESSION_USER        VARCHAR(255) not null,  -- user name
DB_NAME             VARCHAR(255) not null,  -- database name
NAME_STR_METADATE   VARCHAR(2000) not null, -- lines of LDM
TIME_WRITE_LOC      DATE not null,  -- time for current DB
TIME_INTO_GLOB      TIMESTAMP(9),
NAME_PROC           VARCHAR(100) not null, --
{Proc_metadata, Proc_data}
OPERATION           VARCHAR(10) not null,  -- ins, del, update
primary key      (NAME_STR_METADATE, TIME_WRITE_LOC).
```

Thanks to the information stored in the log table, which is automatically formed when the corresponding parameter of the stored procedure of the LDM interpreter is specified [18], the process of recovering incorrectly changed or lost data is simplified, and the procedure for determining users, times and the nature of their changes is facilitated. In addition, the information from the log-table of the changed data can be used in distributed systems when data is propagated (replicated).

It is no secret that an audit procedure is no less important for creating a complete database security system. Actions with critical data should be logged. Therefore to monitor the status, changes introduced to the database, user actions, in addition to using standard DBMS audit tools, on the platform of which the database scheme with the universal basis of relations was implemented, special diagnostic functions, including dynamic analyzers of code coverage implemented in the LDM interpreter, capable of detecting entering incorrect data, as well as triggers that support the logging of operations performed in the database have been developed. Also, for accountability of user actions, data from the log table of the changed data, as discussed above, can be used.

Thus, solving the problem of protecting corporate databases built on the basis of the database scheme with the universal basis of relations, from possible threats, special means (in the form of implemented scheme objects) and the rules for their use were developed in the process of creating this database scheme. These means and rules are based both on common methods and tools supported by the DBMS, on the platform of which the proposed scheme is implemented, and on its own mechanisms developed within the framework of creating this scheme. The means and methods implemented in the DB schema with the universal basis of relations to ensure the security of databases are shown in a systematized form in Fig. 1.

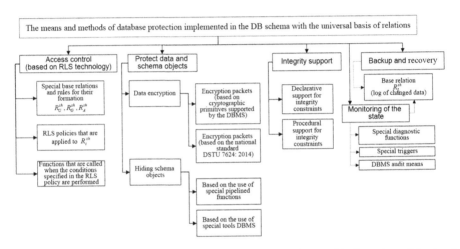

Fig. 1. The means and methods implemented in the DB schema with the universal basis of relations to ensure the security of databases

3 Conclusions

1. To ensure the security of data in databases built on the basis of the database scheme with the universal basis of relations, an approach is proposed of the integrated use of common methods and tools supported by the DBMS, on the platform of which this scheme is implemented, as well as its own mechanisms developed in the framework of creation of the DB scheme that is invariant to SDs.
2. Solving the problem of protecting databases as the most important corporate resource, in the process of creating database schema invariant to subject domains, special means were developed (in the form of implemented schema objects such as triggers, procedures, packages, tables, functions) and rules of their use, ensuring: access control to schema objects; data protection and hiding of objects; data integrity support; recovery of incorrectly modified or lost data; monitoring of the state, changes introduced into the database; logging user actions.

3. Implemented in DB scheme with the universal basis of relations, means and methods of protection allow you to control access to data up to a specific element.
4. The practice of using databases built on the basis of the database scheme with the universal basis of relations, for information systems of different subject domains, in the projects of which it was required to organize reliable, safe storage, adaptation to changes occurring in SD and legislation, timely processing of data, showed that they have a sufficiently high degree of controllability of access to data, cryptographic protection of data, reliability, stability.

References

1. Esin, V.I.: Invariantnaya k predmetnym oblastyam shema bazy dannyh i ee otlichitelnye osobennosti. Radiotehnika: nauch.-tehn. zhurnal. 193, 133–142 (2018). (in Russian)
2. Esin, V.I.: Model dannyh s universalnoj fiksirovannoj strukturoj. In: Materiali mizhnarodnoyi naukovoyi konferenciyi, TAAPSD 2014, pp. 112–116. FO-P Aleksandrova M.V., Kirovograd (2014). (in Russian)
3. Esin, V.I., Pergamencev, Y.A.: Tehnologiya proektirovaniya modeli predpriyatiya na osnove universalnoj modeli dannyh. http://www.citforum.ru/database/articles/udm/. Accessed 26 Mar 2018. (in Russian)
4. Connolly, T.M., Begg, C.E.: Database Systems: A Practical Approach to Design, Implementation, and Management, 6th edn. Pearson Education Limited, Harlow (2015)
5. Groff, D.R., Vajnberg, P.N., Oppel, E.D.: SQL: polnoe rukovodstvo, 3-e izd., Per. s angl., OOO Izdatelskij dom "Vilyams", Moskva (2015). (in Russian)
6. Date, C.J.: An Introduction to Database Systems, 8th edn. Addison-Wesley, Pearson (2004)
7. Kajt, T.: Oracle dlya professionalov: Per. s angl. OOO «DiaSoftYuP» , Sankt-Peterburg (2003). (in Russian)
8. Nanda, A., Fejershtejn, S.: Oracle PL/SQL dlya administratorov baz dannyh. Per. s angl. Simvol-Plyus, Sankt-Peterburg (2008). (in Russian)
9. Grachev, V.M., Esin, V.I., Polukhina, N.G., Rassomakhin, S.G.: Data security mechanisms implemented in the database with universal model. Bull. Lebedev. Phys. Inst. **41**(5), 123–126 (2014). https://doi.org/10.3103/s1068335614050029
10. Esin, V.I., Esina, M.V.: Osobennosti zashity dannyh v bazah dannyh s universalnoj modelyu. Prikladnaya radioelektronika **10**(2), 226–232 (2011). (in Russian)
11. Soroka, L.S., Esin, V.I., Esina, M.V.: Tradicionnye metody i sredstva zashity dannyh, realizovannye v baze dannyh s universalnoj modelyu dannyh. Visnik Akademiyi mitnoyi sluzhbi Ukrayini. Ser.: Tehnichni nauki **2**(44), 7–12 (2010). (in Russian)
12. Esin, V.I., Yurasov, V.G.: Zashita dannyh v baze dannyh s universalnoj strukturoj. Informaciya i bezopasnost. Voronezh, Voronezhskij gosudarstvennyj tehnicheskij universitet. **17**(2), 180–187 (2014). (in Russian)
13. Fedorov, A.V., Pyankov, V.M., Vihlyancev, P.S., Simonov, M.V.: Sistema razgranicheniya dostupa k dannym na urovne zapisej i yacheek. Zashita informacii INSIDE, **3**, 2–4 (2012). (in Russian)
14. Patent 8,131,664 B2, United States, Row-level security in a relational database management system/ Curt Cotner, Gilroy, CA (US); Roger Lee Miller, San Jose, CA (US); International Business Machines Corporation, Armonk, NY (US). N 12/242,241 (2012)
15. Homonenko, A.D., Cygankov, V.M., Malcev, M.G.: Bazy dannyh. KORONA print, Sankt-Peterburg (2004). (in Russian)

16. Methods and systems for transparent data encryption and decryption, United States Patent 7426745. http://www.freepatentsonline.com/7426745.html. Accessed 26 Mar 2018

17. Esin, V.I., Esina, M.V.: Yazyk dlya universalnoj modeli dannyh. Sistemi obrobki informaciyi. **5**(95), 193–197 (2011). (in Russian)

18. Esin, V.I., Esina, M.V.: Interpretator yazyka dlya universalnoj modeli dannyh. Nauka i tehnika Povitryanih Sil Zbrojnih Sil Ukrayini **2**(6), 140–143 (2011). (in Russian)

Author Index

Printed in the United States
By Bookmasters